The Search

A Historian's Search for Historical Jesus

By

Dr. Ron Charles

This book is a work of non-fiction. Names and places have been changed to protect the privacy of all individuals. The events and situations are true.

© 2003 by Dr. Ron Charles. All rights reserved.

No part of this book may be reproduced, stored in a retrieval system, or transmitted by any means, electronic, mechanical, photocopying, recording, or otherwise, without written permission from the author.

ISBN: 1-4107-0367-3 (e-book)
ISBN: 1-4107-0368-1 (Paperback)
ISBN: 1-4107-0369-X (Dustjacket)

Library of Congress Control Number: 2002096474

This book is printed on acid free paper.

Printed in the United States of America
Bloomington, IN

1stBooks - rev. 12/21/02

Table of Contents

AUTHOR'S PREFACE vii

INTRODUCTION xi

I THE QUEST BEGINS 1

> The motivation to begin my search for the historical Jesus and how that search got started. My early efforts. My discovery of the key of truth.

II THE GOSPELS 11

> My detailed study of the Gospels and the motivation that drove me to "consume" every detail of the Gospels.

III ESSENTIAL GOLDEN NUGGETS 16

> The discovery of the nucleus around which my research efforts revolved.

IV AUGUSTAN ROME 29

> A chronological review of the rule of Augusta Caesar at the time of Jesus' birth.

V THE ROME OF TIBERIUS 41

> A chronological review of the rule of Tiberius Caesar at the time of Jesus' ministry, death, and resurrection.

VI HEROD'S RULE 56

> A chronological review of the rule of Herod the Great at the time of Jesus' birth.

VII A CHRONOLOGY OF THE LIFE OF JESUS 60

> A chronological order of the events of Jesus' life that I used as a foundation as I progressed in my research.

VIII SOCIETY AND RELIGION 72

> A look at the society of Judaea and the Galilee at the time of Jesus and the religions and philosophies that existed in Judaea and the Galilee.

IX A SON IN OLD AGE 82

    A review of the birth of John the Baptist; the annunciation to Mary; and Mary's conception of Jesus.

X THE NATIVITY 98

    The birth of Jesus and the mysterious events surrounding his birth.

XI MOTHER OF GOD 133

    A brief history of how the "Mary, Mother of God" dogma became a doctrine of the Catholic Church.

XII INVASION FROM THE EAST 149

    Visit of the magi to the home where Jesus was staying approximately two years after his birth. Joseph flees to Egypt with Mary and Jesus.

XIII SON OF THE LAW 163

    Jesus' silent years including his journey to Jerusalem to become a "Son of the Law" at age 13.

XIV BAPTISM AND BEYOND 178

    Jesus' silent years including his journey to Jerusalem to become a "Son of the Law" at age 13.

XV FIRST YEAR OF MINISTRY 217

    AD 26, Jesus' first partial year of ministry. His first disciples are called. The marriage of Cana. His move to Capernaum.

XVI SECOND YEAR OF MINISTRY 237

    AD 27, Jesus' first full year of ministry. Cast out money changers the first of three times; confrontation with Nicodemus; ministry in the Galilee; centurion's servant healed; arrest of John the Baptist; call of Peter, Andrew, James, and John; the Sermon on the Mount.

XVII THIRD YEAR OF MINISTRY 311

    AD 28, Jesus' second full year of ministry. Religious conference in

Capernaum; call of Levi; healing of man at the Pool of Bethesda; healing of the man with a withered hand; raising a man from the dead in Nain; the death of John the Baptist.

XVIII FOURTH YEAR OF MINISTRY 382

AD 29, Jesus' third full year of ministry. Feeding of the 5,000; Jesus and Peter walk on water; the death of Joseph, the husband of Mary, Jesus' mother; trip to Caesarea Philippi and the transfiguration; faith as a grain of mustard; coin in fish's mouth; and teaching parables in Capernaum.

XIX FIFTH YEAR OF MINISTRY 424

AD 30, Jesus fourth full year of ministry. Trip to Tyre and Sidon; confrontation with Legion; feeding of 4,000; "Rivers of living water;" woman caught in adultery; and healing of woman who was stooped over for 18 years.

XX FINAL YEAR OF MINISTRY 469

AD 31, Jesus' final partial year of earthly ministry and the year of his death and resurrection; prodigal son; the rich man and Lazarus; Lazarus raised from the dead; Zacchaeus and Bar-Timaeus in Jericho; triumphant entries into Jerusalem; cast out moneychangers for second and third time; "Render unto Caesar;" the 10 virgins; Passover feast, the last supper, and his betrayal.

XXI ARREST AND CRUCIFIXION 537

The agony in the garden, Jesus' arrest, his trial, sentencing, and crucifixion.
Peter's denial.

XXII THE BEGINNING 576

The resurrection and post-resurrection.

XXIII EPILOGUE 596

My search continues.

APPENDIX: JEWISH CALENDAR 597

APPENDIX: IDENTIFICATIONS and DEFINITIONS 598

AUTHOR'S PREFACE

When I first began to determinedly study the life of the historical Jesus, I made the mistake of approaching his life from the viewpoint of the current (the past 100 years) commonly accepted tabulated timeframe. In so doing, I felt that it would be a very simple matter to arrange the life of Jesus into a logical chronology that I could use as a foundation for my search for a historical Jesus.

The task seemed at first to be fairly straight forward, based on the currently accepted fundamental premise: Jesus was born of the virgin Mary, perhaps in the winter time, probably somewhere between 4 BC and 2 BC in the town of Bethlehem; his birth was acknowledged by shepherds and wisemen, who worshiped him at the manger site; Joseph and Mary fled with Jesus to Egypt because Herod sought to kill him, where they stayed for a year or two before returning to Nazareth; at age 12 Jesus went to the Temple in Jerusalem with his parents and astounded the religious officials with his knowledge; at age 30 Jesus was baptized by John the Baptist in the Jordan River; he immediately went into the wilderness to be tempted; upon his return from the wilderness Jesus called his first four (Andrew, Peter, James, and John) of eventually 12 disciples, and began his ministry; he had many run-ins with the Jewish religious leaders but he also performed many miracles and taught the multitudes; his ministry lasted just over three years but not quite four years; on the Sunday before his crucifixion he was triumphantly welcomed into Jerusalem; on Thursday he had the Last Supper with his disciples; that night he was arrested in the garden where he was praying; a mid-night trial convicted Jesus and early Friday morning he was condemned to be crucified; Friday morning he was crucified; he died Friday afternoon and was buried; on the following Sunday he raised from the dead; and 50 days later he ascended into heaven. It was all predetermined and all very neatly wrapped in a concise orderly package. Little thinking needed to be exercised on my part because the chronological order of his life had already been adroitly established.

However, as I plunged deeper into the Gospels, I began to see some inconsistencies and some chronology problems with the neat package that had been wrapped by modern fundamentalists. The inconsistencies became so obvious and so discomfiting that I had to re-evaluate what was actual truth based on historical fact and what was presumed truth based on tradition.

Eventually, satisfied that what I had learned and was continuing to learn in the Gospels was correct and factual, I turned my attention to the currently and generally accepted chronological order of Jesus' life to see if in it lay the cause for the inconsistencies. What I found in this chronological order was a foundational base that dated back less than a hundred years. It appeared that the commonly accepted perspective regarding the life of Jesus was grounded in the premise that the Gospels for the most part recorded the same events in Jesus life, but from different authors' individualistic viewpoint. This premise was what has come to be called, "The Harmony of the Gospels." Harmony of the Gospels means that each important event in Jesus' life (excluding the silent years between age 12 and 30) was recorded in at least one of the Gospel texts. If two or more Gospels recorded similar events, a harmony of the Gospels base demands that the two or more Gospel records were actually recordings of the same event, but were accounted for differently based on the author's discretion, interpretation, and audience directed license. That being the case, and if the Gospel recorded events in Jesus' ministry are the most important events that happened during his ministry (the fact that they were recorded at all is because they were obviously the most important events in his ministry), then assuredly most all of these events could have easily fit into a three-year ministry chronological timeframe.

Yet, in today's society it would be ludicrous and irrational to believe that only one woman in any given country, region, area, county, city, or town, had cervix cancer; that only one man had a sick daughter; that only one military officer had a domestic who was sick; that only one bad storm hit a particular area within a three-year span; that any one preacher preached only one sermon on a particular subject; or that anyone (not including at least 12 followers and at times it could have included hundreds of followers) living in the world today is so physically fit that he could repeatedly walk up and down steep hills and through barren desert land, in intense heat or frigid cold, traveling hundreds of miles each year for three years running, so quickly that he ended up walking faster and covering more ground, in less time and with less effort than if he had been riding an animal or driving in a horse-drawn wagon or carriage? Yet, we are led to believe that this was the case regarding the life and ministry of Jesus. Somewhere and somehow logic had to intervene.

Eventually, I became so frustrated with the inconsistencies and the illogical presumptions, that I decided to forget about tradition and everything that I had learned or assumed to be true regarding the life of Jesus, and start all over with no preconceived ideas, no predetermined notions, and no previously established convictions concerning the life and ministry of Jesus.

I again began to study the Gospels in detail. I studied them book by book, chapter by chapter, verse by verse, word by word, letter by letter, and from period to period. With this type of intensive study it did not take long for me to realize that each sentence, each word, and each punctuation mark placed in the Gospels was important and necessary for understanding the Gospel's message. There was nothing written in the Gospels that can be considered irrelevant, secondary, or unimportant.

After I had finished studying each Gospel individually, I went back and comparatively studied each of them and compared each narrative to the narratives of the other three. It was then that I realized that although some of the events in the ministry of Jesus were recorded in more than one Gospel, a large portion was not. Many events were recorded in one Gospel *only*.

Finally, after I had satisfied myself with my comparative study of the Gospel narratives, I began a comparative study of the Gospels and historical documentation, especially Roman history and the writings of Christians and non-Christians alike during the first 10 centuries after Christ's crucifixion.

I read hundreds of documents relating to the person and character of Jesus and reviewed countless chronologies and accounts of his life, ministry, and deeds. Some were complimentary, suggesting that there had never been a man like Jesus in the entire history of the world, that he was a great teacher or the greatest of the prophets, or exalted him to the level of God incarnate; while others were blasphemous, asserting that Jesus was nothing more than a charlatan, magician, mystic cult leader, or wandering vagabond.

Some documents confirmed the Gospel accounts signifying that Jesus raised from the dead, ascended to the Father, and lives today as man's Savior and Lord. While others stand in marked contrast to the Gospels, claiming that indeed he died, but he did not rise from the dead. Instead, his disciples took his body from the tomb and contrived a hoax concerning his resurrection. Other documents claim that he did not die at all. Rather, he survived, recovered from the ordeal, got married (most of these say that Jesus married Mary Magdalene), had children who were the ancestors of the royal bloodline of the Merovingian dynasty, and died an old man.

Hundreds of chronologies, some as recent as the year 2001 while others were centuries old, suggested that Jesus was born anywhere from 25 BC to AD 25, that his mother was anywhere from 12 to 35 years old when he was born, that he began his ministry anywhere from age 24 to age 40, that his ministry lasted anywhere from two years to twelve years, that he was crucified sometime between AD 2 to AD 45, and that he was somewhere between 25 to 45 years of age when he was crucified.

During these years of research I have maintained the premise that the record of Jesus as recorded in the Gospels is non-argumentative truth. But, considering the fact that the Gospels do not give exact dates or years and is sometimes very vague with regard to time spans and time frames and how events that occurred during those times fit within or together with established Roman history, I chose to disregard all chronological assumptions and conjecture concerning Jesus' life and to the best of my ability develop what I hoped would be a logical chronological timetable of the life and ministry of Jesus. The chronological timetable had to fit within the parameters of known Roman history, society, law, and culture. I realized that by doing this I ran the risk of challenging the currently accepted modern chronology of Jesus' life. Nonetheless, I felt an obligation to develop a chronology that I felt most logically and comfortably fit within the established time frame of known Greco-Roman history.

This is not to suggest that all of the hundreds of chronologies developed over the past number of centuries are wrong and the one that I developed, based on my research, is correct. I dare not presume that the chronological record of Jesus' life that I developed is the only one right and everyone else's is wrong. For as I continue my research, I am quite certain that I will modify and adapt my chronology to more easily fit into history's timetable as I discover more and more details about the life of Jesus. However, based on the scant amount of corroborating information that I have discovered thus far (dealing with but "the tip of the iceberg" of events and occurrences associated with the life and ministry of Jesus) I have chosen to chronicle Jesus' life into a format that best fits within the framework of my research documentation.

Although I will undoubtedly spend the rest of my life researching and documenting the life and ministry of Jesus and still only cover a small percentage of the events of his life, and realizing that with all of my efforts I have not even come close to providing a basic outline of Jesus' life, much less a detailed account, I nevertheless felt that I needed to record the details of my pursuit thus far and my experiences relating to that pursuit. The result was this book, *The Search*.

In this autobiographical account of my research, I chronicle Jesus' life and explain how I discovered non-Biblical corroboration that confirms the truth of the Gospel records of Jesus' life and ministry. I have recorded the information as I found it. I have not molded it to fit into a predetermined idea or dogma. Some of the information I found was in marked contrast to the traditional view of Jesus and his ministry. As such, I chose not to take "sides." I searched for the information, found it, and recorded it without any alternative motive except to corroborate the truth of the Gospels. My motive and purpose for this research was and still is, not to attempt to change anybody's mind concerning their perception of the life of Jesus or to discredit any existing ideas or viewpoints. It was merely to find non-Biblical historical resources that would serve to substantiate the truth of the Gospel records within the context of historical truth.

I have chosen to use the authorized or King James Version (KJV) of the Bible when referring to scriptural portions. It's not that I feel that the King James Version is any more accurate than any of the other versions; it's just that I grew up using the King James, so I am familiar with it. In addition, I like the poetic Elizabethan English language in which the King James Version is written.

I would like to express my deep appreciation to Dr. Al Plysier, professor of history at Piedmont College, for encouraging me to complete this autobiographical account. He also was responsible for the final and the most extensive proofreading of the manuscript.

I also want to thank Michelle Thomas, Kim Stuckey, and Laura Wairs for their proofreading and their suggestions. Without their help, this book would still not be complete.

A very special thanks to my wife, Paula, who spent many weeks and countless nights alone over our past 32 years of marriage, while I traveled all over the world researching and collecting information, and spent incessant hours compiling and writing. She is truly remarkable to have put up with so much so that this book could be published.

INTRODUCTION

There are two great creeds that have historically defined and identified the Christian faith—each serving in its own way as a guide to help those who have confessed Christianity throughout the centuries, to stay the course originally established by Jesus and later implemented by his followers: the *Apostles' Creed* and the *Nicene Creed*.

The *Apostles' Creed* was formulated in the 2nd century, probably with the help of Ignatius of Antioch, who suffered martyrdom in Rome during the reign of Trajan (AD 98-117), so that Christians could give clear and consistent answers when asked why they believed in Christianity or believed that Jesus was divine.

The first half of the creed is the most easily recognized part.

> *I believe in God the Father almighty,*
> *Creator of heaven and earth;*
> *and in Jesus Christ, his only Son, our Lord;*
> *who was conceived by the Holy Spirit,*
> *born of the virgin Mary*
> *suffered under Pontius Pilate,*
> *was crucified, died, and was buried.*
> *He descended into hell.*
> *On the third day he rose again from the dead,*
> *and ascended into heaven.*

A disturbing question regarding the creed is not so much what it says, but rather, what it doesn't say. The creed goes directly from Jesus' birth to his death, being totally silent about his life. If logic is the rule, then judging by the *Apostles' Creed*, neither anything Jesus said nor anything he did while living and ministering on this earth is essential to Christian faith.

The *Nicene Creed* is named after Nicea, the city in Asia Minor where in the 4th century, under the supervision of Constantine, the Roman Emperor who was baptized a Christian before his death; Christian bishops officially defined the doctrine of Jesus' divinity.

As with the *Apostles' Creed*, it too demonstrates no interest in the life and teachings of Jesus.

The first half is the most commonly known part of the creed.

> *We believe in one God, the Father, the Almighty,*
> *maker of heaven and earth, of all that is, seen and unseen.*
> *We believe in one Lord, Jesus Christ,*
> *the only Son of God, eternally begotten of the Father,*
> *God from God, Light from Light, true God from true God,*
> *begotten, not made, one in being with the Father;*

through him all things were made.
For us and for our salvation he came down from heaven.
By the power of the Holy Spirit he took flesh from
the virgin Mary and became a man.
For our sakes he was crucified under Pontius Pilate;
he suffered, died, and was buried.
On the third day he rose again according to the scriptures.
He ascended into heaven.

Christians in today's society agree on very little doctrinally. Yet, most seem to agree that the *Apostles' Creed* and the *Nicene Creed* are the foundations upon which modern day Christian doctrine and theology is built. Yet, according to these foundational Creeds, what Jesus did before he died is relatively unimportant with regard to living a life that is pleasing to and acceptable to God. Only Jesus' miraculous birth and sacrificial death seems to matter.

Notwithstanding this common Christian belief, the author of John's Gospel wrote, *"And there are also many other things which Jesus did, the which, if they should be written every one, I suppose that even the world itself could not contain the books that should be written"* (John 21:25). Why would the writer of John imply that all incidences in the life of Jesus were equally important if his birth and death were the only significant events in his life? Why would he say that the deeds and sayings of Jesus during his time on earth could probably not be contained in all the books that existed in the world at that time (more than a half-million volumes) if in fact all of the most important and the most significant events in his life and ministry could comfortably fit into one 20- or 30- page narrative (Gospel) of his life and ministry (modern theological experts propose that the other three Gospel narratives are nothing more than repeats of the one)?

It seems apparent that either the writer of John's statement has exaggerated his point; he has lied about the wealth of significant events associated with the life and ministry of Jesus; or the developers of the current and commonly accepted notions regarding Jesus' life and ministry have grossly underestimated those events. Which supposition is correct? The author of the Gospel of John? Or the developers of the Harmony of the Gospels premise (originating in the 19th century) along with its commonly accepted ideology and chronology of the life and ministry of Jesus?

Presuming that the writer of the Gospel of John is correct, then logic would demand that the deeds and sayings of Jesus would be of utmost importance to the young Christian faith. So much so, that numerous, and perhaps hundreds, of documents would have been produced during the first and second centuries after Jesus' death (and resurrection) attesting to the value placed by the early Christians upon his deeds and sayings. History has proven that such was the case.

Even so today, to suggest that the only thing that matters is the birth, death, and resurrection of Jesus, and all else associated with his life is irrelevant is a misnomer in the greatest sense. That would be like saying that all that matters to citizens of America is that the early American fathers declared independence from Britain and then by the 21st century America became the mightiest nation that the world has ever seen. Nothing else that happened between these two great events—the

American Revolutionary War, the emancipation of slaves, the War between the States, World Wars I and II, the stock market crash, post-war prosperity, the civil rights movement, Vietnam, the assassination of four presidents, the blight of terrorism— matters to American citizens. Yet, without the moldings of the historical occurrences in the middle, the two end events would mean very little. So it was and still is with the life of Jesus.

In today's society, most books on the subject of Jesus are divided into three categories: *scholarly, historical,* and *inspirational.*

Scholars and educators write the *scholarly* books for scholars and educators, complete with footnotes, comments, documentation, comparatives and opinions, assumptions, and hypothesis. The readers of these books are usually comfortable in the world of modern science and philosophy, yet they are curious about why Jesus has become the most influential character of the past 2,000 years.

The authors of the *historical* books feel they have an obligation to be forthright and honest about the life of Jesus, even if such candid treatment of his life sequesters traditional Christian doctrine from modern academia. They seek to reconstruct the life of Jesus by using rigorous historical standards that strips away all theory, conjecture, assumptions, hearsay, customs, and tradition leaving nothing but the basics of the bare bones facts of historical birth, deeds, and death. Because Jesus was a historical figure, who lived in a real world, in a time in the historical past, who confronted real people, and was influenced by historical events that were happening around him, authors of historical books seldom try to confirm truth in anything that does not or cannot pass the rigid tests of genuineness and fact established by the uncompromising standards and application methods of modern historical scholarship. Thus, they insist that historical data is not only the place to start, but also where it all must end. In short, true historical truth allows no latitude for the inclusion of profession, belief, or inspiration in its assessment.

Both *scholarly* books and *historical* books deal primarily with the fact that Jesus was a loyal 1st century Jew from the Galilee, who had a Jewish family, Jewish friends, and many Jewish followers. In essence, the Jews were his friends, even though like the Jewish prophets of ancient days, he, without a doubt, probably did rile against the trappings of the Temple and the Temple cult with its hypocrisy and oppressive purity standards. In addition, they usually assume that Jesus was generally a poor uneducated Jewish Galilean peasant who became an itinerate teacher, whose wisdom was far beyond what should have been a limited academic background, and who had a unique compassion that was an unheard characteristic of the typical Jew during the time of tyrannical Rome's oppression of the Jews.

To the authors of these books, Jesus' relationship to the Romans (except for his crucifixion, which is usually presented as executed by the Romans but instigated by the Jews) was slight if at all, and then only by accident or coincidence. They assume that like his follow Jews in Judaea, he probably resented the Roman oppression, and chose not to associate with them. Nevertheless, if they did come to him, like the centurion in Capernaum (Luke 7:2-10), he did not turn them away. There is little thought and virtually no conjecture that Jesus may have not only been a loyal Jew, but that he was also a loyal Roman subject whose deeds and sayings were greatly influenced by the might of Imperial Rome with its ambience, culture, society, history, and law (In reality, the only thing that Jesus really knew about politics, law, enforcement of the law, and society was Rome. It had influenced the area wherein he was born and ministered for more than 60 years before his birth and would continue to influence it for four centuries after his death. So, in essence, Rome and Roman policy and society were probably, next to his relationship with God the Father, the foremost influences that molded and patterned his life and ministry.).

Unfortunately, both *scholarly* and *historical* books are often unintelligible to the average American reader who does not know the biblical languages, is not acquainted with the history of the area where Jesus lived and ministered, or is not familiar with the time in history in which he lived.

Inspirational books are usually written by Christians to Christians in order to inspire faith. By capitalizing upon the spirit and the intent of the creeds and liturgy, they seek to spiritualize the deeds and sayings of Jesus into a typology reflected in Christian theology, doctrine, and piety. Generally, the authors of inspirational books care little about confirming the authenticity of the Gospel records and choose instead to concentrate upon what affect a particular deed or saying has upon the ultimate issue of Jesus' death, which cleanses us from sin, and the assurance of eternal life because of his resurrection. Because the Gospels are perceived to be the inerrant Word of God, complete and unequivocally accurate within themselves, historical accuracy becomes secondary to spiritual enlightenment. In such an atmosphere, it is not unusual for inspirational writers to denounce as heretical, scholarly and historical books about Jesus.

Authors of *inspirational* books about Jesus usually agree that the Gospel narratives say little about the world in which Jesus lived. So, because the Gospel narratives say so little and the authors of inspirational books feel that no other historical source is needed to ensure spiritual inspiration, most apply the deeds and sayings of Jesus to their current world and present day circumstances and situations, assuming that Jesus probably would have acted or reacted the same way in this modern world as he had originally acted or reacted in his world. But, although certain aspects of human nature remain constant, the modern world in which we live is a far cry from the world wherein Jesus lived.

So, when we evaluate the three most common types of books written about Jesus in today's world, we discover that, for all practical purposes, they address either the history of Rome at the time in which Jesus lived and ministered, the history of the Jews during the time in which Jesus lived and ministered, the events of Jesus' life and ministry and the spiritual implications associated with those events, or the inspirational lessons taught by Jesus and how the lessons apply to us today. Seldom, if ever, do the most common books address Roman history *as well as* the deeds and sayings of Jesus' ministry, much less how they interconnect and influence each other.

The object of this book is to offer a fourth choice. It is neither predominately *scholarly*, *historical*, nor *inspirational*. Rather, it is a book that seeks to understand why Jesus said what he said and did what he did in light of the fact that he was not only a loyal Galilean Jew but he was also a loyal Roman subject, who was probably educated in Greco-Roman influenced schools, who probably worked under the authority of Roman administrators, who ministered under the protection of Roman officials, and who died as a enemy of Rome as mandated by Roman law.

The book is not intended to present Jesus in any lesser light than that of deity. Yet, within the context of known Greco-Roman history, customs, philosophies, and manners of the time in which Jesus lived and ministered. It attempts to show under what circumstances his ministry and popularity grew and flourished in Roman Mare Nostrum and then floundered.

Since more than 60 percent of the deeds and sayings attributed to Jesus in the Gospel accounts relate either directly or indirectly to the fact that Jesus was greatly influenced by Imperial Rome, I felt it was my duty to seek to uncover the history behind the life and ministry of Jesus and how he was most influenced by his Greco-Roman surroundings.

By no means do I presuppose that I have covered even a fraction of the details regarding the life and ministry of Jesus recorded in the Gospels. On the contrary, I have only dealt with a small portion of those events (deeds and sayings)—those that can be historically proven without a doubt. So, although my search for the historical truth concerning the life and ministry of Jesus has been an intensive and extensive quest, I feel that I have only begun to scratch the surface.

The book is *historical* in that it portrays the life of Jesus as it was in Roman Mare Nostrum East (what became known as the region of Palestine and Syria). It is *scholarly* in that it confirms each Gospel recorded event with non-biblical authenticating documentation. It is *inspirational* in that it assumes that the Gospel records are the most accurate records available about the life of Jesus and that the word and deeds recorded in the Gospel narratives have been preserved for two millennia because they were the narratives that God felt would be most spiritually beneficial to this current generation.

This book will seek to discover Jesus' life by filling in the empty center between birth and death of the creedal descriptions of Jesus. It will reach beyond the bare bones skeleton of historical Jesus and will alight firmly upon the fully developed historical epic of *Jesus— the loyal Jewish Roman subject of Roman Mare Nostrum East.*

I
THE QUEST BEGINS

As I ascended the first flight of stairs leading to the small third floor auditorium of the campus library of the University of Texas, I glanced at my watch. I was ten minutes late. The lecture by special guest lecturer, Dr. Richard Link, professor of Classical Roman History from the University of London, had probably already begun.

As quietly as possible, I slipped into the back of the auditorium, accepted a program brochure from the door attendant, and sat down in a seat in the back row.

Although Dr. Link was already standing behind the lectern, apparently he had just been introduced because he had not begun his lecture.

Dr. Link's topic that evening was "Jesus: the Roman subject."

For as long as I could remember, I had had an inert interest in learning the truth about Jesus. Not what the movies say about him, but rather what is true concerning his life and ministry. So, when I read in the local newspaper that Dr. Link was going to be lecturing at the university library on the subject of Jesus, I felt it might be interesting and could be worth attending.

After thanking the head of the university's History Department for his hospitality and the department's invitation, Dr. Link began his lecture by asking the small audience to close their eyes and try to picture a hypothetical scenario, that very well could be more historical than theoretical.

After instructing every one to close their eyes he said, "I want you to use your imagination and picture the events as vividly as you possibly can while I relate the story to you. Now keep you eyes closed the entire time that I relate the story to you. Just imagine yourself as an eyewitness to the events of the story. Picture yourself actually being there. Better yet, imagine yourself as the main character in this story: a Roman solider."

He waited for everyone to close their eyes and then he began to tell his story.

"It is early afternoon of a spring day in the year AD 31 and you are a Roman soldier. But you're not just any Roman soldier, you are a Roman centurion and you're stationed in the Roman province of Judaea.

"Three times each year the Roman authority sets aside a day for the execution of criminals who have been found guilty of sedition. This day was one of those days set aside to carry out those executions. You have been assigned the task of maintaining order and overseeing the execution—this time being carried out in the garbage dump of Gehenna, outside the walls of the city of Jerusalem, located in the state of Judea of the province of Judaea.

"It's an unpleasant task, but one that was necessary.

Now," Dr. Link said breaking into his story line, "Just let your imagination run free, as we follow the thoughts and actions of the centurion as he oversees the execution process."

Dr. Link paused to allow everyone to clear their thoughts and begin the imagination process.

He then closed his own eyes and descended into deep thought. Afterwards he continued.

"From mid-day onward the darkness had slowly made its way east from the western horizon. Now two hours later, the sky had turned completely dark, giving it the appearance of moist black velvet. The darkness had begun innocently enough as it slowly moved from its resting place in the Mare Nostrum to completely engulf the entire Jerusalem region, within a matter of a couple of hours, forcing torches to have to be lit in order to provide light.

"As the northeast wind gusted from off of the surrounding cliffs, gently at first and then gradually increasing in velocity until now the flames of the lighted torches which only slightly pierced the uncanny eerie darkness, fluttered almost horizontal against the blast, the centurion pulled his scarlet cloak tighter around his neck and turned his back to the squall in an attempt to shield himself from the cutting affects of the relentless rush. He then ordered his second in command to increase the number of workers who were keeping watch over and manning the continually burning refuse fires, to ensure that the flames would be contained and not spread as a result of the intensified wind.

"He had never experienced anything like this before. Sure he had endured countless battles with rain, snow, frozen ground, sleepless nights, no food or drink, and marching for days on end only to complete the journey just in time to help defend the Empire against seemingly insurmountable odds. He had even had to engage the enemy at night, with instinct as his only guide. But, never had he had to deal with unpredictable natural forces in which neither he nor any other man had the ability or power to control.

"He had experienced both the eclipse of the sun and the moon, but this darkness was caused by neither. He had *never* witnessed this type of darkness. It was so unearthly; so, mystical and numinous. It was almost like crossing over into the realm of the paranormal and metaphysical—if one believed in that sort of thing. He did not. In fact, unless you count sporadic and extremely infrequent devotion to Mars, the god of war, he was not a believer in any god, goddess, spiritual leader, oracle, prophet, priest, religion, religious leader, or philosopher. He believed in war, fighting to achieve recognition, loyalty to Rome and to its quest, and dedication to and admiration for the Emperor—nothing or no one else mattered, nor deserved his devotion.

"The darkness was so thick and heavy that you could feel it weighing on the body. The scattered torches that he ordered lit an hour ago had done little to relieve the pitch-blackness and the consternation associated with it. No rain. No eclipse. No dense cloud cover. No fog. Just unexplained impenetrable darkness.

"And now, adding to the darkness, for some reason known only to the gods, if in fact they did exist, the wind began to blow from a direction opposite that of the movement of the darkness. Sometime he had never experienced before.

"As he stood with his back to the wind, he wondered how he ever ended up in such an intractable region of Rome's eastern provinces? He had moved up through the ranks of legionnaires, accompanying Tiberius on his conquests in Gaul and Armenia, until finally he had achieved the rank of centurion—commander over 100 of the Emperor's finest and bravest.

The Search

"Although it was true that he had seen enough war to last a lifetime, and that he had spent enough time on the battlefield to more than justify his transfer to a non-war zone, he had not envisioned that he would spend the last years of his military career in the eastern province of Judaea, serving as nursemaid to a cantankerous breed of religiously obnoxious separatists. But, here he was, commanding the guard who had been dispatched by Pilate, Procurator of the province of Judaea, to escort a group of prisoners, probably close to 50 in all, to the garbage dump of Gehenna, the valley where the Roman authorities crucified those who had been found guilty of sedition against Imperial Rome, and to oversee their execution. How degrading! Yet, if for the good and the welfare of Rome, then nothing is degrading. Not even this—this watch commanding over a bunch of more dead than alive, felons!

"As the wind continued to blow, he turned to look at the broken and bloody mass of torn flesh that was once a man, hanging by iron spikes, that had been driven through his wrists, from the wooden cross member. The hanging man was one of five or so who were close enough that he could hear their screams and groans of agony, even over the noise of the bustling wind.

"The criminals had been crucified in a half moon arrangement in five rows. In the first row was crucified three. In the next row, arranged in a half-circle around and behind the first three, about six or eight feet behind the first ones, was crucified seven. In the third semi-circle arched row were crucified 10. The fourth had 13 and the last row had 17. This semi-circle, half-moon, design for capital punishment was typical for those who had been condemned for treason for at least as long as he had been in the army.

"The centurion had taken a position near the middle of the third arched row of the crucified convicts, directly in front of one who had been accused, according to the indictment hanging above his head, of claiming to be a king of the Jews. There he waited impatiently for sundown, when he was allowed to leave that destitute valley of death, reeking from the stench of rotting and burning garbage, rotting flesh, clotted blood, and body waste, and consign those human vermin to the dogs, vultures, and other starving scavengers who hasten the miserable deaths of the criminals by feasting on their decadent carcasses.

"Watching the man on the cross out of the corner of one eye and the small group of mostly women who were standing just outside of the first arched row of crucified criminals out of the corner of his other eye, he became slightly perplexed.

"He had heard of this man, this Jesus, the one who had been indicted as a king of the Jews, off and on over the past two years, since his transfer from the Galilee in the north to Judaea, and for about two years before that when he was stationed in the Galilee. But all that he had heard about him was either good or it was something that he had done or said to the Jewish religious leaders and they spoke about him with contempt. Of course, since he held the Jewish religious with little regard, their insults of Jesus carried little weight with him.

"While he was in the Galilee, he had heard stories about Jesus performing miraculous acts and tales about him controlling the weather. He had heard of his befriending Romans and that he seemed to support the Jews' submission to Rome. He had even heard stories that suggested that he could have even been a Roman citizen by adoption, that many of his teachings were rooted in and founded upon well-known Roman history, Roman philosophy, and Roman customs, and that he used Roman law as if he had been trained as a Roman lawyer.

"That he had not only had a mysterious life but also a mysterious birth; that his birth was known to and acknowledged by Augustus; and that as an adult man he was known in the house of Tiberius, with some even suggesting that he was that Theophus of Tiberius. Others claimed that he was a direct descendant of the ancient Jewish king, David, and that if not a god or part-god; he was at the very least a servant of a god. Of course, to one who did not believe in the gods, such claims meant essentially, nothing. Nevertheless, all of these stories and tales were of little consequence now, for he had been indicted for treason against Rome—a crime punishable by the most cruel and extreme of all deaths: crucifixion.

"Although the sun was totally obstructed by the darkness, he surmised that the time was probably approaching the ninth hour, just three hours short of the time he could leave the valley and go back to his depot and try to forget about the horror of the spectacle of which he had had an unenthusiastic part.

"As he longed for the time to pass by more quickly, he heard the man on the cross groan from deep within— a groan that notified all who heard it that all hope had vanished and hopelessness and despair had taken up residence.

"He turned to look at the naked mass of festering flesh and torn muscle hanging in ribbons from a partially exposed endoskeleton, out of whom had emanated the deep despondent moan. As he did, he saw the quasi-man push against the spikes nailed through his feet, with all of his available strength in order to exhale just enough of the contaminated air that was poisoning his body so that he could utter a few words. With all the strength that he could muster, which considering the circumstances was not much, he cried out in a language that was unfamiliar to the centurion, *"Eli, Eli, lama, sabach tha-ni?"* Although the noise of the blowing wind almost drowned out his cry, it was loud enough for the few who were near to hear.

"Some standing in front of the semi-circle scene of execution began to mock him and mock his anguished cry, while others felt that perhaps he wanted something to drink. The centurion didn't know what to think. And it really didn't matter. He was obviously guilty or else Pilate would not have condemned him. But he still could not help but wonder what this man had done in order to be found guilty of treason against Imperial Rome?

"He stopped a man from approaching the cross, who had dipped a sponge into a pot of bitter wine vinegar intent upon offering it to Jesus. But, as he glanced at the bloody mass hanging on the cross, he thought, 'What difference does it make now?' So he allowed the man to lift the vinegar soaked sponge to Jesus' lips. He didn't watch to see if Jesus had the strength to drink it or not; but, probably not.

"Afterwards, the man returned to where he had been standing and was jeered for offering the vinegar to Jesus. Disgusted at their total lack of empathy, the centurion roughly ordered the few who were mocking to move along and to remove themselves out of ear shot range. He then returned to his position in front of the cross and again turned his back to the penetrating wind.

"How utterly sadistic? What's wrong with these people? These Jews? Even when a man is dying, and it is most definite that he will die, they are not satisfied. They still wanted to jeer and mock. Why? He did not understand that type of resentment and those depths of disdain. It seemed as if everyone in Jerusalem hated this man, this Jesus. He had even been mocked and ridiculed by other criminals and those around him who had been crucified with him. In fact, the only one who seemed to care enough about him to defend him was a malefactor, a homosexual prostitute who had killed his Roman citizen lover while in the midst of their perverted act, who had been crucified next to him. Jesus had spoken kind words to the man after he defended him; words whose meaning the centurion really did not understand, nor did he try or want to understand.

"He recalled that when he was stationed in the Galilee that he had heard that this Jesus had hundreds and thousands who followed him and gathered around him to hear his message of unconditional love and tolerance. In fact, he remembered that he had to on two different occasions, when there had gathered so many people to hear and to be ministered by Jesus, send a sorti to ensure the peace. Fortunately, there was no need for the precaution, for Jesus seemed to have the ability to control the crowds, regardless of the size, to whom he ministered. But, with the never-ending rebellious atmosphere for which the Galilee was notoriously known, the centurion could not be too sure of anything, especially when it involved large gatherings.

"But now, on the day of his crucifixion, the day that he needed his friends more than any other time in his life, there were only a small handful—a man, it was rumored that the man was either Jesus' brother or one of his followers, and a few women, one was obviously his mother—who paid their respects to him.

"Where were all of his friends and followers? All of those to whom he ministered? Where are those who thought of him as their deliverer or king? And what about his family? Not even they? He seemed to have gotten plenty of contemptuous attention from the Jewish religious leaders, especially during the first two or three hours after his crucifixion, before the darkness began to creep in. How is it that they seemed to have the time and made the effort to come to this place and scoff at him, but, his friends and family could not even make an appearance to show their love and support of him?

"As the centurion was trying unsuccessfully to mentally justify the lack of support from Jesus' friends and family, he heard a stirring coming from the direction of the cross. He turned around and looked at Jesus just as he was trying with all of his strength to again, as he had done on a few other occasions, push against the spikes in his feet in order to lift his tattered body enough to exhale and attempt to speak.

"Jesus finally succeeded in lifting his body enough to again speak, or more realistically, what sounded to the centurion to be more like a deep and forced groan, rather than any words that could have been understood or distinguished. Although it was probably as loud as Jesus could confabulate, the groan or words, whatever it was the centurion could not tell, was barely audible over the sound of the blowing wind. And with that, Jesus gave a last short gasp, and then dropped his head against his chest. He was dead.

"At the exact moment of death, the centurion thought he felt a strange jolt originating from deep inside the earth. But, he quickly dismissed it as being nothing more than his imagination.

"The centurion couldn't believe Jesus was dead. It usually took a week or more for victims of crucifixion to die, but Jesus had died in just over six hours from the time he had been crucified.

"Suddenly, as he was about to reach out and place his hand on the pulse in Jesus' foot to assure himself that Jesus was really dead, he felt the earth begin to again move and to shake and rumble under him. This time it was not his imagination. It was real. The ground split open in numerous places and began to vent columns of smoke and intense heat. Moments later, huge boulders began to be ripped from the surrounding rock cliffs and came thundering down the steep rock walls, smashing to the ground in the valley below. Lightning streaked from one end of the pitch-black, yet, cloudless sky, to the other, accompanied by continuous thunder crashes so intense that one would think that the entire earth was breaking apart as they rolled down through the valley.

"Never in his entire life had he witnessed such action by the forces of nature. It was immediate. It was powerful and all consuming, and although it only lasted a few minutes, it seemed to him like the destruction went on for hours.

"He had witnessed earthquakes before as well as deafening thunder, lightning, and the ground splitting open, but never all at once and never with such intensity. And especially not in what appeared to be in response to the death of a mere man who had been condemned for sedition.

"Although the mythology that he had been taught as a child was full of how the forces of nature reacted to various events orchestrated by the gods, or how nature mourned and reacted with violence at the death of this or that god-man or a particular mortal that was part god and who was beloved by a particular god or goddess, but those were all myths. They were stories. Fables meant to entertain and to inspire. They were not meant to be believed, literally. Why would nature care what happened to a mortal? And even if it did care, why would it react in such a devastating way? Maybe it was coincidence? Maybe this destruction was not nature's reaction to the death of Jesus? Maybe it just happened that way? Maybe it was just chance that the earth quaked and responded with such defoliation the instant that Jesus died? Maybe it was all just an unplanned random occurrence?

"But, what if it wasn't? What if all of this was somehow connected to Jesus? What if nature was really reacting to his death? What if the earth and all of nature was weeping because a god had just been killed? And not only killed, but killed by Romans? Romans under his supervision?

"While keeping one eye on the debris falling around him, ready to shield himself from harm if it became necessary, he began to closely study the mass of torn and broken bloody flesh hanging from the cross, that had just moments before gasp his last breath.

"Who was he? Who was this man who did good, yet suffered such a horrible death? Who had thousands of followers, but none so dedicated that they stood by him during his most trying moments? Who was this man who had the character of a noble Roman, but yet he was a Jew? Who seemed to be respected more by Romans than by his own countrymen, yet who suffered death as an enemy of Rome.

" So many paradoxes. So must inconsistency. Too many dilemmas, questions, and ambiguities. Who was he? What was he? Certainly he was a righteous man?

The Search

But could he have been more than mere man? Could it be that the stories of gods and goddesses that he learned and believed as a child, but which he had chosen to reject as an adult, were true after all? Or at least partially true? Could it be that a god could have birthed a mortal? Or that a man could have been part god? Could gods and goddesses actually beget offspring? Could a god actually have a son, who could live as a mortal on earth, and who was recognized as deity by all of the forces of nature? But, if a god or a son of a god, or a man who is part god, would he be able to be killed? And if so, how do mortals kill immortals or half immortals? Why would a god allow his god turned mortal son to be killed by mortals? Who was this man, if in fact he was a man? Or who was this god who could be killed by mortals? Or son of god who was allowed by a god to be killed? What god would allow that? Which one of the many gods that he learned about as a child would allow such a thing? Maybe it was a god that he had not learned about? Maybe a Greek god, a Persian god, an Egyptian god, or a Celtic god? Since this Jesus was a Jewish rabboni, maybe the god who sacrificed his son was the God of the Jews? That would make the most sense, if in fact he were a god or the offspring of a god, or the offspring of the God of the Jews.

"Finally after what seemed to be forever, the forces of nature began to calm down and the darkness began to gradually loosen its deathly hold. But, the centurion hardly noticed. He was preoccupied. He wanted to know why? What? And who? How could this man who was so influenced by Rome, become an enemy of Rome?

"He was still standing at the foot of the cross upon which Jesus hung, wondering and thinking, two hours later. By then, all of the darkness had vanished and the earth's quaking had moderated to calm. He was still there wondering, evaluating, and trying to figure it all out, when just before sundown some high ranking officials came with orders signed by Pilate that allowed them to take the body of Jesus off of the cross and to bury it.

As they carried the linen wrapped body of Jesus away, the centurion made one last walk through the place of execution in the valley of Gehenna to ensure that all was secure, before walking back to his depot in the Antonia fortress. As he walked, he convinced himself that truly this man was not only a righteous man, but that he also must be a god or at least the son of a god and probably the Son of God—the god of the Jews.

"He didn't sleep much that night, nor for many nights thereafter, for after all, he had supervised the crucifixion and the death of he who was a divine Jew; yet, who was very much Roman in style, actions, behavior, demeanor, and fraternization: a divine Roman Jew."

When Dr. Link finished, we all sat in complete silence for a few minutes reflecting on the mental images that he has just painted for us.

Finally, he invited us to open our eyes. "Although this story is of my own fabrication, it very well could have been true.

"In fact, if we use the Gospels as our primary source of a record of the life and death of Jesus, the story follows those narratives very closely."

"But is there more to the life of Jesus than what's recorded in the four Gospels of the New Testament?" Dr. Link asked as an introduction to the remainder of his lecture.

Dr. Ron Charles

The rest of his lecture seemed to center around the validity of what Jesus said—whether he *really said* what the Gospels recorded that he said or the authors of the Gospels instead wrote what Jesus *probably would have, or should have, said* and then over the centuries what was written by these authors has been adopted by the Church as truth and as the actual words of Jesus.

After his fascinating introductory imaginative story, I was excited about hearing the rest of Dr. Link's lecture. Maybe I expected too much for I came away with more questions than answers and more disappointment than contentment.

Even though the lecture was not what I expected, it did succeed in sparking a hitherto untapped interest in discovering the historical truth regarding the life of Jesus—truth that authenticated the Gospel records. Thus began my concentrated search for historical Jesus. A search that has to date lasted for 33 years and has taken me to five continents.

Over the years, I have discovered multiplied thousands of books, documents, and manuscripts that endorse the established traditional viewpoint of Jesus' life. But few of these are harmonious with historical fact.

For the most part, the majority of these conventional sources seemed to agree on several basic points regarding the life of Jesus—points that traditional Christianity established as foundational centuries ago, regardless of whether or not historical fact confirmed the truth of the established foundational points. These traditional points are:

- Jesus was a Jew. He had a Jewish father and mother, Jewish family, and Jewish friends.
- The Jewish people have been one of the most hated and persecuted people throughout world history.
- The events surrounding Jesus' birth are mysterious in the least and miraculous at most.
- Jesus was a Galilean Jew who became a teacher. Judaean Jews hated Galilean Jews.
- Jesus was a Roman subject who spent most of his life in the Roman state of the Galilee, in the Roman province of Syria.
- No known writings of Jesus have survived.
- Jesus was totally free from prejudice and bigotry, yet both were instrumental in his death.
- Although Jesus preached love and showed compassion, neither was available to him during the final days of his life.
- Jesus died by crucifixion (one of the most painful of all deaths) as an enemy of Rome, at the hands of Roman officials, through the instigation of Jewish religious officials.
- All those whom Jesus considered his friends and devoted followers, abandoned him.
- Jesus' grave was empty when it was investigated three days after his death, testifying to the accuracy of his own prophecy that he would rise from the dead.

The Search

- One out of every three people who live on the earth today honor him and claim to follow him.
- The Jesus of the 1st century Galilee (a Roman subject) seemed to be quite different from the Jesus whom came to be interpreted through the Christian ideology, theology, creeds, presumptions, liturgy, art, poetry and prose, and hymnody of the past 2,000 years (a Jesus totally devoid of Roman influence).

Even though these traditional foundational points are fundamental to the Christian faith and are for the most part non-argumentative with regards to doctrinal truth, they cannot pretend to be historical truth. Only substantiated verity can function as genuine truth.

In reviewing documentation written about the 1st century Roman Mare Nostrum East occupation period and how that occupation related to the life and ministry of Jesus, it seems that either the material was written about Rome or from a Roman perspective or about Jesus and his deeds and sayings, with little and no reference to his Greco-Roman surroundings or how Imperial Rome influenced what he said or did.

On the surface there seemed to be very little written that tied the two—the Greco-Rome world and Jesus—together. However, eventually I began to recognize that the assumption was nothing more than a façade used to cloak the fact that Jesus was in fact greatly influenced by his surroundings.

Jesus was both a loyal Galilean Jew as well as a loyal Roman subject. He respected, honored, and sought to safeguard the Law of Moses and the rituals and traditions associated with historical Judaism, but, he also respected and honored the Roman authorities under whose rule he was born and to whom he was subject. And although many of Jesus' followers were Jewish and his authority to teach in the name of God was granted him by the Jewish religious hierarchy, he also had Roman followers which motivated him to use Roman history and philosophy to emphasis points in his teachings and to use his relationship with Roman officials to enhance his ministry. *Benjamites*

The Gospels—Matthew, Mark, Luke, and John in the New Testament of the Bible—are quite insistent that Jesus was more than just a Jewish rabboni who restricted his ministry and teachings to the descendants of Abraham, Moses, and David. Nevertheless, present day thinking implies, irrespective of what the Gospels shows and implies, that Jesus ministered primarily to Jewish peasants and only occasionally did he come in contact with non-Jews.

In today's Christian society, although it is customarily known and accepted that the Romans were ultimately responsible for Jesus' death, beyond that, seldom is Rome or Roman cultural predominance depicted as having even the slightest influence upon the life and ministry of Jesus. Nothing could be further from the truth, for not only are the Gospels a vivid portrayal of Jesus' life as a subject of Imperial Rome, but dozens of non-biblical sources document and authenticate this truth of the Gospel records.

Over the centuries, a great injustice had been propagated with regard to Jesus and his ministry—an injustice that has effectively eliminated a primary factor

(Jesus' Greco-Roman surroundings) that influenced most of the true life and ministry of Jesus. Although Jesus may not have been a Roman citizen by birth in the strictest sense of the word, he was most certainly a loyal and honored (until just immediately before his death) Roman subject, who used that renown for his benefit and the benefit of the ministry in which he was involved.

However, before truth can be authenticated, it first must be resolved how truth can and must be determined.

That resoluteness I found in John's Gospel of the Bible, chapter 18, verse 37. The subject was Jesus' interrogation by Pilate immediately preceding his crucifixion. "T*hat I should bear witness of the truth. Everyone that is of the truth hearth my voice. Pilate saith unto him, What is truth?"*

Roman law would set an accused man free if he had two witnesses to swear to his innocence. But, just like two truthful witnesses could set a man free, so two witnesses who agreed could guarantee a verdict of guilt and three, a sentence of death. Two witnesses could condemn or two could set free. In the ancient Jewish law, two witnesses, confirming the others' testimony, were needed before the court considered the testimony to be truthful. The same system was true for Hindu law at that time, as well as Chinese law, Parthian law, Greek law, Egyptian law, and Arabic law. In all of the courts of law of the most influential governments in existence at the time of Jesus' birth, life, and ministry, truth was established *"in the mouth of two or three witnesses"*(2 Corinthians 13:1).

Therefore, in order for truth to be established, at least two records must confirm one another. In the case of historical documentation, at least two records from the same time period must confirm one another, or if they are from different time periods, a less ancient document must authenticate a more ancient document.

The primary texts that record the life and ministry of Jesus are the four narrative Gospels of Matthew, Mark, Luke, and John. For more than a millennium and a half these Gospel records have been accepted as authentic and undeniable truth by countless millions. However, these Gospel accounts, although separate records which at times record separate and different events, cannot be used as four different authenticating documents. They can only be used as one authenticating document and their separate and individual records of the birth, life, ministry, death, and resurrection of Jesus are one source—only one. Although an event may have been recorded in more than one of the Gospels, still they serve as *only one* witness to the events.

In order for truth to be established, there has to be at least one other source confirming the Gospels' record. So, because the first witness is the Gospels, then the events recorded in the Gospels are the events that must be challenged as truth. In other words, if an event, lesson, sermon, miracle, command, or a mandate is not recorded in the Gospels, it should not be evaluated or scrutinized as truth, since the Gospels are the first witnesses to the truth. If it is recorded in the Gospels, then a search must be conducted to find a second witness, thus fulfilling the legal requirements that established truth at that time in history. If it were not recorded in the Gospels, no further consideration needed to be entertained.

II

THE GOSPELS

My initial research priority regarding the Gospels was directed at trying to find evidence that would either confirm the accepted tradition of who authored the Gospels or identify the true authors of the four Gospels (I did not evaluate the *Gospel of Thomas* or any of the other writings that had been rejected as canon). Very early in my efforts, much to my surprise and somewhat to my unnerving because of a lifetime of traditional teachings, I discovered that it was very doubtful that the Gospels were written by the ones whose name the individual Gospel records bare—perhaps with the exception of the *Gospel According to Luke*.

My first challenge was to investigate *The Gospel According to St. Mark*, probably the earliest of the four Gospels and the text from which both the authors of Matthew and Luke probably got a major part of their information. I found out that the earliest fragments of this Gospel, written predominantly in Greek with some passages written in a Greek/Syriac/Chaldean combination, dated back to perhaps as early as AD 60 but most certainly to AD 75 and was found near Luxor, Egypt in 1961. This Gospel was not only the first of the four to have been written, but it was the one that seemed to be the most chronologically accurate with regard to objective history and how history related to the ministry of Jesus. However, contrary to popular belief, I found that the John Mark who *Acts of the Apostles* says was associated with Paul for a time most likely *did not* write the Gospel that bears the name of Mark.

In AD 130 Papias, the Bishop of Hierapolis, claimed that a John Mark of Canatha had written the Gospel in AD 60, using information that he had received from James, the brother of Jesus, the apostle Peter, and Barnabas. But, based on information that I found at the University of Texas library, it seemed to me that James, the brother of Jesus, and the first acknowledged leader of the sect of the Nazarenes in Jerusalem, who later called themselves "Christians," (the group in Jerusalem was lead by James and a group in Antioch was led by Paul and Peter), was the most likely candidate to have authored this Gospel. It seems that James, less than 15 years after Jesus' death and resurrection, sought first to preserve a permanent record of Jesus' ministry. Second, he sought to use such a record to help and to encourage the newly established Nazarene convert groups, many of whom were former Jews, scattered throughout Judaea. He wrote (using his own personal knowledge as well as information told to him by the apostle Andrew) a "rough outline draft" of the ministry of Jesus. This "rough sketch" was then distributed to all of the Nazarene groups scattered throughout the Roman province of Judaea, with a promise from James that he would be sending a more detailed record of the life and ministry of Jesus as soon as he had written it.

I found that the person to whom James had entrusted the delivery of this outline was a young Greek associate by the name of either Mark, John Mark, or Mark son of John. This rough sketch became known as *A Record of the Service of Jesus the Christ as Written by James, a disciple whom Jesus loved, and Delivered by Mark, a*

Brother and Fellow-Laborer. Before James had the opportunity to write a more detailed record of the life and ministry of Jesus, he was martyred. Hence, the only accurate and authentic eyewitness account of the ministry of Jesus by an undeniably reliable and credible source was in the form of a "rough outline draft" that had most likely been written by James, the brother of Jesus, and had been delivered by an associate of James, a man by the name of Mark.

Within ten years of James' death, his outline document had become known as *The Gospel of Jesus, Written by James, Delivered by Mark*. Within 20 years of his death, the document had come to be called *The Gospel of Jesus Delivered by Mark*. This quickly evolved into *The Gospel Delivered by Mark* and finally, by the end of the 2nd century, into *The Gospel According to Mark*.

Unfortunately, by that time at least one-fourth of James' original outline sketch had been lost. What remained was three-fourths of the original outline text. So, in essence, although Mark was the first Gospel written, it is not, nor was it ever intended to be, a detailed record of Jesus' ministry. Instead, it was intended to be a very rough and a very incomplete record of Jesus' ministry to "tide the Nazarene groups over" until a more detailed record could be compiled and completed by James, the brother of Jesus. Nevertheless, it became the primary reference for the writing of two (Matthew and Luke) of the other three Gospels. Although there can be a convincing argument made in favor of the authors of Matthew and Luke's use of at least one other common source, perhaps a source that has been identified as *Q* from the German *Quelle*, meaning *source*, (which may have been a single document or many different documents), or some other common source that has not yet come to light, Mark's Gospel seems to have been the main source from which the authors received much of their information.

I next investigated *The Gospel According to St. Matthew*. This Gospel seems to have originated at approximately the same time or slightly after Titus, the Roman general, laid siege to the city of Jerusalem and destroyed the Jewish Temple: Herod's Temple. This Gospel may have been the second Gospel written, or it could have been the third. The earliest Greek/Latin fragments of *The Gospel According to Matthew*, dating from as early as AD 140, were discovered in Romania in 1940, and are now housed at the Middle Eastern Museum in Vienna. Although the author of the Gospel is traditionally believed to have been Matthew, commonly identified with Levi, the former tax collector and apostle of Jesus, this belief was not proposed until the middle of the 2nd century, when Cedus, the Bishop of Berea, claimed that an angel had appeared to him and told him that Matthew, the apostle, was the author of the Gospel. More probable is that the second (or third) Gospel was written by a late 1st century or early 2nd century Jewish convert to Christianity, perhaps even an early church leader (two early Saxon texts now housed at Sunderland University in Sunderland, England, claim that a 2nd century disciple of Justin Martyr, named Isador, was the author of the *Gospel of Matthew*). But, whoever was the author, I am convinced that he must have had a remarkable knowledge of 1st century BC through 1st century AD Jewish history, manners, and customs; and although the author did not seek to place the events of Jesus' life and ministry in chronological order, he did preserve the primary teachings, character, and purposes of his ministry. Because the Christians were at that time being martyred by the hundreds, the author probably felt that a permanent record should be made for the purpose of preserving the character of Jesus' ministry, just in case all believers in him were exterminated. For this reason, it is supposed by some biblical historians that this Gospel was the Gospel that was generally read to an assembly of early believers when they gathered for/to worship.

I next investigated the author of *The Gospel According to St. Luke.* I discovered that this Gospel was either the second or the third Gospel to have been written. The earliest fragments of this Gospel, written in Greek, date back to about AD 150. They were discovered in an almost inaccessible cave near Oxyrhynchus in Egypt in 1897. Another fragment of the Gospel dating from AD 180 was found in Bulgaria, near the Macedonian border in 1932. It is now housed in the Rylands Library Museum in Manchester, England. *The Gospel According to St. Luke* was probably written about 20 to 30 years after the death of Paul. But, since the exact year that Paul was martyred is not known, the year in which Luke's Gospel was written can't be determined. Tradition says that besides the *Acts of the Apostles*, Luke, the physician, a companion of Paul, authored Luke's Gospel. Some of the more "questionable" information I found caused me to speculate that if Luke was in truth the author of the Gospel, he probably had help from at least one of his disciples, perhaps one Cedes of Antioch, a disciple who compiled Luke's information from personal interviews. I also think that along with Mark's Gospel, Luke might have drawn information originally set down by either the apostle Andrew or the apostle Philip. Luke himself never gives himself credit for writing the Gospel, even though he had that opportunity when in the introduction to the Gospel, the author dedicates the writing to His Excellency Theophilus, and says that his document was just one of many that have been produced since the time of Jesus' ministry that attempted to record the events of his life. Evidence refuting this tradition is scarce, so I have tentatively chosen to accept Luke as the author. Luke's Gospel is much more technical in content than any of the other three Gospels. It too seemed to be greatly lacking chronologically, although Luke did objectively attempt to weave the life and ministry of Jesus into Roman history.

The author of the fourth and final Gospel that I evaluated was also the last Gospel to have been written: The *Gospel According to St. John*. The earliest fragments of this Gospel, discovered in Egypt in 1935, seem to be the famous Papyrus Bodmer II, written in Greek. Originally, it was thought that the fragments dated back to AD 115, but in 1965 papyologists at the University of Hamburg determined that the fragments had not been written before the mid-3rd century, and most probably in the 5th century. Today these fragments are on display at the Library of Magdalene College in Israel. I also found that there are some theologians who believe that the John Rylands papyrus, dating from about AD 125, contains passages that seem to correspond to passages found in John's Gospel. However, although I do not claim to be an expert in the elucidation of ancient manuscripts, it seemed to me that the form of writing used by the author of the John Rylands papyrus was more comparable to Mark's Gospel.

In researching John's Gospel, I discovered that up until the time of the Council of Bishops held in Toledo, Spain, in AD 1215, it was generally believed by the Christian world that John, the apostle of Jesus, had been killed along with his brother, James, by Herod Agrippa in AD 44. It was at this 1215 Council of Bishops that John was proclaimed to have lived until AD 104; that he had been boiled in oil in AD 95 during the widespread persecution of Christians under Domitian; that he had survived the ordeal only to be exiled to the Isle of Pathmos, a 1st century Roman penal colony located in the Aegean Sea; and that he died of natural causes at the age of either 100 or 104, although no evidence had ever been found to justify the council's proclamations concerning John. It was also at this Council that John "became" the author of the *Gospel According to John, The Revelation,* and the *I, II, and III Epistles of John.* Throughout the middle Ages, controversy raged over who was the actual author of these writings. While most Protestants during and after the 16th century believed that John was killed, along with his brother, James, by Herod Agrippa and that the writings in question were actually written by three different authors, the Catholic Church held to the belief that John, the apostle of Jesus, was the author of all five writings. So widespread was this Protestant belief, that John Foxe wrote in his March 1563 publication, *Actes and Monuments of These Latter and Perillous Days,* "...without a doubt, both James and John were beheaded by Herod Agrippa in AD 44." A 4th century Gnostic manuscript entitled, *The Fourth Gospel,* claims that both *The Gospel According to John* and *The Revelation*, were written in the middle 2nd century by John Presbyter (Prester John), a supposed contemporary of Polycarp, Ignatius, and Papias; if in fact there was such a person as John Presbyter (Prester John), because there is considerable evidence to justify questioning whether John Presbyter ever existed. (During the Middle Ages it was strongly believed that this John Presbyter [Prester John] really did exist and that he was a man worthy of the highest honor and esteem, and that the epistles of *I, II, and III John* were written at the beginning of the 3rd century by a John of Tarentum, a supposed believer in this same John Presbyter [Prester John]).

A Coptic manuscript, found near Cairo in the late 19th century, dating from the 8th century, entitled, *The Gospels of the Canon,* claims that James, the brother of Jesus, was not only the author of the *Gospel According to Mark* but that he also authored *The Epistle to the Hebrews,* and the last three-quarters (which would be the last 17 chapters) of *The Revelation.* The document also attributed the authorship of the *Gospel According to John* and the first portion of *The Revelation*—the first four chapters—to a late 2nd century bishop by the name of John of Illyricum, Bishop of Dyrrhachium, who had presumably dictated the works to a scribe by the name of Nathan of Caesarea, who recorded the dictation as two separate documents. John of Illyricum claimed to have read the actual personal records of James, the brother of Jesus, Bishop of Jerusalem, and that much of his account was based on those records. Some Coptic historians believe that this Bishop of Dyrrhachium very well could have been the actual figure from whose real life and exploits the stories of the legendary John Presbyter evolved.

A 5th century Syriac manuscript attributes authorship for *I, II,* and *III John* to John of Patmos, a disciple of John, the apostle of Jesus, some 20 years after the death of John by order of Herod Agrippa.

Empress Eudoxia, wife of the Emperor of the Roman East, Arcadius, claimed that John Chrysostom, bishop of Constantinople from AD 398 to 403, with whom the Empress had a continual and on-going conflict, was the author of both *The*

Gospel According to John and *I, II, and III John,* as well as the first quarter of *The Revelation.* She further claimed that the latter three-quarters of *The Revelation* had been written at an earlier date than the first quarter; and that Gregory of Nyssa, senior adviser to Emperor Theodosius, had written these latter three-quarters in about AD 382.

After investigating the authorship of the Gospels, concluding that the authorship of the Gospels was a mystery that might never be resolved, I began to dive headlong into dissecting the Gospels in order to determine what was recorded with regards to how Greco-Rome culture and society influenced Jesus, and searching for non-biblical texts that would serve to confirm the authenticity of the Gospel accounts.

Dr. Ron Charles

III
ESSENTIAL GOLDEN NUGGETS

Although I could have spent the rest of my life studying nothing but the Gospels, I at length felt confident enough in my knowledge of the Gospels that I wanted to begin my non-Gospel research. So, adopting the premise that the Gospels were the unchallenged truth concerning the life and ministry of Jesus, and that the truth as recorded in the Gospels was uncompromising and non-argumentative, and that they and they alone are the true and factual sources to which all other non-Gospel sources must be compared, I expanded my search for historical Jesus to include non-biblical texts.

As my journey progressed and accelerated from "baby step" insecurity to all-out unrestrained and uninhibited research, I discovered along the way two golden nuggets of information and advice that have proven to be invaluable and indispensable over the years. It is around the nucleus of these two golden nuggets of advice and information that my research has been fashioned, molded, and formed.

The first golden nugget came in the form of some advice given to me by the most unlikely source; a man named Francis LeBeaux from Boulogue, France.

I remember that I was dead tired when I arrived in Boulogue very late in the afternoon, just as the sun was setting, that early March day. I just wanted to rent a room someplace, anyplace, as soon as possible and go to sleep. The first place I came across was on the waterfront. It was a small inn named *Jean's*.

The inn sat between the boardwalk of the waterfront and a narrow cobblestone street that ran in front of the inn. The inn itself was more like an ancient pub than an inn, although it did have four rooms upstairs that they rented to over-night guests. The inn was constructed of stone with a part-tile and part-timber roof.

Too tired to care what it looked like, I checked in for the night.

The first floor of the old inn was one big open room furnished with three long, maybe 15 to 20 feet long, thick wooden tables, each with bench seats made of split logs running the entire length of the table. They looked to be at least two hundred years old. A huge fireplace with a roaring fire that was kept blazing around the clock, was the only heat in the entire building (in early Spring, no heat was needed during the day, so by early to mid-afternoon, the fire made it uncomfortably warm inside; however, it did get chilly at night, so after nightfall the warmth of the fire felt delightful). A number of pots and kettles hanging in or near the fireplace told me that the fireplace was also used for cooking. The only light for the big room was supplied by two small light bulbs hanging from single wires that dropped from the high ceiling and a few coal oil lamps that were scattered around. There was no bar or kitchen. Food was cooked in the open fireplace so all the guests and patrons could see its preparation and other than water and thick black coffee that had been cooking all day over the open fire, there was nothing to drink but heavy ale, cheap wine, or watered-down rum that was stored in huge wooden barrels lining the back wall.

The Search

Open wooden stairs led from the main room to a wooden balcony that ran across the back wall of the inn, under which the barrels of ale, wine, and rum were stored. The four rental rooms exited onto the balcony. Each room had a small window that looked out over the wharf dock.

The beds were hand hewn heavy wood construction that were at least two hundred years old with goose-down feather mattresses topped by thick, centuries-old hand made quilts, the kind for which Americans would have paid hundreds of dollars to own.

The rooms had no electricity and no plumbing; two or three candles and a coal oil lamp in each room supplied the only light. There were no showers; however, the owner supplied each room with fresh water daily and brought a bucket of hot water with an ample supply of towels every morning. The room rented for the equivalent of $5 per night; that included a nightly supper and the privilege of listening to exciting tales of pirates, smugglers, highwaymen, and swashbuckling adventurers by the inn's owner, Francis LeBeaux, till as late into the night as one dared. In fact Francis, who spoke a heavy accented form of broken English when the occasion demanded it, would talk all night if anyone wanted to listen.

On that evening, I was the only rental guest, although there were a few dining and drinking patrons who came and went throughout the early evening.

When I walked in, Francis welcomed me and told me that if I wanted a room for the night that I should take my stuff upstairs and take my pick of rooms. I did not have to sign in or give any personal information. As I was walking up the open stairs he shouted at me to come back down after I get settled in and have something to eat before turning in for the night. He was serving venison stew, roasted game bird (it looked like partridge or pheasant), and fish soup (I could have any of the three or all three if I wanted), bread, and my choice of drink or hot black coffee.

I thanked him and said that I would be back down to eat shortly. A few minutes later I walked back downstairs and joined three other men seated at one of the long tables. They were already eating. We greeted one another and Francis asked me what I wanted to eat. I had some of the venison stew and roasted bird and washed it down with a big mug full of thick and strong hot black coffee. I was about half finished with my meal when one of the men seated at the same table asked Francis to tell us a story.

As Francis was telling his stories, the entire atmosphere reeked with the memory of smugglers and pirates reminiscent of Jean Lafitte. At any moment I felt as if I would actually see pirates stumble through the doorway with pieces-of-eight in hand demanding a port of rum. Although I was dead tired, I quickly became transfixed as I listened to Francis' stories. After his second story, the three men bid us good night and left the inn, leaving Francis and me alone. I felt like I needed to get some sleep, but Francis was so interesting and so amiable that I could not break away. We ended up spending another two hours talking with one another before he encouraged me to call it a night and go back to my room and get some sleep. During that two-hour conversation Francis told me that the inn was built in 1680 and that it had remained in his family, serving as an inn continuously, since that time.

Francis was a big man, standing well over six feet and weighing 250 pounds or more. He was probably in his mid- to late-50s, had a heavy but trimmed; gray-streaked beard and long hair that reached mid-way to his shoulders. The hair had far more gray than its original dark brown color. Francis had a thunderous voice that had never been taught how to whisper. He lived alone; had never been married. "Never had dee time fo dee women," he told me.

Since I was the only rental guest, Francis treated me like royalty.

I decided to stay for a couple of extra days, so Francis served as my tour guide as we walked all over the little town, and all the while Francis told his non-stop fascinating stories. Those three days were some of the most intriguing and unforgettable that I have ever experienced. In essence, Francis was a 300-year throwback to the days of adventurers and heroes. He was truly a remarkable person; someone I will never forget.

On the second night, as we sat at one of the long tables eating roasted pork, I told him about my search for historical Jesus project. Francis was not a religious man and had not been inside of a church since he was a child, but he was interested in the project. I spent almost the entire evening telling him about my quest and acquainting him with the real personal Jesus, not necessarily the untouchable, impersonal catechism Jesus that he was introduced to as a child.

It was during this conversation that Francis gave me the advice that became one of those two golden nuggets around which I molded my research efforts. The advice was not earth shattering, theological, or philosophical, it was just a simple and friendly word of advice based on his personal knowledge of Europe, having lived in France his entire life. Nevertheless, it made such an impression upon me that it totally revolutionized my research methods, procedures, and strategy. After I asked Francis if he had any suggestions that he felt would help my efforts he told me that I needed to concentrate my research in the smaller towns or in the libraries or cathedrals that were not typical tourist attractions. He said that much of the information that I was looking for could be found in Europe, but that it would *never* be exposed to the general tourist public. He said that the church has made sure that the only documents or manuscripts that the tourist public will ever see are those that support the historical doctrines and the teachings of the church. All others are stored and preserved out of view of the tourists. They could probably be found, but not in the big cities or in the tourist areas. And if by chance some are to be found in the big cities they will not be on display. He told me to go to Reims, Nancy, Orleans, or even Avignon, in France, and the same types of towns in all the other countries of Europe, but that I needed to stay away from the big cities like Paris, London, Berlin, Madrid, and Vienna, unless I was going there just to visit or to be a tourist. "Wheen yo researcher," Francis told me as he gently padded my cheek, like a little boy, "yo must go to plas whir touris is not, or not so much."

The day I left the inn, Francis gave me a big bear hug when I told him good-bye, and then walked away to prevent me from seeing his tears. As he walked away, I knew without a doubt that I had made a friend for life; one that comes along only a few times in a person's lifetime.

Another golden nugget revealed itself not too long after my visit with Francis. However, this nugget wasn't advice, rather, it was the discovery that there had been multiplied dozens, if not hundreds, of non-biblical documents written about the life of Jesus, some dating from the earliest days of Christianity. So, knowing that they had existed at one time gave me hope that many probably still existed. They just needed to be located. This nugget of the knowledge that some of these documents probably still existed came to light the very first time I put into practice what Francis had advised, when I went to Reims, France to visit a church suggested to me by Francis.

The French countryside was enchanting with its early spring grass and rolling hills as I drove towards Reims. Upon arriving I checked into a little hostel across from the town's central parking lot, called the Carege House. It was just two blocks from St. Anne's Cathedral, the church where Francis had told me to begin my new research stratagem.

St. Anne's was originally the primary church of the 13th century Monastery of St. Anne. But by the 18th century the monastery had long since been abandoned and most of it had been torn down, leaving only the church and a couple of smaller buildings intact.

After checking in I walked down to the church. I was amazed at how well preserved the old church was. Obviously, the diocese had paid special attention to its care and upkeep.

Upon entering the church I first took a few minutes to wonder at the beautiful altar and massive architecture of the main cathedral, and then following a small sign that pointed the way to the manuscript library, I walked outside of the main adytum into a long hallway, just off the left side of the sanctum.

I walked all the way down the hallway to the back of the church before seeing another small sign that pointed the way down another hallway that led outside into an open courtyard. In the courtyard, another sign pointed the way to the manuscript library, which was located at the far end of the courtyard. The building that housed the manuscript library was all that remained of the original 13th century monastery.

The manuscript library was much smaller than I had anticipated; however, they did have a fairly impressive collection of letter manuscripts, ancient bound volumes, and leaves of manuscript texts.

When I walked into the library, I was surprised that no one asked to help me. In fact, the two male employees who were seated at an oval shaped desk, looked at me when I entered, quickly put their fingers to their lips signaling me to be quite, and then continued with whatever they were doing. Huge signs were located in conspicuous places that read in French, German and English: SILENCE—NO TALKING PERMITTED.

The manuscripts, text documents, and volumes were on display either on stands or under glass. Beside each display was a brief description written in both French and English, explaining the text's contents. I spent two hours just walking from one display to the other and studying the descriptions of the text or manuscript, before I began my research.

The library had a modern microfiche and film file as well as an old style card catalog. I chose to use the microfiche and film file.

After skimming through the film file for an hour or so, I concluded that although there were numerous texts on the subject of Jesus, few corresponded with truth as presented by the Gospels. Finally, I found a film of a document that looked interesting. It was a two hundred plus page bound, hieotike Latin text.

In reading through the notes that explained the history of the volume, I discovered that the text was the only remaining volume of a three-volume set that had been written by Alphonsus Liguori of Naples, the bishop of St. Agatha from 1762 to 1775, and the author of the noteworthy *Moral Theology*. The entire three-volume set was entitled *Testimonies of the Death and Resurrection of The Light*. The surviving volume was volume number one.

Alphonsus had founded the Order of the Redemptorists in November of 1732. It brought him a certain amount of local notoriety. But when he published his *Moral Theology* in 1748, his prestige catapulted to international status. Alphonsus prided himself in being a scholarly and well-learned educator. As such, he traveled all over Europe and the Middle East researching and collecting data from hundreds of documents and manuscripts. However, no one knew what he was researching or why. Because of his extensive travels, his order suffered extreme internal conflict for years, causing Alphonsus to sink into severe depression. In 1775 Pope Pius VI relieved him of his leadership and allowed him to retire to a private cell in Nocera to recover.

He retired with the huge amount of research data that he had collected over the years and remained there in total isolation and seclusion, except for occasional visits from his trusted aid, Francesco Alfedro (who had been loyal to Alphonsus since his [Francesco's] conversion from Judaism in 1756), until his death in 1787. Just days after Alphonsus died, Francesco died in the same cell; some say the death was self-inflicted. The bodies were not discovered until they were already well decomposed. It was not until after their deaths that it was discovered that during that time of isolation, Alphonsus had written, using the data that he had collected over the years, the contents of what became his three-volume testimonies set; although the pages were not bound until a year after his death when they were sent to Paris.

Apparently it took almost a year for the binding experts in Paris to bind the pages into volumes. Finally by mid-year 1789, the project was complete—just in time for the French Revolution.

The summer and fall of 1789 was a nightmare in Paris. There were riots in the streets. Shops were ransacked and burned, warehouses and storehouses were emptied, government buildings were looted and burned and churches and religious institutions were pillaged and destroyed. One of the victims of the revolutionary riots was the prestigious book binding shop, Rigaud le Grand, that had bound the writings of Alphonsus Ligouri. The volumes had not been delivered back to the abbot of St. Agatha, who had ordered the writings bound, because the abbot had not yet paid for the binding services. So, they were in storage at the shop when it was looted and destroyed by revolutionary rioters. All of the bound volumes in the shop were destroyed except this one volume of Alphonsus' and one written by Jean-Jacques Rousseau. They escaped only because the owner of the shop, Michael Prouse, was in the shop at the time of the looting. He escaped with his life and as he fled, he grabbed the two 'books' in an effort to save them. Prouse fled to the safety of Reims and there gave the books to the monks of St. Anne's for safekeeping. Michael never returned for the books, so the manuscript library at St. Anne's "inherited" them.

The Search

I felt that if the content of the volume were half as fascinating as the history behind the volume, it would be well worth the effort, regardless of its many pages, to take the time and research it thoroughly. As I read I took detailed notes on the document.

Alphonsus began his text by describing how he and Francesco had traveled all over Europe and the Middle East collecting valuable information to document his exposition. He concentrated on early Christian writings and Francesco concentrated on any surviving Jewish documents, including the early Talmuds and letters of instruction and teaching.

He then gave a justification for his infatuation in discovering any and all documents, especially from non-Christian writers, that would confirm the life, death, and the resurrection of Jesus.

He said that because the life, ministry and teachings, death, and resurrection of Jesus was of such importance to the world, he believed there had to be an unusually large amount of non-Christian records that related the events of his life. These records he suspected could be found in court records, letters, histories, legislative records, testimonials, and in the Talmuds and the teachings and testimonials of the Jews.

He reasoned that the Roman Empire at the time of Jesus' life, death, and resurrection was filled with debaters, historians, recorders, and writers, who wrote on any and all subjects brought before them. He also felt that because the Roman court records of that day were so carefully preserved there should be at least a mention of Jesus' life, trial, and execution in the court records.

In addition, he reasoned that the educated Jews of Jesus' time, were of the educated elite of the Roman Empire, and that they meticulously recorded even the slightest detail of any and all events, actions, or judgments that affected even the least influential citizens of Judaea or of the Galilee. These were preserved, many being adopted into and made a part of the Talmuds of Jerusalem, in the great library of the Sanhedrin in Jerusalem. But, most of those records, including the original writings that were absorbed into the Talmuds of Jerusalem, had up until that time (Alphonsus' time), never been found. What happened to the remainder that perhaps numbered into the hundreds (Alphonsus questioned)? He knew that some had been destroyed when the Sanhedrin library was burned. It was also common knowledge that the Jewish religious leaders of the first five centuries had systematically eliminated the name, actions, teachings, and basically, the memory of Jesus from their records, histories, and legislative records. However, not even these revised and edited records had been found.

Many of these records might also have been destroyed when the great libraries at Alexandria, Jerusalem, Rome, Ephesus, Antioch, and Constantinople were ransacked and burned. Pope Gregory IX had cartloads full of Talmuds and Jewish writings burned, and when Rome destroyed Jerusalem, anything and everything of material worth and educational value was taken to Rome. Yet, Alphonsus believed there should be some record among the non-Christians that documented the death and resurrection of Jesus.

Alphonsus wondered about the fate of the library of Serenus Samnaticus. It seems that in the 3rd century, Serenus Samnaticus had amassed a huge library of 1st,

2nd, and 3rd century Christian writings (tradition says that he possessed the actual court documents of the trial of Jesus and of Pilate's report of the trial to Tiberius), Jewish writings, Roman records, and histories from throughout the Empire. At his death in AD 236, he left over 62,000 volumes, out of an estimated 80,000, to his student, M. Antonius Africanus, the son of Gordianus the Great. The remainder were supposed to have been given to one of the teachers who tutored Serenus Samnaticus' children; a man whose name is known only as Proclemius. Nothing is known of the fortune or misfortune of the volumes given to Antonius Africanus or of Serenus Samnaticus' remaining volumes that were supposed to have been given to Proclemius.

Alphonsus went on for another two pages wondering and reasoning about the destiny and fate of numerous known library collections before he concluded that portion by making a list of "knowns." The list enabled him and Francesco to centralize their search efforts and to eliminate areas of research that were not relative.

In order to establish a historical non-Gospel link between the life of Jesus as recorded in the Gospels and that recorded in secular history, I listed Alphonsus' "knowns" in the exact order in which Alphonsus wrote them in his introduction.

He wrote, "It is known that:

+ In the great and ancient libraries of the Empire there were men known as *baalie suphoths*, or 'book-compilers.' These men would take manuscripts of the same or of various authors and bind them between cedar boards and clasp them with brass, copper, steel, gold, or silver clasps.

+ The Jewish rabbi and Pharisee doctor Pseudonymanus Joseph Ben Gorion not only compiled the works of Philo in AD 150, but he also compiled the legal records of the Sanhedrin from the time of Herod the Great until the sacking of Jerusalem in AD 70. These would perhaps have included the records of the ministry of Jesus, but certainly the trial and death of Jesus.

+ Another Jewish rabbi, Ekaba, compiled the writings of Josephus in the 2nd century. He was given the responsibility by the Jewish Council of Rabbonis of editing any mention of Jesus, his teachings, his actions, and his ministry out of the official records of the Jewish state. It is also known that he and his students personally destroyed over 1,000 manuscripts and documents, Christian and non-Christian alike, that mentioned the name of Jesus.

+ About 2,000 Coptic Christian manuscripts have been found that date from the 1st century to the 10th century. Most of these are in Egypt.

+ At least 3,000 documents and manuscripts written in the Iranic, Arabic, and Semitic languages were discovered in AD 953—most dealt with various Christian doctrines and the histories of Christianity from the 1st century to the 7th century, including the life and ministry of Jesus.

+ Lucian of Syria, one of the most respected of all ancient historians, testified to the existence of Jesus and to the documented evidence of the influence of his life, when in a letter written on the death of Peregrinus in 170 AD, he described Jesus as:

> '...the man who had been fixed to a stake in Judaea; ...as one still worshipped for having introduced a new code of morals into life...as that first lawgiver of theirs [the Christians]...and who made them believe that they are all brothers when they have abjured the gods of Greece, and worshipped the crucified man who is their teacher, and have begun to live according to his laws...of which so much has been written of him and his wisdom...of not alone by those his brothers but by our own chroniclers that surely his appeal and his effect will not soon be subdued. '

+ Numerous other historians wrote dozens of volumes about the life, ministry, trial, death, and resurrection of Jesus, and about his influence and the spread of the religious philosophy that bears his name. Among these historians was Quandratus who wrote a defense of Christianity to Emperor Adrian. Other histories were written by Justin Martyr, Tertullian, Vincentius, Cilens the First, Origen (who wrote eight massive volumes on the subject), Duranzo, Rabbi Akiba, Celsus, Aretas (the king of Arabia), and Arcadius, the eldest son of Theodosius the Great, who became emperor in AD 395 upon the death of his father. He was the emperor who divided the Roman Empire into the Western and Eastern Empires. When Acradius divided the Empire, he chose to rule the Eastern Empire from his seat of government in Constantinople and appointed his brother, Honoris, emperor of the Western Empire, with his seat of government in Rome. A war soon developed, ending with the overthrow of Honoris. The events of the war are sketchy, but enough is known so that a conclusion can be drawn. It seems that Honoris wanted his sons to be educated in Constantinople free of charge, giving as a reason that the great library was there that used to belong in Rome (Constantine had taken all but 70,000 volumes to Constantinople. Of the 70,000 that remained in Rome, none were originals. Constantine had many of the documents copied. The copied versions remained in Rome and the originals were taken to Constantinople. It was estimated by Honoris that Constantinople had over 35 million documents, manuscripts, scrolls, and volumes brought to Constantinople. Many were originals of Christian writings of the first three centuries and Roman histories and court records of Rome and its provinces from the time before Julius Caesar until the present [Alphonsus' time]). When Acradius refused, Honoris demanded that the library be divided. Again Acradius refused. War over possession of the library resulted. Acradius conquered the Western Empire, Honoris was killed, and the library remained in Constantinople. It remained there until <u>1204 when the **Christian** crusaders attacked and sacked the ***Christian*** city of Constantinople</u>. The library was set on fire and for six days the heat from the burning books and manuscripts was so intense that it reportedly melted the armor of the crusaders who were burning the books. Only 13 of the 50 massive Imperial Volumes of Constantine escaped the fire and less than 10,000 volumes and manuscripts. It is estimated that as many as 1,000 heroic citizens of Constantinople lost their lives trying to rescue the library contents. It was also claimed by hundreds of historians that the crusaders took more loot and more riches and treasures from the city of Constantinople at that time than all the loot and riches that had been taken from all cities and all conquests of all conquerors and all armies combined, from the beginning of time up until that time. Only the burning of the great library in Alexandria ranks as equal to the tragedy of the intellectual destruction that the crusaders inflicted upon the city of Constantinople, and upon civilization."

At this point I want to pause in my paraphrasing of Alphonsus and interjected a personal note concerning Byzantium.

When in 1261 the Byzantium troops of Michael VIII overthrew the Latin kingdom that had been set up in Constantinople and re-established the Eastern Empire, he and his successors had the library rebuilt and scholars were encouraged from throughout the world to come and be educated in Constantinople and to restock the library. One hundred years later there was a bitter and violent battle between the papal forces of Rome and the defenders of Constantinople over the Christian contents of the library. The battle was called the Battle of Tanze. Eventually the defenders of the library defeated the Pope's army and forced them out of Byzantium. By 1453 when Constantinople fell to the Ottoman conqueror Mohammed II (Mehmet), its library was one of the largest and most influential in the world. Mehmet estimated that there were about one million documents in the library at the time of his conquest. He did not destroy the library. He simply transferred the more precious documents and books, about 200,000 to 300,000, to Hagia Sophia and St. Irene church and hid them. Then he locked the library with its remaining volumes intact. Over the next two centuries more and more volumes were transferred from the library to Hagia Sophia, which had been converted into a mosque. Six times before 1800 the library was vandalized and volumes were stolen. When it was finally demolished and replaced with a park in the 1800s, of the more than 700,000 volumes that had been locked up in the library by Mehmet, less than 1,000 remained. These were transferred to the Blue Mosque for safekeeping.

Let's now return to Alphonsus' "knowns."

"+ It was known that in the year 748 of the Empire which was 330 of the Christian era, Constantine the Great moved his seat of government from Rome to Constantinople, taking with him all of the original copies of all Christian literature known to him, up until that time. The *original* writings of the Scriptures and *original* 1st century commentaries on the Scriptures were rewritten on hieotike (some historians claim that they were written with liquid gold) and were bound between solid gold plates into 50 massive (about 3 feet by 4 feet and 2 feet thick) volumes—the Imperial Volumes of Constantine. Only 13 of these massive volumes survived the purge of the city by the crusaders. When Mehmet conquered the city, he had so much respect for these 13 surviving sacred volumes that he would not allow them to be destroyed. Instead, he had them displayed in glass-covered cases of rare wood and precious stones and had them placed in Hagia Sophia.

+ Constantine left copies of all of the Jewish Talmuds and Sanhedrin records that were in existence at the time of his rule (probably about 30,000 manuscripts and scrolls), including those taken from Jerusalem, and copies of another 40,000 documents, manuscripts, and volumes covering a variety of subjects by hundreds of writers, in the library at Rome. The originals were taken to Constantinople. The Visigoths destroyed the library of Rome in 410, with King Alaric personally torching the building. But before the burning of the library, and while the invaders were busy ransacking other parts of the city, many (about 42,000) of the manuscripts, documents, and volumes were saved and hidden in various basilicas that had been constructed by Constantine the Great: the basilicas of St. Paul located outside of the city walls, of St. Peter, built on Vatican hill, of St. Agnes on the Via Nomentana, and St. Sebastian on the Apian Way. Over the next 12 centuries all of the basilicas except St. Peter's were ransacked and robbed repeatedly. Many of the pillaged documents ended up in and are still being housed at St. Peter's.

+ Justin said that he had personally inspected and studied several Roman judicial and senatorial documents including Pilate's report to Tiberius concerning the trial of Jesus, Pilate's report to the Syrian governor concerning the trial and death of Jesus, Pilate's report to Tiberius and to the Theophus Commission concerning the death of Jesus, Caiaphas' report to Pilate concerning the death and supposed resurrection of Jesus, the Jewish Sanhedrin's report to Pilate concerning the trial of Jesus, Herod Antipas' report to the Theophus ambassadors of Tiberius requesting an investigation of a Galilean Rabboni—Jesus, Herod Antipas' report to Tiberius concerning the life, miracles, and death of Jesus, Herod' Antipas' report to the Theophus Commission and to Tiberius regarding the death of Jesus, Tiberius' report to the Senate concerning the Theophus, and Tiberius' report to the Senate concerning Jesus."

After listing his "knowns," Alphonsus began to describe the Jerusalem Talmud (he did not include the Babylonian Talmuds in his description), more commonly called at that time The Talmud of the Jerusalem Sanhedrin. He began his description by explaining that the word *lamond* which meant "to teach" or "to teach by example," was the root word from which the word *talmud* was derived. Along with the word *lamond*, there were two other words that the Jewish rabbis used in referring to the Talmuds: *shanoh*, which means "to learn" and *gamor*, which means "having learned" or "having ceased to learn." The Jerusalem Talmud, which consisted of numerous Talmuds, was compiled by a group of Jewish scholars led by Johanan bar Nappacha in AD 279. He succeeded Rabbi Yehuda ha Qadosh, who had died in AD 219. From these Talmuds were written by the Jewish rabbis, numerous documents. It was alleged by Pope Boniface II in AD 530 that Johanan bar Nappacha had instructed his compilers to remove not only the name but *all memory and proof of the existence of Jesus* from the finished Talmud. Of course it is impossible to prove such an accusation, Alphonsus admitted.

The most important Talmud of the Jerusalem Talmud was the Mishna. This contains the opinions and commentaries on The Law. Hillel II originally translated the contents of the Mishna in approximately AD 80, after the destruction of Jerusalem. But it was not edited and complied until AD 279 under Johanan bar Nappacha's watchful eye. The Mishna is further divided into the Halachah, the legal and doctrinal material, and the Agada, which contains stories and legends. This Mishna contained the laws from all nations in existence at that time or which at one time existed, that were thought to be compatible with the Laws of God as recorded by Moses, and commentaries upon the Law of Moses and how it related to all of the other laws of other nations.

The next Talmud was the Tosephta. This portion contained the rituals of Temple service as well as the moral regulatory laws of human relationship and morals.

Next was the Mechilta. This book explained the organization and the duties of the Sanhedrin and the Court of Elders and Priests. The Sanhedrin, the legislative body of the Jewish nation, was divided into two bodies, the greater, which had seventy members, and the lesser, which had twenty-four members. The Court of Elders and Priests had twelve members and its chair was the High Priest. This court decided all appeals, and its judgment could not typically be appealed.

The next Talmud that Alphonsus explained was the Saphra. The word Saphra means "corner-stone or foundation rock." This was a large book with quotations from various works of the ancient world. It basically traced the development of and showed examples of laws that have been based on or were related to the Laws given to Moses by God.

Next he described the Talmud called Siphri. It was a book that traced the history of the world up until that time, the time of the compiling of the Siphri, paying special attention to the descendants of Abraham.

The Pesikta and Midrasham were next. These were Talmuds that recorded sermons, ideas, sermon extracts, and words of wisdom from great men of all ages.

Alphonsus mentioned the Nagad, Kikhil, Midrash, and others as well, but he did not elaborate upon them. He finished this portion of his first volume by again writing in Latin, "So foolish to have rejected Light in preference to dark hardness."

The next document that Alphonsus evaluated and commented upon was a letter that he said Francesco discovered in Constantinople. It was a letter written to Eusebius Pamphili (the Arian Bishop of Caesarea and the one who baptized Constantine shortly before the Emperor's death), by Emperor Constantine, concerning the compiling of the Christian Scriptures.

Alphonsus began this portion by giving a brief background to the letter followed by his chronicle the letter.

Although I will continue to paraphrase Alphonsus' record, I will quote Eusebius Pamphili's letter directly.

Alphonsus said that it was a known fact that the Roman Emperor Constantine had transferred to Constantinople all of the original scrolls and documents that had been accepted by the first three centuries leaders of the Christian faith as inspired Scripture. There he had the scriptures compiled and bound into 50 volumes and placed in the newly constructed educational library for public view. Some historians have claimed that the volumes were so large that it took two men to open one of them. Upon completion, Constantine inspected them. As he approved each volume, he dated it and placed his name and official seal upon it.

The volumes were written on hieotike in large, bold, Latin characters. The leaves were bound between thick gold plates and on the front of each was a sculptured figure of a man hanging on a cross, with the inscription, *"Jesus, Son of God, crucified for the sins of the world."*

Eusbius was given the charge of replicating 50 copies of the 50 volumes. These 50 copies of the 50 volumes would be distributed to particular Christian churches within the city of Constantinople and the surrounding area. The copies would not be as large as the originals, about two and a half feet square. They would be written on parchment rather than hieotike, they would be bound between cedar boards rather than gold plates, and the front board of each copy would have a gold inscribed figure of Jesus. The letter that Francesco discovered was the letter that Constantine wrote commissioning Eusebius to prepare the copies.

The following is a quote from Constantine's letter:

> "Victor Constantine Maximus Augustus to Eusebius:
> It happens through the favoring of God our Savior that great numbers have united themselves to the most holy church in this city, which is called by my name. It seems, therefore, highly requisite, since the city is rapidly advancing in prosperity in all other respects, that the number of churches should also be increased. Do you, therefore, receive with all readiness my determination on this behalf? I have thought it expedient to your Prudence to order 50 copies of each of the bound sacred Scriptures, the provisions and use of which you know to be most needful for the instruction of the churches, to be written on prepared parchment, in a legible manner, and in a commodious and portable form, by transcribes thoroughly practiced in their art. The procurator of the diocese has also received instructions by letter from our Clemency to be careful to furnish all things necessary for the preparation of such copies, and it will be for you to take special care that they be completed with as little delay as possible. You have authority, also in virtue of this letter, to use two of the public carriages for their conveyance, by which arrangements the copies, when fairly written, will most easily be forwarded for my personal inspection, and one of the deacons of your church may be entrusted with this service, who, on his arrival here, shall experience my liberality. God preserve you, beloved brother."

Alphonsus concluded the matter of Constantine's scriptures by writing, "Whether Eusebius completed his task is a mystery that will likely never be known, but we do know from the testimony of Jerome in AD 416 that at least six sets of the copied Scriptures were completed and distributed to churches in Constantinople, but because both Eusebius and Constantine had adopted Aryanism as official doctrine, the Church did not recognize the Scriptures of Constantine as authorized. It was not until Jerome had completed the Latin version of the Scriptures in AD 414 that the Church recognized his [Jerome's] translation as the authorized translation of the Scriptures."

As I finished taking notes of Alphonsus' observations it seemed quite obvious to me that there was a wealth of information out there someplace that would serve as confirmation to the truth of the Gospels. It just had to be found. Although I knew without a doubt that some of the ancient documents and manuscripts have been lost or destroyed over the centuries, I was just as convinced that there were other confirming documents out there someplace, perhaps dozens or even hundreds, that have not been lost or destroyed and were just waiting to be discovered.

So, building upon the foundation of the uncompromising truth of the Gospels, and using the nucleus of the two golden nuggets of advice and information around which I molded my research stratagem, I set out to search for and to find as much Gospel-collaborating non-biblical documentation as possible, relative to the life and ministry of Jesus.

IV
AUGUSTAN ROME

Very early in my research, I realized that the Gospels were not written to reflect any sense of a chronological order of the life and/or ministry of Jesus. They seemed rather to have been written so as to emphasize Jesus' teachings and his relationship with God the Father and with his fellow man. They were a *kerygma*, or preaching written down, or maybe even a *kerygmatic* history, rather than an objective history. In addition, I discovered that not only were there the commonly acknowledged missing years in Jesus' life from age 12 or 13 to about age 26 or 27 (age 30 in the commonly and currently accepted chronology), called the silent years or the unknown years, but there were also missing days, weeks, and months in the very midst of his known years of ministry.

Therefore, I decided that I would chronologically arrange Jesus' life in a manner so that I would be able to understand it. This chronicle would then serve as my personal road map that would guide me on my journey to find historical Jesus.

However, before I present the chronological timetable of Jesus' life, I want to paint a picture of the political, social, and religious Roman world into which Jesus was born and in which he lived and ministered.

A half a century before the region where Jesus lived and ministered became a Roman province, it was a Hasmonean state, which would become known as Palestine. It was an area that flourished in an age between empires. Seleucid Syria, under whom the area that came to be known as Palestine had been subjected for almost a century, was in a state of irreversible decline, and Rome had not yet grown strong enough to challenge this eastern remnant of Alexander's empire. Hence, when the Hasmoneans led a rebellion against their Seleucid overlords and established an independent Jewish state, there was not a power in that area strong enough to prevent their expansion.

Before we go any further, I first need to explain about the word *Palestine*. The word Palestine used today to describe a geographical location of ethnic Jewish occupation, generally inclusive of an area that occupied the region of Roman Syria, Judaea, Phoenicia and the region of the Sinai, was not used in connection with this location distinction until the 17th century AD. The word itself comes from the Latin word *Palestina*. This was the name given to the entire region of the eastern Mediterranean, by the Roman emperor Hadrian in the year AD 135, following his suppression of a Jewish rebellion led by the self-proclaimed "messiah," Bar Cochba. This name, *Palestine*, regardless of what today's academia says, was never used to identify Judaea, the Galilee, or any area within the region, until after AD 135, and was not used as a preferred location name until after 1660.

Now, back to the new Hasmonean state.

Within the newly formed state the Sadducee religious sect, with its rigid system of temple administration, became *the* dominant religious power and the Sanhedrin committee of elders (controlled by the Sadducee sect) became *the* dominant judicial body.

The most renowned Hasmonean of this new Jewish state was John Hyrcanus, who ruled over the Jewish state from 134 to 104 BC. John was the third son of the high priest/governor Simon Maccabees and he was consumed with the notion that he had been chosen by God to restore the ancient Davidic kingdom. Claiming that God had given him a vision outlining a plan for the conquest of the region that came to be known as Palestine and the elimination of all foreign religious influence, John set out to forcibly exterminate all foreign cults and heterodox religious sects from "God's chosen land" and to eliminate all who refused to conform to the dictates of his own unique form of Judaism.

Driven by fanatical religious fundamentalism, John and his army of mercenaries, in 130 BC, first razed and destroyed the Samaritan temple that was located on Mount Gerizim and then some years later, in 109-108 BC, he destroyed the city of Samaria itself. He then turned his attention to the Greek city of Scythopolis. He burned the city and massacred all of its inhabitants merely because they were Greek. This slaughter was quickly followed by his conquest of the province of Idumaea, where he massacred the inhabitants of its two main cities, Adora and Marissa, because they refused to reject *their* form of Judaism and adopt *his* form of Judaism.

John's son, Alexander Jannaeus, who was high priest/governor from 104 to 76 BC, took John's policy of expansionism and forced conversion even further than had John. He invaded the Greek dominated Decapolis, as well as Nabataea, the province of Gaulanitis, the Galilee, and Syria. Alexander was thought by most of his subjects to have become mad. This was mainly due to his numerous unnecessary and unprovoked senseless massacres of all who opposed or who he thought opposed his "right of God"—Jew, half-Jew, and non-Jew alike, or any who refused to submit and be converted to the Hasmonean form of Judaism.

Such cruelty led to a revolt by the Jewish people and a violent civil war. The civil war lasted for six years and cost the lives of more than 50,000 Jews before it ended in victory for Alexander. Upon Alexander's death in 76 BC, his widow, Alexandra Salome, reigned in his stead. However, she was neither able to thwart the people's underlying resentment against the Hasmonean dynasty, nor quench the smoldering coals of a second inevitable rebellion. With her death in 67 BC, the quiescent coals burst into flames as civil war again ignited; this time between Salome's sons of succession, Hyrcanus II and Aristobolus II. For the next four years, both sides killed thousands of Jews as the populace aligned itself to support one side or the other of Salome's rivaling sons.

Feeling that the civil war would have no winners, but instead, would continue to eliminate thousands of his countrymen, Hyrcanus II appealed for military help from the newly appointed Roman consular of Rome's recently acquired eastern Asian territories, Gnaeus Pompeius, or Pompey the Great. Antipater, the most able and most powerful Idumaen chief-minister of Hyrcanus, negotiated the agreement with Pompey on Hyrcanus' behalf. In exchange for Pompey's military intervention, Antipater guaranteed that immediately upon the defeat of Aristobolus II, all Hasmonean controlled and administered lands would become subject to Rome. Pompey, in turn, guaranteed that Hyrcanus would be installed as vassal king/high priest of Judea and that both Antipater's family and any other notable Idumaen

The Search

families recommended by Antipater, would be able to flourish unmolested under Roman protection.

In 63 BC, after a three-month siege and after having mercilessly crushed Aristobolus and his forces, which cost the lives of 12,000 Jews, Pompey marched triumphantly into Jerusalem. As pledged, Pompey installed Hyrcanus II as vassal king/high priest, subject to Rome. Hyrcanus in turn appointed Antipater to be governor of the Galilee. On the day that Pompey entered Jerusalem, all of the Hasmonean-controlled lands and territories became subject to and possessions of Rome, bringing to an end the last independent Jewish state for more than 2,000 years.

An underlying, but acute, rivalry soon developed between Antipater and Hyrcanus; a rivalry that would intensify over the next sixteen years. Whereas Hyrcanus sought to consolidate his position by developing a strong relationship with his Judean subjects, Antipater consolidated his position by developing strong relationships with Rome.

By 47 BC, Antipater had become so politically influential that he convinced Julius Caesar, over the objections of the great orator and statesman, Cicero, to dissolve the office of vassal king and bring Judea under direct Roman rule through the office of procurator. Hence, Hyrcanus was removed from the office of vassal king, although he retained the position of high priest, and Antipater was appointed first Roman procurator of Judea. In turn, Antipater appointed one of his sons, the 26-year-old Herod, to be governor of the Galilee, and another son, Phasael, to be governor of Jerusalem.

Herod, who was a lifelong friend of Roman consul, Mark Antony, quickly gained a reputation for being a brilliant politician, a highly efficient statesman, and a shrewd, yet generous, negotiator. Nonetheless, he had also shown himself to be a savage barbarian, seemingly hovering on the brink of insanity, capable of unspeakable cruelties. Flavius Josephus, the Roman/Jewish historian, wrote that [Herod] "...was no king but the most cruel tyrant who ever ascended the throne. He murdered a vast number of people and the lot of those he left alive was so miserable that the dead might count themselves fortunate. He not only tortured his subjects singly but ill treated whole communities. In order to beautify foreign cities, he robbed his own, and made gifts to foreign nations which were paid for with Jewish blood.... Within a few years, the Jews suffered more misery under Herod than had their forefathers at any other time.... In 35 years, hardly a day passed without someone being sentenced to death..."

In 40 BC, turmoil again rocked Judea. A nephew of Hyrcanus II, Antigonus, with the help of the Parthians and many of his own Hasmonean family, seized Jerusalem. He imprisoned Phasael, who committed suicide in prison. He also disposed Hyrcanus from his position as high priest. Soon thereafter, Hyrcanus was found dead in his prison chamber.

When Antigonus marched his Parthian mercenary army north to invade the Galilee, Herod fled to the safety of Rome via Arabia and Egypt. There, he appealed to the Roman Senate for help. They responded by making him *King of Judea*, with the formal title of *rex socius et amicus populi Romani,* which meant *allied king and friend of the Roman people.*

In 37 BC, Herod returned to Judea with a Roman army which, when added to his loyal troops, totaled 30,000 infantry and 6,000 cavalry. He re-took Jerusalem and mercilessly crushed the rebelling faction, massacring thousands of rebels (many of whom were Hasmoneans) and Parthian mercenaries. Afterwards, Herod received the new title of *King of all of the Jews* from Augustus, and Herod's regime was installed as Judea's official ruling body, replacing the office of Roman procurator. He ruled Judea until his death in AD 4.

Throughout his reign, Herod remained the most loyal and the most reliable of all of Rome's Mare Nostrum, or Mediterranean, provincial authorities. He was by far the most rewarding and flattering to Rome of any of their Mare Nostrum rulers.

Herod became known as *Herod the Great*, the same Herod that reigned in Judea at the time that Jesus was born. Through the policies that Herod established, the political direction of the entire region was determined and destined for decades after his death. As a result, throughout Jesus' life, within the region of what came to be called Palestine (maybe with the exception of Jerusalem itself) Herod's influence could be seen and felt in every facet of Jewish life.

Herod never really forgave the Hasmoneans for the part that they played in the 40 BC revolt. Consequently, he waged a 40-year unrelenting war of extermination against the Hasmoneans, although his own wife, Mariamne, whom he eventually ordered executed, was a Hasmonean. She was the great-granddaughter of Alexander Jannaeus. It obviously never occurred to Herod that only a small fraction of the Hasmoneans had actually supported the rebellion (and if it had occurred to him, he did not care), for he waged his undeclared war of extermination against them all, killing hundreds of them and confiscating the material wealth of them all. In so doing, he not only punished all those who he accused of supporting the rebellion, but he also systematically eliminated any who could claim ancestral rights to his throne. By 20 BC, the Hasmonean family was for all practical purposes, extinct.

Herod also forcibly separated the Jewish political state from its religion. His very first act upon assuming power in 37 BC was to execute 46 members of the Sanhedrin, effectively stripping it of its political powers. Throughout the remainder of Herod's reign, the Sanhedrin was nothing more than a religious court, totally separated from political or secular matters. It was not until after Herod's death that the Sanhedrin began to regain limited political influence, mainly resulting from their friendship and cooperation with the Roman authorities. Herod refused to accept the religious post of high priest, successfully divorcing that office from the secular administrative office of the king. Thereafter, the office of high priest became an appointed civil authority position. Under Herod, the House of Boethus was appointed to the office of high priest.

No one could ever accuse Herod of being compassionate or merciful. The opposite in fact has been well documented by the deaths of countless thousands during his reign. Nevertheless, he was a brilliant politician and statesman. He played opposing sides against one another with calculated precision to maintain a somewhat volatile, yet very solid and balanced "Judaic/Roman" administration.

Herod prided himself in the fact that he had humbled the power and influence of the Hasmoneans and the Sanhedrin and had redistributed their power and influence to the Diaspora Jews. In fact, Herod himself considered his assimilation of the Diaspora Jewry into Judean politics as his greatest political accomplishment in Judea. However, he did not restrict himself to Judea in his special treatment of the Diaspora Jews. Throughout the Roman Empire, wherever there was a Jewish community, Herod was there with money, influence, and massive construction projects.

Herod was the best friend that Rome had in the east. Through his unparalleled and unequaled Greco-Roman-style construction projects, he created an undeniably strong physical presence of Roman authority throughout his domain. He built stadiums, circuses, and hippodromes in Sidon, Damascus, Tyre, Antioch, Caesarea Maritima, Samaria, Jerusalem, and Scythopolis, wherein he single-handedly restored the Olympic games to the eastern Roman Empire. He built sea-ports (including the magnificent port of Caesarea Maritima, the capital of Roman-occupied Judea), fortresses, roads, cities, palaces, the wondrously magnificent Jewish Temple in Jerusalem, and equally magnificent temples dedicated to Zeus, Apollo, Bacchus, Venus, Mars, Artemis, Diana, Isis, Osiris, and Mercury, along with scores of other temples dedicated to numerous Roman, Greek, Egyptian, and Babylonian gods and goddesses, as well as temples dedicated to Caesar. He also built canals, waterways, dams, schools and educational institutions, and dozens of fine amphitheaters.

Through Herod's liberal education policy (education was free and mandatory through age 17 for all male subjects and through age 14 for all female subjects), he made his subjects by far the most educated in all of the Roman Empire, including Rome itself. In the 2nd century, Phinehas the Rabbi recorded that at the time of Herod's death, illiteracy among Jewish men did not exist in the Roman Empire and that only the very old Jewish women could neither read nor write. He also noted that there were over 100 Jewish scholars who served as educators, tutors, and authors in the Imperial court and in the household of Caesar, who had been educated under the policies of Herod, and another 10,000 served as educators, tutors, and administrators throughout the Roman Empire. He also noted that at the time of Herod's death, more than half of his male subjects had received or were receiving advanced education beyond that which was mandatory.

However, all of this did not come without a heavy price. During one 12-year period of his reign (25 to 13 BC), Herod taxed his subjects, Jew and non-Jew alike, mercilessly by doubling their tax load every year during those 12 consecutive years. This led to unrest among the people, forcing Herod to suppress the unrest savagely and quickly. His merciless actions cost the lives of hundreds, if not thousands, in each of those 12 years. In fact, Herod's ruthless treatment of his subjects became so well known that eventually his actions caught the attention of Caesar Augustus, who upon hearing of one of Herod's latest atrocities, said in disgust, "it is better to be Herod's dog than his subject."

While Herod was becoming well established as the King of the Jews, Rome's influence continued to grow unchecked under Augustus. A useful reference relating to Rome's rise to power during this period, that I discovered in the University of Chicago library, was a manuscript entitled, *...including Christ*. It was a small 30- to 35-page unpublished manuscript reputed to have been written by the American/English novelist Henry James in 1879.

The manuscript was packed with dates and facts, but the author made no attempt to tie them together. To say that it was a confused muddle of boring reading would be an understatement. It certainly did not reflect the genius of such a masterful author as James. In fact, it was so "non-professional" I seriously doubt that James wrote it. I believe his name was plagiarized and that the true author is an unknown who tried to capitalize upon James' brilliance.

After an introduction, James (or whoever was the actual author of the manuscript) wrote an eight-page synopsis of what was happening in the Augustan Roman Empire just before, during, and some time after the birth of Jesus. After this, he recorded page after page of boring dates, events, and facts in a somewhat chronological listing pattern.

I will paraphrase the synopsis.

Imperial Rome's very nature and government were remarkably the creation of one man with outstanding ability, Julius Caesar's great-nephew and adopted heir, Octavian.

After the defeat of the murders of Julius Caesar and of Mark Antony and Cleopatra, Octavian returned to Rome in about the year 30 BC to become a consul. There he re-established the reality of his great-uncle's power behind a façade of republican devotion.

On January 16, 27 BC, the Senate gave Octavian the honorific title of Augustus. That title, *Caesar Augustus*, became the name by which he is remembered, although he personally preferred the title *princeps*, meaning first citizen.

In 12 BC Augustus became *Pontifex maximus*, the head of the official state religious cult, as was his great-uncle before him.

In the year 9 BC Tiberius, the future emperor, succeeded Drusus, stepson of Augustus, who had died while on military command in Germany, as the Supreme Commander of all Roman forces in Germania (Germany).

Over the next three years, Tiberius was practically unstoppable and undefeatable as he established Roman preeminence in the region of the Rhine River. So successful was Tiberius in Germany that Augustus in 6 BC sent him to Armenia, hoping that he (Tiberius) would be able to repeat his military successes in Armenia also. However, Augustus and Tiberius had a very heated disagreement about occupation policy, and instead of reorganizing Armenia, Tiberius resigned his position and secluded himself in voluntary exile as a private citizen to the island of Rhodes.

It was during this time, probably in 7 BC, that Jesus was born in Judea. That same year, 7 BC, the *Pax Romana*, the imperial peace, was proclaimed and established by Augustus, which successfully removed the threats of barbarian incursion and international strife from the Empire. As a result of the *Pax Romana* and its influence, within the frontiers of the Empire there was order and peace as never before.

In 5 BC several magi representing an eastern coalition appeared in Jerusalem seeking a newborn king; and in January 4 BC, Augustus succeeded in averting war with this eastern coalition. Because of Herod's rash actions, the eastern coalition had made plans to invade Roman Judea. Later that year, 4 BC, Herod the Great died.

By 2 BC, the differences between Augustus and Tiberius were resolved. Tiberius was reinstated and Augustus sent him to Armenia, where he was successful in suppressing rebellion and reorganizing the administrative jurisdiction of Armenia, placing it under the umbrella of "The Clientele" states.

That same year, Rome's leading poet, Publius Ovidius Naso, known as Ovid, was banished by Augustus to the Black Sea colony of Tomis. His crime was that he offended Augustus by implicating Augustus with his graphic erotic verses.

In Rome during this time, Augustus was busy systematically and patiently molding Rome's once erratic hodgepodge government into a well-organized, smooth-running, yet practical imperial administration. This new Augustan government was heavily colored with concern for moral revival, restoring the virtues of ancient Rome, and social reform. Also in 2 BC, in recognition of his efforts and to pay tribute to him as the author and architect of the world's first (and only) ubiquitous peace in history, Augustus was endowed with the title *Pater Patriae*, "Father of his country."

Roman rule under Augustus was unique in that the Roman authorities did not want to interfere with the operation of local customs and traditions. Because the empire and the civilization it carried were unashamedly cosmopolitan, Rome was more tolerant than any empire that existed before it, and in many ways, more than any that have ever existed since.

The empire was never a racial unity whose hierarchies were closed to non-Romans. Only one of its peoples, the Jews, felt strongly about the retention of their unique identities and that distinction rested primarily in religion.

The Augustan government virtually invented town-planning and huge cities as regional governmental administrative centers. The Augustan pattern was reflected in all of the great cities of the empire. It was central to the civilization which Rome sustained everywhere. Although the ancients had large cities, most were capitals of empires.

Augustan Rome transferred the large city concept of the imperial city of Rome into the frontiers and the provinces. Each and every province and frontier region had at least one and usually many cities that served as regional administrative centers, which governed the region or the province on behalf of Rome. Regional populations were encouraged to populate the cities.

There was room in the Augustan Roman Empire for all manner of religious belief and philosophy, provided it did not violate public order or inhibit adherence to the official religious observances sponsored by or dictated by Rome.

Taxes kept the Augustan empire going. It was the one issue in which Rome had zero percent tolerance and accepted no excuses for failure to pay. Tax receipts and the collection of taxes was the one issue that could provoke immediate Roman military intervention quicker than anything else, save open rebellion and insurrection. Every non-Roman citizen man, every non-Roman citizen family, every town, village, and city, every state, and every province paid taxes. No one was exempt. Although not heavy in normal times, when the taxes paid for administration and police and military protection, at times of war or economic hardships they could become unbearable. Every province had the same tax liability based on the economy and provision of the province. Only the emperor had the power to reduce a province's tax liability. As an example, in Egypt, Rome demanded a large portion of taxes to be paid in grain and cotton exports. Less than 30 percent of Egypt's annual tax liability was paid with money. However, in Judaea, where grain was not plentiful, salt, which was plentiful, was collected to satisfy their tax liability. In Judaea, more than 50 percent of its tax liability was paid in salt.

The next four years (from 1 BC to 2 AD) were somewhat uneventful politically, except that in AD 2, one of Augustus' two grandsons, Lucius Caesar, died. This in effect strengthened Tiberius' position as Augustus' successor, since Lucius was the only son of Augustus' wife, Livia, making him Augustus' stepson.

Two years later in AD 4, Augustus' only remaining grandson and bloodline heir, Gaius Caesar, died. The Roman Senate insisted that Augustus immediately designate a legal heir. So, on June 26 of that year, he legally and formally adopted Tiberius (who had recently been given tribunician powers by the Senate), as his son, and named him Tiberius Julius Caesar. Augustus then proclaimed that Tiberius would soon be named as his legal heir. Two months later, Augustus again adopted. This time he adopted the son of Agrippa (Agrippa was probably Augustus' most able general, if not one of the three greatest generals in all of Roman history. He was killed in battle in 12 BC), Agrippa Postumus. Not to be outdone, Tiberius also adopted. He adopted his own nephew, Germanicus, to be his son.

In September, AD 4, shortly after Tiberius adopted Germanicus, rebellion again broke out in Germany. Augustus immediately recalled Tiberius from Armenia and sent him to Germany. There Tiberius subjected the rebelling Langobards and agreed to a pact of non-aggression with the Cherusci. Afterwards Germany was re-established by Tiberius as a Senatorial province, Germania. Using the newly established province of Germania as his base, Tiberius crossed the Rhine and for the next two years waged war on the Marcomanni, who were occupying the area of what became the eastern part of Germany.

In Britain in AD 5, Augustus, submitting to Senate pressure, acknowledged that Cymbeline, king of the Catuvellanui, could be considered king of all of the tribes of Britain, because he had proven his conquest ability on the field of battle.

The years following the death of Herod the Great were years of horror for the people of Judea and the Galilee area. Archelaus, Herod's son and heir who ruled as Ethnarch of Judea, Samaria, and Idumaea, had proven himself to be no less ruthless than his late father. In due course, in late April, AD 6 a delegation of Judean Jews went to Rome to protest against Archelaus and his extreme cruelty and to demand of Augustus, Jewish self-rule.

Augustus, who was a strong believer in his long-standing policy of encouraging local self-rule vassal states, responded to the Judean delegation's petition both positively and negatively. On the positive side, Augustus repudiated Archelaus' Ethnarchship and exiled him to Gaul. On the negative side, Augustus denied the Jews self-rule. Instead, he incorporated the three former domains of Archelaus into a single Senatorial protectorate province: Judaea, consisting of three states: Judea, Samaria, and Idumaea. This new senatorial province would be administered by a Senate-appointed Roman procurator, who would be directly responsible to the Roman governor of the Imperial Senatorial Province of Syria (at this time the governor of Syria was Sulpicius Quirinus).

So, the Imperial Senatorial Province of Syria, under the authority of the Roman Imperial Provincial governor, now consisted of the senatorial district provinces of Phoenicia, the Galilee, Bashan, Ituraea, the Decapolis, Peraea, and the senatorial protectorate province of Judaea. The district provinces of the Galilee and Peraea were administered by the Tetrarch Herod Antipas; the district provinces of Ituraea and Bashan were administered by the Tetrarch Herod Philip; the district province of Phoenicia was administered by the Tetrarch Segirus; the district province of the Decapolis was under the direct administration of the Roman 10th Legion and ranking military authority; and the senatorial protectorate province of Judaea was under the administration of a Senate-appointed procurator.

In addition, three of these provinces were broken down into states. The senatorial protectorate province of Judaea consisted of the states of Judea, Idumaea, and the district of Samaria; the district province of Bashan consisted of the states of Auranitis, Batanaea, Trachonitis, and Gaulanitis; and the district province of Ituraea consisted of the states of Abilene, Panias, and Ulayha.

In July, AD 6, Augustus appointed Coponius to be the Senatorial protectorate province of Judaea's first procurator. He established himself in Caesarea Maritima (a new Roman city where only Roman citizens were allowed to live) on the Mediterranean coast, in the district of Samaria. There, he maintained a Greek/Syrian auxiliary armed guard of 3,000. Later (after the revolt of AD 7) he was also to maintain an armed military garrison of 6,000 auxiliary troops (100 were Roman soldiers) in Jerusalem, with headquarters in the Tower of Antonia, located within the Herod's Temple complex.

Simultaneous to Coponius' appointment, Quirinus deposed the Jewish High Priest that Herod the Great had appointed just before his (Herod's) death in 4 BC and replaced him with Annas. Annas held the position of High Priest until AD 15, when procurator Gratus replaced him with his (Annas') son, Eleazar. In AD 26, Annas' son-in-law, Joseph Caiaphas, replaced Eleazar.

The appointment of a Roman procurator in Judaea caused a violent revolt in Jerusalem in February, AD 7. The enraged Jerusalem nationals took out their wrath on Sabinus, the Roman procurator for the collection of taxes. Fearing for his life, he sought protection and refuge in the palace of Herod in Jerusalem. The rebels surrounded the palace and threatened to burn it to the ground. Leaving a contingent to sentry the palace, the rebels then turned their attention to the Roman citizens and authorities that lived in the city of Jerusalem. The rebels imprisoned the Romans, confiscated their properties, and burned their homes and businesses. In short, the whole city was in violent rabblement from February to June, AD 7.

Simultaneously, a revolt broke out in the Galilee. Judas of Gamala (called Judas the Galilean, the son of the fierce Galilean revolutionary, Hezekiah, whom Herod the Great had executed) led this revolt. Judas and his followers besieged and captured the city of Sepphoris, the provincial capital of the Galilee, located about five miles north of Nazareth, mid-way between Nazareth and Cana of Galilee. He then made Sepphoris his revolutionary headquarters. Judas' followers were called *sicarii* (meaning dagger men), by the Romans; *zealots* (meaning enmity or rebellion), by the Galileans; *Cananaeans* (meaning jealousy or opposition), by the

Judaeans; and *qanna* (meaning rebellion or opposition), by the non-Jewish/non-Roman population.

Upon receiving word that Sabinus was being besieged in Jerusalem and that Judas had started a rebellion in the Galilee, Coponius appealed to Quirinus, the governor of Syria.

In June, AD 7, Quirinus dispatched Coponius and his force of auxiliary troops to Jerusalem, while he (Quirinus) and his troops invaded the Galilee on two fronts: from Ituraea in the north and from the Decapolis in the east.

Coponius, ordering his force of auxiliary troops not to attack the revolting population in Jerusalem, had his forces surround the city, not allowing anyone in or out.

Meanwhile Quirinus invaded the Galilee. He overwhelmed the rebel held city of Sepphoris, captured it, and burned it to the ground. He dismembered Judas (Judas was dismembered over a two-day period in order to prolong his torture) and crucified all of the remaining rebels. He then enslaved the non-rebel population of the city: this was their punishment for allowing the rebels to use their city as a rebel headquarters. Quirinus then turned his forces south (passing through Nazareth) to join Coponius' forces in Jerusalem, in preparation to rescue Sabinus.

On August 19, AD 7, Quirinus' troops joined Coponius' forces on the outskirts of Jerusalem and marched into the city. He first overwhelmed the rebels who had laid siege to Herod's palace, and rescued Sabinus. He then unleashed such a terror upon the population of Jerusalem that Coponius trembled in horror and disgust and refused to take part in this "punishment of Jerusalem," so called by Quirinus. When Quirinus had finished, 5,000 of Jerusalem's population had been executed by "archery firing squad," 2,000 more had been crucified, and another 800 had either been beheaded, pulled apart, trampled by horses, or had been killed in the fighting.

After this ruthless suppression by Quirinus, there was a general calm (except for isolated insurrections) throughout Judaea and the Galilee until the first year of the procuratorship of Pontius Pilate in AD 26, when widespread violence again broke out in the Galilee and Judaea.

James paused in his synopsis and gave a personal footnote concerning Jesus' boyhood.

He wrote, "This rebellion and inexorable cessation by Quirinus doubtless made a tremendous impression upon the 14-year-old Jesus, and probably made an indelible impact upon his life. Can you imagine what was going on in Jesus' mind at this time? One of the most memorable events in his life up to that point had taken place only months before this upheaval (in April AD 6): the celebration of his becoming a *Son of the Law*. With the magnitude of that event still fresh on his mind, he found himself caught in the middle of the most violent insurrection to hit the Galilee since the days of Herod the Great. It was an insurrection so intense that the capital city, Sepphoris, located just five miles to the north of his own home, was left in ashes, and virtually all of its population were either killed or enslaved. And then, after the horror inflicted upon Sepphoris, the governor turned his army south and marched right through Jesus' own hometown on their way to lay siege to the holy city of Jerusalem itself. The world that Jesus had known since he was old enough to remember, had come to an end. Imagine the heartache that he felt when news of

Jerusalem's cataclysm reached Nazareth. In the holy city where he had been honored just months before, lay thousands of dead inhabitants; victims of Quirinus' ruthless suppression of the revolt."

After this, James continued with his synopsis, which I will continue to paraphrase.

It took Jerusalem seven years to recover from Quirinus' punishment. Procurator Ambivius, in his first year (which would have been AD 10), convinced Antipas to begin re-building Sepphoris, and to use the enslaved former residents of Sepphoris as construction laborers. It took ten years for the city of Sepphoris to be rebuilt, but after it was reconstructed, the former residents of the city, turned slave laborers, were freed from their bondage and became freemen under the tutelage of the Roman proconsul at Scythopolis.

Coponius served as Roman procurator of Judaea from AD 6 until AD 10, when M. Ambivius replaced him. It was this same Ambivius who convinced Antipas to reconstruct Sepphoris. He served as procurator until AD 13.

Tiberius was recalled to Germany where he served until AD 6. In that year the Pannonians revolted, so Augustus dispatched Tiberius from Germany to Pannonia (present day Austria/Hungry) to suppress the rebellion.

Tiberius' departure from Germany left void a strong military leadership in the region. Without a strong military presence like Tiberius to keep in check the Gaultic rebels, insurrection was immanent. General Quinctilius Varus was eventually dispatched to Germany in October of AD 8, but by that time the Cherusci had reverted back to the brink of rebellion. Varus, convinced that the Cherusci would not dare rebel against their Roman overlords, chose to ignore the signs of revolt. This attitude eventually led to one of the most disastrous military setbacks in Augustus' reign. In May of AD 9, Varus' Roman army suffered the most devastating military defeat in the history of Rome up until that time. The Roman army, consisting of three legions under the command of General Varus himself, was ambushed in the Teutoberg Forest on the banks of the Rhine River, by the Cherusci tribe under the leadership of the German prince, Arminius. Hemmed in by forests and marshes, the Romans were exterminated almost to the man. Varus committed suicide rather than face Augustus' wrath.

After this disaster, Augustus abandoned his plans for the conquest of all of Germany, even though he kept control of both the Rhine and the Danube frontiers.

Meanwhile in Pannonia, by June of the year AD 9, Tiberius had finally crushed the three-year-old rebellion in that central European region. In January of the following year, Pannonia became a Roman Senatorial province, linking Illyricum on the Adriatic Sea with Moesia on the Black Sea.

Back in Rome in the year AD 10, Augustus announced that for the second time in his rule, peace ruled throughout the Roman world. While Augustus' proclamation may have been true in 7 BC, peace did not rule throughout the Roman world in AD 10. But the proclamation of AD 10 did give Augustus an excuse to begin a massive building program, dedicated to the memory of peace and to the legacy of Augustus, that would as Augustus said, "At my death, leave Rome, a city of bricks, swathed in marble...." This reconstruction of the city of Rome continued under Tiberius for eight years after Augustus' death.

In Parthia (the most threatening power to Augustan Rome's most eastern border) in AD 12, the puissant military genius, Artabanus III, became king of Parthia. Parthia continued to be Rome's primary eastern nemesis throughout the first two centuries AD, and had it not been for the fact that it was devastated by the plague that overran the region from AD 163 to 165, it may have remained Rome's chief antagonist.

In April, AD 13, Augustus appointed Tiberius as his successor by giving him a *proconsular imperium maius*, thus creating joint regency.

On August 18 of the following year, AD 14, Augustus died at Nola at the age of 76.

With that statement, James finished that portion of his précis.

V
THE ROME OF TIBERIUS

After Augustus' death, five significant events took place in quick succession, events that were to shape Tiberius' career and influence the politics of Rome for centuries thereafter.

- First, the Senate, acting on the proposal of the consuls, proclaimed Tiberius to be emperor.
- Second, Augustus' adopted son, Agrippa Postumus, was put to death. Some years earlier Agrippa Postumus had been disinherited by Augustus because of his degenerate ethics, and he was exiled to Planasia.
- Third, Tiberius, as his first duty, proclaimed that effective immediately, the power to elect officials would be transferred from the people (citizens of Rome) to the Senate.
- Fourth, the Senate decreed that Augustus, their *Princeps* (Divus Augustus), had been raised to deification (*consecratio*). They then ordered that Augustus' own recorded chronicle of his reign be displayed on two bronze plates that would be attached to pillars in front of the Mausoleum Augusti (the Field of Mars). This was the beginning of *mandatory* emperor worship. Refusal to worship was a crime.
- Fifth, the legions in Pannonia revolted. This resulted in Tiberius sending his adopted son, Germanicus (the natural son of Tiberius' brother, Drusus the Elder), to Pannonia to put down the revolt. This was the beginning of the brilliant and much-admired career of Germanicus—a career that was to threaten the very office of the emperor itself and which would lead to Germanicus' death.

Along with these five far-reaching events, there were two other events in the year AD 14 that affected Judaea directly.

1. M. Ambivius was relieved as procurator of Judaea, and was replaced by Annius Rufus. Annius Rufus served as procurator until AD 15, when Valerius Gratus replaced him. Gratus served as procurator until AD 26, when Pontius Pilate replaced him (Jesus would have probably been about 33 years of age in AD 26).
2. Quirinius was re-called as governor of the Senatorial Province of Syria and was replaced by Gnaeus Calpurnius Piso. Piso served as governor of Syria until AD 19, when he was re-called by the Roman Senate.

By February, AD 15, Germanicus had successfully suppressed the revolt in Pannonia. Just days after hostilities had ceased in Pannonia, the German coalition of tribes revolted. Germanicus was en route to Rome to accept the position of consul offered him by the Senate, so he was unaware of the rebellion. However, upon his arrival in Rome, he was told of the revolt. Upon hearing the news, he stopped still in his tracks, turned and walked back to his stables, mounted his horse and immediately left for Germany. He sent word to Tiberius by messenger that he had left for Germany. Germanicus' consulship was awarded him in his absence. The German campaign protracted until December, AD 16, when Tiberius ordered the campaign to be discontinued because of excessive costs.

Germanicus refused to heed Tiberius' order and continued the campaign on his own, financed out of his own resources. It was while Germanicus was in Germany with his wife, Agrippina, and his four-year old son, Gaius (the future emperor), that the Roman soldiers nicknamed Gaius, *Caligula*, meaning "little boots," because of the little military boots that he wore. He always hated the name, but it stuck.

Meanwhile in AD 16 in Rome, Clemens, a slave of the slain adopted son of Augustus, Agrippa Postumus, impersonated Agrippa saying that Clemens had actually been the one who had been killed. Clemens sought to overthrow Tiberius. The truth was discovered before any harm came to Tiberius, and Clemens was executed.

AD 17 was by far the most politically active year of Tiberius' reign up to this point. In March, AD 17, an event took place that would not only affect Tiberius for the rest of his life, but also would impinge on and influence the life of Jesus throughout the duration of his ministry. On the night of March 13, while on holiday in Gythium, Greece, Tiberius had a dream in which a man calling himself Genius told him about the birth of *The Theophus*.

Although for years I had heard sketching stories about an influential dream that Tiberius had and about how that dream could have influenced the ministry of Jesus, I had never been able to find enough creditable information about the dream to take the stories seriously or to presume that the stories may have an element of truth in them. It was not until I traveled to Greece that I discovered the first documentation that confirmed the truth of Tiberius' dream.

There in the library of St. Stephen's monastery, part of the monastic community called Meteora (the Meteora comprised a series of monastic buildings, built by Byzantine monks, perched on top of a cluster of detached precipitous rocks), I found the first resource that told about Tiberius' dream of The Theophus.

The brothers (monks) at the monastery had translated every document in the library into Italian, French, Greek, and English and had written a background history for each document, manuscript, and book in the library.

The document that told about Tiberius' The Theophus was a very large three-leaf manuscript, written in French on three large (about 12" long by 32" wide) pages of hieotike, the finest of parchment. The pages were bound by two pieces of cedar and were held together with brass clasps. It appeared to me that these three pages were probably all that remained of a larger text.

As I read the translation and the historical background information and began to take paraphrased notes, my assumption was confirmed. This particular French document was a 14th century French copy of an earlier German document written by Gothard, the 11th century Abbot of the Bavarian monastery of Nieder-Altaich. The original German copy apparently had disappeared during the Napoleonic purge of Bavaria, so all that remained of Gothard's writing was this French re-write.

It seems that the document (the French re-write) had been discovered in Auch in southern France, in 1610 (where it had probably been copied by a 14th or 15th century monk), during a reconstruction project on the old monastery at Auch, two days before a monk from Auch stabbed Henry IV to death. The monk had claimed that finding the manuscript had been a sign that King Henry had to die.

As the story goes, once the supporters of Henry discovered why the monk acted on his murder plot, they became infuriated and for the next three months they rode throughout southern France seeking out and destroying all of the religious manuscripts and documents that they could find. Fortunately, word spread of the intended destruction, so most of the most ancient and valued manuscripts were hidden until the rage had passed. However, the manuscript that had caused all of the problems, the one that I was holding, did not escape. Originally it had been a huge 40-plus page bound document, but only the three leaves survived.

Upon seizure of the document at the monastery at Auch by Henry supporters, each leaf of the document was ripped from it's binding and was burned. The Abbot of the monastery objected adamantly, and pulled three leaves from the fire and ran into the church for safety. The destroyers did not pursue him, content instead in burning the remainder of the document, plus at least a dozen more manuscripts.

Soon thereafter, the Abbot fled for his life to the Meteora monastic community in Greece taking with him the three leaves that he had salvaged. In Meteora's St. Stephen's they have remained.

According to the brothers' historical records, the original document of Gothard was one of three large bound volumes, of which none survive, that Gothard wrote about the rise and fall of Jesus' popularity with the Romans. In it's day, it apparently was a document that even Pope Benedict IX, the Pope who was removed from office and then re-appointed to office on three different occasions, admired—and he admired very little.

The French monk who had copied and re-written the document in French used both sides of large sheets of hieotike and wrote very small. Although there were only three surviving leaves, there was much information written on each of them.

The three hieotike leaves dealt with the dream that the Roman Emperor Tiberius Caesar had on March 13 of the year AD 17, while on a visit to Gythium, Greece. The dream was so profound and so overwhelming that it drastically affected Tiberius and his policies from the time of the dream until the end of his life.

Gothard wrote that the dream consisted of a man in royal apparel appearing before Tiberius. In the dream Tiberius was sitting on his sentencing chair, which he called "the seat of judgment," in the Senate chambers, when the man walked in. Tiberius immediately arose and uncharacteristically bowed before him. The man then addressed Tiberius and told him to rise and to not bow before him for he was but a mere messenger representing and sent by the most ancient of days and always in the present—*I am*. The messenger then introduced himself as Genius. He said that during the reign of Augustus Caesar, *The Theophus* (this name was more of a title, rather than a proper name) was born of a simple virgin maiden within the eastern provinces of the dominion of Augustus. The title *The Theophus* meant,

"King and Emperor forever." It indicated that The Theophus' reign would be one that would last forever and that he, The Theophus, would live for all of eternity.

Genius went on to tell Tiberius that the kingdom of The Theophus would be a kingdom that would encompass the whole earth and one that would last forever. Miracles performed by him, control over and subjection by him over the laws of nature, signs, wonders, and great insight and wisdom would identify The Theophus. Genius then warned Tiberius that he (Tiberius) was not to tolerate worship of himself (Tiberius). Genius then walked out of the chamber.

When Tiberius awoke, he was bewildered, yet he was convinced that the dream was real and true. From that night onward, he determined that he would find The Theophus.

Tiberius became so obsessed with the dream and with his search for The Theophus that he offered automatic and irrevocable Roman citizenship to each and every person living in the state or province in which The Theophus was found. In addition, he said that the state or province would be rewarded by a declaration and would become a ward of Caesar (in essence, that state, province, or nation would lose it's national identity and would become a religious state and the personal property of Caesar, subjacent to Caesar *only*).

Shortly thereafter, Tiberius issued a proclamation stating that he would not receive, nor would he tolerate any form of personal exaltation or worship, and that upon his death he should neither be deified, exalted, nor worshipped. He later revised the proclamation saying that if the people insisted upon offering worship to his honor, that the worship should be directed to Genius, whom he claimed was his guiding spirit.

Not long after this proclamation, Gothard continued, a quasi-religion and religious form of worship developed in collaboration with the search for The Theophus. Huge rewards were offered regularly to any city, state, province, or nation that could prove that The Theophus had been born in their region or was presently living in their region. Additionally, Tiberius sent personally appointed ambassadors from Rome to every eastern province in the Roman world, to interview and appoint trustworthy representatives to search their respective regions continually for any sign that The Theophus lived in their region or that he had been born in their region.

Naturally, this led to a rush of reported messiah, savior, and "holy ruler" Theophus sightings. Claims came in to Rome from every corner of the eastern Roman world. All of the claims had to (as dictated by Tiberius himself) be addressed, investigated, confirmed, and authenticated by the Roman ambassadors appointed by Tiberius. By the time Jesus' ministry began, the ambassadors had at least a two year and perhaps even a three year backlog of sightings and claims from all over the eastern Roman world. Each needed to be either rejected or confirmed as legitimate claims that warranted further, more intense, investigation and examination.

Gothard claimed that the Herodians (the family, followers, and officials of the House and line of Herod), who were devout followers of Caesar and were fanatical in their unconditional, unchallenged, and unquestioned support of Roman policy, especially if it was instituted by Caesar himself, were appointed by Tiberius' ambassadors to head the official search for The Theophus in the Roman province of Syria. It did not matter whether the Herodians believed the dream or believed that there was such a person as The Theophus—Tiberius believed it and that was enough. The Herodians proved themselves monomaniacal in their tireless efforts in searching for The Theophus—efforts that were rewarded repeatedly by Tiberius with privileges, honor, exemptions, riches, tax relief, citizenship, and prestige. In order to remain in Tiberius' good graces and utmost favor, the Herodians became disreputable in looking for signs, wonders and miracles and in quickly investigating any report of any such occurrences within the boundaries of the province of Syria. During the reign of Tiberius, because of their fervent dedication to Tiberius' commission, the Herodians enjoyed the highest level of influence, privilege, honor, and respect with the Roman authorities, and a fear, dread, and honor from the people that was unparalleled in all of Syria. Their word in Syria *was* law. Their actions were sanctioned, and their authority *could never* and *was never* questioned. In fact, during the rule of Tiberius, to question the word, motives, or actions of a Herodian was just as impertinent, just as unacceptable, and just as punishable as questioning Caesar himself.

I stopped reading and sat for a few minutes trying to assimilate what I had just read, before I moved on. If this information was true then it explains the Herodians involvement in the ministry of Jesus. For as long as I could remember I felt and was taught that the Herodians allied with the Pharisees and the Sadducees in efforts to try to trap Jesus so that they could accuse him of some politically seditious or religiously blasphemous activity. Then they could use that action against Jesus so that they could get rid of him once and for all. However, if the Herodians were appointed by Tiberius' representatives to spearhead The Theophus search and investigation efforts in Syria, as this manuscript reveals; then I needed to reevaluate the reason why the Herodians sought Jesus, why Herod, when he was interrogating Jesus immediately before his crucifixion, hoped that Jesus would perform some miracle for him, and the rational behind the Herodians simulated alliance with the Jewish religious leaders. They were not trying to trap Jesus or have him perform like a trained monkey; they were monitoring Jesus' movements, observing his actions, scrutinizing his teachings, and collecting all the information that they could with respect to Jesus, his teachings, and his actions so that they could deliver that information to Tiberius' Theophus commission representatives. Without a doubt Jesus was the one Syrian provincial resident that in all likelihood could qualify as a possible candidate for The Theophus. Therefore intense examination of Jesus by the Herodians was not only de rigueur to ensure a comprehensive analysis, it was an obligatory mandate prescribed by Tiberius Caesar himself.

It all began to make a whole lot sense to me. The Herodians were not religious. In fact they were more agnostic than they were religious. So, why would they join forces with the Sadducees and Pharisees? The answer was now so obvious. They didn't. They only used the Sadducees and Pharisees to provoke Jesus and to force a reaction from him so that they could observe his character and temperament under the most unpleasant situations and the most stressful of circumstances. The Theophus would likely react to any snare set by the Pharisees and Sadducees with patience and would respond to their deviousness with perceptive wisdom. So, how would Jesus respond? Would he respond the way The Theophus would presumably respond? If he did, then Jesus should be further studied and evaluated as a potential candidate. But if he did not, then The Theophus investigation should be focused away from Jesus.

According to my understanding of the Gospel records, it appears that Jesus reacted and responded the way The Theophus would presumably have responded and reacted.

I continued reading the translation of the Gothard manuscript.

According to official documents supplied to the Imperial court of Rome by the Senate of Rome, a prominent Roman citizen by the name of Valleus Paterculus was appointed by Tiberius to head Tiberius' Theophus investigative efforts. Valleus Paterculus was a well-respected Roman historian who was 19-years old when Jesus was born, and from what we can gather from the writings of Priscian and Tacitus, Valleus had been a close friend of Augustus Caesar, who raised him politically by degrees until he became one of the most influential men in all of Rome, during which time he commanded the personal guard of Augustus for 16 years. It seems that sometime between the ages of 35 and 40, Valleus Paterculus resigned his position and retired to his villa to write his *Historia Romania*, although under Augustus and while Vinceus was consul, he retained the office of praetor.

After The Theophus dream by Tiberius, he (Tiberius) created a special commission of 130 ambassadors whose responsibility was to investigate claims from all over the eastern Roman world of potential sightings of or reported actions of The Theophus. If an ambassador reported that the actions or character of one who was under investigation was consistent with the character of The Theophus as understood by Tiberius, the chief ambassador commissioner would be dispatched to the region and investigate the matter himself. If the chief ambassador commissioner felt that more investigation would be necessary, he would go back to Tiberius and report his findings. Tiberius then had the option to dismiss the report or accept the report. If he accepted the report, he again sent the chief ambassador commissioner back to the region accompanied by four Roman Senators, a magistrate from the Roman Treasury, and the chief Roman military magistrate of the region, to further investigate and to interrogate the one who had been identified as potentially The Theophus.

If the chief ambassador commissioner determined that this person was The Theophus, he had the power to announce to the world that The Theophus had been discovered, and the accompanying Senators had the right to proclaim in the name of Caesar and in the name of the Roman Senate that that region or county was from that day forward to be a religious ward of Caesar, and that Roman citizenship would be awarded all of its citizens. The Roman treasury magistrate had the authority to distribute the cash rewards promised by Tiberius and to exempt the country's or region's residents from taxes; and the military magistrate had the authority to declare all of the citizens of the region and their descendants, to be exempt from military service from that time forward.

Tiberius appointed Valleus Paterculus to be the chief ambassador commissioner, head over the 130-member The Theophus Commission of Ambassadors. Although when they began, the ambassadors had little true power, within three years of Tiberius' dream they were conceivably the most powerful group of men in the entire world, perhaps with the exception of the Roman Senate. However, there were some who felt that they were even more powerful than the Senate, although there was never a confrontation between the ambassadors and the Senate to prove which was most powerful or influential.

One thing was certain however, this Commission of Ambassadors lead by Valleus Paterculus did have the ear of Tiberius, and to keep Rome content and satisfied meant to keep Tiberius happy and satisfied. Therefore, not a single Senator, military leader, political leader, religious leader, or influential citizen in either Rome itself or in any of its territories, frontiers, or provinces is recorded to have objected to Tiberius giving The Theophus Commission of Ambassadors unprecedented latitude, indiscriminate power, and unlimited financial resources.

The manuscript stopped abruptly. Obviously Gothard had written more, but it would probably forever be lost.

As I mentally re-assessed the information found in the manuscript, I could certainly understand how Tiberius' obsession with the search for The Theophus probably was a, if not *the*, major factor that motivated and influenced the Roman authority's treatment of Jesus; and how it became a, if not *the*, driving force and rational behind the Jewish religious leader's obsession to eliminate Jesus at all costs.

I discovered a confirmation of Gothard's manuscript and of the authenticity of Tiberius' The Theophus dream while I was touring The Musee Historique Lorraine in Nancy, France.

The museum had quite an impressive collection of Greek and Roman artifacts. While some of the objects were very rare, others were like so many hundreds of other Roman and Greek artifacts scattered around in dozens of museums throughout Europe.

I began my visit to the museum by slowly strolling through the Greek section, followed by the Roman section. It was in this sector that I saw a Roman statue of a kind that I had never seen before; and although I had seen literally hundreds of Roman and Roman era sculptures and statues, I had never seen one like this. It was a statue of a beautiful bare-breasted female figure that was holding a bird in one hand and holding one of her breasts with the other hand. The sculpture was entitled *A Muria of Theophus*. The caption below the title read, *A tribute to the members of the Murias of Theophus as appointed by Tiberius—1st century AD.*

I was astounded. There was the name *Theophus* again. Again I was confronted with evidence of the existence of the belief in and search for, The Theophus, but this time it was in the form of a sculpture rather than a manuscript or a document.

As I studied the sculpture's every detail, a young lady, perhaps 24 or 25 years old, approached me. I had been running my hand across the marble arms of the statue, and this young lady was an employee of the museum. She politely asked me not to touch the work of art. I apologized for touching the statue, and then asked her if she could tell me about the statue.

She began to explain. "Although the designer and creator of the sculpture were unknown, it dated back to the 1st century reign of Caesar Tiberius. It depicted a religious movement that originated from an apparent dream of Tiberius that evolved into a cult religion called *The Murias of Theophus*."

Dr. Ron Charles

_{a cult}

She then continued. " In the 1st century, a member of the Murias confronted Jesus and that the incident was recorded in St. Luke's Gospel of the New Testament, chapter 11:27-28. Then to my surprise, she quoted the scriptural reference.

> *'And it came to pass, as he spake these things, a certain woman of the company [Murias] lifted up her voice, and said unto him, blessed is the womb that bare thee, and the paps which thou hast sucked. But he said, yea rather, blessed are they that hear the Word of God, and keep it.'*

I asked her if she knew anything more about the cult.

She said that she did know a little about it, but she did not know a lot because although at the time it was probably quite a well-known phenomenon that reached every part of the eastern Roman Empire and probably influenced every level of society, the cult only lasted until shortly after the death of Tiberius. After his death, he was deified (contrary to his last instructions) and was proclaimed by Caligula to have become the actual fulfillment of his own dream. So, by proclamation of Caligula, Tiberius became *The Theophus*.

"After this proclamation by Caligula," she continued, "The cult, the religion that grew out of the cult, it's religious rituals, and devotion to the religion rapidly died out until within 100 years after Tiberius' death, the cult of the search for The Theophus and the religious devotion that grew-up around it, had pretty much disappeared and had been forgotten.

"Consequently, all that is known about the religion and about *The Murias of Theophus* is from a few historical texts from that period, a few 1st century Senate reports, three or four state treasury records where funds were appropriated on behalf of the search by The Theophus Commission of Ambassadors, and a few lines mentioned in the biographies of some of those who lived during that time.

"So, as you can probably understand," she said, "because there is so little information available, we have only limited knowledge of the cult.

"But," she continued, "I will tell you what I know."

We sat down on a wooden bench near the sculpture and she began to explain the history of the mysterious religious cult of *The Murias of Theophus*.

She began her explanation by restating the fact that apparently the cult was influential for only a short period of time—actually only during the reign of Tiberius.

"It seems," she continued, "that after Tiberius had his dream concerning The Theophus, Livia, Tiberius' mother, the wife of Augustus (Livia was the mother of Tiberius and the wife of Augustus. Her first husband was Tiberius Claudius Nero. He was the father of Tiberius), claimed that she had been visited by Juno, the Roman goddess who was called 'the queen of heaven, the mother of all gods and devils, the virgin queen, the dove of heaven.' Livia claimed that Juno to told Livia that she, Juno, was the true mother of The Theophus and that Livia was to organize a *murias* (a myriad or a group of 10,000 devotees [the KJV translated this word, *company*]) of devoted prophetesses who would be led by the spirit of Juno and who would roam throughout the eastern empire searching for The Theophus, the son of Juno."

48

"Livia claimed that Juno had told her that she (Juno) had impregnated a young virgin, who lived in the eastern provinces of the empire, with The Theophus, so that he would be born a human and be raised as a man. But Jupiter, her husband and supreme god, had hidden the identity of the young girl from her (Juno) so that she would not be tempted to re-claim him before it was time for him to be revealed as The Theophus. Juno became angry and refused to have any further relations with Jupiter. Jupiter in turn became angry and said that when it became time for The Theophus to be revealed to men and for him to take his position as a god/priest/king, he (Jupiter) would not reveal his (The Theophus') human identity to Juno nor reveal the identity of his (The Theophus') earthly mother to her. Therefore, when Jupiter declared that it was time for The Theophus to be revealed, Juno had to search for him. She sought to accomplish this with the help of the *murias*, which became known as *The Murias of Theophus*."

"Athanasius tells us that on March 20, AD 22 these 10,000 roaming prophetesses of Juno left Rome in search of The Theophus. They were supposed to have been given special insight by Juno so that they would be able to recognize The Theophus when they found him."

"By AD 30, *The Murias of Theophus* cult center had been moved from Rome to the Temple of Juno in Caesarea Philippi. From there, the 10,000 dedicated women, reputed to have been the most beautiful women in the empire, were sent out in search of The Theophus. But by then, the original spirit of the mission had deteriorated into nothing short of roaming religious prostitution."

She continued, "The standard method of operation of members of *The Murias of Theophus* group confirms the biblical record alluded to in Luke 11.

"Apparently when a murias prophetess approached a man of her choosing, she would say in a loud voice for all in the vicinity to hear, *'Blessed is the womb that conceived thee and the paps which nourished thee.'* This pronouncement of choosing was called the *Myriad of Juno*. It was supposed to signify that Juno had recognized the chosen man as a possible The Theophus candidate.

"From a physical standpoint and a social and community point of view, it was a great honor for any man to be chosen by a member of *The Murias of Theophus*. For not only had he been chosen to have a physical sexual relationship with one of the most beautiful women in the world, but he could qualify to receive a reward in gold, if he was chosen as a candidate, that would have been an amount equal to 13 years' wages of an average tradesman or craftsman. That was enough to catapult any man's economic status from one of poverty or mediocrity to that of extreme wealth.

"With his selection by *The Murias of Theophus*, the prophetess commanded the chosen man to repeat these words after her, *'Blessed is the fruit of the queen of heaven.'* After he repeated this sentence, she would come very close to him and speak to him very softly so that only he could hear, *'You have found favor. You are blessed.'*

"It was claimed by these prophetesses," she continued, "That they were the living embodiment of Juno. In essence, they said that the goddess Juno inhabited them, making them, in essence, Juno in human form. And that through a sexual encounter, Juno would recognize her son because if the man chosen was really her son, The Theophus, he would not be able to bring the sexual encounter to completeness because his seed would naturally reject the potential impregnation by him of his own spirit mother. So, after the prophetess spoke softly to the chosen one, they had a sexual encounter during which the prophetess would whisper in his ear personal words of eroticism, supposedly 'inspired' by the queen of heaven.

"If the man completed the sexual union, he would give the prophetess a monetary contribution. Three-quarters of the contribution was delivered to the Temple of Juno in Caesarea Philippi and the remaining one-quarter was allowed to be used by the prophetess for her own personal support.

"If the man did not complete the sexual union but instead stopped the encounter before reaching its climatic end, then this action was perceived to be a sign that the man very well may qualify as a candidate to be recognized as The Theophus.

"The man was then encouraged to accompany the prophetess back to the Temple of Juno in Caesarea Philippi. There he would go through a three-day ordeal of numerous sexual encounters with the three Most High priestesses of Juno. If he successfully endured these encounters without a climatic ending, he was chosen as a Theophus candidate and was given his reward in gold.

"After this three-day ordeal, he was obliged to remain at the Temple of Juno for 30 days, during which time he was regularly tested in the same way. If at any time during the 30 days he failed in that he allowed an encounter to advance to completeness, he was disqualified from consideration. He still was allowed to keep his reward in gold, but he was no longer considered as the possible Theophus.

"Although there was evidence," she interjected, "that on at least four different occasions a man did make it *to* the candidate stage, there is no record that any man successfully made it *through* the candidate stage.

"It was one of these prophetesses, from *The Murias of Theophus* who approached Jesus and challenged him with the *Myriad of Juno*. The challenge was quite unusual within itself, because, seldom, if ever, did a Murias prophetess approach Jewish religious leaders.

"Jesus' response was unique to say the least.

"Paraphrased," she said with a smug smile, "He said that a person is not blessed because of where and under what circumstances he was born or because of to whom he was born. Nor is he blessed because he is proclaimed to be worthy of being blessed or acknowledged as being chosen of God. Rather, a man is blessed who hears the Word of God and then keeps it, or does what the Word says to do."

After I had discovered this information about The Theophus, The Theophus Commission of Ambassadors, and the Herodians part in the search for The Theophus in Syria, things that had been for years clouded and mysterious, began to appear much clearer. Now there was a reason why <u>Jesus told countless people that he healed, not to tell anyone</u>—and it was not because it was not yet time for Jesus to reveal who he really was, as I had been taught all my life—and why he abruptly and without prior notice seemingly arbitrarily left one region and traveled to another, why the Pharisees were so antagonistic, why the Sadducees were so cynical, why the scribes were so sarcastic, and why the Romans seemed to be so accommodating throughout his ministry, up until the last few weeks of his life. If it was well known to these that Jesus was being examined as a possible candidate for The Theophus, then previously unexplained, unjustified, and illogical actions by them and the ensuing reactions by Jesus, can now be logically explained, rationalized, and justified.

I now want to refer again to the Henry James' synopsis that I paraphrased in the chapter entitled **Augustan rule**. But, this time I will begin paraphrasing from about mid-way through the second portion, or second chapter (the chapter entitled *Tiberius*) of his thesis. This particular portion deals with the reign of Tiberius, the Roman Emperor during the time of Jesus' "silent years," ministry, and death.

On May 26, AD 17 Germanicus and his forces had finally subdued the German tribes under the leadership of Arminius. Germanicus was praised throughout the empire as the reincarnation of Alexander. This sent Tiberius into a jealous rage, resulting in his recalling of Germanicus to Rome, and his demanding that Germanicus not leave Rome.

By September, AD 17, Germanicus had patched up his differences with Tiberius, and afterwards Tiberius gave him permission to leave Rome. Germanicus then retired to Nicopolis in Epirus (northern Greece).

Early in the summer of AD 17, kings Archelaus of Cappadocia and Antiochus of Commagene died under mysterious circumstances. Almost immediately, both of these regions were annexed into the Roman Empire. Cappadocia was established as a Clientela state province and Commagene became part of the Senatorial province of Syria.

The following February, AD 18, while he was still retired at Nicopolis, Germanicus became consul for the second time. In July of that year, Germanicus traveled to Armenia as Tiberius' official ambassador, where he installed Artaxias (Zeno) on the throne of Armenia.

Also in AD 18, in July, Herod Antipas founded the spectacular imperial city of Tiberias, located on the western shore of the Sea of Galilee. He had decided that the city of Sepphoris was not an ideal enough site for his royal court, so he decided to build another royal city (he also maintained a residence in the House of Herod compound in Capernaum and one in Jericho), more luxurious and more centrally located. He chose for the site of his new city an ancient cemetery that was located on the west shore of the sea. Antipas named the city Tiberias, in honor of Emperor Tiberius. From that time until his death, Antipas dated all events associated with his rule from the date of the founding of Tiberius, which he considered his crowning and most grandiose achievement.

A portion of the city was constructed with Jewish labor; some of it, forced labor (almost without exception, all Jews who were slave or forced laborers where Judean Jews. There were few, if any, slaves or forced laborers who worked on the city of Tiberias who were Galilean Jews). Little did it matter to Antipas that the Judean Jews were outraged at his desecration of the cemetery. Construction was continuous (24 hours per day) for eleven years, before decreasing to standard work days (12 hours per day) for an additional six years.

In the 2nd century, a speculation arose that gradually evolved into an accepted truth that was unquestioned for more than 1,500 years. This speculation was that Joseph, the father of Jesus, and Joseph's construction business, had worked in Tiberias (under contract, not as forced labors) for ten years. During that time Jesus served as one of Joseph's construction supervisors in Tiberias.

It was also in AD 18 that Herod Antipas and Herod Philip expanded and "nationalized" agriculture. In order to make their realms more productive, improved methods of collective farming were introduced (which increased annual agricultural production by more than 300 percent) and small peasant holdings were incorporated into large cooperative farms, owned and operated by the Herodians. The peasants and former property owners became tenant farmers of the land and were allowed to live on the land. Eighty percent of the crop harvest was paid to the Herodian landowners, while the tenant farmer was allowed to keep 20 percent (although he had to pay taxes on his harvest).

Germanicus stayed in Armenia until September AD 18, when he traveled to the Illyricum port city of Dyrrhachium. He stayed there until January of AD 19. Then without permission from Tiberius, he traveled to Egypt in pursuit of a young (16-year old) Greek beauty with whom he had developed an intimate relationship while in Dyrrhachium. The father of the young lady had sent her to Alexandria to keep her away from Germanicus. When Tiberius discovered that Germanicus had traveled to Egypt without permission (he had to have special permission because Augustus had barred all Senators, consuls, and governmental officials from traveling to Egypt without special permission from the emperor himself. The conflict with Antony and Cleopatra had prompted this action by Augustus, and Tiberius had not as yet effaced the declaration), he became consumed with rage, stripped Germanicus of his consulship, and threatened to have him arrested and executed.

However, a military revolt in Syria soon took his mind off of the Germanicus problem.

Germanicus left Egypt in April, AD 19, and returned to Rome. There he again "patched things up" with Tiberius, promising never again to return to Egypt without permission, and paying a fine for *Contempt of the Regime* that would be equal to $2 million by modern standards. Tiberius restored Germanicus' consul position and sent him to Syria to subdue the revolt.

When Germanicus arrived in Antioch, the administrative capital of the Senatorial province of Syria, in May, AD 19, he discovered that there was enough evidence against Gnaeus Calpurnius Piso, the governor of Syria, to implicate Piso himself as being responsible for fomenting the military revolt. Germanicus dismissed Piso as governor in June, AD 19. Germanicus demanded that Piso leave the province by December of that year and present himself to the Senate in Rome for interrogation.

Piso was furious with Germanicus and swore revenge. That revenge apparently was realized on October 10, AD 19, when Germanicus died in the city of Epidaphne, near Antioch. On his deathbed, Germanicus accused Piso of poisoning him and implicated Tiberius for ordering his (Germanicus') death.

Piso was immediately summoned to Rome to answer charges of treason and murder. The Senate, with respect to Germanicus' deathbed implications, never officially questioned Tiberius, but suspicions of his involvement in Germanicus' death followed him the rest of his life. Tiberius soon found himself friendless and mistrusted. Although Tiberius was a brilliant general and military leader (who had *never* lost a major battle or a military campaign) he was neither an able administrator nor competent ruler.

In February, AD 20, the prosecution of Piso for treason and murder officially began. But in July, in the midst of the trial, Piso committed suicide.

In AD 21 the Gaulic tribes of the Treveri and the Aedui, under the command of the Romanized noblemen Julius Florus and Julius Sacrovir respectively, revolted with an army of 40,000. The revolt was violently suppressed by Gaius Silius, the commander of upper Germany. This corybantic suppression was primarily responsible for the nickname that came to characterize Silius' actions, the *succubus marauder* (the demon despoiler).

In March of AD 22, Emperor Tiberius suppressed the Egyptian and Jewish religious rites, forms, rituals, ceremonies, and methods of worship in all cities of the Empire whose population exceeded 20,000, and whose Egyptian and/or Jewish population exceeded 5 percent of the population. The only cities that were exempted were Alexandria, Jerusalem, Antioch, Damascus, and Cyrene. In these five cities an Egyptian and/or Jewish population could represent no more than 50 percent of the total population. Tiberius commanded the city officials (except for the exempted cities) to burn the religious apparatus of both the Jews and the Egyptians and to enlist every able-bodied Egyptian and Jewish male (age 14 to 40) in the city into military service (in February AD 23 Tiberius partially reversed this demand and exempted both Egyptian and Jewish religious leaders). The remainder of the Jews and Egyptians in the cities were given a choice to either acknowledge allegiance and loyalty to Caesar and remain in their home cities or not and be expelled from the cities.

In May, AD 22 Tiberius banished the astrologers from Rome and every city in the Empire that had a population of 25,000 or more (Corinth and Caesarea Philippi were the only exempted cities). However, three years later Tiberius reversed this proclamation because the astrologers promised that they would not practice their art openly in Rome or any provincial or state seat of administration.

In November, AD 22, the stage began to be set for the ushering in of the greatest threat to Tiberius' rule, in the person of Sejanus. Sejanus, the Roman Perfect who was sole commander of the Praetorian Guard, the most elite troops in the Roman military (the majority of these soldiers were fierce Illyrians. They were feared and respected by all.), began consolidating his Guard by recalling them from all over the Empire, commanding them to mobilize in a permanent camp that he had set up just outside of the city of Rome.

In December AD 22, Tiberius' son, Drusus, who was very influential with the Roman Senate, died under very suspicious circumstances (some Senators implicated Sejanus in Drusus' death). Sejanus quickly moved to fill the influence void that had been left by Drusus. Being very persuasive, Sejanus raised rapidly in Senate influence so that by February AD 23 he was *the* most powerful Senate influence in Rome. In the meantime, his Guard was increasing in number daily, as soldiers continued to arrive in the camp that he had set up, from all over the empire.

In February AD 23, Tiberius declared that all but 2,000 Jews and 5,000 Egyptians would be immediately expelled from the city of Rome, and that the 2,000 (these did not include the 200-300 Jews who were in the employ of the House of Tiberius and the Imperial Court) and 5,000 respectively could only live in a Tiberius designated "ghetto" located within the "city of refuse" (the garbage dump) in the northern sector of the city of Rome (this portion of Tiberius' declaration was reversed by Caligula in AD 39, allowing Jews and Egyptians to settle anywhere in Italy; but it was re-instated by Claudius in AD 42, followed in AD 48 by his decree to expel *all* of the Jews from Rome). Accompanying Tiberius' declaration were strict guidelines wherein the Jewish and Egyptian religions' worship forms and rituals, observances, laws and rules, philosophies, doctrines, sacred writings, and dogmas had to come under the general critique and approval of the regional Roman authorities. In the province of Judaea the Roman authorities collaborated with the Sadducees to ensure compliance. It was into this restrictive environment that Jesus launched his Judaism-rooted ministry.

According to St. Ignatius, February AD 23 was also the month and year that Jesus was baptized by John in the Jordan River. He said that Jesus was 29 years old. St. Caligastia said that Jesus' baptism took place in April or May of the year AD 23 and that he was 30 years old.

By April of AD 23, Sejanus had made his first allegation of treason. This was the first of hundreds that he and his paid associates would make over the next nine years. Publicly, Sejanus preached social reform and social equality. However, his surreptitious intent, goal, and purpose were to weaken Tiberius politically. He did this by gradually eliminating his (Tiberius') support through accusations of treason directed toward Tiberius' friends and supporters, while at the same time maintaining an awesome show of force, through the placement of his Guard. This show of force was meant to convince the citizens of Rome that he, not Tiberius or the Senate, was their true protector and guardian.

It resulted in a political upheaval that could very well have toppled Tiberius' rule, if not for the fact that in AD 27, Tiberius, out of shear disgust and embitterment, abandoned the city of Rome and went into self-imposed retirement on the island of Capri. Although he continued to serve as Rome's emperor, he governed from Capri. Mass trials, mass convictions, countless executions, and unprecedented suicides rampaged for nine years between AD 23 and AD 31. These years are recorded in history as the *Years of Embitterment.*

From April AD 23 until Tiberius' retirement in AD 27, Sejanus made over 700 public allegations of treason and sedition. Of the accused, over 300 were either executed or they committed suicide. However, after Tiberius' retirement in AD 27, Sejanus' allegations exploded to over 9,000. He had 200 associates in his employ whose primary job was to "find dirt" on anyone and everyone, anywhere and everywhere. Each of the more than 9,000 accused was convicted and each was either executed or committed suicide.

It was during this time, in April AD 31 to be exact, that Jesus was convicted of sedition and was executed. It is no wonder that Pilate, even as ruthless as he was, backed off when the Jewish leaders said that if Jesus was not crucified that he (Pilate) was no longer Caesar's friend. This meant that they would accuse Pilate of treason to Sejanus. Since Sejanus' record was very impressive in that most, if not all, of those accused of treason, through whatever means it made no difference to Sejanus (in this case it would have been through the Jewish officials), he took every accusation seriously and moved on the accusations with incredible speed. So, in essence, had Pilate be accused of treason, it is most likely that he would have been immediately stripped of his position and recalled to Rome by Sejanus to stand trial for the crime of treason. Pilate was totally unscrupulous and without moral conscious, but he was not stupid. So, to avoid a potentially devastating move regarding his political future, Pilate submitted to insistence of the Jewish officials.

In an ironic twist of fate, it was in October AD 31 that Sejanus himself was convicted of conspiracy and was executed. Jesus, in fact, may have been one of the last victims of the political fallout that Sejanus had so mercilessly instigated. Sejanus had accused so many that for three years after his death, trials continued for the ones that he had accused in his last days, although, after his death, there were no recorded executions that can be directly attributed to his allegations.

Tiberius was so embittered by the whole ordeal that even after Sejanus' death, he did not return to Rome. He governed the empire from Capri until his death at the Bay of Naples port city of Misenum in AD 37.

With that statement, Henry James ended the second part of his synopsis.

VI

HEROD'S RULE

Although the stage has now been set for what was happening in Rome's political arena during the time of Jesus' birth, life and ministry, I feel that in order to get a well-rounded perspective of the world into which Jesus was born and lived, we need to look at the Judaea political scene, the religious establishment, and society as a whole during the time of Jesus birth.

I discovered valuable information regarding political Judaea at the time of Jesus' birth in a book entitled *The Life of Herod the Great*, written by Elbert Conway, a professor of biblical history at Edinburgh University that had been published in 1876. I found the book in the library of Lancaster University in Lancaster, England. In the book, Conway did not deal with the Galilee so much, but rather he concentrated on Judaea and the state of Judea.

He began his background material by saying that the Judean political climate in 8 and 7 BC was one of instability and oppression; an instability that could trace its roots all the way back to the days of the Maccabean revolt against Syria in 167 BC, but was revived in the year 67 BC, when each of the two "rightful" descendants of the Judean priest-king Hasmonean line, Aristobulus II and Hyrcanus II, both claimed succession to the throne of Judea and went to war against one another to defend each of their respective rights. To the victor went the rulership of Judea.

With the advice and help of Antipater, a Jew of Idumaean descent who had proven his loyalty to the Roman general Crassus, Hyrcanus II had by 63 BC defeated his brother, Aristobulus II, and had set himself up as king of Judaea. However, the rule was short lived. That same year the Roman general, Pompey "The Great" laid claim to Judea and annexed all of Judea to the Roman province of Syria.

Pompey first had Aristobulus II killed. He then appointed his own military aid and close friend, Scaurus, to be *eques* or military guardian of Judea. This was followed by Pompey's appointment of the loyal Antipater, King of Idumea, the mountainous desert area some 25 miles south of Jerusalem and west of the Dead Sea, as governor. Upon Hyrcanus II, Pompey conferred the religious rank of High Priest of the Jews.

By 47 BC, Julius Caesar had secured his position as Triumvirate Consul of Rome, whereupon, he dissolved the office of Judean *eques* and made Antipater *Epitropos* of all of Judea including Idumea, Samaria, and the Galilee; and granted Roman citizenship to Antipater and his family and his descendants forever. Immediately, Antipater appointed his son, Herod, to be Military Perfect of the northern-most sector of his procuratorship, the Galilee.

Herod was unsurpassed in military vigor and heroic qualities. He so impressed the Roman Senate that in 44 BC, the Senate made him Military Perfect of not only the Galilee, but also of Judea and the entire Coele-Syria region as well.

Julius Caesar was assassinated in 44 BC. This was followed by the Roman civil war, during which, in 43 BC, Antipater died. After Antipater's death, Herod became the *unofficial* ruler of Judea. So impressed by his unsolicited management of Judea and of the Galilee were the Triumvirates Octavian (later called Augustus) and Mark Antony, that in 40 BC, during a short placidity of civil war hostilities, Antony, whose Triumvirate-ruled region included the province of Syria, made Herod *Tetrarch* of Judea.

Civil war again erupted in western Rome near the end of 40 BC. Taking advantage of the instability in the west, the Parthians, from the rugged mountain region northeast of Syria, invaded Roman Syria, which included Judea, in 39 BC. Because of the civil war, Rome could not militarily afford to send troops to the east to confront this invasion of Roman Syria by the Parthians, so Antony and Octavian convinced the Roman Senate to grant the title of *King of the Jews* upon Herod. In addition, the Senate gave him the authority, in the name of the Roman Senate, to defend both Judea and the Galilee against the Parthian invasion.

At first, the war for the defense of Judea and the Galilee went badly for Herod. The Parthians captured Jerusalem and installed the Hasmonean, Antigonus, on the throne as ruler of Judea, forcing Herod to flee to Rome for safety. Upon Herod's return to Judea (accompanied by Roman troops), it took Herod three years of continual fighting to retake Jerusalem and to dispose of Antigonus, and another year to completely drive the Parthians out of the Galilee and the province of Syria. But finally, by 34 BC, the task set before him by Antony and Octavian had been accomplished: the Parthians had been driven back to their mountain home, the eastern province of Syria had been saved and restored to Rome, and his (Herod's) rulership as *King of Judea* or more rightly *King of the Jews,* remained secure (although subject to the Roman governor of Syria, the Roman senate, and the Roman Emperor) until his death in 4 BC.

Throughout his reign, Herod remained a friend and ally of Rome, yet he was distrusted and hated by his subjects in Judea (In the Galilee, he was not hated as much as he was in Judea. This was probably due to the Galilee having a far more cosmopolitan population, wherein Jews were in the minority, than did Judea, which had a proportionately larger Jewish population). Because of his Idumaen (Edomite) descent, he was resented by the Hasmoneans (whose rulership he had displaced by Roman proclamation), even though he had married the Hasmonean, Mariamne, the granddaughter of the late Hasmonean High Priest, Hyrcanus II (she was 12-years old when Herod married her, but she was only one of Herod's seven to ten wives [seven are mentioned by name although some historians claim that he had ten wives]. During the height of his rule, it was claimed by some at the time that he was married to seven wives at the same time. His ten wives gave him nine sons and five daughters). Herod was also disliked by both the religious leaders and the typical Judean citizen, and feared by his own family. During his thirty-year reign, he had over four hundred family members killed, including a sister, two wives, and three sons.

Herod was totally void of any moral scruples, yet he was an expert in political flattery and compromise. On one hand, by extreme brutality, he eliminated all of his rivals, including his own wife, the beautiful and innocent Mariamne (she was 20-years old [although most historians claim that she was the mother of at least one of Herod's sons, some others contend that she was still a virgin when she died, with

Herod refusing to consummate the marriage, citing that he would not be defiled by a Hasmonean] when she was put to death by Herod) whom she accused of plotting along with her mother of treason against him; while on the other, he sought to appease the religious community and his Judean subjects by launching grandiose building projects.

In Judea, Herod built new royal palaces in Jerusalem, in Caesarea Maritima, and in Jericho. He built new cities in Samaria and in the Galilee, new ports on the Mediterranean, magnificent forts and castles, and theaters and entertainment facilities throughout his domain. These projects were magnificent, but most historians feel that his crowning construction achievement was the Jewish Temple of worship in Jerusalem. Construction on the Temple begun in 20 BC, at the time of Jesus' death it still was not complete. Yet, it is considered by all who have studied its magnificence to be one of the greatest construction feats known to man. In fact, many historians say that the Temple in Jerusalem, known as Herod's Temple, should have been the eighth wonder of the ancient world and that the ninth wonder of the world is the fact that it was not recognized as the eighth wonder of the world.

Through severe cruelty and ruthless barbarism, Herod crushed the Judean population into submission. In order to guarantee that the Roman Emperor Augustus would look the other way and not see his (Herod's) ruthlessness, Herod annexed Peraea, Gaulanitis, Trachonitis, Batanaea, and Auranitis into his kingdom and then gave them to Augustus as a gift on the emperor's birthday. By the means of this balancing act, Herod, by the time of Jesus' birth, had become the most powerful "home grown" political influence in Judea in more than eight centuries.

In reality, Augustus was probably mired in a no-win quandary concerning Herod. He absolutely despised Herod because of his senseless cruelty, yet Herod was the most able administrator in the whole of the eastern Empire. The Judean area was so vital to Roman trade (it stood at the crossroads of Rome's extensive trade routes and connected three continents. The control of this trade crossroads region was mandatory if Rome was to maintain its control of the east.), that a strong and able administrator was a necessity, not an option. Hence, for the sake of the empire, Augustus compromised his own principles with regard to Herod, and "chose to looked the other way." He had no choice. So, even though Augustus hated Herod vehemently, Herod was secure in his position.

Although it was true that Herod's unpredictable behavior could cause Judea to explode into violence without warning, yet, generally speaking, Herod had made Judea a safer place (safer than during the Hasmonean rulership) and the populous overall were enjoying relative prosperity, due to immense revenues gleaned from Rome's rapidly increasing inter-continental trade business.

On February 1, 7 BC, Augustus Caesar declared that for the first time in the history of the world, peace ruled throughout the world (this claim has since been proven to be true. Between 7 BC and 5 BC is the only time in the history of humankind that total peace "reigned" throughout the world. From east to west, and from north to south, within the limits of the Roman Empire as well as beyond the borders of the Roman Empire, there is no record of any war, conflict, rebellion, or upheaval anywhere.)

However, in the year 5 BC, that all changed when Herod very nearly was the cause of a world war.

VII

A CHRONOLOGY OF THE LIFE OF JESUS

With the Roman historical background regarding the time of Jesus' birth and childhood now established, I feel that the development of a workable chronological order of his life is in order—one that conforms to and fits well within the established and accepted parameters of Roman historical fact.

The following is the chronology that I developed and used throughout my research efforts.

The life of Jesus

8 BC

1. The angel Gabriel appeared to Zacharias telling him that his wife, Elizabeth will have a son in her old age—Luke 1:5-23
2. In Elizabeth's sixth month of pregnancy, the angel Gabriel visited Mary, a virgin from the Galilee. He tells Mary that she will conceive and have a son—Luke 1:26-28
3. Mary goes to live with Elizabeth until after the birth of Elizabeth's son—Luke 1:39-56
4. Elizabeth's son is born. Augustus is Roman Caesar. Herod the Great is king of all of the region that came to be known as Palestine—Luke 1:57
5. Elizabeth's son is circumcised and named, *John*—Luke 1:59-66
6. Zacharias prophesied about John and about the coming Messiah—Luke 1:67-79.

7 BC

7. Mary returns to her home in Nazareth. Joseph, her fiancée, discovers that Mary is going to have a baby—Matthew 1:18-19
8. An angel appears to Joseph in a dream and tells him to take Mary as his wife—Matthew 1:20-23
9. Joseph marries Mary—Matthew 1:24
10. The Roman Syrian district of Judea's turn to pay taxes. Augustus gave the proclamation two years earlier. Cyrenius (KJV) was governor of Syria—Luke 2:1-3
11. Joseph and Mary travel from their home in Nazareth in the Galilee to Bethlehem in Judea, Joseph's birthplace, to register and pay the special tax—Matthew 2:5; Luke 2:4-6
12. During the Passover celebration sometime between April 12 and April 18, Jesus is born in the Bethlehem area—Matthew 1:25; Luke 2:7—
NOTE: *The traditionally accepted date of Jesus' birth and the method*

of reckoning the Christian Era (BC and AD), around which our calendar revolves, was introduced in the sixth century by Dionysius Exiguus, a Scythian monk living in Rome. He made a mistake in his calculations of at least six years and perhaps as much as eleven years. And although over the centuries, numerous historians have proposed the year of Jesus' birth to be anywhere from 17 BC to 14 AD, I have chosen the year 7 BC as the year of his birth, because to me that year seems to be the most accurate and the most logical when known Roman, Greek, Syrian, and Persian history is evaluated and compared to the biblical texts.

12. Consecrated shepherds who were caring for the Passover sacrifice sheep came to where Jesus was born—Luke 2:8-20
13. While still in Bethlehem, eight days after his birth, Jesus is circumcised and named—Luke 2:21
14. Forty days after his birth, Jesus is taken to the Temple in Jerusalem by his parents to be presented at the Temple Redemption Ceremony—Luke 2:22-24 [Leviticus 12:2-8]
15. Prophecy and prayer of Simeon—Luke 2:25-35
16. Acknowledgment of Anna—Luke 2:36-38
17. Joseph and Mary with the infant Jesus return to Nazareth in the Galilee—Luke 2:39

5 BC

18. About two years after Joseph, Mary, and the infant Jesus had returned to Nazareth in the
Galilee, wisemen or magi, following the tumult in the heavens, which they had witnessed in the East, come to Jerusalem in search of the baby king—Matthew 2:8-10 [Daniel 7:13-14 records the prophecy by Daniel that drove the magi to search for the baby king]
19. Herod the Great sent the magi South to Bethlehem to find the baby. Instead they traveled North to Nazareth in the Galilee, following a star that they were convinced was guiding them—Matthew 2:8-10
20. The magi find the toddler Jesus, worship him, and present to him the *Gifts of Ramses*—Matthew 2:11
21. In a dream, God warned the magi not to return to Herod. Instead they were to return to their own countries another way—Matthew 2:12
22. An angel appeared to Joseph in a dream telling him to take his family and flee to the safety of Egypt. They leave immediately for Egypt—Matthew 2:13-15
23. Herod discovers that he has been scorned by the magi and becomes furious—Matthew 2:16
24. Herod orders the slaughter of the infants in a 15 mile or more radius of Bethlehem; this included Jerusalem—Matthew 2:16-18 [Jeremiah 31:15]. This slaughter leads to a potential "world war" between the eastern coalition and Rome.

4 BC to AD 6 (10 years)

25. Herod the Great dies (in 4 BC)—Matthew 2:19. His kingdom is divided between Herod Archelaus, Herod Phillip, and Herod Antipas.
26. An angel appears to Joseph while they lived in Egypt and tells him to take his family and return home—Matthew 2:19-20. It was probably not until 2 BC or later, however, that they actually left Egypt.
27. They returned to live in Nazareth in the Galilee sometime between 2 BC and AD 6—Matthew 2:20-23. At this time Jesus could have been as young as 5 years old to as old as 12 years old.
28. Jesus grew strong and increased in wisdom—Luke 2:40
29. In AD 6, just before his 13th birthday, Joseph and Mary take Jesus and the family to Jerusalem for Passover so that Jesus, the oldest son, could participate in his bar mitzvah, or the *Son of the Law* weaning ceremony. Although Jesus was 12 when they left Nazareth, by the time Passover was over he would be 13 years old, the age in which he qualified to be a *Son of the Law*—Luke 2:42
30. After the *Son of the Law* ceremony, Jesus' parents join a caravan returning to the Galilee. However, Jesus stayed behind—Luke 2:43-45
31. Jesus' parents cannot find him. They return to Jerusalem where they find him in the Temple—Luke 2:44-49
32. Jesus returns to Nazareth with his parents and remains under their authority—Luke 2:51

AD 6 to AD 23

These are years of silence in Jesus' life, commonly called the "unknown years." However, there were important events taking place in the Roman Empire.

- In AD 6 the Roman province of Judaea is formed. The province includes the states of Judea and Idumea and the district of Samaria. The province is placed under the control of a Roman Procurator.
- In AD 7 the people of the state of Judea revolt against the new Roman Procurator. The revolt is mercilessly crushed.
- AD 10 to AD 13—M. Ambivius is Roman Procurator of the province of Judaea.
- In AD 14 Augustus dies. Tiberius succeeds him. Tiberius rules until AD 37. That same year Annius Rufus is appointed Procurator of the province of Judaea. He governs until AD 15.
- In AD 15 Valerius Gratus is appointed Procurator of the province of Judaea. He governs until AD 26.
- In AD 17 Tiberius had his dream concerning The Theophus.
- In AD 18 the city of Tiberias was founded. Much of it is built by Jewish labor.

AD 23

33. Jesus traveled from Nazareth in the Galilee to the Jordan River to be baptized by John, the son of Zacharias and Elizabeth, called "The Baptist."—Matthew 3:13-16; Mark 1:9-11; Luke 3:21-22. Jesus was 30 years old—Luke 3:23
34. After his baptism, Jesus went into the wilderness to be tempted—Matthew 4:1-11; Mark 1:12-13; Luke 4:1-13

AD 23 to AD 26

35. Jesus increased in wisdom, stature, power, and in favor with God and man—Luke 2:52; 4:14
36. For the three years between the time of his wilderness experience at age 30, until the beginning of his ministry at age 33, nothing is known of Jesus' life.
37. During this three year period Jesus grew very powerfully, spiritually—Luke 4:14

AD 26

38. Pontius Pilate is appointed Procurator of the province of Judaea.
39. John called "The Baptist" continued his preaching and baptizing. Literally thousands came to hear him and to be baptized by him—Matthew 3:1-12; Mark 1:3-8; Luke 3:2-18.
40. In the Spring of AD 26, Jesus came to Bethabara where John was baptizing—John 1:28. At that time John denied that he was either the Messiah, the Messias, or that prophet—John 1:24 [Malachi 4:5]
41. Jesus returned the following day to Bethabara. John said to himself, "Behold the Lamb of God," [the Messias]—John 1:29-34
42. Jesus returned to Bethabara the third day. John proclaimed loud enough so that his [John's] disciples, Andrew and John, could hear, "Behold the Lamb of God." These two disciples of John follow Jesus to where he was staying—John 1:35-40
43. Later, perhaps the same day, Simon [later to be called Peter by Jesus—Matthew 16:18], the brother of Andrew, meets Jesus—John 1:41-42
44. The following day, leaving Andrew, Simon, and another disciple of John (possibly John) behind, Jesus travels to the Galilee to search for and find Philip. Philip becomes Jesus' first called disciple—John 1:43
45. Jesus confronts Bartholomew [Matthew 10:3], the Nathaneal. Seems likely that Bartholomew the Nathaneal becomes a disciple of Jesus at that time—John 1:45-51
46. Taking Philip and perhaps Bartholomew the Nathaneal with him, Jesus goes to the synagogue in Nazareth. He reads from Isaiah [61:1-2]—Luke 4:16-27
47. Jesus is rejected in the synagogue and the people want to kill him. He escapes—Luke 4:29-30

48. In late summer of AD 26, Jesus and his two disciples go to the marriage at Cana [it was probably Jesus' sister that was getting married]. He turns the water into wine—John 2:1-11
49. In the Winter of AD 26, Jesus, his two disciples, his mother, and perhaps some of his brothers moved to Capernaum—John 2:12

AD 27

50. Nothing more is recorded about the life and ministry of Jesus until the spring of AD 27, when he attended the first Passover celebration in Jerusalem since beginning his ministry. It has now been a year since John the Baptist had proclaimed, "Behold the Lamb of God"—John 2:13
51. Tiberius retires to Capri.
52. Upon his arrival in Jerusalem, Jesus went to the Temple. There he threw out the money changers—the first of three times that he did this in his ministry—John 2:14-22
53. Jesus remained in the city of Jerusalem for about two months. Many believed on him—John 2:23-25
54. It is during this two month period that Jesus had his confrontation with Nicodemus [late spring of AD 27]—John 3:1-12
55. John's testimonial of Jesus—John 3:13-21
56. Soon after Jesus' confrontation with Nicodemus, Jesus and his disciples leave the city of Jerusalem but continue to stay in the immediate area of Jerusalem and in the state of Judea until the early summer of AD 27—John 3:22; 4:2
57. Controversy develops between the disciples of John and the Jewish religious leaders—John 3:25-36
58. In early summer of AD 27, Jesus and his disciples prepare to return to the Galilee [John 4:1] in order to avoid competition with John's ministry. However, before they leave Judea, John the Baptist was arrested by Herod Antipas and imprisoned at Herod's mountain fortress of Machaerus—Matthew 4:12; Mark 1:14
59. Jesus and his disciples return to the Galilee, traveling through the district of Samaria—John 4:3-4
60. Confrontation with the woman at Jacob's well in Sychar and the revival that follows—John 4:5-43
61. When Jesus and his disciples arrive in the Galilee, they are welcomed with open arms—John 4:45. They go back to Cana—John 4:46
62. A Herodian approached Jesus requesting that he come and heal his son—John 4:46-53
63. The son is healed—John 4:50-53
64. In August of AD 27, Jesus and his disciples went to the Sea of Galilee. There he taught out of Simon's boat—Luke 5:1-3
65. After he had finished teaching, he instructed Simon to launch out into the deep. Simon and his partners catch a haul of fish—Luke 5:4-6

66. Simon, Andrew, James, and John were called by Jesus to be his disciples—Matthew 4:18-22; Mark 1:16-20; Luke 5:8-11
67. Jesus and his disciples entered a synagogue in Capernaum. There he taught and healed a demonic—Mark 1:21-28; Luke 4:33-37
68. Sometime afterwards Jesus and his disciples left Capernaum and returned a few days later. Nothing is known about this time away from Capernaum. However, upon his return he healed a centurion's servant—Matthew 8:5-13
69. Sometime between September and October of AD 27, Jesus healed Simon's mother-in-law of Bubonic Plague—Matthew 8:14-15; Mark 1:30-31; Luke 4:38-39
70. By the fall of AD 27 Jesus' fame was rapidly spreading into all areas of the Roman province of Syria—Matthew 4:24-25
71. Out of shear exhaustion, Jesus sought a place to pray—Mark 1:35
72. He prayed all night. The following morning people began to search for him—Luke 4:42
73. His disciples find him—Mark 1:36-37
74. Jesus takes his six disciples into a mountain [perhaps a cave] and taught them what has become to be known as "The Sermon on the Mount"—Matthew 5:1-7:29
75. Coming down off of the mountain, he healed a leper—Matthew 8:2-4; Mark 1:40-45; Luke 5:12-15
76. Nothing more is recorded about the life of Jesus until the winter of AD 27. Sometime that winter Jesus decided to take his disciples, cross over the Sea of Galilee, and go to Gaulanitis. Before he left a scribe met him, followed by his confrontation with one of his disciples—Matthew 8:18-22; Luke 9:57-62
77. Jesus and his disciples enter the ship. As it sets sail for Gaulanitis, Jesus went to sleep. A storm hits and Jesus calms the storm—Matthew 8:23-26
78. Upon their arrival on the other side of the Sea of Galilee, they are met by two demonics. He delivered the two men. After the men were delivered Jesus and his disciples left the area and went back to Capernaum—Matthew 8:28-9:1
79. Jesus goes into the wilderness to pray—Luke 5:16

AD 28

80. Nothing more is recorded about the life of Jesus until the early Spring of AD 28. At that time he was invited to participate in the great religious conference that was held in Capernaum. At the conference he healed a paralyzed man who was lowered down to him through the roof as he taught—Matthew 9:1-8; Mark 2:1-12; Luke 5:17-26
81. Jesus called Matthew (Levi) to be his disciple—Matthew 9:9; Mark 2:14; Luke 5:27-28

82. Matthew gave a feast in Jesus' honor. Jesus' lessons on new wine, new garments, friends of the groom, and the yoke is easy—Matthew 22:11-30; Mark 2:16-32; Luke 5:31-39
83. While at the feast, a Herodian approached Jesus asking him to heal his dead daughter—Matthew 9:18-25
84. On the way to the Herodian's house, Jesus healed a woman with an issue of blood—Matthew 9:20-22
85. His fame spread—Matthew 9:26
86. Returning to Matthew's house, he healed two blind men and a man who could not speak—Matthew 9:29-34
87. Jesus went into all the cities and towns in the Galilee teaching, preaching, and healing—Matthew 9:35
88. In mid-spring of AD 28, Jesus and his disciples left the Galilee and traveled to Jerusalem to attend Passover—John 5:1
89. In Jerusalem they went to the Pool of Bethesda. There Jesus healed a man who had been diseased for 38 years—John 5:2-47
90. They stay in Jerusalem for a number of weeks
91. At the beginning of the summer of AD 28 his disciples are confronted because they picked corn on the Sabbath. Jesus responded with his "The Lord of the Sabbath" teaching—Matthew 12:1-8; Mark 2:23-28; Luke 6:1-5
92. Jesus healed a man with a withered hand—Matthew 12:9-14; Mark 3:1-6; Luke 6:7-11
93. In mid-summer of AD 28, Jesus chose 12 out of the ranks of his disciples and followers and commissioned them to be apostles. Among these 12 were the 6 original disciples that he had called. They were sent out at this time to minister to Jews in Judaea *only*—Matthew 10:1-15; Mark 3:14-19; Luke 6:13-16
94. Jesus presents his "Sermon on the Plain" to the 12 commissioned and ordained apostles—Luke 6:12-49
95. Leaving the 12 to minister in Judaea, Jesus returns to the Galilee—Matthew 12:15-20; Mark 3:7-12
96. He is accused of casting out demons by the authority of Beelzebub—Matthew 12:24-30; 12:43-45; Mark 3:22-27; Luke 11:16-20; 11:24-26
97. Jesus' confrontation with a woman from the Murias of Theophus—Luke 11:27-28
98. Jesus went to Capernaum. There he healed a centurion's servant—Luke 7:2-10
99. On August 29, AD 28, Jesus traveled to the Roman military town of Nain. There he raised a Roman soldier from the dead—Luke 7:11-17
100. Nothing more is recorded about the life of Jesus until the winter of AD 28, when
   John sent his disciples to question Jesus and ask whether he was the one—Matthew 11:2-6; 11:20-24; Luke 7:18-35

101. In December of AD 28 Jesus attended the Feast of Dedication celebration at the home of Simon the Pharisee in Capernaum. At the feast a woman anointed Jesus' feet—Luke 7:36-50; 11:45-53
102. .At the feast Jesus gave his teaching on the greatest commandment and the good Samaritan—Luke 10:25-37
103. From late December AD 28 to early January AD 29, Herod Antipas celebrated his birthday.
104. On January 3, AD 29, in the midst of the celebration, he had John the Baptist beheaded— Matthew 14:1-2; Mark 6:14-28

AD 29

105. The body of John the Baptist was buried by his disciples—Mark 6:29
106. After John's death and burial, the commissioned 12 returned to Jesus in the Galilee. They told him about John and about their ministry—Mark 6:30; Luke 9:10
107. Nothing more is recorded about the life of Jesus until the Spring of AD 29, when he led his disciples to a fish drying area near Tiberias. There he fed the 5,000—Matthew 14:13-21; Mark 6: 33-44; Luke 9:10-17; John 6:1-14
108. After feeding the 5,000 he sent his disciples across the Sea of Galilee. The first time that Jesus walks on water. Peter walks on water—Matthew 14:24-33; Mark 6:47-51
109. Jesus walks on the water a second time—John 6:14-21
110. The scribes come to Jesus seeking a sign—Matthew 12:38-42
111. Upon the death of Joseph in early summer of AD 29, Jesus' mother and brothers come to Capernaum to get him—Matthew 12:46-50; Mark 3:31-35
112. A few days later, he did go to Nazareth. There he stayed until late October or early November of AD 29. While in Nazareth, he sent out the 12 again. This time they were allowed to minister to all people everywhere, not just to the Jews in Judaea—Matthew 10:16-47; Mark 6:1-13
113. He appointed and sent out 70 more to minister to anyone who would listen—Luke 10:1-16
114. In September or October of AD 29, both the 12 and the 70 return to Jesus in Nazareth—Luke 10:17-22
115. In late October or early November of AD 29, Jesus and the 12 travel to Caesarea Philippi. There Peter confesses that Jesus is the Christ, the Son of the Living God—Matthew 16:13-25; Mark 8:27-28; Luke 9:18-27
116. Transfiguration on Mount Hermon—Matthew 16:28-17:16; Mark 9:1-13; Luke 9:28-36
117. Teaching on faith as a grain of mustard—Matthew 17:17-20
118. In late November or early December of AD 29, they left Caesarea Philippi area and go back to the Galilee—Matthew 17:22; Luke 8:1-3

119. Disciples argue about who is greatest—Matthew 18:1-34; Mark 9:33-37
120. They go to Capernaum. Peter pays special Temple tax for them with a coin found in a fish's mouth—Matthew 17:24-27
121. .Jesus taught the people parables about the sower, the tares, mustard seed, mustard plant, lamp on a stand, leaven in a loaf of bread, household treasure, treasure in a field, the pearl of great price, casting out a net, and the householder—Matthew 13:1-52; Mark 4:1-32; Luke 8:5-18
122. Jesus and his disciples get into a boat and sail to the other side of the Sea of Galilee.
Another storm [either December 30 AD 29 or January 1 AD 30]. Jesus calms the storm—Matthew 8:26-27; Mark 4:35-41; Luke 8:23-25

AD 30

123. .Jesus and his disciples land in the Decapolis. Confrontation with man who came to known as Legion—Mark 5:1-21; Luke 8:27-40
124. They were asked to leave the area. They returned to Capernaum. When they arrived in Capernaum, Jesus is met by Jarius, a Jewish religious official, who asked him to come and heal his sick daughter. While following Jarius to his house, again he is approached with a woman with an issue of blood. He heals her. He continues to Jarius' house and heals the girl—Mark 5:21-43; Luke 8:40-56
125. Nothing more is recorded about the life of Jesus until the early Spring of AD 30. At that time he was confronted by scribes and Pharisees who had arrived from Jerusalem about his disciples not following the tradition of washing their hands—Matthew 15:1-20; Mark 7:1-23
126. After this confrontation, in April of AD 30, Jesus and his disciples travel to the Phoenician cities of Tyre and Sidon. There he confronts a woman whose daughter was possessed by a demon—Matthew 15:21-29; Mark 7:24-31
127. Jesus and his disciples leave Phoenicia and travel overland to the Sea of Galilee. There they sail over the Sea to the Decapolis. In Decapolis he heals a man who is deaf and cannot speak—Matthew 15:29-31; Mark 7:31-37
128. In Decapolis he feeds the 4,000. Afterwards he and his disciples sail back to Dalmanutha—Matthew 15:34-39; Mark 8:5-10
129. Jesus heals a man from Bethsaida—Mark 8:22-26
130. A boy with an evil spirit is healed—Mark 9:15-29
131. In September of AD 30, Jesus' brothers come to him asking him if he is going to Feast of Tabernacles in Jerusalem. The Feast was held September 15-22 in the years AD 30—John 7:2-10
132. After the Feast had begun, Jesus and his disciples went to the Feast. There he made his "rivers of living water" proclamation—John 7:11-44

133. Woman caught in adultery—John 8:3-11
134. Jesus' proclamation about being the light of the world—John 8:12-58
135. In late September or early October of AD 30, a blind man healed when Jesus rubbed mud on his eyes and told him to go wash in the Pool of Siloam—John 9:1-37
136. Jesus' teaching on the good shepherd and my sheep hear my voice—John 10:1-18
137. Jesus and his disciples return to the Galilee from Jerusalem. Nothing is recorded of their activities during this time.
138. In late October AD 30, Jesus and his disciples leave the Galilee and travel to Peraea and Judea Beyond Jordan—Matthew 19:1-2; Mark 10:1
139. Jesus heard about Pilate mingling the blood of Galileans with their sacrifice—Luke 13:1
140. Jesus healed a woman who had been stooped over for 18 years—Luke 13:10-21
141. Taught the lesson on the straight gate—Matthew 7:13-14; Luke 13:24-30
142. In December AD 30, Jesus and his disciples left Peraea and Judea Beyond Jordan and travel to Jerusalem. There on December 25, they celebrate the Feast of Dedication at the home of the Chief Pharisee. While there he taught the parable of the wedding feast—Luke 14:1-24

AD 31

143. In mid-January AD 31, Jesus and his disciples left Jerusalem and traveled back to Judea Beyond Jordan—Matthew 19:2-30; John 10:40-42
144. Jesus taught his lessons on taking up your cross, building a tower, making ready for war, and salt loosing its savor—Luke 14:25-35
145. Jesus teaches lessons on the lost sheep, the prodigal son, the unjust steward, and the rich man and Lazarus—Luke 15:1-17:10
146. In late January AD 31, Jesus and his disciples go to Bethany and he raises Lazarus from the dead—John 11:1-46
147. Nothing more is recorded about the life of Jesus until March of AD 31, when Jesus and his disciples left Ephraim and began to travel to Jerusalem "the long way around"—Matthew20 17; Mark 10:32; Luke 9:51; John 11:54-55
148. .Jesus healed 10 lepers in Samaria. Only one came back to thank him—Luke 17:12-18)
149. .Jesus and his disciples travel through Jericho. There he confronted Zacchaeus, heals the son of Timaeus (Bar-Timaeus), and heals two blind men—Matthew 19:29-34; Mark 10:35-52; Luke 18:35-19:10
150. Parable of the 10 talents—Luke 19:11-27

151. On Tuesday, March 13, AD 31, the first of Jesus' two triumphant entries into Jerusalem—Matthew 21:1-11; Mark 11:1-10; Luke 19:29-44
152. Jesus goes to the Temple and for the 2nd of 3 times, casts out the moneychangers— Matthew 21:12-13; Luke 19:45-46
153. Jesus cursed the fig tree—Matthew 21:18-22; Mark 11:12-26
154. Jesus goes to the Temple and for the 3rd and final time, he casts out the moneychangers—Mark 11:15-17
155. On Thursday, March 22, AD 31 Mary anointed Jesus' feet. Judas complains about the waste—John 12:1-8
156. On Friday, March 23, AD 31, the second of Jesus' two triumphant entries into Jerusalem—John 12:12-19
157. Jesus taught the parables of the two sons, the evil servant, the marriage feast, and the wedding garments—Matthew 21:23-22:14; Mark 11:27-12:2; Luke 20:1-18
158. 158. Render unto Caesar—Matthew 22:15-22; Mark 12:14-17; Luke 20:22-26
159. The greatest commandment—Matthew 22:23-46; Mark 12:18-37; Luke 20:27-44
160. On Saturday, March 24, AD 31, Jesus and his disciples went to the Temple. The lesson o the widow's mite—Mark 12:41-44; Luke 21:1-4
161. Jesus' Olivet Discourse—Matthew 24:1-51; Mark 12:41-13:2; Luke 21:5-36
162. Jesus' teaching on the parable of the 10 virgins and the 5 talents—Matthew 25:1-46
163. The plot against Jesus—Matthew 26:3-4; Mark 14:1-2; Luke 22:1-2
164. On Tuesday, March 27, AD 31, Jesus and his disciples had dinner at Simon the leper's house. Jesus experienced his 3rd anointing. Judas went out that very evening to make a deal to betray Jesus—Matthew 26:6-16; Mark 14:3-11
165. Wednesday, March 28, AD 31, preparations made for the Feast of Passover—Matthew 26:17-19; Mark 14:12-16; Luke 22:7-13
166. The Passover feast and Last Supper held. The establishing of the Lord's Supper—Matthew 26:20-30; Mark 14:17-26; Luke 22:14-39; John 13:1-35
167. Walk to the garden—Matthew 26:31-35; Mark 14:26-31; Luke 22:31-39; John 13:36-17:26
168. Prayer in the garden and Jesus' arrest—Matthew 26:36-56; Mark 14:32-52; Luke 22:39-54; John 18:1-12
169. Trial, flogging, and pre-crucifixion—Matthew 26:57-27:37; Mark 14:53-15:25; Luke 22:54-23:31; John 18:13-19:18
170. Crucifixion—Matthew 27:38-56; Mark 15:25-47; Luke 23:32-49; John 19:16-30
171. Jesus' burial—Matthew 27:57-66; Mark 15:42-47; Luke 23:50-56; John 19:31-42

172. Resurrection and post-resurrection—Matthew 28; Mark 16; Luke 24; John 20-21
173. Ascenion—Acts 1:4-11—and the spread of Christianity

VIII
SOCIETY AND RELIGION

The next area that I feel needs to be clarified is the religious state in which Judaea (the state of Judea in particular) and the Galilee found themselves at the time of Jesus' birth, life, and ministry. I found information about their religious state at the Rococo Library, located at the Mannheim Palace or Schloss in Mannheim, Germany, in a Latin manuscript written in 372 by Pope Damasus I.

Like most of the ancient manuscripts in the library, the Latin manuscript had been translated into German, French, Spanish, and English. According to the accompanied historical information, the manuscript was actually a "school lesson" that had been written by the Pope for his new secretary, Jerome, who later become known as St. Jerome. The seven surviving manuscript leaves were only a small part of a larger, 60-leaf lesson text that dealt with the various types of religions and philosophies that had been present during Jesus' life, and how those influences were still very much alive during that time—the lifetime of Pope Damasus and Jerome.

From the onset the manuscript captivated me. If Damasus was even close to being correct, the religious influences of Jesus' day were just as diversified as the influences in today's world. In fact, if Damasus' information was true, Jesus not only had to deal with a wide variety of religions and religious influences, but some of his teachings and parables very well could have been inspired by those influences, especially those most respected and honored by Romans.

In Damasus' introductory statement he indicated that he would say very little about Judaism. Instead he would focus on the other religions that were active at the time of Jesus' life and ministry.

Damasus wrote that the Greco/Roman Hellenistic social system that was in place in both Judaea and in the Galilee at this time in history, (immediately preceding Jesus' birth, up through his death and resurrection), was a hodgepodge of religious beliefs and religious philosophy. Except for Judaism, which was dominant in the state of Judea, there was no one religious belief or philosophy that was more dominant or more esteemed by the population than any other, during the emperorships of Augustus and Tiberius. A form of Judaism was being practiced (not necessarily the pure Judaism of Moses, but a more Hellenized Judaism that had been influenced by Greek Aristotelian philosophy, Alexandrian Stoic doctrine, Platonic philosophy, and Persian Zoroastrianism, and confined by the political ambitions of the Sadducees and the Pharisees) in both Judaea and in the Galilee. However, there were also dozens of other religions, religious beliefs, and philosophies that were practiced in both Judaea and in the Galilee.

Damasus then listed and briefly described the predominate religions and religious beliefs that were being practiced in Judaea and the Galilee at the time of Jesus.

> 1). *The Greek*, specifically Hellenic, *and Roman cult religions*. These included the worship of and the ritual observances associated with the Greek and Roman gods of mythology, patriots, and tradition. These

were the most ascendant religions in Judaea, excluding the state of Judea and Jerusalem. In the Galilee, these were third-most influential behind Zoroastrianism, and the mystery cults.

2). *Emperor worship.* This was the deification of the Roman Emperor as the symbol of the state and of the state's (the Empire's) immortality. Emperor worship did not become an officially recognized religious practice until after the death of Augustus, but by the time of Jesus' ministry in the province of Judaea (excluding the city of Jerusalem), it had become the second most common religion. In the Galilee, there were hardly enough devotees to this religion to be recognized, yet during the reign of Claudius there was a serious, yet unsuccessful, attempt to establish it in the Galilee.

3). *Astrology.* This pseudo science imported from Babylon, had developed by the 2nd century before the birth of Christ into a religion throughout the Greco-Roman world. It was followed, practiced, and respected in Judaea and in the Galilee, but it was most influential in the Decapolis and in northern Syria.

4). *Zoroastrianism.* This religion, imported from Persia, was probably the most dominant religious belief in the Galilee and in the Decapolis from the 2nd century before the birth of Christ through the 3rd century after his birth. It was so widespread by the 1st century before Jesus' birth, that every region of the Empire of Rome had large Zoroastrian followings. Next to the Greek Platonic and Aristotelian philosophy, Zoroastrianism was the primary non-Jewish religious belief that influenced Christianity.

5). *The mystery religions.* A rash (some historians from that time claim that in Syria alone there were as many as 60 mystery cults active in the 1st century after the birth of Christ) of mystery religions and cults, most imported from Egypt and Babylon sprang up throughout the Greco-Roman world in the 300-year-period between the 1st century before the birth of Christ and the 2nd century after his birth. The mystery cults were 2nd only to Zoroastrianism in influence in the Galilee. In Judaea at the time of Jesus' ministry, their influence was 4th behind Greco-Roman cult worship, Emperor worship, and Judaism (in that order).

Next, Damasus listed the primary philosophies that were dominant in Judaea and in the Galilee at the time of Jesus' life and ministry.

Over the centuries the Greeks, Persians, Assyrians, Babylonians, and Egyptians had produced a multitude of philosophies that were still active in Judaea and in the Galilee at the time of Jesus' earthly life, but five seemed to be most dominant. They did not take the place of religion or worship; rather they were in addition to religion.

At that time, religion and worship were usually recognized as an action *apart* from everyday life. It was a special concentrated effort. Philosophy on the other hand *was life.* It was how a person lived on a daily basis. Four of these philosophies had their roots in the earlier Platonism of the Greeks and one had its roots in Persian Zoroastrianism.

The ones that were rooted in Platonism were:

1) *Epicureanism.* This school of thought was dedicated to the pursuit of happiness. It taught that men could do something to improve their status and condition. It was an extremely optimistic philosophy. It was the most active philosophy in the province of Judaea, excluding the state of Judea.
2) *Stoicism.* The Stoics believed that a controlling Reason-Fate dominated all of nature. They taught that the soul of man was divine, but that it was imprisoned in an evil body of the physical. Man could achieve liberty from the evil body by living in harmony with God (the Universal Mind) and nature, thus virtue became its own reward. The philosophy seemed to have it's major following in the upper classes of both Judaea and the Galilee.
3) *Cynicism.* This philosophy derived its highest recognized influence through the efforts of Diogenes of Athens. The philosophy's core doctrine was that man could save himself, if he wanted to, and if he would. It taught simplicity and virtue and encouraged man to meet death with courage, for a better life lay ahead. It was nondiscriminatory and classless. Paul the apostle was greatly influenced by Cynic philosophy. In Judaea, Cynicism influenced the Pharisees. The philosophy was 2nd only to Eudemos Zoroastrianism in influential philosophy in the Galilee.
4) *Skepticism.* This philosophy said that knowledge was fallacious, and that conviction and assurance was impossible. It was by far the most pessimistic of all of the dominant philosophies. In the Galilee, Skepticism was the most influential philosophy among the Herodians. It had a limited following in the province of Judaea, mainly among the intellectuals and Sadducees.

The one rooted in Persian Zoroastrianism was:

Eudemos Zoroastrianism. As the name suggests, this philosophy had its roots in Zoroastrianism. Although Zoroastrianism was by far the most influential religion of the residents in the Galilee and in all of Syria, Eudemos Zoroastrian philosophy, which is a philosophy rooted in the mystical ascension to God dogma of the religion, had its greatest influence with the higher educated of Syria. This philosophy along with Cynicism was taught in all public education institutions in the Galilee (Eudemos Zoroastrianism teaching was compulsory up to age 17, while Cynicism was optional, but strongly recommended).

Damasus then listed the other minor, yet influential, religions that had devotees in Judaea and in the Galilee.

Hinduism. This was one of the oldest religions in the world. The members of the army of Alexander brought it back from India. In reality, it was not one religion but rather, a family of religions. In essence, Hinduism was so diversified that it's beliefs and practices could be adjusted to absorb all other religious beliefs, practices, philosophies, forms of worship, gods, and doctrines. Damasus claimed that there was a huge Hindu following in upper Syria and in Persia at the time of Jesus.

Hinduism gave birth to *Jainism, Buddhism* and *Sikhism*.

Jainism, unlike Hinduism, was based upon a founder. He was known as Mahavira, born in India in 599 BC. While Jainism did not have a large following, its devotees were primarily in the Decapolis and in Phoenicia during the time of Jesus' ministry.

Buddhism began in India about 500 years before the birth of Jesus. It came out of disillusionment with Hinduism. Its founder was Siddhartha Gautama, born in 560 BC. About 200 years after his death, Buddha began to be worshipped as a god, which was contrary to his teachings. In the Roman Empire during Jesus' time, Buddhism was practiced mainly in Parthania and in parts of Arabia, although there were schools that taught Buddhist philosophy in Cyrene, Cyprus, and in Syria.

Confucianism. This was more of an ethical system than a religion. Chiu King founded it about the year 520 BC. He was born in China about 560 BC and died in 479 BC. In about 200 BC the followers of Chiu King deified him, which was contrary to his teachings. Along with Greek and Zoroastrian philosophy, Confucianism was taught in every school of higher education in the Roman Empire. It produced thousands of Roman Empire disciples. It was thought to have been brought back from China by Greek traders. Jesus was most likely well acquainted with Confucian philosophy.

Taoism. This was part of the required philosophy curriculum taught at all levels of education in Egypt and in Achaea. Lao-Tzu founded it in China in about 600 BC. Whereas Confucianism had practical humanistic ethical teachings, Taoism was more mystical and enigmatic.

Shintoism had exported devotees as far west as Persia and Parthania, and was being taught in the House and Court of Herod at the time of Jesus ministry. Although the House of Herod taught Shintoistic philosophy, it substituted reverence for the Japanese way of life with reverence for the way of life that had been established by Caesar Augustus and Herod the Great.

Damasus concluded his descriptive analysis by saying, "All of these religious and philosophical influences were active in the whole of Syria, especially in the Galilee, during the time of Jesus' life and ministry. To speculate that Jesus was not acquainted with or that his thinking was not influenced by these influences, would, I think, be illogical and presumptuous. Jesus had been taught most of these different religious concepts and philosophies as part of his compulsory education curriculum in schools in Egypt and in the Galilee. So naturally he was well acquainted with them. Our question should not be whether he was acquainted with or influenced by these religions and philosophies, but rather how was Jesus able to garner conceptual truth out of each and then combine and utilize those truths in a way that was not only the *absolute* truth, but was truth that was pleasing to God the Father, and was beneficial to the people to whom he was ministering? In most of these religions and philosophies, there were certain elements of truth. Jesus had the unique ability to discern the truth in each of these influences and he knew how to insert that truth into the *absolute* truth of his message for the overall benefit of those to whom his message was directed. In essence, Jesus was *the* ideal master discerner of truth and the faultless artisan of compilation of that truth, so that the ultimately compiled truth could be presented to man for his overall good and benefit. Quintessentially, Jesus' teachings were neither a compilation of religious ideas nor a conglomeration of heathen religious philosophy and ethics, but rather they were an acquisition of absolute truth as instructed and directed by the Holy Spirit. So, although Paul and John, as well as many of the other first and second century fathers, were without a doubt, influenced by many of these religious and ethical philosophies, Jesus stood alone as a philosophical non-convert. Yet he used the truths of the philosophies whenever they were applicable to or could be adaptable for his purposes."

The next foundational area that I feel I need to address is the social order wherein Jesus lived. I found an excellent resource that revealed this information at The German National Museum in Nuremberg, in a manuscript written by Vincent Strambi, bishop of Macerata and Tolentino, in 1809. Bishop Strambi had been banished by Napoleon because he refused to take an oath of allegiance to Napoleon. He fled to the northern Italian/Austrian border region, where he stayed until after Napoleon's defeat.

The text that Bishop Strambi wrote was originally a bound volume of some 50 pages, but only seven of the original pages survived. The manuscript was written in Latin, but the museum researchers had translated it into German, French, Spanish, and English.

The manuscript was a description of the various social orders that were to be found in Judaea and the Galilee at the time of Jesus' ministry.

Vincent first concentrated on Judaea. I'll paraphrase what he wrote.

At that time [the time of Jesus' ministry] in Judaea, the population was generally divided socially, rather than culturally or nationally. The population of the province of Judaea was roughly 20 to 30 percent Jewish and almost 85 percent of that number lived in the state of Judea. Hence the state of Judea, within the province of Judaea, had a Jewish population that made up 50 to 60 percent of the total population of the state of Judea.

Although the state of Judea Jews were those who identified themselves with traditional Jewish ancestry, it is very doubtful that even 1 percent of those professing Judaism, could trace their ancestry back to *pure* Hebrew bloodline roots. Most had a variety of mixed-race blood in their past, which technically, according to the Old Testament's proclamation of Ezra, would have disqualified them as pure Hebrew/Jews.

The other 50 percent or less of the state of Judea's population was represented by at least 30 other people groups. Because of the "over-population" of Jews in the state of Judea, traditional Jewish dress, customs, religious observances and rituals, speech—predominantly conversational Aramaic with Greek used in business and in writing (the *only* copies of the Hebrew Scriptures, what we now call the Old Testament, available in both Judaea and in the Galilee at this time, were written in

Greek. There were no scriptures available that were written in Hebrew.) and manners—were not only very much in evidence with the Jewish population, but also with the non-Jewish population as well—it is a fact that many non-Jews, especially in Jerusalem, adopted the Jewish lifestyle and mannerisms, and identified with Judaism—and the religious laws that the religious leaders used to control the Jewish populous in the state of Judea, were demanded of these religious leaders, with little or no compromise. Because the Jews were in the majority in the state, the Roman authorities allowed this kind of religious over-lordship of the Jewish population, so long as it did not interfere with their (the Romans) own governmental policies or jeopardize their control over the province. The Jewish religious community was given so much freedom by the Roman authorities that the Jews even attempted to proselyte the non-Jews in the state of Judea, and convert them to Judaism. Apparently they were somewhat successful for it is estimated that in the state of Judea at this time, although the population was just slightly over 50 percent Jewish, well over 75 percent of the non-Roman population identified with either the Jewish religion or with Jewish customs, manners, rituals, celebrations, or observances.

Nonetheless, in the Idumea and Samaria regions, as well as all the other regions other than the state of Judea, of the province of Judaea, where the Jewish population was in the minority, and the Jewish religion was practiced by less than 10 percent of the regions' population, Jewish religious over-lordship, was hardly recognized much less tolerated and honored. Although the ultimate desire of the Judean religious leaders was to extend their right of rule and government to include all Jews, everywhere, the limit of their Roman recognized governing influence, seems to have been restricted to the state of Judea, within the province of Judaea, *only*. In all other areas of the province of Judaea, except for in the state of Judea, there seemed at that time to be no recognizable difference between Jew and non-Jew, except in religious observances.

The categories of the population in Judaea were divided along social and political ranks and orders.

1) The *aristocracy*. They were the upper classes with money and official power.
2) The *patricians*. They were the second level of wealth and political authority.
3) The *esquirian*. They were the level of wealth and authority that was "earned" authority.
4) The *middle class*. Although it was small, it formed the backbone of Judean society.
5) The *proletariat*. They made up the vast majority of the free Judean population. They were the commoners.
6) The *plebeians*. They made up the lowest level of the commoners. It was the second largest free Judaean population group.
7) *Slaves*. They were was by far the largest social group in the Roman Empire, but second to the *proletariat* in the province of Judaea.

The next region covered was the Galilee (after Herod the Great's death this region became part of the Tetrarchy of Herod Philip). The Jewish population of the state of Judea regarded the Galilee and its residents with very little respect. In fact, they viewed the Galilee with utter contempt, referring to it as *Galil-ha-goyim*, which meant *Galilee, the land of the heathen and the uneducated*. The title was meant to be one of contempt—yet with respect to it being the land of the heathen, it was more accurate than inaccurate.

In the Galilee, at the time of Jesus' ministry, as much as 99 percent of the population was from a lineage other than Jew: Syrian, Greek, Persian, Babylonian, Phoenician, Assyrian, Egyptian, or Median ancestry, leaving only one percent who could claim any kind (even mixed blood, or partial Jewish blood line would qualify) of Jewish descent. Even in the population's religious preference in the Galilee, the Jewish religion was in the minority, with less than 10 percent of the population identifying with the Jewish religion. The remainder of the population identified with a score of other religions and religious philosophies.

The Galilean Jews were far more liberal in their religious views and observances than their state of Judea counterparts. The Judean religious leaders had made in-roads of influence into the Galilee over the past half-century, but they did not have even a fraction of the influence they had in the state of Judea, especially in Jerusalem. Although the Galilee did have it's share of Pharisees and Sadducees and religious leaders, enough to make life miserable for whoever crossed them, their political and administrative influence in the Galilee was for all practical purposes, non-existent.

So despised were the Galilean Jews by the state of Judea's religious leaders, that there existed a kind of Galilean proscription that served to prohibit Galilean students from qualifying for rabbi training (education was supposed to be open and free for all except slaves, and discrimination was strictly forbidden, yet there were very rigid qualifications that had to be met before a student could qualify for rabbi training. These qualifications were used by the Judean religious leaders to disqualify Galilean students). If a Galilean Jewish student ever did ascend the religious education ladder to the level of rabbi or rabboni, the event would have been so rare that the occasion would be unprecedentedly historic indeed. In fact, if not for Roman intervention the event would have been so rare that the odds of it happening would be in our modern terminology, a one in a million chance.

Although the Galilean Jews were *far* more liberal and much more compromising in their religious views than the Judean Jews, in the area of politics, they were far *less* liberal and *less* cooperative with the Roman authorities than the Judean Jews. It's a known fact that some bellicose Galilean Jewish nonconformist groups were nationalistic to the point of being extreme in their anti-Roman sentiments. At the time of Jesus' life and ministry, it can be factually argued that the Galilee was a "hotbed" of anti-Roman sentiment. (The Jewish dissidents were only one of as many as 60 or more dissident groups and rebel bands in the Galilee that were actively involved in anti-Roman/revolutionary activities.) It was a sentiment that would ultimately birth the extremely violent Jewish anti-Roman movements of the 1st century. Because the Galilee was so volatile politically, entire legions of Roman soldiers were permanently stationed in the region.

The Search

However, the Romans were not ruthless masters. If a person was not involved in one of the revolutionary groups or if he cooperated with the Roman authorities and was not a troublemaker, he could live a normal, productive and prosperous life in Roman Galilee. In addition, if he befriended the Romans or attempted to diffuse any potential political explosion, or was a known peacemaker (like Jesus), he could rise to a high level of influence in Roman Galilee. So even though politically the stability of the Galilee seemed to be far more fragile than the political stability in the state of Judea, if a Galilean Jew was non-political and non-controversial, the opportunities for him to live a comfortable, prosperous life were far greater than his counterpart in the state of Judea.

Again, as he did with Judaea, Vincent aligned the population of the Galilee along social strata.
1) The *aristocracy*. As it was in Judaea, these were the upper classes with money and official power.
2) The *particians*. They were the second level of wealth and political authority.
3) The *esquirian*. As in Judaea, it was the level of authority and wealth that was earned. The *middle class*. This group in the Galilee was larger than the middle class in Judaea.
4) The *proletariat*. They were the commoners.
5) The *plebeians*. They were the lowest level of commoners.
6) The *slaves*. This was the third largest population group in the Galilee.

A characteristic of the Galilee that seems to be the most obvious is that the region was Greek. True, it was under Roman political rule, but socially and culturally it was Greek. The Greek language was *the* official language of all of the countries, territories, and provinces of the Mare Nostrum—the Mediterranean—area, as well as the official language of the Roman Empire in the East. Greek culture, Greek philosophy, Greek religion, Greek architecture, Greek games, Greek morality and principles, Greek customs, Greek art, Greek educational standards, Greek social order and lifestyle, and the Greek style of dress were the common denominators that united all of the peoples of the Roman Empire in the East. The Galilee was no different than any other eastern Roman province: it, in essence was Greek. Whereas the spoken language in the Galilee was totally and completely Greek, in the state of Judea, Jews spoke Greek in business dealings only, opting instead to speak in Aramaic for everyday conversational language. Even though with the extreme cosmopolitan make-up of the Galilee region in which some native and national dialects and languages were used scantily, Greek for the most part was the official language, both spoken and written, of all of the Galilean populous.

With that the manuscript page stopped abruptly. Obviously there was more that he had written, but it had been lost.

I turned my attention to the last manuscript page.

This last surviving page of Vincent's text probably belonged some number of pages beyond his social strata listing, because it's subject matter was far removed from the social strata theme and seemed to stand alone. It dealt with the distinctive dress styles that characterized Judaea, particularly the state of Judea, and the Galilee.

Again I will paraphrase what he said.

In the state of Judea, the dress styles of the Jews reflected that of historical Jewish tradition and custom. For men that meant unshaven faces, uncut hair, long robes that also served as a head covering (head covering was compulsory), and semi-solid foot wear. For women, long hanging hair, veiled faces, covered heads, a long (ankle length) heavy linen or wool under garment, with a tight fitting wrap-around type underwear, and a long wool outer robe, and either sandal foot wear or no foot wear at all. The remainder of the Jews in the province of Judaea, except for the state of Judea, dressed more like the Galileans, which was, for all practical purposes, Greek.

In the Galilee, the Jews neither segregated themselves nor separated themselves with regards to dress. The only exception perhaps, would be if Galilean Jews traveled to Jerusalem for a feast or for a religious observance, during which time they might have dressed more "Judean."

Jews in the Galilee dressed Greek, like all others in the Galilee region. Typical for men was short or mid-neck length hair. They were either clean-shaven or they had a shorter well-trimmed beard. For everyday, he wore a short (knee or mid-thigh length) short-sleeved dress-type linen or light wool body garment, the year around, with a longer seamless course-woven woolen outer toga robe and girdle support for winter (although woven wool britches were worn by some men in the winter), and for more formal occasions he would usually wear a long flowing white, scarlet, gray, or blue linen toga. If any head covering were worn (normally there was no head covering worn at all in the Galilee), he would wear a small hat of some kind. He also would wear lace-up sandals. A woman typically had either short hair or long hair that was arranged on top of her head to appear short (although it was not forbidden to let the hair hang long, it was not a typical Greek practice to do so). For everyday, a married woman wore a short (knee or just below the knee length) sleeveless or short- sleeved dress-type light linen garment called a *stola* year around, along with brief-type silk or linen undergarments (underwear), with a long-sleeved longer (shin or ankle length) linen or wool outer robe for winter. An unmarried women wore the same dress except that the *stola* was either mid-thigh or knee length, with no undergarments (underwear). For more formal occasions she would wear a sleeveless white shear silk under-garment with a white, blue, silver, or purple long flowing shear silk seamless toga outer-garment. She wore no head covering and wore lace-up sandals.

Joseph and Mary, as well as Jesus and his disciples, would have dressed like this. They would have culturally and socially been Greek with Greek customs and manners, and they would have spoken Greek in their everyday conversation. In fact, when he was growing up, the only time Jesus would have spoken Hebrew was when he went to the Temple (if even then), and the only time he would have spoken Aramaic (if at all) was when he went to Jerusalem.

Mary and her other children would have spoken Greek as their every day language while they were living in the Galilee, but after the death of Joseph, she moved to Jerusalem (she probably moved to Jerusalem in February AD 30).

The Search

Accordingly, when she and the children who went with her moved to Jerusalem (this probably included James, the second oldest who became the leader of the church in Jerusalem, even though he could have also been a disciple of Jesus and probably traveled with him), they spoke Aramaic as their every day language.

That concluded the Bishop Vincent Stambi manuscript and the description of society in Judaea and the Galilee at the time of Jesus' ministry.

IX

A SON IN OLD AGE

A study of the life of historical Jesus must begin with the pronouncement of the birth of John—Luke 1:5-23.

In the first chapter of Luke's Gospel, the angel Gabriel appeared to Zacharias, the priest, to announce that his wife, Elizabeth, who had passed her childbearing years, would have a son. He was to be called John. He became known as John the Baptist or John the Baptiser.

It seems that Zacharias was an ordinary priest, whose class was instituted by David. His primary duty was Temple service. Zacharias' ancestry was Levite of the House of Aaron, through the line of Abijah, according to Nehemiah 12:17.

It seems that at this time in Judea, according to Shillel, a priest serving in Hebron at the time of Herod the Great, there were more than 24,000 priests divided into 24 different priestly orders. Although ordinary priests were allowed to perform temple duties twice during a year, the honor of performing Temple duties was given to an ordinary priest only once in a lifetime. Hence, it was on this occasion, the once in a lifetime opportunity to perform duties in the Temple itself, that Zacharias was found in the Temple, performing those priestly duties. Verses 8 & 9 of Luke 1 read,

> *"And it came to pass that while he executed the priest's office before God in the order of his course, according to the custom of the priest's office, his lot was to burn incense when he went into the Temple of the Lord."*

Before I continue any further I feel it is necessary to give a little background concerning the first chapter of Luke, the primary source of the birth of John and Mary's visit to Elizabeth. According to a 3rd century Arab/Christian tradition, Luke 1:5-47 was written by Luke, the physician, <u>in the Aramaic language</u>, rather than the Greek or Latin, which were Luke's typical writing languages. This tradition explains that the difference in language used by Luke was because this portion of chapter one is <u>a record of Luke's personal interview with Mary</u>, the mother of Jesus. The interview was conducted some 25 years after the death and resurrection of Jesus, probably in Jerusalem. Mary answered Luke's questions in the "language of the hearth," the Aramaic language, the language used by most Judean Jewish commoners of that day. Few Galileans, however, spoke this language. Luke wrote as Mary had spoken to him, in the language she chose to speak, Aramaic, (because she was living in Jerusalem, she spoke to him in Aramaic) rather than her native Galilean Greek dialect. Luke reverted back to the Greek language in verses 48 through 55 of chapter one as he gives, in a hymn of true early church poetry, his own personal tribute and praise to Mary, much of it imitating the Song of Hannah in the Old Testament. Then in verses 56 through 80 of chapter one, Luke again picked up his interview with Mary and wrote in the Aramaic language as Mary spoke to him.

The Search

Now back to Zacharias. The statement *"in the order of his course"* (Luke 1:8) referred to the once-in-a-lifetime opportunity to serve in an official capacity in the Temple. In other words, it was Zacharias' turn to perform his once-in-a-lifetime duties in the Temple. The statement *"his lot was to burn incense"* (Luke 1:9) refers to the practice of drawing lots to determine who would have the privilege of burning the incense (symbolic of prayer) on the Altar of Incense on the Day of Atonement (usually in early October) of that particular year.

Because there were so many ordinary priests, a system of drawing lots for the privilege of burning incense was instituted. Zacharias was very old and he had been waiting a lifetime for this privilege. Needless to say, this was *the* highlight of his priestly career.

Zacharias and his wife Elizabeth were childless. According to Jewish tradition, childlessness to a woman, like sterility to a man, was not only a reproach; it had come to be believed by the people that it was a curse dispensed by God as a punishment for sin (Genesis 16:2; I Samuel 1:6; and Isaiah 4:1). Consequently, although they were righteous and blameless in their service and worship to God, in the eyes of their friends and neighbors, they were perceived to be under a curse from God, as punishment for perhaps some unconfessed, hidden, or inherited sin.

As the story goes, as Zacharias was standing on the right side of the Altar of Incense, the angel (*angelos* in Greek and *malak* in Hebrew; the definition of both is *messenger*) Gabriel appeared to him and told him that his prayer had been answered. What prayer had been answered, is not known. It could have been his private prayer in regards to his wife's barrenness or it could have been the prayers that were being symbolized by the smoke of the incense being burned on the Altar of Incense. But considering that Zacharias had not begun to burn the incense when Gabriel appeared to him, it is safe to conclude that his prayer regarding Elizabeth's barrenness was the prayer that had been answered. Gabriel announced that Elizabeth would have a son and that his name would be called *John*.

The name, *John*, was a Greek name (Ioannes) that means *loved* or *favored*. The Jews in the Jerusalem area had adopted it (Yohanan) during the days of the Syrian domination and had assigned to it a definition that meant *Jehovah shows favor*.

Although Judean Jews had given the Greek name a Hebrew definition, it still seemed strange to me that the angel Gabriel would command that this miracle baby, born into a Jewish priestly family, be given a pagan Greek name. It just didn't make any sense. Why manufacture problems and controversies that need not be invented? John would have enough problems without having to contend with this stigma. Now he would also have to fight this pagan name battle for his entire life. Yet I knew that because it was recorded in the Gospels, I had to accept the story that Mary had dictated to Luke as true. Besides, there was no evidence to prove it false.

However, looking at the story from a strictly logical point of view, it may not have been out of character for the angel to demand that the baby be given a Greek name. At this time in history (Elizabeth probably conceived in either January or February of 8 BC) Rome was the mistress of the known world and the non-compromising will of the Roman Empire was *the* supreme law of the land. This was especially true in the circle of countries that surrounded The Mare Nostrum. But, though Rome ruled supreme politically and militarily, in the everyday life of its citizens and subjects, their culture was Greek. The Greek language was *the* official language of all of the countries, territories, and provinces of the Mare Nostrum area, or Mediterranean area, as well as the official language of the Roman Empire in the East. Greek culture, Greek philosophy, Greek religion, Greek architecture, Greek games, Greek morality and principles, Greek customs, Greek art, Greek educational standards, Greek social order and lifestyle, and the Greek style of dress were the common denominators that united all of the peoples of the Roman Empire in the East. The Roman province of Syria, which included what is now known as the region of Palestine, was no different than any other eastern Roman province: it, in essence was Greek. From Mount Hermon in the north to Beersheba in the south and from Peraea and East of Jordan in the east to the Mediterranean in the west, the Greek way of life was the rule rather than the exception. Only in a few small villages of northern and northwestern Galilee and a few small villages of Judea, could any resemblance of the genuine, historical Jewish lifestyle be seen. Yet, in these villages, Greek influence was easily recognized as the most dominant cultural influence. Even in Jerusalem, the very heart of Judaism, where the local Jews had their Temple of worship to constantly remind them of their Jewish heritage, religious beliefs, and customs, Greek culture prevailed. Only in their religious observances and practices did the Judean Jews separate themselves from Greek cultural influence. So in essence, Jerusalem, like all other major cities in the eastern Roman Empire, was a typical Greco-Roman city: politically dominated by Rome, but Greek in its culture and way of life.

Some six months after Elizabeth conceived, the angel Gabriel was again sent to the region. This visitation is recorded in Matthew 1:18-23 and Luke 1:26-38

One of the most fascinating resources that I found that discussed the annunciation and Mary's virginity was at Emory University's Candler School of Theology in Atlanta. It was a book written by Rev. Charles Chauncy, the leader of the anti-Great Awakening movement, the "Old Light," who pastored the First Church of Boston from 1727-1787. In his *Seasonable Thoughts on the State of Religion in New England*, published in 1743, he criticized the New England revival and defended the anti-revival position. Chauncy apparently published an original edition and then a second edition, a revised edition. The revised edition, published about five months after the first, is about 150 pages shorter in length than the original and is the edition that most theological libraries have. The first edition is more rare than the second with less than 2,000 copies printed. Emory had one of those first editions. The book discussed Joseph and Mary, their espousal and the position that espousal played during the time of Jesus' birth, and Mary's virginity. Much of this information was for some reason edited out of the second edition.

I will paraphrase what Chauncy wrote. He began his chapter number three by quoting from Matthew, Luke and Isaiah.

"Now the birth of Jesus Christ was on this wise: when as his mother Mary was espoused to Joseph, before they came together, she was found with child of the Holy Ghost" (Matthew 1:18).

> "Behold a virgin shall be with child, and shall bring forth a son, and they shall call his name Emmanuel, which being interpreted is, God with us" (Matthew 1:23).
>
> "And in the sixth month the angel Gabriel was sent from God unto a city of Galilee, named Nazareth, to a virgin espoused to a man whose name was Joseph, of the house of David; and the virgins name was Mary" (Luke 1:26-27)
>
> "And behold, thou shalt conceive in thy womb, and bring forth a son, and shalt call his name Jesus. He shall be great, and shall be called the Son of the Highest: and the Lord God shall give him the throne of his father David" (Luke 1:31-32).
>
> "Then said Mary unto the angel, how shall this be, seeing I know not a man?" (Luke 1:34).
>
> "And the angel answered and said unto her, the Holy Ghost shall come upon thee, and the power of the highest shall over shadow thee: Therefore also that Holy thing which shall be born of thee shall be called the Son of God" (Luke 1:35).
>
> "Therefore the Lord Himself shall give you a sign; behold, a virgin shall conceive, and bare a son, and shall call his name Immanuel" (Isaiah 7:14).

Chauncy then continued with an explanation, which I paraphrased.

The traditional Christian interpretation of the Matthew 1:18 setting is that the Scripture *implies* Mary's virginity when it states that she was found with child, *"before they came together."* The Greek word that is used in connection with this statement is *suneithein*. Ever since the days of Alexander the Great, this word was used to intimate two different statements that seem to contradict one another. The first meaning is "before living together." The other meaning is "to come together physically." Hence, this scripture does not give a translation that is clearly defined enough to allow a satisfactory evaluation concerning Mary's virginity. If Matthew 1:18 was the only Scripture that could be used to prove Mary's virginity, then her virginity could not be proven.

Matthew 1:23 and Luke 1:27 are also cited as proof of Mary's virginity. But in each of these references the Greek word used for "virgin" is *parthenos*. The word means "an unmarried maiden, a maid of marrying age, or a young girl." If the use of these references is intended to attest to Mary's virginity, they will prove to be greatly lacking and non-convincing.

Chauncy then evaluated the Isaiah 7:14 setting, which is usually sighted as Christianity's foundation upon which the belief in the virginity of Mary is built. This particular "prophecy" is part of an even larger prophecy, prediction, or presumption made by Isaiah, concerning the destruction of the kings of Syria and of Ephraim before the time that his [Isaiah's] infant son would reach an age of knowing right from wrong. He made the prediction as he was taking his infant son to meet King Ahaz. The prediction did actually come true just three years later, when Assyria invaded Syria, and Pekah, king of Ephraim, was killed by Hoshea. In the midst of this larger prophecy, Isaiah spoke the words recorded in verse 14. In the statement,

"Behold a virgin shall conceive" the Hebrew word that is used for virgin is *almah*. The word means "a young woman or a woman of child bearing age." This word, Chauncy noted, was usually, but not always, used in an analogy in connection with and/or in describing empires, kingdoms, people groups and races of people, social systems, or nations. Of the thirty times that the word is used in the Old Testament, only two times is it used in connection with young women; and in both of those times it is used to describe an unmarried young woman.

Chauncy then referred to another resource from which he had gathered some of his information.

"An intriguing piece of information I (Chauncy) discovered was a copy of a 17th century Middle English reprint of a 12th century Yiddish manuscript that was written as commentaries, giving opinions and appraisals on the text of some of the Babylonian Talmuds. One of the commentaries dealt with the Talmud text wherein the scholarly Rabbi Hezeial ben Judah quotes this very same Isaiah prophecy in connection with the great Persian Empire. He observed that Cyrus the Great often referred to his empire as *The Virgin Kingdom*. Cyrus claimed that he had been given his power of conquest by the stars, more specifically, the constellation Virgo, the Virgin. In addition, Hezeial claimed that this particular portion of Isaiah's prophecy was an allegory that symbolized the future for the people of Israel; that Persia, the Virgin Kingdom, will birth a son, a nation of people, who will be called, *'God with us,'* or *'God's chosen people,'* or the *'people of God.'* He said that because of the proclamation of Cyrus, the nation of Israel was birthed out of the Persian Empire, and that Israel became known as *'God with us' or 'God's chosen people.'*"

I paused to think about this before I continued. Although obviously Rabbi Hezeial would not agree that this portion of Isaiah's prophecy had anything to do with a foretelling of the birth of Jesus, his explanation about Cyrus was believable. It is well known in history that Cyrus did in fact claim to have received his directive to conquer while studying the constellation Virgo and that his did call his empire "The Virgin Kingdom," yet, I had never considered those historical facts in light of Isaiah's prophecy until now. Although now, 2000 years after the birth of Jesus, we can look in hindsight and say that Isaiah was referring to the birth of Jesus, at the time of the birth of Jesus it is logical to see how Hezeial, as well as all those who had lived from the time of Isaiah to the time of Jesus, would have interpreted the prophecy the way that he did. The Israelis called themselves "God with us," or "God's people," or Immanuel. They also called themselves "the first son of the offspring of Cyrus" for at least three centuries after Cyrus proclaimed their right to return to their homeland. In essence, they did look upon themselves as the first son of the Virgin kingdom. So, for Hezeial to record what was being taught at that time concerning the interpretation of this prophecy by Isaiah seems quite logical. *"A virgin shall conceive, and bear a son, and shall call his name Immanuel"*—out of the Virgin kingdom, the empire of Cyrus, Persia, would be birthed a son, the nation of Israel, and they would be called God with us, or the people of God. It seemed to me to be an obvious interpretation of what Isaiah had prophesied. For four centuries after Isaiah gave his prophecy, this interpretation of his prophecy was the accepted. But now, with the birth of Jesus the four-century-old "truth" of Isaiah was changed to reflect the birth of Jesus? I can certainly understand why the Jewish religious leaders rejected this as being a prophecy relating to Jesus.

I then returned to quoting Chauncy.

"I (Chauncy) feel that the translators of the Greek Septuagint, when translating the Isaiah 7:14-16 portion, did in fact correctly translate the Hebrew word that was used in the Hebrew text, *ha-almah*, into the secondary connotation Greek word, *pathenos* (which has come down to us in the King James version as *virgin*), which means 'a young girl just into puberty.' But, when the Greek text was translated back into Hebrew and then into Latin, the translators incorrectly assumed that *patanos*, was the ***primary*** Greek connotation of the word that the original Septuagint translators had translated *pathenos*. *Patanos* meant *'a virgin; a woman who has never had sexual relations.'*

"As such, they then assigned the Hebrew word *betulah*, which also meant *'virgin; or a young woman who has never had relations with a man'*, as the word that should be used in the Hebrew text. By the time of the King James translation, the story of Mary's virginity had become the foundational rock upon which the Roman Church's doctrine had been built. Hence, to translate the Isaiah portion accurately (which would have in effect cast doubts upon the dogma of Mary's perpetual virginity) would have been nothing short of heresy.

"Again," Chauncy noted, "we are faced with the complex problem of having no clear-cut, non-controversial proof of Mary's virginity; at least based on this portion of Isaiah."

"So, when we evaluate all of the Scripture portions that are usually cited as proof of Mary's virginity, only one (although one should always be enough to prove definite fact), Luke 1:34, seems to give the proof that is needed. In this portion of the first chapter of Luke, Mary questioned the angel and said how could such a thing be because, "*I know not a man?*" In Greek, the word that is used to describe this statement is *gignosko*. In Latin, the word is *cognoscere*. Both words imply that she had had no physical relations with a man. The Greek word means, "to produce a child through marriage relationships." The Latin word means, "sexual relations." Consequently, in the Greek, the statement would read, *"I cannot produce a child, I am not married."* In the Latin, the statement would read, *"I have not had sexual relations."* So, after considering all of the traditionally accepted scriptural proofs, only Luke 1:34 attests, without a doubt, to Mary's probable virginity at the time that the angel confronted her."

Chauncy continued by describing the annunciation. "According to the Luke setting, the angel Gabriel appeared to Mary in the city of Nazareth, but it does not say where she was at the time that he appeared. Speculation has ranged from that she was sleeping in her house to shopping in the market.

"However, an 11th century Latin manuscript that I (Clauncy) discovered while in London some twelve years earlier, which was reputed to have been re-writings of a 2nd century writing of St. Ignatius of Antioch, claimed that as Mary approached a fountain in Nazareth to fill her water-pitcher, the angel Gabriel appeared to her.

"Another Latin manuscript dating from the 12th century, said that the angel Gabriel appeared to Mary in her sleep and told her that she would conceive that very night and that she would birth a son and that she had to raise him as a Greek, for his name would be Greek—Jesus.

"An Arabic manuscript written by a scribe named Abid of Damascus in the 8th century says that Mary was impregnated by the spirit of God while she slept and that when she awoke an angel ate bread with her. The angel told her that she had conceived during the night and that the fruit of her womb would be the son of the Most High, and that his named would be called, Jesus.

"Another 11th century Arabic manuscript that was shown to me (Clauncy) by a Turk who was in London trying to sell the manuscript, said that the angel who had appeared to Mary had himself impregnated Mary. More light was shed on this presumption when I (Chauncy) discovered in a 15th century Arabic manuscript, whose authorship was attributed to a scribe named Ismael of Babli, a two line statement relating that as Mary slept, an angel sent from Allah, *"came in unto her [Mary]...and she conceived..."*

"What was most interesting about the two line statement were the words, *"came in unto her"'* because these are the same words that were used by Luke in verse 28 of chapter one.

"I compared the statement in an Arabic/Greek/Aramaic word study lexicon and discovered that the only other time that this particular statement is recorded in the Bible was when Judah impregnated Tamar, his daughter-in-law, recorded in Genesis 38:18.

The Hebrew word *bow* is the word that was used to describe the statement *"came in unto".* The definition of the word is, "to enter, come, come in, to go into, to lead in, to cause to come in, or to enter as with physical relations." As stated, the same term is used in Luke 1:28. If this portion of Luke was written in Greek, the Greek words that were used to describe the statement "came in unto" were *eiserchomai pros.* The words mean, "to come in and go out again, to enter into to the advantage of, to come in to, to come at and to enter."

"If this portion of Luke was written in Aramaic, the words that were used to describe this statement were *metaph prpe.* The words mean, "to enter into with regard to entering, to arise by, to begin to be." Although the Luke definitions seem to be incredulously consistent with the Genesis text, there did not seem to be enough convincing evidence to accept Gabriel's impregnation of Mary as logical or factual.

"I (Chauncy) became further convinced that the Gabriel story was a fabrication invented to discredit Jesus' miraculous birth, when two days later I discovered, quite by accident, an Egyptian manuscript that for years had been housed in Jerusalem, but had been loaned to Queen's College in Cambridge.

"As I was reviewing some 16th century Islamic texts in the college library, I found a manuscript that appeared to be Egyptian Coptic. It was written in Arabic. It appeared to have been misfiled and had been consigned to the Islamic manuscripts sector rather than to the Coptic or Egyptian manuscript sector. The manuscript, probably dating from sometime between the 10th and 15th centuries, was a warning to the Christians in Egypt. It warned that in past times, about two generations after the death and resurrection of Jesus, a group of infidel mystics had fabricated and circulated a story that the virgin, the mother of the Christ, had been impregnated by

The Search

the angel of annunciation, not by the Spirit of God, and that Jesus was not *the* son of God, but rather he was *a* son of God because he had been fathered by an angel. The manuscript went on to warn the Christians that the story was still being circulated at that time, and that they must remain faithful to the truth, regardless of how convincing the lie may be. Needless to say, after reading this, I became even more convinced that the whole story about Gabriel's fathering of Jesus was nothing more than a malicious attack bent on destroying the truth concerning the birth of Jesus.

"With regards to Mary's virginity and the virgin birth of Jesus, I found significant information at Queen's College. I read literally dozens of book segments, manuscripts, and documents that ranged from the early Talmuds to the 1st and 2nd century Christian writers, and from early Arabic traditions to Gnostic spiritualist writings.

"What I discovered," Chauncy continued, "was that the controversy concerning the virgin birth had been on-going from the time of Jesus' earthly life up until the present day (Chauncy's day).

"After studying numerous documents, I concluded that about half of what I had read at Queen's College supported the virgin birth of Jesus, and the other half either flatly rejected the virgin birth as fact, or tried to justify a rejection by explaining away its possibility.

"The authors of the documents that supported the virgin birth generally did not go into detail about why they believed in the virgin birth. It appeared as though they accepted the virgin birth as a matter of fact or as a matter of principle.

"The documents that rejected the virgin birth usually seemed to have attached to their rejection a justification for the rejection and an alternate theory or a so-called, 'historical proof' of what they claimed was the truth about the birth of Jesus. In these non-virgin birth hypotheses, there seemed to be a common thread of quasi-logic. The one thread of 'logic' that all seemed to share was that Mary, a young girl, probably age twelve, thirteen, or fourteen had sexual relations before she was married and that she had become pregnant.

"Some of the stories centered around Mary's supposed rendezvous with a number of men ranging from a Roman soldier to a Chaldean priest, but most seem to suggest a pre-marriage tryst between she and Joseph, her betrothed, resulting in her pregnancy.

"Most of the stories that claimed Joseph fathered Jesus also claimed that after Mary realized that she was pregnant, she and Joseph fabricated the divine conception story to hide the guilt of their pre-martial union.

"Of course," Chauncy continued, "if a person begins his search for the truth about the virgin birth with a pre-determined conclusion of unbelief, then chances are he will eventually find some documentation someplace to justify his conclusion of unbelief."

At this point Chauncy began a series of theological arguments that did not seem to add anything to the proof that he was revealing. So, I skipped all of the theological reasoning and picked up again with Chauncy's retelling of some of the myths associated with Mary's conception.

"Among the Orthodox Jewish community," Chauncy wrote, "a story that is recorded in the Talmud is usually sighted by the non-virgin birth supporters as the 'true' story about Jesus' birth. This story claims that Miriam (Mary), a hairdresser (*plicatricem capillorum mulierum*—the occupation that Jewish tradition gives to Mary) from Nazareth, was given a Bill of Divorce by her husband, Pappos (Joseph), the stone carpenter, because Miriam had committed adultery. She gave birth in secret to Jesus, whose real father was Tiberius Julius Abdes Pander, a Roman soldier, who was born in Sidon in Phoenicia, and who belonged to the Roman legion garrisoned at Nain in the Galilee.

"A Sidonian story circulated in the 2nd century says that Mary was raped by a Roman soldier named Julius Panthar. She conceived Jesus as a result of that rape.

"A Tertullian story circulated during the time of Jesus' ministry says that he was the illegitimate son of a stone mason from Nazareth and a *magdalah* or prostitute, who also served as a hairdresser, from Bethlehem.

"A Jewish tale that originated in Alexandria about the time of Jesus' baptism says that he was the product of an incestuous relationship between Mary and either her father or her brother.

"A Gnostic tradition from the 3rd century says that Mary had offered herself to a Roman knight at the Temple of Isis in Caesarea Philippi during the Last Festival of Summer celebration. As a result, Jesus was conceived.

"A story that seems to have originated in the 4th century in Spain says that Jesus was conceived as a result of Mary being raped by her uncle, Joseph of Arimathea. The story goes on to say that Mary secretly married Joseph of Arimathea after the rape, and that Joseph of Arimathea paid Joseph, a stone mason from Nazareth, to pose as her husband in public. It also says that Mary and Joseph of Arimathea were still secretly married at the time of Jesus' death.

"An early Arabic tradition says that Elizabeth and Zacharias contrived a meeting between Mary and an Arabic prince named Alba-Pand, who was traveling to Egypt and who had stopped in Halleh, the town where Zacharias and Elizabeth were living at that time, to rest for a while before he continued on his way. He made quite an impression on the old couple, so they introduced him to their beautiful niece, Mary, who was visiting them from Nazareth. Mary and the young prince soon developed a physical relationship, resulting in the conception of Jesus.

"A story that seems to have originated in Babylon in the 1st century says that Claudius commanded an investigation be made into the Jewish Messiah question. The investigation was initiated because of the influence and the claims of Theudas, a self-proclaimed Jewish Messiah who claimed to be The Theophus of Tiberius, who incited a rebellion among the Jews in Rome in AD 43. As a result of the rebellion and the investigation, Claudius expelled all of the Jews from Rome in AD 44.

"Claudius demanded that the investigation include all self-proclaimed, as well as publicly recognized, Jewish Messiah claimants, since the rule of Julius Caesar. This included Jesus.

"Included in the information collected about Jesus were accounts of his teachings, his miracles, his death, and the mystery of his birth. The portion of the investigative report that dealt with Jesus concluded that the conception of Jesus was the result of a union between Mary and a Jewish priest by the name of Joseph-ben-Jubal.

"The report said that the priest had raped her at age twelve when Mary had gone to her first purification ceremony at the Temple in Jerusalem.

"The report went on to say that Mary considered Jesus, the son who was conceived as a result of the rape, to be a gift from God; in essence a son of God; presented to her by a priest; one whom the Jews felt was the earthly representation of their God: His will, His purpose, His plan, and His actions; on earth. In order to cover up his involvement with Mary, the priest bribed Joseph, who was working as a stonemason in the construction that was going on in the Temple compound. Joseph was to claim responsibility and was to keep silent about the priest's bribe. In return, Joseph would be 'set-up' in his own business in his hometown of Nazareth. In addition, as part of the cover-up, Joseph and the priest concocted the divine visitation and conception story.

"Another story that likely had its origin in Macedonia about the 2nd century claims that Mary's father and Joseph's father had been close friends in Nazareth, and although Joseph was six years older than Mary, she developed a close friendship with Joseph. One day a Roman soldier raped Mary. She was a virgin. Mary's father responded by killing the soldier, which resulted in the imprisonment and execution of Mary's father. Mary, left homeless, was first invited to live with Joseph's family, followed shortly thereafter by her adoption by her Roman citizen uncle, Joseph of Arimathea, her father's brother.

"At this point the story becomes confusing. One version says that Mary became pregnant as a result of the Roman soldier's rape. Fearing reproach, she fled back to her mother's family in Egypt, asking her close friend, Joseph, to accompany her. There in Egypt, Jesus was born.

"Another version of this story states that Mary did not become pregnant by the Roman soldier as a result of the rape, but that the soldier was killed by Mary's father. Mary's father was in turn executed for the murder of the soldier. After her father's death, Joseph's family took in Mary. While Mary was living with Joseph's family, Joseph and Mary yielded to temptation, resulting in the conception of Jesus. Shortly thereafter, her uncle adopted her. But, fearing that reproach would come upon her uncle, she fled with Joseph (her espoused) to Mary's family in Egypt by way of Edom. In Edom, in the town of Beth-ham, Jesus was born.

"After the birth of Jesus, the two versions again agree, saying that when the couple arrived in Egypt, Joseph married Mary and with the help of Mary's family, spread a story that subtly implied that Mary's pregnancy was of divine origin. Joseph and Mary returned to Edom when Jesus was twelve years old, where they lived until Jesus was about twenty. In Edom, Mary and Joseph's other children were born. When Jesus was about twenty, the family moved back to Nazareth to take over Joseph's family's business. By this time, Mary was no longer implying divine conception; she was openly proclaiming it. Thus, when Jesus began his earthly ministry, the story of his divine conception had been well propagated.

"A variation of this story appeared in the 9th century agreeing with the story about Mary's rape by a Roman soldier and Mary's father killing the rapist. For this act of homicide, he was sentenced to hard labor for the rest of his life in the sulfur mines of Dalmatia. Left without a family because her mother and grandmother were still in Egypt, Mary, at the age of 12, was adopted by the younger brother of her father, her uncle, Joseph of Arimathea, a Roman citizen.

"Because he (Joseph of Arimathea) assumed legal parentage of Mary while she was pregnant, he also became the life-long legal parental guardian of the child that she was carrying (not all of the children that would be born to her, just the one that she was carrying at the time that she was adopted). So, although Joseph and Mary were Jesus' parents, Joseph of Arimathea, as legal parental guardian of Jesus, could also claim life-long paternal privilege. Therefore, through this adoption by Joseph of Arimathea, a Roman citizen, both Mary and Jesus became Roman citizens.

"Except for the rape claim, there seemed to me (Chauncy) that this story had much more merit than any of the others. Although I (Chauncy) do not believe that Mary was raped, I do feel that she was adopted by her powerful Roman citizen uncle, Joseph of Arimathea, after some unknown tragedy or misfortune removed her father from her life. At the time of her father's removal, Mary had just become pregnant with Jesus (her father's removal well may have been the reason why she went to Judea to visit Elizabeth. Until her uncle could adopt her, she had no other place to go. Or, more unlikely, the misfortune could have occurred to her father while she was gone to visit Elizabeth). She was not married to Joseph, and she had no immediate family who would care for her. Hence, her uncle, Joseph of Arimathea, adopted her as his own daughter, making her unborn son, Jesus, his legal son."

With that Chauncy ended the 3rd chapter of his book. A book that if nothing else, was eye opening to anyone who had been raised on the fundamentalist traditions of the past 100 years.

After Mary had received a visit from the angel Gabriel, she left her home in Nazareth located in the Galilee and traveled to Judea to visit Elizabeth. The scripture reference is in Luke 1:39-41.

> *"And Mary arose in those days, and went into the hill country with haste, into a city of Judah; and entered into the house of Zacharias, and saluted Elisabeth. And it came to pass, that, when Elisabeth heard the salutation of Mary, the babe leaped in her womb; and Elisabeth was filled with the Holy Ghost" (Luke 1:39-41).*

During my years of research, one of the most enlightening documents that I read concerning Mary's visit to Elizabeth, I discovered in the British Library in London. The document was a 13th century Old English commentary on the 9th century Latin apocryphal *Protevangelium of James*, compiled by a man who identified himself as Richard of Tadcaster. Tadcaster was a 13th century trading village, long since disappeared, originally located on the River Wharfe in Yorkshire.

I will paraphrase Richard's commentary notes regarding Mary's visit to Elizabeth.

Richard wrote that Luke says that after the angel's visit, Mary hurriedly left her home to go visit her cousin Elizabeth, who was pregnant with John. If tradition is correct, Richard noted, Mary was pregnant when she left her home to visit

Elizabeth. The time of her conception of Jesus probably would have been sometime in July or August of 8 BC.

Richard then described in detail how Mary had other children. This really surprised me because I thought that by Richard's time the Church of Rome had pretty much convinced all of Christian Europe that Mary was a perpetual virgin.

Richard wrote, "The Gospels say that Joseph and Mary had three other sons: Joses or Joseph, Judas, and Simon; and daughters—the number of daughters is not told. But according to the *Protevangelium of James,* Mary had ten sons and four daughters. Along with Jesus, James, Joses, Judas, and Simon, she also had Judas Thomas, Jonas, Judah, Enos, and Levi James. The daughters' names were Miriam, Melkha, Eskha, and Ruth. Of these," Richard continued, "Mary's second son, James, was born in Egypt or in Nazareth immediately before they fled to Egypt. The other sons, (except for Judas Thomas) and daughters were born in either the Galilee, Edom, or Moab."

Judas Thomas, Richard claimed, was a twin of Jesus and was born in Bethlehem, either the same day as Jesus or one day after Jesus was born. He went on to say that this Judas Thomas was the same Judas who betrayed Jesus with a "brotherly kiss of betrayal and death." I will cover more on the subject of Judas Thomas later.

After this description of Mary's other children, Richard returned to Mary's journey to visit Elizabeth.

He said that the Greek word for cousin, *suggenes*, means "countryman." This countryman may or may not indicate blood relative. In as much as Elizabeth's heritage was predominately from the tribe of Levi and Mary's, through her father, was more or less from the line of Judah, it seems unlikely that they were blood relatives. Rather, they were probably close family friends.

For centuries the Roman Church has depicted John the Baptist as a religious "wild man," growing up as a hermit in the desert. According to Luke's passage it seems that Mary went to visit Elizabeth *in a city* in Judah, probably either Hebron (called *'Ain Karim*), about twenty miles south of Jerusalem, or *Juttah,* about five miles south of Hebron. This would indicate that John grew up in a city and then when he reached a certain age he left home to live in the wilderness (he in fact did leave home about the age of twenty-five and did live in the wilderness, from the time he left home until his imprisonment, as a Jewish Hasid Hakamin [a pious Jewish hermit who preached repentance and separation from worldly temptations], and possibly even became a member of one of the hermit religious sects existing at that time: the Essenes, the Qumran monks, the Therapeutae, and the Margherians or some other sect). It also shows that John's social background for the first twenty-five years of his life was in reality urban, rather than nomadic.

Luke records nothing about Mary's long journey to Elizabeth's (from Nazareth to Hebron was approximately eighty miles if Mary traveled directly through the Samaria region. Typically, it would have taken her from seven to ten days to cover this distance.), or about Joseph's reaction to such a hurried trip. Instead Luke immediately takes us to Elizabeth's home and concentrates upon the events of Mary and Elizabeth's meeting.

Luke records that when Elizabeth heard Mary's greeting, the unborn babe, John, leaped in her womb. The Greek word for leaped that is used here is *skirtao*. It means, "birth kick" or "birth pain." It was used when referring to birth contractions. This may or may not indicate, as the church has taught for centuries, that the unborn John recognized the voice of Mary and responded to it. More than likely, Richard speculated, Elizabeth's emotionalism at seeing Mary resulted in a natural birth contraction.

Luke also says that Elizabeth was filled with the Holy Ghost the very moment that Elizabeth heard Mary's verbal greeting. In Luke [1:15], the angel told Zacharias that John would be filled with the Holy Ghost *"from his mother's womb"* In other words; John would be filled because his mother was filled.

Here [in the 41st verse of Luke 1], the angel's promise to Zacharias came true. Elizabeth became filled with the Holy Ghost, which in turn filled the unborn babe John. If this is the case in every instance of the Holy Ghost infilling a mother who is bearing an unborn child, is not known, but it did happen in this incident.

Elizabeth immediately cringed because of the birth contractions. Yet, the pain seemed to be somewhat of a joy, resulting in her salutation of thanks and praise to "the mother of my Lord". It is interesting, Richard noted, that the word Luke used for "mother" is not a word at all, but rather it is a combination of two words from two different languages: *Eloah-theos*.

When we break the *word* down, Richard wrote, and study the definitions, we find that the first part of this word, *Eloah*, is Hebrew. It is a Hebrew form for "God," meaning "God, the Divine One." The second part of the *word*, *Theos*, is the Greek word for "God," meaning "Deity, the Supreme God."

"Why did Luke in this setting use a word for 'mother' that was not even a word, but rather a combination of two different words from two different languages?" Richard asked.

To add even more mystery to Luke's intentions is the fact that the *word* Luke used for "mother" is very close in assemblage to the Chaldean word, *Elothos*, which was used in identifying the female character of the supreme god of the city of Babylon in the third millennium BC, *E-Zida*.

The ancient Babylonians claimed in their religious mythology that *E-Zida* had both male and female characteristics, and both a good and a bad side personality or character. Also the female character of *E-Zida*, *Elothos*, had conceived and given birth to a son, who was called *El-bal*. This son-god, *El-bal*, lived as man on earth and established a worldwide kingdom, long before the founding of Babylon itself. As the legend goes, *El-bal* gave himself sacrificially to *E-Zordoc,* the evil serpent god, to redeem the people of the world, who *E- Zordoc* had captured and was holding for ransom. After three days, *Elothos* raised her son from the dead, and he became the Sun god, the god of all life.

So, taking this ancient Babylonian legend into consideration, (a legend that was well-known to all in the Roman world at this time, including to the Jewish people) it seems quite obvious why Luke recorded Elizabeth's praise in the way that he did.

Elizabeth's acclamation was a praise of thanks to the real, not legendary or mythological, Second person of the Trinity—the God-Head; the Comforter; the One God who conceived; the "God-Mother" of God the Son, her Lord; the One who had just filled her moments before: *The Holy Ghost.* It was *NOT* a praise and tribute to Mary, but rather this was Elizabeth's praise and tribute to the *Holy Ghost*, the "Mother of my Lord," the Second person of the Godhead, Mother of the Third person of the Godhead, the Son. Mary had told Luke about Elizabeth's praise when she was interviewed by him some years after Jesus' death and resurrection, and Luke had written it down as it was told to him, using a "word" to describe "mother" that was easily identified to all in the Empire at that time who would read his Gospel.

Since Luke was writing to a predominately intellectual Greek audience, and not a Jewish audience, he had to use a "word" that was not only an immediately recognized description of the God-Mother, the Holy Ghost, but one that would be non-contentious with the new Christian converts, yet well-known throughout the Roman world. Unfortunately, over the ensuing centuries since Luke's writing, the original descriptive definition, the one that Luke had intended, was lost. I (Richard) personally suspect, it was purposely forgotten or hidden by the church, in order to give "Scripture inaugurated" credibility to the worship of Mary dogma that swept the Roman world from the latter part of the third century, and has now engulfed the whole of Europe.

I had to pause in my note taking." What enlightenment!" I inserted. "Of course! It made sense! Elizabeth was giving praise to the Holy Ghost, the Mother of the Son, her (Elizabeth's) Lord! Of course the Roman Church wanted to mold this into an adoration of Mary. It had no choice if it insisted upon exalting Mary to the position of deity."

I then returned to Richard.

The 12- or 13-year-old (probable—or at the extreme outside 14-year-old) Mary, Richard continued, was astonished by Elizabeth's emotional eruption. She obviously didn't know how to respond, but she felt she needed to say something. Mary's timid and perhaps somewhat fearful response to Elizabeth's praise salutation is recorded in Luke only.

> *"And Mary said, my soul doth magnify the Lord, and my spirit hath rejoiced in God my Saviour" (Luke 1:46-47).*

The next portion [eight verses] of Luke's record is Luke's poetic hymn of tribute. They *ARE NOT* the words of the 12-or 13-year-old Mary. This hymn of praise and testimony to the mother of Jesus is now called *The Magnificat,* because of its first word in a later Latin version. The hymn is strictly a testimonial by Luke. There are *no* grounds for giving so much attention, as many exegetes have done, to the question of whether the statement was spoken by Elizabeth in tribute to Mary or by Mary herself. Neither is correct. It was Luke's own personal tribute.

Luke then states (1:56) that Mary stayed with Elizabeth until the birth of John, probably either in October or November of 8 BC, after which time Mary, now four months pregnant, returned to her home in Nazareth.

The remainder of this portion of Luke's record (chapter one) deals with the birth of John (Luke 1: 57-58); the circumcision and naming of John (Luke 1:59-63); the miracle of the return of Zacharias' ability to speak (Luke 1:64-67); and

Zacharias' prophecy concerning his son, John, and the coming Messiah (Luke 1:67-79).

Luke chooses to remain silent about Mary's return home to Nazareth, the implied controversy (Matthew 1:19) between her and Joseph and the townspeople of Nazareth (if in fact there was a controversy), and the next five months of her pregnancy. Luke doesn't pick up the story of Jesus again until he is almost ready to be born.

The Search

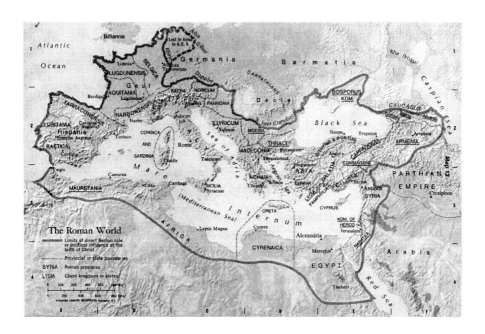

Dr. Ron Charles

X

THE NATIVITY

Throughout the history of Christianity more has been written and spoken about Joseph and Mary than any other married couple in the entire history of the world. But, so little historical facts written about them have been discovered.

One of the most outstanding books that I located regarding the known history of Joseph and Mary was at the research library of Georgia Tech University in Atlanta. It was entitled *The Carpenter's Mentor*.

According to the accompanying notes, the book was published in France in 1661, by special order of Louis XIV. A Count Berini Comeaux of Azay-le-Rideau authored the book. Although the subject of the book was Joseph, the earthly father of Jesus, and Mary, his mother, it was not a typical storybook that told a fantasy tale about Jesus' parents. It was a history that gave "life" to the mysterious person of Joseph and his relationship to Jesus and to Mary while at the same time bringing Mary down from the divine pedestal, upon which she had been placed, to the level of humanity.

According to Count Comeaux, *Joseph*, or *Pappos* in Hebrew, was a genuine Hebrew name, whose origin dated back to the days of the Patriarchs. Christian tradition, or more rightly, Catholic tradition, which has influenced all of Christianity, says that Joseph was a carpenter, a worker in wood. The Muslim tradition calls him *Yusef ben Yarakub, en neggiar*, "Joseph son of Jacob, carpenter, builder of houses." The term, *en niggiar*, was applied both in describing a wood carpenter, as well as a brick mason or stonemason. The Aramaic word for carpenter meant *architect and builder in stone and metal*; the Greek word for carpenter meant, *designer of stone buildings*. The Arabic tradition says that Joseph was a stone carpenter-architect. In what material he actually worked is unclear and immaterial, although by most accounts he was a stonemason. But, what is clear is that he was a master builder. The Count said that he agreed with the majority of his reference accounts and felt that Joseph was a master stonemason, that he and his family had a successful construction business in Nazareth, and that they were probably wealthier than the average Galilean Jewish family of that time.

Count Comeaux then talked about a scroll that was found in 1652 in the Ayasofya Mosque or Haghia Sophia (St. Sophia church) in Constantinople. It was a sheepskin scroll of hagiography that contained the record of two interviews with Joseph and Mary. The interviews were supposed to have been made by Gamaliel, who was said to have been sent by the Sanhedrin in Jerusalem. The record was entitled *Talmuds of the Jews, 27B—Interrogation of Joseph and Mary in Regard to Herod's Child in Bethlehem, Whom He Feared Would be King.*

The scroll revealed that the first interview made by Gamaliel was conducted in Mecca, in the land of Ammon or Moab. The second interview was made some four years later in the Galilee city of Nazareth. According to these interviews, Joseph and Mary, after the birth of Jesus in Bethlehem, returned to Nazareth, their home city in the Galilee. But for fear of Herod, they left Nazareth and fled first to Moab,

The Search

then to Egypt. Upon leaving Egypt, because Joseph feared a possible reprisal by the Roman authorities because of the magi issue and Herod's reaction to their disregard for his authority, they again settled in Moab, in the city of Mecca. There they lived for 18 years, before moving back to Nazareth in the Galilee.

In the interviews, Gamaliel reported that Joseph was a stone workman. Joseph had been taught the trade by his father and had worked in his father's businesses in Nazareth before marrying Mary. Gamaliel felt that Joseph was about 40 or 45 years old, was very tall, and that his hair looked as though it might have been auburn when he was younger. He went on to say that Joseph was a poor talker whose yes was yes and whose no was no. He felt that Joseph was probably disagreeable with his family, and that he and his wife, Mary, had little common ground from which to communicate. He had eight children, seven of which looked very much like him. The oldest, Jesus, looked very much like his mother, Mary. His opinion of the oldest, Jesus, was one of mixed feelings. On the one hand, he said that Jesus was a good worker and that he knew that he had the ability and the professionalism to carry on the family business, having proven his ability and his worth while working in Tiberias; but on the other, Jesus had not, until very recently, shown much interest in taking the responsibility that his position as elder brother demanded, although Joseph felt that that was changing. He got along well with Jesus and wanted Jesus to open a family branch in Capernaum, but so far it had not happened. In reference to the vision it was inferred that he had had of an angel, Joseph said that it was more of a strong thought in the mind, rather than a vision—a thought that said that his elmah had been with child for one month of the spirit of God and that the child would rule over kingdoms. The thought continued by indicating that she (Mary) had been chosen by God and that he (Joseph) must marry her and bring up the child as his own son. When the child reached adulthood he would be chosen by God to bring the kingdom of God to his people. Joseph went on to say that he questioned whether the thought was real or just his imagination, but because of his devotion to Mary, he married her.

Count Comeaux then turned his attention to Mary. Unlike Joseph, a true Hebrew name, the name *Mary* was of Egyptian origin; although church tradition felt it necessary to demand that Mary's lineage be traced as if it had descended from the line of David. The word, *mary*, in the Egyptian language meant, "rebellious" or "one who is apt to rebel." In fact, in Egypt at the time of Mary's birth, a rebellious daughter was often referred to as a "mary." It may indicate that *Mary* might not have been the birth name of Jesus' mother, but rather, a name by which she was called, a nickname; perhaps describing her character as a young child. Over the centuries, an overwhelming number of imaginative apocryphal writings concerning Mary have been produced. Among these were *The Protevangelium of James* and *The Gospel of Pseudo-Matthew*. Both of these edified Mary and portrayed her as having a remarkable and abnormal, yet godly and holy, childhood. It is from the *Protevangelium* that we get the tale that Sepphoris, the Roman city not far from Nazareth, was the birthplace and the early childhood home of Mary. The Gospels themselves say nothing about Mary's childhood. Nothing whatsoever is stated in the Gospels about Mary's life before Jesus was born, except that Luke states she was a virgin; that she was full of grace, *kecharitomene*, which meant "beautiful and pleasing to look upon;" and she was espoused to Joseph.

The scroll that records Gamaliel's interview with Joseph also describes Gamaliel's two interviews with Mary. The scroll records that at the time of Gamaliel's first interview with Mary in Mecca, she looked as though she was about 35 or 40 years old. She had a cheerful, happy, and somewhat mischievous spirit; and she was fair to look upon, although she had birthed eight children who had survived. Gamaliel said that she was rather fleshy with dark brown eyes and dark brown hair, and that her grandmother, Pennel, and her mother, Anna, were of some renown in Egypt, their home country. Gamaliel described Mary's life after she left Egypt, "Leaving her mother in Egypt, Mary was brought by her father to Judea in the days of Augustus. Her father arranged her espousal to Joseph, the son of a wealthy builder of stone buildings and homes in the Galilee, but her uncle, her adoptive father, not her own, arranged the marriage of her and Joseph...." Gamaliel went on to describe the events that led up to the time of Jesus' birth. "She said that she was very young, 12 years old, and frightened when the angel told her that she would conceive and birth a son. Naturally she thought that the son would be from Joseph. Again the angel appeared and told her that she would conceive by the Holy Ghost and that the son will save his people and reign over kingdoms...She did not believe the visions until she began to swell...her father was then put away by the authorities and she left her home to visit friends...it was while she was away that her uncle arranged for her adoption...upon her return, she told Joseph, who decided to put her away for tax purposes...but soon after, Joseph said that a strange but frightening thought made him change his mind and that he had decided that he must marry her..." Gamaliel then gave his own observations: "Mary does not have a good relationship with Joseph, her husband, or with all of her children. Three seem to side with her in disputes that often occur between she and Joseph, although Jesus, the eldest son, usually chooses not to take sides. Joseph has at times told her to leave and not return, but as yet divorce has not resulted...However, on two different occasions she and her oldest, Jesus, have left Joseph and have lived for extended periods with her uncle and adoptive father. She says of Jesus that he was a thoughtful child, who caused very little problems.... He was thoughtful to the point of carelessness at times and is not close to any of his brothers and sisters except Miriam, the second oldest daughter, and at times James, the second oldest son."

In Gamaliel's second interview with Mary, this time in Nazareth, she said of Jesus, "Jesus is always kind to women, which is not the character for most men, but he has little interest in those women of his own heritage...although I know that there is a young woman of Egyptian heritage in Bethany in Judea and another in Scythopolis that he is fond of, in fact I suspect that he will marry the young woman from Bethany, if that occasion presents itself to him...." When asked about the angel's words that Jesus would reign, she laughed, saying that "Jesus has indeed taken his rightful position as elder brother and accepts his responsibility as a provider, along with his father, for the family, but, she wonders whether Jesus will be able to rule his own family, much less a kingdom...." Gamaliel went on to say that "...it seems that like most Galileans, Mary and her husband Joseph care little about the Jewish nation or the Roman oppression...they both seem to be self-seekers interested in nothing concerning our plight.... It seems that his [Jesus'] teacher was a former rabboni whose name was Massalian, of Egyptian estate, who had become a priest and who now lives in the village of Bethany. Massalian says that Jesus is an excellent student, who is thoughtful and pious, and is dedicated to the true purpose of God's dealing with man.... He at times becomes impatient with Jesus because of his obsession with details and because of his desire to apply the Law to daily life, without the benefit of an interpreter.... He too says that Jesus is interested in a young woman in the village and plans to marry her...."

Count Comeaux then began to discuss the history of the set of scrolls, which included the scroll that contained Joseph and Mary's interviews.

He said that how the scrolls got to Constantinople is a mystery, but there is a local tradition that is noteworthy concerning them. It seems that, according to this tradition, more than 300 scrolls of the writings of Gamaliel, including the records of his interviews with Joseph and Mary, were housed, along with hundreds of other scrolls, books, manuscripts, and parchments, at the library of the Sanhedrin in Jerusalem, located near the pool of Hezekiah in the Millo sector of the city. When Titus destroyed the city of Jerusalem, he also destroyed the library of the Sanhedrin. While the library was burning, 13 priests risked their lives in an attempt to save as many of the documents as possible. Nine of the priests lost their lives in the process, but the four who survived succeeded in rescuing more than 60 scrolls, books, parchments, and manuscripts. Among documents that were saved were a small dole of ten of scrolls written by Gamaliel, including the scrolls that recorded the interviews with Joseph and Mary. All others were destroyed. The four priests who rescued the Sanhedrin documents took possession of the testimonials and brought them out of Judea for safekeeping.

A priest by the name of Daniel of Herodium took possession of the ten surviving Gamaliel scrolls and brought them to Apollonia in Illyricum, where he hid them. There they remained in hiding until the first crusade, when in 1097 troops from Raymond, Count of Toulouse's army, while pillaging through the ruins of the city, discovered the scrolls. Raymond took possession of the scrolls and brought them with him to the Holy Land. There in 1099, after the successful recovery of Jerusalem, he left them in safe keeping with the newly appointed king of the Kingdom of Jerusalem, Godfroi de Bouillon (Godfroi, however, did not accept the title of *king*, he instead accepted the title of *Defender of the Holy Sepulcher*— nevertheless, in everything except title, he was the king). Upon his death in 1100, his younger brother, Baudouin, who did take the official title of King of the Kingdom of Jerusalem, succeeded him. He died in 1118. Internal strife and succession turmoil characterized the Kingdom of Jerusalem until 1187, when sultan Saladin recaptured Jerusalem. The scrolls were safely guarded by both Godfroi and Baudouin until the Abbey of Norte Dame du Mont de Sion in Jerusalem was complete under Baudouin's reign. The scrolls were then placed in the abbey for safekeeping and remained there until 1187.

During the siege of Jerusalem by Saladin, a servant of Gérard de Ridefort, Grand Master of the Templars, known only as Philip, fled with the scrolls and hid them in a dry, abandoned cistern, near Acre. They safely remained hidden there until the fourth crusade when in 1191 they were discovered by a knight fighting with Richard I, Coeur de Lion, the eldest son of Henry II, king of England, during the conquest of Acre by Richard. Richard took personal possession of the scrolls as he left the Holy Land to return to England. But, as he traveled through Austria, Leopold, Duke of Austria, seized Richard. Leopold in turn handed Richard over to Emperor Henry VI, who held him for ransom. Upon his arrest, the scrolls were discovered in Richard's possession and were placed in the Monastery of Tegernsee, located in the Duchy of Bavaria, for safekeeping. There they remained until the 13th century, when the monastery was closed. For the next two centuries, the location of the scrolls was a mystery. They surfaced again in 1463 when they were discovered in an underground salt cavern near Damascus by a Turkish salt trader, who took them to Constantinople with visions of selling them for a high price to Muhammad II (Mehmet) "The Great," the Ottoman Turk who had conquered Constantinople in 1453, and had made it his capital. As the trader attempted to enter Constantinople through the ancient Golden Gate and the accompanying Fortress of Yedikule, Muhammad's gate authorities discovered the scrolls, confiscated them, and presented them to Muhammad. He had them encased in a vault in an underground chamber at the church of St. Irene. They remained there until the construction of Topkapi Sarayi (Topkapi Palace) forced the abandonment of some and the removal of many other "religious treasures" that were being housed in St. Irene. Among the treasures that were removed were the Gamaliel scrolls. Mehmet had the scrolls placed and sealed in one of the hundreds of small cave vaults in the lower chambers of St. Sophia. There they remained, forgotten, until their re-discovery in 1652.

That concluded *The Carpenter's Mentor* and Count Comeaux's record of Joseph and Mary.

After the birth of John, Mary returned to Nazareth—at least four months pregnant. Today, it is commonly accepted and presumed, with reinforcement from Hollywood and television, that upon Mary's return to Nazareth there ensued a scandalous controversy involving Joseph and Mary, the townspeople, and the local religious leaders. However, except for a brief mention about Joseph contemplating putting Mary away privately to spare her from being a public example (Matthew 1:19), the Gospels do not give even a hint that such a scandal ever existed. So, if the Gospels were silent with regard to any scandal, and yet the accepted Christian tradition demanded that a scandal did in fact take place, how could I ever find the truth whether or not the scandal actually existed?

I found my answer while researching at Baylor University in Waco, Texas, in a rare book written in 1884 by the Calvinist, Herman Bavinck. In fact the book was so rare that there had only been one hundred copies printed. It was entitled *Scandals*. The book generally exposed in detail the scandals or presumed or accused scandals within the ranks of Christianity from the time of Jesus until the time of John Calvin. Bavinck was supposed to have written a second volume that traced the scandals from Calvin's time until the time in which Bavinck lived. According to the scant information that described the history of Bavinck's *Scandals*, copies of the second volume, if indeed they were published, have not been located.

Bavinck's *Scandals* began discussing the alleged scandal of Joseph and Mary by quoting Matthew 1:19.

> *"Then Joseph her husband, being a just man, and not willing to make her a public example, was minded to put her away privily."*

Bavinck began his exposé saying that this Matthew verse relates to Joseph's contemplation on what to do about Mary. Nowhere does Matthew record Mary's visit to Elizabeth. However, in order to fully understand Matthew 1:19, Mary's trip to Elizabeth, as recorded in Luke, must be placed in the chronological order of events, which is between Matthew 1:18 and 1:19.

By the time Mary returned to Nazareth [probably in November of 8 BC], she was already four or almost five months pregnant, and the baby had probably begun to show. Her return was presumably met with mixed emotions from Joseph and from Mary's father (if in fact her father was not dead or in prison). They would have been delighted to see her after a four or five month separation, but they would have been shocked and disturbed to discover that this 12-year old espoused wife and beloved daughter, had returned to them *pregnant*. "How did Joseph respond when Mary tried to explain to him that she was still a virgin, and that God was responsible for her conception?" Bavinck asked as an introduction to the remainder of his discussion.

"The public scandal because of Mary's pregnancy that tradition depicts," he continued, "May not have ever happened. If these circumstances had occurred in the state of Judea, most definitely, a vicious and perhaps even violent scandal would have developed immediately. But in the Greek-culture dominated, Romanized Galilee, where situations of this nature were not unusual, Mary's condition may not have caused an after thought or even a stir. However, Matthew 1:19 does suggest that Joseph was concerned enough about something that he thought very seriously about nullifying the espousal contract privately. If public scandal was something about which he may not have been concerned, then what was his concern?"

At this time in the Galilee, although the Romans had very lackadaisical laws relative to marriage, there were strict laws concerning taxation. The Roman law of taxation concerning marriage was specific and non-argumentative, and it was strictly enforced to the point of imprisonment if adherence to the law was not followed to the letter.

Within 10 days after marriage the new husband had to report the marriage to the local Roman tax authority and pay a nuptial tax on his new bride. If the tax was not paid within the 10-day period, the tax was doubled daily until it was paid, up to 30 days. If the tax was not paid by day 30, the husband was imprisoned. With the birth of the first, third, and fifth child, another tax was levied. This was a successor tax that had to be paid within the first year of the birth of the child. If not paid within that first year, the tax was doubled every 30 days until it was paid. If it was not paid by the second birth date of the child, the father would be imprisoned and the mother and her children would be sold as domestic servants.

In the case of an espousal followed by marriage, the espousal tax had to be paid sometime within two years of the registration of the espousal documents. After marriage, the nuptial tax was due, but the married couple could deduct from that tax the amount that they had already paid in the espousal tax.

If a woman pledged to be married (an espoused woman), became pregnant before the actual marriage was realized, the espousal tax, the full nuptial tax, and the successor tax were due before the sixth month of pregnancy. If not paid by the sixth month of pregnancy, imprisonment for the man and servanthood for the woman were immediate. If the pregnant woman was neither pledged nor espoused, then the Roman government, making her a ward of the local civil government, levied no tax. She remained a ward until the birth of the child, after which time she could either be responsible for her own livelihood and support herself, or she could be returned to her family.

One of the ways used by Galileans to circumvent the triple-tax-liability was to put the pregnant woman, who was his espoused (or pledged), "away privately." The Romans did not keep close "tabs" on the marriage practices of the Galilean Jews; they left that up to the local authorities. Rome's authorities checked the marriage records only about every 90 days. Thus, if a Jewish man had a pregnant pledged wife or espoused bride and had a good relationship with the local authorities, he could have the pledge of marriage registration or espousal registration documents altered or nullified for a small fee before the Roman authority's scheduled evaluation of the records. The local Galilean authorities called this process "putting her away, privately." By this action the man could avoid paying the full triple-tax that could condemn him and his family to a life of poverty. By "putting her away, privately" he also freed himself from any marriage responsibilities. In short, he was under no obligation to marry the woman, nor was he obligated to support her. But, by doing so, it was almost guaranteed that the child would be born illegitimate.

What Joseph was contemplating, is not known. What is recorded, is that an angel appeared to Joseph in a dream and told him not to be afraid to make Mary his wife.

If Joseph was an honest and "a just man" as the Bible seems to suggest, then it is possible that instead of "putting [Mary] away privately," he may have contemplated subjecting Mary to the "ordeal of innocence". If Joseph was an uncompromisingly dedicated orthodox Jew or a religious leader, then this ritual of the "ordeal of innocence", would have been demanded by the local Jewish religious leaders, although in the Galilee the demands of the religious leaders were always under extreme subservience to local Roman authority. Accordingly, in the Galilee, if Joseph was a typical Jewish Galilean businessman, laborer, or professional, rather than an orthodox Jew or religious leader, it was neither mandatory nor expected that he subject his espoused to such an ordeal. Nevertheless, if he was known locally as an orthodox religious zealot who lived by the strict letter of the Jewish religious laws, (as in the case of Jerusalem Shammaite [or "inner-circle"] Pharisees), then not only was it expected for him to subject her to this ordeal, but he was obligated to do so.

The "ordeal of innocence" ritual began with the woman being asked if she was guilty of promiscuity. If she confessed to promiscuity under the Law of Moses, she would be stoned. But in the Galilee, under the law of Rome, neither stoning nor any other act of capital punishment based on religious law and/or principles was permitted. However, non-fatal punishment based on religious law if administered by the local Roman authorities, was allowed. In this case, she might have to succumb to any one or all of the following Roman forms of punishment: being marred (cut off either her nose, right ear, right hand, right breast, or all four); being abandoned to the streets; being officially pronounced dead, thus condemning her to live as a beggar; or being exiled. But according to Herman Bavinck's evidence, there were very few times in which a woman was subjected to these kinds of punishment in the Galilee. It was more common in the Greek/Roman Galilee during the first century that the guilty woman was simply offered a bill of divorce (Deuteronomy 24: 1-4), and was given a token fine equivalent to less than one day's wages. This relieved the man of any support responsibility, and freed the woman to go on with her life as an independent single mother and that ended the matter.

In the "ordeal of innocence" ritual, if the woman maintained her innocence, and yet was accused by either her future husband or any male member of either his or her household, she had to submit to the "trial of the bitter water that causeth the curse." A priest sent from the Temple in Jerusalem performed this examination.

During the examination the woman who was accused of promiscuity was brought into a local synagogue. She had to stand before the priest who had been brought up from the Temple in Jerusalem. While standing before the priest, he poured blessed water into a pottery vessel and mixed into it a handful of dust from the floor of the synagogue. He then addressed the mixture with ritual incantations, curses, and imprecations. Next he turned to the woman and said, *"If no man have lain with thee, and if thou hast not gone aside to uncleanness with another instead of thy espoused husband, be thou free from this bitter water that causeth the curse. But if thou hast gone aside to another instead of thy betrothed and if thou be defiled, and some man have lain with thee, the Lord make thee a curse and an oath among thy people, when the Lord doth make thy thigh to rot, and thy belly to swell, and this water that causeth the curse shall go into thy bowels, to make thy belly to swell, and thy thigh to rot."* The priest would then write the same words on a parchment, and would then immediately erase the words by plunging the parchment into the bitter water. The water was then given to the woman to drink. If she was indeed an adulteress, the water was supposed to perform an abortive function, after which she was supposed to have been killed, preferably by stoning (Deuteronomy 22:25-28); if she suffered no ill effects, she was held guiltless and was either free to return to her family or free to return to her husband, if he still wanted her.

It is not known what prompted the angel to appear to Joseph in a dream. It seems quite clear, however, that Joseph did not follow through with what he was contemplating.

Bavinck then quoted Matthew 1 beginning at verse 20:

> *"But while he [Joseph] thought on these things, behold the angel of the Lord appeared unto him in a dream, saying, 'Joseph, thou son of David, fear not to take unto thee Mary thy wife: for that which is conceived in her is of the Holy Ghost. And she shall bring forth a son, and thou shalt call his name Jesus: for he shall save his people from their sins.' Now all of this was done, that it might be fulfilled which was spoken of the Lord by the prophet, saying, 'Behold, a virgin shall be with child, and shall bring forth a son, and they shall call his name Emmanuel, which being interpreted is*

> *God with us.' Then Joseph being raised from sleep did as the angel of the Lord had bidden him, and took unto him his wife: and knew her not till she had brought forth her first born son: and he called his name Jesus (Matthew 1:20-25).*

It is not known how long it was after Mary's return from visiting Elizabeth that Joseph had his dream. But if speculation is of any value, I (Bavinck) speculate that the angel appeared to him within a month or two after her return to Nazareth, and a week or so after their marriage.

Bavinck points out that though church doctrine insisted that Mary and Joseph had no sexual relations until after the birth of Jesus, he had found no information that would confirm that doctrine. His position was that whether Joseph had sexual relations with Mary or not, something had frightened him to the point that he feared having any [or any further] relationships with her. This being the case, an angel appeared to Joseph in a dream and told him not to be afraid to *"take Mary your wife"*, or do not be afraid to have sexual relations with your wife. So, following the prompting of the angel, Joseph did renew relations with Mary; they journeyed to Bethlehem; Mary's son was born and Joseph named him, Jesus. Whether or not Joseph believed the Holy Ghost conceived Jesus and that this same Jesus would save his people from their sins is debatable.

At first glance Matthew's account of the angel's visit seems straightforward. There does not appear to be any hidden or strange interpretation—the angel appeared to Joseph in a dream and told him to take Mary as his wife; Joseph married her; they journeyed to Bethlehem; and there the baby was born and Joseph named the baby, Jesus.

But under closer investigation, it is evident that there is some confusion, especially with verses 19, 20, and 24 of Matthew 1, because neither of these three record that Joseph was commanded to marry Mary. In fact, verses 19 and 20 seem to imply that Mary was already his wife, and the thing that Joseph feared was "taking her", or having sexual relations with her while she was pregnant with Jesus. Verse 24 implies the same thing. Nowhere does it specifically say that Joseph married Mary. These Scriptures only **IMPLY** that they are married already; that he first feared to take her; that the angel told him not to fear and to take her; and that he then did take her.

In 1589 an explanation regarding these implications originated, that has become widely accepted. The explanation says that since Joseph and Mary were espoused, then it was permitted for each of them to claim to be "husband" or "wife" and that they were recognized as such. Furthermore, the explanation claims that this is the reason why the words "husband" and "wife" are used in the biblical reference to Joseph and Mary, even though they were not actually married. But, nowhere in the history of the Jews, the Greeks, or the Romans is such a thing even suggested, much less practiced. In fact, the opposite was typically true in Roman subjected countries. If Rome followed the same taxation policy in the Galilee that she carried out in all other subjected countries, for taxation purposes it was not permitted to claim marriage unless you were actually married. Nor was it permitted, under penalty of a very hefty fine plus a double tax, to be identified as being married (to be addressed as husband or wife) unless you actually were married. So, according to well-known historical evidence and very accurate Roman tax records, this explanation has no factual foundation.

Bavinck concluded, that in evaluating this sexual relations interpretation, the following scenario may have developed: Mary, the 12-or 13-year-old virgin, conceived Jesus by the Holy Ghost; she immediately left home and went to visit Elizabeth; she stayed with Elizabeth until after the birth of John, Elizabeth's son; Mary returned to her home; Mary was adopted by her uncle; Joseph married Mary thus subjecting himself to the Roman triple tax; he became frightened for some unknown reason, and determined not to have sexual relations with Mary; the angel appeared to him and told him not to be afraid to have relations with her; they went to Bethlehem where Jesus was born.

With regard to espousal and espousal arrangements, Bavinck wrote that espousal was a very serious commitment for Jews during the time of Joseph and Mary, with specific laws that governed age, procedure, and the espousal ceremony. Since the days of Ezra, the lawful age for espousal for a Jewish man was 17. If the man was beyond the age of 19, espousal or engagement (*qiddushin* or *erusin*) was *not necessary*. But between the ages of 17 and 19, espousal was *mandatory*.

Consequently, if Joseph was a follower of the Jewish religious and ethics laws, and if he was indeed espoused to Mary, then we can conclude with certainty that he was at least 17-years old and not over 19-years old. The legal age for espousal for a woman was determined by her own biological clock. A woman became eligible for betrothal upon reaching puberty, signified by her first menstrual cycle, which normally occurred about the age of 12 or 13. Immediately after her seven days of ritual cleansing, which was required upon entering puberty, she became eligible for marriage. At that time, her father, oldest brother, or oldest surviving male next of kin registered her name as being eligible for marriage at the local synagogue. Any man looking for a wife could then negotiate with the young lady's father, or the one who registered her, to marry her. If the young man was between 17 and 19 years old, he had to first submit to a period of espousal. If he was over the age of 19, he could negotiate for marriage.

"The young lady's name remained on the register of 'young ladies eligible for espousal or marriage' for two years. If she was not espoused or married within two years of her registration, her name was removed from the rolls for a period of one year, after which time it was placed back on for an additional one year and six months *only*. If she was not espoused or married during the 18-month period, she would be proclaimed by the local synagogue leader as being 'not fit for marriage.' This pronouncement usually was a death sentence to her chances of ever getting married. But, for most young Jewish ladies, this 'curse' never occurred. In fact, for most Jewish young ladies in the Galilee at this time, a young woman's future husband was probably chosen for her well in advance of her puberty ritual, (there are examples of husbands being chosen and being committed to the family of the girl as early as her sixth birthday) and betrothal negotiations on her behalf were begun by her father or older brother, the very day after she completed her initial seven days of purification. More than likely, Mary was 12- but no older than 13-

years old when she became espoused to Joseph. This was just three months before she would receive a visit from the angel, Gabriel.

The custom of the Jewish people when negotiating to secure a bride for a son, illustrates just how serious betrothal really was to them. Even though, as noted earlier, espousal was not necessary if the man was over the age of 19, it was still required that the would-be-bride present a dowry to the family of the groom-to-be, and that the man, regardless of his age, sign a betrothal covenant and registered with the local authorities. A minimum 40-day wait (there are recorded instances where the wait lasted five years or more—the length of this waiting period was dictated by the girl's father if the man was age 19 or less; it was negotiable if the man was age 20 or older) was then required after the betrothal documents had been registered, before the marriage celebration could be performed, making the marriage official and allowing the couple to live together as husband and wife. If the husband-to-be was under the age of 19, it had to be determined by the father of the bride that the potential husband truly did have enough means to provide for the bride. Once it had been determined that the young man had acquired sufficient means to make it possible for him to provide for the bride, the father of the young man would contact the father, older brother, or oldest male next of kin of the girl to whom the son was pledged to be married, and betrothal negotiations began. The son's father would call in a man to act as a deputy for him and his son. This deputy was called 'the friend of the bridegroom.' This man was fully informed as to the dowry the young lady was willing to pay her groom's family. Then, together with the young man's father (if 19 or younger—if 20 or older, the man represented himself) and an elder of the family, he would go to the home of the young woman. The son's father would announce that the deputy would speak for the party, and then the bride's father would appoint a deputy to represent his family. Before negotiations began, a drink would be offered to the visiting group. They would refuse the drink until the mission for which they had come was complete. When the two spokesmen faced each other over bread, the negotiations began. There had to be consent for the hand of the young woman and an agreement on the amount of dowry that was to be paid by her. When these were agreed upon, the deputies would arise, exchange congratulations, accept a drink of wine, and drink together to seal the agreement. The next step was to draw up the betrothal contract.

At that time, betrothal was not a simple promise between a man and a woman that they pledge to marry. Rather, it was a legal contract, signed in the local synagogue, witnessed by the president of the synagogue, an elder of the village council, and an elder from each family of the couple that was to be married. The document was then permanently recorded and filed in the local synagogue. The betrothal contract was so binding that if the future husband died before the marriage, the future wife would have the full status of a widow. After the document had been witnessed and filed, the pledged husband and wife usually continued to live with their respective parents while preparations for marriage were being made.

Bavinck then deviated from the historical aspect of espousal and began to interject his own opinion.

"While this was the traditional Jewish custom (particularly in Judea) of how the pledged bride and groom were to conduct themselves," Bavinck wrote, "and certainly the most moral way, in the Galilee of Joseph and Mary's time, it was seldom the typical way. Some Galilean Greek literature suggests that because of the 'without restraint' moral attitude of their Roman overlords a Jewish pledged bride and groom in the Galilee actually lived together for up to a year before the actual marriage celebration took place. Whether this was the case with Joseph and Mary, will probably forever remain shrouded in mystery. If they did conform to the accepted practice of the day in the Galilee, they probably did, in fact, live together before the actual marriage ceremony; very much like the espousal customs in some Muslim influenced countries today."

Bavinck then went back to the subject at hand: the marriage preparations of a typical Jewish marriage.

"The marriage preparations could have taken up to a year or longer. Traditionally (historical Jewish tradition only—not in common every day practice in the Galilee at that time) and lawfully (Jewish religious law, not Galilean civil law) during this time of preparation, any physical relations were forbidden between the espoused couple, under a penalty of pronounced adultery and the punishment that accompanied the pronouncement, in reality, pre-marital physical relations were in fact the norm in the Galilee more than the exception. Yet, according to the religious law, if such relations did take place during this time of preparation, either the groom or the family of the groom could demand a Bill of Divorce (such bill was the only legal document recognized by the religious law that would nullify a contract of espousal or betrothal), witnessed by the same people who had witnessed the betrothal contract; exactly as if the couple were actually married; and filed in the same synagogue where the original betrothal contract had been filed."

Bavinck again diverted and inserted a personal note.

"The husband or the family of the husband were the only ones who could seek divorce. According to both the Jewish religious and civil laws, it was not permitted for a woman to seek divorce. Under Jewish *civil* law, a man could divorce a wife or nullify a betrothal contract simply by stating to his wife in the presence of three witnesses, 'I divorce you. I divorce you. I break all ties with you. I am relieved of your care.' He neither had to have the statement in writing nor did he have to file a Bill of Divorce at the synagogue. But, as stated earlier, under Jewish *religious* law, a Bill of Divorce had to be filed at the synagogue. Notwithstanding, Jewish *civil* law was the *only* Jewish law recognized, acknowledged, and honored by the Roman government. Jewish religious law was not. Hence, filing for divorce was legally neither required nor necessary under Roman occupation."

Bavinck then went back to his discussion of the preparation time.

"During the 40 days to one year or more period of time between the betrothal contract and the actual marriage celebration," Bavinck continued, "the pledged husband usually busied himself with building a house for his bride, while she continued to build-up the financial dowry that she had to present to the father and family of her groom-to-be. In addition, the bride, during this time, usually learned from her mother and from the mother of the groom-to-be, the art of being a wife and a mother. In Mary's case, it seems probable that her father (Christian tradition calls him, Joachim) and her mother (Christian tradition calls her, Anne) had separated for some unknown reason, for both Mary's mother and her grandmother had remained in Egypt while she (Mary) and her father moved from Egypt and settled in the Galilee (Mary's sisters, Salome and Miriam, [the only sisters of Mary that are mentioned in the Gospels. Salome was the mother of James and John, making James and John cousins of Jesus], may have remained in Egypt and moved to the Galilee somewhat later, or they too could have moved with Mary and her father; we do not know for sure). Hence, Mary would have to had learned from her uncle/adoptive father's wife, from Joseph's mother, from some close relative, or from Joseph's mother and her father's new wife, if in fact he and Mary's mother were divorced, and if he had married again."

With that statement, Bavinck concluded.

The next event associated with the birth of Jesus was the tax-census and Joseph and Mary's journey to Bethlehem. This tax census has come under extreme scrutiny over the past 100 years with some theologians and historians claiming that it never happened, while others insisting that it did. Because I began with the preconceived opinion that Luke's record of the tax census was true and non-argumentative, I was able to totally disregard any resources that argued against the historical fact of a tax census at the time of Jesus' birth, and concentrate my efforts on resources that confirmed the Gospel account.

By far the most significant resource that I discovered was one that I found at Cambridge University's Magdalene College library. In fact throughout my years of research Magdalene College was repeatedly referred to as having the world's *only* known authentic resource that reported the official tax and census during the time of the birth of Jesus. It was recorded on an untitled manuscript fragment labeled simply MSCL125.

According to accompanying historical background information, the manuscript fragment was all that survived of a letter written by Epiphanius, Bishop of Pavia in the year 490. The letter was originally sent to Clotilda, who was to later become the wife of Clovis, King of the Salian Franks, in answer to a question asked by Clotilda. She had asked Epiphanius how the census that caused the Virgin to travel to Bethlehem was conducted, considering there were at least three civil authorities that ruled over the area of Jesus' birth at the time of his birth. Epiphanius, claiming to have relied upon legal documents that had once been housed at Emperor Alexander Severus' private library in Mainz, gave an answer that if not totally correct, at least gave a logical explanation regarding seemingly conflicting historical reports from the era.

After an introduction and the typical flattering and well wishes and a long statement of adoration dedicated to the Virgin and to the son, Jesus, Epiphanius began his answer to Clotilda's question by quoting a portion of Luke.

> *"And it came to pass in those days, that there went out a decree from Caesar Augustus, that all the world should be taxed. (And this taxing was first made when Cyrenius [Quirinus] was governor of Syria.) And all went to be taxed, every one into his own city. And Joseph also went up from Galilee, out of the city of Nazareth, into Judea, unto the city of David, which is called Bethlehem; (because he was of the House and the linage of*

David:) to be taxed with Mary his espoused wife, being great with child" *(Luke 1:1-5).*

I will paraphrase the remainder of Epiphanius' letter.

After quoting from Luke, Epiphanius continued by explaining that as a result of the long Roman civil war following the murder of Julius Caesar, coupled with the expenses incurred by putting down the revolt of Pannonia in the 15th year of the reign of Augustus, which would have been 12 BC, Rome's fragile financial stability was dubious. Because of this volatile financial state, Augustus in 9 BC made a decree that said that in conjunction with the customary 14-year census (scheduled to begin in 9 BC), there would be another special tax-census throughout the Empire, and that this special tax census would be applicable to every non-Roman male subject in the Empire. In addition, Augustus proclaimed that it would be assumed that every woman (both Roman and non-Roman) who was or would become with child, at the time that the area where she lived had to pay the tax, would birth a male child (irrespective of whether she did in reality or not). Therefore, every woman in the Empire who was pregnant at the time that their regions would be taxed, over the next three years, had to pay a tax on her unborn child at the town of either her husband's or father's birth.

Epiphanius then explained how the Roman consul, Publius Sulpicius Quirinus (whom Luke calls Cyrenius), had been appointed governor of Syria by Augustus that same year, 9 BC, and that at the time both the region of Judea and the region of the Galilee were part of the Imperial Province of Syria. He then said that two years later, in 7 BC, Quirinus ordered a tax-census. In addition, in 7 BC Herod the Great demanded that each Jewish descendant male age 15 to 60 register between March and June of that year, and be taxed in the city of his birth, and that each non-Jewish descendant male age 15 to 60 register and be taxed at either Jerusalem, Caesarea Maritima, Caesarea Philippi, Bethsaida, Beersheba, or Scythopolis.

He then explained the sequence of events that led to Joseph being taxed as a result of this special tax-census.

1. Augustus made the decree in 9 BC that a special tax-census was to accompany the routine 14-year census. The tax-census demanded that all non-Roman males between the ages of 15 and 60 were to pay a special census tax at the time of their routine registration, and all women were with child at the time that the region was taxed, over the next three years, were to pay a tax on the unborn child. Each imperial province would in turn arrange a method whereby its tax obligation would be paid, with a deadline of three years for the completion of the tax-census worldwide. Each Imperial Provincial governor would be responsible for the collection of the special census tax in his own province.
2. By 7 BC, it was the province of Syria's turn to be taxed. Quirinus, the governor of the Imperial Province of Syria, ordered the decree into effect and delegated the implementation of the census tax to his four

Tetrarchs who governed the four regions of the Imperial Province of Syria.
3. Herod was not only the proclaimed "King of the Jews," but he was also the Tetrarch of the regional province of Judea, which was one of the four regions that made up the Imperial Province of Syria. Herod chose to implement the tax-census in his region by demanding that each non-Roman citizen Jewish male age 15 to 60 register at the city or village of his birth (or closest city or village to the place of his birth), and that each non-Jewish non-Roman citizen male register at an appointed city (either Jerusalem, Beersheba, Caesarea Maritima, Caesarea Philippi, Scythopolis, or Bethsaida), that would serve as an area census headquarters (for both Jew and non-Jew males who resided in Herod's region, but whose city of birth was outside of the Tetrarchy of Herod, then the male was to register at Caesarea Maritima). Herod ordered that individual registration and payment of the tax was to begin in March of that year, 7 BC, and was to be completed by the end of June of that year, 7 BC.
4. Herod divided his Tetrarchy into 15 taxing districts, with each district responsible for its own registration process. Each taxing district established by Herod was given a specific time limit (approximately seven days) to complete its registration process, so that the registration and tax-census for all 15 districts would be completed within the four-month period (March to June) established by Herod. Within the four-month period, all of the non-Roman citizen males age 15 to 60 within the Tetrarchy of Herod had to be registered and taxed.

Because of this, Joseph, the non-Roman non-citizen, Jewish husband of Mary (who may or may not have been a Roman citizen through adoption), had to wait for the official census bidding of the district wherein Nazareth, Joseph and Mary's home city, was located, before he could travel to his birth city and register himself as well as Mary's unborn child (as per Augustus' proclamation).

Because each district had only seven days to complete their individual registrations, and considering the fact that Bethlehem, the birth city of Joseph (where the record of his birth was cataloged), was a minimum of three to as much as six days journey from Nazareth, Joseph was obliged to leave for Bethlehem as soon as he had received his registration orders. The district in which Nazareth was a part likely received its registration orders sometime in April of 7 BC. Upon receiving his tax-census bid, Joseph took Mary (because Mary was with child and her unborn child would also be taxed, she had to accompany Joseph) and immediately left for Bethlehem. But, unfortunately for Mary, their appointed registration time corresponded with her delivery time. As they journeyed closer and closer to Bethlehem, it became apparent that Mary's child would not be born at home in Nazareth, but rather, in a strange city, with strange surroundings, far from both friends and family, and in the midst of a national Jewish celebration: Passover.

Bethlehem (the Hebrew adaptation of the word meant *"the house of bread"*), the traditional birthplace of King David, was located about six or seven miles south of Jerusalem. The village was known before the Israelite conquest under Joshua as Beth-Lahamu, *"the house of Lah."* Lah was an early Babylonian god worshipped by the area Canaanites before the conquest. The name of the village was probably changed from Beth-Lahamu to Bethlehem in about the year 1570 BC, the year that Joshua renamed many of the southern hill country villages.

As they approached Bethlehem, it would have become quite obvious to them that the city's available accommodation space was extremely limited. This probably caused them to seek accommodations in a northern "suburban" area of Bethlehem (between Jerusalem and Bethlehem), probably near the little village of Ramat. The lack of accommodation space could have been caused by the ordered tax census, but more likely the accommodation shortage was due to the housing demand placed upon Bethlehem because of pilgrims traveling to Jerusalem for the observance of Passover. In 7 BC, the Passover celebration would have been observed in April.

With this statement, Epiphanius' manuscript abruptly ended. Obviously the last portion of the letter was missing and no effort had been made by the historians who had written the manuscript profiles to "speculate" on what the missing part may have said. Nonetheless, Epiphanius had shed light upon what up until that time had been to me a very confusing series of seemingly unrelated tax census events, decreed by three different Roman authorities, spread out over a two-year period.

The Gospels do not tell us anything more about Joseph's (and perhaps Mary's son's) registration. But by closely examining Luke's record of the birth of Jesus it appears that perhaps Joseph and Mary had been in Bethlehem for a day or two before he was born. This would have given Joseph enough time to register and pay his (or their) tax before Mary gave birth.

> *"And so it was, that, while they were there, the days were accomplished that she should be delivered" (Luke 2:6).*

While researching at Rice University in Houston, Texas, I found an intriguing document relating to the birth of Jesus that compelled me to re-evaluate some of my most time-honored "yuletide" traditions.

The document was a sermon or a teaching lesson that had been written by Marcel LeRue Dimireaux, a French Catholic priest who fled France during the days of Napoleon's rise to power and settled in Prussia. There he renounced Catholism and joined a splinter group of Protestant reformists who called themselves, *Purstrictists*. They sought to purge Christianity of all traditions, dogmas, and doctrines that they felt diverted from a pure and strict interpretation of the Scriptures. He spent the last 12 years of his life, after fleeing France, writing sermons and teaching lessons whose purpose seems to have been to discredit the conventional traditions of the Church. The title of this sermon or lesson was, "The Place of His Birth." I will paraphrase what he wrote.

Marcel said that it seems that Bethlehem, at the time of the birth of Jesus, because of its close proximity to Jerusalem, was a major supplier of accommodation space during the seven-day Passover celebration. In the year 7 BC, the year of the birth of Jesus, the full moon of the 14th of Nisan, the beginning of Passover would have been on April 12. The celebration would have lasted until April 18.

Considering Joseph and Mary arrived in Bethlehem at the height of the Passover season, it is most logical to assume that the reason why *"...there was no room in the inn..."* was because of the overcrowded conditions due to the vast influx of Passover celebrates into the city. Sometime during the week of April 12 to April 18, 7 BC, Jesus was born.

Marcel then explained about the inn that had no room. This inn was a *caravansary* or *geruth*. It was a fenced enclosure built especially for travelers, with sheds or small houses encircling the inside perimeter of the enclosure. These sheds or small houses were partitioned off into rooms. In some caravansaries, the sheds or small houses were built on raised platforms, while in others the sheds or small houses were built at ground level. The animals of the travelers were housed in the fenced open courtyard, while the travelers themselves stayed the night in the sheds. Within the fenced open courtyard was a large wooden or stone enclosure (box) or a large dugout area (similar to a shallow pit) that was filled with animal feed, wheat straw, and corn shucks. This large enclosure or shallow pit was called a *manger*. Its primary purpose was to serve the feeding needs of the animals that were being housed in the courtyard. It is not known how big this particular manger was, but it had to have been large enough to service the animals that had accompanied all of the travelers that the inn could accommodate. Still, it was not an uncommon practice to allow travelers to sleep (either free of charge or for a very minimal fee) for the night in the manger, if there was no more accommodation space for them in the sheds.

Logic would demand, Marcel continued, that the location of the actual spot where Jesus was born has long since disappeared. Traditional Orthodoxy identifies his birthplace with a cave near the town of Bethlehem; while traditional fundamentalism says that he was born in a stable. The Gospels neither confirm nor deny either. In fact, the exact location of Jesus' birth did not even become an issue until 200 years after his birth, when Justin Martyr made a cynical statement saying that the exact spot of Jesus' birth would be revealed to the one to whom God chose to reveal its location. One hundred years later, Martyr's jest had evolved into a divine prophecy which Emperor Constantine I, "The Great", encouraged by his mother, Helena, claimed as his "right" as *the* one chosen by God. So, to "confirm" the authenticity of Martyr's "prophecy," Constantine in AD 313 confiscated the pagan shrine of the cult of Adonis-Tammuz built at the mouth of a cave near the town of Bethlehem, one that had been revered as a shrine for centuries before the birth of Jesus. He re-named the cave and shrine, *The Basilica of the Nativity*, and proclaimed that the basilica marked the actual spot where Jesus was born. Although the original shrine that became *The Basilica of the Nativity* has been destroyed and rebuilt, and destroyed and rebuilt and embellished a second time, it is still honored today by millions in Orthodoxy as marking the spot where Jesus was actually born.

The stable fable, venerated by fundamentalists, is not quite as old as the cave story. It dates back to the days of St. Francis of Assisi. He insisted that Jesus was born "...in the likes of a wooden shelter." Years later, John Calvin claimed that "...my Lord and Savior has indicated that He was born in a wooden cattle shelter known as a stable." Calvin felt that this stable was similar to the ones that were scattered throughout the Swiss Alps during Calvin's day. From that time until the present Calvin's *stable* has become an intricate and irreplaceable ingredient of the fundamentalist's nativity tradition.

But, according to Luke, Jesus was most likely born in neither.

> *"And she brought forth her first born son, and wrapped him in swaddling clothes, and laid him in a manger; because there was no room for them in the inn" (Luke 2:7).*

In this passage, as well as verses 12 and 16 in the same chapter of Luke we find only that Jesus was born and that he was wrapped in swaddling clothes (bandages tightly wrapped around a newborn baby [Lamentations 2:22 and Ezekiel 16:4]. Since this was the typical Egyptian method of caring for newly born babies and Mary's ancestry was Egyptian, wrapping Jesus in swaddling clothes was not unusual. However, it would have been unthinkable for a devout Judean Jewish family to wrap a newborn in this manner). Jesus was then laid in a manger. Based on cultural and social tradition, Joseph and Mary probably spent the night at the inn (joining many other like travelers), in the open courtyard of the *geruth*, because all of the housing sheds were occupied. They probably intended to join others in sleeping in the courtyard manger, but sleep likely failed them because Jesus was born there in the manger where they were seeking to rest.

Although Luke is totally silent on the details concerning Jesus' birth, much embellishment of that "holy moment" has been and is continuing to be circulated as if it were factual. "For this cause," Marcel wrote, "I feel it my purpose and obligation before Jesus Christ my Lord to correct the misleading and to rebuke the wrong.

"Let it be known that from the Holy Ghost of God, my Father, that outside of the fact that Jesus' conception was a miraculous, humanly inexplicable event, all else, (except for the angels' appearance to the shepherds and the wisemen's visit to the young child, Jesus) associated with his birth, childhood, and life up until the time of his earthly ministry, was *natural, normal, typically human,* and *non-miraculous*. Mary had a normal pain-riddled, non-miraculous delivery of a normal baby boy (except that he was divinely conceived). The baby grew into childhood; a normal, non-miraculous, typical childhood; and the child grew into normal, non-miraculous, adulthood. It was not until Jesus was about to be launched into his earthly ministry that the non-conventional and the miraculous became a part of his life. The matter has now been settled. It need not be opened for question."

Marcel then turned his attention to the day on which Jesus was born. He said that although the Western Christian world celebrates the birth of Jesus on December 25, and the Eastern Christian world celebrates it on January 6, neither history nor logic confirm either date as the date of Jesus' birth. In fact, until the 4th century, the dates most commonly accepted for the birth of Jesus were March 28, April 18, 21, or 22, and May 20 or 29. By the 5th century, things had changed.

In the East, the Christian church, convinced that Jesus had lived exactly 30 years, calculated backward from the date of his death, which they claim was April 6. They assigned him twenty-nine years and three months of actual life, and nine months of gestation time. Thus, according to the eastern Christian church, the nativity fell on January 6.

In the West, when in 313 AD Constantine I (the Great) issued the "Edict of Milan" granting religious tolerance for all religions and freedom of religious choice, Christianity immediately catapulted into the religious forefront. As a result, uproar developed regarding the future observance of the centuries old religious rituals of Rome's many pagan gods. To appease the pagan devotees, Constantine encouraged the absorption into Christianity of many holidays that had been, up until that time, days observed for and devoted to, and the celebration of many of Rome's pagan gods. Thus, December 25 became the date of Jesus' birth, by imperial edict, replacing the celebration of the sun god, Sol Invictus.

The original celebration of the sun god began with the winter solstice (this falls between December 21 and December 25; in fact, the sun begins to gain precisely on December 25, after the sign of the Virgin has reached the horizon) and continued for 12 days (hence, the origin of the medieval European practice of celebrating the 12 days of Christmas), with December 25 recognized as the day in which the sun was re-born.

Accordingly, with Constantine's edict, the celebration of the sun god was absorbed into Christianity, and December 25, the birth date of the pagan sun god, became the birth date of Jesus, the Son. True to form, Constantine the Great was the first emperor to celebrate the birth of Jesus on December 25. By the time Theodosius made Christianity the official religion of Rome in 395 AD, December 25 had already been officially adopted by the western Christian church as the date of Jesus' birth.

"However," Marcel continued, "I am not a legalist when it comes to dates and times. I celebrate Jesus' birth on December 25 because it commemorates his birth and because it is the date that is recognized and celebrated by our society as his birth, even though I know without a doubt that he was born sometime during the month of April. If I were to choose to not celebrate his birth on December 25 just because it is a former pagan holiday, then I think I would have to go into the mountains and live the life of a hermit, communicating with no one. For if you research the origin of the names of the days of the week and the months of the year, and then research the day of the week or date of the month or day of the year that some pagan god, goddess, or emperor was honored or celebrated, you will discover that virtually every day of every month of every year was dedicated to some pagan entity. This means that we can either celebrate because we choose to commemorate; whether or not we know historically if the event actually did take place on that date, or whether that particular day was some day of ancient pagan celebration; or we can isolate ourselves from society, knowing that this is really the only way that we could truly be free from any 'pagan holiday' celebration, commemoration, or observance. I choose not to do that. I choose instead to live my normal life, and celebrate simply because I want to commemorate."

This ended Marcel's sermon.

Another aspect of the birth of Jesus is one that was a matter of great controversy for centuries. I would like to briefly discuss that at this time. It has to do with the existence of Judas Thomas, the presumed twin of Jesus.

The Search

I was first introduced to Judas Thomas while researching at Tulane University in New Orleans, Louisiana, in a modern reprint of a set of sermons and commentaries reputed to have been written by Fantinus, the 10th century Abbot of the Greek community of St. Mercury in Calabria.

Tradition says that Fantinus had a vision of St. Andrew, who instructed him to renounce his position and become a wandering teacher. So, after having served as an Abbot for more than 13 years, he quit and spent the next 30 years of his life as a nomadic teacher. The 20 or so sermons and commentaries were all that remained of the more than 100 instructive commentaries that he wrote on the simplistic way of life.

Two of the commentaries dealt with specific issues concerning the birth of Jesus. One attempted to downplay the Roman Church's rationalization of the assertion that because Mary was a perpetual virgin, that even in child-birth God had made it possible for her to maintain her virginity and that this miracle so surprised the Roman mid-wife, Salome, who had helped deliver Jesus, that she became the first Roman believer in Jesus and in the Virgin.

It was in the other commentary of the two that dealt with the birth of Jesus, that I was introduced to *Judas Thomas,* the supposed twin of Jesus. Apparently, in early medieval times, an acknowledgement that Judas Thomas as a real person, was readily accepted. But by the 7th century, because of an intense suppression effort by the Roman Church, there were few who referred to him, openly.

Although Fantinus' mention of Judas Thomas was very brief, it was enough for me to become curious. According to the manuscript, not long after Mary had returned to Nazareth from visiting Elizabeth, Joseph of Arimathea adopted Mary (who was five months pregnant with Jesus) and gave her permission to marry Joseph. They were wed shortly thereafter.

The marriage was consummated; resulting in the conception of Judas Thomas, even though Mary was already pregnant with Jesus (Fantinus inserted into his record that Joseph of Arimathea did not adopt Judas Thomas even though Mary bore him. At the time that Mary was adopted by Joseph, she was with child with Jesus, so he was the only child adopted by Joseph of Arimathea when Mary was adopted). In essence, Mary conceived Jesus through the Holy Ghost, and she conceived Judas Thomas through her union with Joseph. So, at the time that she and Joseph went to Bethlehem, Mary was carrying "twins." As God had already predetermined, so says Fantinus, Jesus was born first, in the exact fulfillment of time, as a perfect full-term baby. But after Jesus was born, Judas Thomas was immediately born thereafter (whether immediately thereafter or a day or two later, we cannot say), but he was born as a premature baby. However, because he was born at the same time as Jesus, Judas Thomas had no premature ill effects. Thus Judas Thomas became known as the twin of Jesus; an assertion that the Roman Church could not allow to stand. Therefore a concentrated effort was made to stamp out the memory of Judas Thomas.

I discovered another book resource that discussed the Judas Thomas issue while researching at The University of Texas-Arlington, in Arlington, Texas.

The book was an oversized leather-bound volume that was about an inch thick. It was entitled *These are They*, written by Peter Thomas, a monk who lived in

Salzburg in the 16th century. The book was written in English and the accompanying notes that told the history of the book, said that this particular volume was an 1827 leather-bound English reprint of the original. The original had been written in German and was said to have been crudely bound between two oak boards and held together with leather cords.

According to the notes, Peter Thomas had been one of the clerics selected to represent the Catholics at the Catholic-Protestant peace talks in Augsburg, Germany in 1555. A peace accord was signed between the two religious factions on October 3, 1555. After the peace was formalized, Peter chose to remain in Augsburg for a while before returning to Salzburg. He was never heard from again. What became of him, nobody knows. In January 1556, when his cell in Salzburg was cleared of his personal items, his original board bound manuscript was discovered. The archbishop of Salzburg took immediate possession of the manuscript. That is the last that anyone saw of it until it reappeared in Munich at the beginning of the 19th century. There the manuscript was reprinted and translated into English and French. Each translation was bound in leather.

It appeared that *These are They* was a collection of biographical sketches featuring people who influenced the life of Jesus and who had influenced early 1st and 2nd century Christianity. Peter Thomas claimed that the sources of his information were the writings of Ignatius of Antioch, Justin Martyr, and Gnostics tradition. As I skimmed the book I became increasingly aware that in my studies of the writings of both Ignatius and Justin Martyr, which are still available today, I had found nothing that corresponded to the information that Peter Thomas said that he used in his biographical sketches. So, it seemed obvious to me that Peter Thomas either used texts by Ignatius and Justin Martyr that have long since disappeared or he fabricated the facts and added their names in an effort to bring credibility to his writings.

Of the personalities that Peter Thomas included in his manuscript, it was the biographical sketch of Judas Thomas (whom Peter claimed was his ancestor, if there really did exist such a person), which he concentrated on most.

According to Peter's speculation based on his research information, Joseph married Mary not long after her adoption by her uncle, Joseph of Arimathea, which was shortly after her return from visiting Elizabeth.

Although Roman Church doctrine insisted that even after they were married, Mary and Joseph had no sexual relations, he (Peter) had found no information that would confirm that doctrine. His position was that whether Joseph had sexual relations with Mary or not, something had frightened Joseph to the point that he feared having any [or any further] relationships with her. Peter felt that after their marriage, they consummated the marriage, resulting in Mary's conception of Judas Thomas through her union with Joseph. But she was already with child with Jesus by the Holy Ghost, so Joseph became extremely frightened and refused to have any further sexual relations with her. This being the case, an angel appeared to Joseph in a dream and told him not to be afraid to *"take Mary your wife"*, or do not be afraid to have sexual relations with your wife. So, following the prompting of the angel, Joseph did renew relations with Mary; they journeyed to Bethlehem; and there the full-term baby Jesus was born as well as the pre-mature baby, Judas Thomas. Hence, the story spread that Judas Thomas was Jesus' twin brother.

Peter then very subtly, yet brazenly, reprimanded the Roman Catholic Church for having suppressed the story of Judas Thomas since the 7th century. In fact, he lamented that the 7th and 8th century remnants of Gnostic followers (in the 7th century these Gnostics were in hiding because "war" had been declared upon them by the Catholic Church) claimed that all references to Judas Thomas had been removed from the Scriptures by the Church because his existence would prove that Mary was not a perpetual virgin. So potentially threatening was Judas Thomas to the doctrine of Mary's perpetual virginity that the church propagated a story that claimed that when Mary was visiting Elizabeth, the mother of John the Baptiser, Joseph had a sexual encounter with Mariam, the sister of Mary, and as a result of this encounter, she became pregnant with Judas Thomas. The church further contended that Mariam accompanied Joseph and Mary to Bethlehem where she gave birth to Judas Thomas either the same night as Mary gave birth to Jesus, or a day or two after Jesus' birth. The church claimed that Mariam died during childbirth and that Joseph and Mary absorbed Judas Thomas into their family, as Jesus' brother. As time went on the story evolved and Judas Thomas became Jesus' twin brother. In this rendition, Peter Thomas points out that the earliest 7th century record of the story claims that the sexual encounter between Joseph and Mariam happened after Mary's return from her visit to Elizabeth and after Joseph discovered that Mary was pregnant. He further pointed out that the later 8th century traditions identify Mariam as a servant of Mary.

Peter then expresses his own beliefs concerning Judas Thomas. "I think that Mary was a virgin when Gabriel announced to her that she would conceive Jesus. Being pregnant, she immediately left Nazareth and went to visit Elizabeth. If there was such a person as Judas Thomas, then I think that he was conceived as a result of a liaison between Joseph and Mary's servant girl or her sister, while Mary was away. When Mary returned and after her adoption by her uncle, Joseph married her [Mary] and paid the Roman triple tax. They consummated the marriage, but something happened during the encounter that so frightened Joseph that he became convinced that he should not have relations with her again. An angel appeared to him in a dream and told him that it was permitted to have relations with his wife. However, he still did not until after Jesus was born. Mary's servant or sister may or may not have accompanied them to Bethlehem, but she did have her baby close to the same time that Jesus was born in Bethlehem. She did in fact die during childbirth and her son, Judas Thomas, was adopted by Joseph and Mary."

Peter ended his discussion of Judas Thomas by stating that there is not enough information to conclude without a doubt that there was a person by that name. Nor is there enough evidence to prove that he did not exist or that he was not the brother of Jesus. What is known is that Mary, the virgin, conceived Jesus by the Holy Ghost before she had married Joseph. She and Joseph were married, Jesus was born, and Joseph named him Jesus. Anything beyond this is purely speculation.

By the time I had finished reading the book and taking a few notes, I didn't know what to think. The story had its interesting points, but to me it just seemed to be to absurd to be true. So, I "filed it away" in my mind, as one of those rare situations that could be possible but because of a total lack of authenticating documentation is most unlikely.

The next major event to take place with regard to the birth of Jesus was the visit of the shepherds to the birth site. This event is recorded in Luke 2:8-18.

> *"And there were in the same country shepherds abiding in the field, keeping watch over their flock by night. And, lo, the angel of the Lord came upon them, and the glory of the Lord shone round about them: and they were sore afraid. And the angel said unto them, fear not: for, behold, I bring you good tidings of great joy, which shall be to all people. For unto you is born this day in the city of David a Saviour, which is Christ the Lord. And this shall be a sign unto you; ye shall find the babe wrapped in swaddling clothes, lying in a manager. And suddenly there was with the angel a multitude of the heavenly host praising God, and saying, glory to God in the highest, and on earth peace, good will toward men. And it came to pass, as the angels were gone away from them into heaven, the shepherds said one to another, let us now go even unto Bethlehem, and see this thing which is come to pass, which the Lord hath made known unto us. And they came with haste, and found Mary, and Joseph, and the babe lying in a manager. And when they had seen it, they made known abroad the saying which was told them concerning the child. And all they that heard it wondered at those things which were told them by the shepherds" (Luke 2:8-18).*

It was at the University of Istanbul in Istanbul, Turkey that I discovered a manuscript that talked about the shepherds who were witnesses to Jesus' birth. The manuscript was one of two that University of Istanbul archaeologists had discovered hidden deep within the underground vaults of the church of St. Saviour Chora. The manuscript was apparently written in the first half of the 15th century by a Regimold of Iconium. It was a compilation of what he felt was the most accurate record of the shepherds' visit, outside of the Gospels.

Regimold began the manuscript by quoting Luke's record (Luke 2:8-18) of the shepherds' visit and then he explained their visit.

Regimold wrote that Luke says that there were shepherds in the area who were notified of Jesus' birth by an angel. Not only was the angel's appearance to the shepherds most significant, for it gives at least two confirmations of the time of year, springtime, during Passover season, when Jesus was born.

The first confirmation corroborates the season, or time of the year. The second corroborates a specific month of the year for certain, and perhaps even the day in that month.

This first confirmation rests in the fact that in Judea at this time, flocks of sheep were allowed to graze out of doors from mid-spring, after the rainy season had ended (the rainy season ended in mid-March) up till the early fall.

The second confirmation deals with the kind of sheep that were being watched by the shepherds and the location of the shepherd's watch during that time of year.

The Search

The area known as the *Hills of Ramat*, just north of Bethlehem, about three miles south of Jerusalem, was a small area of lush (in the spring time) rolling hills. Many years ago the High Priest in Jerusalem had set the area aside. The Hills of Ramat were under the jurisdiction and protection of the High Priest.

It was in this area that the Temple priests housed for 10 days (three days before Passover week, plus the seven days of Passover week) the flock of sheep that was to be used as Passover sacrifice animals, during the seven days of unleavened bread (Passover week). It was probably near here that Joseph and Mary stayed the night, and where Jesus was born.

The shepherds mentioned by Luke were the *sanctified shepherds of the seed of Jacob* who were chosen by the High Priest to be responsible for the care and the safety of the holy and sanctified sacrificial Passover sheep that would be sacrificed during that year's Passover celebration. To every seven sheep was assigned a sanctified shepherd, a Levite, and a presbyteroi rabbi (an elder rabbi) of the line of Zadok. The shepherd would care for the sheep, the Levite would see to the sheep's ritualistic cleanliness; and the presbyteroi would choose the sheep to be sacrificed.

It was to the sanctified shepherds, the Levites, and the presbyteroi rabbi that the angel of the Lord appeared and proclaimed the birth of Jesus. To these men who were well trained in the religious rituals of the Jews and who were knowledgeable of the prophecies and expectations concerning the prophesied Christ, the Savior and sacrificed redeemer, the announcement came as quite a shock. Some of them (Luke indicates that it was the shepherds that went to investigate and not the Levites or presbyteroi rabbi) immediately left the *Hills of Ramat* to go and investigate what the angel had said.

We have no idea how long they searched, but considering the enormous number of Passover travelers occupying the area, it could have taken them a good part of the night to locate the newly born baby.

Finally they found the inn where Joseph and Mary and the newly born baby (all three of them) were lying resting in the large dugout manger located in the inn's open courtyard (they were three out of probably many who were sleeping in the large open manager). After the shepherds had confirmed that what the angel had told them was true, they left the inn and began to enunciate all over the area, what the angel had announced to them concerning the new born babe.

Notice that nowhere does Luke record that the shepherds either bowed before or worshipped the newborn babe, Jesus. The tradition of the shepherds worshipping at the manger dates back to the days of St. Jerome. In a letter that he wrote to a Julian of Damascus, he first introduced the idea.

The appearance by the angel was certainly an unprecedented and unusual event, but it is doubtful that the shepherds would have left the *Hills of Ramat* to investigate had not the angel proclaimed that this newborn babe was a *Savior* and that he was *Christ the Lord*. The statement by the angel was the fuel that propelled the shepherds onward to locate the birthplace of the Savior.

At this time in the history of the Jews, there was great anticipation concerning the imminent arrival of two great Jewish deliverers. One of these anticipated deliverers was a religious leader, a Savior; he was called *Messias*. The other anticipated deliverer was a social and political leader, a Christ; he was called

Messiah. Hence, two deliverers were anticipated: *Messias* and *Messiah*. One was to come to free his people (the Jews) from their sins; the other was to come to free his people (the Jews) from their oppression and re-establish the ancient kingdom of David. No one was expecting both *Messias* and *Messiah* to come as one person, in the form of a baby.

The strong belief in an anticipated arrival of two Jewish deliverers, Regimold continued, was confirmed in 1379. In that year Venetian explorers who were investigating a cave on the island of Corfu, located just off the western coast of Greece and at that time a Venetian possession, discovered a four-inch diameter boat skin scroll. The scroll consisted of seven letters that had been written in Hebron, in the 1st century, about 20 years after the crucifixion of Jesus, by the great rabbi Hillel the Third. The scroll was sent to a rabbi living in Antioch by the name of Josh ha Rushi. An unknown Islamic scribe had translated the entire set of seven letters in the 10th century into Arabic, and had entitled them *The Hillel Letters Regarding God's Providence to the Jews*. The letters were then hidden and forgotten until 1379, when they were discovered.

The seventh of these letters was extremely long and dealt with, among other things, the issue of the anticipation of two Jewish deliverers.

In the letter Hillel wrote,

> "...not only was the expectation of a remarkable personage universally prevalent among the Jews at the time of the birth of Jesus of the Galilee, called by his followers The Christ, of which no evidence exists, that I have found, in either our histories or our association with this Jesus or our esteemed leaders of our reverent estate that should confirm such a decree affirmed upon him by his followers, but the phraseology was already in use which designated what he was to be and accomplish. There was at the time a Messianic phraseology derived from different parts of the writings of the prophets which embodied and expressed all their anticipation...this much was certain, that there was to be a Messiah, there was to be a new dispensation, and there was to be an anointed prophet of sacrifice...a Messias.... No one knew precisely how each was to appear, or how it would be. Imagination, of course, was set to work, and each one for himself formed his own, and made whatever passage of the prophets he choose to be descriptive of the persons and the office. Not only the imagination, but also the passions were concerned in the formation of these expectations. The one, whom we call Messias, was thought to be a religious reformer, and the new state of things to be a condition of higher religious perfection.... The universal expectation among the Jews seems to have been that he was to be a prophet like unto Moses, but greater...who will save us from sin. Another was Messiah...a great personage whose coming was shortly expected as a king...greater than any who had sat upon the Jewish throne. It was this expectation that followed the Galilean Jesus through his itinerancy...and even after his death and supposed resurrection (so claimed by his followers), his pupils claimed this expectation and this hope.... One idea of his kingdom...was that he was not only to reign over

The Search

the Jews, but was to destroy all other nations... it is also anticipated that this Messiah should never die.... This confident expectation of the Jews had already no little political disturbance. It was this proud anticipation of universal conquest that made them so restive under the government of the Romans. That they who were destined to reign over the world...and whose King Messiah was to have the heathen for his inheritance, the uttermost parts of the earth for his possession, who was to break with a rod of iron, and dash them in pieces like a potter's vessel...should be in vassalage to a foreign power, was more than they could bear...."

After quoting this portion of Hillel's letter, Regimold continued with his treatise.

When the angel announced that the Savior (both *Messiah* and *Messias*), which is Christ (*Messias*) the Lord ("soter" or military deliverer; *Messiah*), had been born in Bethlehem, the city of David (the long anticipated birth place of *Messiah*, the son of David), the holy men watching the sanctified sheep, were confused, shocked, amazed, afraid, anxious, delighted, and bewildered all at the same time. Could the angel mean that both *Messias* and *Messiah* had been born? Or did the Angel mean that just one of them had been born? Confusion drove them to go to Bethlehem and investigate. They were obligated to do nothing less.

After finding the babe with his mother and his earthly father, they spread the news about what the angel had said, then returned to the *Hills of Ramat* to prepare for Passover.

For centuries, Regimold continued, the only sources, outside of the Bible, that attempted to record anything about the shepherds' visit to the manger that night, were grossly embellished fabrications. They were written for the purpose of solidifying Mary's exalted position of "Blessed Virgin." It was not until 1224, when numerous scrolls entitled *The Senatorial Courts of Tiberius Caesar, and by the Sanhedrin in Jerusalem* were discovered by soldiers of Theodore I, the ruler of the Despotate of Epirusin in a forgotten, centuries old, underground vault in the burial catacombs of Janina, that we procured what may be the first authentic, non-embellished, account of the birth of Jesus and the shepherds' visit.

One of the scrolls had four separate manuscript entries. Two of these were of special interest because they dealt with the birth of Jesus and the shepherds finding the baby Jesus. One manuscript was entitled *Jonathan, the son of Heziel, interview with sanctified shepherds of Ramat* and the other one was entitled *Letters of Melker, Priest of the Synagogue at Bethlehem. Sanhedrim, 88B, by R. Jose, order No. 2.*

The first entry, the *Jonathan, the son of Heziel...*manuscript, was supposed to have been an interview conducted by a chief scribe named Jonathan (who had been sent by the Sanhedrin in Jerusalem), with three of the sanctified shepherds who were watching over the sanctified Passover sheep the night that Jesus was born. The shepherds told Jonathan,

> "...it was the third watch of the night when we were awakened by a bright light as bright as the light of day.... All at once the night seemed to be filled with human voices saying, *Glory! Glory! Glory to the Most High God!*

> *Happy art thou Bethlehem, for God hath fulfilled His promise to the fathers; for in thy chambers is born the King that shall rule in righteousness! The Savior, which is Christ the Lord!* Their shouting would rise up in the heavens, and then would sink down in mellow strains, and roll along at the foot of the mountains, and die away in the most soft and musical manner; then it would begin again high up in the heavens, in the very vaults of heaven, and descend in sweet and melodious strains...the light would seem to burst forth high in the heavens, and then descend in softer rays and light up the hills and valleys, making everything more visible than the light of the sun.... They said that it shown around the whole city, and some of the people were frantic until the priest Melker, came out to the people clapping his hands in joy and addressed them saying that this thing was of God and was a fulfillment of prophecy.... They went into the city and found a young mother with her new born baby and her husband resting in a feeding closure for animals. We felt in our hearts that this babe may be the cause of such joyous praise...."

The second entry was a letter that Melker the priest had written to the Sanhedrin in Jerusalem. In the letter he stated,

> "...the night that the heavens shone like the sun of day 18 guardians of the sanctified Passover sheep approached me in the streets asking me where the child lay who caused such a commotion in the heavens. I told them to search the city until they had found a child that had been born that night. They returned to me near daybreak saying that they had found the [baby] to the north of the city near Ramat and related to me a story which the very young mother had told them concerning an angel who had appeared to her saying that the child was a gift from God. That he would rule his people.... Afterwards some returned to the flocks while the others spread the news of their discovery throughout the hill country. After some eight days I sent for the mother, to have the babe circumcised. At that time she repeated the same story to me.... I am informed that she could have been tried by law because she could not give a better evidence of her virtue than to claim her child was gifted from God, but that she and her husband had residence in the Galilee, where such stories and claims give no rise for question. If she lived in Judea she could have been stoned according to the Law, although I must admit that I can think of no other case that such apparent divine manifestations, manifestations to which I was witness, were seen on the occasion of the birth of her son. In the past I have examined at least 20 different young women who claimed to be virgin and who claimed to be with child of the spirit of God. But none had accompaniment of such manifestations as was witnessed that night in Bethlehem...had not she fled back to the Galilee with her husband, a stonemason's master in Nazareth of the Galilee, no doubt she would have been presumed innocent.... even in Judea and Jerusalem."

The Search

"It cannot be proven without a doubt," confessed Regimold, "that these were authentic records, I believe there is certainly more validity to them than in the hundreds of other embellishments (excluding the Gospel accounts) that materialized during the first thousand years after Jesus' birth."

With that, Regimold's record of the shepherds' visit to the birth site of Jesus was concluded.

After Jesus was born, we know that Joseph and Mary stayed at least eight more days in the Bethlehem area. The Gospels do not record whether they had to stay in the open courtyard of the inn those eight days, but most likely they did not. Eight days after his birth, Jesus was taken to the local priest and was circumcised and named.

> *"And when eight days were accomplished for the circumcising of the child, his name was called Jesus, which was so named of the angel before he was conceived in the womb" (Luke 2:21).*

I found an excellent source concerning the ritual of circumcision while I was researching at San Jose State University in San Jose, California. But rather than a book or a manuscript, the source was more like a spiral notebook. In reality, it was a medical text written by Dr. Feltan Lipinski, a Jewish surgeon who in 1882 when he was 32 years old, had fled Poland for America, for fear that the Russian pogroms would spread to Poland. When he arrived in America, he had nothing. He had to start his life all over again; and had he not discovered a link between bacteria, sanitary conditions, and infection, chances are he would have vanished into obscurity. But, in 1912, when he was 62 years old, he made three medical discoveries that revolutionized the fight against and the treatment of infection: 1) that amputation could be avoided if infection could be prevented; 2) that infection could be prevented if specific kinds of bacteria that attacked an open wound could be killed; and 3) that it was difficult for bacteria to exist in a sanitary environment. After his death in 1919, his journal research notes were published under the title *The History of Sanitation, Infection and Disease*, and were bound in spiral notebook fashion. Although there were over 1,000 copies published, only nine were known to still exist. San Jose State had one of the nine.

A Dr. Howard Burnstein wrote the introduction to the text. In it, Dr. Burnstein claimed to have been a colleague of Dr. Lipinski in his research. He also claimed that although Dr. Lipinski was Jewish by birth, he had spent his whole life as a non-religious agnostic. Then in 1914, just five years before his death, he became a Christian through Dr. Burnstein's influence. Dr. Lipinski began to read the Bible and discovered that God had given many specific commands concerning cleanliness, sanitation, and the prevention of disease. Dr. Lipinski also became fascinated with the fact that God was a personal God who cared about the welfare of men, even to the point of giving them health and preventative medicine instructions.

The editor of the notebook organized Lipinski's material in such a way that the first portion dealt with medical treatment and sanitation in ancient times. This was followed in section two by explaining how that biblical sanitation instructions and medical procedure could have made an impact upon sanitation conditions in the medieval ages, if they would have followed the instructions. The notebook concluded with sanitation and medical treatment from the beginning of the Napoleonic era to the end of the 19th century.

It was in the biblical emphasis section, the second section, that I found information about Jesus' circumcision and the first few days after his circumcision. Under a chapter (chapter four of section two) entitled "Circumcision—More Than Religion," Lipinski traced the history of the ritual of circumcision and argued that the practice was more than a religious ritual; it was actually a preventive medicine and sanitation practice, instituted by God to prevent disease. It was in this chapter that Jesus was presented, relative to his own circumcision.

"According to Hebrew law," Lipinski wrote (Genesis 17:10-11; Leviticus 12:3), "all male children were to be circumcised on the eighth day after birth. In Jewish religious ritualism, this was reputed to have been a token of the Abrahamic Covenant. A local priest usually performed the circumcision and it was on this occasion that the child was named. In the Galilee, because of its predominate Greek influence, and because in the Galilee the Jews were in the smallest of minorities, circumcision was not such a mandatory ritual for them. In fact, very few Jewish males, less than one percent, were circumcised in the Galilee at this time. But, considering that Jesus was born in Judea, it was most advisable for his parents to follow the Jewish birth rituals. Hence, Jesus was most likely circumcised by the local priest, at which time he was named *Jesus*. I'm sure that the priest was somewhat amazed that the infant's parents named him *Jesus*, a Greek name; yet considering they were from the Galilee, he was probably not surprised".

Lipinski then began to go into a long explanation regarding Jesus' name that seemed to be totally unrelated to the theme of the text. This led me to believe that perhaps an editor somewhere along the way had added this portion after Lipinski's death. He began his explanation by quoting three portions of Scripture.

> *"And she shall bring forth a son, and thou shalt call his name Jesus: for he shall save his people from their sins" (Matthew 1:21).*
>
> *"And behold, thou shalt conceive in thy womb, and bring forth a son, and shalt call his name Jesus. He shall be great, and shall be called the Son of the Highest: and the Lord God shall give him the throne of his father David" (Luke 1:31-32).*
>
> *"And the angel answered and said unto her, the Holy Ghost shall come upon thee, and the power of the highest shall over shadow thee: Therefore also that Holy thing which shall be born of thee shall be called the Son of God" (Luke 1:35).*

He then continued by saying that for years Christians had taken for granted many things that may or may not have been true. But because they had evolved over the centuries to become a part of the traditional Christmas story, they have come to be accepted as fact.

"The Matthew text, Matthew 1:21," he wrote, "Says that this son of Mary will save his people, or the people of his lineage, from their sins. The word save in the Greek is *sodzo*; it usually implied 'salvation from sin, sickness, or spiritual conflict through personal sacrifice.' Although this verse says that he will save his own people, the Jews, Mary was commanded to name her son, *Jesus*, a Greek name; hence, identifying him with a 'barbarian' people, rather than with the Jews.

"Some theologians have tried to show that the Greek name, *Jesus*, is the same as the Hebrew name, *Yehoshua* or *Joshua*, which in Hebrew means 'salvation,' but there does not seem to be enough substantial evidence to prove this conjecture to be true.

"All that can be proven is that the name, *Jesus, is a Greek name* that until the 4th century AD had a Greek definition. The name meant 'eternal, eternity, or for eternity.' This seems to correspond with what the angel said when he told Mary that her son would (in the future) be called *Emanuel*. The word *Emanuel* is a Persian word that was borrowed by the Greeks, and came to mean 'God eternal or God with us for eternity.'

"Alexander the Great was praised as *Emanuel* after his conquest of Persia's emperor, Darius. Seleucus I, founder of the Seleucid dynasty, came to be called *Emanuel* by the citizens of the city of Babylon. Marius, the Roman general, upon his return to Rome after his victory over the Kingdom of Numidian, was proclaimed to be *Emanuel*.

"It was not until the 4th century, that St. Basil declared that the name *Emanuel* meant 'salvation' or 'God who is with us—salvation.' No one knows why he changed the definition of the word, but his new definition stuck. It is now the commonly accepted definition for the meaning of the name, *Emanuel*.

"So, Mary was told to name her son the Greek name, *Jesus*. Yet, she was also told that he would be the Savior to his own people, the Jews, and not the Greeks: *very confusing*. Except for the fact that the angel had told her to do it, there seems to be no explanation why Mary would name him, *Jesus*. Unless, like in the case of the naming of *John*, Greek names were the common and accepted more than the exception in the Galilee, at this time in history. If there was some other reason or justification for naming him *Jesus*, it appears to have been lost to us.

"When we look at the Luke texts, the confusion becomes even more prevalent. In verse 31 of chapter one, again the angel said that Mary's son was to be named *Jesus*. Verse 32 and verse 33 say that he will be great and will be called (in the future) the *Son of the Highest*. It also says that the Lord God will give to him the throne of his father, David, and that his kingdom will last forever, without end. In verse 35 the angel says, that that Holy thing (interesting that he said *thing* and not *son* or *person*) which shall be born will **ALSO** be called the *Son of God*. Therefore, what we have is that verse 31 says that he will be called *Jesus*; verses 32 and 33 say that he will be called the *Son of the Highest* and that the Lord God will give him the throne of David, and his kingdom will last forever, which implies Messiahship; and verse 35 says that he will also be called the *Son of God*. If he will be called the *Son of the Highest* and **ALSO** the *Son of God*, then who is the one whom the angel referred to as *Highest* to/of whom Jesus will be His *son*? And who is the Lord God who will give him the throne of David?

"The term *Son of the Highest* in Greek is *huios hupsistos*. Its root comes from the Chaldean. It means, 'a son—the off-spring of man and of the highest regions of the Most High God of all Gods.' It was first used by Chaldean magi in Babylonia and then by Zoroaster priests in Persia to describe their God who had been selected by the eternal God Superior, the supreme God of all of the Gods in all of the universes (they taught that there were four universes), to come to earth and to be born a man and rule the people of earth.

"Xerxes was said to have self-adopted this title, and then forced the Zoroaster priests, under penalty of death, to officially proclaim him the *Son of the Highest*.

"The apocryphal *Book of Enoch* claims that this title, *Son of the Highest*, was a reference to the Christ, although apart from the Christ-implied reference in Luke 1:32, the Gospels themselves never make that claim.

"The term *Son of God* in verse 35 is translated in the Greek, *huios theos*. It means, 'a man, the offspring of a man of a Godhead.' It refers to a god's beginning of human life on the earth.

"St. Ignatius, Bishop of Antioch during the reign of Roman Emperor Trajan, in a letter to the Magnesians, wrote that sonship referred to Jesus' humanity, not his deity. As God, He had no beginning, but as man he had a beginning. When he left his position as God and became man, he at that moment had a beginning and became the human offspring of the eternal Godhead. In the realm of heaven, God had no son, for sonship is human and refers only to Jesus' humanity. Only on earth was he Son of God; he was a man without sin, in whom God could reside. *Jesus* was his human name on earth. Now that he is again in heaven, his name is not Jesus, for he is no longer a man, he is again God, the third member of the Trinity.

"Whether Ignatius had it right or not," Lipinski continued, "we may never know until we meet our maker face to face ourselves. But I do think that he was on the right track. The angel did say that he would, in the future, be called the *Son of God*. He was in fact a man in whom the Spirit of God resided, and is today called, and has been called since shortly after his resurrection, the *Son of God*.

"Now back to verse 32. Who is the Lord God who gives him his kingdom that will last forever? The term is translated in the Greek *kurios Theos*, which means, 'the God who is the possessor, owner and master.' Yet, the term is not Greek in origin, but rather it has its roots once again, in the Chaldean. The word was used to show that a particular geographical region was under the control of a particular and specific, god-master. The angel messenger used the term when he appeared to and addressed Daniel, regarding the angel's 21-day delay in coming to Daniel, due to spiritual combative interference by the prince of the kingdom of Persia. This suggested that the spiritual forces that controlled the geographical area of Persia, had delayed him for 21 days.

"By the angel Gabriel's use of this term to Mary, he implied that the Supreme God had given another spiritual power mastery over the region which had been the kingdom of David. That spiritual power will in turn, give or forfeit, his mastery control of that region, over to the *Son of the Highest*. Although this may or may not be what Luke had intended the statement to mean, we cannot and we must not guess or draw non-fact based conclusions. Hence, if we take the statement literally for what it says, we have no choice but to accept as fact the literal interpretation.

The Search

"In essence, the angel said to Mary that her son would reign over the geographical region of the old kingdom of David, and that his kingdom would last forever. Now almost 2,000 years later, we can speculate that the angel may have been referring to a spiritual kingdom, whose center of influence is the region of David's old kingdom: Israel and the surrounding area. This in fact has happened. The so called 'Holy Land', and Jerusalem in particular, is the spiritual center of three of our civilization's most influential religions: Christianity, Islam, and Judaism, and for years seems to have been the center of the world's attention."

That concluded the chapter entitled "Circumcision—More Than Religion," and it gave me a mountain of fuel that catapulted my quest for knowledge about Jesus from one of continuous flame to one of roaring inferno. It now seemed so obvious to me that God the Father had planned every tiny detail of man's redemption with perfect precession with zero percent tolerance, even down to something as simple as the naming of Jesus.

Although chapter four entitled "Circumcision—More Than Religion" had concluded, someone in the past had inserted two more hand-written pages into the notebook, between the conclusion of chapter four and the beginning of chapter five.

The hand-written notes began, "Accordingly, the next event for Jesus after his circumcision was his trip to the Temple in Jerusalem." The author of these two pages then briefly explained the events that took place before and after Jesus was taken to the Temple in Jerusalem. The author began by quoting Luke's record of the event.

> *"And when the days of her purification according to the Law of Moses were accomplished, they brought him to Jerusalem, to present him to the Lord; (as it is written in the Law of the Lord, every male that openeth the womb shall be called Holy to the Lord;) and to offer a sacrifice according to that which is said in the Law of the Lord, a pair of turtle doves, or two young pigeons" (Luke 2:22-24).*

The author continued by writing, "According to the Law of Moses (Leviticus 12), a mother was considered unclean, just as with her menstrual cycle, for a period of seven days after childbirth if she had birthed a male, and 14 days if she had birthed a female. After the seven-day period, she still had to remain isolated, not touching any holy thing and not being allowed to enter the Temple for an additional 33 days, if she had given birth to a son, and 66 days if she had borne a daughter. After this time had run its course, she was expected to travel to Jerusalem (if she lived in the Galilee she could go to a synagogue in Capernaum) to undertake her own purification ritual by offering the appropriate sacrifice: a lamb as a burnt offering and a young pigeon or turtle dove as a sin offering. In case of poverty or if she was not from a direct Hebrew bloodline, a turtle dove or a young pigeon could be substituted for the lamb as a burnt offering. Considering Mary presented the least expensive offering, it was either because she was not of pure Hebrew blood (which would be the case if her mother or grandmother were Egyptian), she and Joseph were poor (unlikely if Joseph was a master stonemason), or they did not bring enough money with them to buy a lamb.

"In addition to the purification ritual for the child's mother, if the newborn male was the first child, the father of the child was required (Exodus 13:11-16; Leviticus 12:2-8) to redeem the child from the Lord, in what has come to be called the Redemption Ceremony. According to Numbers 18:15-16, the first born son was sacred to the Lord and had to be redeemed from the Lord for five shekels (about 20 days' wages for a common laborer) payable to the presiding priest. Afterwards, the priest would bless the baby as he concluded the Redemption Ceremony.

"Although this was normally the extent of the ritual and ceremony, in the case of Jesus, two unique events occurred before the actual ceremony began.

"Luke tells us that there was a man by the name of Simeon (Christian tradition says that this Simeon was the father of Gamaliel, the teacher of Paul, and was the son of the great teacher, Hillel), who was living in Jerusalem at this time and that he was anxiously anticipating the coming of the Messiah. Luke goes on to say that Simeon was a devout man and a just man and that the Holy Spirit was upon him. And the Holy Spirit had promised him that he would not see death until he had seen the Christ. It seems that on the day that Joseph and Mary brought Jesus to the Temple to be presented to the Lord, the Holy Spirit led Simeon to the Temple also. He seems to have been there already when the parents arrived, for verse 27 implies that Simeon met them upon their arrival at the Temple. Simeon took the baby from the parents, probably from Mary, and held him in his arms, and recognized the baby as being the one whom the Holy Spirit had promised that he would see before he died. He then prophesied while holding Jesus that the babe would be a light to the Gentiles and would be a glory to the Jews.

"Joseph and Mary were totally taken back by the words of Simeon," the unknown author continued, "but they said nothing. Simeon obviously sensed their apprehension and blessed them individually. He concluded by again prophesying, this time to Mary, telling her that Jesus would truly be a light to many and a stumbling block to others and that her own heart would be pierced, meaning that she would suffer extreme anguish because of what would happen to her son.

"Their being joined by an elderly prophetess by the name of Anna immediately followed this event. She too agreed that the babe was the promised redeemer, and told everyone in Jerusalem who would listen, that she had seen the redeemer.

"After they had concluded their ritual duties in Jerusalem, Joseph and Mary took the infant Jesus and returned to their home in Nazareth, in the Galilee. By this time it was probably near the latter part of May or early June of the year 7 BC."

This ended the unknown author's hand-written addendum to chapter four.

Nothing more for two years is recorded in the Gospels concerning Jesus' life. However, I discovered a manuscript at the University of Toledo in Toledo, Ohio that helped me understand what was happening in the area that came to be known as Palestine, during that two-year Gospel silence.

The manuscript was a 13th century French copy (it was accompanied by an English translation) of an earlier Latin manuscript—no trace of the original remained—written in about the year 400 by a Roman Senator by the name of Pammachius. Pammachius had married the daughter of St. Paula and was a devoted friend of St. Jerome. He and St. Fabiola founded a hospice for pilgrims at Porto. The manuscript was actually an explanatory commentary addressed to Jerome, clarifying the political state of Herod's kingdom immediately following Jesus' birth, but before Joseph and Mary fled with him to Egypt.

About three-quarters of the way through the three-leaf document, I found Pammachius' words so intriguing that I feel that I should quote them directly.

"Upon their [Joseph, Mary and the babe Jesus] return to the Galilee from Bethlehem and Jerusalem after the birth of Jesus, they had heard that Herod the Great had decreed following the Passover celebration of that year [7 BC] the initiation of a great four-month long summer celebration and feast to commemorate the declaration of world peace by Caesar Augustus. From Panias to Idumaea and from Peraea to the Mediterranean, Herod proclaimed a kingdom-wide celebration. For four months, beginning with the first signs of summer (probably in May or June) his subjects were relieved of their kingdom tax burden (this did not include taxes paid to Rome—it applied only to taxes that were paid to Herod), and every night, in every principal city of his kingdom, from sun-down to sun-up, free food, wine, and entertainment was provided for whomever chose to accept it. This four-month celebration was followed by another one of Herod's famed grandiose building surges, which spread to all corners of his kingdom. During this period of massive construction 100 percent of all able-bodied Jewish workers were employed. It is the first and only time that this occurred in the history of the Jewish people. Note that these projects were not constructed by slave labor. All workers were paid employees of Herod.

"Because of the four-month long celebration and the enormous construction efforts of Herod that followed, comparative peace and prosperity throughout his kingdom was the rule rather than the exception. Throughout that entire two-year period, in every city, town, and village in every area and region of Herod's kingdom, there was peace and prosperity. Then came the ambassadors to Judea representing the kingdoms of the East and peace and prosperity was no more to be."

That was all that was written in the body of the manuscript, but as I was about to return the manuscript to its place, I noticed that someone had written something in the manuscript margin. The words were written in Latin. The writer identified himself simply as a 14th century Cluny servant of the Lord.

The "Cluny servant of the Lord" wrote on the manuscript margin that it was probably during this two-year period of peace and prosperity that Joseph's family business expanded from one of simple local carpentry or stone masonry to one of regional weighty [heavy] construction. During this two-year construction and prosperity onslaught, the Galilee became more aligned with Greek culture, much more than it had been previously, so much so, that in most communities all traces of traditional Jewish culture vanished, never to rise again. Even in the few communities where Judaism did meagerly survive, it had to fight fearlessly just to preserve its scant existence. Nazareth probably fit into this latter category.

Nowhere in the Galilee was Judaism politically influential or culturally consequential, nor was there any place where Judaism experienced any significant growth. On the contrary, Judaism in the Galilee, at the time of Jesus' infancy, was nothing more than a shell and a memory of the once proud social order that in former times had referred to itself as *God's chosen people*.

For all practical purposes, within two years after Jesus' birth, except for a handful of scattered pockets in less than a dozen villages where Orthodox Judaism was trying desperately but with little success to persist, Judaism survived in name only in the Galilee.

In the midst of this semi-Judaistic to non-Judaistic environment was the young child, Jesus, raised. So, because Herod's kingdom was enjoying a season of unprecedented peace, it appears that nothing of major political consequence occurred during the first two years of Jesus' life. So ended the marginal notes of the Cluny servant of the Lord.

XI

MOTHER OF GOD

Before we leave this portion of Jesus life and continue on into his unknown years, I feel that it is important to explain how many of our current traditions regarding Jesus and the Virgin Mary have developed.

Actually the story of how I discovered much of this information starts on a mid-morning Swissair flight that I was taking from Zurich to big, expansive, dirty, yet exotic and ancient, Cairo, Egypt.

As I sat down in my coach class seat, I immediately noticed that my seat back was stuck in a permanently down position. Because the seats had to be upright for take-off, the flight attendant moved me from my coach seat up to an empty first-class seat. Needless to say, I did not object. She seated me next to a very distinguished looking gentleman. Once I got settled and the flight was off the ground, we introduced ourselves. The gentleman's name was Dr. Richard Hawkinson. He was a professor of Cultural Anthropology at the University of Toronto in Toronto, Ontario-Canada. As we talked, our conversation eventually turned to my search for historical Jesus quest. Dr. Hawkinson did not claim to be a Christian, in fact he said that he was actually non-religious; however, he was fascinated by my search for historical Jesus efforts and the research potential associated with it.

For more than three hours Dr. Hawkinson and I discussed many traditional Christian doctrine, dogmas, and theories and it was evident that Dr. Hawkinson had a commanding knowledge of the Bible and the dogmas and traditions of Christianity. When I wondered out loud about the origin of some Christianity traditions and dogmas, Dr. Hawkinson's reply followed by an explanatory observation added a new wrinkle to my research emphasis.

Dr. Hawkinson said, "I want to be real honest with you. Some Christian traditions and dogmas were introduced in a calculated effort to destroy what you as believers in the Christian faith now perceive as truth, and particularly in an effort to counter-balance that calculated destruction effort."

I was somewhat taken aback by Richard's statement, so I asked him to elaborate.

He responded by saying, "What you have to do with your research is to address and confront three fundamental quasi-theological tenants that have led to this array of what is in reality, false dogmas and doctrines; dogmas and doctrines that have for centuries been used to enslave multiplied millions of people. These three fundamental tenants that you must confront are: (1) The virgin birth of Jesus (2) The divine mother and incarnate son and (3) Mary, the mother of God.

"If you don't address these you cannot hope to intelligently approach a rational justification for believing what you profess and have no grounds for projecting your beliefs to others.

"Although we do not have enough time before we arrive in Cairo to discuss all three tenants, I think I do have enough time to cover at least one; at least partially anyway. For the other two, you'll have to find the information yourself. But, I think I have given you enough to go on, so that you can get on the right path to do the necessary research to get the information for yourself.

"Let's look at the virgin birth first. If you will recall your traditional Old Testament ideology, the promise of God way back in the Garden of Eden was that the *head* of the serpent, typically identified throughout Judeo/Christian history as Satan or Lucifer, or more rightly, the Luciferian system, would be bruised or crushed, by the seed of woman. In other words, it is supposed that God proclaimed that the Luciferian system's head would be crushed by a woman's offspring. The offspring would supposedly be conceived without the accompanying necessity of the physical seed of a male.

"It is now assumed by most 'mystics' and dogmaisticism/ideological historians that the Luciferian hierarchy could not and would not allow the miraculous arrival of the obliterator of their system. Hence, the Luciferian hierarchy launched a two-front, opposite extremes assault in an effort to neutralize God's proclaimed vengeance strategy and hypothecation. One front would concentrate on the denial of a virgin born redeemer/extirpator; the second would concentrate on the acceptance of a virgin birthed redeemer. On the one hand, the virgin birth would be mocked and ridiculed; while on the other, the virgin birth would become a foundational mainstay of Christian doctrine, and of virtually every religion and religious philosophy in the world, both Western and Eastern.

"Let's look at the denial focus first," he continued. "If a person or a belief or a philosophy chooses to deny the virgin birth of a redeemer, in this case Jesus, then that person or belief or philosophy must deny three foundational Christian beliefs. The first is the belief in divine conception and the second is the belief in virgin conception and birth. The denial in turn opens the door to and welcomes with open-arms a multitude of justifications and explanations that seek to explain away the ideology of Jesus' miraculous birth, which is one of the basic foundations upon which the Christian faith is built. The Bible must also be rejected as the unerring Word of God Supreme. In these fundamental beliefs are eliminated, there will arise dozens of hypothesis, explanations, and justifications that seek to fill a spiritual, psychological, or emotional void with logic, that can, in reality, only be filled with faith.

"Accordingly," Dr. Hawkinson continued after the stewardess had asked us to buckle our seatbelts because we were preparing to land, "It is safe to say that the Luciferian power structure has been phenomenally successful in portraying to the intellectual world the utter impossibility of a virgin birth and the ridiculousness of trying to accept as fact, such an absurd notion. It is unfortunate for those who espouse the Christian belief, that many who choose to deny the virgin birth, justify their denial on the Bible itself. I wish I had the time to cover the Biblical justification in more detail, but if I did, I would not have the time to talk about, the second front of the Luciferian attack. It is an effort to neutralize the first of the three tenants; that of the virgin birth.

"Now let me quickly cover the high points of the second front, before we land. Although the second front of the Luciferian attack, the acceptance of the virgin birth of Jesus, is the opposite extreme of the first front, the denial of the virgin birth, the second front has become just as devastating to the belief in a true divine conception and the virgin birth of a redeemer/Messiah, as the first front. The second front centered around the introduction of a virgin birth myth in the foundational beliefs of virtually all known ancient, as well as present day, religions, religious philosophies, and religious beliefs. Consequently, the attribution of a divine father to a human or of a divine conception and virgin birth became, early in mankind's religious history, neither remarkable nor impossible. By the time the *true* virgin birth did occur, the event had been so deeply rooted in religious lore and mythology, that it was, for the most part, rejected by the Jews as nothing more than just another myth about another virgin birth of another human savior whose actual father was a god, and who was born for the purpose of bringing deliverance to an oppressed people. Examples of the effectiveness of this second front, the virgin birth acceptance front, are seen in the ancient, (both past records and present records), histories, and religious myths of many of our past and present Western and Eastern societies: Greek, Roman, Hittite, Babylonian, Illyricum, Chinese, Hindu, Norse, American Indian, Egyptian, and scores of others. All you have to do is take the time to study the myths of these cultures to understand the universal acceptance of such a belief.

"In western mythology, the Greek hero, Perseus, was said to be the son of the virgin, Diana, and the Greek's chief god, Zeus. Hercules was the son of Alcmene, a mortal woman, sometimes depicted as a virgin, and the god, Zeus. Aeneas was the son of the goddess, Aphrodite, and a mortal man. Achilles was the son of a sea nymph married to a mortal man. Roman history taught that the virgin, Rhea Silvia, conceived Romulus, the mythological founder of Rome, and his brother Remus, by the god of war, Mars. Even historical figures were said to be of divine origin: Pythagoras, Plato, Aristotle, Alexander the Great, Julius Caesar, Cyrus the Great, Augustus, and dozens more."

"Now," he continued as the plane touched down, "in oriental mythology, the allusion made by Luke the Evangelist in his record of Jesus' birth, to divine intervention associated with that birth, readily agrees with Eastern myths which envisaged God in terms of luminous radiation, gusts of wind, or gathering clouds. In India, the story of Krishna the savior, closely resembles in detail, the birth of Jesus: the annunciation to the virgin, Jasoda; the incarnation of the god, Vishnu; the adoration of the shepherds; persecution by the rajahs, who ordered the killing of every male child born on the night of Krishna's nativity, and so on. Right here in Egypt, at the Temple of Luxor, south of here, is portrayed the annunciation of the god, Thoth, to the virgin Isis; the conception of Horus; and the subsequent homage paid to Horus and Isis by many of Egypt's other gods. In the worship of Mithras, Mithras himself, in the form of light, entered the body of a virgin, and he himself was subsequently born of that virgin in a cave, just after the winter solstice. In Buddhism, a god who appeared in the form of a cloud conceived Buddha, the Enlightened One.

"Examples of a virgin birth can easily be identified in the mythological religious foundations of cultures throughout the world: from the Aztecs and the Mayans to the Eskimos, and from Japan, Australia, and Korea to South America and Africa. Little research is needed to discover that the virgin birth myth has not only been spread world-wide but has cut across all cultural boundaries and all historical time tables. In short, this Luciferian, two-front assault seems to have worked flawlessly, and it would have worked to absolute perfection had it not been for a small, yet determined, group of followers of Jesus, who launched a counter-attack so furious in the first two centuries AD, that the Luciferian plan was almost halted in its tracks and was nearly neutralized.

"To repudiate this counter-attack, the Luciferian hierarchy had to move quickly in order to re-establish and re-organize it's plan of attack. Hence, the second tenant of the Luciferian deception plan: the divine mother and incarnate son, was introduced in an effort to counter-attack the offensive assault of the first and second century early Christian church fathers."

Just as Dr. Hawkinson had finished his statement, the plane rolled to a stop in front of the disembark gate. He again apologized that he was not able to elaborate upon the other two areas that he had introduced, but I was confident that I would eventually find the information in all three of the areas that would serve to corroborate Dr. Hawkinson's observations.

As we left the plane, I walked towards customs while Dr. Hawkinson walked towards the gate where he would board a plane for Nairobi, Kenya where he was scheduled to speak at a historical conference. As we parted, I thanked him for his insight and his observations, telling him that he had made me realize that there was much more hidden regarding the religion based on the person of Jesus than was allowed to be exposed to the public. I told him that the research project would not have the same simple focus that it had; that from this time forward the accentuation of my research would be designed to expose deception and reveal absolute truth.

I spent about two weeks in Cairo doing a lot of research and visiting some of the tourist sites, but found little in the way of authenticating documentation. So, I decided to fly to Damascus, Syria and do some research in the Damascus Museum, one of the finest in the Middle East.

The Damascus Museum was located next to the beautiful Taqiah Mosque in the western part of the city, the area called "new city" by the locals.

The Museum was originally built by the French back in the 1920's, and has become world renowned for it's ancient Babylonian, Assyrian, and Persian artifacts and exhibits, as well as it's extensive Islamic history sector. In addition to these four cultures, the museum also has displays and artifacts from virtually every civilization and culture that had ever occupied the Tigris-Euphrates Rivers area from the 7th millennium BC up to the 6th century AD, as well as artifacts from such cultures as the ancient Indus, Hindu, Hittite, and Hurria. Along with this wealth of ancient artifacts and displays, the museum also housed one of the most comprehensive ancient manuscript and cuneiform tablet research libraries in all of the Middle East.

To my great surprise and delight, I found a virtual gold mine of manuscripts and tablets in the museum that dealt with the subject of the virgin divine mother and incarnate son issue. Issues that Dr. Hawkinson had not had time to address on the plane to Cairo. Because the museum had already translated most of the ancient manuscripts and cuneiform tablets into Arabic, French, and English, I had no problem reading the manuscripts and tablets and accompanying descriptive information.

The Search

Most of the manuscripts and tablets that I read were ancient Babylonian, Sumerian, Akkadian, Assyrian, Hindu, Seminite, and Roman works, dealing with subjects that ranged from history to mythology and religion, and from military campaigns to politics. I spent a week studying in the manuscript library and another three days doing research in the Islamic history sector.

In so doing, I began to develop an understanding of how effective the divine mother and incarnate son portion of the Luciferian assault had been conducted through the ages. I also began to piece together a picture of how this portion of the assault evolved and how it was designed to work. Although some of the information I discovered was a little hard to believe, I found too much evidence to suggest that it was mere legend, myth, or fabrication; it was frightenly true.

By reading the Babylonian, Akkadian, and Sumerian tablets, as well as the commentaries on those tablets, I discovered that upon the death of Nimrod, the king of Babel, in about the year 4599 BC, the divine mother and incarnate son myth began to be implemented through the efforts of Semiramis, Nimrod's mother/wife queen. By 4550 BC, the mythological doctrine of the divine mother and incarnate son was firmly entrenched into the ancient Babylonian religious mysteries. Fifty years later, in 4550 BC, the myth had been exalted to become the principal foundation upon which ancient Babylon's entire religious system was built.

From Babylon the doctrine spread rapidly until by 4000 BC it had penetrated every religion and religious system of the ancient world. There was not a single nation, social system, culture, or race that was left untouched or undefiled by this Babylonian religious doctrine.

By studying numerous Assyrian and Seminite tablets, I discovered that in Egypt, the divine mother and incarnate son became known as Isis and Osiris.

In India, they became known as Isi and Iswara. In Asia, they were known as Cybele and Deoius.

In early Rome, they were known as Fortuna and Jupiter-puer. In Greece, they were known as Ceres or Irene and Plutus, and in China they were known as Shing Moo and her holy child. There just was too much evidence to not suggest that from this Babylonian foundation evolved countless mythological tales, religious beliefs, and worship rituals representing every culture and every social system in the known world.

As the centuries rolled by, cultures were re-molded to fit the current social order of a specific nation, race, or group of people. Along with this cultural re-molding came a re-molding and re-shaping of religious myths and religious beliefs. Hence, the names of mother and child, their representation, their duties and powers, and their purposes, also underwent changes that conformed to the evolving cultural changes.

Accordingly, Semiramis in Babylon evolved from mother/wife queen, to divine mother, to Rhea—the mother goddess who derived her glory, power, and deity from her son. From Rhea she evolved into Ashta, the undefiled, and then she evolved into Nin, the perpetual virgin. From Nin, she evolved into Juno, the virgin dove, the breath of God, and then by 350 BC, she had evolved into Alma, the virgin mother of God and the immaculate conceiver, the holy spirit of God.

Semiramis' son/husband, Nimrod (Nimrod was the illegitimate son of Semiramis, whose father was unknown; or if he was known his identity had been hidden) the martyred king of Babel, evolved from the son of the unseen father, to the son of miraculous birth. From the son of miracle birth, he evolved into Ninus, the son of the virgin mother. From Ninus, he evolved into Tammuz or Iaachus, the son who was sacrificed. Then he evolved into Kronos or Baal (Bal or Bel), the son who became and is, god. From Kronos, he evolved into Phoroneus, the mighty deliverer. Then he became Zero or Zeroastes, the only seed of woman who can emancipate. Next he became Ben-Almet-Ishaa, the redeeming son of the virgin of salvation, and finally, by 280 BC, he had evolved into El-Bar, the son of god, the crusher of the serpent, of the seed of the virgin mother.

This same kind of human-to-deity evolution took place in Greece, Rome, the cultures of Asia Minor, China, India, Mexico, early Europe, South America, North America, Egypt, Africa, the Mesopotamian cultures, Canaan, Australia, Indo-China, and Japan. For this reason, amazing similarities in personality, character, physical appearance and attributes, and duties and responsibilities can be found in virtually all gods and goddesses, regardless of people groups, race, culture, social system, nation, kingdom, or time in history.

It became obvious to me that by the time of Jesus, the Babylonia-originated doctrine of divine mother and incarnate son was so deeply entrenched into the various paganistic religious systems and rituals that the thought of such a doctrine penetrating Orthodox Judaism was a blasphemous sacrilege to the Jews. Such a doctrine should not be tolerated by anybody, for any reason, at anytime.

With the help of the research that I did in the Islamic history sector of the museum, I discovered the information that I needed to consummate the final pieces of the picture puzzle of the Luciferian assault design. It was the information that I collected in this sector that showed me how the divine mother and incarnate son deception was still very much alive and was working it's influence in today's modern world.

Much of the sector dealt exclusively with the rise and history of Islam, but it also included a wealth of information relative to Islam's relationship to the Jews, the Pope, and Christianity in general. It showed how those relationships had fluctuated from mutual respect and admiration to extreme abhorrence.

One of the most surprising discoveries that I made was the honor and praise that the Muslims had given 1st century Orthodox Judaism and the 1st and 2nd century Christians, for their efforts in neutralizing the deceptive and blasphemous doctrine of the divine mother of God. The early Muslims acknowledged with pride that as a result of the dogged immovability of Orthodox Judaism of the 1st century against the doctrine of divine mother and incarnate child, coupled with the 1st and 2nd century early church evangelist's spread of the Gospel, the 4,600-year-old Babylonian doctrine of divine mother and incarnate child had been stopped. The doctrine had to retreat to the ever increasing tide of the Gospel of Christ. So successful was the offensive movement of the Gospel in the Roman Empire, that by the 4th century AD, the very foundation of the once dominate Babylonian paganism lay crushed, never to rise again in it's original form. Although it still maintained a

The Search

stronghold in other parts of the world including China, India, and parts of Africa, in the Roman Empire, the doctrine's influence had become non-existent.

So powerful and so rapidly had the Gospel tidal wave spread throughout the Roman world that the Luciferian-doctrine war machine had been caught off-guard. It had to re-organize. It took three centuries for the Luciferian hierarchy to re-organize and implement a new design of the old Babylon plan and purpose—one that would be just as effective as the original design. The new design would again center on the adoration and the exaltation of the virgin mother. This time not only would she be exalted to a level that was equal to the son, she would be exalted *above* the level of the son.

According to most, if not all, of the early 1st and 2nd century Christian writings, it seems that Mary was given little, if any, consideration in doctrine or ritual observance. She was honored as the mother of Jesus, but beyond that, she was not regarded as anyone special. In fact, for the first three centuries after Jesus' birth, the church took little interest in Mary's life, whether she had more children besides Jesus, what might have happened to her after Jesus' death and resurrection, or her perpetual virginity.

As a matter of fact, according to the information that I collected there in the Islamic history section of the museum, Mary did not become a "perpetual virgin" until John Chrysostom proposed the idea in AD 399. He said that Mary must be, "called a virgin *ante partum, in partu, post partum,"*—hence, *perpetual virgin*.

Not unexpectedly, it was also during the 4th century that Constantine I, Constantine the Great, prepared the way for Christianity to become the official state religion, thus insuring that Mary would indeed climb that pedestal to deity. As it turned out, after obtaining official recognition from Emperor Constantine I, Christianity absorbed as equals the whole mass of pagans who had never been converted. So, as not to provoke the new pagan "Christians," the state recognized, approved, and brought into this new official state religion (Christianity) the foundational and fundamental doctrines of the traditional pagan religions, along with much of their worship rituals.

One doctrine that was demanded by the new "Christians" was the doctrine of the mother-goddess. They insisted that it be continued by whatever means necessary to maintain it.

In the Roman world at that time, the goddess cult that was given the most devotion was that of the Great Mother of Phrygia, followed by the cult of Isis, and then the cult of the Phoenician goddess, Astarte. When Christianity became officially recognized by the state, instead of rejecting and resisting the mother-goddess cult worship, Christianity absorbed it. As a result, Mary was elevated to the level of the goddesses. Many statues of Isis and the Mother of Phrygia were transformed into statues representing Mary and many of the epithets that were formerly assigned to Isis and Astarte, such as Redemptress, Savior, and Virgin Mother, became epithets of Mary.

Among the goddess characteristics that were adopted in the progression of Mary's exaltation was the attribute of *perpetual virginity* was the one that seemed to be the most obvious pagan trait, and the greatest insult to God's plan for man's redemption.

The idea of Mary's perpetual virginity as introduced by John Chrysostom in AD 399, became an official observance of the church in AD 575 by proclamation of Pope Benedict I. In AD 583, Pope Pelagius II again proclaimed the "fact" of Mary's perpetual virginity and issued a Papal Bull declaring the obligation to defend the "doctrine" by force of arms if needed. By AD 599, "defending the doctrine by force of arms," as advocated by Pelagius, had evolved into an offensive tool to justify Gregory I's demand to "bring all infidels under the protection of The Virgin, even if an infidel had to forfeit his life in order to ensure his salvation." Then in AD 649, at the Latern Council, the proclamation of Pope Benedict I became an official dogma of the church. In AD 675, the Tolentino Council confirmed the dogma as an official foundational and fundamental doctrine of the church.

As Mary "evolved" into *the perpetual virgin*, The Virgin Mother, Joseph, the husband of Mary and earthly father of Jesus, became an impotent old man. Jesus' brothers and sisters became either his cousins or his step-brothers and step-sisters from a former marriage of Joseph's.

Another pagan trait that made its way from pagan idiosyncratism, to "Christian" dogma, to church doctrine, was the *Mother of God* notion. It was a doctrine that, in my opinion based upon the historical information that I found in the Islamic sector of the museum, was *the one thing* that actually caused the creation of, the belief in, and the rapid spread of *Islam*—absolute submission or resignation to the will of Allah.

The stages through which Mary evolved to become the *Mother of God* began at the first Council of Nicaea in AD 325. It was at the Council that a foundational doctrine was established that said that since Jesus was the Son of God, then Jesus must in fact be and actually was/is, God. The Council participants argued that because of Jesus' position as Son of God, then he in fact is part of the Holy Trinity and was actually, God on earth. Hence, through Council proclamation, Jesus became God.

The Council's true motive may very well have been to bring honor, praise, and exaltation to Jesus, yet an unforeseen problem soon developed with respect to Mary. Could the mother of Jesus (*christotokos*), who was God the Son, a member of the Holy Trinity, be the mother of God (*theos-theotokos*)? If Jesus was in fact God, then how could God (*theos-theotokos*) owe His origin to a woman, unless that woman was divine as well?

The argument seemingly was settled by proclamation at the Council of Ephesus in AD 431, when Mary was proclaimed to be *Deipara* or "The Divine Virgin, The Mother of God." From that time on, Mary, Mother of God, began to occupy the divine pedestal that before the Council of Ephesus had been reserved only for God the Father, God the Son, and God the Holy Spirit.

The proclamation at the Council of Ephesus was rapidly adopted as doctrine throughout the world of Christianity. Hence, while in the eastern Roman Empire the faithful created the Feasts of: Mary's Annunciation, Mary's Purification, The Sleep of the Mother of God, and The Nativity; in the western Roman Empire they built churches in Mary's name and to her honor and dedicated them to her.

Concurrently, new and/or expanded attributes were ascribed to Mary. Those that just 100 years before had belonged exclusively to the pagan goddesses Isis,

Ceres, Minerva, the Great Mother of Phrygia, Astarte, and Venus (which the specific attributes of redemption, regeneration and mediation), were r to Mary (thus was conceived the dogma that through Eve was wrought fall, and through Mary mankind's redemption and salvation was assured). Temples that once belonged to and/or were dedicated to the goddesses were rededicated to the adoration, exaltation, and worship of Mary.

Over the next century the "Mother of God" doctrine was steadily propagated but it was not until the papacy of Gregory I (The Great), who was Pope from AD 590 to AD 604, that the doctrine began to be pushed dogmatically and militantly upon the "...peoples whose faith in The Virgin is lacking in guidance or absent in practice."

Gregory made many proclamations that in effect neutralized the first four centuries of solid doctrinal foundation that had been laid by the early Christian evangelists. By far the most devastating was when upon securing his position Gregory declared that "Every man, every woman, and every child will, under penalty of death, give The Blessed Virgin her rightful place in their lives." He enforced this proclamation by force of arms.

In the West, the populous more or less acclaimed Gregory's edict, and adopted the Mary, Mother of God doctrine, as canon. But in the East, especially in the Arabian Peninsula, an uneasy undercurrent that soon developed into a religious upheaval so intense that a violent rebellion against Gregory's "forced blasphemy" resulted in the creation a new religious philosophy met Gregory's writ. The religious philosophy spread so rapidly that for more than 1,000 years it threatened the very existence of Christianity itself: the religion of Islam.

Upon realizing what I had discovered, I just sat in amazement. According to this information, the creation of the Islamic religion had been totally preventable. Had the 3rd and 4th century Christians merely followed the simple instructions of Jesus and the example laid down by their predecessors of individual, faith-based, personal conversion, rather than trying to convert the whole world by edict and proclamation, chances are the Islamic religion would have never been born.

Through the untiring efforts of the early Christian evangelists of the first three centuries a strict monotheism, based on the Judaist doctrine of a one and only true God, had been established. It supplemented the ancient axiomatic eruditions of pagan religious worship, all the way from the Mediterranean Sea to the Indus River and from the Black Sea to the Arabian Peninsula. In Arabia by the mid-fifth century the worship of multiple gods and goddesses that had been so prevalent for two millennia had begun rapidly to give way to the worship of a one all-supreme God. (The names of the goddesses were Al-Lat, Al Uzzah, and Al-Manat. They represented respectively the Sun, the Virgin mother of Allah, the goddess of life, death, and redemption; Venus, the goddess of love and fertility; and Fortune, the goddess of destiny and knowledge.) The Arabic tribes called their one all-supreme God, *Allah*.

The god that was originally known as Allah was the ancient supreme god of the Semitic people, the descendants of the Arabic people. The Arabic tribes adopted the name *Allah* for the name of their one and only God Supreme.

So effective were the efforts of the early Christian evangelists, that by AD 550, the Arabic world, led by a group of monotheist converts known as *banifs*, had not only embraced the Jewish based Christian doctrine of monotheism, but had adopted the fundamental truths of the Christian doctrine as proclaimed by the early Christian evangelists. The truths adopted by the Arabic tribes and taught by the banifs were: (1) there is only one true God. (2) The one true God chose the descendants of Abraham to be the recipients of His principles, His plan, and His purpose. (3) A segment of Abraham's descendants, the Hebrews or Jews, rejected God's love, principles, and standards. (4) This segment, the Hebrews or Jews, were in turn sent a divine messenger in the form of a man, born of a virgin: the prophet Jesus, the son from God. (5) This messenger, the prophet Jesus, the son from God, lived a life of perfection on earth and gave his life as a sacrifice for the Hebrews. (6) The Hebrews rejected that perfect sacrifice of God. (7) In turn, God raised Jesus from the dead and established him as the perfect sacrifice for all of mankind. (8) God then exalted him to the position of "My precious sacrifice—My Son." His position as Son is everlasting and eternal.

"I want to point out real quick," I interjected before I continued with my notes on the creation of Islam, "that the last statement, point number eight, was included in the very earliest versions of *The Imrans*, the traditional third sura of *The Koran*, but began to be omitted from *The Imrans* in versions of *The Koran* by the late 7th century."

I then continued with my notes.

By the time of the papacy of Gregory I, "The Great," Arabia was on its way to becoming an eastern stronghold of Christianity. Then came Gregory's declaration of blasphemy, as it was called by Caliph al-Ma'mun, some years later.

Because the Arabic tribes were new arrivals to monotheism, Gregory viewed them as "infidels at heart." They were not worthy of occupying the same level of esteem as inceptive Christians or Jewish converts to Christianity. Hence, the Arab tribes were grouped together with all other "infidels and barbarians," becoming one of the primary focal points for the forced observance of Gregory's directive.

At first, the banifs, who were the unofficial religious leaders of Arab tribes, did not realize that the Arabs were included in Gregory's infidel distinction. It was not until Gregory issued his *Verdict of Separation* in AD 600, wherein he named the Arabic tribes in his list of infidels and barbarians, that they fully realized that the Arabs had been classified as infidels and that it was demanded of them that they worship Mary, the "Mother of God," under penalty of death.

During the past 100 years, the banifs had successfully guided the Arabic tribes through the troubled waters of paganism, and the worship of multiple gods and goddesses, into the refreshing calm of the Jewish based, Christian inspired doctrine of monotheism, and the worship of the one and only true God.

Now, Gregory I, the recognized earthly master and leader of the Christians, had seemingly regressed back into paganism and demanded that all people everywhere worship a goddess known as Mary, the earthly mother of the perfect sacrifice and God's son, Jesus. Mary, Gregory claimed, was the Mother of God, and she must be worshipped under penalty of death. The entire scenario reeked of the old Arabic pagan worship of Al- Lat, the virgin mother of Allah, the goddess of the sun, the worship that they had abandoned, in favor of the worship of the Christian God and the acceptance and practice of fundamental Christian truths.

The banifs sought to keep Gregory's edict from the Arabic people but they did not succeed. By the year AD 601 too much information had already leaked out to enable them to maintain their silence. When the banifs finally did make public Gregory's proclamation, a general upheaval erupted sending shock waves from one end of Arabia to the other.

The unrest convinced the banifs that they either had to take a stand, or face the possibility of open rebellion by the people against them and their teachings. So convinced were the banifs of the truth of monotheism and of the beliefs that they had been teaching, they chose to stand on the side of strict monotheism, against the implications of Gregory's decree.

The rallying cry of the Arabs became, *"How could Allah, the One God, God Supreme, be born of a woman?"*

In AD 602, when word got back to Gregory that the Arabic tribes had taken a stand against him, he became furious. He responded by issuing an avalanche of edicts and decrees directed specifically at the Arabic people and their banif religious leaders.

Gregory claimed that he spoke for God Himself. He claimed and proclaimed fanatically, that he was God's (whenever Gregory addressed the Arabs, he would use the name *Allah* for God) one and only voice of communication to man. He claimed that *every* word that he spoke was in reality God (Allah) Himself speaking and that *every* word had to be followed and obeyed without question, under penalty of death. In addition, he claimed that not only were his spoken words the actual words of God (Allah), but also his written words were the same as God (Allah) writing them Himself, and that whatever he declared or decreed was divine law, just as though God Himself had verbally decreed it to mankind.

Over a short span of just three months in AD 602, Gregory "The Great" set the stage for the creation of Islam, by issuing a rash of decrees bent on bringing under submission the rebellious sentiments of the Arabs. Among the dozens of papal proclamations that were decreed, there were 14 that were most responsible for alienating the Arabic people. These 14 were: (1) Mary, the mother of Jesus, was, is, and always will be, a virgin: perpetual virginity. (2) Mary was sinless throughout her life, and she too was born of a virgin. (3) Mary ascended into heaven bodily, upon death. (4) Through Mary, The Blessed Virgin, man has the assurance of redemption and salvation. (5) Mary, "The Heavenly Dove," "The Queen of Heaven," is man's mediator before God, man's comforter, and man's intercessor. (6) Mary was, is, and always will be the Mother of God. (7) Through Mary, man can have all sins forgiven. (8) Jesus was born of the sinless, virgin Mary. (9) Jesus was born divine, knowing from the time of his birth, his mission and purpose. (10) Jesus is, was, always has been, and always will be, God. (11) Jesus, as God, was not subject to the same desires, limitations, convictions, shortcomings, or temptations that mankind has to face. (12) Mary is equal to God the Father in veneration and must receive adoration worthy of her position *before* adoration of God the Son can be offered. (13) Mary stands as an equal to God the Father, God the Son, and God the Holy Ghost, but must be worshipped and exalted *before* worship to the Trinity can be offered, so that the Trinity, undefiled, can receive worship. In essence, Mary is the one who purifies man's attempted worship and transforms it into the pure worship that can be accepted by the Trinity. (14) Since man is basically a vile creature, he is not worthy to come to God on his own behalf or worship Him without mediation. Hence, worship must be directed to Mary who in turn will transfer the worship to God. Sins must be confessed to Mary who will in turn mediate to God on behalf of the sinner.

The more arrogant and insistent that Gregory became in trying to force submission by the Arabs, the more defiant the Arabs became in their monotheistic stand. To them, Gregory's decrees were steadily becoming less Christian and increasingly becoming more pro-Mary.

Gregory ensured strict adherence to his decrees by sending armies far and wide to enforce obedience. Throughout the ostensible pagan world, by way of Gregory's force of arms, nations, peoples, cultures, and societies reluctantly submitted to the "will of God," so-called by Gregory, and adopted Gregory's decrees as law and religious doctrine—but not in Arabia. In Arabia, Gregory's ruthlessness had the opposite effect. As each new anti-God/pro-Mary, proclamation was decreed; the banif inspired Arabs became increasingly more anti-Mary and anti-Pope.

Originally the Arabs were not anti-Christian. On the contrary, they had adopted as their own, fundamental Christian truths and doctrines, including the acceptance of Jesus as God's son who was sacrificed. In fact, historical evidence shows that the Arabs at this time, considered true Christianity, the Christianity of the first three centuries; the no pope, pre-Constantine Christianity, to be the true religious doctrine, in every aspect, for all of mankind.

As Gregory became more belligerent, the banif-led Arabs became more anti-Pope. Since the Pope claimed to be *the* spokesman for all of Christianity, the Arabic tribes began to develop an anti-Christian sentiment. They did not despise, hate, or resent Christians or Christianity; they despised, hated, and resented the Pope and his blasphemous Mother of God doctrine.

In the year AD 604, the year of Gregory's death, the banifs countered Gregory's assault by issuing their own standards of worship, doctrine, and tenants of faith, and began to preach these new tenants throughout Arabia.

This should have opened the eyes of the so-called Church and its leadership, but it did not. Throughout the next six succeeding popes: Sabinianus (604-606), Boniface III (607), Boniface IV (608-615), Deusdedit (615-618), Boniface V (619-625), and Honorius I (625-638), Gregory's militant and uncompromising edicts were ruthlessly enforced, to the shame and disgrace of Christianity.

The banifs addressed a number of areas in their principles, but there were five major points that they adopted as fundamental doctrine. (1) They rejected that the one true God Supreme, Allah, had a mother. In conjunction with this first point, they added that if Mary, the earthly mother of Jesus, was proclaimed by the Pope to be the Mother of God, then Jesus would have to be rejected as both Son of God, and God as part of a Trinity. In fact, if the Pope said that the Trinity was the true Godhead, then the entire concept of a Trinity would have to be rejected as false. Because they rejected *anything and everything* that the Pope proclaimed or decreed, when the Pope said that Jesus was God and that Mary was the Mother of God, they automatically rejected it as false. In other words, if the Pope said that it was true, then the banifs demanded that the direct opposite must be true, because the Pope cannot speak truth. (2) The Pope had decreed that the Virgin Mary *must* be accepted as the Mother of God and that she must be worshipped as such, or else Jesus *could not be accepted* as the Son of God. True to course, because the Pope had demanded worship of Mary or else Jesus could not be accepted as the Son of God, the banifs had no other alternative but to reject Jesus as the Son of God, because they could not and would not submit to the worship of Mary. (3) They rejected the perpetual virginity of Mary. They did accept the fact that Mary conceived Jesus when she was still a virgin, but after his birth, she did not maintain her virginity. (4) They rejected as false doctrine, *anything and everything* that the Pope said, decreed, or wrote, especially if the Pope claimed that what he said or wrote was the actual words of God. (5) They chose to develop religious guidelines along the old Jewish example of laws, rules, and observances rather than the Christian example of faith and liturgy.

By AD 608, the Arab people, having been vigorously evangelized and instructed by their spiritual leaders, the banifs, since AD 604, had ubiquitously adopted a brand new religious philosophy. It had as its principal elements, both Jewish and Christian doctrine, yet it was unique in that it rejected all of the supplemental elements of Judaism and Christianity. These were the elements that had been added by decree over the past seven centuries to the foundational beliefs of both religions.

In the midst of this massive religious upheaval, on the night of the 27th of Ramadan (the ninth month of the Muslim calendar), in the year AD 610, a man in his early 40's, who became known by the name of Mohammed, was said to have been visited by an angel while he lay sleeping in a cave on Mount Ira about three miles from the crossroads city of Mecca. It was a night that was to alter his life, and through him, divert the course of history.

Mohammed was the posthumous son of Abdullah bin Abdul-Muttalib, of the tribe of Quarries. He was born in the city of Mecca in about the year AD 570. His mother, Amish, died when he was still a young child, so he was brought up first by his grandfather, then by his uncle, Abu Tallinn. As a youth, he accompanied his uncle as they traveled the trading caravan routes from Mecca to Syria. On one such trip to Syria, at the age of 12, tradition says, Mohammed met a Christian hermit who prophesied that he would be a great prophet and that his influence would be felt worldwide.

At the age of 25, Mohammed married Khadija, the daughter of Khuwailid, a rich widow 15 years his senior. Their marriage produced four daughters.

From the time of Mohammed's youth, he had been greatly influenced by Christian hermits who were living in the deserts of Syria, as well as by the banifs who's teachings were founded in the principles preached by the Christian evangelists of first three centuries. He had been influenced so much that by the time Gregory made his Mary, Mother of God decree, Mohammed's beliefs were closer to true, undefiled Christian standards than most of those who openly proclaimed to be Christian. Had the decree never been made, chances are Mohammed would have become a Christian believer. But, Gregory changed all of that.

In AD 604, when the banifs began preaching their newly ameliorated religious philosophy, Mohammed willingly picked-up the banifs' mantel of reform. Over the next six years, the banifs had such an influential impact upon Mohammed that he began to isolate himself from the routine of typical daily life. He found himself more and more, being led into a life of sequester and solitary prayer and meditation. For hours he would contemplate and reflect upon the teachings of the banifs and search the Jewish scriptures and the Christian writings, looking for real truth, man's true purpose, and man's destiny, and how that destiny related to Allah, God Supreme Almighty.

By AD 610, Mohammed was a semi-hermit (in practice only-not in fact), isolating himself for days at a time in the mountains near Mecca, praying, studying, and meditating. It was while he was in the midst of one of these times of isolation in the mountains, that, according to Muslim tradition, the world's destiny was changed.

As the story goes, in the month of Ramadan, on the night of the 27th Mohammed fell asleep while meditating. While he was sleeping, the angel Gabriel appeared to him in a dream (some versions say that the angel Gabriel appeared to him in a vision while he was meditating) and commanded, *"Mohammed, recite!"*

He replied, "What shall I recite?"

The order was repeated three times, and then the angel said,

> *"Recite! In the name of thy Lord who created,*
> *Created man from a clot.*
> *Recite! And thy Lord is Most Bounteous,*
> *Who teacheth by the pen,*
> *Teacheth man that which he knew not."*

Thus, were revealed the first fragments of the *Koran* or *Qur'an*. The word in Arabic means, *The Recital*, held by those of the Islamic faith to be God's [Allah's] eternal and infallible word.

When he awoke, the words it is said seemed to be "inscribed upon his heart."

After that experience, Mohammed firmly believed that he was a messenger of God, sent forth to confirm previous scriptures that had been given by God to the Jews and the Christians, through His chosen prophets. *The Koran* says that the Jews disobeyed God by rejecting God's love and plan and sacrifice, thus they corrupted the scriptures, and the Christians had disobeyed God by corrupting the true worship of God by allowing other personalities [Mary] to be worshipped before Him, and that they had divided themselves into schismatic sects. Having thus gone astray, Mohammed felt that God had appointed him to bring them [the Jews, Christians, and the descendants of Abraham] back to the right path, to the true religion preached by Abraham, Moses, and Jesus. Thus, was Islam created.

Over the next 22 years, Mohammed's Koranic revelations followed each other at brief intervals. At first Mohammed memorized the words himself. Then they were committed to memory by professional remembrances. Just before his death, the revelations were set down by a scribe, and after his death, during the caliphate of Omar, the second Caliph, the revelations were collected and arranged into suras, or chapters. Under the caliphate of Othman, Omar's successor, the revelations were bound in book form.

Throughout the 22-year period (Mohammed died on June 8, AD 632), Mohammed spread his revelations and doctrine (on occasion, by force of arms) to his ancestral people, to Christians who were willing to listen and stand against the Pope, and to the Jews.

After the death of Mohammed, Islam soon followed the same path as all other religious ideologies. What began as a simple, straightforward philosophy, fragmented into schismatic alliances and the followers of Islam rallied around the different philosophical religious viewpoints of the different caliphs who succeeded Mohammed. Even today the fragmentation of Islam is evident in the various sects of Islam, such as the Sunnites and the Shi'ites, scattered around the world.

It quickly became very obvious to me that the Pope and his forced doctrine of the exaltation of Mary as Mother of God, was not only responsible for the founding and the rapid spread of the Muslim religion, but I feel like the blame for the death of multiplied millions of Muslims, Jews, and Christians alike, in the so-called *Holy Wars*, lies squarely on the shoulders of Gregory I, "The Great," and his successors over the next 1,000 years who maintained his non-compromising standards. Gregory wanted so much to instill the worship of Mary into Christian doctrine, that he was totally blinded to the fact that there was well-grounded opposition to his position. That opposition could not only alienate nations, or groups of people from the Christian faith, but it had the potential of causing a full-scale rebellion against him in particular, and against Christianity in general; because he was blinded, he pressed forward unrelentingly.

Islam and Christianity are so similar. The main difference *IS* the position of Jesus. Christians accept Jesus as Son of God, Redeemer. Muslims accept Jesus as God's prophet, and God's perfect sacrifice, hence 'a son of God, redeemer.' Yet the followers of both religions have been manipulated and told that they are *very* different. These manufactured differences have led to politically motivated 'Holy Wars' of forced conversion and expansion on both sides, which ultimately cost the lives of millions. In just over 100 years after Mohammed's death, the Caliphs, or successors of Mohammed, had extended the Islamic faith from India to the Atlantic coasts of Africa and Spain.

By using the Mother of God dogma as it's keystone doctrine, the post-4th century church leadership literally re-wrote the Holy Scriptures to incorporate Mary's newly attained virtues, attributing inspiration for such additions to the Holy Spirit.

The assumption of Mary to divinity led to the necessity of excluding any sin in her, including original sin. True to form, in 1476, Sixtus IV, in his *Cum Praecelsa*, proposed that the doctrine of Mary being sinless, be added as an article of faith. Then in 1546, at the Council of Trent, an official proclamation was issued that proclaimed that Mary was immune from all sin, even venial sin. Thus, the doctrine of the *Immaculate Conception* was birthed. Finally in 1854, Mary's long journey from humble maiden to sinless virgin consummated when Pius IX made Mary's sinlessness an official article of the church.

After Pius' proclamation, the next logical step intended to confirm Mary's deification, ascension into heaven bodily at the time of her death, as did Jesus, her son, [hence, like Jesus, her tomb is also empty or at least in her case it *became* empty] was only a matter of time. In due course, in 1950, Pius XII declared as an article of faith, the doctrine that Mary at death was assumed into heaven bodily. This was followed in 1954 with the announcement of the endowing of the Feast of Mary the Queen, which celebrates her inferred deity.

The Mother Queen was now a goddess, and as such, she had to be given the ability to mediate and to forgive sin. So, in 1958, at the Mariological Congress of Lourdes, Mary was granted the ability to mediate and to forgive sin. This was re-confirmed in 1964 by Paul VI. Hence, Mary the virgin mother-goddess had in just over 1500 years, evolved from simple mother of Jesus into mankind's primary mediator and redeemer.

Hence now, at the dawning of the 21st century, it looks as though the Luciferian hierarchy's chosen path of neutralization of the truth by infiltration and deception has worked to perfection. In fact, both Luciferian fronts have worked with such distention, that doubt and confusion regarding Jesus, his birth, his life, and his ministry is, in today's world, the norm more than the exception.

XII

INVASION FROM THE EAST

The next Gospel recorded event in the life of Jesus took place about two years after Joseph had taken his wife and infant son back to Nazareth in the Galilee. During the two years since Jesus' birth, during which time Joseph and the family lived in Nazareth, Joseph had gained quite a reputation—thanks to Herod's two-year long continuous massive building venture—as one of the Galilee's greatest master stonemasons and Joseph's heavy construction business enterprise had began to blossom. Also during this two-year period Mary likely had at least one other child, probably James.

It was during this unprecedented time of prosperity and immense building endeavors throughout the kingdom of Herod the Great that magi arrived from the East, uninvited, in Jerusalem, demanding to see the newly born King of the Jews. This was the beginning of the end of the kingdom's two-year prosperity run.

Every year Christmas nativity scenes throughout the Christian world would be incomplete without a representation of the three wisemen, bearing gifts in hand, bowing before the manger and worshipping the newborn King. However, quite a number of years ago while visiting a beautiful church library in Augsburg, Germany, the library of the twin Catholic/Protestant church of St. Ulrich and St. Afra, I discovered a document containing some very convincing information that to me proved that the wisemen did not arrive in Herod's kingdom seeking the new born king until some two years after the birth of Jesus.

The document was bound, but it was not a book in the true sense of the word. It was a journal of personal notes that had been written by the Swiss theologian Karl Barth, sometime after 1932. Barth had never published any of the material nor had anyone else. Apparently the notes had much to say about a variety of subjects, the least of which was a warning to all German-speaking people of Europe regarding Hitler's rapid rise to power. Barth, fearing that the notes would fall into the hands of the Nazis, gave them to his brother, who at that time lived in Innsbruck, Austria. When it was apparent that Hitler was going to take control of Austria, the bound volume of notes was secretly taken to the church of St. Ulrich and St. Afra and hidden in a vault in the church. After the war, Barth, who had other projects that were occupying his time, donated the volume to the church library.

As I scanned the hand written notes of Barth, I was amazed at his depth of understanding and reasoning relative to true Christianity and the true Great Commission. Although he had a lot to say about the "mad-man Hitler and his party of demons," he did not dwell on them, instead he focused much of his attention on various theological and Christian reasoning disputes and analysis, the history of Christian thought and doctrine, and the basis and justification for current Christian thought, tradition, and dogma.

Addressing the justification of Christian dogma and tradition theme, Barth wrote page after page of notes about his discoveries apropos to the part that wisemen played in the story of Jesus' nativity.

He began his discussion of the wisemen by saying that there was relative peace throughout Herod's kingdom during the two years immediately following the birth of Jesus, but by 5 BC, that had changed. He then quoted Matthew 2, beginning with verse one.

> *"Now when Jesus was born in Bethlehem of Judea in the days of Herod the king, behold there came wise men from the east to Jerusalem, saying, where is he that is born King of the Jews? For we have seen his star in the East, and are come to worship him. When Herod the king had heard these things, he was troubled, and all Jerusalem with him. And when he had gathered all the chief priests and scribes of the people together, he demanded of them where Christ should be born. And they said unto him, in Bethlehem of Judea: for thus it is written by the prophet, and thou Bethlehem, in the land of Juda, art not the least among the princes of Juda: for out of thee shall come a governor, that shall rule my people Israel. Then Herod, when he had privily called the wise men, enquired of them diligently what time the star appeared. And he sent them to Bethlehem, and said, go and search diligently for the young child; and when ye have found him, bring me word again, that I may come and worship him also. When they had heard the king, they departed; and lo, the star, which they saw in the east, went before them, till it came and stood over where the young child was. When they saw the star, they rejoiced with exceeding great joy.*
>
> *And when they were come into the house, they saw the young child with Mary his mother, and fell down, and worshipped him: and when they had opened their treasures, they presented unto him gifts; gold, and frankincense, and myrrh. And being warned of God in a dream that they should not return to Herod, they departed into their own country another way. And when they were departed, behold, the angel of the Lord appeareth to Joseph in a dream, saying, arise, and take the young child and his mother, and flee into Egypt; and be thou there until I bring thee word: for Herod will seek the young child to destroy him.*
>
> *When he arose, he took the young child and his mother by night, and departed into Egypt: and was there until the death of Herod: that it might be fulfilled which was spoken of the Lord by the prophet, saying, out of Egypt have I called my son.*
>
> *Then Herod, when he saw that he was mocked of the wise men, was exceeding wroth, and sent forth, and slew all the children that were in Bethlehem, and in all the coasts thereof, from two years old and under, according to the time which he had diligently enquired of the wise men. Then was fulfilled that which was spoken by Jeremy the prophet, saying, in Rama was there a voice heard, lamentation, and weeping, and great mourning, Rachel weeping for her children, and would not be comforted, because they are not. But when Herod was dead, behold, an angel of the*

Lord appeareth in a dream to Joseph in Egypt, saying, arise, and take the young child and his mother, and go into the land of Israel: for they are dead which sought the young child's life.

And he arose, and took the young child and his mother, and came into the land of Israel. But when he heard that Archelaus did reign in Judea in the room of his father Herod, he was afraid to go thither: notwithstanding, being warned of God in a dream, he turned aside into the parts of Galilee: and he came and dwelt in a city called Nazareth: that it might be fulfilled which was spoken by the prophets, he shall be called a Nazarene" (Matthew 2:1-23).

After quoting the Scripture reference, he continued.

About two years after the birth of Jesus, wisemen or magi, suddenly appeared in Jerusalem, demanding to see the newly born king of the Jews.

Herod was in Jerusalem at this time. It is not known why he was in Jerusalem, because his capital and governmental seat was in Caesarea Maritima, although he did make it a point to come to Jerusalem during the Passover season (and occasionally during other celebrations), when there was trouble, or when he wanted to inspect his construction projects. Although it is not known under what circumstances he was in Jerusalem at this time, we can speculate that it may have been because of the Passover. So, if logic, protocol, and ethics were to rule, the wisemen probably traveled to Caesarea Maritima first, and then learning that Herod was in Jerusalem, they traveled to Jerusalem to meet with him.

"Yet," Barth stated, "The age-old questions have not yet, even to this day, been answered to everybody's satisfaction. 'Who were these wisemen, or magi; where did they come from; and why were they there in Jerusalem?'"

In addressing these questions, Barth first pointed out that the visitors to Jerusalem were not kings. That particular Christian tradition was based on a late 13th century misinterpretation of Psalms 72:10 & 15. Rather, they were magi. The word *wisemen* is a Greek form of the word, *magi*, from which we get the word "magician."

Magi, at the time of the birth of Jesus, were astronomers, interpreters, teachers, physicians, Zoroastrian priests, scientists of their day, astrologers, court historians, royal counselors, administrators, and governors. They were also used as official emissaries and ambassadors representing the respective king and ruler of their country or empire, to/in another country. In short, magi were sent by their particular ruler, in the ruler's stead, to a foreign country, with the full power of attorney to speak and/or act on behalf of that individual ruler or emperor. Not only did they represent their respective ruler in a foreign country, they *were the ruler*s of their individual and particular country, kingdom, or empire while they were in that foreign country.

At this time in history, magi were actively involved in the courts of the kings/rulers/emperors of the Indus and the Kushan empires in India; the Parthian empire; of the Han dynasty in China; in Persia; in Babylonia; and in Arabia. Because the Bible does not say how many individual magus left their specific country or kingdom in search of the young child, we can only assume that magi representing several, if not all, of these empires and countries, visited Herod in Jerusalem.

What brought them to Judea? By this time in history, and for five centuries before this time, Daniel, the captive Jew who rose to prominence in Nebuchadnezzar's Babylon, had become and was still the most respected of all Chaldean magi. His reputation was such that within 300 years after his death, he had been exalted to the position of deity. Because of the great respect and honor that all kingdoms and empires in the East had for Daniel, and because of their unfaltering faith and belief in his writings, to the point that his writings were considered divine, the disciples and priests of Zoroaster together with the Chaldean magi, interpreted Daniel's writings in such a way, that they were eminently expecting a savior and world leader to arise in the region of Roman Syria (Judea). They believed that this leader's dominion would be worldwide and his rulership would last forever.

Daniel wrote hundreds of scientific, social, philosophical, and prophetic documents while in the court of Babylon and Persia, but the document that conceivably excited these magi the most is the portion that is recorded as Daniel 7:13 & 14 in our Bible: *"I saw in the night visions (stars and constellations), and, behold, one like the Son of man came with the clouds of heaven, and came to the Ancient of Days, and they brought him near before Him. And there was given him dominion, and glory, and a kingdom, that all people, nations, and languages, should serve him: his dominion is an everlasting dominion, which shall not pass away, and his kingdom that which shall not be destroyed"* (Daniel 7:13-14).

In addition, Persian history claims Zoroaster was a student of Daniel, and that Daniel had revealed to him that when a formerly unrevealed star appeared in the constellation Coma, it would be a sign that the King of kings had been born in the region of Jerusalem. So, through their own method of interpretation, these magi had concluded that this particular prophetic writing of Daniel would be fulfilled during the declared *pax Romana* of the Roman Emperor Augustus.

The assertion by Daniel, coupled with an unprecedented pandemonium in the heavens so prophesied by Daniel to Zoroaster, and which had been witnessed by the magi, convinced them that indeed Daniel's prophetic *new world ruler* had been born.

As royal counselors and confidants of their respective rulers, the magi were in the position to convince their rulers that to insure the continued existence of their individual monarchies and to guarantee their (the empire's or kingdom's) friendship with the newly born and future all-powerful world ruler, they (the magi), representing their rulers, must give allegiance, obeisance, and reverent homage to this newly born ruler.

Barth said that he discovered through his own research that enough ancient documentation had survived that showed without a doubt that the magi did succeed in convincing these most powerful rulers of the East, to give their allegiance to this new-born world ruler (when the magi who represented their respective and individual empires and kingdoms gave their allegiance, it was the same as a king or emperor himself giving allegiance).

Barth then broke from his flow and wrote, "Before I get back to the documentation that I discovered confirming the main purpose of the magi first want to cover some of the documentation that deals with this pandemonium ... the heavens that so electrified these magi. It excited them so much that they traveled thousands of miles in search of the cause and purpose for such a tumult."

I'll first point out the corroboration that Barth discovered which seems to confirm such an event in the heavens, and then I'll cover his synopsis of the matter. I will quote this portion directly from his notes.

"According to the medieval astronomer, Johannes Kepler, a conjunction of Saturn and Jupiter in the constellation Pisces, took place in April of the year 7 BC.

"An acquaintance of mine, the German astronomer, Dr. P. Schnabel, while deciphering cuneiform texts in Babylon in 1925, confirmed the find by Kepler when he discovered that not only did the conjunction of Saturn and Jupiter in the constellation Pisces take place at that time, April 7 BC, but that on the same side of the sun an alignment of a total of six planets fanning out over a 15° arch, also took place in April of the year 7 BC.

"The Italian astronomer, Ricciotti, says that with this conjunction and alignment, three comets would also have been seen over Judea in the spring of 7 BC. Also, seven combined eclipses of the sun and moon would have been visible from Judea during the year 7 BC.

"Vespiani, the second century Roman astronomer, said that, 'Mercury, Venus, Mars, Jupiter, and Saturn aligned with the earth in the constellation of Pisces during the Passover of the Jews in the year that Jesus, whom his followers called the Christ, was born.'

"The 4th century Arabic astronomer, Agobid, wrote that, 'At the time of the birth of the prophet Jesus, over the city of Jerusalem could be seen for 30 consecutive days, brilliant comets streaking across the sky.'

"Pherialious, the Greek-Roman historian/astronomer of the 2nd century said, 'The tumult in the heavens with comets, alignments, eclipses, and conjunctions that accompanied the birth of the one whom the sect of Christians call Christ, surely must indicate that his was truly of miraculous birth; even the heavens testify of him.'"

Barth then made a personal comment, "If any of these reports are true, (and why shouldn't they be? For what motivation would these astronomers have in deceiving or falsifying their own research reports?) is it any wonder that the wisemen, magi/astronomers/astrologers, of the East set out to investigate and to search for the one whose birth was responsible for such a heavenly display, that had been, up till that time, unprecedented, and has remained up till this present time, unprecedented?"

He then returned to his discussion of the travels of the magi.

The Matthew account does not say how many magi came to Judea in search of the new ruler. Based on the types of gifts that were mentioned in the Matthew account, western Christian tradition maintains that there were three and eastern Christian tradition says that there were 12. Although there have been numerous western and eastern apocryphal writings that seem to corroborate their respective traditions, in reality few of these traditions can be confirmed by any reliable historical record.

However, there were some well-respected non-Christian non-Jewish historians who lived during the time of Jesus' birth and life (or immediately thereafter) who did accurately record the events related to the magi's visit to Jerusalem. Their writings can be considered authoritative, nonbiased, and non-prejudiced. These historians were Su-Ma- Chen, the Chinese/Persian historian, who actually accompanied the magi caravan and recorded as one who was an actual eye-witness; Barborus, the Parthian historian; Hue-Lo, the Greek/Chinese historian, who was living in Jerusalem when the magi arrived; Tacitus, the Roman historian; and Sueronius, the Latin historian.

Su-Ma-Chen wrote that he accompanied as the designated Persian court historian for a caravan of 100 ambassadors, along with servants, officers, and military escorts, sent by the kings of the Empire of Parthia, the nine kings of the Kushan Empires of the Indias, the Han Empire of China, the kingdom of the Babylonians and of the Arabs, and the kingdom of Persia to Roman Syria in search of the new King of the Jews born in Judea at the time of Augustus.

Barborus wrote that a great caravan of camels, ambassadors, and astronomers, sent by 13 kings of the East, during the days of Publius Quirinus, passed continually through the Ester Gate in Damascus from sun-up to mid-day, as they journeyed to Jerusalem to seek an allegiance with and to give homage to the newborn emperor, thought to be born in Judea of the Romans.

Hue-Lo wrote that there was only one time in history that the great empires of the East united under a single purpose: this was when the new king was born in Syria at the time of the tumult in the heavens, during the time of the *pax Romana* declared by the great Roman Lord Augustus, under whose governorship of Syria was of Quirinus.

Tacitus recorded that when Quirinus was governor of Syria and Herod was king of Judea, a caravan of more than 800 laden camels arrived from an eastern confederacy of 13 kingdoms, uninvited, in Jerusalem searching for a king whom they claimed was born in Judea, whose birth had been announced by the tumult of the stars. They reported that among the great and the wise of the East, there was a persuasion that in their great and ancient books of their priesthood and holy men, it was written that at this precise time, the East should become mighty, and that those issuing from Judea of Syria should rule the world. Herod, fearful that his dominion would become a battleground between Rome and this confederacy, received them with caution. In Rome's Senate, fear spread like a fire. The greatest kingdoms of the East had united and had invaded the kingdom of Rome. The Senate did not trust Herod. They feared that his uncontrollable brutality would instigate war between the two greatest powers on earth.

Sueronius, the Latin historian, said that 28 months after the affray in the heavens, testified to by our own (Roman) astrologers, during the days of Augustus, a caravan of a thousand camels, armed escorts, and emissaries, one unequaled by any known in all of Rome, seized upon the city of Caesarea Maritima and then upon the city of Jerusalem, to the great distress of Herod, whom the Senate gave the title of King, and of the city. Royal ambassadors from 13 eastern kingdoms had united and had traveled this long way to be allied to the world ruler whom they say had been born during the affray in the sky at the time of the extra tax census commanded by Augustus and executed by Publius Sulpicius Quirinus. Herod, feeling an obligation to protect the succession of Rome, and not knowing that in the East an ancient and constant opinion prevailed that it was destined there should issue at this time from Judea those who should obtain universal dominion, killed more than 40 infant males in the district of Judea, attempting to abolish the new emperor, one year before Herod's death.

Barth continued with his own observations. I will quote him directly.

"It seems obvious to me that as per these dependable and trustworthy historians, what happened is that the rulers of the great kingdoms of the East united in order to give their allegiance to the great world emperor, whom even the heavens declared was great and mighty. They had sent their ambassadors (court magi) to Roman Judea to search for a new emperor. It took them more than two years from the time they first witnessed the tumult in the heavens, until they arrived in Judea. Having invaded the Roman Empire, uninvited (considered an act of war), they felt it necessary to follow diplomatic protocol and to present themselves to the Roman officials who governed that area. Hence, they arrived in Caesarea Maritima, the governmental seat of Judea. Discovering that Herod was in Jerusalem, they journeyed to Jerusalem, and presented themselves to Herod. Both Herod and the *entire city of Jerusalem* were terrified. Here, representatives delineating the rulers of the greatest empires of the East, whose combined kingdom's land area, population, and military strength was many times greater than that of the Roman Empire, traveled for more than two years and more than 2,000 miles, to invade the Roman Empire with a caravan of at least 800, to as many as 1,000 camels; more than 100 ambassadors representing at least 13 different Eastern kingdoms and empires; a large military escort; all of their needed servants, physicians, technicians, and caretakers; state officials and ministers; and court historians and scribes; demanding that Herod take them to see the new world emperor, the King of the Jews. For the first and only time in history, 13 of the eastern world's greatest empires allied and united to fulfill one purpose. It's certainly not surprising to me that Herod was terrified and *all of Jerusalem with him.*"

"Needless to say," Barth continued, "Herod was in a volatile situation. If he did not play his cards right, his life would be considered worthless from four different directions:

1) If it was true that a new king had been born, who even the empires of the East knew as *King of the Jews*, why had not Herod reported it to Rome? Hence—*TREASON*.
2) The invasion by the eastern confederacy was without prior notice. It was a total surprise, and Herod was not ready. He would have to answer to Augustus for his lack of preparation, and for allowing this invasion. Hence—*TREASON*.
3) Herod's domain could be the battlefield for the greatest war ever to be conceived in the minds of men, up to that point; a war between the greatest confederation of the eastern powers ever to exist, against the

greatly feared Roman Empire. Why had not Herod notified Rome that such a battle was developing? Hence—*TREASON*.

4) If a new king was born in Judea, who would become the king of the Jews? Why had Herod allowed this newly born king to live, seeing that he would have to assert his authority over Rome's appointment in order to fulfill that position? What if an allegiance was solidified between this new king and the eastern confederacy, in the very heart of Roman Judea? It would, in essence, relinquish that entire area to the confederacy. Hence—*TREASON*."

Herod was trapped, he had to do something and he had to do it fast. To give himself some breathing room he inquired of the Jewish Sanhedrin if such an event was anticipated. The Sanhedrin confirmed that a world ruler was expected to be born and he was to be born in the town of Bethlehem in Judea.

Herod felt that he had to eliminate this threat to his throne and to Rome, preferably before the representatives of the eastern confederacy had an opportunity to form an allegiance with the new king. He sent the magi to Bethlehem and asked them to return to him immediately upon their discovery of the location of the babe, so that he could "*go and pay homage to him also.*"

Herod's true intent was most likely to have the babe somehow eliminated—either by death, exile, or kidnapping—preferably without the magi knowing about it. Obviously, if they were to find out that Herod had eliminated the king to whom they had just given their allegiance probable war would be immediate.

According to Matthew, the magi left Jerusalem, heading south to Bethlehem. However, as they traveled to Bethlehem, they (the magi) again saw one of the same heavenly signs that they had seen two years previously. They saw it in the sky north of them. They took this as a directive sign and immediately turned north to *follow the star.*

The phenomenon led them into the Greek dominated region north of Judea, called the Galilee, to the city of Nazareth.

Over the city of Nazareth, the "star" seemed to stand still, before disappearing entirely.

Probably leaving their huge caravan outside of the city, the magi found the house where Joseph, Mary and the two-year old toddler, Jesus, lived. Inside the house, the magi, representing their respective kingdoms, presented the toddler with gifts (ancient historians have identified these three particular gifts by the distinction of *The Gifts of Ramses*) that were intended to solidify a political allegiance between the new king and the eastern confederation. These same particular gifts were given to Ramses the Great, Xerxes, Alexander the Great, Hannibal, Tigleth-Pilser, Cyrus the Great, and Antripitus as an indication of solidification of alliances with powers that were considered their equal or greater, or with whom they feared. The gifts were gold (to acknowledge the recipient's royal position as king), frankincense (to acknowledge the recipient's position as the highest of all priestly orders of his kingdom's religious system), and myrrh (to acknowledge the recipient's deity or his god/man position—a position that all of the above mentioned recipients claimed for themselves).

The Gospel of Matthew says that after the presentation of the gifts, the magi were warned by God in a dream not to return to Herod in Jerusalem. So they and their immense caravan returned to their native countries, leaving directly from Nazareth.

After the departure of the magi's caravan, an angel appeared to Joseph in a dream and told him that Herod would seek to kill the child. The angel told Joseph to take his family and flee to Mary's ancestral home, Egypt. There they were to stay until it was safe to return.

Herod may not have intended to immediately harm the infant, at least not so brazenly that the magi would have known about it. But then the magi refused to return to Herod, and instead returned to their countries immediately by an alternate route (Herod as yet probably did not know that the magi had turned north to Nazareth), he became furious. He thought that they had gone to Bethlehem, so when he received word that the caravan had departed from the Galilee, he was extremely insulted that they had not followed the appropriate protocol and had not officially dismissed themselves from him at his court. They had instead returned to their respective kingdoms, leaving directly from the Galilee, without receiving Herod's official discharge. The magi had probably been gone for days or even weeks before Herod was told of their departure. It was doubtless out of fear that Herod was not told. It was widely known that on occasion, Herod, during fits of rage, would 'kill the messenger' bearing bad news. Hence, the best way to spare one's life was to avoid being the precursor of bad news. Herod felt as if he had been mocked, belittled, and treated with contemptuous disrespect by the ambassador/magi.

He also may have discovered that the magi had indeed made an alliance with the child-king, sealed by the immutable *Gifts of Ramses*, the most honored and universally recognized of all diplomatic endorsements of allegiance between accordant powers. If this was true, Herod realized that according to the eastern confederacy the alliance that they made with the child-king not only dissolved Herod's kingdom but also placed his realm under their jurisdiction.

Neither his kingdom nor the whole of the Roman Empire was a match to this confederacy, so he dared not take out his wrath upon the returning caravan. However, he could not and would not let their insult go unavenged.

Thinking the child-king was still in Bethlehem, (Herod probably felt that the magi had made the agreement with the child when he sent them to Bethlehem. He likely did not know that they had made the allegiance when they went to Nazareth. He also probably did not know whom the child was, that he lived in Nazareth, or who his parents were in Nazareth. He felt that the reason why the magi went home from the Galilee was so they would not have to return to him in Caesarea) Herod turned his wrath upon the male children, age two-years and below, in the area surrounding Bethlehem, including Jerusalem.

This slaughter was supposed to have taken place during the months of September and October of the year 5 BC.

Livy recorded that over a period of 50 days Herod killed one male child below the age of two every day in the region of Bethlehem and Jerusalem.

Sueronius wrote that Herod's slaughter of the infants was not restricted to Bethlehem and not restricted to Jewish babies. His crime reached beyond

Bethlehem to include Jerusalem, Hebron, Herodium, Juttah, Ramah, Bethany, and Emmaus; and involved the destruction of 11 Jewish infants, but many Greek, Syrian, Egyptian, Idumaen, and Arabian infants as well, and that even infants in and of the house and court of Herod were not immune to his butchery.

Ignatius of Antioch wrote that when Augustus learned of Herod's ruthless and senseless slaughter, it was said that he kicked over an image of Mercurius (Mercury) and cried in utter disgust in a loud voice, "It is better to be Herod's ass, than to be his son or subject."

One of the first resources that Barth had used years before he wrote the information down in his volume of notes, was a manuscript that he had studied while on an investigative visit to the Vatican library in 1922, shortly after Mussolini became premier of Italy. The scroll that Barth studied was one that had originally been found in the year 1660, in a forgotten underground vault of the Vatican I library. The scroll was entitled, *Herod Antipater's Defense*. It was a copy of a much more ancient manuscript that was entitled, *Herod Antipater's Defense Before the Roman Senate in Regard to His Conduct at Bethlehem*. The original manuscript was alleged to have been the actual records of Herod's defense before the Roman Senate and Augustus in regard to his action in slaughtering the innocents.

Barth recorded the words of Herod's defense:

> "...My guards told me that a large caravan of over 1,000 camels and an armed escort of one thousand infantrymen from an allied association of all of the eastern empires beyond the Euphrates had entered the city of Jerusalem and had caused the whole city to fear destruction at the hands of the eastern armies or by the armies of Rome defending the city.... Their kings' representatives appeared at my gate, at least twenty or more sent by their emperors. They were in search of a babe who they say had been born king of the Jews. I told them that I ruled the Jews under Caesar Augustus. They said that the babe would rule after me.... I sent them away and told them that I would send for them in three days after I investigate.... The excitement in the city had grown until it was intense and I sensed a rebellion of fear. I felt that if left to itself, nothing would be able to control it. I called the Hillel court, which read out of the Law and the prophecies of the Jews that a king was to be born of a virgin in Bethlehem. Out of the writings of Daniel, the respected Chaldean magician, whom they of the East call divine, they read that his kingdom would be worldwide and that it would last forever. They also said that the spectacle witnessed in the heavens signaled the birth of the new king.... Although this spectacle was nothing but a phenomenon of nature, and the thing a delusion, it did not better the condition I was in. A man will contend for a false faith stronger than he will for a true one, from the fact that the truth defends itself, but a falsehood must be defended by its adherents: first, to prove it to themselves, and secondly, that they may appear to be right in the estimation of their friends. But the fact is, this case is about as follows: The Roman taxation was cutting off the support of the priests, and they were hurtful under it. Again, the double taxing—that is, the tithes to the priests

and the tax to the Romans, although my own taxes had been excused for almost two years—was bearing heavily on the common people, so that they could not stand it, and the priests saw that one of them would have to go unpaid; and, as they saw the Romans were the stronger, they wrote these things in the Tosephta, and read it daily in all their synagogues and their temple, that the Jewish mind might be prepared for the event, knowing that they could magnify a mote into a mountain, when it came to anything outside of the common laws of nature, and knowing that if they could get the common people to believe in the things there would be no end to their fighting. And from all appearances the excitement was fast driving the people that way. It had already become a proverb with the children of Bethlehem and Jerusalem that the Jews had a new king, that neither Caesar nor Herod would reign any more, that they would have to pay no more taxes to keep up the Roman government. Such talk and sayings were among the poorer classes of society. So I saw an insurrection brewing fast, and nothing but a most bloody war as the consequence.... In my honest judgment it was best to pluck the undeveloped flower in its bud, lest it should grow and strengthen, and finally burst, and shed its deadly poison over the empire and impoverish and ruin it forever...I have no malice toward infants. I took no delight in listening to the cries of mothers.... No! I saw nothing but an insurrection and a bloody war were our doom, and in this the overthrow and downfall, to some extent, of our nation..."

The last few years of Herod's life were a nightmare for his subjects in Judea, and for his own family as well. He was always suspicious and accused almost everyone and anyone, including his oldest son, Antipater, and his second son, Herod, of treason and attempted insurrection. During the last year of Herod's life, 4 BC, he was stricken with a number of serious illnesses: intestinal cancer, ulcers, swelling of the legs, respiratory problems, bone cancer, and probably a brain tumor. He suffered more during his last year than in the previous 69 years of his life.

Knowing that Herod's illnesses were incurable, and that his death was only a matter of time, two Jerusalem rabboni, Judas ben Sariphaeus and Mattathias ben Margalit seized the opportunity to incite their followers to revolt. Though bedridden, Herod still had enough state of mind to put down the rebellion. He had the two rabboni burned alive and had 40 of their accomplices strangled. He then disposed of the High Priest, whom he accused of knowing about the plot, but doing nothing to prevent it (records show that the High Priest did in fact know about the plot and chose to look the other way), by having him tied to a stake with a corpse. The High Priest died as the corpse decayed. The disposal of the High Priest was reported to have been on March 13, 4 BC, during an eclipse of the moon. The High Priest died on March 23, one week before Herod's death.

In the midst of this last nightmarish year of Herod's life an event took place that was to dramatically change the social and political climate of Judea. On January 18, 4 BC, Caesar Augustus received an emissary at his court in Rome, who had been sent by an eastern coalition of 13 kingdoms who were at that time preparing and mobilizing an army of more than 500,000 on the great plain that lay between the Chouspus River in the Zagros Mountains and the Tigris River. The emissary's message was that the coalition intended to invade the eastern borders of the Roman Empire through the region of Judea in less than one year's time, and that he (the emissary) had been given the authority to declare war on Rome in the name of the alliance. The emissary went on to say that the reason why the declaration of war had been instituted was that word had reached the coalition that Herod had killed the new king, spoken of by the divine Bel-tesh-Azzar (Daniel), to whom they had made alliance through their court representatives, just seven months previously, in order to expand his kingdom to beyond the Euphrates River.

Augustus was said to have been beside himself when he learned of the coalition's intent. He issued an immediate response, which has come down to us in the records of Irenaeus, who was appointed Bishop of Lyons in AD 177. A segment of his great work *Demonstration of the Apostolic Preaching* was entitled "Augustus Thwarts World Conflict". In this, Irenaeus recorded that Augustus sent a reply back to the eastern kingdoms by their emissary, saying that Herod was a mad-man who acted independently in his butchery; that he had the approval of neither Augustus nor of the Roman Senate when he acted; and that it cannot be confirmed that a male child to whom the eastern empires had pledged allegiance was among those children that had been killed by Herod. Augustus then explained that Herod was near death and that he was not mentally capable of governing his kingdom, consequently Augustus himself would issue a proclamation within 30 days that would demand the immediate dissolving and re-districting of Herod's kingdom. Finally, Augustus said, if the coalition would reconsider its intent, he (Augustus) would pledge that Rome would investigate the validity of the report that a male child with whom the eastern coalition had pledged its allegiance had been killed, that Rome would not seek expansion into territories beyond the Euphrates River, and that duty-free trade with the coalition would be operative for 10 years from that date forward.

"We really have no idea what happened after that," Barth wrote, "But there is no record of an invasion. Considering that such an invasion of Rome would have been the same as a world war today, I'm sure there would have been some record if it had occurred. So, I think Augustus' reply first pacified the coalition; and then when they (the coalition) saw that he (Augustus) was a man of his word, they were satisfied to the point of calling off the invasion.

Augustus had made a commitment to avert war, so he had to follow through with it. Accordingly, on February 18, 4 BC, just 40 days before Herod's death, Augustus proclaimed that within 100 days or upon the death of Herod, whichever came first, Herod's kingdom would be divided between not less than three, and not more than five successors, whom Herod was to choose without delay. Seven days before Herod died, Augustus had grown impatient with Herod's procrastination and sent word demanding that Herod either name his successors within two days, or Augustus would place the entire kingdom under direct Roman procuratorship. Thus, just five days before he died, Herod was forced to divide his kingdom. He had already imprisoned his oldest son, Antipater (the very day that he made his choice of succession, Herod had Antipater, his oldest son, killed for treason), and had banished his next oldest, Herod. For that reason, Herod chose his three youngest sons to be his heirs. Archelaus was given Judah (which included the region of Samaria) and Idumes. Archelaus ruled as the Roman Ethnarch (this was a higher office than Tetrarch) of these areas until AD 6. Herod Philip was given Iturea, Trachonitus, Gaulanitis, Auranitis, and Batanea. Philip served as Roman Tetrarch (directly below the rank of Ethnarch) of these areas until AD 34. Herod Antipas was given the Galilee and Peraea. Antipas served as Roman Tetrarch of these areas until AD 39. A fourth region, Abilene, was carved out of Philip's region about a year after Herod's death, and was given to Lysanias, as a proffer for peace. Although Lysanias was not related to Herod the Great, he was related to Philip through Philip's wife. Lysanias was also given the title of Roman Tetrarch.

By this time, just five days before his death, Herod was increasingly tormented by uncontrollable frenzies, brought on by his atrocious sufferings that would last for hours at a time. During these fits of madness and wrath, Herod condemned hundreds to death, including his own son, Antipater; 400 of his most trusted friends; 300 of his most able administrators; and many more hundreds who were unfortunate enough to have been seen, heard, or thought of by Herod during those last miserable days. Finally on the evening of March 30, 4 BC, as Passover preparations were about to begin, at the age of 70, Herod died in the midst of some of the most excruciating pain that he had ever endured. Athananasius, Bishop of Alexandria from AD 328 to 335, said that it was a fitful end to a life of one who had himself caused such pain and torment.

Barth concluded his notes by writing, "Herod's death set off a rebellion among the people that broke out simultaneously in Judea, Peraea, and the Galilee. The Temple compound in Jerusalem became the rebel's mobilization headquarters (they felt that even Herod's successors would respect the sanctity of the Temple). Within two days of Herod's death, Archelaus proved that he was no less ruthless than his late father. He had his troops surround the Temple and massacre everyone on the premises. Three thousand were killed that day, including many innocent Passover celebrates. This was only the beginning of many atrocities that would soon be attributed to Archelaus."

After the death of Herod the Great (in 4 BC), according to Matthew 2, verses 21 through 23, Joseph was again instructed in a dream to not only leave Egypt and return to the Palestine region. But, in light of the bloody chain of events associated with Archelaus, Herod's son who succeeded him as ruler of Judea, it is not at all surprising that Joseph chose not to return to his homeland immediately. When he did decide to return, he chose not to take his family to Judea. Instead he took them to the opposite end of the region and settle in his hometown of Nazareth, in the Galilee. The Galilee was an administrative district set up by Pompey, whose administrative governing council was located in the western Galilee Roman city of Sepphoris.

We don't know how long after the angel appeared to Joseph instructing him to return that he and the family actually left Egypt. A 2nd century Cappadocia Christian account that I discovered while researching at the Cairo University in Cairo, Egypt, stated that while in Egypt, Joseph made quite an impressive name for himself as a master stonemason. His primary building focus was on large facilities constructed on behalf of the Romans in the Egyptian cities of Babylon, On, and Memphis. So, when the angel appeared to Joseph in 4 BC, he was understandably hesitant about closing down his thriving business in Egypt and moving back to his homeland. But when Augustus levied a tax on all new and future heavy-construction projects in February, AD 4, eight years after the angel had appeared to him, Joseph felt that it was probably time for them to leave Egypt. So, he took his family and returned to the Galilee, arriving in Nazareth in September of AD 4. Jesus would have been about eleven years old.

Another account that I found at the Cairo University, originating in 3rd century Arabia, confirms the visit by the angel to Joseph in a dream in 4 BC, and also confirms that Joseph had a business enterprise in Egypt. This account states that Joseph left Egypt in January of AD 6, because he received word that his brother, whom he had left in charge of the construction business in Nazareth, had moved the business from Nazareth to Moab and had asked Joseph to join him there and help him with the business. So, considering that since Augustus had levied his construction tax almost two years earlier, Joseph's business profits had steadily diminished, he decided to accept his brother's offer. So, leaving Egypt, Joseph settled his family in Moab. Upon the death of Joseph's brother, this account continued, which occurred during Jesus' 20th year, Joseph moved the construction business and his family back to Nazareth in the Galilee, arriving in Nazareth in June, AD 13.

XIII

SON OF THE LAW

The next major event in Jesus' life took place in April, AD 6, when he was 13 years old. That is when he became a *Son of the Law* (Luke 2: 41-52). Actually he was 12 years old when he left his home to travel to Jerusalem with Joseph and Mary to participate in the *Son of the Law* ceremony, which was suppose to be celebrated during the Passover of his 13th birthday. It was while they were in Jerusalem for Passover, actually sometime during the last three days of the Passover celebration, that he turned 13 and was allowed to participate in the celebration.

While I was visiting a friend in Sur, Lebanon, I ran across, strictly by accident, an ancient document whose subject was this biblically recorded incident. I was actually researching the Old Testament hero, Joshua, at St. Andrew's library, when I stumbled upon the ancient manuscript.

Deogratias, Bishop of Carthage from 436 to 452, had written the leather manuscript in Latin. It was addressed to Genesius of Clermont who had died in AD 450. Therefore, it seemed obvious that the manuscript had to be written before 450.

It appeared the manuscript was a portion of what was at one time an even larger manuscript. Apparently Genesius had contacted Deogratias and had asked his opinion on a number of questions concerning Jesus, his life and ministry, and about specific apostles of the early church.

This manuscript was Deogratias' response to Genesius, answering his questions. The majority of the manuscript containing the answers to his questions was missing, but there were answers to two of his questions that had remained intact.

The two questions that he answered with accompanying comments related to: (1) Jesus at the age of 13 confounding the doctors of the Law in the Temple, when Jesus officially went through the ceremony to become a *Son of the Law*; and (2) information about Joseph of Arimathea.

The manuscript began by recording the biblical account (Luke 2:41-52) of the ceremony in Jerusalem, when Jesus became a *Son of the Law*.

> *"Now his parents went to Jerusalem every year at the feast of the Passover. And when he was twelve years old, they went up to Jerusalem after the custom of the feast. And when they had fulfilled the days, as they returned, the child Jesus tarried behind in Jerusalem; and Joseph and his mother knew not of it. But they, supposing him to have been in the company, went a day's journey; and they sought him among their kinsfolk and acquaintance. And when they found him not, they turned back again to Jerusalem, seeking him. And it came to pass, that after three days they found him in the Temple, sitting in the midst of the doctors, both hearing them, and asking them questions. And all that heard him were astonished at his understanding and answers. And when they saw him, they were amazed: and his mother said unto him, Son, why hast thou thus dealt with us? Behold thy father and I have sought thee sorrowing. And he said unto*

them, How is it that ye sought me? Wist ye not that I must be about my father's business? And they understood not the saying which he spake unto them. And he went down with them, and came to Nazareth, and was subject unto them: But his mother kept all these things in her heart. And Jesus increased in wisdom and stature, and in favor with God and man" (Luke 2:41-52).

Afterwards, Deogratias went immediately into his explanations.

Apparently Genesius had asked Deogratias about this event in Jesus' life—the *Son of the Law* ceremony.

Deogratias responded by writing, "We have no idea where Joseph and his family were living at this time. Luke [2:41] says that they went *up* to Jerusalem. If they were living in Moab at that time then geographically, Jerusalem would have been up. If they were living in Nazareth, then topologically, Jerusalem would have been up from Nazareth. Further down in Luke [2: 51] it seems to indicate that they first went geographically down, perhaps to Moab, then from there they turned and went geographically up to Nazareth."

After this opening statement by Deogratias, and before he went into an explanation about the ceremony itself, he began talking about the typical education of a Jewish boy during the time of Jesus' boyhood.

Deogratias said that since Jesus was not raised in the typical Judean Jewish society, his education was not typical Judean Jewish. During his first 11 years Jesus was educated as an Egyptian, of Roman occupied and controlled Egypt.

Deogratias felt that both Jesus' mother and his father probably taught him as much of the traditional Jewish manners and customs, as well as the Law of Moses, as they knew. Their knowledge was probably limited since they were from the Greek dominated region of the Galilee. Generally speaking, Jesus' first years of formal education were Greek dominated and Roman controlled, Egyptian education.

It is true that Herod had raised Jewish education to the highest possible level throughout the eastern Roman Empire, in Egypt. However, separate or segregated education was not allowed. Hence, all children regardless of ethnic, cultural, or historical background, had to be educated in the state controlled Greek/Roman/Egyptian schools. Joseph and Mary knew enough about the Jewish religious customs that when Jesus reached the age in which the Law commanded that he become a *Son of the Law*, they did not hesitate to fulfill their obligation by him.

Deogratias then returned to the *Son of the Law* ceremony.

It was not unusual for Jewish men and women to come to Jerusalem from all over the known world to commemorate the annual celebration of Passover. Children were not allowed to participate in the formal celebration. In Jesus' case, as the first-born son, he was not allowed to participate in the celebration until after he had been through the *Son of the Law*, Bar Mitzvah, investment ceremony, which occurred during the Passover celebration of the year that he reached his 13th birthday.

The *Son of the Law* ceremony was performed in the Temple in Jerusalem. Ever since the days of Ezra had signified a young man leaving childhood and entering manhood. In essence, he was ceremonially and officially, weaned.

Deogratias then briefly explained the weaning ceremony.

Since the time of Ezra, Orthodox Jewish mothers suckled their first-born son every Sabbath until they were 13 years old and had been invested as a *Son of the Law*. This was the accepted practice for Judean Jewish mothers, but the extreme exception for Galilean Jewish mothers (in fact, the Galilean residents considered the practice degrading and held the Judean Jewish mothers who practiced it in disdain). We are not sure which direction Mary chose, but chances are, she conformed to the Galilean ways regarding this tradition, much like she and Joseph had with most other Jewish traditions.

The "nursing until age 12 or 13" was not for every child, only the first-born son. Ezra started it, and it became a tradition. Every Sabbath, just before sundown, the mother would nurse the first-born son until after his Bar Mitzvah, which signified the weaning of the child, and his passing into manhood.

At that time in the history of Jerusalem (AD 6), a typical Passover celebration would draw in excess of 3 million Jewish celebrates. This did not include the hundreds of merchants and vendors, the non-Jewish sightseers, the Roman authorities, the Roman military, or a multitude of other non-Jewish residents and/or visitors. For a 12- or 13-year-old boy, his first participating Passover visit to Jerusalem would have been quite a momentous event.

During his first participating Passover of a *Son of the Law* candidate, the young man was allowed to participate in the first three observances: Pesah, on the 14th of Nisan, the day the Passover lamb (or sanctified sheep) was killed; the holy convocation, on the 15th of Nisan, the most solemn period of the Passover; and Matsoth, the 16th of Nisan, the day of the sheaf offering that celebrated the first harvest. It was on Matsoth, that the father of the son—in Jesus' case, Joseph—paid five shekels in redemption money (Numbers 3:47 and 18:16—this gave him the legal right of fatherhood), marking the beginning of the young man's Bar Mitzvah, or the *Son of the Law* ceremony.

On the day following the ceremony, the new *Son of the Law* was allowed to attend teachings held by the most prestigious rabbonis and rabbans of the day, and to attend commentary teachings held by local rabbis. These teachings were presented beneath the arcades of the Temple. During this time the new *Son of the Law* was allowed to remain in the Temple (all day and all night if he wanted to) for the remainder of the Passover celebration. He was not allowed to address the rabbonis and rabbans or to question them. He was, however, allowed to question the rabbis who were presenting the commentary teachings.

Luke implies that Jesus spent the remainder of the celebration discussing and asking questions of the rabbonis and rabbans, or as Luke states, the "doctors of the law."

"How was it that a 13-year-old boy was allowed to question this prestigious group of teachers?" Deogratias asked the question.

"One theory that has been voiced for at least 100 years," Deogratias wrote, "Is that Luke's record contends that Jesus, after becoming a *Son of the Law*, was allowed to attend the teaching meetings of the Sanhedrin, who during Passover traditionally met in the Temple compound. But again, how did a 13-year-old boy manage to spend at least three and maybe as many as five days with the teaching

Sanhedrin, considering that their meetings were closed to all who were not members?"

Luke tells us that Joseph and Mary packed up to begin their journey home thinking that Jesus was likely somewhere in the returning caravan, probably with kinfolk. The caravan traveled a one-day's journey, which ranged in length from as few as eight miles to as many as 30 miles. At camp that first night, Joseph and Mary discovered that Jesus was not with them. They immediately returned to Jerusalem and finally found him after searching for three days. Whether or not the three days included the one-day that it took them to return to Jerusalem is unclear. If so, Jesus was missing for four days; if not, he was missing for five days.

If Jesus was truly allowed to stay in the Temple compound for the three to five days that remained in the Passover celebration, then we know where he ate and slept for those days. He must have known that his parents had left to return home, especially if they opted to return home before the celebration had concluded. If he did not stay in the Temple compound, where would a lone 13-year-old boy sleep and eat in a city overflowing with more than three million people for those three to five days?

At this point Deogratias introduced Joseph of Arimathea.

The Bible says very little about Joseph of Arimathea. We know that he was a very rich, secret disciple (Matthew 27:57) of Jesus who claimed the body of Jesus from Pilate and had him buried in his own tomb. He was a member of the Sanhedrin (*honorable counselor*—Mark 15:43) and he had not consented to the Sanhedrin's decision to have Jesus crucified (Luke 23:50-51). Beyond these few references, little more is recorded about Joseph of Arimathea in the Bible.

According to eastern Christian Church tradition, Arabic tradition, the Jewish Jerusalem Talmuds, early British tradition, and *Roman Senatorial Annals and Chronologies* dating from that time, Joseph of Arimathea, a Roman citizen by conferance, was the younger adopted brother of the father of Mary, the mother of Jesus (First century Christian tradition says that Joseph of Arimathea was adopted by Joseph's father when Joseph of Arimathea was a small boy of eight or nine, after he was orphaned when both of his parents, his older brother and his older sister were killed in a ship wreck) This made Joseph Mary's uncle and Jesus' great-uncle. Joseph had a natural daughter, Anna, whom Mary called *consobrina* or blood-cousin.

These traditions also all agree that for some reason Mary's father was either imprisoned or was killed, leaving the pregnant Mary, fatherless (she was pregnant with Jesus at the time of her father's displacement). Joseph, Mary's uncle stepped in and legally adopted Mary. Under Roman law when he adopted Mary, her unborn child was automatically adopted also. So, in essence, Mary became the adopted daughter of Joseph of Arimathea and Jesus, when he was born, automatically became the adopted son/grandson of Joseph of Arimathea. This made both Mary and Jesus, legal Jewish Roman citizens—Jewish by birth, but Roman by adoption.

Joseph, the husband of Mary, was the earthly father of Jesus and the natural father of all of Mary's other children, but Joseph of Arimathea was Jesus' great-uncle, adoptive grandfather, and legal adoptive father.

The Jewish Talmuds and *Roman Senatorial Annals and Chronologies* refer to Joseph of Arimathea as *Joseph de Marmore*. This was a Roman title of honor that was given to a Jew of Jewish royal bloodline (whether he was from the line of David, the Hasmonean, or the line of Herod, is unknown), who had proven himself loyal to Rome and had been granted Roman citizenship. This honor automatically made all of Joseph's children, heirs, and direct descendants Roman citizens too. The title, *Joseph de Marmore*, accompanied by a town designation (Arimathea) meant, "Joseph, the Great Lord of Arimathea."

According to Early Church (first two centuries after Jesus' resurrection) tradition, Joseph was said to have been one of the richest Romans and *the* wealthiest Jew, in all of Syria with residences in Rome, Corinth, Arimathea, Jerusalem, Jericho, Damascus, Caesarea Maritima, Massilia on the coast of Gaul, and in Britain near the town of Venta.

Gildas Badonicus, the early British historian, referred to Joseph of Arimathea as *Nobilis Decurio Britianniea Provinus*. *Nobilis* was a title given to Roman provincial Senators. *Decurio* was the title of authority given to a Roman Senator whose pre-eminence was with the Empire's mining districts. *Britanniea Provinus* identifies the Roman province of Britain. In other words, Gildas Badonicus claims that <u>Joseph was *the* Roman provincial Senator who represented the Roman province of Britain, and he was *the* Imperial Minister of Mines and Mining for the Roman Empire</u>. This coupled with the fact that Joseph was the member of the Jewish Temple Sanhedrin that was appointed by and represented Rome and Roman interests, made him a powerful uncle/grand-uncle/father/grand-father.

According to Roman law, as well as Jewish law, only the next of kin could claim and bury a victim of capital punishment. Traditionally, the remains of the victims of capital punishment were cremated. So, how was it possible for Joseph of Arimathea to claim the body of Jesus?

According to Deogratias, there were two possible means whereby Joseph could claim Jesus' body.

One, if Joseph was a Roman Senator and the Imperial Minister of Mines and Mining for Rome, is it any wonder that he had direct access to Pontius Pilate when he claimed the body of Jesus? Joseph was far more significant in the eyes of the Roman authorities than Pilate.

Second, if Joseph was the uncle of Mary and Mary's legal guardian/father by adoption, as well as the great-uncle, grandfather, and adoptive father of Jesus (which he could prove), he could legally, by right of Roman citizen parentage, claim Jesus' body, even though Jesus had been crucified for treason against Rome (under Roman law only Roman citizen parents or Roman citizen spouses could claim the body of a Roman who had been convicted of treason against Rome. Bodies of non-Roman who had been convicted of treason were not allowed to be claimed).

Deogratias then asked a hypothetical question, which he followed with a factual answer.

He asked, "If Joseph of Arimathea was a Roman Senator and if he was as powerful as stated, why did he not stop the crucifixion of Jesus?"

He then answered the question.

In the fifth year of Tiberius' reign, the Praetorian Perfect, Sejanus, moved his guard to the outskirts of Rome and encamped there, refusing to withdraw until all of his demands for social equality had been met. During that time there were numerous accusations and counter accusations of treason and disloyalty, resulting in the death of thousands through mass executions and numerous suicides. This condition continued until Sejanus' execution in October of AD 31. These crisis years were called *The Years of Embitterment*.

In the midst of this crisis, Tiberius became so incensed with the whole ordeal that he withdrew from Rome and retired to the island of Capri. He remained there, governing from Capri by courier, until his death in AD 37.

It was during this crisis time that Jesus was crucified. So fragile was the stability of the government of Rome during that time that each and every accusation and suspicion of treason was treated with the utmost earnestness. Hence, during *The Years of Embitterment*, entreaty in cases of high treason, by decree of Tiberius, could be appealed to and the ruling overturned by the emperor *only*.

Since Tiberius had isolated himself and would not accept *any* audience from *any* official, except for the Theophus commission of ambassadors, the repeal of a death sentence for treason was impossible. During the days of Tiberius' self-proclaimed retirement from public duty, more than 9,000 allegations of high treason against Rome were enunciated to Sejanus or on behalf of Sejanus by provincial governors or procurators. One of these was the allegation against Jesus. Everyone of the accused was found guilty and each sentenced. About 4,900 out of the 9,000 who stood condemned were executed and that included Jesus. If Joseph had protested the death sentence against Jesus it would have done no good. Without a provision for appeal to Tiberius, all hope of a repeal of Jesus' death sentence was dashed. Hence, Jesus was condemned the very moment that he was accused of treason, and no one could do anything about it.

Deogratias then returned to the subject of Joseph of Arimathea.

In the Gospel of John (19:26), while on the cross, Jesus gave the care of his mother to *"the disciple whom he loved."* For more than 300 years after the time of Jesus' crucifixion, it was assumed by the church, that Jesus at that moment had transferred care of his mother from himself back to either James, his natural brother; Lazarus, whom he had raised from the dead; or his/her adoptive father, Joseph of Arimathea, the disciple (Matthew 27:57) who Jesus loved with *agape* love or with the highest form of personal relationship love, like a father-son type of love.

It was not until the late 4th century that Anastasius of Rome claimed and proclaimed that Jesus was addressing John his disciple, the presumed author of the Gospel of John in this portion of the Gospel of John. However, Anastasius was most likely wrong, for why would Jesus instruct his younger cousin, John, to care for his mother when he had so many brothers and sisters and Joseph, her/his adopted father, still living?

Deogratias continued.

The reason why Jesus was a stranger to his own people, in that very few knew who he was, was because he and his mother, Mary, had lived with their uncle/father, Joseph of Arimathea, for 12 years (from Jesus' age 17 to age 29), in both Judaea and Britain, because of a family conflict between Joseph, Mary's husband, and Mary.

Mary and Jesus left Joseph, her husband, and went to live with Joseph of Arimathea, at his home. While living there, it is presumed that Jesus traveled with him on his many trips to and from Britain.

"Joseph of Arimathea," Deogratias wrote, "Was one of the richest men in all of Roman Syria and especially in the Roman province of Judaea. He owned virtually all of the metals shipping trade between Syria and Europe and especially between Judaea and England.... because Joseph was the Minister of Mines and Mining for the Roman Empire as well as a Roman Senator representing Britain, a great deal of time was spent in England. Joseph, hence Jesus, could travel anywhere mines were being worked to sell ore and minerals to the Roman Empire, especially in England.... making Jesus a virtual stranger to the Galilee...that would explain why most of the Jews had questions about who he was. Even his cousin (if indeed he was his cousin), John the Baptist did not recognize him (John 1:31)...Jesus was required to pay the 'stranger and wanderer's tax' recorded in Matthew (17:24-27).... Bartholomew the nathaniel who lived close to Nazareth had no idea who Jesus was...in reality, Jesus was known by very few in the region of his own home town. that could explain why a 12 year old boy could so astound the great professors of the Law in Jerusalem, yet nothing more is recorded about this astounding young man until he neared age 30. If he had remained in the Judaea or the Galilee area, surely more would have been written about this boy phenomenon.... Jesus at age 30 was more of a resident of Britain than he was a Galilean resident because he had spent more time with his countrymen in Britain than he had spent with his Jewish countrymen in the Galilee....The traditions of Glastonbury say that Jesus had blue eyes and either auburn or medium brown hair and was kept somewhat short according to the Greco-Roman standards of that day. They also said that he and Mary, his mother, had built a home on the south end of Lake Glastonbury, near the home of Joseph, and had lived there for some time on two different occasions. At the completion of the second stay, they left Britain to return to the Galilee when Jesus was 29 years old. The city of Glastonbury is located near the headwaters of the Thames River near Bristol, within the region of the Silurian Kingdom, the center of Druidic worship...."

Roman Senatorial records show that the Roman Senate appointed King of Britain, Arviragus, "Allotted to the Roman Senator Joseph, said by the infidels to be of Arimathea, in Judaea, and by Joseph to be the adopted father of Mary his niece and her son, Jesus, and his followers, 12 hides [just over 1900 acres] of land in Joseph's Senatorial provincial district of Glastonbury. This gift was given to Joseph in the name of the Roman Senate as compensation to Joseph for the wrongful death of his adoptive son, known to his followers as 'the Christ', during the reign of Tiberius. It was on this land that Joseph built a church wherein the cup [the legendary holy grail] was housed and in whose courtyard the tree of thorns (tradition says that this tree grew as a result of Joseph planting one of the thorns taken from Christ's crown of thorns) grew."

Bernard, Bishop of Lyons, wrote that, "Five years after the death of Jesus, Joseph of Arimathea and 11 others including Mary, the mother of Jesus, Joseph's adoptive daughter, settled in Glastonbury after sailing first to Massilia [Marseilles], then passing through the whole of Gaul, arriving at the channel of Britain on the morning of the celebration of the birth of Augustus. "

The statement that Deogratias attributed to Bernard, Bishop of Lyons, concluded Deogratias' record of Joseph of Arimathea. He then returned to describing the *Son of the Law* ritual.

Deogratias felt that it was through Joseph's influence that Jesus had his opportunity to debate the Sanhedrin doctors of the Law. Jesus, as well as Mary and Joseph, her husband, probably stayed with Uncle Joseph at his residence in Jerusalem. When they were to return to the Galilee, the first caravan stop very well may have been Arimathea, some 18 miles north of Jerusalem, on the main road that led north to the Galilee. It is most probable to assume that Mary and Joseph had given permission for Jesus to accompany Uncle Joseph back to Arimathea, anticipating meeting Joseph and Jesus when they arrived. Obviously Joseph and Jesus were delayed in Jerusalem, so Joseph and Mary went back to investigate what had happened.

When they did finally find Jesus, he was in the Temple debating with the doctors of the Law. They scolded him, to which he replied that he was doing his father's business. Deogratias says that Jesus was referring to the *Law*. This was a ritual in which a young first-born son became a *Son of the Law*. Hence, Jesus is saying to his earthly father and his mother that he was doing what he supposed to be doing, which was being about his father's, the Law's (since he had just become a *Son of the Law*, then his father was the Law) business, or the business of doing as the doctors of the Law did at that time—debate, comment upon, and teach the Law. They, like he now was, were officially *Sons of the Law*. As such, the Law was not only his father, but it was their father too.

The statement made by Jesus had nothing to do with any type of premonition, knowledge, suspicion, or conjecture that he was doing his heavenly Father's business. He was not implying that he was the Son of the Heavenly Father. It is unlikely that he suspected such a thing. He was simply saying that he was exercising his position as a *Son of the Law*, and that the Law was now his father. In essence, he was trying to sprout his wings and be a man, as many 13-year-old young men will do today, yet he was still a child emotionally; too old to play with toys and too young to act responsibly as an adult.

Jesus submitted to his earthly parents, went back to Nazareth with them, and was subject to them.

This ended that portion of Deogratias' document. The remainder of the document dealt with Jesus' probable education.

Deogratias continued by writing that since the days of Alexander the Great, formal education had played a vital role in the life of a typical Jewish boy. When Herod the Great was appointed king, he viewed education vital and he demanded it as an indispensable ingredient of a young Jew's up bringing.

By the time Jesus was born, Herod had set into place a well-organized and systematic educational program throughout his domain. Herod made mandatory some curriculum yet he gave the states the freedom to customize a good portion of their educational requirements to fit their culture, their social system, and their customs. Therefore, the education for a Jewish boy in the Galilee at the time of

The Search

Jesus' boyhood would have been inherently different from the education that a Jewish boy received in the state of Judea.

In the state of Judea (not the province of Judaea—only the state of Judea. Education in the province of Judaea was similar to that offered in the Galilee), the formal education for Jewish children began at age six and was compulsory for boys up to age 13 and for girls up to age 10. The children were taught in a local synagogue classroom setting by qualified Jewish teachers, who had been approved by the Roman authorities. During this first phase of education a young Jewish boy in Judea was taught the Law, the Creedal statements (the Shema), the Psalms, the prophets, the history of the Jewish people, the laws of sacrifice, etiquette, music, writing, arithmetic, poetry, gymnastics, geography, the Greek language, the Latin language, Roman history, Roman law and government, Greek history, and Persian history. School was in session all year long, six days a week, eight hours per day.

At age 13, a higher education was available for all boys who desired to become a priest, a rabbi, a teacher, or a scribe. If a boy chose to continue in his education, it was mandatory for him to go through the Bar Mitzvah ritual on the day of Matsoth (during the Passover celebration) of the year in which he turned 13. In higher education, students were taught on a ratio of five students to one teacher. The teacher was a member of the Rabbinate. Here the student was allowed to discuss questions about the Law with the Pharisaic teachers. He also learned geometry, economics, medicine, Latin, the Greek language, the Hebrew language, Roman religion, Roman law, Roman poetry, Roman philosophy, Greek philosophies, and Persian philosophy. He received an in-depth study of Leviticus, Deuteronomy, Numbers, and Psalms. Learning an occupation was another part of the student's higher education. The occupation was usually the same as the student's father's occupation or profession.

At age 17, the boy graduated from higher education and had to decide whether or not he wanted to continue with an even higher education. If he chose to continue his education in the state of Judea, he had one of four options: (1) He could go to a Roman school where he could learn the political structure of Rome, thereby assuring himself of eventually attaining some type of Roman "governmental occupational" position. (2) He could enroll in a Roman military school. Here he would be trained in the art of war. After graduation he would be joined to a Roman legion as part of the legion's auxiliary support. (3) He could choose to enter the priesthood and begin training toward that goal (becoming a *nathael* first then later becoming a *nathanael*) or (4) he could choose to be a teacher and enroll in one of the two Judean Rabbinate schools.

If the young man chose to enter the priesthood, he would move to the Temple complex in Jerusalem and there for the next 28 years, he would be trained in the office of a priest. Throughout his 28 years of training, various goals were achieved: at age 30, the young priesthood student, the nathael, became a nathanael, or an auxiliary priest; and at age 45 he became eligible to become an independent priest. After serving as an independent priest for 10 years, he became eligible at the age of 55, to become a chief priest. Five years later, at the age of 60, he became eligible to become the High Priest. All priests and all official temple servants, with the exception of the scribes, belonged to the religious sect of the Sadducees.

171

It was highly unlikely for a young man to enter the priesthood unless he had Sanhedrin "kinsmen" connections or was from a priesthood aristocratic family (the priest positions were normally passed down from father to son). The student would have to be recommended for priest training by the High Priest, and he had to be approved by the government of Roman. Because the school of priests graduated only 25 nathaels per year, it was difficult to get into this school, even if a young man had Sanhedrin or bloodline priesthood connections.

If a young student chose the teaching route after higher education graduation, he had to enroll in one of the two available Rabbinate schools: the school of Hillel or the school of Shammi. For the next eight years (until age 25) the young man lived at the school and was taught along with the Law and the scriptures, the Mishan (the opinion of respected interpreters of the Law), the Midrash (commentaries on the whole scriptures), the Torah (the Law), the oral traditions and decisions on the Law passed down from the time of Moses (these were later called The Talmuds), Greek and Roman history, governmental regulations, Greek philosophy, and governing religions.

After four years of education, at age 21, the brightest of the students were chosen to be tutors. These students were employed as private tutors to other students. After four years it was mandatory for the young teacher trainee to join the sect of the Pharisees.

At age 25 the young teacher-trainee graduated from the Rabbinate school as a rabbi. He then remained as an understudy to a local rabbi for five years before he was permitted to "launch-out" on his own (at age 30) as an independent rabbi.

Upon graduation from the rabbinate school, the *top* (only one student—the top student) student in the graduating class had the option to go further in his education rather than submit himself to be an understudy of a local rabbi. He could choose to either begin his training to become a rabboni, or he could choose to begin his training to become a scribe, or a lawyer of the Law.

If he chose to begin training to become a rabboni, he had to submit to another five years (until age 30) of extensive training by a personal tutor, a rabban (Grand Master—<u>Gamaliel was a rabban</u>). Included in this extensive training was extended travel with the rabban in accompaniment to the world centers of civilization such as Egypt, Babylon, Persia, and Greece. After these five years of personal training, the student had to go through a brutal three-day question and answer session before the Sanhedrin. If he passed, he was given the title of *Rabboni*.

After becoming a rabboni, the student could choose to become a rabban by submitting to an additional 12 years of training under the direct tutoring of the Rabboah of Innan, the highest level of rabban authority. There was only one position of Rabboah of Innan (According to Jewish tradition, Innan was supposed to have been the angel who had been sent from God to teach Adam all knowledge and all intellectual wisdom), at a time, and he occupied that position for life. Before his death, the Rabboah of Innan was required to select from the ranks of the rabbans, his successor. At the time of Jesus' ministry, the Rabboah of Innan was Ezariah II, son of Hurran of Azotus.

If a student chose to begin training to become a scribe after rabbi school graduation, he would move to the Temple in Jerusalem where for the next five years he was taught to interpret the Law by a personal tutor, a *soferim* (a Doctor in the Law). After this five years (at age 30), he would be classified as a scribe (lawyer of the Law). If he wanted to become a soferim (a doctor of the Law) he had to submit to an additional 10 years of personal tutoring by a Sadducee member of the Sanhedrin.

These were the typical educational requirements for a young Jewish boy in the state of Judea.

The following are the educational requirements for a Jewish boy in the Galilee.

Unlike the state of Judea, where Judaism influence was dominant, the Galilee's Jewish population was only a minuscule fraction of the population whole, and the educational requirements reflected that fact. The Galilee was extremely cosmopolitan, with no one ethnic group or race dominant over any other. As such, education was under the *direct control* of the Roman authorities. Because the Galilee was compiled of numerous peoples, cultures, ethnic groups, and races, the Roman authorities allowed limited ethnic education up to the age of 12, if that education did not interfere with the prescribed Roman educational agenda. In the Galilee during the time of Jesus' educational training, education in Jewish (or any other culture and ethnic groups including Persians, Babylonians, Arabs, Syrians, Phoenicians, etc.) culture, religion, law, philosophy, and customs was optional education allowed to be taught by Roman approved Jewish tutors during the first two hours of the education day up until age 12 *only*. The remaining six hours of education per day was compulsory under the directive, control, supervision, and authority of the Roman educational officials. After age 12, ethnic education was not permitted.

In the Galilee (as well as in the province of Judaea, excluding the state of Judea), education began at age five and was compulsory (compulsory but not rigidly enforced) for boys up through age 17 and for girls up through age 12. Except for the first two hours of the teaching day, education was conducted in Roman built schools. For a Jewish child in the Galilee, the first two-hour optional education segment of the day was conducted either at the local Jewish synagogue or at Roman approved central locations.

During the allowable seven years of optional ethnic education (two hours a day until age 12), the young student, a young Jewish student in Jesus' case, was taught the Law, the Shema, the Psalms, the prophets, Jewish history, Jewish philosophy, Jewish manners and customs, Jewish ethics, laws of sacrifice, the origins of Judaism, and limited portions of what became the Talmuds. This was far less than the Jewish education that was available to a Jewish student in the state of Judea. For this reason Judean Jews considered Galilean Jews to be "unlearned in letters," or unlearned in the Jewish ways and customs.

This is the reason why the religious leaders in Jerusalem on the day of Pentecost said of the Galilean apostles of Jesus that they were unlearned (Acts 4:13). It wasn't because they were uneducated. They were educated. In fact the Romans insisted that the Galileans received the best education available at the time. It's that they were not educated in the Jewish ways and customs.

During the 12 years of a Galilean boy's compulsory Roman education (up until age 17) he was taught etiquette, music, the art of war, all forms of mathematics, poetry, gymnastics, wrestling, athletics, geography, the Greek language, Latin, Greek and Roman culture, Greek and Roman manners and customs, Greek and Roman philosophy, cultural philosophy, the history of the world, Roman history, Roman law and government, Roman diplomacy, Persian history, the study of world religions, the study of world philosophies, economics, trade and merchandising, architecture, engineering and construction, art, agriculture and animal husbandry, speech and oratory, writing and communication, the history of religion and philosophy, and the history of ancient civilizations. The teacher-to-student ratio was usually about four-to-one.

Upon completion of the compulsory education at age 17, a young Galilean Jewish graduate had a number of choices: he could start to work in an occupation or profession, continue his education in a number of Roman universities scattered throughout the Empire, attend a Roman political school to train for Roman politics, go to a Roman military school to train for the military, attend a Roman trade school to be trained in a trade or profession, try to go into priesthood training (but the chances of a Galilean being approved for priesthood schooling was greater than one in a million), or choose to pursue teaching or rabbi training.

If a student did choose to pursue the teacher or rabbi route of higher education, the Roman authorities demanded special consideration for Galilean students. Since the Rabbinate schools were all located in the state of Judea, it was impractical for a student in the Galilee to travel all the way to the state of Judea in order to enroll in the school. Because of this, the Roman authorities demanded of the Rabbinate schools that they each allow a total of 10 Galilean students per year to be enrolled in their schools. These Galilean students did not have to go to Judea for their training. Instead, they were under the eight-year directive of Judean Rabbinate school-appointed personal tutors who set up residences in the Galilee. Each invited no more than two students per year to live with the tutor at his residence in the Galilee where he would personally tutor and train the students. In AD 11, when Jesus was 17 years old, there were a total of nine Rabbinate school-appointed tutors who were living in the Galilee and training Galilean rabbi students. The subjects that they taught were the same as those taught in the Judean Rabbinate schools.

Upon the completion of his rabbi training at age 25, a Galilean rabbi student had to submit to five years of understudy, just like his Judean counterpart. Also like his Judean counterpart, each year's top rabbi student in the Galilee had the opportunity to advance to either rabboni training or scribe training. Here again, the Roman authorities intervened. They demanded that if the year's top student decided to pursue rabboni training, either a rabban chosen by the rabbinate school of the Roman authorities choosing, or a qualified and Roman approved member of the Sanhedrin was obligated to establish a residence in the Galilee so he could be the personal tutor of the rabboni student. If the top student chose to follow the path of a scribe, the Sanhedrin was obligated to establish Galilean residence for a soferim so that he could personally tutor the young scribe student. Joseph of Arimathea well could have been the Sanhedrin/Roman appointed soferim to the Galilee at the time of Jesus' educational training.

This was as far as the Roman intervention went. If after this the young man chose to pursue training to become a rabban or a soferim, he had to move to the Temple in Jerusalem.

Interference by the Roman authorities into the religious education of rabbis and scribes was a major point of contentious dissension between the Roman authorities and the Judean religious leaders, and also between the Judean rabbis, rabbonis, and scribes, and their Galilean counterparts.

Taking all of this into consideration, it seems quite obvious that Jesus' education was far more Greco-Roman than Jewish, especially since the first few years of his education was Roman/Greek/Egyptian, allowed no formal provisions for the optional ethnic teaching that was allowed in the Galilee.

With that the manuscript of Deogratias came to an abrupt end. It seemed logical to assume that there was more, but it had obviously been lost, destroyed, stolen, or had disintegrated centuries ago.

After the incident in Jerusalem when Jesus became a *Son of the Law* at age 13, Luke 2:51-52 tells us that Jesus returned to Nazareth with his father and mother and remained subject to them. During that time he grew in stature, and increased in wisdom and favor with God and man. Beyond that, the Gospels record nothing more about the life of Jesus until his baptism in AD 23 when he was 30 years old.

On the other hand, because of this silence in the Gospels, many writers over the centuries have felt it necessary to "fill in the gaps" on what they presume was really happening in Jesus' life. In my many years of research on the life of historical Jesus I have come across literally hundreds of stories concerning these hidden or unknown years. These have included legends that tell of Jesus' travels to the New World and his preaching to American Indians; his search for truth with Persian priests, Indian gurus, Buddhist monks, or Nepalese holy men; his studying Confucianism in the royal courts of China; his numerous miracles that ranged anywhere from making water come out of rocks to stretching wood, to turning trees into soldiers. Yet in this horde of accounts, stories, and legends I found nothing that would add anything of value to what was recorded in Luke—that Jesus' life for the next 17 years was not unusual, not miraculous, or out of the ordinary. It was a typical life of a typical young man who went to school, became a rabbi and then a rabboni, and learned a trade by helping his father in the stonemasonry construction business.

I like what Henry James said in his book ....*including Christ*, about Jesus during this 17-year period. He said, "Contrary to popular portrayal, I [Henry James] do not believe that Jesus lived his life in virtual solitude, walking slowly over the hills of the Galilee, day in and day out, with perhaps a lamb in his arms, in total seclusion, meditating and contemplating the things of God and the future of mankind. I think he was far more 'normal' than that.

"I think that if he did live in the Galilee and was reared there, he fit in well with the typical Galilean of his day. I think he worked hard in his father's stone-masonry business, building public buildings, places of worship including Jewish synagogues, Roman baths, government buildings, amphitheaters, residences, and anything else that his father's business was contracted to construct.

"I think that he had friends and that he communicated with and had association with his family and relatives including among many others perhaps, his Uncle Zebedee and his cousins, James and John, whom he called the *sons of thunder*. It is very conceivable that he might have known or at least seen or become aquatinted with many of the ones to whom he later ministered and who he healed.

"So likely is this scenario that the only way that it would not have been so, is if Jesus was away from his Galilean home for extended periods of time, perhaps traveling, maybe, with his great-uncle and adoptive father, Joseph of Arimathea. This is the *only* way that he would not have been acquainted with his countrymen or they with him. During these years, Jesus may or may not have been acquainted with those who were later identified as his friends in the state of Judea. If he was, it is most likely that he was not as close to them as he was to his own Galilean countrymen.

"But whatever the case, I [James] think that he was a normal young man who had a normal childhood. He had relatives, some of whom were very close to him, and some with whom he had a less than enthusiastic desire to become close. He had chores and duties. He attended school. He went to work. He played sports and games. He had friends, some were very close, and some were nothing more than acquaintances. He may have even had a girlfriend. He probably had to be disciplined by his parents and like all children who grow into adulthood; he learned by his mistakes. He may have felt that his life was more than the norm and that there truly was something, the magnitude of which was yet to be realized, special about him and his relationship with God.

"Concerning Jesus and the Son of God issue; whether as a boy he knew that he was destined to be man's savior and knew his mission to man, I [James] do not think that Jesus knew any of this while he was growing up. While he might have suspected that there was something different about him, especially if his mother ever told him about the strange events that had surrounded his birth and his early childhood (the Bible seems to imply that she did not tell him, she instead kept all those things to herself, hidden in her heart), I do not think that he ever concluded that he was of divine nature, was commissioned to be the savior of the world, or was the long awaited Messiah/Messias until after his baptism in AD 23 and wilderness experience, immediately thereafter.

"I [James] think that Jesus grew up like a typical Galilean of his day, no more——no less.

"It was not until after he had submitted himself to the mission to which he was appointed by his Father that he came into the full realization of his divinity, his position, and his mission.

"From the time of his baptism in AD 23 until the launching of his ministry in AD 26, Jesus had three years to realize and try to comprehend his mission. Early in the year AD 23, Sejanus was rapidly becoming the most influential political figure in Rome. At this same time in the Galilee, temporarily insulated from the political turmoil in Rome, Jesus began preparing for a jaunt to the Jordan River.

"This trip would signal his embarkation upon a pilgrimage that would culminate in the redemption of man and in his own death and resurrection."

The Search

XIV

BAPTISM AND BEYOND

In AD 23 John the Baptist was rapidly climbing the stairway of popularity and prestige. He was Judea's first "big name evangelist and prophet" in over 500 years. From all over Judaea, Peraea, the Galilee, and the Decapolis people by the thousands flocked to the desert regions surrounding the Jordan River to listen to the preaching of John the Baptist and to be baptized by him. In the words of Dr. Billy Graham when he spoke at the North American Conference for Itinerant Evangelists held in Louisville, Kentucky, the atmosphere that surrounded John's rise to prominence was a "cross between a medieval carnival, an evangelist crusade, and a Great Awakening camp meeting. It was new and refreshing and exciting."

John the Baptist was typical of the reclusive desert dwellers of his day. He wore a loin garment made of camel leather and ate the common desert dwellers' food of locust and wild honey.

He preached that entrance into the kingdom of God was by repentance only. This was contrary to the Pharisee's belief that entrance was based on a person being pre-chosen by God to enter the kingdom of God; and that they (the Pharisees) had been chosen first by God.

John also preached that public baptism was necessary to show true repentance. Baptism as taught by the Pharisees was a prerequisite to confirm that a person had proselyted from his or her religious convictions and had to become a believer in the Jewish religion. So, John's message was novel and inspiring.

It was into this atmosphere that the 30-year-old Jesus preceded when he journeyed from his home in Nazareth to the Jordan River in the spring of AD 23, to be baptized by John.

Like most of the events of Jesus' life, I discovered a multitude of legends, stories, and myths associated with John's baptizing of Jesus. Some of the stories would have made excellent Hollywood fiction. Yet they all seemed so shallow, predetermined, mystical, and seemingly "out of step" with what I felt was the truth of the Gospels. The Gospel records are so pure and direct. They did not have to rely upon mysticism and numinous phenomenon, nor did they have to create a fantasy world aurora around the person of Jesus to get their point across that this was indeed the first step of Jesus' short but intense journey that quickly evolved from God's anointed servant and messenger to man's savior.

I read so many accounts about John the Baptist and Jesus' supposed association with him and the strange and mystical events that accompanied Jesus' baptism that I was beginning to doubt whether anything genuine and authentic had ever been written that would corroborated the simplicity of the Gospel records of Jesus' baptism.

Finally in 1991 I found what I was looking for in the National Library of the country Albania.

The library located directly behind the Palace of Culture in Skanderbeg Square in downtown Tirana, Albania. There I discovered a book written in 1603 by the

French bishop, Francis of Sales (it had been translated into English and German) entitled *Baptism and Sanctification* that answered many of my questions regarding the baptism of Jesus.

In the book, Francis first presented background material dealing with the accepted baptism practices during Jesus' day, followed by the probable methods of baptism used by John the Baptist, and concluded with a proposed dramatized scenario of the baptism of Jesus.

Francis began with a 20-page introduction of adoration and praise to Christ, the Pope, and the Catholic Church and an apology in advance that some of the information that he discovered was contrary to the practice of baptism then adopted by the Roman Church. For the sake of the preservation of historical knowledge, he had recorded the information as he had discovered it, without comment or elaboration,

Francis discovered that in the year 1095 Anselm of Canterbury, the Archbishop of Canterbury, claimed that Jesus was baptized on the day of the celebration of his (Jesus') birth, in April, in the year of our Lord, AD 23. He (Anselm) said that Jesus traveled from the Galilee to the Jordan River to be baptized, and that the exact location of his baptism is not known.

Francis then quoted Matthew (3:1-17 and 4:1):

> *In those days came John the Baptist, preaching in the wilderness of Judaea, and saying, repent ye: for the kingdom of heaven is at hand. For this is he that was of by the prophet Esaias, saying,' the voice of one crying in the wilderness, prepare ye the way of the Lord, make his paths straight.' And the same John had his raiment of camel's hair, and a leathern girdle about his loins; and his meat was locusts and wild honey. Then went out to him Jerusalem, and all Judaea, and all the region round about Jordan, and were baptized of him in Jordan, confessing their sins.... Then cometh Jesus from Galilee to Jordan unto John, to be baptized of him. But John forbade him, saying, I have need to be baptized of thee, and comest thou to me? And Jesus answering said unto him, 'suffer it to be so now: for thus it becometh us to fulfill all righteousness.' Then he suffered him. And Jesus, when he was baptized, went up straightway out of the water: and, lo, the heavens were opened unto him, and he saw the Spirit of God descending like a dove, and lighting upon him: and lo a voice from heaven, saying, this is my beloved son, in whom I am well pleased. Then was Jesus led up of the Spirit into the wilderness to be tempted of the devil"* (Matthew 3:1-17; 4:1).

Francis continued by explaining the message and ministry of John the Baptist.

John was exceptional. The message he preached, although it had been taught and practiced in the Hasid Hakamin communities for decades, was a message that the average citizen in Judaea and the Galilee area had never heard. Not only was it a novelty for them to hear a man speak who had perhaps been a part of one of the communities, but the message that he brought was also novel in that it was one with which they had never before been acquainted. Consequently, through the novelty of the man (his dress, his character, his personality, and his mystique), his message, and his mannerism, literally thousands from all over the area that is now known as Palestine, flocked to hear John and to be baptized by him.

Francis side tracked a bit and wrote that it is not clear whether or not John knew Jesus at the time of Jesus' baptism. Logically speaking, if they were bloodline cousins, then they probably would have at least been acquainted with each other. However, if his mother and Elizabeth were nothing more than compatriots and friends, there is a possibility that they were not acquainted with one another. This, coupled with the fact that after baptizing Jesus, John continued to preach and baptize for the next three years, just like he had been doing before Jesus' baptism, seems to imply that John did not fully recognize Jesus, at the time of his baptism, as either the Messias or the Messiah. In fact, the followers of John, known as Mandeans (the earliest Christians were called Nazarenes), continued to survive even after John's death and on into the 2nd century.

After this, Francis returned to his original thought.

A portion of Matthew (15th verse of Matthew 3) seems to indicate that in Jesus' case, a specific baptism ritual was not only expected, but was demanded of John by Jesus (this implies that although John generally used a particular type of baptism ritual for all who came to him, in Jesus' case, John used another type of baptism ritual that was specifically demanded by Jesus, rather than the ritual that John was accustomed to using with all others).

This special and unique ritual demanded by Jesus was probably much like the intense baptism rituals that were demanded as an introductory initiation for the new priests in Ezra's day or the ones that were typical for inductees into the religious mysteries of Persia, Babylon, India, and post-Babylonian Egyptian Judaism—the same rituals that were being practiced secretly in many of the religions at that time.

These Jewish rituals called the *suffering of baptism* varied somewhat from religion to religion, but generally they were similar.

In the days of Ezra, the suffering of baptism initiation ritual for candidates into the priesthood included literally burying the candidate in the ground (not in a tomb) for a period signifying the death and burial of the old self and the old way of life. After an unspecified but extended period of time, the candidate was dug-up signifying being raised into a new way of life. There are records that report the deaths of some of these candidates because they were buried too long. How long the typical candidate was buried, is not known, but it was common for a candidate to be unconscious when he was retrieved.

By the time of the Maccabean revolt the practice of burying in the ground had been replaced by "burying" in water. This practice consisted of holding the candidate under water until he passed out. This signified his death and the burial of the old self. The candidate was then raised out of the water and revived, as a sign of being raised into a new life of dedication to the priesthood of God.

In 7 BC, Caesar Augustus outlawed all forms of the initiation by baptism for all non-Romans of all religions under the rule and authority of Rome, including the suffering of baptism associated with Judaism, under penalty of imprisonment. However, for *Roman citizens* who wanted to conform to a particular religion's ritualistic requirements or initiation and induction rites, these restrictions by

Augustus did not apply. So, although non-Romans were not allowed to participate in the Jewish suffering of baptism rituals, Roman citizens were under no such restriction and could participate in the ritual.

Hence, by the time Jesus was baptized, the particular baptism ritual demanded of John by Jesus was illegal to non-Romans and had been prohibited for some 30 years.

Although this does not prove that Jesus was a Roman citizen, circumstantially it strongly suggests that he very well could have been or at the very least had a very strong connection to the Roman authorities. If he was not a citizen or if he did not have special permission from high ranking Roman authorities, he would have been breaking a direct law instituted by Caesar Augustus himself. Knowing Jesus' respect for authority, it is doubtful that he would have purposefully disregarded the law of the land or contemptuously disobeyed the decree of Augustus.

The initiation of baptism was at the time of Augustus' prohibition decree a standard practice for most eastern religions, and had been since before the days Abraham and Hammurabi.

Jewish tradition claims that the suffering of baptism ritual was originally introduced by Shem, the son of Noah, in commemoration of Noah's ordeal of "passing through the waters of suffering." Over the next number of centuries, from the Shem-inspired origin, the practice of baptism diversified as it was adopted into the rituals of various religions throughout the world.

At the time of Augustus' imposed restriction, although there were perhaps as many as 200 different variations of the practice of baptism. The three most commonly used forms of the initiation by baptism were: (1) the suffering of baptism used by the Jews that has already been discussed; (2) being buried in sand for one full day and night, leaving only the head exposed (this was used in conjunction with initiation into the priesthood of Jainism and Zoroastrianism); and (3) the initiation practice that has been identified as the "trial by fire and water" practiced by many of the Greek, Babylonian, and Syrian cult religious sects. In this initiation the inductee was set on fire and then he was thrown into water and held under until he passed out.

Because of Augustus prohibition decree, the only type of Jewish baptism that was at that time allowed by the Roman authorities for non-Romans was called by the Pharisees "purification of the spirit." This consisted of a quick, total immersion of the person in water; or a partial covering of the person by sand, or the dipping of the upper part of the person's body into the water and having the person drink part of the water while his head was under the water.

Although it is generally accepted that Jesus was baptized by John in the Jordan River (the name *Jordan* was an old Sumerian name that meant "piss" or "piss drain." The Jordan River had served as a sewage disposal channel for centuries and was by the time of Jesus' baptism putrefyingly polluted.), as stated in the Matthew and John settings. The Luke setting approaches the baptism from a different position.

Luke (chapter 3) says (in verses 19 and 20) that Herod had arrested John before Jesus' baptism (which is recorded in verse 21). If this is true, then we have no record of who really baptized Jesus. Over the centuries, the commonly accepted justification for this difference is that either the Luke setting is incomplete. A large segment of the baptism record in Luke was either lost or destroyed. This made the Matthew and the John settings the more accurate record of Jesus' baptism; or John submitted to Jesus' request and inaugurated him into the ministry with the suffering of baptism ritual first, and then Jesus was re-baptized in the Roman accepted form sometime after John's imprisonment. Thus, Jesus was baptized as was permitted him as a Roman and as was expected of him as a Jewish religious leader.

After his baptism, Jesus was led (or driven as is suggested by the Gospel of Mark) into the wilderness for a continuation of his ritualistic rabboni training in self-discipline and spiritual awareness (this was typical for all rabboni hopefuls—rabboni training with a private rabban was for 5 years. Two years into the training the rabboni hopeful was initiated by baptism followed by his isolated wilderness challenge of extended fasting and prayer), being tempted in virtually all important aspects of his physical, emotional, psychological, and spiritual life. This time of isolation in fasting and prayer was usually established by the rabban under whose authority the rabboni in training was subject. But generally, the time of isolated prayer and fasting selected by the rabban was not less than 10 days and not more than 50. Nonetheless, Jesus' situation could have been different than all other rabboni hopefuls in the past three decades. All other Jewish rabbonis in training over the past 30 years were initiated in the "purification of the spirit" baptism ritual, which was far less physically challenging. Jesus, on the other hand, was initiated through the suffering of baptism ritual which would have left his body extremely weak and exhausted.

I discovered an excellent account of Jesus' wilderness experience in a book entitled *The Cost of Leadership,* while researching at the Palace du Palais' historical reference archives in Avignon, France. The walled city of Avignon was the seat of the papacy during the Church's period of schism in the 14th century. The Palace du Palais was the former papal residence.

The Cost of Leadership was written by Hans von Dohnaniy, the brother-in-law of Dietrich Bonhoeffer, the great anti-Nazi Lutheran theologian, who was executed by the Nazis in April of 1945. Hans sought to bring Dietrich into the plot against Hitler. Whether Dietrich actually did participate is uncertain. But, he was implicated, accused, and then was executed. After Dietrich's death Hans went into seclusion. There while in seclusion, he wrote the book. Rather than a novel or reference book, *The Cost of Leadership* seemed to be more of an essay that traced Jesus' experience in the wilderness, after his baptism.

I will paraphrase what von Dohnaniy wrote.

Immediately after the baptism of Jesus, the Gospel of Mark says that Jesus was driven by the Holy Ghost into a harsh and desolate wilderness area to be tested. Most present day (late 1940's) theological historians agree that this was probably the wilderness surrounding the Dead Sea area. The Mark 1 and Luke 4 record of this experience says that Jesus fasted for 40 days and nights, during which time he was continually tested. The Matthew 4 setting says it was after his 40 days of fasting that he was tested. By these three Gospel records we are forced to conclude that Jesus fasted for at least 40 days during which time he was continually tested in numerous areas. However, there were three areas in which he was unequivocally tested: (1)

turn stone into bread, (2) bow down and worship the tempter, and (3) seek protection from angels. How many times these three temptations tormented Jesus is unknown, but what is known is that these three were presented during the 40 days of fasting and at least once after the initial 40 days of fasting.

It is common knowledge, von Dohnaniy continued, that if a person is healthy, if he or she drinks a lot of fluids, and if he or she expels minimal energy, anyone should be able to fast for 40 days. But Jesus' situation may have been different. He had just concluded the taxing ordeal of the suffering of baptism, which would have left his body in a severely weakened state. Next, he was forced into the hot, dry and physically trying desert, which would have been overwhelming.

In the course of a "normal" fast, or a fast that does not take into consideration all of the other traumas that Jesus had to endure, a person usually loses his or her desire for food (hunger leaves) after five days. After 10 days, all solids will have been eliminated from the body, and a person's secretion and perspiration is greatly reduced. By day 15, spiritual sensitivity is greatly increased and the person becomes in-tune with his or her body, mind, and spirit. By day 20, the person will have eliminated most of his or her body poisons, making the breath very sweet. Also, by day 20 he or she must increase fluid intake. If not, they will begin to have uncontrollable hallucinations. On days 40 through 45 hunger returns with extreme agony and starvation begins to set-in.

There is much speculation about the events surrounding Jesus' wilderness experience. This speculation has evolved over the centuries into scores of opinions and conclusions. Of course the most commonly accepted belief, taught by the Catholic Church and adopted by the non-Catholics, is that Jesus was actually tempted by Satan, the prince of darkness, in an attempt to "short-circuit" his (Jesus') mission.

Alfred Glastonbury, the 19th century English theologian turned mystic, in his *Reflections on the Nature of the Mind* concluded that the temptations of Jesus were those that were in his own mind, brought on by hallucinations. In short, he said, Jesus was in conflict with himself over the mission that he had been called to do— that his spiritual self wanted to answer the call, but his emotional self did not.

The 18th century German Christian historian Raymond Billsbugh said in his *Recovery of Truth* that Jesus was not tested by a spiritual evil force called Satan, but rather by an evil human being, a person, probably a renegade religious hermit, who mocked and tormented Jesus while he (Jesus) was attempting to become spiritually enlightened.

Other opinions that von Dohnaniy discovered dealt with the possibility that the temptations of Jesus were strictly symbolic and that they were nothing more than spiritual and emotional upheavals that Jesus had to go through as part of his spiritual maturity progression.

Among those who believe that the temptations were orchestrated by Satan, just as the Gospels record, there are differing opinions why these specific temptations were used, and not others, or why these three were used over and again, rather than multiple temptations.

All opinions seem to agree that the tempter is the one who first mentioned the possibility of Jesus being the Son of God (Jesus at this time had never made that declaration or assumption about himself), but the agreement seems to stop there. While most present day (1940's) evangelicals and fundamentalists choose to take the position that the three particular temptations were used to symbolically test Jesus' power of miracles, his position and rank of Messiahship, and his power over death, von Dohnaniy admitted that he had not found enough recorded evidence to confirm or to refute that there are grounds for belief in such an opinion.

Von Dohnaniy then turned his attention to evaluating the three-recorded temptations. The fact that Matthew and Luke record them chronologically different, he commented, matters little. The difference only implies that Jesus was tempted on more than one occasion with these same temptations. The first temptation is the one in which both records agree—turning stone into bread. In association with this temptation, Jesus was first confronted with the issue of doubt regarding his Son of God position: *"If thou be the Son of God, then..."*

The first temptation dealt with the physical body's craving for food, and with Jesus' miraculous abilities as the Son of God. Jesus overcame this temptation by quoting Deuteronomy 8:3. *"...That he might make thee know that man doth not live by bread only, but by every word that proceedeth out of the mouth of the Lord doth man live."*

The second temptation, or third, whichever account one chooses to use as a resource, was when Jesus was taken into (implying that he was taken into a cave or a cavern or within a mountain) a high mountain and was shown all the kingdoms of the world and the glories of those kingdoms in a moment of time. It implies that Jesus was shown in a split-second of time all of the kingdoms, empires, and dominions of the world: past, present, and future. It was meant to appeal to Jesus' natural man's vanity to rule and his ego for power. Complete rulership and dominance was offered him if he gave his allegiance to the self-proclaimed Prince of the kingdoms of the earth, Satan. How this revelation of past, present, and future was achieved, we do not know. What mountain was used, we do not know. Many theologians during the first 10 centuries after Christ's resurrection did not feel that this mountain was located in the area of Judaea at all. Consequently, it could have been any mountain in the world; Mount Sinai, Mount Everest, Pikes Peak in America, or even Mount Ararat [this was von Dohnaniy's personal choice]. Again, Jesus overcame the temptation by quoting Deuteronomy. This time it was Deuteronomy 6:13 and 10:20. *"Thou shalt fear the Lord thy God, and serve him, and shalt swear by his name"* (Deuteronomy 6:13). *"Thou shalt fear the Lord thy God; him shalt thou serve, and to him shalt thou cleave, and swear by his name"* (Deuteronomy 10:20).

In the final of the three temptations Jesus was taken to the holy city (Luke identifies this city as Jerusalem, Matthew does not identify the city), and was invited to stand on a pinnacle of a temple, and was ordered to cast himself down, because God would send his angels to protect him. It has been argued that Herod's Temple had no pinnacle, so this could not have been Herod's Temple, but this does not mean that Jesus could not have been taken to any other "holy site" in Jerusalem (Jerusalem at this time had many "holy" temples and places of worship representing numerous religions, religious practices, and religious philosophies). Also, it has been argued that this temptation may not have happened in physical Jerusalem at all, but rather in a location that was considered to be a holy place, hence the term "Holy Jerusalem," implying a place that was holy to God or to spiritual powers and spiritual authorities in general.

If this is true, Jesus could have been taken to any number of cities that had temples or places of worship or to any site that was considered "holy." There has been much justifiable speculation over the centuries that Jesus was taken to the top of the Great Pyramid in Egypt, for thousands of years proclaimed by many in the ancient world to be the most "holy" site in the world.

Of course all of this is speculation and serves nothing more than to increase further speculation and to isolate opinions. To prevent such speculation and opinions from becoming tools that can be used to discredit or cast doubt upon the accurate record and the authenticity of the Gospels, we must be satisfied to conclude that Jesus had to go through a long period of physical and emotional turmoil and temptation—turmoil and temptation that was designed to, and had the potential of, destroying his mission to mankind. That the temptation served as a test wherein Jesus successfully overcame all odds and obstacles and victoriously launched himself into the commission for which he was chosen, seems obvious, von Dohnaniy concluded.

He then continued. "This fact is more than obvious from the view-point of the 2nd century Jewish historian/medical doctor, Ekaba of Tiberias, when he wrote in his essay, *Non-truth of Jesus as Messiah*, '...Jesus came back from his forty days' retirement with a scheme of religion entirely new. It differed from everything that had gone before in being spiritual and universal...his pupils claimed that the Law was given by Moses, but grace and truth came by Jesus after his forty days of retirement and years of isolation and training...But the system that he proposed, though perfect in its ideals within itself, existed nowhere but in his own mind...thus he launched upon the world a religious scheme that was good, but one that would not or could not work within the framework of the existing religious scheme.'"

After his days of temptation, von Dohnaniy continued, the Gospels record nothing more about him for three years (until AD 26), except that he increased in the power of the Spirit (Luke 4:14), and in wisdom and stature, and in favor with both God and men (Luke 2:52).

What Jesus did during this three-year period is not known. Perhaps he stayed at home in Nazareth and helped his father with the construction business. Perhaps he traveled throughout the country getting acquainted with and becoming friends with many of the Roman officials, Herodians, Jewish officials, and religious officials, or maybe he returned to school. Maybe he used this time to get to know his friends and relatives more intimately. Some claim that he followed John the Baptist and became one of his disciples.

Perhaps Jesus became involved in local politics. If so, he would have probably moved to a more politically conducive atmosphere such as Sepphoris (the capital of the Galilee), Scythopolis (the administrative capital of the Decapolis), or Capernaum (the regional center of commerce). For centuries many Bible historians believe that during this three-year period, Jesus traveled throughout the Roman Empire, the Near East (Egypt, Syria, Armenia, Asia, Parthorum, etc.), the Middle East (India, Persia, etc.,) and the Far East, learning and gaining knowledge. They claim that this is the reason why the Gospels seem to imply that he was not well known in the region of the Galilee. That is why the people, even among his followers, asked and questioned who he was and where he was from. In fact, this idea was alluded to in letter number three, of the famous *Hillel Scrolls* written by Hillel the Third.

In that letter Hillel wrote, "...afterward this Jesus from the Galilee returned from the days of his retirement...and in order to mature his former training in the histories and in the philosophies of the Grecians, the Romans, and of the Egyptians...he felt it time to sojourn in the east, so to learn from the great thinkers of Zoroaster, the magi of Chaldea, and the rhijas of Arabia and of the Indias..."

Another document indicates that he either went the opposite direction, or else he traveled to both regions and each record only records the travels of one segment of his over-all journey.

A 1st century Roman named Lucius, von Dohnaniy continued, who was a Senator under Claudius, wrote in a letter commenting on Claudius' expulsion of the Jews from Rome, [a letter that is currently (1940's) secure in the Chancel of Roman Archives in Compioni, Italy]

> "...they (the Jews) are a people who are totally void of honor and pride. None must be allowed to inhabit the same region as Romans. All but one has shown reason why they should not be eradicated from off of the earth. This one I received while on the imperial business of Tiberius Claudius Nero Caesar in Scythopolis during the expurgation of Sejanus. A one Jesus, the son by adoption of our Briton provincial Senator called in the barbarian tongue, Joseph, who served by appointment of Augustus as Imperial Minister of Mines, who (Jesus) was accused of treason and crucified for such offense by Judaean Procurator Pontius Pilate during the days of Tiberius, although I have found no cause for such means, but for the sake of the honor of Caesar, must be of necessity, who was contracted to build the Acreopolisium circus in Scythopolis. With talent that can only be compared to the greatest of that of Athenea and Egypt, he built the circus in two years that to others of his trade and race would have finished in five. So pleased was Coporius (the administrative governor of the Decapolis) that a feast in honor of the occasion of its completion was ordered for the Day of Augustus. This stonemason, Jesus, was to be celebrated. He refused the honor, instead was content to feast with the workers of his employ. My imperial representation was such that I could have demanded his honor, but chose to tribute instead his desire for no glory. Upon which time, through my persuasion, this stonemason, Jesus, accompanied me to Rome, where he lived in the home of his adopted father, Josephius Maximus (Joseph in the barbarian Jewish tongue, our Senator and Imperial Minister of Mines), and learned the ways of Rome and was taught in the histories of the world by the Senate historians and philosophers of my own choosing. I cannot but believe that had he not returned to his home region, the Galilee of Syria, at the time of the appointment of Pontius Pilate, he would have become a Senator in fact for

the Empire. Such a loss is to our regret and to the shame of the race of the Jews. For he and he alone is of all of his race worthy of life sustained."

A fact that may give a sense of authenticity to these speculations is that at this time in Roman history, trade routes had been established all over the known world. Roman merchandisers and traders had exploited virtually every corner of the known world.

According to *The Periplus of the Erythraen Sea*, a book written in the 1st century by either a Greek or Alexandrian sea captain that describes in detail the extent of Rome's first century trade ventures, Roman traders traveled from Japan to Spain and from Africa to Britain and to what is now northern Russia.

Consistent with Matthew 3:1-12, Mark 1:3-8, and Luke 3:2-18, von Dohnaniy continued, John the Baptist's ministry during the three years of silence in Jesus' life, reached such a height that literally thousands from all over the area came to hear him and to be baptized by him. "But whether Jesus was a part of that ministry is a notion that will probably never be corroborated."

With that statement, von Dohnaniy's concluded the portion of his book that dealt with Jesus' wilderness experience.

Another option that needs to be considered about the seemingly three "lost" years between Jesus' wilderness experience and the beginning of his ministry is the training that he had to have been followed in order to become a rabboni. It's quite logical to assume that the 5 years of mandatory rabboni training most likely included these three silent years.

I found a source that seemed to confirm the rabboni training speculation when I was studying at the library of the Albright Institute in Jerusalem, Israel.

There I discovered a book written in 1836 by Jacob Lowpinski, a rabbi from Poland who had turned Christian. The book was entitled *Rabbonis in Training*. It described the educational requirements and expectations of a rabbi who sought to advance to the position of rabboni.

As I skimmed the contents of the book, I settled upon the third chapter, a chapter entitled "Jesus' probable training." Lowpinski introduced the chapter by saying that Jesus' rabboni training partially took place during the so-called silent years, between his baptism and wilderness experience in AD 23 when he was 30 years old, and the beginning of his ministry in AD 26, when he was 33 years old.

Lowpinski continued by tracing the typical educational requirements that were necessary to become a rabboni, and then he used that factual information to draw a conjectural conclusion.

Lowpinski said that if a young student wanted to be a rabbi he had to enroll in one of the two available Rabbinate schools: the school of Hillel or the school of Shammi. For the next eight years the young man lived at the school and was taught the Law and the scriptures, the Mishan, the Midrash, the Torah, The Talmuds, Greek and Roman history, governmental regulations, Greek philosophy, and world religions.

After eight years, the student graduated from the Rabbinate school as a rabbi. He then remain an understudy to a local rabbi for five years before he was permitted to be an independent rabbi.

Upon graduation from the Rabbinate school, the top student in the class had to either begin his training to become a rabboni, or to begin his training to become a scribe—a lawyer of the Law.

If the graduate chose to begin training to become a rabboni, he had to submit to another five years of individual training by a personal tutor, a Rabban. Included in this individual training was extended travel with the Rabban to the world centers of civilization. At some point during this individual training time, the rabbi was expected to submit to the ordeal of baptism initiation and to a time of extended fasting—from 10 to 50 days—in total isolation (usually in the desert, the rugged hills of Judea, the wilderness of Peraea, or the rolling hills of the Galilee region). This was supposed to prepare him for his ineluctable service for God. After the five years of comprehensive personal training, the student had to go through an interrogation before the entire Sanhedrin. If he survived this brutal interrogation, the High Priest gave him the title of Rabboni (John 20:16). After becoming a rabboni, the student could choose to become a Rabban by submitting to an additional 12 years of training under the direct tutoring of the Rabboah of Innan, the highest level of Rabban authority.

If Jesus, Lowpinski continued, followed the traditional path of rabboni training, during those five years of intensive individual training, then Jesus was trained by a personal rabban. Two years into this training, Jesus would have submitted to the ordeal of the baptism initiation (obviously Jesus chose to have John the Baptist baptize him, which was his option. It did not matter to the rabban who performed the initiation. All that mattered was that the student submitted to the ordeal). In Jesus' case, the period of isolation and fasting lasted for at least 40 days and took place in the wilderness, perhaps in the wilderness of southern Judea. It was during this time that he went through his time of temptation. After these two experiences, if the typical rabboni training was followed, Jesus returned to the rabban and submitted to another three years of training, which included extensive travel to almost all of the centers of civilization through out the known world: Egypt, Parthia, Rome, Greece, Persia, Syria, and perhaps India. While at these centers of civilization, typically, the rabboni-in-training learned the culture, traditions, history, and religious philosophies of the land, from the rabban who was accompanying him as well as from native teachers.

I paused for a moment to think about what Lowpinski had written. If Lowpinski was correct, then there is a great probability that Jesus' baptism and subsequent fast and wilderness experience was part of his rabboni training. In fact it was a mandatory part of that training. If true then this certainly sheds a different light on why Jesus needed to be baptized. It had nothing whatsoever to do with his baptism being an example that we as Christians should follow, as the commonly accepted notion presumes. Whether he had ever sinned or not, baptism was a mandatory part of Jesus' five-year rabboni training. He had no choice if he wanted to fulfill his rabboni training requirements.

I then returned to paraphrasing *Rabbonis in Training*.

Lowpinski confirmed that Jesus most likely followed the typical rabboni training by referring to a letter that had been written in the 2nd century by a Jewish doctor named Ekaba, who alluded to the 1st century rabban, Hillel the Eminent.

Lowpinski quoted Ekaba, who quoted Hillel as saying, "Afterward, Jesus returned from his retirement and fasting ...and to mature his rabboni training in the histories and in the philosophies of Achaia, Rome, Egypt, Persia, and Hindus, his rabban felt it time for he and Jesus to sojourn in the eastern lands, to learn from the philosophers of Zoroaster, the magi of Chaldea, the rhijas of Arabia, and the shaman of the Indias..."

Lowpinski then gave his personal opinion concerning Jesus' so called three silent years of adulthood. "To me (Lowpinski) it seems quite obvious that the reason for the three years of silence was that Jesus was in the midst of his five years of rabboni training. He began that training two years before his baptism and time of isolation and it continued for three years after his baptism and wilderness isolation experience. Then upon completion of that rabboni training, Jesus again appeared on the scene, as a Rabboni, authorized and sanctioned by the High Priest."

After completing his personal comments, Lowpinski concluded the chapter, "Jesus' probable training," by briefly describing what was happening in the Roman Empire at the time that Jesus was in the midst of his five years of rabboni training. As I read Lowpinski's description, I was amazed at how closely his information matched the research data that I had already collected.

Lowpinski make clear that in Rome in AD 25, Sejanus accused the historian Cremutius Cordus of treason. Rather than face a humiliating trial, the great historian committed suicide. Sejanus then ordered all of Cremutius Cordus' works to be destroyed.

In the spring of AD 26, Pontius Pilate was appointed Roman Procurator of the province of Judaea. He ruled from the new port city of Caesarea Maritima, but maintained residences in Jerusalem, Scythopolis, and Antipatris. Pilate was a ruthless governor who regarded the Judaeans with utter contempt. That year the Jews of the Galilee and Judaea openly and violently rebelled against their Roman overlords. The rebellion was proliferated by Pilate when he set up images of Augustus and Tiberius in cities throughout the state of Judea, and when he brought images of the emperors into Jerusalem. These acts resulted in a riot, which Pilate suppressed with extreme ruthlessness.

Later that same year, Herod Antipas divorced his wife and married his niece, Herodias, the wife of his half-brother, Herod Philip of Rome. This act prompted John the Baptist to denounce Herod Antipas publicly for marrying Herodias, incestuously and illegally. Three years later, on January 3, AD 29, John the Baptist was beheaded.

Also that same year, Agrippina, the widow of Germanicus, the adopted brother of Tiberius, who publicly accused Tiberius of responsibility for the death of her husband, was arrested by order of Tiberius and was banished for life to Pandateria. Afterward Sejanus ordered the arrest and imprisonment of her sons, Nero and Drusus.

With that, Lowpinski concluded "Jesus' probable training," of his book *Rabbonis in Training.*

The Plain of Esdraelop located in the Galilee. The Roman military town of Nain was located on the slops of the hill in the far background. The ruins of the Augustan Way military highway is located at the foot of the hill running left to right----Israel.

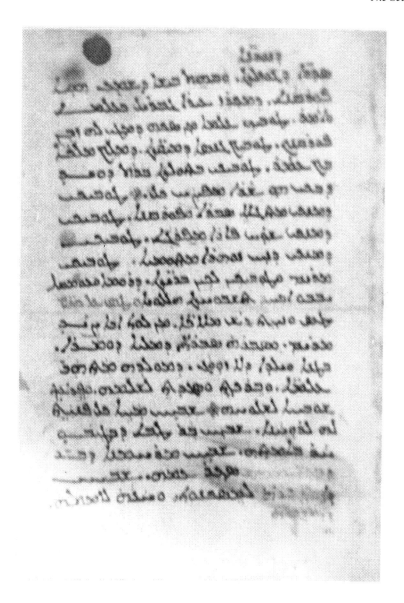

Original Syriac manuscript describing Gabriel's announcement to Mary that she will birth a son. It was written by Eusebius of Caesarea in about the year AD 330—Armenia.

The pyramid of Khafra (foreground) and the Great Pyramid of Cheops (behind)—Egypt.

The village of Hallstatt. Salt mines located in the mountains overlooking Hallstatt provided Rome with more than half of her annual salt needs during the reigns of Julius Caesar, Augustus, Tiberius, and Caligula—Austria.

Dr. Ron Charles

A modern Israeli military installation located on the ancient salt flats of the Dead Sea (Salt Sea). More than half of the state of Judea's tax load to Rome was paid in salt—Israel

The Search

The Rhine River near where Julius Caesar encouraged his troops with his "yoke is easy" speech on the night before they crossed the river to conquer the remainder of Gaul----Germany.

The city of Jerusalem looking west from the Mount of Olives—Israel.

The Dome of the Rock built over the ancient site of the Jewish Temple of worship in Jerusalem. It is the second most holy site for Muslims—Israel.

Dr. Ron Charles

Ruins of the walls of Herod's Temple in Jerusalem are in the background. Ruins of a Byzantine wall are in the middle, and ruins from the crusades era are in the foreground—Israel.

The Search

The Sea of Galilee looking east from Tiberias. The Golan Heights is in the background—Israel.

The southern outlet of the Sea of Galilee looking east—Israel

The Search

Ruins of a synagogue in Capernaum. The visible ruins date back to the 3rd century AD, but the foundation dates to the time of Jesus—Israel.

The Jordan River just south of the southern outlet of the Sea of Galilee—Israel.

The probable wilderness where Jesus was tempted. It is located near the Dead Sea—Israel.

Dr. Ron Charles

Continuing archaeological investigations in Jericho—Israel.

City walls of Jerusalem constructed by Herod the Great—Israel.

The Garden of Gethsemane on the Mount of Olives—Israel.

The Search

The Via Dolorosa in Jerusalem. The route that tradition says Jesus took to the place of crucifixion—Israel.

The hill traditionally identified as Mount Calvary by Protestants—Israel.

The Search

The valley of Gehenna as it looks today. It was in Gehenna that Jesus was crucified. It was the garbage dump of Jerusalem during the time of Jesus—Israel.

The Garden Tomb or Gordon's Tomb. Many Protestants believe that this could be the tomb of Jesus—Israel.

The Search

The resting place in the Garden Tomb where the body was placed—Israel.

The traditional site of the Upper Room in Jerusalem. Here, according to tradition, is where Jesus and his disciples had the Last Supper and where the church was established on the Day of Pentecost when those who were gathered there were filled with the Holy Ghost. The existing structure dates to the 12th century. However, the foundations of the structure may date to the time of Jesus—Israel.

The Search

The Eastern Gate in Jerusalem. It is through this gate that tradition says the Messiah will enter Jerusalem at the end of the age—Israel.

Dr. Ron Charles

A crusader castle foundation in Jerusalem—Israel.

The Search

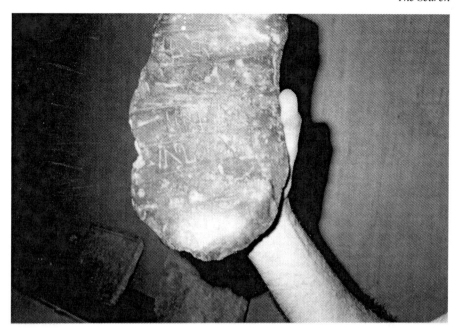

A burial stella identifying the burial place of Titus, indicating that he had died because of his refusal to deny Christ in the circus (amphitheater) of Dyrrhachium—Albania.

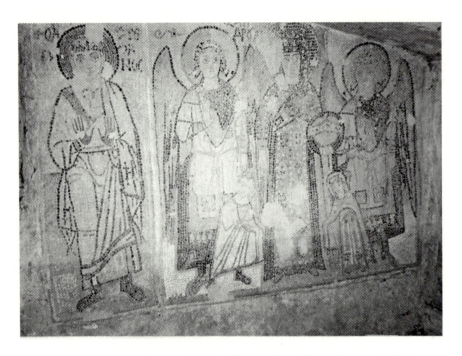

Byzantine mosaics in the amphitheater of Dyrrhachium dedicated to those who had lost their lives for the cause of Christ. Titus is depicted at the foot of Gabriel, the angel in the middle—Albania.

XV
FIRST YEAR OF MINISTRY

(AD 26)

In the Spring of the year AD 26, the year that Jesus' executioner, Pontius Pilate, became Procurator of the Roman province of Judaea, probably sometime after his 33rd birthday, Jesus completed his rabboni training (a man had to be at least 33 years old before he could hold the position as rabboni and be officially recognized by the High Priest as a rabboni).

Upon completion of his training and his becoming a High Priest accredited rabboni (John 20:16), Jesus left his home in the Galilee and journeyed to Bethabara, where John the Baptist, the person who had solemnized his (Jesus') rabboni initiation baptismal ritual three years previously, was still preaching and baptizing (John 1:28). There John looked at Jesus and announced to himself and to those standing near, *"Behold the Lamb of God!"* John 1:29-40). Afterwards, he returned to the Galilee (John 1:43, Luke 4:16) to continue his ministry.

The *"Behold the Lamb of God!"* pronouncement was shortly followed by Jesus' call of the first of his disciples: Philip (John 1:43), a Greek from the city of Bethsaida, in the Galilee, with whom Jesus had probably been acquainted for some time.

While researching at the University of California at Los Angeles (UCLA), I found an excellent resource that discussed in detail the events surrounding John the Baptist's *Behold the Lamb of God* proclamation and the calling of Jesus' first disciples.

I spent a number of hours studying in the university library's rare books and documents section before discovering a book that can only be described as extraordinary. The book was entitled *The Calling*. It was a rare leather-bound volume written by the historical theologian, Fredrick Shelley of Scotland, in 1822, and was published in 1851 by Shelley's grandson, after his (Shelley's) death. The book so rare that there are only 30 copies known to exist. The UCLA library had one of the 30.

The book was about 450 pages in length. In it Shelley described the calling of the first disciples of 40 different leaders. These leaders included Jesus, Lao-tzu, Confucius, Siddhartha Gautama (known as Buddha), Zoroaster, Plato, Francis of Assisi, Zeno, and others. Of course, the portion that interested me most was the section dealing with Jesus' calling of his first disciples. Shelley claimed to have gotten his information from ancient sources, but he did not identify those sources. So, although the information seemed bona fide, with no distinguishing sources, I was left to speculate on the credibility of Shelley's information.

I read the section that dealt with Jesus' first disciples through once and then went back and read it a second time. This second time through I took paraphrased notes.

Shelley began his section on Jesus by stating that John the Baptist was typical of the hermit desert dwellers of his day. He wore a loin garment made of camel leather and ate the common desert dwellers' food. He preached that entrance into the kingdom of God was by repentance only and that public baptism was necessary to show true repentance.

According to the Gospel of John, chapter 1, verse 28, Jesus left the Galilee and went to see John the Baptist near Bethabara Beyond Jordan, on the east side of the Jordan River.

Whether Bethabara Beyond Jordan was a location, a region, or a village is not known. The 29th verse seems to imply that the day that Jesus arrived, John did not see him, or if he did see him, he did not recognize him. This would have been logical because he had not seen Jesus since he had baptized him some three years previously.

It was not until the next day, when Jesus returned to the same place, that John the Baptist saw him, and seemed to recognize him. Verse 31 implies that John did not know him (Jesus) when he had baptized him (Jesus) three years before. But this time, he did recognize Jesus and realized that he had been sent from God to fulfill a specific mission for the redemption of man from sin. It was on this day, the second day, when Jesus went to where John was baptizing, that John made a silent proclamation to himself, *"Behold the Lamb of God which taketh away the sin of the world."*

After John recognized him, it is apparent that again Jesus left the area.

Then the third day, Jesus again returned to where John was baptizing. Jesus was probably there for quite some time, unknown to John. At about 4:00 in the afternoon (John 1:39) as Jesus turned and began to walk away, John saw him. However, this time, when John saw Jesus, he proclaimed openly and loudly enough so that at least two, perhaps more, of his disciples heard him, *"Behold the Lamb of God!"*

Jesus did not stop. He kept walking, but as he walked on, two of John's disciples (one was named Andrew [a Greek name] and the name of the other is not known) who had heard their master proclaim *"Behold the Lamb of God"* began to follow Jesus. Seeing them following him, Jesus turned around and asked them what they wanted. They responded by asking him, "Where do you live? or Where are you staying?" Jesus told them to follow him and he would show them. Apparently they stayed with Jesus the remainder of the day.

Later that evening, or perhaps a couple of days later, Andrew found his brother, Simon Peter (Simon was a typical Hebrew name, but Peter was a Greek name. Since Andrew was also a Greek name, there seems to be an indication that Simon and Andrew's mother may have been Greek. It was a common practice at that time that if the father and mother were from two different races or ethnic cultures, the oldest son would have a first name of the father's heritage background, and a second name of the mother's. The second son would have the first name of the mother's heritage background and if he had a second name, it would be from the father's background. So, if Simon was the oldest son and Andrew the second son, and if their father was of Hebrew heritage [the father's name was Jonas, a Hebrew name. This indicates that Simon and Andrew's father was probably of Hebrew heritage.] and the mother of Greek heritage, then the oldest son would have a Hebrew first name and a Greek

The Search

second name; and the second son would have a Greek first name. Thus, the brothers were named Simon [Hebrew] Peter [Greek] and Andrew [Greek]).

Simon may have been in John's company or Andrew may have had to go all the way back into the Galilee, where he lived, to get him, this is unknown. What is known is that Andrew found Simon Peter and told him that they had found *Messias*, or the Christ. Although Simon Peter might not have been convinced, he was curious enough to follow his brother to where Jesus was staying. There Andrew introduced Simon to Jesus.

Jesus responded to Andrew's introduction by telling Andrew's brother that though his name was *Simon*, meaning a reed, in the future he would be called *Cephas*, an Aramaic word that means a chip of granite rock. It was not until two years later that Jesus began to address Simon by the name of Cephas. This reed to rock analogy as it pertained to Simon became Jesus' living allegorical teaching statement and an example representing a believer's spiritual maturity progression.

Following Andrew's introduction, Simon and Jesus became friends. But contrary to tradition, Jesus did not call Simon to be his disciple at that time.

It is unknown whether Andrew, Simon, and the other disciple of John, (the one who is not named), spent the night with Jesus. What is certain is that the next day, the day after Jesus met Simon, he (Jesus) left the area and traveled back into the Galilee.

There in the Galilee, perhaps in the city of Bethsaida, he (Jesus) actively searched for and found Philip, a Greek. Philip was from the city of Bethsaida, the home city of Andrew and Simon.

The fact that Jesus searched for Philip indicates that he probably knew Philip and that he (Jesus) purposely searched for him until he found him.

Upon finding him, he (Jesus) asked him (Philip) to be his disciple by saying "*Deute poiso mou*" (*come after me*—This was a typical 1st century formal invitation that a Galilean rabboni made to a potential disciple or student). It seems to be quite ironic that the first disciple called by Jesus was neither a religious leader nor a Jew; he was a Greek—very unusual!!

Whether Philip joined Jesus immediately is not known, although John 1:45 seems to imply that Philip did not join him immediately. Instead he searched for and found his friend, a nathanael (*Nathanael* was not a proper name; it was a title), perhaps named Bartholomew (Matthew 10:3) meditating under a fig tree, probably in Bethel.

A *nathael* was a rabbi who had been approved to begin his preparation for the priesthood; a *nathanael* was a rabbi who was in the midst of his training for the priesthood. He had already completed his schooling and was a practicing apprentice to a priest.

Priesthood legend says that the nathanael who had been chosen by God to become the High Priest, who would recognize the Messiah, would be given a vision as a confirmation that he had been selected. The vision was supposed to be given by God while the nathanael was sitting and meditating under a certain fig tree, called the "tree of meditation," in Bethel, the supposed place where Jacob had his vision of a stairs or a ladder reaching to heaven, with angels ascending and descending the stairs or ladder. The vision that the nathanael was supposed to have was one in which he would see Jacob's ladder and the angels ascending and descending.

If he had this vision while meditating under the tree of meditation, it was a sign that he had been selected by God to be the one who would recognize the Messiah, and who as the High Priest would represent or be a spokesman for the Jewish people to the Messiah. Every nathanael for the past 300 years who had a deep desire to become that High Priest had followed this ritual.

This nathanael, the friend of Philip, was no different than any of the other hundreds who had sat under the same fig tree in Bethel before him, except that this nathanael was the one that had been selected to receive a special introductory revelation: the revelation of that long awaited redeemer.

When Philip found the nathanael, he told him that they had found the one about whom Moses and the prophets had written, the Messiah (Deuteronomy 18:15-18), in the person of Jesus of Nazareth.

The nathanael responded by quoting a familiar annotation of that day, "Can anything good come out of Nazareth?"

Philip did not respond to the "tongue-in-cheek" pun; he simply told him to come and see.

The statement by the nathanael was a well-known joke in Syria at that time; a joke that had a historical basis. It seems that during the days of the kings of Israel, the shear cliffs that were in the area that became known as Nazareth, was the primary site where limestone was quarried until the Assyrian and Babylonian conquests. During the days of the Jewish captivity, there was no quarrying done in this area.

But, during the time of Alexander the Great, quarrying was renewed in order to supply building materials for Alexander's building projects. A tower, a *nazarat*, was constructed on top of one of the cliffs, overlooking the Great Plain (the Plain of Esdraelon) to guard and oversee the quarrying endeavors. Eventually, a small community arose around the tower whose inhabitants were employed in the quarrying of the limestone. The community became known as "the house of the tower", or *Nazaratha*. The term was later shortened to *Nazareth*.

After the death of Alexander the Great, the quarrying, though not completely halted, was greatly reduced. But by then, the small community had grown into a small village. To insure that the village maintained its existence, even though the quarrying, which was the lifeline of the community, had diminished, the village inhabitants began to encourage the surrounding communities to discard the carcasses of animals that had died and the refuse from animal slaughtering in the old abandoned quarry pits around the village of Nazareth. These communities would pay to have the animal carcasses and waste eliminated. As a result, Nazareth became known as an animal carcass and waste disposal site.

Within two hundred years, Nazareth would evolve into *the* major refuse and disposal site for not only the Galilee, but for Judea and Samaria, and for all of Syria as well. The people of the town made a good living by working in the quarries (about 20 percent of the town's population worked in the quarries) and in the disposal sites (about 75 percent worked in the disposal sites). Some historians who lived during that time claim that the average citizen of Nazareth made more income than any other average citizen in any other city or town in all of the eastern empire. Some estimates claim that a resident worker of Nazareth made more money in one day than most residents in other cities made in five days. But this good living did not come without a price. Nazareth became *the* joke of Syria (hence, "does anything good come out of Nazareth?") and it became a derogatory slang word for anything that was despicable, dirty, diseased, putrefying, or unclean.

The citizens of Nazareth provided a great and undeniably necessary service to Syria and to Roman occupied Judaea, the Galilee, and the Decapolis; one in fact that was absolutely mandatory. The service rendered by Nazareth was so noteworthy that in the year AD 48, Caesar Claudius granted Roman citizenship to the city officials of Nazareth and to their families from that time forward and for all generations thereafter. Yet, it still was the butt end of countless jokes and vulgar statements. Judaea's and the Galilee's relationship with Nazareth became one of love-hate. They needed Nazareth, but hated what the city represented.

Another problem with the "garbage dump" was that because of the high level of lead contamination and bacteria putrefaction the area became a breeding ground for numerous diseases and infections, both physical and mental.

Thus, Nazareth became synonymous with both physical and mental sickness and disease, and its name became an annotation that referred to and described any plague, epidemic, and pestilence in the area.

When Jesus saw the nathanael, Philip's friend, Jesus spoke first and identified the nathanael as an Israelite indeed (this term was often used to identify dedicated priesthood students) with no guile, or with no deceit. It meant that this nathanael was outspoken, yet honest.

The nathanael questioned Jesus on how he knew him. Jesus responded and said that even before Philip found him under the fig tree, he saw him.

Jesus' response was enough to convince the nathanael that Jesus was the Son of God, the Messiah.

Jesus then told the nathanael that he would see great things, and that he would in fact see Jacob's ladder, the thing that all nathanaels longed to see in a vision, but that the angels would be descending upon him, Jesus. This meant that he, Philip's friend, had indeed recognized *The Messiah*, and that he, Jesus, was that Messiah.

This nathanael, the friend of Philip, is not referred to again in scripture unless he is in fact Bartholomew (John 21:2 lists a nathanael who was from Cana in Galilee—whether this was Philip's friend is doubtful, but it is possible. More than likely the nathanael mentioned in John 21 was a nathanael who joined the disciples after Jesus' death, but before his resurrection).

The Gospel of John never indicates that Jesus called this nathanael to be one of his disciples. It is assumed that he was, but it is not known for sure. If this nathanael was Bartholomew, then Jesus called him to be a disciple. If this is Bartholomew and if Jesus called him to be a disciple at this time, then he was the first Jew called, but the second disciple called.

"For argument's sake," Shelley wrote, "I will assume as fact that this nathanael was Bartholomew and that he was called to be Jesus' second disciple. Both he and Philip followed Jesus from that time forward.

It was not until August, AD 27, that Peter, Andrew, James, and John were called by Jesus to be his disciples, almost a year and a half after the call of Philip and Bartholomew (if this nathanael was Bartholomew)."

With that statement Shelley completed the portion of his book that dealt with Jesus' calling of his first disciples.

Soon after Jesus had asked Philip to be his first disciple and had confronted the nathanael, whose name was probably Bartholomew, the three of them traveled to Jesus' home town, Nazareth, which seemingly was not Bartholomew's favorite town in the Galilee. Because we do not know where they were when they began their journey, we don't know how long it took them to get to Nazareth. They could have already been somewhere in the Galilee or they could have been back in Judaea near Bethel.

On a Sabbath, after their arrival in Nazareth, Jesus and the two disciples went to one of the local synagogues. There in the synagogue, Jesus, as was his privilege ever since he had been consecrated a rabboni by the High Priest, stood and addressed the worship participants.

While researching at the School of Theology library of the University of Leipzig, I came across some enlightening manuscripts. One of the manuscripts, written by Jacques LeFèvre, addressed this event in a synagogue in Nazareth.

The University of Leipzig was spread all over downtown Leipzig, Germany. During the divided Germany days, Leipzig had been the 2nd largest city in East Germany. At that time and still today, the University of Leipzig was/is one of Europe's premier universities. More known for its superior music and biological sciences education, I was surprised to find listed on the main university directory, a School of Theology. The school was located on Email-Fusch Street, a short distance southeast of the Rosental Zoo, which was a good ways (too far to comfortably walk) northwest of the main campus. Although it was not the best school of theology I had ever visited, considering that for decades the university had been held hostage to the philosophies of communism, both the school and its small but superb library, were quite impressive.

In 1523 Jacques LeFèvre, a historian who was serving at the university in Paris, wrote a manuscript that addressed Jesus' Sabbath day synagogue confrontation with the residents of Nazareth. According to the accompanying manuscript background information, the surviving two-pages of the manuscript were the only pages remaining of LeFèvre's larger 34-page French translation of an original 40-page Latin manuscript.

The Langobard, Paulus Diaconus, a court historian for Charlemagne, had written the original Latin text entitled *Christos de Admonito*, in 789. Diaconus had bound the 40-leaves between gold-plated cedar boards and presented it to Charlemagne as a Christmas gift. *Christos de Admonito* was a collection of stories, based on historical fact, of Jesus' life while he lived in Nazareth. The surviving two pages of LeFèvre translation of the original Latin text dealt with Paulus Diaconus' record and his analysis of what happened at the synagogue in Nazareth when Jesus returned to Nazareth after his baptism by John the Baptist.

The Search

The portion of the Gospel of Luke that Diaconus used as his text was chapter 4, verses 16-30. I won't quote the entire text; just enough to get an idea of what Diaconus is talking about.

> *"And he came to Nazareth, where he had been brought up: and as his custom was, he went into the synagogue on the Sabbath day, and stood up for to read. And there was delivered unto him the book of the prophet Esaias. And when he had opened the book, he found the place where it is written, the spirit of the Lord is upon me.... And he closed the book, and he gave it again to the minister, and sat down...and he began to say unto them, 'This day is this scripture fulfilled in your ears'.... And they said, 'Is not this Joseph's son?' And he said unto them, 'Ye will surely say unto me this proverb, physician, heal thyself: whatsoever we have heard done in Capernaum, do also here in thy country. And he said, verily I say unto you, no prophet is accepted in his own country'.... And all they in the synagogue, when they heard these things, were filled with wrath...." (Luke 4:16-30).*

I will paraphrase LeFëvre's translation of Diaconus' *Christos de Admonito*.

How long Jesus and his two disciples were in Nazareth before they visited the synagogue on a particular Sabbath day, is not known. What is known is: (1) because of Jesus' rabboni position, he was allowed to actively participate in Sabbath ceremonies; (2) apparently Jesus had been participating in these Sabbath ceremonies since his return to Nazareth after completing his rabboni training and his being anointed a rabboni; and (3) that on that particular Sabbath, as was his custom since his return from rabboni training, Jesus, accompanied by his two disciples, went to the synagogue to participate in the Sabbath ceremony.

The ceremony progressed typically and smoothly that Sabbath day up until the time that Jesus spoke.

A typical Sabbath day ceremony of Jesus' day began with the congregation (men and women were separated) standing in the sanctuary and chanting psalms. Afterwards, an elder in the community, wrapped in his *tallith* (prayer shawl), began to read from the Ten Commandments. This was followed by the pronouncement of the *Shema* (the prayer of Hebrew monotheism), which was composed of passages from the Pentateuch. When the prayer was complete, the same elder chanted the *berakoth* (benedictions—today called the *Shemoneh Esreh* or the Eighteen Benedictions). After each benediction was pronounced, the standing congregation responded by saying in unison, "Amen." The service then ended with the *Bareku*, one of the Jew's oldest prayers, the elder and the congregation speaking alternately. After this, the *shammash* (the sacristan of the synagogue) took from a wooden *aron* (an ark or wooden chest) a parchment scroll of the Pentateuch and the prophets, and located the place where the oral reading should begin. He then waited for a rabboni (if a rabboni was not present, a rabbi would be acceptable; if neither a rabboni nor a rabbi were present an elder male member of the congregation could qualify) to volunteer to read from the parchment. The readings were to be presented in order, from one Sabbath to the other, as prescribed and dictated by the High Priest in

Jerusalem. All synagogues everywhere read the same passages on any given Sabbath. It was estimated that it would take 12 years to finish reading the entire parchment scroll in the order in which the High priest had dictated. After reading the text, the rabboni would be seated and would make comments about the text and then entertain questions regarding his comments. Afterwards, the congregation was dismissed.

On this particular Sabbath, Jesus, the rabboni, volunteered to read and to make comments. The *shammash* handed Jesus the scroll opened to the passage in Isaiah that was scheduled to be read on that Sabbath. But instead of reading the pre-selected High Priest dictated passage, Jesus searched for and found another passage that he wanted to read. The portion was a Messianic prophecy uttered by Isaiah over 750 years before that time, the portion that we now identify as Isaiah 61:1-2. After he read the passage of Isaiah, he rolled-up the scroll, handed it back to the *shammash*, sat down, and prepared to make comments.

The people were quite surprised that Jesus had read a text out of order and they did not understand why he had done it. What Jesus had done could have been perceived as an act of defiance, that carried with it a penalty that would have banned him from participating in rituals and ceremonies conducted in that synagogue for the rest of his life),

After he had seated himself, his first words were that this 750-year-old prophecy had been fulfilled in him that very day, before their very eyes. In essence, he was saying to his home town neighbors and friends, that this prophecy relating to the Messiah, voiced by Isaiah over 750 years before—a prophecy that had been preached and whose fulfillment had been expected for more than seven centuries—had that day been fulfilled in him, a young man who they all knew and who's father was Joseph, with whom they were closely associated.

The fact that the people asked whether Jesus was Joseph's son, LeFëvre continued, a question that was asked in present tense, indicated that Joseph was probably still alive. It is unlikely that Joseph was present that Sabbath in the synagogue.

If we look at this event logically, Jesus made some major mistakes if he had any desire to make a good impression or if he wanted to increase his following or be accepted by the local residence and the local religious community.

His first mistake was when he read the scriptures out of order. The second was made when (in verse 23) he quoted a well-known proverb. The proverb was not just any proverb; it was a proverb of Cicero, a well-respected "pagan" Roman Senator who had died in 43 BC. The occasion for Cicero's proverb was documented, and was well known by even the most uneducated of the residents of Nazareth. The occasion, on which this proverb was first spoken, was Cicero's defense before the Roman Senate in 51 BC, when he was accused of disloyalty by Mark Antony (who later had Cicero murdered). When asked by Antony why he, Cicero, felt that he had the ability to preserve (soothe or massage with ointment) the tormented souls of the beleaguered and floundering citizens of Rome, Cicero replied, "You, my most esteemed Antony, will say of me, 'Physician (embalmer or preserver) preserve your own self, not us. For what you have heard done in Capri, do so as well in Rome.'" (Cicero had been sent to Capri by Julius Caesar in an attempt to secure the loyalty of the region. They had initially pledged their support to Pompey during the civil war. In Capri, Cicero had not only prevented a riot by his oratory, but he had convinced them to pledge their allegiance to Caesar rather than to Pompey.) So moved was the Roman Senate by Cicero's defense that he was unanimously acquitted of all suspicion.

Jesus used this same proverb, changing the name of Capri to Capernaum and the name of Rome to his own country. But the intent was left unchanged.

It was bad enough that Jesus defended his actions, but to use within the holy sanctuary of the synagogue, a proverb of the pagan Roman Senator Cicero in his defense to justify his actions, was inexcusable. In essence, Jesus felt like he was being condemned without cause, just like Cicero felt he had been condemned without cause.

But Jesus did not stop there for in verse 24 he rubbed salt into the open wound by making his third calculated "mistake." He quoted a well-known aphorism originally spoken in 335 BC by the renowned pagan Greek philosopher Aristotle when he said, "No prophet is accepted in his own country." How dare Jesus quote a pagan Greek philosopher in the very midst of the holy synagogue?

But he wasn't finished yet, for then he had the audacity to compare himself with and to claim equality with two of the greatest and most respected prophets in all of Jewish history: Elijah and Elisha. He finally ended his barrage by saying that just like Elijah was not sent to a Jewish widow, but rather, to a pagan widow from the pagan Phoenician city of Sidon; and Elisha was not chosen to heal a Jew of leprosy, but rather, he was chosen to heal a commanding general of pagan Syria, so they, the people of his own community will be rejected by God in favor of pagan people and pagan nations and that the pagans were far more qualified to receive the blessings of God than they, the ones who called themselves, *God's chosen people* (so taught the Pharisees).

After that the people rushed Jesus and seized him, intending to throw him off of a cliff into one of the quarry pits. Had they succeeded in their attempt, Roman citizen or not, they would have been called into question for killing another Roman citizen.

But the Bible records, *"he passing through the midst of them went his way."*

How he escaped this sure death, is not known. But it happened. How was it accomplished? All that is know for sure is that it must have been done through a miraculous, an unexplainable, and beyond natural mechanism that by-passed both the laws of time and space.

With that statement, Lefèvre's manuscript of the rewrite of Paulus Diaconus' *Christos de Admonito* ended. It's unfortunate that only two pages of his translation had survived.

After this event at the synagogue in Nazareth, the Gospels are silent regarding Jesus' life until the late summer of that year, AD 26. It was then that he and his two disciples attended a wedding ceremony in Cana, just north of his hometown of Nazareth. The Gospel of John says that it was at this wedding that Jesus performed his first miracle: turning water into wine.

Although I found scores, perhaps even hundreds, of stories, commentaries, sermons, and assumptions that attempted to shed light on the unusual events surrounding the wedding in Cana and Jesus' first miracle, none was more bizarre than the document I found, as if by predetermination, as I was driving through the town of Antakya in southern Turkey.

I had left Iskenderun, Turkey mid-morning on a Sunday, planning to drive the 40 or so miles, up the steep, narrow, and winding mountain road to the town of Antakya (also called Hatay), located on the Orontes River, not far from the Syrian border. Antakya, the New Testament city of Antioch, is the capital of Turkey's Hatay province. The city (Antioch) was founded in 300 BC by Seleucus I. Pompey the Great conquered it for Rome in 64 BC. By 40 BC it had become a very important trade center for the eastern Roman Empire.

It remained a major economic and trade center for first the Roman Empire, then the Eastern Roman Empire (Byzantine Empire), the Crusaders, the Seljukes, and finally the Ottoman Empire for more than one thousand six hundred years, before its commerce importance began to decline. Because the modern city only occupies a small portion of the original city, numerous Greek, Roman, Crusader, and Ottoman ruins and remains can still be seen. I intended to stop for a while in Antakya and visit some of the ruins, and then continue on my way toward the Syrian border. However, as I drove through the town on my way to the ruins, just as I passed an old mosque, I had a flat.

I pulled into a vacant lot next to the mosque and began to prepare to change the flat. But, I discovered that there was no air in my spare tire. It was Sunday and although most of the town residents were Muslim, whose holy day is Friday, the town still honored Sunday as a holy day for Christians. This had been dictated and decreed by Mehmet the Conqueror as a memorial to the historical part that the city played in preserving the Christian faith against overwhelming and in some cases seemingly insurmountable odds. That decree was still being honored after more than 500 years. However, it was bad for me because all the businesses in town were closed, which meant that I was stuck. I had no way of getting the tire repaired, no way of getting air for the spare, and no way of buying a new tire until the next day, Monday.

There was no one around, and I had no idea if there were any hotels around. I locked the car and started walking toward the mosque. When I got just about even with a door leading into the mosque (it was not the main entrance but a door near the main entrance) the door opened from inside, hitting me and startling me. The man who had opened the door from inside had not seen me, so when the door hit me, he was startled too. After we had both figured out what had happened, we had a good laugh.

The man recognized that I was either European or American, so he spoke to me in a formal style of English that made my English seem yokel. It soon became obvious that this man was much more clever and genteel than I had originally assumed.

He first introduced himself. His name was Amad. He was the mullah or "priest" at that mosque. The mosque was originally an Orthodox church that had been built in the 6th century. Its original name was the Church of Saint Barnabas. Mehmet the Conqueror had turned it into a mosque back in the 15th century. I responded to his introduction by introducing myself.

The Search

He asked if he could help me, so I told him about my tire problem. Amad said that everything was closed and that I would not be able to get the tire repaired until the next morning. I asked him where the closest hotel was located, but he responded by saying that because I had broken down in front of the mosque, that it was a sign that Allah demanded that he (Amad) take care of me. He told me that I must come to his home, eat his food, and would stay with him and his wife until the tire was repaired. I dared not offend him, so I accepted his invitation/demand. We became good friends that day.

We walked back to the car, where I picked up my duffel bag "suitcase" and briefcase. While I was getting these, I noticed that Amad had crossed the street and was talking to a young man. Within a couple of minutes both of them crossed the street and walked over to the car where I was waiting. Amad introduced me to the young man, his name was Izerim, and told me that he (Izerim) had consented to watch the car for the rest of the evening until we returned the next morning. I later found out that Amad had paid Izerim the equivalent of about $20 US to stay there all night and watch the car.

We then walked to Amad's house, which was about four blocks from the mosque. As we walked, Amad asked me why I was in Antakya. I told him that I was an American historical researcher and that I was on my way to Syria, but that I first wanted to stop and visit the old ruins of Antioch.

He asked me what I was researching. I told him that I was searching for information that would help me to confirm the Gospels concerning the life of Jesus.

Just before we entered Amad's home, we stopped and he told me that since I was a historian searching of information about Jesus, he wanted to show me an ancient manuscript that he had found almost 30 years ago, when a gas explosion damaged part of the foundational structure of the mosque. He explained that one of the support columns in the lower basement of the mosque was badly damaged by the explosion, and that while he was surveying the damage, he found a small cavity that had been concealed for centuries by the column.

Inside the cavity he found a pottery jar containing two parchment scrolls and one fleece manuscript. He said that both the scrolls and the sheepskin manuscript were written in Greek. Amad said that he never told anyone about the scrolls and manuscript for fear that they might be confiscated. During the next 10 years or so, he deciphered and translated into Turkish the fleece manuscript and one of the scrolls.

After Amad had explained how he had found the artifacts, we both entered his home. He introduced me to his wife, Betra, and told her in English (obviously for my benefit) that I would be staying with them for a day or two. She bowed her head in submissive agreement and then walked quickly and quietly to the back of the house to prepare a mid-afternoon lunch.

Amad excused himself and within about ten minutes returned carrying the two scrolls and the fleece manuscript. The scrolls were so fragile that I did not want to handle them, so I asked Amad to unroll one of them. As Amad attempted to unroll the one, pieces of the parchment broke off and crumpled beneath his touch. The one that he unrolled was the scroll that he had partially translated into Turkish.

I suspected that the scroll probably dated back to at least the time of the building of the church in the 6th century, for the jar that contained the scrolls and manuscript had been hidden beneath one of the original support columns of the church.

Amad explained that the scroll began with the author of the text introducing himself. "Apparently," Amad continued, "the scroll was a long letter that had been addressed to a group of people in the city of Patara in the small Roman regional province of Lycia, located on the Mediterranean Sea just south of the larger regional province of Galatia." Since I knew that an earthquake had destroyed the city of Patara in AD 93, the scroll had obviously been written some time before that time.

Amad explained that the author of the scroll letter was a man who identified himself as "Lucius of Iconium of Lycaonia, a slave and unworthy servant of my risen and living Master." Evidently Lucius was a 1st century Christian. In the part of the scroll that was most legible, was a message of encouragement to the worshippers in Patara, urging them to remain devoted in their faith, even to the point of death by decree of Emperor Domitian. Also decipherable was a eulogy to "our brother in the faith, Titus, who had been martyred in "the blood games of Domitian in the circus at Dyrrhachium."

I knew that ancient Dyrrhachium was present day Durres, Albania. Located in Durres were the ruins of a 1st century Roman amphitheater (circus) where local tradition claims St. Titus, the companion of Paul, was martyred. Dyrrhachium was the site of numerous 1st, 2nd, and 3rd century martyrs, and many were killed in the amphitheater games. The first record of Christian participation in the games at the amphitheater in Dyrrhachium was not until AD 86, during the emperorship of Domitian, a good nine years after the traditionally accepted date of the death of Titus. Although Titus may have been martyred in Dyrrhachium, he may or may not have been martyred in the amphitheater, as local legend claims. But, if there was any truth to the local Durres legend of Titus' martyrdom, the Titus eulogized in the scroll might be the same Titus who was martyred according to the Durres legend.

The scroll was fascinating, but the sheepskin manuscript interested me the most.

Amad unrolled the sheepskin manuscript as well as his Turkish translation of the manuscript and began to explain. "This sheepskin manuscript was written in Greek and appears to be a letter of petition addressed to the Roman state administrative magistrate located in the city of Sepphoris. Although this sheepskin manuscript was placed in the vault beneath the column before the column was set in place in the 6th century with the building of the Church of St. Barnabas, I feel that the style of writing is more compatible with 1st century Roman texts. So, the manuscript could date back to the time of Jesus' life."

Again I was amazed at Amad's sophistication and intelligent as he began reading his Turkish translation and I began taking paraphrased notes.

The letter requested that the Roman magistrate in Sepphoris intervene in a commercial dispute between a Jewish woman from the Galilee city of Nazareth and a Roman merchant from the Galilee city of Cana. It seems that the Jewish woman from Nazareth had ordered from the Roman wine merchant in Cana, 30 ephah (about 180 gallons or 660 liters) of wine, divided equally between *kalos* wine and *halos* wine (15 ephah of *kalos* wine and 15 ephah of *halos* wine), for the occasion of the wedding of her daughter which was scheduled to be held in Cana during the month of Elul (late summer, about August). The wine was to be delivered directly to the wedding celebration.

When the wine delivery was made, only 12 ephah (5 ephah of *kalos* and 7 ephah of *halos*) were delivered instead of 30, although the Jewish woman had in advance for 30 ephah. She wrote that this shortage of wine could have been troublesome had not her son, a rabboni and the older brother of the bride, produced an additional 27 ephah (162 gallons) of *kalos* wine. (She did not say how he produced the wine.) Afterward, she continued, when she returned to the Roman merchant with her son, the rabboni, and her husband, who owned a stonemasonry construction business in Nazareth, for remuneration of her money, the merchant, refused to make restitution. She went on to say that she and her rabboni son along with two other of his brothers were planning to move to Capernaum in order to expand their construction business to that city, so she not only requested on behalf of her husband permission from the magistrate for her, her rabboni son, and the two other brothers, to make the move to Capernaum in order to open-up a construction branch of the family business, but also begged his intervention into the dispute with the merchant in Cana so that the affair could be settled before their anticipated mid-winter move.

"Neither Mary's name nor Jesus' name," Amada continued, "were mentioned in the manuscript, yet the events that were recorded in the document were suspiciously similar to the events that took place at the marriage celebration at Cana, attended by Mary, Jesus and his disciples, and recorded in your Bible's Gospel of John, chapter 2."

I was amazed by the sheepskin manuscript and by how closely it resembled the story of the marriage at Cana. Whether the document was authentic or a very well crafted fabrication and embellishment will probably never be known. Nevertheless, Amada felt that chances were more favorable than not that the manuscript was either an original (AD 26) or a copy (probably about AD 35) of an original letter written by Mary the mother of Jesus, before she and Jesus' moved to Capernaum.

Although by now I should not have been surprised by anything concerning Amada, I was taken back to hear how well aquatinted this Muslim mullah was with the details concerning the story of the wedding at Cana and Jesus' miracle of turning water into wine performed at the wedding. Cana was located about seven or eight miles north of Nazareth and about three miles directly north of the Roman city of Sepphoris, the capital of the Galilee,

He said that the marriage traditions represented in the story of the marriage at Cana are still practiced in Muslim countries. He then took a few minutes and told me about the present day Muslim marriage traditions.

Afterwards, Amada continued his explanation of the wedding at Cana by quoting from memory (again to my surprise) the portion of John 2 that told about the marriage.

> "And the third day there was a marriage in Cana of Galilee; and the mother of Jesus was there: and both Jesus was called, and his disciples, to

> the marriage. And when they wanted wine, the mother of Jesus saith unto him, they have no wine. Jesus saith unto her, woman, what have I to do with thee? Mine hour is not yet come. His mother saith unto the servants, whatsoever he saith unto you, do it. And there were set there six water pots of stone, after the manner of the purifying of the Jews, containing two or three firkins apiece. Jesus saith unto them, fill the water pots with water.... this beginning of miracles did Jesus in Cana of Galilee...." (John 2:1-11).

According to this portion of the Christian holy writings," Amada said, "the marriage took place about three days after a conflict in a synagogue in Nazareth involving Jesus. Jesus and his two disciples attended the marriage. In this same portion of the Christian writings, it is stated that the mother of Jesus was there. The word that was translated *there* by the Anglo-Saxon translators of the King James Version of the Christian writings was the word *soryi*. The word meant "sponsor or patron or initiator." In this case the word was used to indicate that the mother of Jesus was the sponsor or the one in control of preparation—the one who was sponsoring and preparing the marriage celebration.

"If it is true that Mary was the sponsor of this marriage celebration, and if we look at the traditions in place at that time regarding Jewish marriage celebrations, then the celebration was in honor of the marriage of the daughter of Mary, the sister of Jesus.

"At that time," Amada continued, "According to tradition, the mother of the bride was the one who had the responsibility of organizing the marriage feast and preparing for the celebration. The celebration was normally held at the home of the parents of the groom, or at a place chosen by the parents of the groom. So, Mary was in charge of the celebration preparations. If the groom was from Cana, then the wedding celebration would be held in Cana.

"If tradition was honored by Mary and followed, then Jesus, the oldest brother, was responsible for giving the wedding feast benediction and the *"Be fruitful and multiply"* blessing to the newlyweds.

"Typically, the celebration and feast began at sun-up. At that time (at sun-up) the first of five courses of food—fresh and dried fruit, olives, bread, garlic seasoned olive oil, and cheese— was served with *kalos* wine. *Kalos* means "sweet, beautiful or clear." *Kalos* wine was sweet strained wine whose sugar had not yet turned to alcohol. This portion of the feast normally lasted most of the morning. Near mid- or late- morning, the second of the five courses—various vegetable, seed, and bean dishes— was served. Throughout the rest of the afternoon and evening the other three courses were served. All of the last four courses were served with *halos* wine. *Halos* means "less sweet or worse." The sugar in halos wine had begun to ferment into alcohol.

"After all five courses had been served, the older brother (in this case it would have been Jesus) stood and while addressing the couple, gave the feast benediction and the marriage blessing.

"After this, the bride and groom excused themselves from the feast and went into isolation for the next month. Western Christians get their "honeymoon" tradition from this custom. After the bride and groom were sent off with much gayety and exultation, the guests were invited to stay and celebrate well into the night.

"For the next seven days," Amada continued, "food and wine were continuously served and guests and friends were invited to come and go as they pleased and to bring gifts for the newlyweds.

"Sometime during the first day's celebration, because Mary had been 'short-ended' on her wine supply, (according to the sheepskin manuscript, Amada inserted), Mary ran out of wine. She told Jesus about the shortage hoping, that since he was the older brother and perhaps a co-sponsor, he would do something to avert catastrophe.

"Jesus responded by saying that it was not appropriate for him to tell the guests about the wine because it was not yet his time to address the people. In unspoken, yet obvious, implication, he told Mary, his mother, 'Wait until it is my turn, and I have given my benediction, then I can and will do something about it.'

"Whether or not Jesus waited until it was his turn to give the benediction, or he responded immediately to her request, is not known. All that is known is that he did respond to his mother's need in a way that probably she had not anticipated.

"She probably felt that after Jesus had completed his benediction, he would either go to the wine merchant there in Cana and find out where the wine was that was supposed to have been delivered to the wedding, or he would go purchase more wine. It probably never entered her mind that he would meet the need for wine by miraculous means.

"Located at the house or place where the celebration was being held," said Amada, "were at least six stone water troughs. These were used to cleanse implements during times of religious celebrations or observances. The troughs each held about 27 gallons or just over 102 liters, of water. Jesus told the servants to fill the troughs with water. (It probably took them a long time to carry enough water to fill all six troughs with 27 gallons of water each, or a total of 162 gallons.) After they had filled the troughs, he told them to dip some of the water out and serve it to the 'governor of the feast.' The governor of the feast was the one who was the public spokesman representing the groom. He kept things on schedule. He was usually the 'best-man' or 'friend of the bride-groom' and was usually either a relative of the groom, a close friend of the groom, or the highest-ranking non-religious Jewish official in the community.

"After the wine was served to the governor and after he tasted it, he was amazed that Mary had chosen to serve *kalos* wine twice. *Kalos* wine was usually served only in the morning, with *halos* wine being served for the remainder of the feast.

"He also commented that she had kept the best of the *kalos* wine until then. Whether the governor was irritated by the 'out-of-order behavior' and uncharacteristic procedures is not known. All we know for sure is that he was most astounded by Mary's choice in serving of the best *kalos* wine at that time. The Christian writing of John concludes the event by saying that the miracle at Cana was the beginning of Jesus' miracles. Therefore, the multitude of records that tells of Jesus' boyhood miracles are, according to this writer, John, nothing more than fabrications."

That ended Amada's explanation of the miracle of Jesus turning the water into wine. But Amada was not finished yet.

He re-rolled the sheepskin manuscript and his Turkish translation of the manuscript and set them aside, as he waited for me to complete my notes. Upon my completion, Amada sat very quietly and looked me directly in the eye and asked, "How strong is your Christian faith? Do you think it is strong enough to withstand non-traditional controversy? Can it stand strong against perceived biblical evidence that soundly contradicts the commonly accepted and traditional view of Jesus?"

Before I answered I searched my soul for a few minutes so that I would answer honestly. I then responded, "I feel that through my research efforts I have discovered enough earth-shattering, controversial information about the life of Jesus that not much of anything could shake my undying faith in him, his mission, or his message."

"Although I am Muslim, "Amada responded, "I do admire your determination to remain faithful to your beliefs and strong in your resolve."

Again, for at least the 4th or 5th time Amada took me totally off guard. What he said so shocked me that I could not respond. For so long I had been of the opinion that although Muslims respected Christian's beliefs, they did not honor them or admire them. Now this Muslim "priest" in one full sweep destroyed all of my preconceived ideas and assumptions. It mystified me how he could say that he admired my faith and my determination.

Yet, I knew by now that Amada was truthful and straightforward. He said nothing that was not honest and truthful and refused to give compliments strictly for the purpose of making someone feel good. What he said, he meant. So, although I did not and could not understand, I accepted his admiration as his true and honest feelings about my unwavering faith in Jesus.

Sensing that I as groping for a response, he continued talking. "Because you are strong in your faith and feel that it can't be moved or threatened, I feel like I can share a Syriac document with you that dates back to about the 5th century."

He then excused himself and returned a few minutes later carrying a small leather scroll. "I found this leather scroll in the same vault but was unsure whether I should tell you about it. Now I feel that I can.

"This scroll's subject is also the wedding at Cana, but from a different perspective. I think that in order for me to explain to you what it says, I first need to quote the references in John that the 5th century author used to justify his assumptions."

Amada then quoted the John portion.

> "When the ruler of the feast had tasted the water that was made wine, and knew not whence it was: (but the servants which drew the water knew;) the governor of the feast called the bridegroom, and saith unto him, Every man at the beginning doth set forth good wine; and when men have well drunk, then that which is worse: but thou hast kept the good wine until now" (John 2:9-10).

He then explained what the document said. "The argument presented in this Syriac manuscript is that the governor of the feast called out to the bridegroom and complemented him for serving the best *kolas* wine of the feast. Since the servants knew that Jesus had made the wine by turning water into wine, they told the governor who was responsible for the wine. Once the governor found out who was responsible for the serving of this wine, he wanted to thank him personally. Do you understand where I am going with this?" He asked me.

I sat for a few seconds thinking and then it dawned on me, "Yes. I do. You are saying that this manuscript is suggesting that Jesus is the bridegroom and that this was his own wedding."

"That is right, " Amada answered and then continued, "The manuscript says that the reason why Jesus told his mother that it is not my time is that he was telling her that he could not leave yet or do anything about it because he was getting married. That after he and his bride depart, then he can take care of the problem. Also it suggests that the reason why Mary could tell the servants that they needed to do whatever he said was because it was his wedding and he was the bridegroom.

"However, " he continued, "there is a major problem with this assumption. The wedding celebration was traditionally held in the home of the parents of the groom or in a place prepared by the parents of the groom, yet in the town where they lived. Mary and Joseph lived in Nazareth and the wedding was in Cana. This means that the groom's parents lived in Cana, not Nazareth.

"Although this was a glaring mistake that the author of the Syriac manuscript had not addressed, the document caused quite a commotion in the Christian communities of Cappadocia, Cilicia, Syria, and Armenia in the 5th and 6th centuries. But by the 7th century the Eastern Roman church in Constantinople had successfully suppressed the story and had renounced the manuscript as a vicious attacked against the undefiled holiness of the virgin unmarried Christ."

"And I would agree," Amada said, "What about you?"

I told him that I too agreed. But the manuscript does show that stories had been circulating about Jesus for centuries in an attempt to discredit his life, from the earliest beginnings of Christianity. I then thanked him for sharing it with me.

Amada then picked up the last scroll and unrolled it. It did not seem to be as fragile. As he read the manuscript, I again took paraphrased notes.

"This scroll," Amada began to explain, "according to the opening sentence, was written by a scribe, who was court transcriber for Alexus Rufus, judicial tax administer for the district of the Galilee, under Tiberius Claudius Nero Caesar. I won't go into a lot of detail concerning this scroll. I'll just say that it confirmed through new resident tax records that in the winter (the month of Tebeth) of AD 26, the rabboni Jesus from Nazareth in the Galilee, his mother, two of his brothers (perhaps his sisters went too, but according to the Gospel of Mark [6:3], it seems that his sisters may have stayed in Nazareth. Maybe implying a family split, Amada interjected), and two non-family companions moved to Capernaum in the Galilee and opened a stonemasonry business."

"That is all that needs to be said about this scroll," Amada said as he re-rolled it and set it aside. "But I have a few more things that I would like to tell you that I have discovered. So you can write them down if you want."

I told him that I would write them down and told him to go ahead and start talking.

Amada began by saying; "Capernaum in the Galilee was located in the fertile plain of Gennesaret that extended from the northern part of the Sea of Galilee around to the eastern part of the Sea. In that plain there were many towns and villages, both large and small. There Jesus carried on the bulk of his early ministry. One of the larger cities in the region was Capernaum. It was a tax customs post for the province of Syria. The city became Jesus' vocational as well as his ministry headquarters.

"About three miles north of Capernaum was Chorazin, a small farming village. Almost directly across from Capernaum, on the left bank from where the Jordan River enters the Sea of Galilee, was the fish-processing town of Bethsaida. Next to it was the newly built city of Julias, built by Herod Philip in honor of either the daughter of Augustus, Julian or the daughter of Julius Caesar who was also named Julian. In reality, by the time Jesus moved to the area, Capernaum, Bethsaida, and Julius had all but merged to become one large cosmopolitan area.

"There is no record that I have found that indicates that Joseph, the husband of Mary, moved to Capernaum with the family. If, in fact, Joseph were a master stonemason or an architect that specialized in stone construction, it would have been most logical and probable that he would not choose to leave his business in Nazareth or the stone quarries of Nazareth.

"In AD 756 John of Damascus said that Joseph, the earthly father of Jesus, was a stonemason/architect and that he constructed many buildings of stone in the new Roman imperial city of Tiberias, in Capernaum, in Scythopolis, and in Magdala. He said that Jesus was Joseph's construction supervisor on many of the construction projects (which could explain Jesus' good relationship with the Roman authorities) in Tiberias and that he represented Joseph in a new stonemasonry business that Jesus established in Capernaum on Joseph's behalf.

"Tertullian, the 2nd century apologist, said that Joseph was responsible for the construction of numerous buildings in Capernaum and in the new city of Bethsaida Julius, the city built by Herod Philip in honor of Julian, the daughter of Augustus.

"The apocryphal *The Gospel of Philip,*" Amada continued," says that Jesus was a master stonemason and engineer, having been taught the trade by Joseph, his father. He gave the reason for Jesus moving to Capernaum as a business decision. He said that Joseph had been contracted by a Roman centurion in Capernaum to construct a synagogue in Capernaum. Jesus was given the responsibility of supervising the completion of the construction of that synagogue. This Gospel also claimed that this was the same synagogue funded by the Roman centurion whose servant Jesus later healed (in August of AD 27—Matthew 8:5-13). If this is true, then perhaps Joseph sent Jesus to Capernaum to either oversee the completion of the project or to give the final inspection and approval, so that the synagogue could be opened for business. It is even conceivable to assume that Jesus had been sent by Joseph to open a [branch] construction enterprise in Capernaum. But whatever the case, we know that Jesus did move to Capernaum and that Joseph probably did not, and that Joseph, his reputation, his work, and his accomplishments were well known, even in Capernaum.

The Search

"Nothing more is recorded about Jesus' activities (from the winter of AD 26 when he moved to Capernaum) until the spring of AD 27 (probably the month of Nisan—about five or six months after he had moved to Capernaum), when he attended his first Passover celebration in Jerusalem (John 2:13). It is quite conceivable to conclude that the reason why nothing is recorded is because he was busy finishing the construction of the synagogue."

"That is all I have to say. Do you have any questions?" Amada asked me.

I had hundreds of questions but did not know where to start. Amada was truly amazing. He was a true intellectual, accompanied by dignity, honor, and scruples. He is like no one I had ever met before or since. Although he had not projected that demeanor, I truly felt inferior and felt that I could not ask him any questions. So I told him that I had nothing to ask at that time, but I might later.

For the remainder of the evening we talked about other things and never brought the subject of the manuscripts up again. The next day Amada helped me buy a new tire for the ground and repair the spare tire. By noon I was leaving Antakya heading for Syria.

As I drove, my head was swimming because of information overload. Not only was I in awe of Amada and his endowment but also the information from the manuscripts that he had shared was revolutionary to my traditional thought process.

In one short afternoon I had learned that the wedding at Cana was probably Jesus' sister's wedding, Mary was the sponsor of the wedding, there were two different types of wines served, Mary's wine order had been "short-changed," Jesus was responsible for giving a benediction at the wedding, Jesus and Mary along with some brothers and his disciples moved to Capernaum, and perhaps opened a branch of the family business in Capernaum, and that Jesus was the construction supervisor over the construction of a synagogue in Capernaum that had been funded by a Roman centurion. For all practical purposes, all of this could easily be collaborated by the Gospels or at least by reading between the lines of the Gospels, yet all seemed to be either contrary to or in addition to the currently accepted assumption concerning the wedding in Cana and Jesus' first miracle of turning water into wine.

For the remainder of the day I seemed to be in a daze as I thought about all that had transpired in the last couple of days. In fact even now, it is hard for me to reconcile how the information written in the manuscripts translated by Amada could be so logical and seemed to confirm the record of John's Gospel, yet the information seems to have never made it into the thinking of our current mainline traditions regarding the marriage in Cana. Why? I do not know. Although this information could have been threatening to the dogma of Mary's perpetual virginity, it was not threatening to the deity of Jesus nor was it so controversial that it would weaken traditionally accepted dogma. So, why has it remained such a mystery? And why is it still not considered as factual materials that need to be included in the marriage of Cana story? As yet, I have not found answers to those questions.

The next major event in the chronology of Jesus' life did not take place until the spring of AD 27 when he attended the Passover celebration in Jerusalem. We have no Gospel record of what was happening in Jesus' life from the time he moved to Capernaum to the time that he journeyed to Jerusalem—a period that could have been as much as five months. It is quite conceivable to conclude that the reason why nothing is recorded is because he was busy finishing the construction of the synagogue.

XVI
SECOND YEAR OF MINISTRY

(AD 27)

The next major event in Jesus' life did not take place until the spring of AD 27 when he attended a Passover celebration in Jerusalem. Although in the life of Jesus during this time there was silence, there was plenty of activity on the Roman political scene.

One of the most atypical resources that covered what was happening in Rome at this time I discovered at Oxford University's St. Edmund Hall. The resource was not a document, book, or manuscript. It was a bound set of about thirty ancient maps, with an explanation of each map in a one or two page description following each map. The entire resource was untitled, but in the introduction page it was claimed that a monk named Arthur of Durham during the reign of Henry V, which would have been in the early 15th century, compiled the maps. It was the only known set of these particular maps in existence.

One of the maps was quite interesting to me in that it was a map of the city of Rome showing the encampment locations of Sejanus' forces during the reign of Tiberius Caesar. Although Sejanus claimed that the troops were encamped around the city of Rome to protect the city against the threat of rebellion, these forces were effectively holding Rome hostage to the desires and demands of Sejanus during the time of Jesus' ministry. The map's two-page explanation gave it a sub-title: *AD 27- The Years of Embitterment—Tiberius Flees*. It then explained the sub-title by stating that in AD 27, the year after Jesus began his public ministry, Tiberius fled Rome and settled on the island of Capri.

After this sub-title clarification by the writer, his explanation continued by him quoting the Scripture reference in Luke that identified the time that Jesus began his ministry. He then quickly changed subjects and began to tell about the political state in Rome at that time; the time of the beginning of Jesus' ministry.

The writer began his explanation by saying that the launching of Jesus' ministry is well documented by the Gospel of Luke, chapter 3, verses 1 and 2.

> *"Now in the fifteenth year of the reign of Tiberius Caesar, Pontius Pilate being governor of Judea, and Herod being Tetrarch of Galilee, and his brother Philip Tetrarch of Ituraea and of the regions Trachonitis, and Lysanias the Tetrarch of Abilene, Annas and Caiaphas being the High Priests, the Word of God came unto John the son of Zacharias in the wilderness" (Luke 3:1-2).*

He then clarified the scripture portion.

The ministry of Jesus began during the 15th year of the reign of Tiberius Claudius Nero Caesar (42 BC-AD 37). Tiberius had become Emperor upon the death of Augustus, on August 19, AD 14. If we subtract from that year the two years that Tiberius ruled in collaboration with Augustus, we have the probable launching of the ministry of Jesus sometime between August 19, AD 26 and August 19, AD 27.

The writer then detailed the political condition of Rome at the time of the launching of Jesus' ministry.

In the summer of AD 26, Emperor Tiberius left Rome and retired for four months to Campania, at the prompting of Sejanus. During his absence, Sejanus quickly consolidated his allies and began to "flex" his political muscle, accusing all that opposed him of sedition and treason. Upon Tiberius' return to Rome, he was so disgusted with the political state and with the total lack of responsibility on the part of the Senate, that in February of AD 27, he set up a Prince's Council to be the guardian of political affairs in Rome, while he moved his court of administrative rulership permanently to the island of Capri, off the coast of Naples. In so doing, he literally left the fate of the city of Rome in the merciless hands of the ruthless Sejanus, who quickly moved into the power vacuum left behind when Tiberius moved to Capri.

From Capri, Tiberius "ruled" the Empire. However, because he had little contact with Rome, many of his decisions were unwise. They were mainly motivated by revenge and embitterment, rather than by what were good for the overall welfare of Rome. Among those unwise decisions was one in which he declared that from the "Day of Augustus," August 14 of the year that he moved to Capri (AD 27), until his death, he would not overturn any governor's judgment of sedition or conviction of treason.

Up till that time, Tiberius was known for his fair judgment and mercy in that he had overturned a provincial governor's conviction of treason on numerous occasions, when he felt that a conviction was unjustified or that it had been based on vindictiveness rather than justice. However, from this time forward until his death, there is no recorded account of the overturning a governor or procurator's allegation of sedition or conviction of treason. This was all propagated by the mass hysteria associated with the accusations of Sejanus.

During the first few months of his voluntary exile, Tiberius was inundated with requests for a judgment veto, or an overturning of a conviction of treason, so much so that he became overwhelmed. To rid himself of the stress and responsibility, he ruled that he *would not* exercise his power to overturn *any* conviction. Whatever the governor, the procurator, or the Senate declared, would be the final decision—*period*. Thus, in the case of Jesus, no appeal was made for the overturn of his conviction because such an appeal would have fallen on deaf ears.

With that, the explanation and description of the map ended.

Now back to Jesus.

The year AD 27 marked Jesus' first full year of ministry. Although he began his ministry in the spring of AD 26, this first full year of ministry was a time that Jesus began to be recognized as a true servant of God, which caused his popularity to begin to rise.

Klausner, a Jewish historian, in his *Jesus of Nazareth*, summarized one Jewish Talmud record about Jesus' ministry during the year AD 27. Klausner wrote:

"That his name was Yeshua of Nazareth; that by some accounts he was a Roman by adoption of our Roman representative to our honorable Sanhedrin, Joseph; that he performed miracles and beguiled and led Israel astray; that he mocked at the words of our wise; that he expounded Scripture in the same manner as the Pharisees; that he had five close disciples, but many followers; that he had said that he had not come to take from the Law or to add to it; he cleared the Temple of merchandisers during the Passover which happened on a Sabbath, causing a commotion that caused fear of revolt; he healed the sick; he neutralized the power of the demonic; and he taught as a Rabban with authority, although he was not a Rabban but a rabboni newly anointed by Caiaphas, the High Priest."

It had been approximately one year since John the Baptist had proclaimed, *"Behold, the Lamb of God..."* and Jesus was now ready to expand his ministry from its base in Capernaum. The Passover in Jerusalem would be his first contact with non-Galileans since his ministry began.

We don't know when Jesus and his disciples left for Jerusalem or when they arrived, but according to John 2:14 it appears that the Passover was in full swing by the time they arrived in Jerusalem. Upon their arrival in Jerusalem, he and his disciples first went to the Temple.

When they arrived at the Temple Jesus became furious with the merchandizing that was going on inside the Temple compound. Obviously he was not surprised at what he saw because it had been this way for more than 100 years, in fact the same thing was going on when he became a *Son of the Law* 20 years before. But this time, he became enraged at what he saw.

This seems to suggest that perhaps Jesus had maintained a smoldering resentment for the past 20 years about what was happening within the Temple compound and that now, since he had a certain amount of authority because of his rabboni position, he premeditatively felt it was the time to do something about it.

On the other hand, there is enough information to speculate that although he knew what had been happening in the Temple compound for the past century, this time when he saw it so blatant, anger overwhelmed him instantaneously and he reacted to the deliberate disrespect for the Temple of God, without thinking twice about it and perhaps without realizing that he could have caused a riot by his actions.

Although this was the 1st of three different times that Jesus drove the merchandisers out of the Temple compound, he did not do it over a period of three years. He drove out the merchandisers one time during the Passover of AD 27, but did not do it again until the Passover of AD 31 when he did it twice within two days. If he had a premeditated resentment then logic would demand that he would cleanse the Temple of the merchandisers every year. But since he waited four years between the time of his first cleansing of the Temple until his second cleansing, it seems to suggest that it was a non-premeditated action resulting from his revulsion to the people's blatant disregard for God's holiness and disrespect for Him as their God. Another explanation that has been voiced sporadically over the centuries is that Jesus made such an impression the first time that they dared not try it again for four more years. But if this were true, then why in AD 31 would Jesus have to repeat the action twice over a period of two days?

My knowledge of Jesus' cleansing the Temple compound of the moneychangers and merchandisers was greatly expanded by a man that I met in Rotterdam in The Netherlands, at a bi-annual convention of the *Society for Investigative Truth*, Dr. Olav Gates, a brilliant professor of Ancient Middle Eastern History at the University of Oslo.

Olav said that he had considered himself somewhat knowledgeable of Roman Syria, from the Roman point of view. However, he knew very little from the Jewish prospective and nothing at all about the Temple cult of the Jews and their obsession with the physical temple structure until he read a satire originally written in about the year AD 65, by Junius Juvenalis, a Roman satirist.

In AD 630 Reneaux Fursey, the former Jewish educator turned agnostic historian, translated the satire into French and incorporated it into a teaching that Fursey presented at the monastery at Lagny-on-the-Marne near Paris. The topic of the original satire was the weakness of the God of the Jews who stood by and did nothing while one man drove *His* worshipers (not pagan worshipers) from *His* Temple. "Fursey," Olav said, "incorporated the incident into one of the most convincing teachings on the true purpose of Jesus' calling."

Olav was not a Christian, nor did he have any strong religious persuasion, yet Fursey's teaching had convinced Olav that there truly was something unique and special about Jesus.

Before he went any further Olav quoted the scripture portion that recorded this first of three times that Jesus cleansed the Temple of moneychangers and merchandisers.

> *" And the Jews' Passover was at hand, and Jesus went up to Jerusalem, and found in the Temple those that sold oxen and sheep and doves, and the changers of money sitting: and when he had made a scourge of small cords, he drove them all out of the Temple, and the sheep, and the oxen; and poured out the changers' money, and overthrew the tables; and said unto them that sold doves, take these things hence; make not my Father's house an house of merchandise. And his disciples remembered that it was written, the zeal of Thine house hath eaten me up" (John 2:13-17).*

After quoting the scripture portion Olav said, "The temple was built by Herod the Great and it was huge. He began its construction in 18 BC, and at this time, when Jesus made his first Passover visit to the temple since the beginning of his ministry, construction was still going on.

The Temple stood east of the main city on the plateau of a hill now called Mount Moorish. It was built very near the spot where Solomon's Temple once stood.

"This site is today occupied by *The Dome of the Rock* and the sacred courtyard that surrounds it, *The Harem*. The Dome was built over the site where Muslim teaching says that Mohammed ascended spiritually into heaven."

He continued.

"Herod's Temple appeared as an irregular series of three levels, progressively higher and smaller. At the center of the highest level was the sanctuary, a reproduction of the one that was originally built by Solomon. Without a doubt, Herod's Temple dominated the city.

"Inside the sanctuary stood the Altar of Incense, the seven-branched Monorah, and the golden table on which the priests placed shewbread. Behind a pentagonal door, always covered by a thick heavy veil, was a small dark room, the Holiest of Holies, which only the High Priest was allowed to enter, once a year, on the Day of Atonement. A vestibule reserved for the priests, called the Priest's Court, surrounded the sanctuary. The court was separated from the larger area (about two acres) that surrounded, it by a wall. This was called the Men's Court. In this court, all *male* (only) Jewish worshippers could gather. A second stairway with 15 steps led down to the lower platform, the Women's Court, which was considerably larger, just over four acres. A second stairway, with 12 steps, which encircled the Women's Court on all sides except the west side, led down to the great 35 acre trapezoidal shaped courtyard, called the Gentile's Court. The court was open and accessible to and for all worshippers. The court's two longest sides measured 1,640 feet (almost a third of a mile) and 1,050 feet respectively. The Royal Portico bound the court on the south. On the east, it ended at a line of 162 huge pillars of white marble, which became known as Solomon's Portico. This was the only part of the original Temple of Solomon that survived destruction by Nebuchadnezzar of Babylon more than 500 years before. Nebuchadnezzar commanded the Portico to remain as a permanent reminder of the former splendor of the Temple and as a warning showing what happens when rebellion is fomented against Babylon.

"Solomon's Portico had three colonnades, which was called the Merchants Quarter (*Hanuyoth*). Here vendors and merchants by the hundreds would lease space in order to sell sacrifice animals, food goods, incense, oil, wine, grain, and both religious ritual and secular merchandise of all kinds. Their presence was common during feasts, celebrations, and religious observances. On the north side of the Temple complex was built the Tower of Antonia, the Roman military headquarters in Jerusalem.

"The entire temple area was teeming with thousands of people during the Passover celebrations. During a typical week of the Passover celebration, on any given day, at any given moment, the Court of the Gentiles *alone* (not including the other courts and gathering areas) housed comfortably more than 200,000 to 300,000 participators. In addition, there were merchants from throughout the Empire; tourists by the multiplied thousands; the 6,000 to 8,000 auxiliary soldiers attached to the Roman military; the 100 Roman regulars; the 1,300-man Temple Guard (it was not permitted outside of the Temple complex except by special order of the High Priest and with permission from the Roman authorities); the 15,000-25,000 priests (this number may have include many hundreds of nathanels); the moneychangers (tradition says that there were at least 10,000 to 25,000 moneychangers operating during each Passover); the animal merchants (Josephus says that as many as 200,000 animals were sacrificed during the celebration—all of these had to be purchased from the High Priest approved animal merchants); and the general merchandisers. Dionysius Exiguus, Denis the Little, in AD 530, estimated that the number of people that attended the AD 31 combined Passover celebration, Jesus' last Passover, the one in which he faced death, was well over 4 million.

"Along with all of these multitudes," Olav continued, "the chief priests allowed the Court of the Gentiles to be used as a 'short-cut' so people could pass from one side of the city to the other, without having to go all the way around the Temple complex. The merchant or traveler would pay a fee to the chief priest stationed at the main gate and then they would be allowed to pass through the Gentiles' Court 'short-cut.' This was a very lucrative tax-free (Rome did not tax religious institutions nor their revenues) form of revenue for the High Priest and the Temple. So, needless to say, during times of celebration and festive commemoration, the Temple complex was literally over-flowing with thousands of people.

"It seems that going to the Temple might have been one of the first things that Jesus did upon entering the city. When he arrived, he was appalled and infuriated by all of the commercialism and merchandising. He found some rope and braided a whip; all the while, his fury was growing more intense. Finally, he had had enough. He began to react by forcibly driving the merchandisers and moneychangers out of the complex, kicking over the money tables, and setting the animals free.

"What is amazing about this incident is that in the midst of all of these thousands of people, not a single person, not even a Roman soldier—nobody—attempted to stop Jesus. He continued for perhaps hours, making a tremendous disturbance, yet he remained unchallenged and unmolested.

"In essence, Jesus was countermanding a tradition that had been authorized by the High Priest himself (hence, endorsed by God Himself—so taught the priests and Sadducees) and had been acknowledged as Godly and Holy by the people, for decades. Now, all of a sudden, a newly commissioned rabboni, from the Galilee of all places, took it upon himself to make a whip and use it to disrupt the Holy Passover observance, and countermand a direct imprimatur from the highest Jewish religious authority in the whole of Judaism, by physically driving out of the Temple all of the merchants, animals, and money changers, and by kicking over the tables of the money changers. ("Can you imagine the mad rush as hundreds of people scurried to collect the thousands of loose coins that scattered all over the floor when Jesus kicked over all the tables?" added Olav.) Yet, not a soul laid a finger on Jesus. But why, one could ask.

"Maybe it was because of his good relationship and high standing with the Romans. Maybe it was because they feared him or were afraid to confront him physically. Maybe it was God's protection. Maybe it was because there was so much confusion within the Temple that no one really knew who was to blame for the disruption. But, whatever the case, Jesus was left completely unchallenged.

"As I have already mentioned, Jesus' actions in the Temple could have gone on for hours. Yet, nothing was done to or about Jesus, except that the Jewish religious leaders, probably the Sadducees, questioned him. They wanted to know by what authority he did this?

"I (Olav) can certainly understand the Sadducees' concern. What gave this Galilean rabboni the right and who gave him the authority to provoke the Roman authorities and cause their anger to come down upon them? As a rabboni, was he acting on behalf of the High Priest, or was he acting on his own?

The Search

"Jesus did not answer them in the way that they expected him to answer. He said if they destroyed this temple (He was probably was pointing to himself), that in three days he would raise it up.

"Although they may have understood perfectly what he was implying, they disregarded his implication and concentrated instead upon the physical temple wherein they stood. Perhaps they chose to tactic Jesus from this perspective because he was a well-known builder and would know how long it would take to construct such a building. Or maybe they just chose to challenge him on grounds where they felt they had the advantage.

"They told him that the temple had been under construction for 46 years, (up until that time—so they claimed) so how could Jesus rebuild it in three days. Jesus did not respond to their sarcasm. He probably just walked away and out of the temple area.

"As I have already said, this was Jesus' first cleansing of the Temple. The other two times took place during the AD 31 Passover celebration in the last two weeks of his life of freedom, when there were even more people in Jerusalem than there were at this first time.

"This first cleansing of the Temple was also Jesus' first encounter with the extremely powerful Sadducees. There would not be another *major* confrontation with the Sadducees until the last two weeks before he was tried for treason and crucified—more specifically when he cleansed the Temple twice within a period of 10 days."

After Olva finished, we discussed this incident in Jesus' life for quite some time—I asked questions and Olva answered my questions. I had always viewed this cleansing of the Temple as a minor occurrence in Jesus' life (I also thought that he did it only once in his ministry; I did not know that he did it three times), but once Olva had finished explaining how miraculous the event actually was, I was astonished.

After Passover, Jesus and his disciples remained in the city of Jerusalem for about two months. During those two months of ministry, in which he taught and performed many healing miracles, many hundreds in Jerusalem believed on him. So many in fact that he began to be distinguished by the powerful Sadducees (whose notice probably prompted Jesus to leave the city of Jerusalem) and the Pharisees.

The Pharisees became so curious that one of their most distinguished representatives, Nicodemus, paid Jesus a visit. Whether Nicodemus had been sent by the Pharisees, by the Sanhedrin (in which he was a member), or he was representing himself and was curious about Jesus, we do not know. All we know is that sometime during the two months that Jesus and his disciples were in Jerusalem; Nicodemus visited Jesus one night, acknowledging that it was well known that Jesus had proven himself to be a servant of God.

Thanks to a security guard at the Church of Notre-Dame-des-Victories-du-Sablon, located near the fine arts complex, in Brussels, Belgium, I learned more about Nicodemus' conversation with Jesus than I was at that time prepared to mentally digest. Because of the information overload, it took me at least three months to fully realize the true implications of the information that I had collected.

The Church of Notre-Dame-des-Victories-du-Sablon was a beautiful example of 15th century Gothic architecture and I was looking forward to visiting the church library to see if they had any materials that could be useful to my research efforts.

While touring the church, I struck up a conversation with an elderly (maybe 65 or 70 years old) security guard, who spoke English like a native Englishman. His name was Roger VanRavenswa. Before long our conversation turned to the search for historical Jesus project. Roger explained to me that on a level below the one upon which we stood was a very large rare book and ancient manuscript research library that was used only occasionally by some of the local university professors (this was not the church library that was open to tourists; this was a private, off-limits research library). He asked me if I wanted to see the area.

I immediately said that I did want to see it. As we were walking down the steps to the library level, I asked Roger if I would be permitted to do any research while there. Roger said that that it would be no problem, but that he would have to consult with the acting rector/bishop of the church, whose office was on the same level as the rare book research library.

Upon our exit onto the level that housed the library, Roger asked me to wait just outside of the door of the library, while he went to the rector/bishop's office to ask permission for me to study.

Within a little while, Roger returned with the needed permission. He said that I would be allowed to investigate two (2) books, documents, or manuscripts of my choosing, under specific conditions to which I had to agree. I could not take anything from the library; I could not take photographs; I could not use any recording devices; I could research that day only and had to be finished by 10:00 p.m. closing time; and that Roger had to accompany me. However, I could take longhand notes. I agreed to the conditions and asked Roger to lead the way.

Roger led me into the small (compared to the church library that tourists see) but well stocked, natural finished solid maple-wood rare book research library. The library had the old fashion card catalog filing system. However, not only were the documents cataloged by author and subject, but also by key words and primary focus of the document. In essence, each resource was cross-referenced four ways.

Not knowing exactly where to start, I looked up the key words: *Gospels, Jesus, ministry*, and *Roman*, and then cross-referenced the listed documents. There were four resources to which at least any three of the four key words applied. One was a very large book about two inches thick that detailed the life of Catherine LaBouré, whose holy vision inspired the striking of the "Miraculous Medal." Because of its size and its subject matter, I quickly eliminated that book.

The second of the four resources was a book that had been written by Louis Bertrand, the Spanish missionary to the American Indians, in 1579. It was mainly an account of his missionary efforts. Although tempted to take the time to read it for its historical value, I knew that I just did not have the time.

The third of the four was a letter manuscript written in Latin by Pope Innocent III in 1210, giving pre-approval to the efforts of Francis of Assisi in attempting to get official approval for his newly formed brotherhood. I felt certain that this letter would not be beneficial to my research efforts.

The fourth resource was a bound seven-page velum document written in Latin in 1140 by an Irish teacher, Malachy O'More, which was near the time that O'More was appointed Archbishop of Armagh. The document was a retelling of the story of Jesus' confrontation with Nicodemus, and O'More's varied opinions concerning that confrontation.

As I was reading through the document, Roger told me that he (Roger) might be of some help to me, if I trusted him. I questioned what he meant to which he responded, "I know Latin very well, and it would save you a lot of time if you will allow me to read the document to you orally, and then you can make your notes based on what I read. Of course you will have to trust my translation abilities."

Needless to say I was pleased and told him that since I do not have enough time to do both, I welcomed his help and would be honored if he would read the document so I could take notes.

He started by first giving a brief explanation concerning the document. Then he began to translate the document vocally.

"It appears that this document was a lesson about Jesus' confrontation with Nicodemus, that O'More used to teach students who were studying for the priesthood. In quickly skimming the lesson it seems to me that O'More had a much better grasp on the true picture of this confrontation than anything I have ever read or heard before. But, in the margin of the final paragraph of the opening introduction written in black ink and sealed with a red ecclesiastical seal, is an interesting statement. The statement says that because of O'More's opinions regarding Nicodemus and the way he presented the concept of being born-again, this document has been removed from the Church's list of recommended theological education documents. The document may be used as history, but not as a theological or a Church doctrinal resource. It is dated and sealed, September 13, 1933. I guess that means that up until 1933, the document was used as a doctrinal resource approved by the Church. But in 1933, the Church changed its mind and stripped it of its approved doctrine and theological training status."

"So, let's read it and find out why the church changed its mind. Must be something powerful." Roger said with a smirk.

He began to verbally translate the Latin document into English. "It was during the first two months while Jesus ministered in the Jerusalem area, that Nicodemus came to him at night. This confrontation took place in the late spring, the month of Ziv (Iyyar) in AD 27. The Gospel of John 3:1-12 records the confrontation.

> *"There was a man of the Pharisees, named Nicodemus, a ruler of the Jews. The same came to Jesus by night, and said unto him, Rabbi, we know that thou art a teacher come from God: for no man can do these miracles that thou doest, except God be with him. Jesus answered and said unto him, verily, verily, I say unto thee, except a man be born again, he cannot see the Kingdom of God. Nicodemus saith unto him, how can a man be born when he is old? Can he enter the second time into his mother's womb, and be born? Jesus answered, verily, verily, I say unto thee, except a man be born of water and of the Spirit, he cannot enter into the Kingdom of God. That which is born of flesh is flesh; and that which is born of the Spirit is*

> spirit. Marvel not that I say unto thee, ye must be born again. The wind bloweth where it listeth, and thou hearest the sound thereof, but canst not tell whence it cometh, and whither it goeth: so is every one that is born of the Spirit. Nicodemus answered and said unto him, art thou a master of Israel, and knowest not these things? Verily, verily I say unto thee, we speak that we do know, and testify that we have seen; and ye receive not our witness. If I have told you earthly things, and ye believe not, how shall ye believe, if I tell you of heavenly things? (John 3:1-12).

"Nicodemus was a highly respected Jewish rabboni, a member of the Pharisee sect, and a member of the Sanhedrin. Some historians have claimed that he was one of the very powerful Jerusalem Shammaite Pharisee, but I [O'More] have found nothing to confirm that assumption. According to 1st century tradition, he was a close friend and Sanhedrin associate of Joseph of Arimathea (Joseph represented Rome and her interests), the reputed adoptive father of Mary and Jesus, and one of the three wealthiest men in Jerusalem.

"We have no idea why he came to Jesus by night. The church has heaped, in my opinion, an undue amount of criticism upon Nicodemus for coming to see Jesus at night. Perhaps his justification was in fact because of shame, as has been speculated by the Church for centuries. But there is nothing that I (O'More) have read in God's Word that confirms that assumption. It could have been because he was busy himself in the day, and night was the only time that he was free. Jesus himself was quite busy all day long, so night may have been the *only* time that he was free. It is unlikely that he came to Jesus at night because he was afraid of the Sanhedrin. He was not afraid of the Sanhedrin; he later stood up to the entire Sanhedrin body and defended Jesus.

"In John's Gospel 3:2 there is a strong implication that the Sanhedrin was the body that actually sent Nicodemus to meet with Jesus. If this is true, he was probably sent because he was a friend of or at least an acquaintance of Jesus through Jesus' great-uncle/adoptive father/grandfather and Nicodemus' friend, Joseph of Arimathea. Although Joseph was a Jew who could trace his royal linage back to Solomon, he was also a Roman Senator representing Britain, he was the Minister of Mines and Mining for the Roman Empire, and he served as the Roman appointee and representative to the Jewish Sanhedrin.

"If the Sanhedrin did send Nicodemus, they probably did so because they wanted to know who Jesus actually was, and what justified his actions and revolutionary teachings. The visit of Nicodemus was probably a fact-finding visit. Obviously the powerful Sadducees were exasperated with Jesus because of the events that had occurred in the Temple during Passover (his first cleansing of the Temple compound), and it was a *major* mistake to be at odds with the Sadducees. Hence, every effort to heal the rift or at least to get an understanding of the reasons for the schism or the break in relations and communication between them, the body who had ratified his ordination as rabboni by the High Priest (the Sanhedrin), and him, was well worth it. It was to the advantage of the Sanhedrin, whose membership was largely composed of Sadducees (at least 70 percent were Sadducees), that peace be maintained in Jerusalem. The Sanhedrin may have guaranteed Pilate and the

Roman authorities that this type of disturbance [Jesus' cleaning
would not take place again; hence, the meeting with Jesus was
guarantee.

"According to this John 2:2, the Sanhedrin acknowledged tha
teacher sent from God and that God was with him, for no one could d
that he did unless God willed it and unless God was with him. Yet, Jes   ...ed to
be defiant of any and all of the *rules* that had been approved and/or instigated by the
High Priest himself, who was *the* acknowledged representative of God to and for the
Jewish people on earth. In fact, what had propagated this investigation was the
disturbance that he (Jesus) had instigated during the most widely celebrated of all
Jewish observances.

"So, how could a man be sent from God and yet blatantly defy the rituals of
worship and the allowances set forth by the High Priest, God's *one* and *only* official
representative to the people? The High Priest claimed that he was God's one and
only representative. He also claimed that he had the right to distribute his authority
through rituals, laws, and regulations, to others, to act on his behalf and in his stead.
Hence, the Sadducees and Shammaite Pharisees (especially the Jerusalem
Shammaite Pharisees) claimed that they were acting on behalf of God, because the
High Priest, to act on his behalf, had given them that authority. In essence, what the
Sanhedrin was saying was, how can a man (Jesus) be from God and yet defy God's
chief servant (so the High Priest was called by the members of the Sanhedrin) and
his proclamations and allowances, proclamations and allowances prescribed by God
Himself (so claimed the High Priest)?

"In the Gospel of John chapter 3 verse 3 Jesus did not respond verbally to
Nicodemus' probe and comments. This, plus the presumed incomplete statement
(claimed by many theological historians) in verse 12, has prompted theologians and
historians for centuries to speculate that all of Jesus' conversation with Nicodemus
was not recorded. These same theologians and historians insist that a large portion,
perhaps even the majority, of the conversation is missing from the text that we have
presently (O'More's day and time). I (O'More) have to agree. I think that at least
half of the conversation between Jesus and Nicodemus is missing. Obviously the
writer of the Gospel of John, probably John Presbyter [Prester John], if there was
such a person, (or a disciple of John Presbyter), either did not feel that the entire
conversation was important enough to record or much of the conversation has been
lost over the centuries. Considering that the conversation with Nicodemus took
place a good 70 to as much as 200 or more years before it was recorded by John,
there is a good chance that much of the conversation had been lost long before the
writer of John's Gospel recorded it. But whatever the case may be, Jesus did not
respond directly to Nicademus' inquiry. Instead he told him that he must be *born
again* to see the kingdom of God.

"Nicodemus had neither asked to see the kingdom of God nor had he made any
inquiry about the Kingdom of God. Obviously this *born again* response by Jesus
took Nicodemus by surprise, for this was neither a Jewish teaching nor a Jewish
philosophy.

"Both the term *born-again* and the *death and reborn* philosophy had their
origins in the ancient Babylonian religious mysteries. The term, as well as the

...osophy was foundational teaching of many ancient and present day (O'More's day) religions and religious philosophies including Egyptian mysticism, Zoroastrianism, Hinduism, Buddhism, and many variations of the Greek and Roman religions. Both the term *born-again* and the *death and reborn* philosophy were not unknown but they were not a part of the Judaic religion.

"Nicodemus was disarmed by Jesus' statement and perhaps that was Jesus' purpose. How was it that Jesus could have progressed all the way to the office of rabboni and hold to such pagan beliefs? Nicodemus probably thought. Did he hide his true beliefs and convictions? Did he deceive our most esteemed religious leaders? How is it that the High Priest and the Sanhedrin did not know that Jesus espoused this pagan doctrine? Was Jesus just trying to disarm him? Did he really believe this twice born dogma? Or was he just testing him (Nicodemus)?

"The word that Jesus used for '*see*' was the Greek word *eidon*. The word translated means 'to perceive fully' or 'to comprehend' or 'to understand completely, without codicil'. It *does not* mean 'to see' as in natural eyesight. Nor does it refer to either seeing heaven or going to heaven. What Jesus meant when he used this word was that 'unless you are born again you can neither understand nor comprehend the things of God, the over-all plan of God, the purpose of God, or the concepts and principles of God and His kingdom, as it relates to the hearts of men, to the future, and to His universal harmonious plan.' In essence, the word had nothing whatsoever to do with salvation.

"Unfortunately there is a movement now (O'More's day) that teaches that *salvation, saved, born-again, redemption, forgiveness of sin, name written in the Lamb's Book of Life, repentance, confession of sin, cleansed, new creation, washed in the blood of the Lamb, new creature, remission of sins, child (sons) of God, true believer, conversion, born-again believer, born-again Christian,* and probably many others, are words and phrases that actually mean the same thing: *salvation*. Nothing could be further from the truth.

"For the first 1,000 years after Jesus' resurrection, these words or statements had different meanings. It was not until this past century (11th century) that the same meaning was applied to all of these words and statements.

"In fact," Roger continued as he translated verbally the Latin text, "very subtly over the past 100 years, a number of words and phrases that previously had different meanings began to be used interchangeably in the Word of God in reference to salvation. In due course, these different words and phrases evolved to the point whereby now, at this present time, they are identified and recognized as having the same definition and same meaning.

"A simple word study would be more than adequate to show and to assure that the words and statements have different meanings, yet fundamental factions in the Church have blindly accepted the premise that these different words and phrases are not only alike, but that they all mean the same thing.

"Let's look at one feature of this ridiculous assumption. The Church agrees that salvation was made possible through the shed blood and death of Jesus, the Son of God; and that eternal life with him was assured upon his resurrection. Yet at the time that Jesus had his conversation with Nicodemus, he had neither shed his blood and died, nor had he been resurrected. So if born-again and saved mean the same thing, how was Nicodemus to be saved, seeing that the provision whereby his salvation could be assured had not yet been made available?

"Nicodemus asked, and rightfully so, how can a man be born again? The question that Nicodemus asked should probably be rephrased to read 'explain what you mean by this doctrine whose roots are in mystical paganism.' He was not asking 'how can it be done?'

"Since this twice-born or born-again philosophy had been taught for more than 2,000 years by almost all pagan religions, Nicodemus wanted clarification as to what Jesus meant. Was he saying that the pagan philosophies were correct after all? Was he saying that the death, burial and resurrection ritual that most pagan religions and religious philosophies espoused and had practiced for a millennium was right? Nicodemus needed clarification for himself as well as for the members of the Sanhedrin who had sent him.

"Jesus went on (John 3:5-7) to explain to Nicodemus, that he, Nicodemus, must be born-again if he was to be able to perceive the true things and plan of God: the Kingdom of God. Basically Jesus was saying that it was good that Nicodemus believed on him and acknowledged that he was sent from God and that he (Nicodemus) was a Godly man and knew the Law and the principles of God, but there were steps to be taken and a level to which Nicodemus should seek and strive to advance. If Nicodemus took the steps he would enter into a new arena of understanding and spiritual awareness and reach the level of the perception of the kingdom of God, God's over-all plan for the universe and all of it's inhabitants. But to get to that level the first step he had to take was to be born-again.

"Jesus' message was similar to the message that John the Baptist was preaching—that in order to advance into the fullness of God's eminent plan, a person had to be born of water (or naturally), as well as be born of the spirit (or from above).

"The phrase, *born-again*, implies that death is a prerequisite. Death must occur before there can be a re-birth. A person must die before he can be re-born. Jesus later confided to his disciples that this death is a violent death (Jesus addressed the subject of born-again three different times in his ministry: the first was to Nicodemus, the second time was to three apostles at the Transfiguration in AD 29, and the third was to his apostles in AD 31 when Jesus was telling his apostles about taking up their cross daily), a 'take up your cross' type of death. It is agonizing, humiliating and dreadful, and is executed alone, for God seemingly forsakes and forgets the person who experiences it. He suffers an excruciatingly slow and torturously overwhelming anguish—physically, emotionally and spiritually.

"There is far more here than what the fundamentalists of the Church would have us to believe.

"In the antithesis, Jesus implied that, if Nicodemus was content to live a life of spiritual mediocrity and be respected by the people and honored for his spiritual authority, there is nothing wrong with that. Where he was spiritually was acceptable. But if he wanted to experience and perceive the fullness of God's plan, purpose and kingdom, he must face the harsh born-again experience. The born-again experience is not salvation. It is a separate and independent experience from the salvation experience. It is the end result of a disciplined maturing process that usually takes years of faithful commitment. It is a hard and emotionally devastating process. But it would be worth the hardship if Nicodemus chose to pursue it.

"That is all that our Irish bishop has passed down to us in this document," Roger said as he abruptly ended his translating, "although I am sure that is not all that he wrote. But we only have these seven surviving pages of his much larger text," Roger said as he laid the document down on the table.

I finished with my notes and sat back in my chair. My head was swimming. I had been taught my entire life that when you say that you had been saved it meant that you had been born again. But O'More said all the way back in the 12th century that it was just a century before that that particular belief began to surface. Up until the 11th century, it was taught and believed that there was first, salvation. Salvation was attained with confession of sin, believing Jesus had risen from the dead, belief that he was the Son of God and that through him one could have forgiveness of sin and salvation from eternal death. But after salvation there was another experience that those who were saved could choose to strive for, but it had nothing to do with salvation. It did not guarantee salvation nor did it guarantee eternal life. Only salvation through faith and belief in Jesus Christ and in his sacrifice for the remission of sin could guarantee eternal life. This separate and independent occurrence had to do with spiritual maturity and discipline. It was called the *born-again* experience. It was an experience in which a person dies (not physically, but rather emotionally, spiritually, and psychologically) to *all*, through a horrifying death cycle (depending on self discipline, this could take from days to years to complete). After the death cycle was complete, the born again experience could be realized.

Logically, O'More had a point. Why would Jesus tell Nicodemus that he had to be born again if born again meant the same as salvation, and if the provision for salvation was through the death of Jesus and the assurance of eternal life through his resurrection, was not to take place for another four years from that time? If born-again and salvation was the same and meant the same, how could Nicodemus be born again since the provision for salvation had not yet been provided?

It seemed that O'More gave a convincing argument and a compelling warning, yet it fell on deaf ears. Had the influential leadership who had the power and ability to take a position against the Church, took heed in the 12th century and stood against the swelling tide of doctrinal contamination and compromise, chances are the confusion associated with born again and salvation that has developed since, would have never matured. Nevertheless, they did not heed the warning nor did they attempt to stand against the Church and force it to correct the pretext.

As a result, since the 12th century—in just over 9 centuries—the assertion that born-again and salvation are one in the same experience and that when a person is saved then he or she is actually born-again, has evolved from a tentative assertion into an entrenched and ingrained doctrine of fundamentalism and evangelicalism.

Nevertheless, it would seem that if this were true—that there is a salvation experience and then there is a separate born again experience to those who choose to strive for that goal—that at least some of the more renowned of our present day theologians would have recognized this truth. Within the past 250 years the Christian world has been blessed with some of the greatest Holy Spirit influenced theological minds in the history of the Christian faith. Surely at least one of these spiritual giants would have discovered the truth concerning salvation and born again, if they were in fact different. However, to my knowledge, this notion has neither been discussed, debated, nor has it even been a consideration at any time during the past 250 years. So, either the 12th century schemers who conspired to cover up the true meaning of salvation have done a remarkable job at deceiving the whole of modern Christianity, or the idea that salvation and born again are two different experiences was invented for some unknown or unrevealed reason in a effort to deceive the simplicity of salvation as explicated in the Gospels.

So, I came to the conclusion that I, at that time, not convinced that salvation and born again are two different experiences. I preferred to adopt the position that the new birth is an assurance of salvation from eternal death and damnation. After receiving the assurance of salvation, an individual can choose to advance through levels of spiritual maturity. This process of growing and maturing in the Lord is known as discipleship. Although my position was not so uncompromising that I would refuse to consider optional notions, I felt that I had not discovered enough reliable and reputable documentation to convince me that the past few hundred years accepted born again view was not the true principle of salvation that Jesus originally intended.

"Born again is not the only thing about this John portion that will surprise you, " Roger said somewhat apprehensively, probably not knowing how I would react.

I told him that he might as well tell me because I couldn't become any more stunned than what I was at that moment.

At that, he continued, "Ever since the mid-1700's, when Rev. Sylvester Connolly, the pastor of Manchester Congregational Assembly, claimed that the Apostle John had appeared to him in a dream and told him that Jesus was the author of John 3:13-21, this portion of scripture has been acknowledged as a continuation of Jesus' conversation with Nicodemus. But before that time, and ever since the original drafting of the Gospel of John up until the dream by Rev. Connolly, it had been assumed and taught that John 3:13-21 was John's personal testimonial of Jesus. So, the actual historical events relating to Nicodemus ended with verse 12, and they do not pick back up until verse 22. The entire affirmation between verse 13 and verse 21 (including John 3:16-17) is not Jesus speaking about himself in foresight about what is to come, it is John's testimony about Jesus—who he was and what he had done for mankind—written some 70 to as much as 250 years after the events actually took place."

"So, John 3:16 was not spoken by Jesus?" I asked.

"No." Roger responded, "It was written *about* Jesus *by* John. That doesn't make it any less true, but it was not spoken by Jesus himself."

Again I had to think about what Roger had just said. As I was sitting there thinking, a young lady walked up to our table and whispered into Rogers ear. He shook his head and the lady walked away. A few minutes later Roger said that he had an emergency with which he had to deal, so we would have to leave.

I asked him if everything was ok. He said that all was fine, but that he had to take care of a pressing issue. It was obvious that he did not want to talk anymore about it.

He apologized for having to leave earlier that planned.

I told him that no apology was necessary and that I had learned enough during those couple of hours that my mind would be spinning for days.

In reality, it was spinning for months. It took many days of researching, reading the Nicodemus story and all of John 3 over and over again before I finally came to grips with the fact that O'More very well may be right, and if he was, then many of the traditions that I had been taught all of my life could in reality be lacking in unqualified truth.

After many weeks of studying John 3, I realized that it was a likelihood much of Jesus' conversation with Nicodemus was missing from our current biblical text and that if O' More was in fact correct, then (1) salvation and born-again are two different experiences; (2) salvation is necessary and mandatory for forgiveness of sin and to ensure eternal life; (3) one must choose to become involved in the born-again experience; (4) the born-again experience is not salvation, it neither brings salvation, nor does it guarantee eternal life. It is more of a spiritual maturing process; (5) in order to clearly know and understand the kingdom of God—God's will, purpose, and plan—a person must be born-again; (6) the born-again experience is an agonizing death and rebirth cycle that is not for everybody. It is only for those who are willing to give up and forsake *all* that this world has and has to offer in order to know, realize, and understand the plan of God fully. It takes extreme discipline and non-compromising dedication; (7) if one chooses *not* to progress to the born-again experience, he or she is not any less saved or any less guaranteed eternal life, nor will their personal and intimate relationship with Jesus be jeopardized or threatened. They can still grow in the Lord and still serve the Lord with all that is within them. However, they will generally never advance beyond level four of the seven levels of spiritual maturity (level four is the highest level that 95 percent of all ministers, pastors, evangelists, teachers, and theologians attain), unless they submit to the born-again ordeal. Without the born-again experience, he or she will never be able to fully understand and see (comprehend) the spiritual things of God and the will, purpose, and plan of God.

With these realizations, I completed my in-depth study into John 3 and chose to concentrate my research into other areas of Jesus' life. It was obvious to me that I could have spent decades researching John 3 *only*, but if I had I would never have learned some of the most remarkable facts about the ministry of Jesus.

Jesus and his disciples stayed in Jerusalem until the later part of spring. He probably would have stayed longer, except for the fact that the powerful Sadducees in Jerusalem began to look at him inquisitively, wondering whether he was someone to be taken seriously and feared or just another religious zealot whose flash of influence and popularity would probably dissipate as quickly as it appeared, if they just left him alone and did not acknowledge his existence. Jesus chose to not tempt his nemesis, electing instead to leave Jerusalem and avoid conflict. Soon enough he would have to contend with them, why challenge them before it was time to do so?

Although Jesus left the city of Jerusalem, he did not leave the area. For another month or so, until early summer, he and his disciples stayed in the surrounding Jerusalem countryside and in the state of Judea. It was while he was ministering in the countryside that a controversy developed between the disciples of John and a

Jewish religious leader, probably a Pharisee (John 4:1). Apparently the controversy related to John as compared to Jesus.

John at that time was baptizing in Aenon near Salim (John 3:23). Aenon was located west of the Jordan River in the district of Samaria, about 55 miles northeast of Jerusalem. John was not baptizing in the Jordan River at Aenon, but rather in some of the many clear springs in the area.

John's disciples came to him (John) complaining that Jesus was baptizing more people than John and that people by the droves were coming to Jesus to be baptized.

Note that both John 3:22 and 26 says that Jesus was himself baptizing, but John 4:2 says that Jesus did not baptize, that only his disciples were baptizing. How can this apparent contradiction be justified? Unless we read between the lines of John's record, it can't be justified. So, by taking assumptive liberties, we can conclude that perhaps Jesus was baptizing during the time period indicated by John 3:22 and 26, but by the timeframe represented in John 4:2, he no longer was baptizing because of the controversy about purification between the Pharisees and the disciples of John, and how it related to Jesus' baptism practices. The same controversy is recorded in John 3: 25 and 26.

Responding to his disciples' complaint about Jesus, John the Baptist gave his unconditional and unqualified support for Jesus and for his ministry, by saying, *"He must increase, but I must decrease"* (John 3:30).

When Jesus heard about the controversy with the Pharisees, Jesus decided that he and his disciples would leave Judaea and return to the Galilee in order to prevent competitiveness. But as he was preparing to return to the Galilee, John the Baptist was arrested by Herod Antipas and was imprisoned at Herod's mountain fortress of Machaerus located about 10 miles east of the Dead Sea and about 35 miles southeast of Jerusalem.

After John was arrested, Jesus and his disciples left in haste for the Galilee, passing through the district of Samaria.

Before we continue with the chronology of Jesus and his trip back to the Galilee, I feel that it is important to give a few details concerning John the Baptist's arrest and imprisonment.

By far the most thorough corroboration of the Gospel record of John's arrest and imprisonment came from a Muslim Jordanian acquaintance of mine by the name of Dr. Mehmet Abassi, who was living in Israel and teaching at Hadassah College in Jerusalem. Dr. Abassi is probably the foremost expert in the Middle East on the history of ancient Moab and Ammon, but his passion is John the Baptist lore.

"Herod Antipas," Dr. Abassi began, "was called a 'lover of the quiet life' (*agopon ten esuchian*) by Josephus, the Roman/Jewish historian. Although he may have been scholarly and easy-going when compared to his brother, the ruthless Archelaus, Antipas was very protective of his family and his private life, especially when that private life came under scrutinizing attack.

"To illustrate the extraordinary means in which he would go to protect his privacy, in AD 27 he left his magnificent palace in Capernaum and installed himself in his garrison at Amathus in Peraea, south of Bathabara, where John the Baptist had been ministering, to lead a war against his father-in-law, Aretas, king of the Nabateans.

"Antipas had married Aretas' daughter, Zolleras, a few years before. She was called 'the bent beauty' because of a disease that left her bent over, yet she was considered one of the most beautiful women in the world.

"However, when Antipas was in Rome visiting his brother, Philip, he fell in love with Philip's wife, Herodias. The two brothers worked out a financial agreement that would make Philip wealthier and would send Herodias back to the Galilee with Antipas.

"Aretas became furious when Herod divorced Zolleras (in either AD 26 or AD 27), and had her sent away to Machaerus in Peraea. Aretas pledged to 'take the matter up with Caesar.' Herod in turn, became furious with Aretas, saying that he would not be threatened for doing as he pleased with his wives. Herod responded by raising an army and by setting up an invasion operations headquarters in Amathus. Rome remained neutral in this affair claiming that the whole thing was below the dignity of Rome.

"I do not want to go into all of the events surrounding those years that Antipas traveled back and forth between Capernaum, Sepphoris, Machaerus (where the two sides met in negotiations numerous times), and Capernaum" Dr. Abassi continued. "I will just say that by AD 29, Herod had married Herodias and had paid Aretas 5 talents of gold [approximately $2 million in today's currency] as compensation for divorcing Zolleras.

"In March of AD 29, less than 60 days after the death of John the Baptist, the military operations were called off by Herod after he had suffered a decisive and humiliating defeat at the hands of the army of Aretas. Many people at that time said that Herod's defeat was the God of the Jew's vengeance upon Herod because of the death of John the Baptist.

"After the defeat, Herod returned to Capernaum. It was also during this time that Zolleras was healed of her disease. Many claimed at that time that Jesus healed her.

"Shortly after Herod had set up military operations headquarters in Amathus, John the Baptist, who was ministering in the region, began to criticize publicly not only the invasion efforts, but also the cause and the reason for the invasion: Antipas' adulterous private life. John would not be quite. He frankly accused Herod of breaking the laws of divorce and adultery established by Augustus. He proclaimed that he should be held accountable just like any other Roman citizen or Roman subject. Finally, Herod had John arrested and placed in prison in the dungeon belowground at the spectacular Machaerus fortress.

"The Machaerus fortress was where Zolleras lived at least six months out of the year, she probably had no knowledge that John the Baptist had been arrested and placed in the dungeon at Machaerus until after he had been there for a while. Tradition says that she was away from Machaerus visiting her father in Nabataean and that Herod was in residence at Machaerus when John was arrested. Generally, Herod stayed at Machaerus when Zolleras was away in Nabataean, especially when he had his garrison at Amathus were on war alert.

"When Zolleras returned and discovered that John was in prison, she ordered that he could have unlimited visits from his disciples and that he was to be fed from her own table. Zolleras was a great admirer of John and supported his condemnation

The Search

of Herod. She did not have authority to free John but she did begin a process of appeals to the Roman authorities to secure his release.

"She also began a process of appeals to the Roman authorities, on behalf of John, to secure his release. However, the appeal process would probably not be complete until the late winter (December AD 28 or January AD 29). John was officially arrested for treason, because he spoke against the military operations of Herod. But in the minds of all in Herod's court, it was assumed that John was arrested because he dared to criticize Herod's personal life by accusing Herod of breaking Augustus' law of adultery, which forbade divorce and remarriage, by a woman.

"When John was put into prison, his disciples scattered. Jesus and his disciples also distanced themselves from John as fast as they could by leaving Judea and returning to the Galilee."

"While John was in prison at Machaerus he was told about the great things that Jesus was doing. Jesus healed the sick, he cast out demons, he taught profound truths and preached that the kingdom was nigh, he walked on water, he cleansed the lepers, he calmed the storms, and he was invited to the great religious conference in Capernaum. These reports were exciting and encouraging. They seemed to support the assumption that Jesus was the one who was to come.

Dr. Abassi had much more to say about John the Baptist, primarily about his death. However, chronologically, John's death did not take place until December AD 28 or January AD 29. So, I will discuss more of what Dr. Abassi shared with me regarding John the Baptist in the chapter entitled **The Third Year of Ministry.**

Shortly after John's arrest, if not immediately after his arrest, Jesus left Judaea with his disciples and returned to the Galilee by way of the district of Samaria. As they passed near the city of Sychar, Jesus stopped to rest at Jacob's well, while he sent his disciples into the town to buy food for their mid-day meal. There at the well, Jesus confronted a woman who had come to the well to draw water.

I found some convincing early Christian documentation that confirmed John's record of Jesus' confrontation with the woman at the well, while helping a friend, Aziz Afifi, identify some ancient manuscripts in Sur, Lebanon.

Aziz was a general contractor in the city of Sur. I had met him about five years before when I had traveled to Sur from Israel to visit the ancient ruins of Tyre. Aziz was one of the contractors working on a new visitors' center near the ruins. I spent three days in Sur studying the ruins. During that time, Aziz and I became good friends. Now, five years later I was driving from Turkey to Israel and decided to go to Sur and visit Aziz.

When I arrived at Aziz's house, his wife told me that he was working at the Church of St. Thomas. Apparently, about three weeks before I arrived, there had been a flash flood in Sur that damaged many of the ancient landmarks. One landmark that was damaged was the Church of St. Thomas; an Orthodox church built in the 8th century. Part of its foundation had been washed away. The bishop of the church, Bishop Amazim Ohan, had contracted with Aziz to repair the foundation of the ancient church.

When I arrived at the church, I couldn't find anyone. It would stand to reason that if Aziz and his construction team were doing repair work on the church that I would have seem someone there. But the church was totally empty of people. Finally after repeatedly calling for Aziz, I saw him crawl out from a hole in the floor of the church near the far north wall. Aziz recognized me and greeted me warmly.

I asked him what he was doing and where were all of his employees. He then told me that the day before, while digging out dirt that had been carried under the foundation of the church by the floodwaters, he had discovered an underground vault that probably dated back to the time of the church's construction in the 8th century, or before. The cut-stone sealed entrance to the vault had been partially broken.

He removed enough of the stones to squeeze himself into the vault. Upon entering, he noted that the vault was about three meters square and about two meters in height. Inside the vault he found early Christian amulets, pieces of jewelry, and four bound volumes. Each volume was made of leather sheets bound between two cedar boards, held together with small leather cords, half of which had deteriorated. Obviously these articles had been placed in the vault before the church was built, because the vault was incorporated right into the church foundation. That meant that the artifacts dated at least back to the 8th century, and probably older.

Realizing that what he had found could be valuable, Aziz ordered the work halted and reported to the bishop what he had discovered. The bishop told Aziz to send his crew home for holiday and that he would not need them for at least three days. The bishop then told Aziz that the church would pay the employees' salary for the three days that they were on holiday. After his workers had gone home, the bishop told Aziz that he could not take any chances. If there was anything of monetary value hidden in the vault and the Lebanese officials found out about it, they would expropriate everything that was found, citing national treasure conservation as their justification.

"The bishop and I," Aziz said, "cleaned out the vault carefully and took the charms, jewelry, and board books into the church and hid them in the church safe in the bishop's private office. He was planning to contact an archaeologist friend in Istanbul to ask him to come and evaluate them, but now since you are hear, you might be able to tell us if they are authentic or if they are of any value. The bishop seemed to think that both the early Christian trinkets and the bound volumes were at least 3rd century and perhaps even 2nd or 1st century."

I told him that although I was not an expert in ancient artifacts, I would try my best to date them and evaluate their authenticity.

Aziz led the way to the bishop's office. The bishop had just returned from a trip to the city. Aziz introduced me to Bishop Ohan and told him about our friendship, my on-going historical Jesus research project, and my willingness to evaluate the artifacts.

Bishop Ohan welcomed me enthusiastically, saying that a friend of Aziz' is also a friend of his and that if Aziz places his trust in me, then so does he.

The bishop then invited Aziz and me to sit at a wooden table located at the end of his office opposite his desk. After we were seated he opened his safe that was located directly behind his desk, and retrieved the articles that Aziz had discovered in the vault beneath the church. He brought them to the table and invited me to take my time studying them.

I first took an hour or so to study the amulets and trinkets. Without a doubt these looked to me to be 1st or 2nd century Christian.

I then began to examine the volumes. Each of the four volumes consisted of sheepskin leaf with a text written in Latin, bound between two cedar boards. The first leaf of each volume explained that the text was a Latin re-write of a lesson originally written in Greek by Vitus of Sicily, who I knew died in AD 303. The re-write in Latin was by Bartholomew, servant of Damian, Bishop of Tyre. I also knew that Damian, Bishop of Tyre had died in AD 710. One of the volumes was made up of six sheepskin leather leaves; two volumes had eight leaves; and one volume had 11 leather leaves.

Bartholomew, servant of Damian, claimed in each of the first page introductions that he had re-written Vitus of Sicily's lessons word for word, as I studied the texts, it appeared to me that due to numerous changes in writing style throughout the documents, that Bartholomew had inserted into Vitus' lessons some of his own thoughts.

I carefully examined each volume. Finally, after a couple of hours, I told the Bishop and Aziz that it appeared to me, even though I did not even pretend to be an expert, that the volumes were indeed authentic Latin re-writes of texts that had been written earlier, and they appeared to date back at least 1,000 years. Therefore, they may be the actual re-writes of Bartholomew, the servant of Bishop Damian of Tyre. The six-leaf volume was a lesson describing the annunciation of Gabriel to Mary, the mother of Jesus. One of the eight-leaf volumes told the story of Emperor Constantine's conversion to Christianity and his baptism before his death. These would probably not benefit my research efforts. The other two, however, the 11-leaf volume and the other eight leaf volume, were fascinating. The other eight-leaf volume was a lesson concerning Jesus' calling of Philip to be his disciple. However, the information added nothing to what I had already found. The 11-leaf volume was a lesson using the events of Jesus' confrontation with the woman of Samaria at the well of Jacob as the setting.

I asked Bishop Ohan for permission to take notes of the two volumes. He willingly agreed and even volunteered to read the texts so I could concentrate on taking notes. I thanked him for his offer and welcomed his help. I paraphrased as well as directly quoted as he read.

After reading silently for a few minutes, the Bishop was ready to begin translating the 11-leaf Latin volume out loud. He started by giving the scriptural reference that served as Vitus' text for the lesson. "In our Bible," Bishop Ohan said as I began taking notes, "the text is the 4th chapter of the Gospel of St. John."

He then gave a paraphrased translation, which I partially quoted and partially paraphrased. "Jesus had been ministering in the state of Judea with his disciples. Shortly after his confrontation with Nicodemus, Jesus found out that the Pharisees were upset about his increase in popularity. So he decided to go back to the Galilee the quick way, through Samaria. The area of Samaria was one that was generally by-passed by Judean religious leaders if it was possible.

"The Romans did not separate the area of Samaria from the rest of Judaea. To Rome, the entire area from the fortress of Malata and the city of Beersheba in the south, to the border of the Galilee in the north, and from the Jordan River east, to the Mediterranean Sea west made up the Roman province of Judaea. The Jewish religious leaders from the state of Judea drew a line of separation that isolated Samaria from the state of Judea, just north of Jerusalem (some historians, the Bishop inserted, claimed that the line of separation was drawn just south of Sychar and Mount Gerizim).

"The reason why the area of Samaria was considered 'off-limits' to many Jewish religious leaders in the state of Judea was because the area was occupied by a mixed population of Israelites and descendants of Assyrian colonists (at that time these included descendants of Assyrians as well as Parthians, Syrians, Egyptians, Persians, Scythians, Babylonians, and Medes) who had settled there during the Assyrian domination. Although the civil laws and civil authorities were subject to Roman authority, Rome allowed a certain amount of latitude because the Samaritans had proven to be a cooperative people and had willingly submitted to Roman rule. Because they were a mixed-breed people whose majority representation seems to have been Parthian, much of the civil and domestic regulations that governed four of the major hill cities of the Samaria area—Sychar, Shechem, Samaria, and En-gannim—were Parthian in nature, culture, domestic make-up, and style. This seemed to be a good compromise that kept all the people in those cities, regardless of national origin or decent, content and cooperative. The remainder of Samaria, as a non-separated part of the province of Judaea, was very much Greco-Roman in domestic laws.

"The Samaritan Jews professed Judaism, but they had broken all religious relationships with the state of Judea and Jerusalem, and refused to be a part of the cult of the Temple in Jerusalem. Approximately 20-30 percent of the total population in the four major hill cities of the area of Samaria was Jewish. The remainder of the area classified as Samaria had a Jewish population of less than 5 percent.

"As Jesus and his disciples traveled through Samaria (whether by animal or on foot we do not know, but logic would say that they traveled by animal), they stopped at Jacob's well, just south of the city of Sychar. The city was about 30 miles north of Jerusalem, located just east of Mount Ebal, and a little northeast of Mount Gerizim. Here at Jacob's well, Jesus rested, while his disciples went into the city to buy some food for their mid-day meal.

"Jacob's well was about 20-30 meters deep and about 3 meters in diameter," the Bishop added. "It maintained a constant 3-4 meters depth of water year around, regardless of climatic conditions.

"The city of Sychar," he continued, "At one time (about 800 BC) was a small concentration of mud-brick hovels, where the city of Shechem forced drunks and reprobates to live. The name *Sychar* was one of utter contempt and it meant 'drunkard' or 'good for nothing.' By the time of Alexander the Great, the negative stigma had been forgotten and the city of Sychar had grown to surpass Shechem in population. Tradition says that Jacob's well was the exact well that was dug by Jacob and into which Joseph was placed by his brothers.

"The two mountains that were within view of Sychar: Mount Ebal, the northern most, and Mount Gerizim, were only about a mile or two apart, and were aligned north and south. Mount Gerizim was called *The Mount of Blessing* and Mount Ebal was called *The Mount of Cursing*. It was at Mount Gerizim that Jotham addressed Israel as recorded in Judges [9:7].

"In about the year 332 BC, Sanballet, the governor of Samaria under the Persians, the one who opposed Israel under Nehemiah [Nehemiah 4:7-28], pledged his allegiance to Alexander the Great. Alexander in turn gave Sanballet permission to build a temple on Mount Gerizim to serve as a place of worship for the local Samaritans, so that they would not have to go all the way to Jerusalem to worship at the Temple in Jerusalem. Sanballet built the temple and appointed his son, Manasseh, High Priest of the new temple.

"Before long worship at the new temple on Mount Gerizim rivaled worship at the Temple in Jerusalem. Soon there developed rival priestly offices to the priests in Jerusalem. The priests in Samaria accepted the Pentateuch as their Holy Book, but rejected all else that the priests in Jerusalem accepted as canon. A great and heated controversy developed between the Jewish religious leaders in Samaria, predominately in the four major hill cities, and the Jewish religious leaders in Judea, especially in Jerusalem.

"The rivalry became so intense that in 129 BC, John Hyrcanus destroyed the temple that Sanballet had built on Mount Gerizim. This only widened the gap of hatred and hostility between the two factions. By the time that Jesus' ministry began, the rift between the two was so wide that it was for all practical purposes, irreparable.

"During the reign of Herod the Great, the Sadducees and Pharisees in Jerusalem developed a set of rules and regulations on how Jewish religious leaders (especially those in the state of Judea) were to relate to Samaritans.

"The Sadducees and Pharisees, especially the Pharisees in Jerusalem, tried to force the general Jewish population throughout the region (the Galilee, Judaea, and the Decapolis) to observe the restrictions as well, but they only had limited power to enforce the restrictions with the Jewish religious leaders in Judea.

"In fact, in reality their power of enforcement was restricted to the city of Jerusalem *only*. So the Jewish population in the state of Judea as a whole, and most certainly the non-Jewish population in the state of Judea, and the general population in the province of Judaea, *did not* honor the restrictions. Only the Jewish religious leaders in the city of Jerusalem and a few in the state of Judea outside of Jerusalem honored the restrictions. The Galilean and Decapolis Jews, the Romans, the Greeks, or any other ethnic, social, or religious group of people who lived in Syria also *did not* honor the restrictions.

"These regulations forbade," the Bishop continued, "a Jewish religious leader (Sadducee, priest, Pharisee, rabboni, rabbi, rabban, or Jerusalem scribe) from having any type of communication with any Samaritan, even if the Samaritan was in Judea. Travel into Samara was strictly forbidden under penalty of the religious leader being stripped of his position for two years and scourged (it is very unlikely however that the Roman authorities would allow this type of punishment). Travel all the way through Samaria carried a penalty of stripping the religious leader of his position for five years and scourging him. Traveling into Samaria and talking to a Samaritan while in Samaria carried a penalty of stripping the religious leader of his position for life, scourging him, and imprisoning him in the Temple prison confines for two years. Traveling into Samaria and talking to a Samaritan woman carried the same penalties with the addition of having properties confiscated and have the person's name removed from the Temple rolls, making him an outcast from Jewish society. Travel into Samaria and staying the night in Samaria meant that the religious leader would forfeit his life, his properties and possessions would be confiscated, his family would be imprisoned, and they would be social outcasts for five generations.

"The regulations seemed to be even more of an insistence with regard to the Jewish Samaritan population in the four major hill cities of Samaria, mainly because they had adopted the civil laws of Parthia (with Roman approval) as their domestic laws rather than the Roman/Greek standard that Jerusalem had adopted.

"There is only one recorded incident of death relating to the religious 'law' restricting association with the Samaritans that happened under Roman rule, the Bishop continued to paraphrase. It happened in AD 13.

"In that year, a young rabboni by the name of Zerabbel was forced to stay two nights in Shechem because of a physical injury. This young rabboni was a personal friend of Ambivius, the Roman Procurator of Judea at that time. As per the religious "law" regarding the Samaritans, the young rabboni, Zerabbel, was killed upon his return to Jerusalem. The Temple authorities confiscated all of his properties and possessions, and his family was imprisoned. When Ambivius heard what had happened, he became outraged and ordered the immediate release of the rabboni's family from prison and a return of all of his property and possessions to his family. He then had 60 Judean Pharisees, 20 Sadducees, and 5 priests imprisoned for 10 days. Afterwards, he had them all strangled to death.

"Jesus had traveled with his disciples the 30 miles or so from Jerusalem, and they were tired, thirsty, and hungry. Because Jesus was from the Galilee, he had no animosity against the Samaritans, nor did his disciples, who were from the Galilee also. Although Jesus was aware of and was familiar with the regulations imposed by the Jewish religious leaders in Jerusalem, they did not govern him nor did he honor their regulations regarding the Samaritans. Therefore, he did not hesitate about traveling through Samaria.

"The woman that he met at the well about noon, after his disciples had gone into the city to buy food, apparently did not know that he was from the Galilee (although his dialect should have betrayed him, unless he spoke to her in Greek or Syriac). When she saw the distinctive blue thread in the tassel of his garment belt which identified him as a Jewish rabboni, she assumed immediately that he was a rabboni from Judea and most likely from Jerusalem, because it was unlikely that a rabboni would hail from some other place than Judea. As such, she felt that he would most likely fall under the restrictions of the religious "law" regarding the Samaritans. It probably never crossed her mind that he may not be from Judea. Not only was she surprised that he was there at the well, but she was doubly surprised that he initiated a conversation with her.

"It was socially unacceptable in Parthian domestic law for a lone man to initiate a conversation with a lone woman, unless he was interested in her as a potential wife," the Bishop added.

"It could easily be said ('and it has in fact been both said and taught through out the centuries,' Bishop Ohan inserted) that this woman was the reason that Jesus came to Samaria, but the Bible does not suggest that nor does it imply that. In fact, there is not the slightest implication to suggest that Jesus' talking to this woman was planned and pre-meditated by him.

"Jesus first explained to the woman about the eternal spiritual living waters that he could give her, wherein her spiritual self would never again thirst for satisfaction. She responded sarcastically, assuming that he was talking about natural water, telling him that if he had that ability, he needed to give her that water so she would never thirst again. Jesus then told her to call her husband. She responded by saying that she had no husband. Jesus then revealed to her that she in fact had been a wife to five men and that the man with whom she was living, was not her husband.

"There has been much speculation. It has been assumed that the woman was a 'woman of the world,' a harlot, or at the very least, a 'loose' woman who was an outcast from her community. But there is no evidence to confirm this assumption. The assumption is usually justified by saying that the woman came to the well by herself at noon to draw water, when woman usually came in groups to draw water in the morning. She came at noon, alone, because none of the women of the city wanted to be associated with her. However, the Gospel of John does not say that she came alone. There could have been many women who were at the well beside her and Jesus. Women generally drew water twice a day, either in the morning, at noon, or at sundown. However, there is no indication by Jesus or judgment by Jesus that the woman was a harlot or an immoral woman. The fact that she had been a wife to five husbands is cited as another reason for the assumption."

Bishop Ohan then paused in his translation and added a personal note. "Some years ago I discovered that in the Parthian culture a woman had many more rights than women did in Roman or Greek culture. In Roman or Greek culture a woman was not allowed to divorce; only a husband could divorce. According to the divorce law implemented by Augustus, if her husband divorced a woman, she could not remarry as long as her former husband lived, under penalty of being classified as an adulteress and outcast from society. In Parthian culture, a woman was not allowed to divorce during the first two years of marriage, but after two years she had that right. She could divorce and remarry up to a maximum of five times during her lifetime. This meant that she could have a different husband every third year, and have up to five husbands. This did not include husbands who were lost due to death or ones who divorced her. If for example, a woman had married and divorced five husbands, was widowed twice, and was divorced by three husbands, she would have had ten husbands, and still not be considered immoral or 'loose' according to Parthian cultural standards. Nevertheless, after marrying and divorcing the fifth husband, she was not permitted to marry again. However, she was allowed to share living quarters with a male relative or friend without breaking the civil and domestic laws of Parthia. So, since Sychar had placed itself under the authority of the domestic laws of Parthia, the woman at the well was within her legal rights to have had five former husbands and to be living presently with one that was not her husband. This being the case, she was neither immoral nor was she a harlot. She was simply an unhappy woman who seemed unable to find happiness in marriage."

After these personal comments, the Bishop resumed translating.

"Jesus' knowledge of her convinced the woman that he was a prophet of God. As such she seized the opportunity to ask him a question that had been plaguing the Jews of Samaria, especially in the four primary hill cities, for centuries—where is the most acceptable place to worship God, Mount Gerizim or the Temple in Jerusalem?

"Jesus did not answer her question directly. He said that true worship is worship that is true to the individual, regardless of where it is offered or when it is offered. True worship, worship in spirit and in truth, is personal worship that is true to the individual. It is the type of worship that conforms to each individual's personality. It is the outward expression, within the confines of the person's personality, of that which is deep within the individual; that which is truly the person and not an adoption of a form that is not truly that individual's personality. It is the type of worship that is not restricted to a specific time, place, situation, or circumstance. It is an outward manifestation of that which originates deep within the worshiper.

"The woman was not satisfied with Jesus' answer. She disregarded it by saying, 'It does not matter because when the Messiah gets here, He will tell us the truth. He will tell us where is the acceptable place of worship.'

"Jesus then disarmed her by telling her that he was that one, that Messiah, for whom both she and the people had been waiting.

"At that time, the disciples of Jesus returned and the woman ran back into the city and told the men about Jesus, encouraging them to go see for themselves.

"The word that was used for *men*, implies that these men were 'city authorities;' therefore she went back into the city and told the city's ruling authorities about Jesus. There is no implication whatsoever that she reported to the men because she was immoral and had a better relationship with the men than with the women of the city," the Bishop added.

"As Jesus looked up and saw the great number of people coming out of the city toward him to see for themselves all that the woman had said about him, he gave his great evangelist challenge to his disciples about *'the harvest being white unto harvest—now'*. Jesus and his disciples stayed in Sychar two more days and ministered to the people."

Bishop Ohan then looked up and said that this concluded the lesson on the woman of Samaria. I thanked him and stayed the rest of the afternoon taking to Aziz and the Bishop about the artifacts and manuscripts and about Jesus' interaction with the woman of Sychar.

After the two-day revival in Sychar, Jesus and his disciples continued on their journey back to the Galilee. Upon their arrival, they were welcomed with opened arms (John 4:45). Obviously, the details of his ministry in Samaria and Judaea had preceded him.

Soon after his arrival in the Galilee, Jesus and his disciples traveled to Cana, where the last time he was there, or the last time that we have record that he was there, was when he turned the water into wine. The Gospel of John does not tell us why Jesus went to Cana; perhaps he wanted to visit his sister and new brother-in-law, whose wedding he was likely attending at Cana when he turned the water into wine, and who probably lived in Cana.

But what we do know is that while he was there, word rapidly spread throughout the Galilee that Jesus was in Cana. Even the House of Herod in Capernaum received the news that Jesus was in Cana, located in the hill country about 20 miles southwest of Capernaum.

According to the John 4 setting, a member of the House of Herod, a Herodian, who had a sick son in Capernaum, had heard that Jesus was in Cana. So, the Herodian set off for Cana to find him.

I discovered insightful and valuable information that confirmed John's Gospel account while I was researching at the outstanding academic library of Ain Shams University in the heart of downtown Cairo, Egypt.

At the Ain Shams library I discovered a two-page velum (written on front and back), 13th century Arabic manuscript that the accompanying explanatory notes claimed was a rewrite of a sermon originally written by Gothard, the 11th century abbot of the Bavarian monastery of Nieder-Altaich, and delivered to an assembly of clergy on the occasion of the 10th anniversary of Gothard's appointment as abbot of Nieder-Altaich.

The notes said the sermon was based on the healing of the son of the Herodian who had traveled from Capernaum to Cana in search of Jesus. The Arabic scribe, who translated Gothard's sermon, called himself, Babos, servant of Qalawun, master of Egypt, defender of Allah and of His prophet, Mohammed.

Gothard began by saying that the scriptural text for his sermon was found in John's Gospel (John 4:46-53). He then explained that although a similar event was recorded in the Gospels of Matthew (8:5-12) and Luke (7:1-10), the episode recorded in John and the one recorded in Matthew and Luke are completely different events occurring at two different times, separated by months, if not years.

> *"So Jesus came again into Cana of Galilee, where he made the water wine. And there was a certain nobleman, whose son was sick at Capernaum. When he heard that Jesus was come out of Judea into Galilee, he went unto him, and besought him that he would come down, and heal his son: for he was at the point of death. Then said Jesus unto him, except ye see signs and wonders, ye will not believe. The nobleman saith unto him, sir, come down ere my child die. Jesus saith unto him, go thy way; they son liveth. And the man believed the word that Jesus had spoken unto him, and he went his way. And as he was now coming down, his servants met him, and told him, saying, thy son liveth. Then inquired he of them the hour when he began to amend. And they said unto him, yesterday at the seventh hour the fever left him. So the father knew that it was at the same hour, in the which Jesus said unto him, they son liveth: and himself believed, and his whole house" (John 4:46-53).*

Gothard explained that Jesus and his disciples had just completed a stay in Jerusalem and the state of Judea, and had returned to the Galilee by way of the region of Samaria.

Upon his return to the Galilee, he and his disciples went to Cana to reside for a while. There they were welcomed openly. Cana was located in the Galilee's hill country, a hard day's ride, maybe two, on horseback traveling southwest from Capernaum.

Capernaum, a predominately Roman/Greek city, served the province of Syria as a provincial tax center and center of commerce for the region. Population estimates for Capernaum at the time of Jesus' ministry ranged from as few as 5,000 to as many as 300,000 for the greater Capernaum area. Some historians feel that Capernaum was nothing more than a quaint fishing village, whereas others feel that it was the largest and most influential city in that area of Syria.

Gothard was convinced that it was a very large city because Herod Antipas, the Roman Tetrarch of the Galilee who prided himself in retaining residences in most of the major cities of Syria, maintained an enormous walled residence palace complex in the northern suburb of the city. Herod Antipas resided in the palace complex as well as the vast majority of the Herodians—the House of Herod. Herod's administrative seat of government was originally located at Sepphoris. However, after the completion of the imperial city of Tiberias, he officially moved his seat of government to the city. Yet, he was so attracted to Capernaum that he conducted at least half of his official business from his estate in Capernaum, and regularly "shuttled" between Tiberias and Capernaum.

The writer of the Gospel of John says that a nobleman heard that Jesus had returned from Judea and that he was residing in Cana. The Greek word used to depict this man, *basilikos*, which St. Jerome translated as "nobleman" in the Vulgate, was an official title that was used by the Syrian Roman authorities for officials and members of the royal line of Herod—Herodians. The word indicated that perhaps this "nobleman" was a prince of the family of Herod or at the very least an official, or a down the bloodline relative of the family. In any case, he was a Herodian.

This Herodian had heard in Capernaum that Jesus was in Cana. The writer of John says that the Herodian left his palace home in Capernaum and traveled the 20 miles to Cana in order to convince Jesus to return to Capernaum and heal his (the Herodian's) son, who was sick and was at a point of death.

Gothard speculated that the Herodian, representing the "search for the Theophus commission", was probably sent to Cana to investigate Jesus, who had already performed miracles in Cana and in Judaea, to see if he perhaps could qualify as a possible candidate for The Theophus. The Herodian then would report his finding to the ambassadors in Rome. If they felt that Jesus and his activities needed further examination, they would schedule a time to come to the Galilee, from two to five years from that time, and examine the evidence regarding Jesus.

The Gospel of John setting indicates that the Herodian went to Cana to convince Jesus to heal his son. So, which version was correct—Gothard's or John's?

The scribe who translated the document wrote a comment in the margin stating that he felt that both versions were correct. The Herodian's son was sick. Yet, the search for The Theophus, through Imperial decree, had to take precedence over anything, everything, and everybody—even family. Therefore he was required to leave his son, who was near death, in Capernaum and travel to Cana to investigate whether Jesus could be The Theophus. He had no choice in the matter.

Nevertheless, he might have reasoned that the trip to Cana would give him the opportunity to accomplish both of his goals. Since Jesus was a Jewish resident of the Galilee, it was unlawful and forbidden to refuse the Herodian's demand to return to Capernaum for cross-examination, unless Jesus was in fact a Roman citizen in which case he was not under any obligation to obey the Herodian. Then if Jesus really was a miracle worker, his son could be the object of Jesus' scrutiny. In this way, his son would then be healed and the Herodain's job and purpose would be fulfilled.

It is not known when the Herodian left Capernaum for Cana or how long it took him to get there. Apparently before he left Capernaum, the boy had taken a turn for the worse, and as he left, the boy was at the point of death. Thus, when the Herodian arrived in Cana he was truly concerned about the welfare of his son. He finally found Jesus about 1:00 in the afternoon, whereupon he asked Jesus if he would come with him back to Capernaum to heal his son. Jesus responded with a question/statement with which he intended to determine the motive of this prince of Herod. Was he representing The Theophus commission? Was his insistence nothing more than a fishing expedition in an attempt to fulfill his search for The Theophus obligation? Or was his petition a sincere request exemplifying a true need?

The Herodian responded by answering back, sir, this is not a game. It may be true that my commission is to search for The Theophus through the investigation of signs and wonders, but my request is not a trick. This is not a Tiberius mandated treasure hunt for a mythical ruler; this is reality. My son is dying and if you do not come and heal him, then he will surely die.

Jesus did not return to Capernaum with him, but instead he sent the Herodian away telling him to return to Capernaum because his son was alive and healed.

If Jesus was a Roman citizen, he was under no obligation to obey or submit to the Herodian. But, if he was not a Roman citizen, Jesus violated a number of Roman restrictions by his refusal to accompany the Herodian back to Capernaum.

First of all, if Jesus was not a Roman citizen, he deliberately disregarded the licit statute of authority of the Syrian Roman administrators. As such if the Herodian chose to do so, he could have had Jesus arrested and imprisoned and perhaps even severely punished for his lack of obedience.

Second, this is the first time that Jesus had ever dealt with a Herodian directly and the first time that any Herodian directly confronted Jesus. According to the prescribed law dictated by Herod Antipas, whenever a Herodian directly addressed a non-Roman citizen, the person who was directly addressed by the Herodian was required to bow his or her upper body to the Herodian in honor and submission, and respond with downcast eyes. Obviously, Jesus did neither. In addition, Jesus responded in a way that could have been perceived by the Herodian as contemptuous, which again was punishable by imprisonment or death.

Third, if the Herodian had declared Jesus to be under investigation by the commission of The Theophus, then if Jesus was a non-Roman he would have had to submit to interrogation at the Court of Herod located in Herod's palace complex in Capernaum; he would have had no other choice. It was the law. However, it appears that Jesus was not confronted with that demand.

Fourth, Jesus unceremoniously sent the Herodian away with a promise saying that the boy was alive—it is very unlikely that the Herodian would have tolerated this unless Jesus was a Roman citizen of some renown. Even more amazing, the Herodian who had just then met Jesus face to face and in all probability knew nothing about him or his teachings, accepted Jesus' words without question and believed without reservation. Without even a hint of fact or proof that the boy was indeed healed or was recovering, the Herodian turned, and with ineradicable trust in Jesus' words returned to Capernaum. This was unusual for a Herodian. By their very nature, they were skeptical. They believed no one and had a much-justified reputation of being heartless and fearful. They had faith in or believed in or respected and honored no one, no god, no religion, no law (except those that were specifically declared and demanded by Caesar), no rules or regulations, no government (except the emperorship of Caesar), and no institution (except that of Caesar). In short, they were arrogant and proud, and agnostic in their spiritual beliefs. Yet, they were totally dedicated to Caesar.

Fifth, Jesus endangered his own life by sending the Herodian away. This act probably as much as anything else in the ministry of Jesus, made the residents of the Galilee wonder about him and fear him and his influence and power. If he was not a Roman citizen then for sending the Herodian away, Jesus could have been executed on the spot on the grounds of insubordination and rebellion against the authority of Caesar, or he could have been arrested and sent to prison without a trial, for the rest of his life. Yet, Jesus suffered none of these consequences. Why? We do not know. Perhaps Jesus was a Roman citizen of some renown or at the very least he was respected, highly regarded, and honored by Romans of high renown. Perhaps the Herodian believed that Jesus really was The Theophus. Perhaps he believed Jesus' words and was not yet convinced about The Theophus issue. Perhaps he hoped that Jesus was right; or perhaps he wanted to wait and see whether or not Jesus was right before he reacted. All that is known is that Jesus sent the prince back to Capernaum with word that his son was alive; and the Herodian returned.

Can you imagine the mental and emotional war that was going on inside of the Herodian as he made his way back to Capernaum? He journeyed to Cana to order Jesus to come back with him, knowing that possibility Jesus would heal his son if he came back, and that there would be numerous eyewitnesses to the miracle, which would substantiate his claim that Jesus was The Theophus. Jesus did not return with him so his best-laid plans had come to naught; and he had no assurance, other than Jesus' word, that the boy would survive. He probably felt that he had failed his son and he had failed Caesar and the commission search ambassadors. This turn of events could have dire consequences for him and his family.

On the way back to Capernaum, his servants who had been sent to find him met the Herodian. They told him that his son was healed. He asked them what time it had happened. They told him that it happened about 1:00 in the afternoon the day before. It was the exact time that Jesus had told him that the boy was healed.

Gothard goes on to say that the Herodian believed and his whole house believed [John 4:53]. However, it is not stated in whom or in what they believed. Did the Herodian and his house believe in Jesus? Did the Herodian believe in Jesus' miracle? Did he and his family believe that Jesus was in reality The Theophus? Jesus had refused to come back with him, so he had no witnesses to collaborate the fact that Jesus was responsible for the miracle. In truth, if Jesus did not want to be revealed as The Theophus, this was the way to do it. Did he believe that Tiberius was telling the truth about the dream? Did he believe in the dream? Did he believe in Tiberius? Was the family that believed his immediate family or was it the entire House of Herod? We are not told in what or in whom the prince and his family believed or what "all the family" means. We do know that from the time a report was given of a Theophus sighting until the Roman ambassadors arrived on the scene to examine and authenticate the claim, it took from two to five years. We know that from this time (summer of AD 27) on until the last few months of his earthly ministry (spring of AD 31), except for a couple of instances, the Herodians remained relatively quiet in their relationship to Jesus. It was not until the final few months of Jesus' ministry that Herod sent for him, that Herod actually searched for him, and that the Herodians joined with the Sadducees in questioning him, interrogating him, and closely examining his every move. It indicated to Gothard that there had been pressure placed upon the Herodians concerning Jesus and his potential examination as a candidate for The Theophus.

"This," Gothard wrote, "coupled with the fact that we learn from the now extinct writings of Francesco Magri, Bishop of Burgos from 810 to 833, that less than a year after Jesus' death, ambassadors representing Tiberius' Theophus Commission arrived in Jerusalem and questioned Herod Antipas, Caiaphas, the Jewish Sanhedrin, and Pilate about Jesus, his works and miracles and his death, forced me (Gothard) to conclude that it was not coincidence that the sudden interest in Jesus' activities by the Herodians took place about four years after the miracle healing of the son of the Herodian. If in fact the Herodian did report the event to the commission and the commission in turn felt that more investigation was necessary, it would have been from two to five years before they would have arrived in the area in order to investigate Jesus." The remainder of the document had been destroyed so Gothard's comments came to an abrupt end.

For the next couple of months, nothing more is recorded about the life of Jesus. What he did that summer we do not know.

It was not until August that we find Jesus on the shores of the Sea of Galilee, or as Luke 5:1 states *"the lake of Gennesaret,"* preaching to a crowd of people. It was at this time that Jesus called Peter, Andrew, James, and John to be his disciples. It was also at this time that one of the few unexplained miracles associated with Jesus was recorded by Roman historians and chronologists.

It was at the National Museum in Luxembourg City, Luxembourg, that I was shown documentation that affirmed not only their—Andrew, Peter, James, and John—calling (Matthew 4:18-22; Mark 1:16-20; Luke 5:1-11) but also this unusual and unexplainable event that convinced them to leave their business and to immediately follow Jesus.

The documentation was a book that had been written by a Lutheran pastor, Rev. Dr. Louis Henrii Ranhugel, in 1890, entitled *The Miracle of the Call*. The book was based on a well-known sermon that Rev. Dr. Ranhugel had preached when he addressed the European Lutheran Missions Board conference, which was held in Ausburg in 1888.

The biblical texts that Rev. Dr. Ranhugel used were Luke 5:1-11 and Matthew 4:18-22. The setting was the western shore of the Sea of Galilee, a large lake in the Galilee known for it abundance of fish. It is 700 feet below sea level, about seven and a half miles long at its longest point and three and a half miles wide at its widest point.

Rev. Dr. Ranhugel wrote that Jesus had been preaching to a large throng of people, and they had begun to crowd him so much that they were pushing him into the water. He asked to use Peter's boat in order to push out a ways from the shore and preach from the boat. Peter, who was cleaning his nets after fishing all night without catching anything, agreed. So, Jesus got in the boat, pushed out into the water, and finished his sermon.

After the sermon was finished, Jesus told Peter, seemingly as payment for allowing him to use his boat, to launch out into the *deep* and fish. The Sea of Galilee had three depth distinctions: the *shore*, which was from the shoreline to about 200 feet out from the shore, had a maximum depth of about four feet; the *deep*, which was from about 200 feet from shore extending out for about another half mile to close to a mile, had a depth that gently increased from about four feet to about twenty feet before sharply falling off into the depths; the *depths*, the center of the lake, had a depth, at the time of Jesus, of upwards to 600 feet, although in 1888 the maximum depth was about 180 feet. So abundant was the fish supply in the lake that on any given day there were 100 or more fishing boats vying for its treasure of fish.

Jesus told Peter to *"launch out into the deep,"* or about a half mile to a mile off shore, and to let down his nets (plural). Peter, who had just finished the tedious and time consuming task of cleaning his nets and laying them out to dry, and who probably was tired and did not want to be bothered, objected to Jesus, saying that they had fished all night and had caught nothing. Nevertheless, Peter submitted to Jesus' command, but he said that instead of letting down his nets (plural), he would let down his net (singular). So, he loaded up his gear again and launched his ship.

The day was going to be one that neither Peter, his brother Andrew, nor his partners James and John, Jesus' cousins, would ever forget.

The classical historians Suetonius Tranquillus, Tacitus, Paolo, and Marcus Valerius Martialis, forever etched the day, August 11, AD 27, in the annals of recorded Roman history. They recorded that on this date the Sea of Galilee, or the Lake of Gennesaret, experienced an event that Paola called the "bubbling up of the sea" and that "...the event was foreseen and presaged by a Jesus from the Galilee of Syria, a religious teacher of the Jews, the adopted son of Joseph, the Jewish royal who was Rome's citizen senior senator representing Britain and the emperor's

Minister of Mines, and who (Jesus) was the only Roman citizen of renown under examination by the Theophus Commission of Tiberius."

The event on the lake as well as the auguring of the event by Jesus was witnessed by members of the Theophus Commission sent from Rome; Marcus Omerigus, a Senator from Rome; Claudius Maximus, a special tax envoy sent from Tiberius to investigate reports of Jewish rebel sabotage of the Roman salt tax; Marcus Antonious Somintous, the commander of the portion of Roman 7th Legion stationed at Nain; and Herod Antipas. They had all accompanied Herod Antipas to the city of Tiberias work site that day. Tiberias was located on the western shore of the lake, just a few hundred feet south of where Jesus was teaching. Herod wanted to show-off the new city of Tiberias that was then under construction, hoping they would take word back to Tiberius, keeping Herod in good favor with the emperor.

Thousands of years before that day, the rifting of the Jordan River valley took place. Into one of the deep lava pits that the rifting had created began to pour millions of tons of water from the higher levels. Over the centuries, eventually the continual flow of water began to fill the huge lava pit. This water-filled lava pit became the Sea of Galilee or the Lake of Gennesaret.

A shallow crust of rock (water-cooled lava and melted rock) formed at the bottom of the pit, sealing off the molten lava, allowing over a period of time, the water in the continuously filling pit, to cool. Over the years a deep lake developed. As the lake filled, the water spilled over into the surrounding shallow areas and formed a ledge (less than 20 feet) called the *deep*, before dropping sharply toward the center of the lake, called the *depths*. Because the fish bred in the shallow *deep* and then returned to the *depths*, the best fishing was in the *deep*.

At least once and perhaps as many as six or seven times every five to ten years on the average, an event at the Sea of Galilee occurred that was an unprecedented act of nature. The event was on one hand frightening, yet on the other hand, was profitable. At times the event took place two or three times within one month's time and did not occur again for ten years or more. At other times it occurred once every year. Sometimes the event would take place two or three times per year for six or seven years straight, then not again for nine or ten years or longer. The last time the event took place was in 1848 [based on current records, the last time the event occurred was in 1967]. The 1848 event was unanticipated and came without warning.

The "bubbling up of the sea" was caused by pressure that built up below the surface of the shallow rock crust at the bottom of the lake. As the pressure built, cracks began to develop in the shallow rock crust. As the pressure increased, suddenly and without warning, the crust split open. A huge bubble of sulfuric gas and boiling hot water exploded from the broken crust and gushed to the surface. As the enormous bubble broke to the water's surface, the cooler atmospheric air was rapidly and violently forced outward. As the hot bubble ascended skyward, the cooler air rushed back in with gale force velocity causing immediate and unexpected storms in the middle of the lake. If any ships were unfortunate enough to be in the *depths*, or in the middle part of the lake, when this bizarre act of nature assaulted the Sea of Galilee, they would experience severe turmoil and a devastating "sea storm." The catastrophe was unprecedented in all of the natural disasters in that region. Near the shore or in the *deep*, ships were safe because the ledge protected them. In fact, on the shore and in the *deep* regions of the lake, there were little or no consequences whatsoever as a result of the "bubbling up of the sea."

As the boiling hot water burst towards the water's surface, fish by the thousands feverishly tried to escape the hot water by franticly swimming from the *depths* into the shallow ledge, the *deep*. If a fisherman happened to be fishing in the *deep* when this event took place, within a matter of minutes he would be inundated with so many fish that he could likely match his entire year's catch within minutes. There are reports that fish have been so plentiful during this event that commercial fishing nets would snap and if a person wanted to he could presumably walk to shore by walking on the fish.

It was this event that caused Simon to harvest so many fish so quickly. Moreover, if he had followed Jesus' specific command, the resulting catch would have been even greater than it was.

"The question then," Rev. Dr. Ranhugel continued to explain, "Becomes not how did Simon catch so many fish, but rather how did Jesus know that the *bubbling up of the sea* was about to take place, seeing that it was unpredictable and happened completely unexpectedly? It is true that the event normally took place in the spring or summer, and it was in the summer (August) that this one took place. But the event usually happened without warning so quickly, that to try to predict when it would occur would have been impossibility—yet Jesus did it."

The predicting of the event so impressed Simon and Andrew, Simon's brother, and their business partners, James and John, Jesus' cousins, that at Jesus' bidding, all four immediately left their business and followed Jesus. And it so impressed the Roman officials present that they insisted that the event be recorded in the permanent records of the histories and annuals of Rome.

The Rev. Dr. Ranhugel concluded the book with a statement that seemed contrary to anything I had ever been taught about the disciples.

"Peter, Andrew, James, and John, were personally called by Jesus to be his disciples or followers, but at that time they were *nothing more* than four out of many—perhaps hundreds—who became followers (disciples) of Jesus. They may have had (as did Philip and the nathanael, if in fact the nathanael of John 1 was actually called to be one of his disciples) 'Jesus' ear,' but they did not occupy a special inner circle position at this time. They did not attain a special position until three of the four (Peter, James, and John) were selected by Jesus to accompany him to the Transfiguration, which occurred quite some time after they had been appointed apostles (Luke 6). Even in their selection as part of Jesus' twelve apostles, they were picked out of a multitude of other disciples."

Not long after the "bubbling up of the sea" and the call of Peter, Andrew, James, and John, Jesus and his disciples returned to Capernaum. On a particular Sabbath day not long after they had returned to Capernaum, they went to a synagogue and Jesus began to teach. Jesus' knowledge and his authoritative teaching style amazed the people. But while he was teaching, a man who had an unclean spirit entered the synagogue and disrupted his teaching (Mark 1:21-28; Luke 4:33-37). Jesus responded by casting the unclean spirit out of the man.

I was supplied documentation that validated the Gospel records of this incident as well as a payload of additional information about the power structure of the Luciferian system while researching at the University of Chicago.

Dr. Harriet Blanch, a strong Christian who served her church, North Side Assembly, as Education Director, and was the Director of Research and Investigative Resources at the University of Chicago library, became so fascinated with my search for historical Jesus research project that she spent an entire afternoon and evening helping me find corroborating documentation that confirmed the truth of the Gospels.

One of the most exhaustive books that she picked-out for me was one that dealt with the power structure of the evil spirit world, using this incident of Jesus' confrontation with the man who had an unclean spirit at the synagogue in Capernaum, as the foundational text upon which the author of the book built his thesis.

According to Dr. Blanch, Gustave Doren, a former Methodist pastor turned writer and painter from London, wrote the large, 600-page, leather-bound volume in 1880. Doren was a contemporary and friend of Charles Spurgeon. The book was entitled *Not Against Flesh and Blood*. Doren claimed that a large part of the book, especially portions that dealt with a Luciferian system's line of authority, were paraphrased segments of a document written by Polycarp, Bishop of Smyrna from AD 150 to 155, who was martyred in AD 155. Early Church tradition claimed that Polycarp was a personal disciple of John the Evangelist. Doren said that Polycarp's document was entitled *Divisions*. "To date," Dr. Blanch said, " I have not found a single copy of this document or a copy of a copy of it. All that is known about this document is what the early church fathers, Tertullian and Origen, have written. Although they did not go into detail regarding the document, they did acknowledge the fact that Polycarp had written a document entitled *Divisions*, about four years before he was martyred, and that it was supposed to have been distributed to Christians in Italy and Greece, warning them of the subtle and deceptive evils that were at work in the court of Antoninus Pius, the so-called 'Gentle Aristocrat.'"

The book covered a variety of subjects. However, its primary focus was on the levels of authority in the evil spirit world, which continually war against the levels of authority in the godly spirit world. The section that I felt was most interesting was the portion where Doren sought to prove that Jesus knew about the evil levels of authority and that he correspondingly fought against those evil levels of authority.

Doren referred to Jesus and his ministry throughout the book. But the first one-quarter of the book, the portion that dealt with Jesus' experience in a synagogue in Capernaum, was the portion that I felt better enhanced my research goals.

Dr. Blanch was gracious enough to "wade through" the book for me and to identify areas that would be beneficial to me, while I took notes of her quotes of Doren and her observations and opinions regarding what he had written.

Doren began the first quarter of his document by quoting the Bible references that he used as his foundational text, Mark 1:23-28 and Luke 4:33-37.

> *"And there was in their synagogue a man with an unclean spirit; and he cried out, saying 'Let us alone; what have we to do with thee, thou Jesus of Nazareth? Art thou come to destroy us? I know who thou art, the Holy One of God.' And Jesus rebuked him, saying, 'Hold thy peace, and come out of him.' And when the unclean spirit had torn him, and cried with a loud voice, he came out of him. And they were all amazed, insomuch that they questioned among themselves, saying, what thing is this? What new doctrine is this? For with authority commandeth He even the unclean spirits, and they obey Him. And immediately His fame spread throughout all the region round about Galilee" (Mark 1:23-28).*

> *"And in the synagogue there was a man, which had a spirit of an unclean devil, and cried out with a loud voice, saying, 'Let us alone; what have we to do with thee, thou Jesus of Nazareth? Art thou come to destroy us? I know thee who thou art; the Holy One of God.' And Jesus rebuked him saying, 'Hold thy peace, and come out of him.' And when the devil had thrown him in the midst, he came out of him, and hurt him not. And they were all amazed, and spake among themselves, saying, what word is this! For with authority and power He commandeth the unclean spirits, and they come out. And the fame of Him went out into every place of the country round about" (Luke 4:33-37).*

"The setting of this event," Dr. Blanch began, "was when Jesus and the six (at this time) disciples that he had called, were in Capernaum. On the Sabbath day in late summer of AD 27, they went to a synagogue in the city. Perhaps it was one in which Jesus was involved with its construction, or perhaps it was another one. Historians from that time claim that Capernaum had four synagogues along with numerous temples dedicated to a variety of gods, goddesses and religions. Worship facility estimates in the city range from as few as twenty to as many as a hundred or more representing dozens of religions and religious philosophies.

"Before Doren began his elaboration on the Luciferian system, he first explained in semi-detail the strange events that happened in the synagogue in Capernaum on that Sabbath Day. For the most part he concentrated on the Luke 4 setting.

"At the time of Jesus' ministry exorcism was well known and practiced by a few Jewish priests and by a select number of Pharisees. Polycarp claimed that Solomon originally set down the principles and techniques of exorcism. It was said that during Solomon's reign, so effective was the art of exorcism that Solomon had a school/clinic established for the study, education, and practice of exorcism. The institution claimed a clientele of thousands from every part of the known world. Where Solomon and the exorcists of his day learned their art is unknown. There is enough evidence to presume that it was either divinely given, or it was learned from studying the ancient texts of the Babylonian religious mysteries.

"By the time that Jesus began his ministry, most exorcism was performed by specially appointed exorcists who had been appointed by the High Priest to perform exorcism on behalf of and by the authority of the High Priest. They were chosen from the ranks of the most experienced elder Pharisees and priests. These exorcists did not include non-appointed priests, Sadducees (who for the most part did not believe in demon possession, but who did believe that there was an evil force that could use men in an effort to accomplish its goals), rabbis, rabbonis, or non-appointed Pharisees. Since Jesus did not have the official title of exorcist, his acts of exorcism did not have the blessings of his religious overlords. Whatever he did, he did of his own accord. Consequently, his exorcism could have been, and rightly so from their point of view, interpreted by the religious hierarchy as rebellion and insubordination. This could have been cause, if the religious leaders chose to pursue it, for Jesus' dismissal from his position as rabboni, his immediate and total exclusion for life, from synagogue worship participation, and his excommunication.

"The typical exorcism ritual at Jesus' time was a fractional ghost of the original exorcism ritual practiced in Solomon's time, and it was far less effective. It was not instantaneous, like was so often the case in Solomon's time.

"At the time of Jesus, exorcism would normally be a long, drawn-out, and agonizing process that lasted at least five or six days, upwards to seven or eight months. The primary method of exorcism was to strip the demonic naked and bind the victim in chains. Each time the person became violent and uncooperative, the exorcist would douse the demonic with frigid water that had been blessed by the exorcist priests, until he or she calmed down. This was accompanied by a never ceasing oral recitation of the Law of Moses, the words of the prophets, the Psalms, and the proverbs of Solomon. Four exorcists would each take a shift reading, so that the reading would never stop. In addition, each day two priests would come and take turns reciting the prayers and lamentations of David, Isaiah, and Jeremiah, for upwards to ten hours a day.

"Eventually, the demonic was supposed to calm down and return to normal. Maybe he did and maybe he did not. History has little to say about the effectiveness of this process, but it was generally assumed that the method was effective in only a fraction of the exorcism cases.

"Doren points out that the demonic at Capernaum recognized Jesus immediately upon his (the demonic's) entering the synagogue. The demonic first attempted to discredit Jesus by associating him with the refuge city of Nazareth, and then he sought to slander him by saying that he knew him, implying that Jesus was in league with or in partnership with the demon.

"Doren further contends that according to the Luke setting, the demon was an evil or unclean spirit of a devil. This implied that the evil spirit possessing the man was a servant of a higher level of evil authority, a devil."

"It appears," interjected Dr. Blanch, "that Doren was suggesting something contrary to today's assumptions. Today, those who believe in demons, feel that there are demons that can possess people. Sometimes they are called demons, sometimes devils, and sometimes evil spirits. They have a leader named Satan, who is also known as The Devil and Lucifer. But Doren believed strongly that the three entities were different from each other and that there existed some type of evil level of authority."

"Now let's get back to Doren," she said.

"Doren now begins to lay the foundation for an explanation of the Luciferian hierarchy and how it worked. Again he repeated that he had compiled (or plagiarized, Dr. Blanch inserted) the vast majority of his information from Polycarp's *Divisions*.

"He said that although at the present time (1880), there seemed to be a feeling that all evil influences were one in the same, but called by different names: demons, devil, evil spirit, The Devil, or Satan, evidence produced by the writings of the first three centuries' church fathers indicate otherwise. These writings show that there was then and still is today, and has been since before the creation of Adam, a well organized and extremely disciplined and effective, evil hierarchy and an impressively systematized line of authority that rule, control, and operate the evil spirit world.

"In the first century, the Pharisees, priests, and rabbis called evil influences in general by the Hebrew word *mazzikim*. The word meant 'evil spirits' or 'evil influences' and 'harmful forces.' But whenever they referred to specific evil influences, they used a Greek, Latin, or a Chaldean word or phrase to identify them. The phrase for demon was *pneuma akatharton* (Chaldean). The word for devil was *daemonium* (Greek), and the phrase for evil or unclean spirit was *spiritus immundus* (Latin). Each of these had a different definition to reflect the specific and individual kind and type of evil influence.

"Doren then listed the three evil influences in order of authority, breaking down each group into specialized classes or *castes* (as he called them).

"Although devils, demons, and evil or unclean spirits monitor, observe, and torment all humans throughout the earth and function and perform their respective responsibilities worldwide relative to all humanity. Doren said that he concentrated almost exclusively upon their dealings and relationships with believers in Christ rather than with all of mankind. He did this because Polycarp dealt exclusively with believers.

"I now," Dr. Blanch said as she looked up from the book to make sure that I knew actually what she was going to do next, "will go much more slowly so that you will be able to write down all of the information. I will list the levels of authority in the way and manner that Doren listed them." She then began to narrate.

"DEVIL (*Daemonium*)—This is the highest level of the three 'working' levels of authority. Devils receive their authority directly from the Luciferian hierarchy.

> Within this class there are four castes, or levels of authority and superiority. He listed them in order of superiority and gave a brief explanation of their purpose and function. Although most of these names have come down to us in their Latin, Greek, or Hebrew form, the word origin was actually Chaldean.
>
> *Diabolos*—The word means adversary, accuser, and slanderer. This devil caste is first in superiority within the devil class. They continually stand before God and constantly accuse true believers, who in their (the Diabolos') opinion, have failed. They are the only devil caste that does not

come into earth's atmosphere. This caste has three levels of authority within its ranks.

1. *Dilos* is the highest-ranking level within the caste. The level is the one that deals directly with God in presenting a case against and accusing believers.
2. *Daalos* is the next level of authority. They are responsible for organizing and developing a case against a believer.
3. *Daima* is the lowest level. They are the devils that collect the slanderous information about a believer from observing devils and present the information to the *Daalos*.

Disaliuon—The word means ruler or dominion. This devil caste is second in superiority within the devil class. Their responsibility is to control and seek to rule specific geographical locations on earth (called strongholds). These locations could include cities, countries, areas, regions, provinces, states, groups of countries, people groups, and even political or religious groups and/or philosophies. Like Diabolos, their power is unmatched by any normal human power on earth. Their power can only be neutralized and defeated by a powerful spiritually mature authoritarian believer or group of believers who have attained a spiritual maturity level far above the typical levels of maturity for which many Christians strive, attacking the stronghold directly. This caste also has three levels of authority within its ranks.

1. *Dissali* is the highest level of authority. They rule and control a large area or people group, such as an empire, country, or a race of people.
2. *Dosimia* is the second highest level of authority. They rule a region within the area controlled by the *Dissali*, such as a province or a state within a country or a national group of people.
3. *Desmoni* is the third level of authority. They rule a district within the region controlled by a *Dosimia*, such as a city or a clan or family unit.

Diamonion—The word means observer and tempter. This devil caste is third in superiority within the devil class. They observe true believers and continually monitor each believer's actions and reactions to various temptations that they impose upon the believer. If a believer does not resist a particular temptation, but rather entertains or harbors it and allows it to remain in mind, a demon that specializes in that particular type of temptation (we will cover this later, Doren noted) will be assigned by the observing devil to that believer. The demon will continually torment and harass the believer with that temptation as well as other temptations that are similar to the temptation, to which the believer has yielded, in an all-out effort to cause the believer to sin or to commit iniquity. If the believer does yield to the sin, the demon will attach itself to the believer and will harass the believer day and night with this and other temptations, in an effort to cause the believer to distance himself from God. The demon will remain attached until the believer resists the temptation and refuses to yield to the sin. If the believer yields and thereby sins, the observing devil that assigned the demon to the believer reports the believer's failure and iniquity to an accuser devil, who in turn prepares a slander of the believer to be presented before God, accusing the believer of sin and failure. The *Diamonion* is divided into three levels of authority.

1. *Demus* is the highest level of authority. They are the ones who deliver the information about a believer's failure to the *Daima*, and they select the various temptations that will be presented to a believer based on a believer's past failures and weaknesses.
2. *Deema* is the second level of authority. Whenever a believer shows a weakness to a particular temptation or shows acceptance of a temptation, they begin a concentrated bombardment of that temptation or similar temptations on the believer. Whenever the believer begins to incubate the temptation rather than reject it, the believer is turned over to the authority of a *Das Maus*.
3. *Das Maus* is the third level. The demon that specializes in the temptation wherein the believer shows a weakness is under the direct control of a *Das Maus*. This devil also records every action and reaction of the believer to the concentrated temptation and if the believer yields to the temptation and either sins, trespasses, transgresses, or transacts iniquity, it is immediately reported to the *Deema*, who passes the failure on to the *Demus*.

Diasalos—The word means power spirit or strength. This devil caste is fourth in superiority within the devil class. These devils are evil warriors. They fight against the warrior angels of God and against powerful believers who threaten the other three castes. These devils also stand guard over observing devils and protect them against the more powerful believers who have the ability to recognize the observer devils for who they are and who have the power to force the observing devils to leave a specific area or to leave a believer alone. Although part of their responsibility is to protect *Diamonion*, whereby they must honor the wishes of a *Diamonion* when it comes to their protection, they are not under the direct control of the *Diamonion*. Instead, they are under the direct control of the *Disaliuon*. The *Diasalos* are divided into three levels of authority much like the levels of military authority.

1. *Dia Nunus* is the highest level of authority. This would be equivalent to a general or a high-ranking officer.
2. *Dammia* is the second level of authority. This would be equivalent to a subordinate officer.
3. *Deiaslo* is the third level. This would be equivalent to a fighting warrior or soldier.

"Doren next discussed DEMON (*pneuma akatharton*)—This evil influence is the second of the three 'working' levels of authority. They work exclusively under the directive of the *Deema* and the direct command of the *Das Maus*. Their main function is to torment a believer in an effort to cause a believer to fail before God. Their secondary function is to cause as many humans as possible to forsake the true Godhead and to seek their own way of life and salvation. Incapacitating believers is the number one priority. Tormenting all of humanity is their secondary priority.

Within this class there are four castes, but Polycarp did not say whether one level was superior to another. So Doren simply listed them and explained the duties and responsibilities of each, without speculating on the levels of authority.

Diamon—The word means evil possessor of feeling. These demons specialize in emotional tormenting that includes hopelessness, loneliness, worthlessness, faithlessness, guilt, depression, and self-condemnation. If an observing devil tempts a believer with an emotional temptation, and if the observing devil determines that a believer has yielded to or is sympathetic to the temptation, then an emotional demon, a *diamon*, is assigned to that believer to torment him [or her] with an unrelenting bombardment of that and like temptations. If the believer yields to the temptation, the demon attaches itself, like a leech, to the believer and will harass the believer regularly with the temptation, while draining him [or her] of his [or their] faith in God and his [or her] spiritual life. **THIS IS NOT DEMON POSSESSION** (taking up residence). **RATHER, THIS IS DEMON OPPRESSION** (harassment and torment). **NOTE**: *THIS DOES NOT MEAN THAT ALL EMOTIONAL PROBLEMS ARE CAUSED BY DEMON POSSESSION OR OPPRESSION.* Although, continual yielding to the temptation could eventually lead to possession of a non-believer by that particular demon, the likelihood of demon possession of a believer is near zero. The demon leech that has attached itself to a believer can be dislodged and eliminated from the life of a believer, by that believer resisting the leech through prayer and by the power associated with the name and authority of Jesus, by the believer dealing with the emotional hurts that have resulted from the attachment, and by the believer eliminating the past traumas that encourage and feed the emotional leech. Non-believers on the other hand will have a very difficult time eliminating this attached oppressing leech. In fact, it is impossible for a non-believer to dislodge the leech through his own power, efforts, or abilities. Possession (taking up residence within an individual) of a non-believer by an emotional demon is normally accomplished by two means: continually yielding to the temptation which results in repeated and habitual sin or iniquity; or justifying an acceptance of the continual yielding to the temptation as a normal personality trait and characteristic and an unchangeable way of life (i.e. *this is just me—you have to accept me the way I am-I am the way I am and I'm not going to change*).

Sair—This word means mind manic. These demons specialize in psychological problems such as schizophrenia, hysteria, phobias, bitterness, inferiority, deep depression, self-destruction, intense hatred, despite, and chronic non-forgiveness. <u>**NOTE**</u>: *AGAIN THIS DOES NOT MEAN THAT DEMON OPPRESSION OR POSSESSION CAUSES ALL PSYCHOLOGICAL PROBLEMS.* A major portion of these types of problems is caused by past traumas that have occurred in a person's life, and many times have absolutely nothing to do with demon activity. However, there are most definitely sair leeches that *can* cause these types of psychological problems. While these demons seem to be more active with respect to non-believers than believers, they do torment believers on occasion.

Shed—The word means flesh manic. These demons specialize in disease and sickness that affects the physical body. Again, **THIS DOES NOT MEAN THAT DEMON OPPRESSION OR POSSESSION CAUSES ALL DISEASE AND SICKNESSES.** In fact, demon oppression or possession *is not the cause of most of these diseases*. But on the other hand, there are most definitely *shed* leeches whose specialty includes the infliction of humankind with every disease and every sickness that has ever been known to humankind or that does or has ever, had the possibility and capability of affecting humankind.

Shair—The word means enchantment worship. These demons specialize in filling the spiritual need of humankind. There are shair that specialize in every philosophy, belief, religious practice and doctrine, dogma, philosophical ritual, spiritual experience, worship ritual, and "inner man" fulfillment that has ever been or ever will be known to humankind. The shairs' primary function is to use all of their power and influence to steer attention away from, discredit, downplay, belittle, compromise, change, degrade, cast doubts upon, and corrupt the life, teachings, example, actions, methods, authority, position, and purpose of Jesus Christ.

"The third class of the three 'working levels' of evil influences that was discussed by Doren is EVIL (UNCLEAN) SPIRIT (*spititus immundus*). Evil spirits, although third in the Luciferian working levels of authority, in many aspects are equal to demons in that they are under the direct control of devils. Evil spirits serve under the authority of *dammia, deiaslo,* and *desmoni* devils.

There are four castes within the class of Evil Spirit, but again Doren did not specify whether one is superior over another, because Polycarp did not specify.

Rialos—The word means emissary. These evil spirits are messengers who coordinate and deliver communication between devils, between devil and evil spirit, and between evil spirits. The *rialos* travel along earth's geophysical force fields that are called ley lines. They also direct demons where they are supposed to go on assignment.

Dialolos—The word means to guard one's land. These evil spirits are responsible for making sure that territory claimed by the *desmoni* or *dosimia* devils remains under the devils' control. They are, in essence, security guards who work under the direct command of the *dammia*. If powerful believers threaten a physical land territory, these evil spirits will defend the territory for the devils until *deiaslo* arrive to take up the all out fight.

Milos—The word means to prevent; to travel. These evil spirits are responsible for intercepting a believer's prayers, meditations, or projections that they feel would be a threat to the kingdom of Lucifer or the Luciferian system and its plan and purpose.

Reialos—The word means presence. These evil spirits reside in a specific geographical location, city, territory, region, area, or country. They do not leave that area unless they are forced to leave by powerful believers. They are, in essence, permanent residents who are at all times subject to the beckoning call of that area's controlling *desmoni* or *dosimia*. They are a permanent work force that have the "physical" power of desmoni but lack the authority of desmoni. They are totally and completely subject to the area's ruling *desmoni*, and do whatever is commanded of them by *desmoni*, *dosimia*, and *dissali*."

"Doren went on," Dr. Blanch continued, "to explain the difference between devils, demons, and evil spirits. Again he repeated that he claimed to have received the bulk of his information from Polycarp. He said that devils are beings that were created by God in the beginning. They were originally angels, but they became participants in the Luciferian rebellion against God, resulting in their being cast out of heaven. As such, they became the 'fallen angels.' Since they were created angels, they cannot nor do they have the ability to possess people. Like angels, devils have different levels of authority, as has already been mentioned. They work under the authority of and on behalf of the Luciferian hierarchy.

"Demons are the disembodied souls of the past unrighteous or evil inhabitants of the earth (these lived before the establishment of the new social order by Noah. Some feel that these might have been pre-Adamite earth inhabitants; some feel that they might have been former inhabitants of the earth destroyed during Noah's flood; still others feel that these demons are the spirits [not the souls] of creatures that were created by God who were near human or humanoid, but were not human; and others feels that they are the disembodied souls of the inhabitants of earth who joined the Luciferian rebellion against God [not the rebel angels, who became known as devils, but rather the population that inhabited and resided on earth and who joined in the Luciferian rebellion]). The demons, because they are evil disembodied souls, have to have a body to possess in order to function at their maximum ability level. Whoever they were or how they came into existence, no one really knows. What is known with assurance is that these demons are disembodied souls or spirits of some ancient, now extinct, earth inhabitants: souls that must have a body to possess in order to function at their highest potential. Demons are the evil forces that directly influence humankind either by oppression or possession.

"Evil (unclean) spirits are also created beings. Perhaps they fit in the same category as cherubim. They joined the Luciferian rebellion and became evil forces subject to the Luciferian hierarchy. They do not possess. They are messengers, emissaries, guards, and/or caretakers. They normally reside at and are permanently restricted to a specific geographical area or region, unless they are cast out and forbidden to return to that area.

"Doren then turned his attention to the Luciferian system. But before he began he added a disclaimer saying, 'The following description of the Luciferian system was not gleaned from the Polycarp document. Polycarp merely stated that the system existed. For information about the Luciferian hierarchy I have relied upon the writings of the 18th century Luciferian, Adam Weishaupt and the 18th century Satanist, Sir Francis Dashwood. From their writings I learned the names and identities of the Luciferian system's highest levels of authority. Whether these are truly the actual names and identities of the Luciferian hierarchy cast or whether these mentioned are the total number of players in the Luciferian system's drama, I cannot say. But for the sake of knowledge and scholastic enlightenment I present them as these 18th century devotees have intended and proposed.'

"He said that Adam Weishaupt and Sir Francis Dashwood claimed that the Luciferian system has a four-level hierarchy, much like the levels of authority within the hierarchy of the Christian religion. It culminates with a Luciferian godhead or trinity. Again it is much like the Christian Godhead or Trinity.

"The three highest levels of authority very seldom directly intervene in the lives of humankind or directly intervene in the politics of human government. Only the lower levels regularly trek between earth and the universe that became Hate. They claimed that Hate is one of the four interconnected universes. The three higher levels of authority leave the direct intervention responsibilities to the devils that occupy the earth and who have these responsibilities. These three highest levels of authority are more concerned with the progression of the over-all Luciferian plan, which is in direct opposition to God's overall plan. However, the details of the implementation of the process and function of that plan are left to the earth occupying devils and their underlings. In short, these three higher levels of authority very seldom, if ever, come to earth and influence earth directly. That responsibility is left up to those spirits who have been commissioned to do that particular job. They instead normally remain in the universe that became Hate and rule through their under-authorities from there. The universe that became the universe of Hate is one of four universes. The universe of Hate is the universal home of the Luciferian monarchy. It is the universe of total and complete evil.

The Search

"The lowest level of these higher levels of authority is the level that the biblical apostle Paul described as *powers*. There are 25 ruling *powers*. They periodically, but consistently, shuttle back and forth between earth and the universe that became, Hate.

"Dashwood claimed that the devils, demons, and evil spirits that occupy or reside on the earth cannot travel from one place to another on earth unrestricted. They have to travel along the geophysical force fields or geophysical energy lines, sometimes called ley lines that reside in/on/under/above the earth.

"All of the ley lines on earth are divided into and concentrated in 12 geographical power regions on earth. Within a particular geographical power region, the devil, demon, or evil spirit can travel as it wills and chooses, as long as it is along ley lines that are located within that power region. However, if the devil, demon, or evil spirit wants to move from a particular power region to another power region, it must exit that region through the region's 'exit gate' and enter another region through that region's 'entrance gate.'

"Each of the 12 regions has one exit gate and one entrance gate. Doren then gave an example: Let's assume that a demon is residing in a region that included all of Africa. The demon can travel along ley lines throughout Africa as often as is necessary and as it sees fit. Now let's assume that the demon is commanded by an overseer devil to move to a new residence. A residence that includes, let's say, Europe. In order for the demon to travel from Africa to Europe, he will have to exit the power region that included Africa through that region's exit gate and then enter the power region that includes Europe through the entrance gate of the power region that includes Europe. Once in, he can travel along that power region's ley lines as often as he chooses, unless he is forbidden to do so.

"The *dissali* who reside on earth within specific areas and politically control areas within a power region are under the direct control of the first level of upper Luciferian hierarchy; the *power* level. In addition, the *dia nunus* who reside on earth within a specific area and who militarily control the same areas that the *dissali* control politically, are also under control of the first level of upper Luciferian hierarchy; the *power* level. There are 25 power authorities: 12 authorities rule over and supervise the activities of the *dissali* and 12 authorities rule over and supervise the activities of the *dia nunus* who operate in the 12 power regions.

"Within one of the 12 *power* regions there might be numerous *dissali* and *dia nunus* controlling multitudinous areas or people groups, yet they (the *dissali* and *dia nunus*) are ruled by only two *power* authorities in each *power* region: one authority rules the political activities and one authority rules the military activities (war efforts against powerful believers and godly warriors) within a *power* region. So, in all 12-*power* regions of earth, 12 *power* authorities rule politically and 12 *power* authorities rule militarily.

"The 25th *power* authority rules the activities of the *diabolos* who continually accuse believers before God. Authority levels relative to the activity of *diabolos* accusation and slander have no need to go beyond the *power* level of upper authority.

"Dashwood claimed that he knew the names of at least three of these *power* authorities. Their names are Mith, Swast, and Hexas.

"The second level of higher authority within the Luciferian hierarchy was what Paul called the *principality* level. There are eight *principality* authorities and they rule the 24 power region authorities.

"Although earth-residing devils, demons, and evil spirits must travel and are in fact restricted to travel along the thousands of *power* region regional ley lines only, no such restriction is imposed upon God's angels in general and His warrior angels in particular nor are travel restrictions placed on either those powerful believers in Christ who have advanced into the *highest levels* of spiritual maturity, the power level of Luciferian upper authority, or the three highest levels of the Luciferian hierarchy. They can either travel by the regional ley lines and/or along quadralefian leys.

"Both Dashwood and Weishaupt claimed that there are four quadralefian leys and ley points."

"According to Anton Levey, the late Satanist from California," Dr. Blanch noted, "the quadralefian leys seem to be the *super highway* leys of geophysical forces. They are direct lines that connect all points in the 12 *power* regions. Travel on the quadralefian leys is at, or greater than, the speed of light. They not only extend over the surface of the earth, but they also reach from the deepest depths of the earth to the farthest outreaches of earth's atmosphere."

"Quadralefian points," Dr. Blanch added, "seem to be gates that are both in *and* out gates. It is also through these quadralefian points that the above mentioned angels and warrior angels can travel from universe to universe and from throne domination to throne domination."

"Now back to Doren," she said.

"The 12 *power* regions were divided into four *principality* divisions consistent with and centered around the four quadralefian points. One political *principality* authority and one military *principality* authority governs each of these divisions. Each political *principality* authority governs three political *power* rulers and each military *principality* authority governs three military *power* rulers. These *principalities* seldom involve themselves directly with the daily affairs of earth or humankind. Most of their energies are spent governing from the Luciferian throne domination.

"Weishaupt claimed that the names of some of the *principality* authorities are Gelal, Pazuzu, Lilit, Xastur, Baphomet, Azag-Thoth, Ustur, and Nattig.

"The third highest level of the Luciferian hierarchy was the level that Paul called *dominions*. There are four *dominion* authorities.

"The four *principality* divisions are divided into two *dominion* federations. Within each *dominion* federation is one quadriferrian. A quadriferrian is a gate that leads directly to or from the universe that became Hate.

"Whenever earth-residing devils, demons, and evil spirits come under attack or are subject to intense resistance, they lose much of their power and effectiveness and must be 're-charged' or rejuvenated. In addition, demons who do not have a body to possess and to feed off of or have been 'cast out' of the body that they once possessed, or have been detached from a body to which they were attached, quickly lose their power and effectiveness. They too must be revitalized. Furthermore, all must have regular 're-charges' in order to function at their maximum potential on earth. The re-charging and rejuvenation is accomplished in the universe that became, Hate.

"The quadriferrian is the gate by which the evil influences can leave earth and go into the universe that became Hate and by which they can return from that universe back to earth. There is only *one* 'out' quadriferrian and only *one* 'in' quadriferrian. Dashwood claimed that the 'in' quadriferrian is located at the Giza Plateau in Egypt and that the 'out' quadriferrian is located near ancient Dyrrhachium in the country of Albania.

"The *dominion* federations are centered around these quadriferrians. Each *dominion* has a political *dominion* authority and a military *dominion* authority. Their primary responsibility is to maintain order, security, discipline, and the highest level of efficiency within their *dominion* federation and especially at the quadriferrian point, to insure that each and every evil influence received the appropriate amount of attention to allow it to function at its maximum level of effectiveness.

"Again, Weishaupt claimed that he knew the names of the dominion authorities: Humwawa, Maluka, Mithras, and Ankh.

"Doren then inserted his own opinionated footnote by saying, 'These points (the quadriferrian points) have a higher concentration of evil influences than any other place on the surface of the earth. For this reason, the two quadriferrian locations have been in the forefront of evil oppression for thousands of years, and the people of the region in which a point is located have been enslaved by poverty, war, subjugation, and oppression more often and more vehemently than any other people who have ever lived. However, they will also receive the highest concentration of God's might and power when the time is right and when the time has come to close those gates and commence God's 'Holy War' upon the evil influences that are left trapped in the earth. The evil influences will not be able to escape back to the universe that became, Hate, nor can they receive reinforcements and help from the universe that became, Hate. They will be trapped. Then the warriors of and the power of God will annihilate them.'

"The highest level of Luciferian authority, the Luciferian godhead, is the level that Paul called *thrones*. The level consists of three all-powerful, all superior, supreme spirits to whom all evil authorities, rulers, governors, devils, demons, and evil spirits are subject. They rule with an iron hand of discipline and demand absolute obedience from all of their subjects.

"The first supreme *throne* is Satan who was originally an angel called Lucifer, which means 'holder of the light,' or 'guardian of the holy fire of God.' He was an angel created by God and became an archangel of God. But, he rebelled against God and led a violent overthrow attempt against God. He was defeated in battle and was cast out of heaven. Sometime after this rebellion, but before the birth of Jesus, he changed his name from Lucifer, 'holder of the light,' to Satan, 'angel of light,' 'giver of light,' 'son of the morning,' and 'the morning star,' in an attempt to humiliate and to slander Jesus. When Jesus came to earth and lived as a human, he became known as and was proclaimed as, *'the bright and morning star'* and *'the light of the world.'*

"Satan is the *throne* of the Luciferian trinity that is the god and founder of all deceptive, irreverent, unholy, man-centered, and/or false religions, philosophies, beliefs, doctrines, rituals, and practices.

"The second supreme *throne* in the Luciferian trinity is Belial. Belial is the evil god who deals with and controls conflicts and disturbances in all areas of inner emotions and psychological sensitivity.

"The third supreme *throne* in the Luciferian trinity is Leviathan. Leviathan is the evil god who deals with and controls conflicts and disturbances in the areas of knowledge and intellect.

"The complete *throne level* of the Luciferian godhead took on the title of and is known as, Lucifer, holder of all of humankind's light: physical, emotional, psychological, and spiritual. Hence, whenever Lucifer is referenced, the name implies the **whole** Luciferian godhead and power structure including all levels of authority.

"With that statement Doren concluded his discussion of the Luciferian power structure." Dr. Blanch said. She then asked me if she could take a few minutes and read ahead a little to see if anything else would be helpful to me with regard to Jesus' experience at the synagogue in Capernaum. I told her that I had no objections because it would give me some time to catch-up on my notes.

After reading for a while she concluded with, "For the next two hundred or so pages Doren goes into great speculative depth about how the Luciferian system works and how it influences humankind. He even presented a theoretical power structure of the Trinity and the Godly system. He claimed that he received the skeleton of his information from Polycarp, and that from Polycarp's skeleton, he developed his hypothetical theory. He listed levels of authority and godly spirits and their presumed authority positions and functions, for not only earth and humankind, but for other solar systems and other universes. He further claimed that there were at least four different universes: the universe that became known as Faith, the universe that became known as Hope, the universe that became known as Love (the solar system wherein earth is a part is located in this universe of Love), and the universe that became known as Hate. He said that in the universe that became known as Hate, the *throne level* of the Luciferian system is located."

Although the portion of Doren's latter information, the portion that Dr. Blanch had read and commented on, seemed to be logical and believable to me, most of the information relating to the Trinity and the Godly system was abstruse, speculative, enigmatic, and mystical. So much so that Dr. Blanch and I both felt that the information was too inconsistent with my key of truth mandate to be seriously considered.

With the completion of Doren, my research at the University of Chicago ended.

But my contemplation on what I had learned did not end. Doren had introduced me to so much of the spirit world that I had never even thought about before, much less heard about. Levels of authority? Devils, demons, evil or unclean spirits, and they're all different rather than all being the same? Universe of Hate? Four different universes? Power levels? It was all too much. Although it stands to reason that the kingdom of evil would be organized just like God's kingdom and if in fact Lucifer the arch-angel was cast out of heaven and he became Satan the evil, the adversary of

God and good, then why not a orderly and systematic order of evil hierarchy? One that is divided into levels of authority, accountability, and responsibility? Why not divide the earth up into regions, with each region having is own power level? Why not geophysical power highways? If God created them from the beginning, why couldn't they be used for transport in the spirit world? The questions kept coming over and over, all night long. I never did get satisfactory answers to any of my questions. I thought about Jesus' dealing with demons, about Daniel's confrontation, about the man Legion, and about the Isaiah, Jeremiah, Ezekiel, Genesis, John, I Corinthians, and The Revelation portions that dealt with the issues of Satan, the Devil, spirits of evil, Lucifer, the prince of this world, and the Prince of the Power of the Air. In them I could see how Doren or Polycarp or whoever pulled all the information together, could have theorized an evil hierarchy based on justifiable conjecture and presumption to it's most extreme speculative degree—yet a theory founded in enough factual evidence to conclude that it could be either reality or fabrication. The mystery evil hierarchy scenario reminded me of the search for Noah's Ark: for those who believe, no proof is necessary; for those who don't believe, no evidence will ever be proof enough; and for those who ride the fence, they must decide whether the evidence presented is enough to prove truth, or serves only it deepen speculation, supposition, and uncertainty.

So, even to this day, I am not sure about what I believe regarding this issue. The Bible definitely states that devils, demons, Satan, Satan's kingdom, and evil exist. Therefore, I believe that they exist. I believe that evil influences mankind; I believe that demons possess; I believe that the forces of evil war against the forces of good; and I believe that the souls of mankind are a prize sought by both the kingdom of God and the kingdom of Satan. But how evil influences mankind, how it wars against good, how demons and devils fit in, how and why the souls of mankind are prized to the extent that war is waged for their conquest, or how Satan's kingdom is administered and governed, I do not know. Doren gave a convincing argument, but I still have far too many unanswerable questions to conclude that Doren is without a doubt accurate and correct.

Sometime shortly after his confrontation with the demonic at the synagogue in Capernaum, Jesus and his disciples left Capernaum for a few days. Where they went, what they did, or exactly how long they were gone is not known. But we do know that by approximately the first or second week of September they were back in Capernaum.

Upon their return, Jesus was approached by a centurion who had a sick servant whom he wanted Jesus to heal (Matthew 8:5-13).

I discovered a book explaining this miracle by Jesus at Franklin College, located in Lugano, Switzerland. Franklin College is a four-year American liberal arts college located on top of a hill in Lugano, overlooking the gorgeous lake and the lakeside portion of the city.

The book was entitled *Sacrificia de Jesus*. It had been written in 1637 by John Eudes of France, the founder (in 1643) of the Society of Jesus and Mary.

The book was actually an anti-Semitic treatise, in which John Eudes went into great detail to show how Jesus ministered to and on behalf of Romans, tax collectors, outcasts, and Herodians instead of the Jews.

Eudes began his treatise by reprinting the biblical reference where the centurion's servant narrative was recorded, Matthew 8:5-13.

> "And when Jesus was entered into Capernaum, there came unto him a centurion, beseeching him, and saying, Lord, my servant lieth at home sick of the palsy, grievously tormented. And Jesus saith unto him, I will come and heal him. The centurion answered and said, Lord, I am not worthy that thou shouldest come under my roof: but speak the word only, and my servant shall be healed. For I am a man under authority, having soldiers under me: and I say to this man, go, and he goeth; and to another, come, and he cometh; and to my servant, do this, and he doth it. When Jesus heard it, he marveled, and said to them that followed, verily I say unto you, I have not found so great faith, no, not in Israel. And I say unto you, that many shall come from the East and West, and shall sit down with Abraham, and Isaac, and Jacob, in the kingdom of Heaven. But the children of the kingdom shall be cast out into outer darkness: there shall be weeping and gnashing of teeth. And Jesus said unto the centurion, go thy way; and as thou hast believed, so be it done unto thee. And his servant was healed in the selfsame hour" (Matthew 8:5-13).

Eudes claimed that this centurion's name was Rustus Flabian and that he was the senior Roman centurion in the military district that included Capernaum. His servant's name was Nehem. Nehem was a Galilean Jew, who was a brilliant financial manager. Nehem was Rustus' financial manager for all of his affairs. Under Nehem's masterful management, in just 10 years Rustus had become, next to the royal family of Herod, the wealthiest man in all of the northern Galilee. To reward Nehem for his brilliance, Rustus Flabian granted him his freedom and told him that he would give him anything that was within his power to give.

The one gift that Nehem requested was for a new synagogue to be built in Capernaum, a synagogue in which the Galilean Jews would be proud to attend. Nehem's wish became Rustus' command.

Rustus, wanting the most professional and qualified building contractor available, inquired at Sepphoris, the regional capital, for the name of the finest builder in the region. He was referred to Joseph in Nazareth. Rustus traveled to Nazareth and contracted with Joseph to build the synagogue, but the timeframe imposed by Rustus for the synagogue's completion prohibited Joseph from personally over-seeing the project. Therefore, Joseph sent his son, Jesus, to Capernaum to begin construction on the synagogue; who although was of Jewish birth was Roman by birth adoption. This was in the year AD 21.

Jesus actively worked on the synagogue for four years. Then in AD 25 he reduced his role to that of an overseer and construction manager. It allowed him more freedom of movement. Whereas in Nazareth he was looked upon with suspicion and contempt, in Capernaum, Jesus was respected and welcomed with opened arms. So, when Joseph proposed to Jesus in the winter of AD 26 that he move with his mother and brothers to Capernaum and replace the temporary construction "office" with a permanent "branch" of his (Joseph's) construction business, Jesus jumped at the opportunity.

Construction on the synagogue in Capernaum was completed about six months after Jesus moved to Capernaum. On the day that the synagogue was dedicated to the Lord, Nehem was to be the guest of honor.

As Nehem was riding to the synagogue celebration, his horse suddenly became frightened and threw him off. When he hit the ground, either his neck or his back was broken, paralyzing him from his neck down. Since Rustus was on military assignment, he was not able to attend the celebration, and he was not aware that Nehem had not showed up for the dedication. No one knew what had happened to Nehem, and apparently no one tried to find him.

The dedication began without Nehem and lasted most of the day. It was not until late in the afternoon that Nehem was found lying face up on the ground, unable to move. He was taken to Rustus' home to die. Months later he was still alive—paralyzed with his life slowly slipping away, yet refusing to die.

Rustus had been favorably impressed with Jesus' character, his professionalism, and his principles, and with how Jesus exercised his authority on the job site. In addition, Rustus had been hearing varied reports about Jesus' non-construction supervision activities: teaching, casting out demons, and performing miracles of healing. In September, AD 27, when Nehem's condition had deteriorated to the point that Rustus was convinced that his servant was going to die, Rustus searched for and found Jesus, who was just returning to Capernaum after being away from the city for a few days.

Since Jesus had dealt with Rustus in business for almost five years, Jesus knew him well and perhaps he even knew his servant, Nehem. Thus, when Rustus requested for Jesus to heal his servant, Jesus did not hesitate. He said that he would come to Rustus' house and heal Nehem.

But to Jesus' surprise, Rustus stopped him and said that he was not worthy (the word translated _worthy_ actually meant _clean_ or _holy_ or _spiritually pure_) enough for Jesus to come to his home. It indicated that he felt that in matters that were spiritual or that were out of the realm of human power and/or understanding, Jesus was superior. Rustus recognized Jesus' authority and his power in the domain of the spirit and the region that is beyond and outside of human power, authority, understanding, or reason. Because Rustus lived by the law of authority and obedience to direct orders, he did not hesitate to recognize Jesus' authority in the realm that was beyond human control. As such, he was confident that Jesus did not have to come to his house; all he had to do was give a command to a servant or a disciple and send him on his behalf, or for that matter even give a verbal command against the unseen powers, and the powers and the forces beyond the realm of humankind would obey without question. It implied that Rustus believed without a doubt that Jesus had authority not only over sickness but also over death.

Jesus was amazed by Rustus' faith in him. Perhaps Jesus had never seen this side of Rustus. All of his dealing with Rustus up to this point was strictly from a business vantage point. Jesus then let everyone within earshot know that he was favorably impressed with Rustus' faith. In fact, he had not found this much faith in any Jew in either the Galilee or Judaea. The comment made by Jesus was a slap-in-the-face to the Jews who were present. But Jesus went further and said that people like Rustus who could be found in all areas of the Roman world would actually qualify to be a part of the Kingdom of Heaven before the Jews. Many Jews, he said, would not make it at all. Instead, these Roman world non-Jews would take their place. The Jewish religious leaders, who felt that they were assured a place in the kingdom, just because they were Jews, would be rejected from the kingdom.

Jesus then quoted a passage from the Roman poet, C. Valerius Catullus' (87-54 BC) epigram entitled *Annals of Truth*. The epigram's main theme was the fallacy of thinking that just because a person is a Roman citizen that he is above the law, is above punishment for wrongdoing, and is beyond reproach. He said that those Romans who take advantage of the poor and helpless, who do not respect the government or its authority, who break the law, who despise the righteous, and who place their Roman citizenship rights above the welfare of one, slave or free, citizen or non-citizen, who they can help but refuse to do so, should not inherit the privileges of Roman citizenship but rather, should be placed in the darkest and most vile of all prisons and be placed under a sentence of torture for the remainder of their life.

Jesus quoted Catullus insinuating that many of the Jews were cut from the same cloth as those Roman citizens who Catullus condemned in his writings. These Jews will like Catullus' Roman citizens be *'Cast out into outer darkness: there shall be weeping and gnashing of teeth.'* It was a quote that had been written by Catullus.

Jesus quoted Catullus because he was a well-known Roman poet and his works were mandatory study for any Roman who would serve in authority, including centurions. Both Jesus and Rustus knew the story well. So, because Rustus could relate to the story and understood it, Jesus used it, regardless of the negative repercussions that may have resulted from any Jewish religious leaders who could have been standing nearby listening.

The incident with Rustus is the first recorded event in which Jesus directly ministered to or healed on behalf of a Roman. Rustus was not common Roman; he was a centurion. A centurion was a Roman military captain who had authority over 100 soldiers, which was a 60th part of a Legion.

The Roman army at this time, AD 27, consisted of 30 active Roman Legions and the same number of reserve Legions. Each of these was supplemented by a numerically equal number of three types of auxiliary legions: cavalry, light-armed, and archers. A Roman Legion was under the authority of a Roman Senator who was called an Imperial Legate. Under the Senator were six military tribunes. Under each tribune were 10 centurions. The total complement of a Legion consisted of 6,000 men. All of these were Roman citizens. At this time in the history of Rome, The Empire had 180,000 active military personnel and 180,000 reserve personnel. All of these were Roman citizens. Likewise, there were an additional 540,000 active auxiliary military personnel and 540,000 reserve auxiliary military personnel. Although there was not a complete Legion stationed in Judaea (in AD 70 the Roman 10th Legion was sent from Syria to Judaea, but in AD 27 there were no complete Roman legions permanently stationed in Judaea), there were three legions stationed in Syria: one in central Syria, one in the Galilee, and one in the Decapolis. In Judaea, there were 100 Roman soldiers stationed at the Antonia fortress in

Jerusalem (These 100 were 'battle seasoned' crack veteran troops who were at the disposal of the Roman Judaean procurator. During special observance days or celebrations the procurator himself was obligated to be in Jerusalem. During these times he would summon to the city at least one and perhaps even more cohorts from the area to serve as a deterrent against rebellion and to guarantee peace and order.) with an additional 1,500 stationed in areas around the Jerusalem region, and 600 stationed in Caesarea Maritima. The remainder of the Roman military presence in Judaea was auxiliary units.

Legionaries were heavy infantry and were supplemented by the auxiliary units. Auxiliaries were not Roman citizens like the legionnaires, but they could earn citizenship after 25 years of service. Although auxiliaries were not Romans, they were under the command of Romans. The auxiliaries were grouped into regiments or cohorts of 500 strong. Each regiment was divided into five cohorti and a Roman centurion commanded each cohorti. The regiments were commanded by Roman perfects. Two auxiliary regiments made a tribunal. A Roman tribune commanded these. There were two cohorts named in the New Testament: the Italian Cohort and the Augustan Cohort.

The auxiliary units that were stationed in the Galilee/Judaea region were made up of non-Jewish Syrians, Greeks, Persians, Samaritans, Galileans, Nabataeans, Galatians, Phoenicians, and Egyptians. All were volunteers and were proud to be associated with the Roman military machine. They were treated with respect and were treated as equals by the Roman commanders. They were paid well, compared to the living standards of the majority of their countrymen, and they received a small retirement from the Roman government if they had served for 30 years or more. Seldom did the Roman authorities have problems of rebellion, insubordination, desertion, or refusal to fight with the auxiliary units. Most revolts or desertions, which were also seldom, were within the ranks of the Roman legions, where military service for Roman citizens was compulsory. If an individual had a physical handicap he was exempt from serving. The length of compulsory service was a minimum of three years up to as much as seven years depending upon the political state of The Empire. After the compulsory time was served, a soldier could volunteer to re-enlist up through the age of 60 in five-year service segments."

After finishing this description of the Roman military, Eudes' concluded his record of this particular miracle by Jesus.

"Imagine what the Pharisees thought when Jesus said openly to whomever was in the area and whoever could hear, that a Roman centurion, whom the Judean religious leaders considered evil, had more faith than any and all of those who considered themselves to be God's representatives of God's chosen people. Jesus went on to say that there would be those who come from the empire's western most parts (Romans, Greeks, Illyrians, etc.) and the eastern most parts (Persians, Parthians, Arabs, etc.) who would see the kingdom of heaven *long before* the 'holy and righteous children of God' (as self-proclaimed by them), the Pharisees, that is— if they (the Pharisees) were to see it at all. He concluded by saying that the people the people *from pagan countries*, would be the ones who would sit down with the ancient Jewish fathers in the kingdom: it **would not** be the Pharisees.

"Jesus' prophetic statement has literally occurred. Multitudes in the lands of the West and of the East came to believe in Jesus as their Christ and Messiah before the destruction of Jerusalem and the subsequent dissolving of the Jewish state, and many more multitudes have done so since that time. At the same time, the Pharisees as a sect and as an identity suffered destruction because of their refusal to believe.

"After this, Jesus sent the centurion away saying that the servant was healed. The servant was restored completely."

Upon concluding his statement Eudes' account ended.

After Rustus' servant, Nehem, was healed, Jesus and his disciples again disappeared from recorded history. They did not re-emerge in Capernaum until two and perhaps three weeks later—just in time to greet the Bubonic Plague that was rapidly spreading west from Parthia and Mesopotamia.

Roman history records that tens of thousands were stricken with the potentially deadly disease. However, only one plague victim of note was recorded in the annals of Christian history: Simon Peter's mother-in-law—the lady that Jesus healed in late September or early October, AD 27 (Matthew 8:14-15; Mark 1:30-31; Luke 4:38-39).

I discovered an account of the healing of Simon Peter's mother-in-law at Ankara University in Ankara, Turkey. The manuscript was written in Latin, but it had been translated into Arabic, Turkish, English, and Greek.

Disibod, an Irish monk/bishop and the founder of a monastery in Germany called Disibodenberg wrote the manuscript in AD 670. It is the only surviving manuscript out of dozens that Disibod was supposed to have written. Tradition says that Disibod wrote dozens of sermons about the miracles of Jesus and the parables of Jesus. But out of those dozens only one survived: the account of the miracle of the healing of Simon's mother-in-law.

As I read, it soon became obvious that Disibod's sermon was not just a typical retelling of an event in Jesus' life and an application of that event to daily life. Instead, Disibod went into great detail describing the historical background of the event and how that episode related to the customs and manners of Jesus' day, without being restricted and regimented by the espoused church dogma and doctrines of his day. It seemed that Disibod could have been one of the few theological "free thinkers," who was at least 1,000 years ahead of his time.

Disibod began his sermon by stating that this healing miracle of Jesus was recorded in the Gospel of St. Luke.

> *"And he arose out of the synagogue, and entered into Simon's house. And Simon's wife's mother was taken with a great fever; and they besought him for her. And he stood over her, and rebuked the fever; and it left her: and immediately she arose and ministered unto them" (Luke 4:38-39).*

"In September and October of AD 27," Disibod wrote, "we know that the bubonic plague made an appearance in Syria and more specifically in the Decapolis and the Galilee area, having spread west from Parthia. Many workers laboring on the new cities of Tiberias and Julias that were at that time being built with the help of Jewish labor, died from the plague. This resulted in construction being halted until the plague had subsided. Simon's mother-in-law, who lived in Capernaum, may have been exposed to and become infected with this most fearful of plagues.

"The most dreaded diseases in the Galilee/Decapolis regions at that time were dysentery, malarial fever, skin eruptions, smallpox, pruitus, leprosy, eye diseases, blindness, diseases of Venus (venereal disease), deafness, decay of organ and skin (cancer), swollen and painful joints (arthritis), woman's organ problems, hysteria, the disorder of the nerves, convulsion disease (epilepsy), lung and heart disorders, and the plague.

"In the Galilee/Decapolis districts those afflicted with these or any other disease were treated (both medically and emotionally) as you would suppose one should be treated.

"But in the state of Judea," Disibod continued, "these diseases would have been considered curses of God for punishment of personal or inherited sin. The word that was used in Judea for any of these diseases was *het* or *hattaah*. The word represented guilt for sin or of breaking some religious rule or ritual, as well as the consequence of breaking the rules. The religious leaders taught in Judea that as the consequence of breaking the laws and rules, God inflicted the disease as punishment. As such, in the state of Judea the cure for any of these diseases was held to be possible only if God granted His pardon and remitted the penalty for the sin that had been the cause for the curse of the disease. This in turn could only be sought through special rites of purification and through offerings given at the Temple in Jerusalem.

"The outbreak of bubonic plague was looked upon as an unfortunate tragedy by residents (both Roman and non-Roman alike) and officials in the Galilee and the Decapolis and was treated as such by them. By January of AD 28 the plague had run its course and had taken the lives of over 3,000 people as it spread across Syria. Shortly thereafter construction work was resumed on the cities.

"In the state of Judea, the Pharisees claimed the epidemic was God's punishment upon the people, because the Jewish workers who were working on the cities of Tiberias and Julias had submitted to the Roman authorities and had consented to construct the cities rather than refuse to work. The Judean Pharisees felt that it would be better to refuse to work, thus facing death by the Romans, than to work for the Romans on these 'imperial' cities.

"It appears that Jesus was in a synagogue in Capernaum (perhaps he was praying or maybe it was the Sabbath Day) when he was summoned to Simon Peter's house to heal his mother-in-law.

"Jesus, knowing the true nature and cause of the disease, did not demand repentance from Simon Peter's mother-in-law, nor did he demand specific rites or purification rituals. He simply healed her of the disease, showing no fear of the infectious disease, knowing that she had been stricken through no fault of her own.

"It is not known how many people Jesus healed who were infected with the disease. What is known is that the disease exited the Galilee/Decapolis areas much more rapidly than in times past when the disease struck the region. We also know that work on the cities was resumed by November of that year—seemingly an impossibility without some type of divine intervention."

Dr. Ron Charles

Disibod concluded by writing, "After Jesus had healed Simon's mother-in-law, and perhaps countless others, of the dreaded bubonic plague, his fame spread throughout Roman Syria—the Galilee, the Decapolis, Perea, Auranitis, Bashan, Batanea, Gaulanitis, Ulatha, Trachonitis, Ituraea, Abilene, Phoenicia, Samaria, the district of the cities of Salome (cities of Jamnia, Azotus, Ascalon, Phasaelis, Archelais, and Gaza carved out of the west coast of Judaea), Judaea, Idumea, and Nabatea—healing all who came to him of all manner of diseases and sicknesses (Matthew 4:24-25)."

In the midst of this abrupt outpouring of emotion and compulsion by the people in the region, in late October or early November, Jesus felt it necessary to take his disciples away from the crowds and to minister to them privately, teaching them things that they would need to know in order to help him minister to the needs of the people. Most of the things that Jesus taught them, they had never heard before. The teaching was so different and the things he said were generally contrary to the things the Pharisees and scribes had taught them. This first of two primary teachings that Jesus gave to his disciples privately (this time to six particular disciples, the second time to the 12 who had been selected to be his apostles) have come to be known as *The Sermon on the Mount*.

Although in my research I found a mountain of information that had been over the centuries written about the Sermon on the Mount and thousands of sermons that had been preached using the Sermon of the Mount as foundation text, the most convincing documentations I discovered were in two locations—the Hebrew University in Jerusalem, Israel and the University of Ioannina's Museum of Middles Eastern Anthropology in Ioannina, Greece.

I had been researching at the Hebrew University library for two days and was unsatisfied with what I had found. I decided to try it for one more day, and then if I did not find anything that I felt worth while, I would drive down to Be'er Sheva' and visit Ben Gurion University. On this last day of research at the Hebrew University, Dr. Abram Luwenstein, the head librarian of the university's climate controlled rare books and manuscripts vault, and whom I had gotten to know over the past couple of days and had shared with him my search for historical Jesus project, as soon as I entered the library that day asked me to accompany him to the vault room, he had something that he wanted to show me.

I followed him to the vault and sat down at one of the long reference study tables. Dr. Luwenstein excused himself and returned a few minutes later carrying a large volume about two feet-square. The volume consisted of two oak boards, and between them was bound with brass pins, about one inch thick, a large number of velum leaves.

According to Dr. Luwenstein, Peter Abelard had written the volume in French, in about the year 1123. This was before Peter Abelard had been elected Abbot of St. Gildas de Rhuys in Brittany. The title of the volume was *Theologia Historia*. He said that until yesterday, the volume had not been available because it was being translated into Hebrew, Arabic, and English. So, not only was I able to study the original text, I could read the English translation as well. However, he told me that it was not yet available for public view. The volume and the translations had been given to him for his approval. So, he could not afford to have me study it for no more than just a few hours.

Realizing how valuable the volume was to the university, I contented myself with looking through the original for about a half hour, and then allowing Dr. Luwenstein to replace it. I then used the newly translated English version of the volume for my research.

The *Theologia Historia* was an attempt to trace the development of Christian theological thinking from the foundation of Jesus' teachings up until the time of the volume's production, AD 1123.

Dr. Luwenstein, who was Jewish by birth, was open-minded when it came to the historical person of the man, Jesus. Realizing that I could easily spend weeks "digesting" the huge volume and knowing that my time was limited, Dr. Luwenstein suggested that I concentrate on one particular area that apparently had been a hot theological issue during the time of Peter's writing: Jesus' teaching on the straight gate, as presented in the Sermon on the Mount.

Peter Abelard began his treatise by quoting St. Augustine who said that the *Sermon on the Mount* was probably not a single sermon, but rather it was a compilation of sermons that Matthew took and summarized into a series of maxims. The series of maxims was followed by explanatory illustrations and parables that Jesus used to emphasize the maxim. They were taught by Jesus during the first two to three years of his ministry.

Peter then quoted the scriptural setting of the straight gate maxim.

> *"Enter ye in at the strait gate: for wide is the gate, and broad is the way, that leadeth to destruction, and many there be which go in thereat: Because strait is the gate, and narrow is the way, which leadeth unto life, and few there be that find it" (Matthew 7:13-14)*

After he quoted the scripture, he began his explanation. I paraphrased what he had written.

The word translated *enter* is the Greek word, *agonizomai*. It means to agonize as in a wrestling match or against a foe, or to labor fervently.

At the time of this lesson on the straight gate, as taught by Jesus, consecrated shepherds, priests, and Levites had the responsibility of raising herds of sheep and lambs. Out of these herds would be selected the sheep and lambs that would be sacrificed during Passover. Every seven years a new herd of consecrated sheep was started. Since God demanded that the animals to be sacrificed must be strong and healthy, a method was devised whereby the strongest and healthiest would be chosen every seven years. The ones selected and their offspring would provide the needed sacrificial animals for Passover for the next seven years. An appointee of the High Priest supervised the selection of the sacrificial sheep and lambs every seventh year in the Hinnom Valley, just south of Jerusalem and north of Bethlehem.

The selection process took six days. All day long from sunup to sundown, herds of sheep were led into the Hinnom Valley. Midway through the valley the High Priest appointee would stand on a platform at the junction of a "Y" in the path. Here two gates would close the two paths. The left gate was a very wide gate and the path leading to it and from it offered little resistance and gradually ascended to the pastureland at the top of the hillside. The right gate was different in that it was narrow. It was so narrow that a full-grown sheep could barely squeeze through it, and to get to that gate the sheep had to immediately begin a narrow and steep climb. The sheep that passed through the narrow gate had to continue on a steep unrelentingly climb that was so narrow that only one sheep at a time could walk on the path. In other words, they had to climb in single file until they reached the top of the hill.

When the entire herd had congregated around the appointee's platform he would order both gates to be opened at the same time. The sheep that went through the wide gate and wide path were sold to merchants for butchering and for wool, once they reached the top of the hill. The ones that went through the narrow gate and continued on up the steep and narrow path without falling off or turning back were selected to be the consecrated sheep when they reached the top. They were worthy to be the chosen for God's purpose.

Peter explained that Jesus was trying to tell his disciples (six at that time) that they had a choice. They as his sheep could choose to follow the path of least resistance and minimum spiritual hardships, the way that most followers of Christ will follow. On this path there is room for Christ as well as all other religions and religious philosophies to stand beside him. But at the end of that path destruction awaits. However, if they chose the narrow path, the path that has room for one, Jesus and he only, the path that is agonizing and challenging, and go through the narrow gate, the gate through which only the individual can fit, not the individual with all of his burdens and worldly cares and possessions, they will be rewarded with eternal life.

I was intrigued by Peter's insight on the issue of Jesus being the only way to inherit eternal life. Dr. Luwenstein said that he too admired how well Peter was able to emphasize his point, even in the very midst of the iron-fisted rule of the Church of Rome.

I then wrote a personal note relative to what Peter had written. "If Peter's insight is correct, Jesus was saying that on the wide path there is room for him, for the Pope and the organized Church, and for Buddha, Tao, Confucius, Krishna, Eastern Mysticism, New Age, Transcendental Meditation, and anything and everything else that is intended to relate to man's spiritual nature. The walk up that path will continue undisturbed and unchallenged until it comes to a destructive end. However, on the narrow path there is room for Jesus *only*. But, behind him multiplied millions can line up. It is a path that is agonizing and non-compromising, but if a person maintains his walk up that path behind the leader, Jesus, eternal life is guaranteed at the end."

After I had finished adding this personal note to my notes, Dr. Luwenstein said that he had to return the translation. I thanked him for the unusual privilege that he had given me.

The second intriguing documentation regarding the Sermon on the Mount I found at the University of Ioannina's Museum of Middles Eastern Anthropology in Ioannina, Greece. It was an eight-leaf velum manuscript written on front and back. Each page was lamented between plastic. The university had translated the original

Latin text into Greek, English, and French and had included brief historical background information about the manuscript.

According to this information the eight-page manuscript was all that remained of a larger—100 or more pages written on front and back—document written in 1241 by Alexander of Hales, the author of the world famous and most renowned *Summa Universea Theologiae*. Alexander had acknowledged authorship of the document in the first paragraph of the first page of the eight surviving pages. He had dedicated the document to Duns Scotus, whom Alexander called "a worthy adversary," with an apology to the reader for his writing such a long document discussing every aspect of the sermon given by Jesus called (in his day), *"Jesus sermon as delivered to his disciples on the mount."*

As I read the English translation of the manuscript, it soon became obvious that Alexander of Hales *was not* the typical Catholic scholar of his day, who accepted without question all dogmas and philosophies declared by the church hierarchy. Also amazing was how Alexander used historical background information to explain the spiritual points and practical applications that Jesus tried to emphasize in the Sermon on the Mount. It was a tragedy that the vast majority of the document had either been lost or destroyed forever. If the surviving eight pages were any indication of Alexander's comprehensive insight, the original document must have been the most exhaustive examination of the Sermon on the Mount that had ever been written up until that time, and perhaps of all time.

Alexander began his text by assuming that his readers knew where the Sermon on the Mount was recorded in the Bible. But for the benefit of those reading this book, it is recorded in the *Gospel According to St. Matthew*, chapters five through seven.

Alexander did not approach the Sermon on the Mount in any systematic manner. In other words, he did not go verse-by-verse, chapter-by-chapter, or subject-by-subject. It was as if he was addressing individual subjects and answering a series of questions about the Sermon on the Mount that had been asked of him in no particular order—questions that have long since been lost. So, although it appears that Alexander just skipped around throughout the three chapters, he maintained a constant sense of awareness, knowing exactly what and how Jesus was trying to teach his disciples.

"In the late fall of AD 27 Jesus took six of his disciples into a mountain. This seems to indicate that perhaps he took them into a cave or a cleft of the mountain in order to teach them. The teaching was neither directed to a crowd or to the multitudes nor to his 12 disciples.

This was the first of many times that Jesus and his disciples isolated themselves in order for him to teach them. Although all of this sermon may not have been spoken at this particular time the portion known as the beatitudes and the principles for greater righteousness was most likely taught by Jesus at this time."

It appeared that Alexander's discussion of the beatitudes had been lost or destroyed because the first thing that he discussed is when Jesus described his disciples as the salt of the earth and the light of the world. This is found in Matthew 5: 13-14. He took each of the analogies and described them separately.

He first discussed the analogy of Jesus' disciples being the salt of the earth. In essence, Jesus was saying that his disciples were the most precious of all elements and the preservers from spiritual decay. Alexander then explained the historical setting behind such a statement.

"It was Alexander the Great who first used salt in large quantities to preserve meat during his long military campaigns, as he and his troops set out from Macedonia to conquer the known world. By the time of Julius Caesar, salt had become such a mandatory element in Roman life that it was considered by most citizens of wealth and renown to be more precious than gold, or at least as precious as gold. It was in so much demand throughout the Roman Empire that military expeditions were sent to the far corners of the world in search of, and countries were conquered for the sake of, salt. Rome was shaft-mining salt primarily in what is now Austria. But, Rome also mined salt in Africa, Anatolia, Greece, and Gaul.

"The Empire's largest concentration of exposed (non-shaft) salt reserves was in the area of the Dead Sea (the Salt Sea) salt flats located in the province of Judaea. This area had so much salt and salt was in such demand throughout the Empire that the province of Judaea was allowed by Rome to pay a large portion of its provincial tax burden to Rome in the form of salt. The salt was collected, transported overland, and loaded onto awaiting ships in Ascalon, Caesarea Maritima, Joppa, and Tyre. From there the salt was shipped to Rome. The ships would normally travel to Rome in large caravans of 20 to 30 ships from each of the four ports. After a ship was loaded with salt, it was covered to prevent water contamination of the salt. A loaded ship remained anchored in port until enough ships had been loaded with salt so that a caravan could be formed to take it to Rome.

"At that time in the state of Judea of the province of Judaea and in the Galilee, there were numerous bands of revolutionaries who wanted to overthrow their Roman overlords by whatever means possible. Hence, at every opportunity, the revolutionaries sabotaged Rome's policies, laws, and administrative and military efforts. Consequently, as the covered salt-laden ships were resting at anchor in harbor waiting for a caravan to be formed, the rebels would sneak aboard the ships and under the protection of night would mix dirt with the salt. This is what Jesus meant by the *salt losing its savor*. It meant that dirt in the salt had caused the salt to lose its usefulness. When the shipment arrived in Rome, the salt was ruined. It had too much salt to be any good for soil and to much soil to be any good for salt. At that time the Romans were building roads all over the Empire. The unsavory salt, or the salt and dirt mixture, was worthless for anything except to be used as road fill. In a literal sense Jesus said that the mixture was good for nothing except to be trodden under foot of men.

"The analogy was used by Jesus to teach his disciples that they must be pure. They must not allow the things of the world (symbolized by the dirt) to mix with their life of discipleship (symbolized by the salt). To God, these disciples were most precious in His eyes. Hence, they cannot allow themselves to be compromised by the things of the world. This compromise would result in having too much of God (salt) to be any good for the world (dirt) and too much of the world (dirt) to be any good for God (salt). They must not compromise."

Alexander next explained what Jesus meant when he identified his disciples as being lights of the world, and that a light set on a hill cannot be hid. This portion of the Sermon on the Mount is found in Matthew 5:14.

"Jesus probably," he wrote, "pointed to the warning city of Acaba, north of Cana of the Galilee, which could have been seen from the cave if the cave was located on the north side of the mountain, when he began his analogy.

"During the days of the Maccabean revolt and continuing up through the reign of Herod the Great, square-shaped walled warning cities were built on the highest points of specific surrounding areas. These squared-shaped walled warning cities existed throughout Herod's kingdom. They were situated in such a way that one warning city could be seen faintly from another warning city. The cities were to serve as warning sentries to all of the cities and towns in the surrounding area, warning them of approaching or impending danger. Because a warning city was built on top of the highest point in the area, it could be seen from anyplace in the area. During the day, the warning cities warned of impending danger by displaying large red or yellow banners. In the days of Herod the Great the banner of peace [as it was called] was yellow and was always waving above the North wall. If a red banner waved above the North wall it meant than an enemy had been sighted. Red banners waving above the North and East walls meant that an enemy was advancing toward that area. Red banners waving above the North, East, and West walls meant that the area was under attack. Red banners waving above all four walls meant that the regional warning city was under attack or siege (because these cities were used to warn an entire area, they were normally the first cities in an area to be attacked or brought under siege). If all banners on all walls had been lowered, it meant that the city had fallen.

"Nighttime warnings were different. If all were at peace, a torch would be burning above the North wall. If two torches were burning on the North wall it meant that an enemy had been sighted. If there were two torches lighted on the North wall and one on the East wall, it meant that an enemy was approaching the region. If two torches were lighted above the North wall, one on the East, and one on the West wall, it meant that the region was under attack. If two torches were lit on the North wall and one apiece on the other three walls, it meant that the city was under attack. If all torches were extinguished, it meant that the city had fallen.

"Jesus was trying to point out with the analogy that his disciples were like regional warning cities built on hills and they had an obligation to warn. They had no choice, just like the warning city had no choice. That is the reason why the cities were built. Their sole purpose for existence was to warn. Whether the city officials liked it or not or whether the residents liked it or not didn't make any difference, this was their responsibility and purpose for existence. They had a choice to live in the warning city or not. But once they made the choice to live in the city, they were obligated to be the region's warning city; that was their purpose. They were to give off their lights in order to warn and to guide. Jesus told his disciples that they too were warning cities. Their commission was to warn and to guide. They had a choice to accept his invitation to follow him, but once they made that decision, they no longer had a choice—it was their obligation, their commission, and their purpose for existence. They were like cities built on hills. They could not hide their light, they could neither choose not to give forth their light, nor allow their light to go out. Too many people were looking to them for hope, help, and guidance. It did not matter whether they wanted to be on a hilltop pedestal or not, the fact that they were disciples automatically placed them on a hilltop pedestal. As such, each was commissioned to be a warning city."

After this, Alexander skipped a segment and settled on a portion where Jesus said in verse 17 of Matthew 5 that he had not come to destroy the law, but rather to fulfill the Law. Alexander tried to explain what Jesus meant when he said that. The word that Jesus used that we have translated *fulfill*, is *plerosai* or *pleroun*. *Plerosai* meant, "to bring to a conclusion" and *pleroun* meant "to confirm" or "to ratify." Therefore the statement by Jesus actually reads, *"I am not come to destroy or abolish the Law, but rather, to establish and to defend the eternal validity of the Law."*

Alexander then began to explain the Law, so that his reader could understand what Jesus was talking about.

"The whole of the first five books of God's Word, the Pentateuch, was called *The Law*, or *The Torah*. However, little by little, the Torah was supplemented by oral traditions, the *Mishnah*, which was later codified by the patriarch Judah ha-Nasi at the end of the 1st century AD. Portions of the *Mishnah* finally developed into the *Talmuds*. At the time of Jesus' ministry, the Pharisaic rabbonis had already put together 613 precepts of the *Mishnah*, the majority of which were compiled by Hillel. These precepts, both affirmative and negative, were differentiated between major and minor precepts according to their intrinsic importance. So devoted were many of the Pharisees to these precepts that often they viewed the keeping of the *Mishnah* as mandatory for the complete keeping of *The Torah*, or *The Law*. This practice was what Jesus opposed so forcefully. He believed that these legalistic Pharisees had wandered far from the true faith by becoming too formalistic and too attached to the 'letter of the Law,' or the oral traditions based on commentaries on the Law, the *Mishnah*, rather than the Law itself or the spirit of the Law. So, Jesus said that he had not come to destroy the *Torah*, but rather he had come to defend the validity of the true *Law* and not the validity of the *Mishnah*."

Again Alexander skipped several verses and settled on where Jesus made a statement concerning divorce.

"Jesus' statement is confusing unless one is aware of the historical background regarding his statement and the history behind the act of divorce at that time in the Roman Empire.

"The original Law of Moses allowed divorce for the man only. He could divorce his wife by simply saying to his wife in the presence of at least one witness, 'I divorce you; I divorce you; I divorce you.' The man was allowed to marry again. In fact, he could divorce and remarry for as many as 15 times. But out of those 15, he could not marry more than three women who had previously been divorced by their husbands or were widows. However, a woman was *never* allowed to divorce under *any* circumstances.

"Divorce among the Persians was allowed by either the husband or the wife. A husband could divorce by stating his desire in the presence of three non-related and non-biased witnesses. A wife could divorce by stating her desire to the local governor. Among the Persians there were only two causes whereby divorce would be allowed: for adultery or unfaithfulness, and for abandonment or leaving the partner for a period of 60 days or more, except for cases of military commitments, employment or business commitments, or sickness.

"With the Syrians, divorce was allowed for men *only*. Syrian law permitted a husband to divorce his wife only for the cause of adultery, abandonment, failure of his wife to obey him, or the wife's speaking to her husband in public without being spoken to by her husband, first. If a man divorced his wife she had to submit to the ordeal of public ridicule by being forced to walk through the streets of her city, nude, with a red-painted face. Afterwards, she was considered to be an unclean adulteress. Hence, the only way that she could support herself was through family or government assistance (government assistance was available to all divorced women unless their divorce was caused by her adultery or infidelity), begging, or prostitution. She was also forbidden to remarry. If any man did marry her, he would be considered an adulterer.

"Among the Parthians, divorce was allowed by the woman in cases of abandonment or fornication by her husband. Fornication was identified by the Parthians as having sexual relations with animals, with the man's own blood-line daughter, with another man, with children under the age of ten, with as many as 12 women at a single setting, or in a holy place. A man could divorce for any reason that was considered justified by the local magistrate. The Parthians allowed the man to remarry as many times as he chose to marry and to have as many wives as he wanted to have. A woman could have five divorces during her lifetime. After having five husbands and five divorces she could live with and be supported by another man, but she could not marry him.

"In the Roman Empire, the woman had a far more respected position than in any other social system at that time. The woman essentially an equal partner with the man in marriage. Rome's system was the first system to require its subjects (this was not a requirement for Roman citizens) to marry through the authority of a written contractual agreement (this was strictly enforced by the Romans in all subjected nations). This agreement could be either a marriage contract or an espousal contract. As such, a written bill of divorcement was required to nullify the written contract of marriage or espousal. Divorce was granted by the Roman authorities *only*. (Roman magistrate records from approximately 30 BC through AD 40 show that in the province of Judaea during that 70-year time period there were 2,317 divorce petitions made to the Roman authorities, but only 13 divorces had been granted. That low number was probably a reflection on the harsh anti-divorce law that Augustus passed in 14 BC). Both the man and the woman who were petitioning for divorce had to appear before the Roman authorities and present their cases, after which the Roman authorities decided whether or not to grant the divorce. In the case of Jews, the Romans allowed the two parties to first be judged by the local Jewish religious authority. This Jewish religious authority would then pass his recommendation on to the Roman authority so that he could make a judgment concerning whether the divorce should be granted or not. For Roman subjects, divorce by a man was usually justified for reasons of adultery by his wife (sexual relations with a married man who was not her husband), fornication (sexual relations with animals, with the same sex, with ones own relatives or family members, with Roman officials or military personnel, or with religious leaders), or refusal to obey and/or honor her husband. Divorce by a woman Roman subject was usually justified for reasons of her husband's adultery, fornication, abandonment, refusal to support the family, or refusal to support a widowed mother.

"According to the divorce law of Augustus passed in 14 BC, if either a Roman male subject or a Roman male citizen divorced his wife, the divorced wife would be registered by the Roman authorities as an adulteress and would be forbidden to remarry unless it was by special permission of the local Roman governor or military head. If permission was not granted, which was usually the case, and she had no other means of income or funds from which to support herself, she could register with the Roman authorities as either a beggar or a prostitute. As such, she was permitted to make a living by these means. If any man, subject or citizen, married a woman who had not been granted permission by the Roman authorities to remarry, he would be classified by the Roman authorities (according to Augustus' 14 BC divorce law) as an adulterer and would subject himself to a hefty fine as well as a triple tax burden for three years. If he was not able to pay the fine or the tax, he could choose to be imprisoned for three years instead of having to pay the fine and tax. This punishment was not due to the fact that he was classified as an adulterer, but rather, that he disregarded the decision of the Roman authority that had passed judgment on the woman that he had married.

"A divorced man had the right to remarry three additional times, but he could not marry a divorced woman unless she had been granted permission to remarry, nor could he marry a member of his former wife's family.

"When we look at Jesus' words (Matthew 5: 31-32) we can quickly see how he combined all of the dominant laws and regulations governing divorce into a pointed statement that basically said, 'Augustus' law is the law of the land. Do not break it. Do not concern yourself with what the laws of Moses, or the laws of Syria or Parthia say regarding divorce, Augustus' law is the law and it must be honored.'"

The next portion that Alexander attempted to explain was Jesus' attack against the decades old teachings of the Pharisee hierarchy. It is recorded in Matthew 5:44-45.

"Ever since the religious sect of the Pharisees was established and especially since they had gained renewed significance after the death Herod the Great, the highest levels of the Pharisee sect had regularly drilled into the heads of the Pharisaic students studying to be rabbis and rabbonis that they had been chosen to be and were set apart as *the* children of God. Because they had been chosen to be *the* children of God, they must at all times maintain a life of holiness and purity, and stand against evil. From this concept of purity, they took the instructions that God gave Moses about writing details in a book and then reviewing those details with Joshua on how He will totally eliminate Amalek from off of the face of the earth (Exodus 17:14-16) and the instructions that Moses gave the Israelites concerning the total destruction of the nations that were then inhabiting the land of Canaan, and began to build a doctrine that said that God hated evil nations (nations that opposed, defeated, or subjugated the Jews) and wanted them all destroyed, so it was extremely pleasing to Him that they (the children of God) also hate evil nations.

Since Rome to the Pharisees represented the most evil of the evil, they felt justified in not only hating the Romans, but wanting them utterly destroyed; doing everything in their power short of outright insurrection and rebellion, to make sure that the Romans knew that they were hated by the Pharisees.

"Jesus, however, adopting some of the foundational principles of the ancient philosophy of Confucius and of Zoroaster regarding unconditionally loving and trying to understand ones enemy (a teaching that both of the Jewish schools of the rabbis had adopted as doctrinal truth), told his disciples that the Pharisees were wrong to hate the Romans, whom they considered their evil enemies. Instead, they needed to *love the Romans*. This I am sure did not set well with Jesus' disciples who had been raised under the iron heel of Rome. The disciples had been taught by the religious leaders that they must hate the Romans in order to be pleasing to God. They also felt they had a right to hate the Romans because they (the disciples and their friends and family) were the oppressed and the Romans were the oppressors. It is not recorded how the disciples reacted. But it is possible that they greatly objected to Jesus rational (that all are equal in the eyes of God and that He is not a respecter of persons, giving both blessings and curses to the righteous as well as the unrighteous, as He saw fit in the overall fulfillment of His plan and purpose) and his instructions. They also could have had the attitude that loving Romans was easy for Jesus, who was probably either a Roman citizen himself or at least a resident who was highly respected by the Roman authorities. So, in a sense, loving Romans was easy for him, but not so for the common Galilean resident, as where his disciples."

The next area that Alexander commented upon was the portion in which Jesus sternly warned his disciples about giving so that man could acknowledge them. It is recorded in Matthew 6: 1-4. The accepted practice of that day (in the local synagogues to an extent, but in the Temple compound especially) was to announce the giving of alms to the poor and needy. In the Temple three collection receptacles were set up in three different areas of the temple complex. The most prominent collection box, a solid gold ornamented box, was set up in the Men's Court or the Court of Israel, near the Corinthian Gate that led to the Priest's Court. The second most prominent collection box, a plain silver-plated cedar box, was located in the Women's Court near the Nicanor Gate that led into the Men's Court. The third collection box was a plain fir wooden box that was located in the Court of the Gentiles (Alexander added, 'This is where the widow gave her two widow's mites, about which Jesus taught his disciples a lesson on humility.'). Those who had a small amount to give would place their gift in the plain wooden box located in the Court of the Gentiles. A larger gift was placed in the silver-plated box located in the Women's Court. A telecaster, would call attention to the gift by first crashing cymbals and then announcing the amount of the gift and the name of the giver. The largest gift was placed in the gold box located in the Men's Court. A telecaster announcing the news, shouting the name of the giver as well as the amount given, recognized the gift. This was accompanied by a lengthy anthem of trumpets and the crashing of cymbals, followed by great applause by the men who had gathered in the Men's court. Jesus told his disciples that those men who wanted the praise of other men had truly received their reward. They are hypocrites, or actors who wear false faces, whose total identity comes from the superficial audience from whom they seek recognition. God will not reward their gift because they have received already all the reward that they will ever receive. Jesus did not say that they would not receive a reward, because the law of sowing and reaping is *always* in operation. But rather than receiving their reward from God, whose rewards are based on the attitude of the heart, they would receive the superficial rewards of men, whose rewards are based on facade, pride, and pretense."

Alexander emphasized this fact further by commenting on Jesus' statement about mammon. This was the last of Alexander's Sermon on the Mount commentaries that had survived. It is recorded in Matthew 6: 24.

"The word, *mammon*, is a Semitic word of uncertain origin, and it was used in the 1st century BC through 1st century AD by Syrian/Greek school masters and teachers when they wanted to accentuate the concept of 'substitute god.' Jesus used it in telling his disciples that they cannot worship God and a substitute god."

I paused and thought about this for a moment. I have always thought that Jesus was talking about money or wealth when he used the word mammon. But according to Alexander, Jesus was talking about anything or anybody that takes the rightful place that God should occupy. That could definitely be money, but it could also be wife, children, job, education, recreation, the work of the Lord, or anything that serves as a substitute for God in our lives. This seems to be more in line with other teachings of Jesus, for not only was he concerned about a person who would allow money to get in the way of his or her relationship with God, he was concerned about those who would allow anything or anybody to get in the way of his or her relationship with God.

Alexander continued. "Jesus said that his disciples would have to fight this temptation throughout their lives. He wanted them to be totally absorbed in God. They however were often absorbed with ministry, the needs of the multitudes, keeping schedules, political rightness, religious observance, the attitude of others, as well as money."

Alexander went on the say, "Whenever they substituted those things for God, they would begin to worry about those things, feeling that they needed to control them. But if they kept themselves focused on God and keep God first and foremost in their lives, they did not worry because they knew that God would take care of them. In addition, if there is something else occupying the position that God should occupy, a person cannot rightfully worship God the way He demands to be worshipped. In essence, they cannot worship God and a substitute god at the same time."

That concluded Alexander's manuscript. I sat there in the library for another hour or so contemplating all that Alexander had written, wishing that I had had the opportunity to read Alexander's entire Sermon on the Mount document. I'm sure it would have been inspirational. Unfortunately, the world has lost a true masterpiece. With all the information that I had gathered about the Sermon on the Mount, Alexander's manuscript was far superior than any and all others.

After teaching the disciples, Jesus and his disciples came down off of the mount. A great crowd met them. It is not stated whether the man came out of the crowd, or if he was by himself, but soon after Jesus and his disciples came down off of the mountain, a leper came up to him and fell down before him and worshipped him (Matthew 8:2-4; Mark 1:40-45; Luke 5:12-15). These scriptural portions all seem to imply that the leper was part of the huge crowd and Jesus' confrontation with him took place in the midst of the crowd. This is the first recorded incident where Jesus was worshipped, and the first recorded instance of Jesus dealing directly with a leper.

Apparently Jesus received the adoration without objection. The leper told Jesus that if he willed, he could heal him. The word translated *wilt* in each of the three scriptural setting is the Syriac word, *sqarui*. It had three meanings: *choose, plan, and want to*. So, the leper said either, *"If you choose," "If it is in your plan,"* or *"If you want to."* By looking at this leper's statement, we can't determine which of the three he was saying. But when we consider Jesus' answer as he touched the leper, *"I will; be thou clean,"* which was a statement that included elements of three different languages—Greek, Persian, and Latin—we can understand the context clearly. Jesus' response which has been translated in our Bible, *"I will; be thou clean,"* should have more rightly been translated, *"I choose to heal you because it is within my plan and I want to do it for you. Be clean."* Instantly the leper was cleansed.

Jesus then told the man not to tell anyone, but rather go to the priest and be pronounced clean by him, as instructed in the Law of Moses. If this event took place in the midst of the crowd, there certainly would have been a multitude of witnesses. So, why did Jesus tell him not to tell anyone? Hundreds already knew because they had witnessed it.

It seems that there were probably two reasons why Jesus warned him against telling. First Jesus wanted the man to follow the rules and rituals established by Moses regarding the pronouncement of leper cleansing, so that he would be officially welcomed back into society. Second, Jesus did not want the man to tell anyone how he had healed him: neither the words he used nor the technique. Since Jesus had used neither the traditional Jewish and Pharisaical methods for cleansing lepers nor methods that would have been acceptable to the Sadducees and order of the priests, he felt it best to prevent controversy by strongly suggesting to the man that he say nothing about how he was cleansed.

However, the man did not keep quite. He told everybody. As a result it was no longer comfortable for Jesus to enter into the cities. Why? We do not know. On one hand perhaps because of this healing miracle, crowds coming to him to be healed became so big that the cities could not comfortably contain them without bringing the wrath of the Roman military upon them (especially in the Galilee where Pilate had decreed that large assembles were strictly forbidden). On another it could be that the healing had caused such resentful controversy among the cosmopolitan population of the Galilee, with its dozens of religions and religious philosophies, especially among the multitude of varied religious leaders, that Jesus was not safe to enter the cities: he had to spend time away from the cities until things cooled down. Since the Gospels don't tell us why Jesus could not go into the cities, and only that the healed leper spreading word about his healing by Jesus had been the cause of him not being able to go into the cities for a while, we are forced to speculate.

What we do know is that from that time until mid-winter, nothing is recorded of Jesus' life, activities, or ministry. The next we hear about him, he and his disciples were about the cross the Sea of Galilee and sail to Gaulanitis, in order to get some relief from the huge crowds who had been following him (Matthew 8:18-22; Luke 9:57-62).

While Jesus and his disciples were on the west side of the Sea of Galilee preparing to sail to Gaulanitis, located on the east side, a scribe approached him about becoming one of his disciples, followed by two of his disciples coming to him regarding questions about their inheritance (this was the first of two times Jesus was approached by these disciples concerning their inheritance. The second was in AD 29; just under two years from the first time they approached him). Afterwards Jesus and his disciples launch out into the Sea of Galilee where they are almost capsized by a storm (Matthew 8:23-26). Jesus calmed the storm. When they did finally get to the other side, Jesus was confronted by two demonics (Matthew 8:28-9:1). He healed them both.

I found some interesting information concerning these events in Avignon, France, in another book written by Hans von Dohnaniy, the brother-in-law of Dietrich Bonhoeffer, the Lutheran theologian executed by the Nazis in April of 1945, entitled *Inheritances*.

Von Dohnaniy's *Inheritances* was written in essay form. It was probably written as a lecture or a sermon. Its primary focus was on the superiority of a heavenly inheritance over any type of earthly inheritance. He used many different well-known and well-documented inheritance settlements from history—Alexander, Mehmet the Conqueror, Ramses II, Xerxes, and others. Also included in his essay were two different scriptural passages from Luke's Gospel in which Jesus confronted the issue of earthly inheritance.

A secondary focus of the essay was on Jesus' miracle of calming the storm that hit the sea as they were sailing to the other side.

The setting in which Jesus dealt with inheritance was recorded in Matthew 8:19-22 and Luke 9:57-62. The occasion was in the winter of AD 27.

"According to both the Matthew 8 and the Luke 9 setting," von Dohnaniy wrote, "It appears that as Jesus and his disciples were preparing to board a ship to cross the lake, he was approached by a scribe who said that he wanted to follow Jesus as one of his disciples. Jesus answered the scribe saying that he had no home and that if he (the scribe) wanted to be a disciple, then he too, like Jesus, must be willing to give up his home and all that he has in order to follow him. It is not recorded whether the scribe followed him. However, upon hearing his answer, Jesus was approached by two of his disciples. Second and 3rd century church tradition says that these two disciples were none other than his cousins, James and John, the sons of Zebedee."

Zebedee, Jesus' uncle, was very wealthy and owned his own fishing business. Apparently he had either become sick or he was elderly, and it was assumed that he would soon die. James and John were both concerned about their inheritance in the event of Zebedee's death.

One of them approached Jesus and said that he would follow Jesus without question, but he wanted to wait to follow him until after his father died, so that he could oversee the distribution of Zebedee's estate to ensure that he received his portion. Jesus responded by saying, *"Follow me. Let the dead bury their dead."*

Jesus' statement *"Follow me,"* is self-explanatory. It means, "do not let the affairs of this life distract you from your call and mission. Come and follow me." However, the second portion is more confusing unless we take into consideration the possibility that the King James translators mistranslated the word. In the KJV the word that is used in Jesus' response is *metha*. This is an Aramaic word that means, "the dead." But, many of the earliest manuscripts, including the Vulgate, translated the word as *matha*, which is an Arabic word that means "the villagers."

"If this translation were correct, then Jesus would have responded by saying, *"Follow me. Let the people of your father's village bury him."* This seems much more logical," von Dohnaniy concluded.

"This was," he continued, "immediately followed by the other brother asking Jesus for permission to go back home and tell the family good-bye. In reality what this implied was that these brothers wanted to go back home to make sure that all was in order, in the event that Zebedee died while they were gone with Jesus. They wanted to follow him, but they wanted to hold on to the security of their inheritance of Zebedee's estate. They wanted to make absolutely sure that they got their share.

"Jesus answered the brother by saying that no man having put his hand to the plow and then going back is worthy of the kingdom of God (Luke 9:62). This means that if you say and claim that you have given up *all* to follow me, you must honor that commitment. If you claim that you have given up all for me and then change your mind and choose instead to become involved in the past life or the things of the world, then you are not worthy to be part of my apostolic disciple corp. It is okay to be involved in the things of the world in addition to being a follower of me. But if you have said and claimed that you are willing to and have given up *all* in order to dedicate yourself totally and wholly to my apostolic discipleship service, totally committed and dedicated to ministry for me, then you must not turn back to the former lifestyle or former encumbrances of the world and it's political and economic system. If you are my apostle, and have voluntarily given up *all* to ministry for me, then keep your word and be the apostle that you claim to be. If you do not want to make that commitment, but instead just want to be my servant, friend, and follower, that is fine. But do not claim that you have given up *all* to follow me, and do not claim to be a totally and solely dedicated disciple.

"Jesus had decided to sail with his disciples over the Sea of Galilee to the district of Gaulanitis, north of the Decapolis. While sailing, they fell victim to a storm on the lake. They landed in the Decapolis, near the city of Gergesa (Jerash)."

Von Dohnaniy then broke from his subject matter and described the Decapolis.

"The Decapolis was a league founded by Alexander the Great and his successors in about 323 BC. The league consisted of 10 major cities that had actually been in existence in the region for centuries before Alexander. By the 1st century AD, the term Decapolis referred to both the major cities (each of these cities had a population of over 20,000) and to the region (including all cities, villages, and towns) in which the cities were located. Pliny furnished the earliest known list of these major cities. He listed Scythopolis/Beth-shan, Hippo, Philadelphia/Rabbath Ammon, Gergesa/Jerash, Gadara, Pella, Dion, Canatha, Raphana, and Damascus. By the 1st century AD, four of these cities were of great importance to Rome. They were Gadara, Scythopolis/Beth-shan, Pella, and Abila (each of these four had a population of over 30,000 but less than 100,000).

"The city of Gergesa was also important to the Roman military because it supplied a large portion of the food supplies used by the Roman 10th Legion. Gergesa had large corn and wheat fields, large fish drying areas, and they raised huge herds of pigs. Almost 100 percent of the families in the city of Gergesa were employed by the Roman military to supply food for the 10th Legion who controlled that area, as well as the Legions stationed throughout Syria.

"Pompey the Great had conquered the region for Rome in 63 BC, forming it into a Roman territorial league. Pompey made Scythopolis/Beth-shan (this was the only major city of the Decapolis located on the west side of the Jordan River) the capital and regional court of the league. At the time of Jesus' ministry, this was still the case.

"The region was vital to Rome's military control of the entire region of Syria. The Decapolis was under the direct military control and supervision of the Roman 10th Legion, which allowed it a form of self-reliance and independence. Although the region was under the direct military control and protection of the Roman 10th Legion, it governed its own civil matters under the authority of the Roman Syrian governor.

"Its population was a mix of Syrian, Greek, Parthian, Roman, and Jew (a very small percentage, probably less than one percent, was Jewish). Although the region was under Roman domination and the cities were considered to be Roman cities, the region was very much Hellenistic Greek in its culture. The dominant religious convictions in the region were Zoroastrianism and Greek philosophy. Judaism was practiced by less than two percent of the population."

After describing the Decapolis, von Dohnaniy returned to his subject.

"In Matthew 8:23-34 we read about Jesus' dealing with the two demonics. Jesus and his followers were on the west or northwest side of the Sea of Galilee and he wanted to go to the east side of the Sea, so he and his disciples arranged passage on a large Roman troop carrier sailing ship. It was a ship that was typically used by the Roman military in that part of the eastern Empire for transporting troops on smaller inland bodies of water or large rivers. Such troop carriers, operated by a Roman military crew, were common on the Sea of Galilee at this time. Again, this was not a small fishing boat. It was a large troop carrier sailing vessel that was sailing to the east side of the Sea of Galilee to the Roman military district of Gaulanitis, located north of the Decapolis. The military district of Gaulanitis was under the direct authority of the Roman 10th Legion and the towns and villages in the district were peopled by Romans and those who worked for or on behalf of the Roman military.

"We do not know why Jesus wanted to go to Gaulanitis (perhaps he was just trying to escape the crowds), or why he booked passage on a Roman troop carrier transporting Roman troops to Gaulanitis.

"While it was not customary for a Roman military troop carrier to allow non-military people to sail with them, it was also not unusual to accommodate Roman citizens of some renown, or well respected friends or relatives of renowned Roman citizens. If the military was not in a state of war or conflict, if there was enough room on board to safely carry the troops as well as a small number of passengers, and if the troop commander gave his permission, non-military Roman passengers (and non-Romans who were accompanied by a Roman citizen) could book passage if no other 'commercial' vessel was sailing in that direction. By the fact that they were allowed to book passage obviously means that Jesus and his disciples met all of the criteria.

"Almost immediately upon setting sail, because he was totally exhausted, Jesus went below deck where the sleeping quarters were located, and went to sleep.

"While he was sleeping, a massive storm unexpectedly blew up. The word that Matthew used to describe this storm was *seismos*, a Greek word that meant earthquake or earth tempest. In essence, there was a tremendous upheaval in the Sea of Galilee caused by an earthquake. This word usage was the same as that used in the story of Jonah.

"Some theologians have taught that this upheaval in the Sea of Galilee was an unnatural event caused by Satan in an attempt to kill Jesus. But I (von Dohnaniy) believe that it was a natural event—a natural earthquake that takes places periodically along the fault line on which the Sea of Galilee rests. If Satan had caused it then Jesus would have rebuked Satan rather than the storm and the forces of nature. Jesus always went to the cause and the root of problems and corrected them and fixed them at their place of origin. Therefore it is logical to assume that the storm was a natural occurrence, not a bizarre attempt by Satan to kill Jesus.

"Nevertheless, we do know that all on board were terrified from his disciples to the soldiers to the crew. From the disciples' point of view, they could have been suspicious of the cause of this storm—the same type of storm that overcame Jonah when he was running from God. In fact in Jonah's case, the storm was a direct result of his disobedience to God. Although the disciples did not say this to Jesus, their words betrayed their thoughts. They rushed downstairs and awoke Jesus with the terror stricken cry of *'Don't you care that we perish?'*

"The words the disciples the same words, according to Jewish tradition, that the crew members of Jonah's ship used after they discovered that the storm was caused by Jonah's God because of Jonah's disobedience.

"Here these disciples of Jesus used the same cry indicating that perhaps there was a deep down question about whether Jesus had displeased God; that this time he had gone too far. Without a doubt Jesus had taught and performed contrary to the law of the Sadducees and Pharisees, which they (the Sadducees and Pharisees) claimed was against the law of God. He had ministered to Romans and had healed Romans, the oppressors of God's chosen people (so claimed the Pharisees). He had accepted the praise and adoration of the people. He had used pagan history and mythology as allegories in order to stress particular points in his teachings. He had collaborated with tax collectors and sinners. He had countermanded direct commands of the Sadducees and proclamations by the High Priest himself. He had defied the inner circle of the Pharisees, calling them hypocrites. Maybe enough was enough. Maybe now he had to pay for his defiance and insolence. Maybe the only hope for their survival would be to throw Jesus overboard, like the crewmembers did with Jonah.

"From the Roman's point of view, the battle hardened soldiers, many of whom had faced and had overcome the most powerful enemies of the Empire in the east, were now facing an enemy that they could neither fight nor defeat. They were at the mercy of the forces of nature that had resolved themselves to destroy them. They could do nothing but prepare for the worst of the cataclysm and hope for the best end possible.

"The disciples awakened Jesus in fear and desperation. 'Jesus help us. Is this your fault? Do something. How can you sleep? Do whatever you need to do to save us.'

"Jesus awakened and asked them, *'Why were you so afraid to wake me? Why were you so irresolute? Why were you afraid to face your fears, questions, and suspicions? Why were you so timid about confronting me so that I can prove to you my authority?'*

"Jesus was then faced with a dilemma. Of course he could calm the storm. But he had to do it in such a way that not only would his disciples be reassured that their faith in him had not been a mistake; but he also needed to relate to the Romans that made up the vast majority of the occupants. He wanted them to know that he was their friend and deliverer as well as a friend to his disciples. He wanted them to know that he could relate to them and their fear, and he desired for them to be at peace and know that all would be fine because he was there with them and that he was in complete control of the situation.

"Tactitus," von Dohnaniy continued, "records how Julius Caesar was asleep in the sleeping quarters of his troop carrier as he and his troops were making a dangerous crossing from Apollonia to Brindisi. Mid-way through the crossing an unexpected storm arose. The crew and the troops were convinced that they would sink so they rushed downstairs and awakened Caesar. He rushed on deck and first encouraged the pilot of the ship and told him to hold steady and not to fear. He then turned to his troops and encouraged them by saying, 'Have no fear. Caesar is with you. <u>Peace be with you. Peace I leave with you.</u>' Soon thereafter the storm subsided and his troops were once again convinced that their general, their leader, was a special gift to them from the gods.

"This story was taught as part of Roman history in every Roman school in the Empire. To the Roman soldier, the story had a special meaning because it implied that the gods took part in the selection of the highest levels of the military leadership of Caesar's army. In essence, it was a story that proved that Caesar and his army had been chosen by the gods at that time in the history of the world to bring liberation to the oppressed, freedom to the enslaved, and enlightenment to the uncivilized through military conquest of the barbarous tribes and cultures.

"As Jesus stood on the deck of the ship in the midst of the raging storm, he stretched out his hands and with a loud voice thundered the same words that all Romans learned in school growing up and reiterated in their military training—the very words used by Julius Caesar some 100 years before that time, save the use of Caesar's name. Instantly the storm calmed at Jesus' command.

"Jesus could not have said anything more comforting for both his disciples and for the Romans. For the storm to obey and to cease it's rage was something that convinced every Roman to the last man that Jesus truly was a chosen vessel of the gods for that time in history, and convinced his disciples that he was indeed a special servant, if not in fact the very Son of the most high God, the Messias, the Christ, and the Theophus of Tiberius. Their awe was rivaled only by their bewilderment as they reflected upon what had just happened and by whom it was accomplished.

"The ship sailed the remainder of the journey to Gaulanitis in relative peace and calm. Yet nobody who was on board that evening would ever forget the astounding events of that trip. The ship landed on the eastern shore and all of the occupants disembarked. The Roman garrison was located north of the city of Geresa, so upon disembarking, the troops that had accompanied Jesus on the hair-raising journey likely headed north, in a different direction than did Jesus and his disciples who were continuing their travels to the city of Gergesa.

"Gergesa was located on top of the Golan mesa, about two miles inland from the east coast of the Sea of Galilee. It was located on about the same latitude as Tiberias, which was located on the west shore of the Sea of Galilee. The area north and east of Gergesa, as far as the eye could see, was used for growing corn. The area south was used for raising wheat, and in the area west of the city huge areas had been set aside to raise pigs. All of these served as the primary food supply for the Roman 10th Legion. The town as well as the entire region was employed by the Roman military, which paid the people quite well for their services. So, because of their employment arrangements with the Roman military, Gergesa at that time was thriving and was probably the wealthiest town in the district.

"Two demon possessed men ran out screaming at Jesus as he and his disciples approached the region. The area where this happened is located northwest of Gergesa. In the area there were three large caves in the side of a mountain that were used as a penal colony. The prisoners were former Roman soldiers who had committed murder or other crimes of violence while serving in the eastern Empire. These former soldiers had been declared insane and thus were not responsible for their crimes. As two of these insane, demon possessed men ran out to challenge Jesus, Jesus stood his ground and commanded the demons to come out of the men. The demons asked permission of Jesus to enter into a herd of pigs that were grazing in the area. Jesus gave his permission, so the demons departed out of the men and possessed the pigs. The pigs then went wild and ran the two miles or so to the Sea of Galilee and ran off of the mesa into the water and drowned.

"The event caused quite a commotion in Gergesa resulting in either the officials of the city or the Roman officials under whose administration the city officials served, to come out of the city to where Jesus was located, and confront him. More than likely the officials of the city and not the Roman officials came out to confront Jesus. Seeing that a portion of the city's livelihood had been destroyed by Jesus and fearing what the Roman military might do as a result of the destruction of their food supply, the officials demanded that Jesus leave their area. Apparently the local Roman authority, who could have been the commander of the troops that had accompanied Jesus and his disciples on the journey over the Sea of Galilee the previous evening; did not reprimand Jesus nor was the city of Gergesa punished. It appears to have been one of those 'just drop the subject' issues.

"We do not know what became of the two criminals who now were no longer demon possessed, nor do we know how long Jesus stayed in the area before he and his disciples returned to Capernaum. It is not known if the Roman commander authorized a private return of Jesus and his disciples to Capernaum, or he gave permission for Jesus and his disciples to accompany the troop carrier upon it's return to Capernaum to pick up more troops and transport them across the Sea. Nevertheless, Jesus and his disciples were granted permission to sail back to Capernaum on a Roman troop transport vessel."

That ended the portion of von Dohnaniy's book that dealt with Jesus and the events surrounding his trip across the Sea of Galilee and back to Capernaum.

Nothing else is recorded about Jesus' life, activities, or ministry for the remainder of the winter, except that he went into the wilderness to pray (Luke 5:16). This implies that perhaps Jesus stayed away from people for the rest of the winter, choosing instead to pray and meditate in private, away from everyone, including his disciples.

The next we hear about Jesus is that he has been invited to speak at a great religious conference that was held in Capernaum in the spring the following year, AD 28.

XVII

THIRD YEAR OF MINISTRY

(AD 28)

For many years I thought the place where Jesus healed the paralyzed man who was let down through the roof of the house, was at the home of Peter or one of Jesus' other disciples, probably because Hollywood presented it that way. But, based on information that I found in Cairo, Egypt, that notion could not have been further from the truth.

I remember that I was visiting Fustat, the barricaded-off Coptic Christian area of the city of Cairo. I first toured the Ahmed Ibn Tulun Mosque, claimed by many to be the first mosque built in Cairo, located just outside of the Coptic area. From there I walked down and visited The Church of St. George; St. Sergius Church, built over the spot where Joseph, Mary, and Jesus were supposed to have stayed for a month after fleeing to Egypt; St. Barbara's Church was next; and then Ben Ezra synagogue, where Jeremiah is thought to be buried. After that I visited the Hanging Church or El Muallaka, built over part of the old Roman fortress of Babylon, and the Coptic Museum. The churches were beautiful, but I enjoyed the museum most.

The museum was simple, but the displays of paintings, sculptures, tapestries, and other artifacts were exquisite. The one painting that attracted me the most was of a man turning his back on a table full of coins and was titled *Matthew Forsakes All*.

I was so impressed with the painting that I stopped and studied it for a long while. Finally after about a half hour of studying the painting, the overseer of that section of the museum walked up to me and interrupted my concentration by asking me in broken, yet good English, if he could help me by telling me more about the painting. I accepted his offer and encouraged him to tell me all he knew.

He began his explanation, "The painting is the work of a St. Catherine's monastery monk named simply, Benjamin. The painting dated back to the year AD 648. Apparently Benjamin was so moved by a sermon delivered by John Climacus, the abbot of the Mount Sinai monastery, pertaining to a religious conference in Capernaum where Jesus was invited to speak, and his subsequent call of Matthew, that he wanted to remember it permanently in the form of a painting, which Benjamin planned to present to John Climacus. But before Benjamin finished the painting, John Climacus died; he died in AD 649. After John's death, Benjamin left the monastery and lived as a hermit in a cave at an unknown location in the desert.

"No one knows exactly when Benjamin died, but in AD 670 his bones were discovered in a cave in the Sinai desert. Along with the bones, some personal belongings, a last will and testament, the painting (which he had finished), a handwritten re-write of John's sermon, and a testimonial of how the sermon had changed his life and had inspired the painting, was found.

"The painting has been housed," the overseer continued, "in various locations in this area since it's discovery."

The overseer then asked if I was interested in reading Benjamin's testimonial and his re-write of John's sermon. I told him that if it could be arranged, I definitely wanted to read them.

I followed him to his office where he retrieved a volume that was near the top of his bookshelf.

We both sat down at the table and the overseer began to read and translate the Latin text into broken English.

Although Benjamin's testimonial was fascinating, I decided not to include it in my notes. However, I felt that Benjamin's re-write of John Climacus' sermon was so intriguing that I felt obliged to paraphrase it as the overseer translated.

"The scripture portion that John Climacus used was the Luke setting of the event (5:17-29). However, he did not quote the portion. He only made references to portions of the scripture setting throughout the sermon. Apparently John was a great admirer of Origenes Adamantius (Origen), the head of the Catechetical School in Alexandria, for he used him and his historical records liberally throughout the sermon. John set the stage for the events of that day in Capernaum by quoting directly from Origen's historical records.

"He said that according to Origen, in the spring of the 17th year of the reign of Tiberius (AD 28), the emperor ordered a great religious conference to be held in Capernaum. The conference was to be the crowning event of Tiberius' search for The Theophus in Roman Syria.

"Other religious conferences were held throughout that year in other parts of the eastern Empire—wherever claims of The Theophus had been reported. Apparently Tiberius had been convinced that the true Theophus would reveal himself that very year at one of these great religious conferences that were to be held throughout the eastern Empire. There were a total of 28 religious conferences held that year throughout the eastern Empire. This was the first and the only time that these massive inter-religious conferences were allowed to be held in the Empire. Since there had been reports of numerous sightings of The Theophus in Syria, specifically in the Galilee, Tiberius ordered the religious conference for the province of Syria to be held in Capernaum.

"Throughout the eastern Empire the religious conferences typically lasted three days. Representatives from every religion and religious philosophy in the region were invited. There were numerous discussion groups and the exchange of religious ideas continued non-stop throughout a conference. To each conference there were six guests invited by Caesar's Religious Delegation, the commission appointed by Tiberius to organize the religious conferences, to be special speakers. One special speaker addressed the attendees at mid-day and another addressed them at sundown, for the three days. The Tiberius Theophus commission had identified each of these six as a potential Theophus candidate. They typically were from different religious backgrounds. Jesus, a Jewish rabboni, was one of the six special guest speakers invited to address the Capernaum conference.

"Origen claims that this was the largest religious conference in which Jews were allowed to attend in the history of the Roman Jewish nation. Never again were they allowed to meet in this type of setting. Jewish religious leaders from all over the Galilee and Judaea attended the conference (so claims Origen—this confirms the Gospel of Luke's account) along with leaders from every other religion and religious philosophy in the province of Syria, attended the conference.

"For the Jews, there was at least one representative for each of the 198 towns and cities in the province that had a synagogue, plus the 40,000 priests and religious leaders who lived in Judaea (32,000 of these lived in the state of Judea). Origen claimed that there were more than 70,000 people who attended the religious conference in Capernaum—this included the religious leaders, their families, and visitors.

"The conference was held at the huge *Foria Consortium*, a large open-air, marble column-lined auditorium with a roof and four roofed porches, built much like the Parthian in Athens, Greece. At least 30,000 people could stand in the main facility and another 20,000 people could stand under the porches. The *Foria Consortium* was built by Herod the Great and had become the 'Herod residence complex' in Capernaum. The gathering was one of the many conferences and celebrations that were held at the *Foria Consortium* before it's destruction by the Romans in AD 130.

"Origen claimed that Jesus was the only Jewish born religious leader invited to address the conference. Jesus spoke at mid-day on the second day and had the largest audience of all those who had been scheduled to speak. He estimated the crowd that Jesus addressed to be well over 70,000. The consortium was full and people were gathered in the streets on all sides of the consortium.

"No doubt," John Climacus continued, "Jesus was greatly ridiculed and resented for his participation in this religious conference. Although any one or all of the Jewish leaders would have readily accepted the invitation to speak and would have considered it a great honor to address the conference, they probably regarded Jesus' involvement as condescending. The fact that Jesus was invited to speak and that the crowd he addressed was the largest of the conference suggests a number of things: (1) he was well known by the attendees; (2) he was well known by the Romans who had invited him; (3) he had been identified by Tiberius' Theophus Commission as a potential Theophus candidate; (4) his invitation had been approved by Tiberius Caesar himself. Hence, his ministry and acts were known by/to Tiberius; and (5) of all of the thousands of accomplished and capable religious leaders in the province of Syria, only one Jew, the non-traditional and non-compromising rabboni who lived right there in Capernaum had been chosen by the venerable Religious Delegation of Caesar to address this once in a lifetime conference—Jesus.

"Origen described the manner in which a speaker addressed the conference attendees. He started by giving his address. This could be a long speech or a short one. He then opened the assemblage for questions, answers, commentaries, and discussions, which lasted the remainder of the afternoon or evening. It was during this portion of the program that the events of Luke 5:18-19 took place.

"Jesus was answering questions and discussing issues related to healing, some men arrived at the conference carrying a man on a *somorti*. A *somorti* was a couch, but it was a very special kind of couch. It was an extremely expensive Roman celebration or commemorative couch: the type that was usually given as a gift by the exceptionally wealthy Roman aristocracy to those whom they favored or who had proven themselves loyal to Caesar or to the Roman cause. Many times wealthy Romans arrived at special events or celebrations being carried on a *somorti* by porters. Considering that few Jews and other non-Romans were wealthy enough or loyal enough to Rome to possess this type of couch, it is safe to say that the man who was being carried on the *somorti* was a Roman, a Roman ally, a Herodian, or a wealthy Roman sympathizer. He did not arrive to be an attendee or to participate in the discussions. He arrived in order to be healed by Jesus—the man was paralyzed.

"When the porters arrived at the conference bearing the paralyzed man, they attempted first to squeeze through the crowd in an effort to get to Jesus, but it was impossible. Finally, with no other alternative, they hoisted the man on top of the roof of the huge auditorium and began to rip a hole in the roof in order to let the man down through the roof so that Jesus would heal him.

"It probably took several hours," John Climacus continued, "for the porters to make a hole in the thick tile roof of this massive auditorium big enough for the *somorti* to fit through. Yet all the while Jesus continued to teach and to discuss, and no one left the conference. Considering the length of time that it took to accomplish this task, the Roman authorities would have had time to arrive and to stop the porters. But the porters were not stopped and it indicates that the paralyzed man was a high-ranking Roman. While a hole was being made in the roof of the auditorium, Jesus continued to teach and discuss and no one left the conference.

"The abbot now breaks from his story line to interject a personal note identifying who this paralyzed man could be," the overseer said. "Do you want me to read his personal note or shall I move on to the rest of the sermon?"

I told him that I wanted to hear everything John wrote.

The overseer then explained John's opinion regarding the identity of the paralyzed man.

"According to Georgory Thaumaturgus, the 3rd century bishop of Neo-Caesarea, the *Day of Tribute* for the eastern Empire, August 29, was scheduled to be held that year in the military city of Nain in the Galilee. The Senator from Rome, who was scheduled to attend the *Day of Tribute* special ceremony, representing the Roman Senate and the emperor, was the highly esteemed and politically feared Lucenius Appolonius, thought by many to be the most distinguished member of the Senate. (There is much information that tells of Lucenius Appolonius' political influence and power, yet all that is known about his physical condition is that he became paralyzed and made a miraculous recovery while on a trip to Syria on behalf of Tiberius.) The Senator and his lavish entourage left Rome in late February AD 28 bound for Caesarea Maritima. From there they would travel overland to Capernaum. In Capernaum the Senator would be the guest of Herod Antipas and would stay at the Herod residence complex until the *Day of Tribute* (August 29), when he and his entourage, along with Herod Antipas and his company, would travel to Nain.

"In route to Caesarea Maritima Lucenius Appolonius and his caravan came under attack by pirates. The pirates were successfully repulsed, but the senator was shot in the back by a pirate's arrow. The caravan was within a day's sail of Caesarea Maritima, so the Senator demanded that they continue on. Upon their arrival in Caesarea Maritima, the Senator was treated by the best doctors that the area had to offer, but to none avail. By then, Senator Lucenius Appolonius was paralyzed from his neck down. Nevertheless, he insisted on being transported to Capernaum so that he could attend and represent Tiberius and the Senate at the *Day of Tribute* ceremonies.

"Lucenius Appolonius arrived in Capernaum just days before the great religious conference was scheduled to begin. Georgory Thaumaturgus claims that it was this paralyzed Senator who had been healed by Jesus. Apparently he had been told by some of the Herodians while he was a guest in the residence complex of Herod, that Tiberius' Theophus Commission as a possible candidate for The Theophus had investigated this Jesus who had been asked to address the religious conference. There was no better way to demonstrate if this Jesus was a worthy candidate for The Theophus than to see whether he had the power to heal one that was paralyzed. If he could heal a paralyzed man, then the miracle would weigh heavily in his favor once it was time for the selection to be made by the Theophus Commission.

"If truly Senator Lucenius Appolonius was the paralyzed man who was brought to Jesus, Georgory Thaumaturgus argued, it would explain why no one questioned his order for the roof of the auditorium to be torn apart. It might also be why Jesus was invited to the *Day of Tribute* celebration, which was held later in the year, and why the Pharisees were so angry with Jesus for forgiving the man from his sins. Lucenius Appolonius was the Senator in charge of the *Day of Tribute* in Nain. It is not certain that the Senator was the paralyzed man who was healed by Jesus; however, there is much evidence that it was."

"At this point John returns to his sermon." the overseer said as he paused for a moment.

He then continued to read and translate the sermon from the point where he had left off.

"Luke indicates that because of the multitude of people, the porters were not able to get to Jesus, so they climbed on top of the roof of the auditorium and began to tear the tiles off of the roof. If this auditorium were typical of the construction of that day, the tiled roof would have been between a half cubit and a cubit thick (12" to 26").

"Finally after what might have been hours, the men had a hole large enough for the *somorti* to fit through. They lowered the man down through the roof and right in front of Jesus as he was addressing the attendees.

"Jesus was amazed at the faith demonstrated by the men who presented the paralyzed man before him. But, rather than healing the man right away, Jesus looked at him and told him, *"Man, your sins are forgiven."* The word that Jesus used that was translated *'man'* was the formal Greek word, *anthropinos*.

"This word was seldom used in general conversation and was forbidden by Roman law to be used by a non-Roman if the non-Roman was addressing a Roman (this means that only Roman citizens were allowed to address other Roman citizens with this word). It was an extremely ceremonious word used to describe or when addressing a citizen of high political rank in Rome and a man of honor who deserved the highest level of esteem, obeisance, and admiration. It was a word that encompassed the highest level of all that was honorable and praise worthy. It was exclusively a Roman word of obeisance to be used by Romans in addressing highly esteemed Romans. In the 100 years before that time, the word, *anthropinos*, had been used publicly only three times to describe the most venerable of senior senators in Rome, those who had proven their loyalty to Rome as well as their compassion for the citizenry of the Empire. In 42 BC, Julius Caesar used the word in describing Cicero and in 23 BC, Augustus Caesar used the word to describe Cicero, some 20 years after his death. In AD 26 Tiberius Caesar used the word to describe Lucenius Appolonius. Now here, Jesus used the same word when he addressed the paralyzed man, who very well could have been this same Lucenius Appolonius, telling him that his sins had been forgiven.

"Some scribes and Pharisees who heard Jesus forgive the paralyzed man from his sin were quite upset with Jesus. However they did not say anything openly. They dared not, seeing whom the man was. They considered Jesus' actions inexcusable because:

1) Only God can forgive sin. No man can say that sin is forgiven, and no man can forgive sin.
2) The Pharisees taught that paralysis was a curse imposed by God as punishment for some appalling sin. Therefore only God could heal whenever He chose to heal and whenever He chose to erase the curse for sin.
3) This man was more than a hated Roman oppressor; he was, next to Caesar, the highest-ranking official of their oppressors. If Jesus had any feelings for his countrymen at all, he would curse this man rather than forgive him. Besides, since the man was probably cursed for sins he had committed against them, God's chosen people, God had seen fit for the sin to remain and not to be forgiven. It was obvious to them that God was punishing him for Rome's oppression of the Jews.

"The scribes and Pharisees said nothing, but Jesus knew their thoughts and knew their hearts. He also knew that because they believed paralysis was a curse of God, that only God could remove the curse and thus bring healing. So, he asked them, which is easier, to heal or to forgive sin? Of course they felt that neither could be performed or accomplished by a man. They did not answer him.

"Upon their refusal to answer Jesus, he made a statement for the first time in reference to himself. He told them that so they would know that the Son of Man had power to forgive sin. He said to the man to take up his *somor*, a thick wool fleece throw or cover that was placed on top of the *somorti* to help prevent bed sores and to help absorb perspiration, and walk.

"The term translated *'Son of Man'* was a Hebrew phrase, *ben-adam*. It could also have been an Aramaic phrase, *ben-nasha*. Both were phrases that meant *'a man born to another man.'* It was a phrase that referred directly to the progression of high priest succession, historically through the line of Levi. Hence, the current high priest was called a *ben-nasha* or *'son of man.'* As such, he was in a position to sacrifice the sin offering demanded in the Law of Moses for the people as a whole.

The Pharisees claimed that the Messias would not only be a 'son of man' but he would be the 'Son of Man' or in other words, he would be the ultimate High Priest through the succession of the Levites.

"Here Jesus implies that he is the ultimate High Priest, the Son of Man. Then to prove his point, he healed the man and told him to pick up his *somor* and carry it back to where he was staying. The Pharisees taught that Messias and Messias only had the right and the ability to forgive sin, reverse a curse imposed by God, and heal the cursed in a single action. They taught that this was the one undeniable characteristic that would identify Messias to the Jewish people and the one that would prove without a doubt that he was the true Messias.

"So," John Climacus continued to argue, "when Jesus healed the man he that he had been given the ability by God to heal, that he had the authority to reverse a so-called curse that had been imposed by God Himself, and that he had the authority to forgive sin—even the sin of a hated Roman."

I want to pause with recalling Benjamin's re-write of John Climacus' sermon and insert some information that I discovered in Heidelberg, Germany that relates to Jesus' Son of man claim.

I spent an entire afternoon at the Heidelberg University—about three hours alone at the Buchausstellung der Universitat, the University Library. The library housed an invaluable and extensive collection of a variety of medieval artifacts, including historical and religious manuscripts, illustrations, jewels, art, and original manuscripts of medieval poetry and songs.

Although there were very few manuscripts that would be considered strictly religious, there was one that was of special interest to me. It was a letter written by the Anabaptist reformer Menno Simmons; to his friend Dirk Philips in 1541 after he (Simmons) had fled to northern Germany, in defense of his (Simmons') book *The Foundation of Christian Doctrine.*

The letter defended his Anabaptist position and gave a variety of arguments defending his opinions concerning Jesus' exalted position as Son of God/Son of man. Although the entire nine-page letter was fascinating, I took particular interest in the last of his (Simmons') arguments defending Jesus' Son of man position. Although originally written in German, it had been translated into English, French, and Spanish.

Simmons used as his text a portion of scripture that we identify today as Luke 5:24:

"But that ye may know that the Son of man hath power upon earth to forgive sins, (he said unto the sick of the palsy,) I say unto thee, Arise, and take up thy couch [somor], and go into thine house."

Simmons argued that this was the first time that Jesus had referred to himself as the Son of man. He then pointed out five different facts and forged a resolution based on those facts, with regard to the reason why Jesus proclaimed himself the Son of man.

1. On certain occasions, Pharisees characterized both the anticipated Messiah and the High Priest as the Son of man.

2. The Hebrew term for Son of man (ben-adam) the Greek term (*beshamar*) and the Aramaic term (*bar-nasha*), all meant 'a man born to a man'.
3. The Chaldean term (*en-allha*) means 'a man born to another man'. This term was used by Daniel to describe the coming world ruler whose kingdom would last forever.
4. Jesus used the term, Son of man, in foretelling his death and resurrection and when speaking of his position as judge.
5. Jesus claims that the Son of man was equal to God, when he implied that only God could both heal and forgive sin. So, to show that the Son of man could also forgive sin, he healed the man let down from the roof by his friends. Both healing and forgiveness of sin could be done only by God."

Simmons concluded his remarks on the defense of Jesus' claim to be the Son of man, by saying that Jesus was identifying himself with Daniel's world Messiah ruler as well as claiming that he, a man, had been selected by God Himself to enter into the office of High Priest of the most High God.

I will now return to John Climacus' sermon as re-written by Benjamin.

"It is certainly understandable," John Climacus said and Benjamin wrote, "why the people who witnessed the miracle performed by Jesus at the conference were amazed and why they were filled with fear. Did the healing of the Roman signify that Jesus was in fact the Theophus for whom Tiberius was looking? The miracle certainly would speak well in favor of Jesus' pretension, if in fact he was chosen to be the Theophus. Was Jesus now making a statement of support for the Romans? If so, then he could not have picked a more convenient time and a more opportune setting. As the news rapidly spread, confusion followed in its wake. The man Jesus has the ability to forgive the sins of Romans and God apparently favorably accepts this. Have the Romans now become God's chosen people? If so, then nothing would be impossible for them. Had God's patience with the Jews finally reached the breaking point and as a result he in that has chosen pagan Rome over the Jews as His special nation?

"Fear and excitement coupled with confusion and idolization swept rapidly among the gathered conferees, spilling into the streets and moved through the city, while Jesus' candidate position as The Theophus catapulted to the highest level. With one miracle that could not be denied or explained away, Jesus instantly secured the admiration of the Roman hierarchy, the Roman military, the Roman citizens, the Herodians, the non-Roman non-Jewish population, the religious leaders of countless other religions and religious philosophies, the Roman religious, as well as many of the Jewish religious leaders and Jewish populous (especially those outside of the state of Judea). At the same time it solidified the disdainful contempt the powerful religious enemies from the state of Judea and from Jerusalem, had for Jesus.

"As Jesus left the conference, a huge crowd followed him—some out of curiosity, others out of adoration, and still others out of arrogance hoping to find a flaw in his actions or his character which could be used to slander or ridicule him.

Yet, all followed out of fear, not knowing who he really was or what he was really trying to prove or accomplish."

John Climacus continued with his picture type description of the event. "While Jesus was totally immersed in a flood of admiration, glory, honor and disdain from the massive crowd that followed him, he passed a receipt of customs, the office where taxes were collected. Jesus stopped and looked at an exceptionally wealthy tax collector by the name of Matthew or Levi, the son of Alphaeus (Mark 2:14) the Levite. Because his mother was Greek, his given name was Matthew. His father was of Hebrew lineage. His family name was Levi."

"Here John broke from his story of the call of Matthew," the overseer said, "and explained the tax system in which Matthew was involved."

John began his explanation by identifying the different tax districts.

"Capernaum lay just inside the Tetrarchy of Herod Antipas at the boundary that separated the Tetrarchy of Herod Philip and the Tetrarchy of Herod Antipas. Because it was located on the main trade route that connected the Mediterranean coast with Damascus, it served the Roman province of Syria as the primary seat of customs where Roman taxes were levied and collected on all transit goods. These were collected by Roman military personnel and were used for the support of the military and for the support of the Empire. None of the tax funds were used for the benefit of the local governments or local economy enhancement.

"Because of its location, Capernaum also served as the local customs center where taxes were levied by both Herods on goods passing through their territories. Herod Antipas levied four types of taxes: (1) there was a transit tax on all transit goods, whether imports or exports from the area or passing through the area. This tax was collected by a Roman provincial official and was sent to Rome to support the local Roman authorities; (2) there was an additional transit tax on all outgoing transit goods—exports from the area. This tax was collected by an official representing the House of Herod and was used to support the administration of the Tetrarchy of Herod; (3) there was an additional transit tax for incoming transit goods—imports into the area. This tax was collected by an official representing the House of Herod and was used to support the House of Herod Antipas; and (4) there was a tax levied on all production in the surrounding area. This was called the center of production tithe. There were five other production tithe centers in the territory of Herod Antipas and four other centers in the territory of Herod Philip. Capernaum was the primary center in Antipas' territory where the other five would present their tax receipts four times each year. Caesarea Philippi was the primary center in the territory of Herod Philip. The production tax was the one tax that angered the area populous, especially the radical Jewish faction, for it was a discretionary tax levied as per the whims of the district tax assessor (this assessor served either in Capernaum or Caesarea Philippi). The assessor was normally a national or a resident of the area. He would not be Roman. However, the Roman Council of Economics, under the direct jurisdiction of the Tetrarch, would employ him. The production tax was levied on an individual's income production (this included a person's harvest, catch of fish, harvest of grapes, wine production, wool production, etc.) and/or as personal property tax. It was levied against an individual as often as the district tax assessor felt was necessary, for a much as he felt it necessary. Forty percent of this tax was used to provide supplies for the occupying Roman military. Twenty percent of the tax was distributed to the various towns, villages, and cities of the Tetrarchy at the discretion of the assessor and was used locally by those towns for their local governmental administrations. The remaining 40 percent was used at the discretion of the district assessor as he thought necessary and appropriate. As a result, the assessors usually became incredibly wealthy because they typically levied taxes far beyond what was necessary or needed, allowing them to keep the balance between what was actually spent and what was collected.

"Herod Philip levied five taxes. Along with the four levied by Herod Antipas, Herod Philip levied an occupancy tax. This was a yearly tax that was levied on every non-Roman property owner and/or tenant.

"In the province of Judaea, the district tax assessor was under the direct supervision of the Roman procurator. The assessor was responsible for collecting all taxes in his assigned district. The district seats were Jericho, Caesarea Maritima, Jerusalem, and Ascalon. All taxes collected in Judaea went to the Roman authorities who in turn distributed the funds as needed with 20 percent going to Rome, 20 percent going for the support of the local Roman authorities, 20 percent going to support the occupying Roman military, 20 percent to be distributed to the towns and cities at the recommendation of the district assessor, and the remaining 20 percent to be used at the discretion of the tax assessor.

"Along with these taxes, the High Priest levied a mandatory tax (Temple tax) in the state of Judea (Although this tax was mandatory for Jews living in the state of Judea, it was a voluntary tax for the remainder of the Jews living in Judaea and those living outside of Judaea. However, it was strongly suggested through intimidation—threat of being disfavorable to God or ostracization—that all residents of Jewish lineage pay this tax or Temple tithe). The Sanhedrin levied a similar tax, called The Judgment Tax, and taxes were levied by local authorities to support education, construction, and maintenance.

"In essence, at this time in history the residents of the province of Judaea and of the Galilee were paying approximately 40 to 50 percent of their income, production, and worth in mandatory taxes, another 10 to 20 percent in strongly suggested taxes; and the residents of the state of Judea were paying 60 to 70 percent of their income, production, and worth in taxes.

"As Jesus and the enormous crowd following him passed the customs house, Matthew, a district tax assessor (called publicans) for the territory of Herod Antipas, was busy collecting taxes. As with all of these district tax assessors, all people—especially the people of his own race and lineage—hated Matthew with a hatred that could only be matched by their hatred for their Roman overlords. Rabbi Gellial called these tax collectors, 'despised bloodsucking vermin who fatten themselves on the innocent blood of their fellows.'

"Jesus stopped in front of Matthew, in full view of the huge crowd of his adoring spectators, and invited Matthew, the despised and hated tax assessor, to be one of his disciples.

"Immediately and without hesitation, Matthew left all and followed Jesus. The phrase meant that Matthew made an about face and changed directions. He left all:

his life, his profession, his wealth, his position, and his potentially profitable Roman future, to follow Jesus.

"If Jesus was concerned about his reputation and about his approval with the average resident, his invitation to Matthew would not help his cause. Certainly it would strengthen his position and his standing with the Roman authorities, but the respect that he had gained with the average resident would likely forever be damaged.

"In one mighty maelstrom Jesus plummeted in the eyes of the common people from the highest levels of prestige and honor to the lowest levels of contempt—a friend of tax collectors. His action probably did not set well with the remainder of his followers and potential followers who were in Capernaum. These were people who very well may have been victimized in the past by Matthew.

"Although the Word of God does not tell us how the people reacted, one can speculate. The Pharisees and the enemies of Jesus, saw their glimmer of hope at disposing him, return from its near death position following the great healing just moments before. Jesus' invitation rekindled their spark of indignation and their attempt at isolating Jesus from the people was strengthened instantly.

"To those who feared that Jesus was aligning more and more with the Romans, this did nothing to extinguish those fears. Those who saw in Jesus a savior who would free them from political and economic oppression, the invitation began a process that would ultimately smother that hope.

"Although Jesus still was very popular at this point and was honored and respected by large numbers of disciples and followers, this action was the first step in the long journey that ended with his death. Ironically, it came just minutes after the event that served as the crowning glory of his earthly ministry and aggrandizement.

"To show his appreciation, Matthew gave a feast in Jesus' honor," the overseer said as he continued reading Benjamin's rewrite of John Climacus' sermon.

"To that feast Matthew invited all of his friends who, by the typical standards of the common resident of the Galilee, were not worthy of friendship. Because Matthew was a tax collector, the only friends that he had were Herodians, Roman tax assessors, Roman military personnel, Roman officials, and other tax assessor colleagues. Consequently, the feast was very much a Roman feast, complete with all of the Roman traditions and grandeur. Although the guests were predominately Romans, Matthew had invited some of the local Pharisees to the feast, who had in turn invited Judean Pharisees who were visiting from Jerusalem, to join them.

"John claimed that there were well over 100 guests at the gathering. These did not include Jesus, his disciples (probably from six to nine at this time), or Matthew and his family. Of that number, only 11 were Jewish residents. Out of that small number of Jewish residents, six were Pharisees.

"The Pharisees called the Jewish tax collectors *ame ha-erets*, which modern translations have translated, *'sinners.'* The original word meant, *'men of dirt, scum, fool, reprobate, or good for nothing.'* The 1st century AD rabboni, Hamel of Hebron, said that these tax collectors that worked for the enemies of God and robbed God's own people were the refuse of men, and had no conscience. Another

1st century AD rabboni, Jonathan Jeconiah of Adora, said that *'they deserved to be split in two, like a fish.'*

"It was this type of person, so thought the Pharisees, who Jesus called to be one of his followers. How disgusting and repulsive. Now, it was this same type of person, along with the evil and diabolic Roman oppressors, from whom Jesus accepted an invitation to dine. Nothing could be more contemptible to them.

"At that time," the overseer continued, "The Middle Eastern law of hospitality said that you became a friend for life with whomever you ate. So Jesus, by accepting the invitation, in effect was saying, *'I choose you for my friend for life,'* pertaining to all who were there at the feast. This so incensed the Judean Pharisees who were present that they were willing to try anything so as to accuse him of committing an iniquity; just to appease their lustful, resentful vendetta.

"While Jesus and his disciples were dining with the guests at the feast, some of the scribes and Pharisees from Jerusalem who had been invited complained to his disciples that they should not be eating with sinners and tax collectors. But, they dared not question Jesus or challenge him. He was the guest of honor and even they, as unscrupulous as they were, still respected the law of hospitality. In addition, Jesus had already shown his power and his refusal to 'play' by the expected and Pharisaical dictated religious rules. So, they indirectly challenged him by challenging his disciples.

"They belligerently asked Jesus' disciples why he ate and communed with tax collectors and sinners. The disciples did not answer them, but Jesus did. He told them (Luke 5:31-32) that the people who are healthy do not need a physician and that he did not come to call the righteous. Rather, he came to call the sinners to repentance. The word translated *'call'* meant to *'pull together into a company as with a Roman army or to assemble a fighting force.'* In other words Jesus said that he did not come to raise an army of those who considered themselves righteous and sinless. Instead he came to the sinner—much like a physician leaves the healthy behind and goes to where the sick are located in order to treat them—to call them to repentance.

"They continued to indirectly challenge Jesus by questioning the actions of his disciples concerning fasting, comparing them and their actions to the disciples of John the Baptist. They despised John the Baptist, yet they knew that Jesus admired him. What hypocrisy!

"Jesus again answered on behalf of his disciples using an analogy based on a popular practice of his day. In addressing them he said, *hoi hyoi tou nymphonos*. The term meant 'children of the nuptial bed' or 'friends of the bridal chamber.' The statement alluded to the young friends of the bridegroom who attended him and accompanied him all the way to the marriage bed. After the bride and bridegroom had dressed in their bed apparel, the friends would stay in the room, but would hide behind a sheet. They remained hidden until the marriage had been consummated and the groom had produced a soiled sheet showing and proving to his friends that the marriage had been consummated. Cheering and shouts of joy followed this by the friends. Afterwards the friends returned to the marriage feast.

"When the feast was concluded the young friends who had accompanied the bride and bridegroom to the nuptial bed, would go into a traditional three days of grieving and fasting because their friend had abandoned his former life with them in preference to a life of marriage. Thereafter, one by one the friends would return to the new home of the groom and his bride and would commit their friendship to him and his wife, and give gifts to show their support for his new lifestyle. By using this analogy Jesus was telling the Pharisees who were pestering his disciples that now was not the time for his friends, his disciples, to grieve and to fast. Now is the time for joy. There will come a time when his friends, his disciples, will feel lonely and betrayed and then they would fast (this happened between the time of his death and his resurrection), but for now they must rejoice and be glad.

"In Luke 5: 36-39 Jesus continued with his rebuke of the Jerusalem scribes and Pharisees by comparing their doctrines to his teachings. He told them that trying to incorporate his teachings into the doctrines of the Pharisees was like sewing a piece of unshrunk woolen cloth onto a garment whose cloth had already been shrunk. It looks fine and acceptable until it is challenged or comes under scrutiny, like the cloth being washed or allowed to dry out in the hot sun. It soon becomes obvious that they are not compatible. If left unseperated, the challenge will destroy the old (the already shrunk) cloth (the doctrines of the Pharisees). If the old doctrines were to survive, they should not mix with the doctrines of Jesus. The doctrines of the Pharisees have survived to this day (John Climacus' day), and to this day (John Climacus' day), the teachings and doctrines of Jesus are still separated from them.

"Jesus followed the cloth analogy by saying that his teachings were like unfermented wine and that his new unfermented wine had to be housed in new wine skins or wine bottles (spiritual institution: not a religion or a religious philosophy) so that the teachings (the new wine) and the wine skin (the spiritual institution) could grow and mature together. If the new wine (the teachings and doctrine of Jesus) was placed in old wine skins (the religious institution of the Pharisees), then when the new wine began to ferment (grow and mature) there would be no room in the old wine skin for expansion. There would be zero percent tolerance for the natural growth progression of the new wine. Hence, the old wine skin would break and both the skin (wine bottle) and the new wine would be destroyed. He continued by saying that if people voluntarily refused to forsake the old wine skin, they would neither like nor accept the new.

"With that, John Climacus, ended his sermon and Benjamin ended his rewrite," the overseer concluded. He said that if I did not need his help any longer, he had to leave and attend a previously scheduled meeting. I told him that I no longer needed him and thanked him for his help.

I sat there for a few minutes collecting my thoughts and reviewing my notes. Without a doubt the conference in Capernaum and Jesus' call of Matthew seemed to be the turning point of his ministry. With his performance at the conference, Jesus could have ascended the highest levels of human honor, exaltation, and prestige, in the eyes of both the local populous and the Romans alike. Instead, he choose to separate himself from that prestige in order to minister to all regardless of their social standing, ethnic background, political loyalty, or religious conviction.

At the feast sponsored by Matthew, Jesus gave another meaningful teaching. One that John Climacus had not addressed in his sermon: the lesson about his yoke being easy.

I discovered some fascinating material regarding this particular lesson by Jesus while researching at the Universidad del Valle de Guatemala in Guatemala City, Guatemala.

While viewing some of the ancient manuscripts the university's library had displayed in glass cases, I saw one that intrigued me. I asked the head librarian if I could study it. He told me that I would not be allowed to handle the manuscript itself but that I could study the manuscript translation that the university's Faculty of Education Department of Linguistics and Languages had transliterated. They had interpreted the manuscript into Spanish, modern English, and French. Along with the translations, they had written a brief background relating to the history of the manuscript.

The manuscript was a single leaf that was primarily written in Old English, with portions written in Latin (written on the front and back of the leaf). According to the historical background information, the manuscript was made from linen laminated on sheepskin, and had probably originally consisted of four leafs. However, only that one remained, and it was damaged to the extent that only about a third of it was legible.

Erconwald, bishop of Essex London, had authored the manuscript in about the year AD 678. Untitled, the manuscript's theme seemed to concentrate on how Roman history had shaped and influenced the Gospel. The background information did not speculate on why the manuscript had been written or to whom it was written. Considering the historical tone in which this surviving leaf of the manuscript was written and the historical knowledge that Erconwald seemed to assume from his audience, it appears that perhaps the manuscript was the only surviving portion of a history lesson that was intended to be presented to religious educators of Erconwald's day.

Erconwald made numerous references and explanations, supported by examples, of how Rome's declaration of war against Christianity had actually been the catalyst that caused its rapid spread throughout the Empire, and how Roman politics had actually been the primary influence that had molded early Christian ethics and principles. However, there was only one noteworthy reference to Rome and how it directly influenced Jesus' ministry. It was Jesus' lesson on the easy yoke and the burden made light introduced by Jesus at the feast give in his honor by Matthew.

Erconwald began this portion by quoting the scripture reference that recorded the lesson (Matthew 11:28-30).

> *"Come unto me, all ye that labor and are heavy laden, and I will give you rest. Take my yoke upon you, and learn of me; for I am meek and lowly in heart: and ye shall find rest unto your souls. For my yoke is easy, and my burden is light."*

"The occasion of this call by Jesus," Erconwald wrote, "was a feast that had been given in Jesus' honor by Matthew or Levi, the tax collector after his call by Jesus. It took place in Capernaum in the Galilee. The best biblical account of the events of the feast is recorded in St. Luke's Gospel (5:27-39). However, this particular lesson recorded in St. Matthew's Gospel (11:28-30), was not recorded by St. Luke.

"To that feast Matthew invited all of his friends: Herodians, Roman tax officials, Roman military personnel, Roman officials, and other tax assessor and tax collector colleagues.

"Matthew had also invited some of the local Pharisees to the feast, who had in turn invited Judean Pharisees who were visiting from Jerusalem, to join them. We do not know why they were invited. Perhaps they were invited because Jesus was a rabboni and it was not customary for a rabboni to attend a ceremony or special occasion, especially if sinners or Romans were holding it, without being held accountable by elder members of the Pharisee sect from Jerusalem. Therefore patriarchal Pharisees were obliged to attend the feast.

"There were well over 100 guests at the gathering," Erconwald continued, "which did not include Jesus, his disciples, or Matthew and his family.

"During the feast," Erconwald wrote, "Jesus addressed numerous issues including his own ministry purpose. He told many stories and gave a number of allegories. Among these were the storied lessons of the friends of the bridegroom, new cloth on old clothes, new wine in old wine skins, and the easy yoke.

"I (Erconwald) believe it (the easy yoke) to be the most consequential lesson that he taught at that time. Jesus made the statement concerning the easy yoke after the guests had finished eating, the entertainment had concluded, and the guests were reclining on dinner couches. One of the Roman officials inquisitively asked Jesus why he expected Matthew to give up all—his occupation, wealth, prominence with the Romans, and political prestige— and follow him, seeing that the burden that had been placed upon the people of the Galilee by both Rome and Herod was already more than an average person could bare; and even more so if one had to give up his profession and all of his wealth to follow him.

"A deathly silence fell upon the feast room as all awaited Jesus' response." Erconwald wrote.

"Since Jesus was in the company of Romans, his answer had to be stated in a way to which the Romans could relate. He could not give an answer based on Jewish tradition, the Law of Moses, the sayings and writings of the prophets, or the history of the Jewish people. He had to answer them on their level within an arena and frame of reference to which they could relate.

"After a long silence, during which time Jesus contemplated his answer, he made a profound statement—one to which they all could relate. It was a well-known allegorical statement from a well-known event in Roman history."

Erconwald at this point detailed the history behind the statement made by Jesus.

"In Julius Caesar's chronicles of his conquest of Gaul, he recorded that he, Caesar, had said this same thing when he addressed his troops in Gaul.

"The Roman army of Julius Caesar was far more than a fighting force. They were also engineers and masters of construction who built roads, bridges, fortifications, towns, encampments, dams, aqueducts, harbors, causeways, and canals as they conquered.

"Jochium the Third, the great 2nd century Jewish scholar, said '...the Roman army of Julius Caesar was the most terrible object that has ever trod the earth. It was a vast human machine of destruction contrived for the subjugation of the world, instinct with intelligence, shielded from assault by an almost impenetrable armor, disciplined to withstand any and all onslaughts, and animated with a courage which was best displayed in the shock of ruthless battle. When we hear of a Roman army camp of Caesar, we cease to wonder how that nation under his leadership has carried conquests from the sands of Egypt to the borders of the world north, to the skirts of the Arabian desert. After the age of 17, every Roman son was liable to be enrolled and sent to war at any time. When he arrived at the camp he entered on a course of life in which ease and luxury were altogether unknown. He commenced a disciplined lifestyle in which hardship, affliction, and adversity were occurrences of daily activity no more laborious than such would be expected an skilled worker in service to his employer, who along with at any instant would embrace a call to arms challenge with imperious resolve. The Roman armed forces of Julius Caesar commonly marched in full armor array, geared for battle at an instant, as was fitting 50 Roman miles in a single day, after which, they built defense encampments, complete with protection trenches and embankments. After completion of which they could retire for the night. The army, Caesar himself included (he lived as his army lived and worked like his army worked), averaged merely four hours of nightly sleep, and eating little more than handfuls of parched corn, rough ground bread, dried fish, dried pork, and one cup of sour wine or beer.'

"In spite of all of the hardships and difficulties, under Julius Caesar's masterful command, this army won battle after battle in Gaul. Yet in the face of all of Caesar's success in Gaul, the Roman Senate wanted more from his army. Their attitude concerning Caesar's army was best affirmed by Lucincus when he argued before the Senate, '…the yoke of hardship and discipline must never be lifted from our forces of arms or else Gaul will not be subjected, yet even now he (Caesar) wants more, even now he wants leisure and luxury, even now he wants to drain the treasury for his own self gratification. My resolve is for denial from this honorable body and a demand for rapid conquest... Then our consul can bring his army back to Rome for their leisure.'

"Caesar and his army had been fighting in Gaul for six years, since 58 BC. After six years of constant fighting, winning victory after victory, the dedicated and victorious army of Julius Caesar lay on the threshold of the total conquest of Gaul. However, they were totally exhausted and they had run out of food, except for a few bags of damp and spoiled parched corn. Their military wages had been cut in half by the Senate and none of them had seen their families since they had arrived in Gaul. There had been no free time, no holidays, and no days dedicated to rest for more than six years.

"Caesar had sent a request to the Senate for a restoration of his army's wages that had been cut, and that those wages should be distributed to each soldier's family rather than giving it to the soldier himself. He also asked for more dried fish, pork, and beef, more bread, and more parched corn or at the very least, enough money to buy food for themselves from local Gaultic sources. In addition, he asked for a 15-day holiday, so that his troops could be rehabilitated.

"Lucincus, who led the opposition against granting Caesar's request, responded in writing to Caesar on behalf of the Senate. He wrote that the Senate refused to pay the back wages until after the conquest of Gaul was complete (the army never did receive their past wages). The Senate could not send food, but would permit Caesar and his soldiers to plunder the local residents and the countryside for food. Then Lucincus demanded on behalf of the Senate that each soldier send one-half of his current wages, which had already been cut in half, to the state treasury to help finance the repair of the defenses of the city of Rome. In addition, Caesar's request for a 15-day rest holiday was denied.

"When word of the Senate's response reached the encampment of Caesar's tired and wearisome troops, a demoralizing discouragement began to spread from man to man. In the midst of this wave of discouragement, Caesar called his troops together on the banks of the Rhine River, on the night before they were to cross the river to confront a numerically superior confederation of Germanic barbarian tribes, and explained the grievous situation in which they found themselves to his troops.

"He began his address by reading to his troops the request that he had made to the Senate. He then read the Senate's response, as written by Lucincus. Next, he assured them that he would pay for the food that was needed out of his own resources, and that he would also pay to the state treasury, out of his own resources, the total amount that was required by the Senate, to help fund the repairs of the defenses of the city of Rome.

"Although the soldiers raised their voices in protest," Erconwald continued, "Caesar would neither allow them to pay a single penny for supplies and provisions nor to satisfy the defense repair tax demand of the Senate.

"He followed this announcement with a speech that was so sincere and so touching that it, in effect, permanently bound his army and its loyalty to him for the rest of his life. So loyal were these troops and so dedicated were they to Caesar and to his every wish and desire, that they became known as *fanistums* from which we get the word, fanatic.

"Standing on a large boulder near the south bank of the River Rhine (near present day Wiesbaden, Germany), Caesar began his appeal and words of encouragement by stretching out his arms to his soldiers and saying, 'You have labored and you have won. You have successfully defeated your enemy times multiplied. Now you are heavy laden; all of you. You who are burdened—come to me. Come to Caesar. Come and affix yourself to me. Come to me and I will give rest to your distressed and troubled soul and to your wearied body. Throw off the yoke and the burden that has been placed upon you by your most honored Senate and take my yoke upon you. Learn of me. Learn of my proffer to you. My yoke is easy and my burden is light. Come after me. Follow me. Caesar will bring rest to your body, peace to your soul, and will warrant you conquest over your enemies.'

"After that night, Caesar's army fought for him like demented savages. With the battle cry ever on their lips, *'For Caesar we fight! For Caesar we live! For Caesar we die!'* they went on to conquer, against unimaginably overwhelming odds, the remainder of Gaul and part of Germania, and then they turned south intent upon laying siege to the city of Rome itself.

"This historical event was well known to all Romans, as well as most other nationalities in the Empire, and was well documented and taught in schools throughout the Empire as part of the history of Rome. What better way could Jesus show his work, his mission, and his personal concern to those whom he chose or whom he called to follow him, than to use this well documented historical event as an analogy, typifying his ministry. To Matthew's friends, who themselves were either Romans or were in the employ of Romans, this analogy was impeccable. They understood it perfectly and could relate to it.

"However," Erconwald said, "the Pharisees who attended the feast, viewed the analogy with utter contempt; causing the already fragile relationship they had with Jesus to degenerate even more. How dare this rabboni use a pagan and evil Roman historical event as an analogy applicable to himself and his mission? This was unforgivable in their eyes."

With that statement, Erconwald ended the account of Jesus and the yoke made easy lesson. Then with no introduction and no notice, he began discussing another subject that seemed to relate to the martyrdom of Ignatius of Antioch. Only the first two lines were legible. The rest of the manuscript had been ruined.

When I had finished reading the translation of the Erconwald manuscript, I was convinced that without a doubt this was one of the most amazing documents that I had studied about Jesus' teachings since my research began two decades before.

Soon after Jesus had finished with his lesson on the easy yoke, a Herodian arrived at Matthew's house and approached Jesus and asked if he would come and raise his daughter from the dead (Matthew 9:18-25).

One of the most unusual resources verifying the Gospel record of this event, I discovered at the National Autonomous University of Mexico in Mexico City. In fact, it was a type of resource that I had never seen.

The resource was a large but thin book that detailed and explained the history of artifacts that were on display at the 900-year-old monastery Cartuja de Miraflores, located in Borgos, Spain. The book consisted of drawings of the artifacts that were on display at the monastery and a detailed explanation of the history of the artifacts, written in Spanish, French, and English. The book was attributed to no specific author. The University's rare document research staff had determined that authorship was probably by a number of different monks who resided at the monastery over a period of 200 years in the 17th and 18th centuries. The drawn and detailed artifacts portrayed in the book were all early Christian, and included a variety of relics whose depiction served to support various assertions and dogmas claimed by the church.

The document began with an index, listing the artifacts and giving a very brief description of each. The index indicated the volume detailed 15 different artifacts, however only seven drawings representing seven different artifacts remained. Of those seven, only two had an accompanying detailed description of the artifact that had survived.

The remaining drawings of the seven depicted relic artifacts were: a chip of bone that was supposed to have been a part of the thigh bone of St. Hippolytus; a piece of cloth that was supposed to have been a shawl said to have been used by Elizabeth to wrap John the Baptist; a mud brick that was supposed to have been from the home of Clement; a piece of a dagger that was supposed to have belonged to John Chrysostom; a cutting of hair that was supposed to have been hair from the daughter of the Herodian that Jesus raised from the dead, recorded in Matthew

(9:18-25); and a piece of cloth that was supposed to have been a part of the garment that the daughter of Jarius was wearing when Jesus raised her from the dead, recorded in Mark (5:22-43).

The description that survived was a single portrayal of the last two artifacts drawn and depicted: the cutting of hair and a piece of cloth. The description was entitled *Risen from the Dead*. This first incident involving the daughter of the Herodian was claimed by the description to have occurred in February of AD 28. The second, the raising of Jarius' daughter, was said to have occurred in the winter of AD 30.

According to the description, the two relics apparently made their first appearance in Spain in 1055. They were the possession of King Ferdinand. The relics disappeared in the 13th century and did not surface again until after the anti-Semitic rebellion in Barcelona in August of 1391. Fearing for their lives, the Jews of Barcelona had fled to the royal castle. There they were besieged by an anti-Semitic mob and many were killed. Following this purge, the relics were found in the ruins of a house that had been used as a synagogue in the Jewish ghetto of Barcelona. Afterwards the relics became the property of Ferrant Martinez, the temporary administrator of the diocese of Seville. The relics remained in Seville until 1519, when they were given as a gift to the newly elected Holy Roman Emperor Charles V of Spain, by the city of Seville. He had them placed in the monastery of Cartuja de Miraflores in Borgos for safekeeping, earmarked for the emperor's private enjoyment. In 1918 the monastery placed the relics on permanent public display.

The descriptive record of the biblical story pertaining to the two relics was surprising in that it went into minute detail about not only the biblical events but also the customs of that day associated with the two different healing events of two different girls, occurring two years apart.

Although the healing of the Herodian's daughter and Jarius' daughter were separated by two years, I will address both of the healings at this time in order to compare and differentiate between the two events. I will refer back to this explanation when we reach the chronological order of Jesus' life where Jarius' daughter was raised.

The Matthew 9 setting (the Herodian's daughter) occurred in February, AD 28, in the city of Capernaum. Jesus and his disciples had been invited to a feast at the home of Levi or Matthew, the tax collector. Just as Jesus had concluded telling the guests (who were predominately Roman and friends of Romans) about his allegory of his yoke is easy and his burden is light, a Herodian, a member of the legislative order of the House of Herod, showed up at the feast and interrupted him. The Herodian of John (4: 16-49) probably referred him to Jesus.

As an official of Herod, doors were never closed to him. He could come uninvited to any home or any event, without even a hint of objection from the homeowner or the event master. Because the Herodians were considered the guardians of the peace and the protectors against sedition for the Roman authorities in the region, they would show up unannounced regularly at events where a large number of people were gathered. Therefore, it was not surprising when the

Herodian showed up. What was surprising was that the Herodian upon finding Jesus worshipped him.

The monks stated that according to the Scriptures, the Herodian's daughter had already died. She was at his home, probably in the luxurious royal compound of the House of Herod in Capernaum, receiving the customary lamentations from the official mourners.

Knowing that his daughter was dead, this Herodian searched Jesus out anyway, and asked him to accompany him to his home and to raise the girl from the dead. This is the first time that anybody had asked Jesus to raise anyone that was known to be dead, and the first time that he attempted it. The last recorded evidence that anyone had been raised from the dead was at least 800 years before, so there was no reason to believe that Jesus would be the one to accomplish it, unless the Herodian was convinced that he was The Theophus.

Jesus said that he would come and heal the Herodian's daughter. His disciples followed him; but outside of these few, there was no crowd.

Along the way, Jesus healed a woman who had an issue of blood.

Before I continue with the raising of the Herodian's daughter, I want to describe the two recorded healings of two different women who had an issue of blood.

I discovered information about these healings in a sermon written by the Calvinist John Edwards who ministered at Trinity Church in Cambridge from 1664 to 1680, that was on display at St. John's College Church Museum. His sermon focused the comparison between the healing of the first woman with an issue of blood recorded in Matthew (9:20-22) and the second woman recorded in Mark (5:25-34) and Luke (8:42-48).

"There were many women," Edwards began, "in the Syria region at this time that suffered from a condition that seemed to be very similar to cervix cancer of today (Edwards day). At that time, rather than cervix cancer, they called the disease an issue of blood. According to the Syrian/Roman historian from the 3rd century AD, Euccessius, one out of every 1,000 women in Roman Syria during the reigns of the first seven Caesars, suffered from some form of *'Venus issuance'* (female problems, such as cancer, that usually became active after the birth of a child).

"Leviticus (15:19-28) gives the Law of Moses' restrictions concerning a woman who had an issue of blood, or cervix cancer, or a similar disease. To these restrictions the Pharisees in the state of Judea in the province of Judaea had added their own restrictions, until the burden placed upon the Jewish women in the state of Judea who suffered from these diseases was not only unrealistic, it was intolerable as well.

"In Judea after the birth of a child, if the woman continued to bleed for seven days, she was proclaimed to be unclean. Anytime, not just at childbirth, that a woman hemorrhaged, she was considered unclean if the bleeding did not stop within seven days. If after seven days of isolation she was still bleeding, her new baby would be taken from her, because she would be considered unclean and would defile the newborn baby. A nurse chosen by a priest would from that time until the mother was proclaimed to be clean, take care of the child. The mother was forbidden to touch the baby or to see the baby until after she had been pronounced clean.

"After seven more days of isolation, she had to present herself to the priest to determine if she was clean. If she was still bleeding, she had to stay in isolation for 40 more days. After 40 days, if she was still bleeding, she had to be isolated for an additional 120 days. If after 120 days she was still bleeding, she had to go into permanent isolation, reporting to the priest once a year. If after 12 years she was still bleeding, she was considered to be cursed by God and unworthy of healing. At that point she was officially pronounced dead by the priest. Her name was removed from the rolls of the living and the street became her home. She was forced from that time forward to beg for her food. It was forbidden for her to touch anyone or for anyone to touch her. If she touched anyone or if anyone touched her, they were considered unclean and were required to submit to a 21-day cleansing ritual. If a person did not submit to this, that person who touched her or whom she touched would be considered unclean and would be judged to have inherited the woman's curse. Because she was the living dead, the most degrading of all degrading things that she could do was to touch a religious leader. So debasing was this action, that if it did happen, it was expected of the religious leader (according to the religious laws of the Sadducees and Pharisees) to either have the woman bound and flogged on the spot (in all provinces and districts of Syria except for the state of Judea, the Roman authority was the only authority permitted to flog) or have her immediately banished to the garbage dumps of either Nazareth or Gehenna.

In the days *before* the Roman occupation, the woman could have been killed on the spot without so much as a single word of protest or judgment. But under the Romans such action was forbidden. But, likewise, if the religious leader did not act conformably as dictated by the 'laws of the Sadducees and the Pharisees' and condemn the woman who had touched him or whom he had touched to be flogged or banished to the garbage dumps, he would inherit her curse. The woman was considered dead, thus she was the most unclean of the unclean. Her family disowned her, she had no friends, and the priest told her that God had cursed her and had forsaken her. And the greatest of all tragedies was that she had not been able to hold, touch, or even see her baby since he was seven days old.

"The two women that are recorded in Matthew 9, Mark 5, and Luke 8 had been suffering from the issue of blood for at least 12 years. Thus the priest had already pronounced them dead. They were probably begging for a living and were isolated from all of the living. They were not permitted to touch, to talk to, or to associate with anyone. They existed in a hopeless and irreversible situation.

"The setting regarding the healing of the two women is similar, but the events are different. The following are the differences between the two incidents:

The woman in Matthew 9 searched for Jesus saying that if she could touch the hem or blue tassel of the rope that served as a belt for his garment, which indicated that he was a rabboni, that she would be healed. The woman in Mark 5 and Luke 8 did not search for Jesus; she was in the crowd that was following after him. In addition, she did not say anything about touching the hem of his garment.

When the woman in Matthew 9 touched Jesus, he turned and immediately saw her and knew that she had touched him because there was no crowd around. In

Mark and Luke Jesus had to stop and ask, 'Who touched me?' because there were so many people around him that he did not know who had touched him.

- The woman in Matthew 9 was not healed when she touched Jesus. She was healed after Jesus told her that her faith had healed her. In the Mark 5 and Luke 8 setting the woman was healed immediately upon touching Jesus' garment.
- Nothing is recorded about the woman in Matthew 9 spending any money on medical treatment. In Mark 5 and Luke 8 the woman had spent all that she had on medical treatments that did not help her. She in fact, became worse.
- The woman in Matthew 9 did not come to Jesus trembling because he knew immediately who had touched him. In Mark 5 and Luke 8 the woman came to him trembling from fear for she knew that she had broken the so-called 'Law of God' by touching a rabboni.
- The woman in Matthew 9 was healed as Jesus was going to the home of a Herodian whose daughter was dead already. The woman in Luke 8 and Mark 5 was healed when Jesus was going to the home of Jarius, a leader of one of the local synagogues. His daughter was not yet dead. She did not die until Jesus took time to stop to heal this woman. As he finished healing the woman, a messenger from Jarius' house arrived saying that his daughter had died.

"In neither case did Jesus care that he had been touched by the unclean woman who was the walking dead. The women had special needs and Jesus allowed himself to be used to meet their needs, whether or not his actions were acceptable to the Jewish religious leaders of the state of Judea.

I will now return first to the raising of the Herodian's daughter followed by the raising of Jarius' daughter.

"When Jesus, the Herodian, and Jesus' disciples arrived at the Herodian's home, the official mourners were in the midst of their lamentation ritual, with their flutes squealing at high pitch and their voices wailing. Jesus sent all of the mourners out, saying that the girl was not dead, but only sleeping. However, the mourners knew that she was dead. She had died even before her father had gone to find Jesus. By this time, she could have been dead for hours.

"The mourners mocked Jesus, not because he tried to comfort and to give assurance, but because he said that she was sleeping. The word that Jesus used that has been translated *'sleep'* meant *soul rest*. The word implied physical death, but soul and spirit life. In other words, the body was dead—but the soul lived on.

"This soul rest concept was totally contrary to the beliefs of the Herodians at that time. The Herodians were for all practical purposes atheistic or agnostic, yet they did believe that at death the soul immediately went to a place of testing, trial, and disquisition in the center of the earth; it was not a place of rest (this ruled out any possibility of being 'raised from the dead'). Here, the Herodians believed, the soul was put through a series of trials and was judged by an inquisitor panel of the departed fathers to determine whether the soul was worthy to enter into the restful realm of the dead. If not, the soul would be cursed to wander the interior of the earth in total darkness and isolation for all of eternity. The notion implied by Jesus, that the soul can enter into immediate rest or that the soul does not immediately descend into a place of judgment, was not only foreign to the Herodians, it was totally contrary to their beliefs and ideology.

"Jesus was not disturbed or shaken as the mourners laughed him to scorn. After they all left, Jesus was left alone with the girl. He did not speak to her. He merely took her by the hand, and she rose up, alive. It was a miracle and the news of it spread rapidly."

The monks commented that if Jesus wanted to keep his identity a secret or if he wanted to keep silent the fact that he was the fulfillment of Tiberius' Theophus vision, this was not the way to do it. For the Herodian at least, there was no doubt that Jesus was that Theophus.

"The raising of the second girl, Jarius' daughter, is recorded in Mark (5:22-43). It took place in the winter of AD 30, about two years after the raising of the Herodian's daughter. Jesus and his disciples had just returned from Gadara in the Decapolis where he had healed a man of demon possession. This man has become known as Legion.

"With their return to Capernaum, Jesus and his disciples were welcomed by a huge crowd of joyous people. Jarius, a ruler, or an official ritual overseer of the people in a local synagogue, was among those who met him as he docked.

"Upon Jesus' exit from the ship, Jarius immediately approached him and told him that his 12-year-old daughter was sick and was dying. Jesus did not answer him or speak to him; he merely turned and he and his disciples began to follow Jarius to his house. A huge crowd followed them as they made their way to the house.

"On the way, Jesus again healed a woman with an issue of blood (comparatively referred to earlier).

"As Jesus was healing the woman with an issue of blood, a messenger from Jarius' house arrived and told Jarius that it was too late; the girl was dead. After hearing this, Jesus spoke to Jarius for the first time, telling him not to worry, but to believe. He then forbade anyone from following him and Jarius any further, except for Peter, James, and John."

At this point the monks interjected a personal note saying that Jarius most likely needed Jesus' encouraging words because he probably felt that if Jesus had not stopped and taken the time to heal the bleeding woman, he could have made it to his house before his daughter died. But he did stop, and now his daughter was dead.

"When they arrived at Jarius' house, the professional mourners were already there and had begun their ritual lamenting. Seeing all of this, Jesus told them, like he did in the case of the raising of the Herodian's daughter two years previously that they needed to be quiet because the girl was only sleeping.

"This time the word Jesus used that has been translated as *'sleep'* was a Syriac word that meant *'soul occupation of space.'* It implied that the soul of the girl had not departed. Whether he meant that her soul had not departed her body or that it had not departed the land of the living to dwell in the eternal after-life, is not known.

"Whatever the case, they laughed him to scorn as the mourners did in the case of the raising of the Herodian's daughter.

"Jesus responded by telling them to leave the room. He then took Jarius, the girl's mother, Peter, James, and John into the room where the girl lay. He took her by the hand and said, *'Talithacumi.'* Mark's Gospel states that this word meant, *'Damsel, I say unto thee, arise.'*

"The word *Talithacumi* is actually a Chaldean word that was used by the Babylonian Chaldean magi as part of a long post-death incantation that was spoken over a Babylonian king or a priest who had died, and who had been approved by the High Priest of Marduk to receive the post-death incantation from the High Priest. The incantation was spoken over the dead body, giving permission for the soul to proceed to the after-life and to the abode of the gods, with a guarantee of a prosperous and peaceful after-life.

"They believed that the common man entered the after-life within four days after death because he, the common man, was no threat to the gods, but because the king and the priests were considered embodiments of the gods on earth or at least representative of the gods, these dead souls were supposed to have been viewed by the gods as possible threats to the gods' divine power. Consequently, the dead bodies of kings and priests had to receive special approval from the High Priest in order to receive the incantation, and then the incantation had to be spoken over the body within two days of death in order for the soul to receive special permission to enter into an after-life of peace in the abode of the gods. If the incantation was not spoken, or if the dead king or priest did not receive an approval of the High Priest to receive the incantation, it was said that the soul would walk aimlessly throughout the earth, searching for someone who had the power to give it (the soul) permission to proceed to the after-life. If no one was found who had the power to allow it to proceed to the after-life, the aimless soul would try to possess, torment, and control a human body, preferably a king or a priest, hoping that upon his (the one being controlled) death it (the controlling soul) could then proceed to the after-life.

"The Chaldean word *Talithacumi*," the monks continued, "actually meant, *'I say to thee, 'Soul, arise and proceed.'* It is obvious that although the Babylonians knew the right words to say, they had no clue how to use them or how to apply them correctly—Jesus did.

"The girl responded by rising and walking. Jesus told the onlookers to give her something to eat. This insistence by Jesus that the girl be fed has led some to conclude that the girl was actually in a diabetic coma, rather than being dead. However, Mark's Gospel states that she was dead. Whatever the case, Jesus healed her and raised her from either death or certain death, and she became completely healed and whole—immediately.

"Jesus charged them not to tell others what they had witnessed. It is important to note that Jesus did not warn them to keep quiet about the healing. He was concerned that they not talk to anyone about the methods and techniques that he had used to heal. If they did, their safety would be jeopardized for allowing such procedures to be performed, because Jesus' means and methods of healing were in conflict with the commonly accepted practices and healing rituals and customs of the Jewish religious leaders, and Jarius was a local synagogue leader.

The Search

"After the healing of Jarius' daughter," the monks wrote, "nothing more is known about Jesus' ministry or activities for at least two or three months. But it seems quite obvious that Jesus' raising of the two daughters are two different events, performed two years apart."

With that, the monks' description of the two relic artifacts concluded.

I now will return to the monks' portrayal of the aftermath of the first healing from death—the healing of the Herodian's daughter.

"The news that Jesus raised from the dead the Herodian's daughter, immediately spread like a wind-driven fire through the city and throughout the region (Matthew 9:26).

"After the young girl was raised, Jesus and his disciples returned to the feast being held at Matthew's house. On their way back to the house, two blind men (perhaps they were members of the same family; maybe even brothers) began to follow them and to scream at the top of their lungs, *'Thou Son of David (Messiah) have mercy on us.'*"

Again the monks interjected personal thoughts. "If they were blind, how did they know that this man was Jesus, unless the word had already begun to spread about the Herodian's daughter? Whatever the case, they rightly sought his help."

The monks then continued.

"The type of blindness that these men had, along with leprosy, some forms of deafness, some nervous disorders, and some specific kinds and forms of lameness or paralysis, was believed to be a curse placed on an individual by God because of past family sins that the person had inherited. Most of the Jewish religious leaders, particularly the Pharisees, at that time taught this belief. They placed this type of blindness (having a film over the eyes [these people were called 'cloud eyes' or 'white eyes']) in the same category as demon possession. Those affected were called the 'children of Satan.'

"This type of curse was said to be a permanent curse placed upon the family of the victim, by God, and that after the curse was placed, God would forsake the family and would turn them over to Satan so they would be tormented for all of eternity from generation to generation. The family members were forbidden to ever look at or speak to a religious leader, to ever attend a religious ceremony, celebration, function or event, to ever step foot into a religious facility, to ever buy or possess any religious symbols or materials, to ever pray, to ever quote or read any religious writings, and to be involved in any religious observance or ritual, or they would face the penalty of an immediate death sentence. These restrictions were passed down from generation to generation.

"At this time, the hatred exhibited for these people was acute. A Jewish religious leader would kill such a person for talking to him or looking at him in spite of the fact that the leader would have to answer to the Roman authorities for his act of murder. This religious leader believed that he had done a valuable service for God by killing that one who had dared defile one who was anointed of the Lord.

"It was taught that this curse would and could never be removed, regardless of how good and righteous the succeeding family members were. Only God could remove the curse. The High Priest himself would not even attempt to intercede to God for a family who had received this curse (the curse came to be known as the generations curse), nor would any other priest or religious leader ever consider speaking to them, looking at them, or showing mercy, kindness, compassion, gentleness, or friendship to any of them, much less pray or intercede for them. So fanatical were the religious leaders in regards to the victims of the generations' curse, that they classified them as children of Satan himself, not worthy of life.

"The respected rabban, Joseph ben Gambel said about 50 years before this time that if such a one even spoke to an anointed of the Lord (religious leader such as a Pharisee, Sadducee, priest, rabban, rabboni, or rabbi) that the anointed of the Lord was obligated to immediately take the life of that 'child of the devil' on the spot, to prevent him from polluting the children of God with his evil speech.

"The High Priest, Caiaphas, taught that if by chance the religious leader did not take the life of the cursed who had talked to him, or if that religious leader talked to or acknowledged or showed kindness to the cursed, the religious leader himself would inherit the cursed one's curse, and that he (the religious leader) would from that time forward, and his family for generations to come, also be considered a child of Satan.

"It was further taught that each generation would have at least one family member who would carry the sign of the curse for unforgivable sin. In the case of these men, it was blindness.

"The blind men appealed to the Son of David, the Messiah, the anointed one, to intercede to God on their behalf, so that God would have mercy on them and would forgive them (Matthew 9:29-34). They continued to follow Jesus and the disciples all the way to the house of Matthew, without Jesus acknowledging them.

"When they arrived back at Matthew's house, in front of the entire gathering, Jesus broke with the accepted tradition and practice, totally oblivious to the storm that could possibly ensue, and spoke to the blind men for the first time since he encountered them. He asked them if they felt like he was able to do what they had asked him to do. Jesus was not referring to whether they believed that he was able to heal their blindness, but rather if they thought that he was able to appeal to God on their behalf and to receive mercy and forgiveness from God.

"They answered that they did believe that he was able to do it. Jesus then touched their eyes and said that according to their faith (not his faith or his ability), be it unto you. Jesus touched them, spoke to them, looked at them, and interceded on their behalf. All of these were against the instituted rules to be enforced by the High Priest. The breaking of just one could have cursed Jesus for life (so the religious leaders felt), and could have jeopardized his life as well as the lives of the two blind men.

"As an outward sign that the men had been forgiven by God, Jesus healed their blindness. In front of all of the guests, the disciples, and the Pharisees who were present, the men were healed. This indicated that God had reversed the curse and that Jesus truly was God's anointed who served as God's agent. It was the first record of Jesus healing this kind of blindness.

"Jesus then warned them not to tell what had happened. The word that Jesus used that has been translated *'warned'* was *embrimaomai*. It meant *'a demand of high degree; a threat; to charge at risk of displeasure.'* The thing that Jesus warned them against was not the healing. There were dozens if not hundreds of eyewitnesses to the healing miracle. What he warned them against was telling anyone about the method and techniques that he used to perform the healing, and the fact that he did have the ability to remove the so-called generations' curse and to not only forgive present sin but also to forgive the sins of the past committed by past generations. By warning them, he was not concerned about *HIS* safety; he was concerned about *THEIR* safety. In Judaea their lives would have been in extreme danger. It was only because they were in the Galilee that they were able to survive the wrath of the Jewish religious leaders.

"The healed men did not do as Jesus had commanded. They immediately went out and found a man (probably a friend or relative) who they thought was also a generations' curse victim and brought him to Matthew's house to be healed by Jesus. The outward sign indicating the man's perceived curse was not blindness, it was muteness. However, this man was in fact actually possessed by a demon. He was not a generations' curse victim. Jesus responded by casting the demon out of the man, and the man was healed. The men immediately went out and told everyone, even at that late hour of the night, how Jesus had forgiven them, had reversed the curse, and had healed them.

"The people at the feast were amazed at what Jesus had done and at his total lack of fear, saying that such a thing had never been seen in that area before. The Pharisees who were at the feast were not so receptive. They accused Jesus of casting out demons through the power of the prince of devils.

"Jesus said nothing in his defense, for he knew what the High Priest taught and he knew that these Pharisees were responding to his actions in a way that was expected for them."

With that statement the book ended. No conclusion. No finale. The book just ended. Perhaps the monks wrote more and it has been lost, or perhaps they intended to write more and never got the opportunity. Whatever the case, those last words ended my research efforts at the National Autonomous University.

For the next couple of months, until mid-spring of AD 28, Jesus went into all the cities and towns in the Galilee teaching, preaching, and healing (Matthew 9:35).

In mid-spring, Jesus and his disciples left the Galilee and traveled to Jerusalem in order to celebrate Passover (John 5:1).

In the midst of the Passover observance and celebration, a special ceremony was conducted at the Pool of Bethesda annually called the *Ritual of God's Grace*. Jesus and his disciples attended this special ceremony. Although the ritual was conducted every year during Passover, and we know that Jesus attended at least three different Passover celebrations during his ministry years, the Gospels record only one time that Jesus attended the *Ritual of God's Grace ceremony*—it was during the Passover of AD 28.

It was at the small but extraordinary research library of the Albright Institute in Jerusalem that I found documentation that substantiated the Gospel of John's account of the events that occurred at the *Ritual of God's Grace* ceremony during Passover of that year.

The corroborating resource was a book entitled *Bethesda*, written in 1819 by Dr. Moshe Weizmann. Dr. Weizmann was a Jewish historian who in 1819 was living in Switzerland, but had visited Jerusalem in 1808. While he was in Jerusalem, he recorded stories of miracles ascribed to the healing attributes of the pool. Numerous pen and ink sketches that related to the various stories accompanied the stories.

As I skimmed the contents of the book, I noticed that chapters one and two related to the same event. Chapter one told the history of the pool and the pool's source of water, which dated back to David's day. Chapter two described Jesus' healing a man at the pool. The remainder of the book was interesting, but there was little more that I could use, with regard to my research.

I will paraphrase what Dr. Weizmann wrote as well as quote him direct.

Dr. Weizmann introduced the book by saying that the most famous of all miracles associated with the Pool of Bethesda actually had no connection with the pool itself. It took place on the High Sabbath before Passover, when Jesus and his disciples went to the Pool of Bethesda (John 5:1-16), which meant *"place of mercy,"* to attend the *Ritual of God's Grace* ceremony, which at that time took place each year on the High Sabbath immediately preceding the Passover. Dr. Weizmann then introduced the contents of the book.

Chapter one began with Dr. Weizmann's description of the location of the pool. He said that the pool, also called the Sheep Pool, was located near or next to the Sheep Gate. The Sheep Gate was the gate through which the blood from burnt sacrificed animals and the corpses of non-burnt animals were discarded during Passover. Only one out of every 100 animals that were killed for sacrifice was actually burned as a sacrifice. The corpses of the other 99 were discarded through the Sheep Gate into the Kidron Valley, where the poor collected them for food. The day before Passover, the gate was used as an animal entrance through which the animals that were to be sacrificed would enter into the Temple complex, after they had been washed in the Pool of Bethesda. After the animals that were to be sacrificed were washed, the High Priest declared the pool off limits as a source of water retrieval, until after the *Ritual of God's Grace* was completed.

"The *Ritual of God's Grace* had its origin in the days of King David," continued Dr. Weizmann, "some 1,000 years before the time of Jesus, when Zidok was Priest. After David's adultery with Bath-Sheba he discovered that he had been infected with a venereal disease. The Talmud says that over a period of five days from the time that David initially sent for Bath-sheba, he had sexual relations with her 28 times. Afterwards she returned to her home for two days and then David sent for her again. This time she stayed for 10 days during which time he had sexual relations with her an additional 50 times. The Talmud argued that her pregnancy was a miracle imposed by God as punishment for adultery on both her and on David. This may not be far from the truth because Bath-sheba was in fact in the midst of her monthly purification ritual, meaning the end of her menstrual cycle, when David saw her and sent for her. Considering the fact that this was the least likely time during which she could have become pregnant, her conceiving was probably quite a surprise to both her and to King David. It is doubtful that Bath-sheba gave him the venereal disease. The Talmud records that David contracted the disease as a result of a relationship with a harlot in Gerar. Falling into a state of acute depression after he had received word that the prophet Samuel had died, he went to Gerar in an effort to soothe his emotional hurt. This same Talmud says that

Bath-Sheba was actually infected by David, rather than the reverse, and that the Lord healed her of the disease two years after David had infected her, so that she would be able to conceive and bare Solomon. Sometime after he had discovered that he had a venereal disease, David wrote a Psalm that became known as the 38th Psalm. Although David called the Psalm, *'the Song of Years,'* Zidok the Priest called it *'The Lament of the Diseased.'"*

Once a year, at the time of the Passover celebration, Zidok would accompany David to the brook of Camiel, the place where tradition said David first saw Bath-Sheba. This brook was the source of water that serviced the Pool of Bethesda, built by Herod the Great. When they arrived at the brook of Camiel, Zidok the Priest would pour a drink offering of sour wine followed by a cup of blood from a sacrificed lamb mixed with water from the brook, into the brook as he quoted the *"Lament of the Diseased,"* the 38th Psalm. The ritual became known as the *Ritual of God's Grace*. It was offered in supplication to God yearly by Zidok the Priest on behalf of David, as an act of "penance" for his sin of adultery and murder.

According to rabban Rab Judah's statement in the Talmud, Zidok performed this ritual every year. Then at on *Ritual of God's Grace* ceremony, 38 years after the death of Samuel, the prophet who anointed David to be king, in the midst of the ritual when Zidok was pouring the mixture into the brook and was quoting the 38th Psalm, David was miraculously healed of his disease.

After David's healing, the place became known as *Beth-shalom*, the place of peace, and became a pilgrimage destination for those who were suffering from various forms of venereal diseases.

Solomon had a small but elegant chapel built on the spot, which from that time until its destruction by the forces of Babylon permanently housed a priest who was responsible for administering the *Ritual of God's Grace* to the diseased pilgrims. Upon Jerusalem's destruction by Babylon, the chapel was destroyed and the ritual was abandoned.

With the return of some of the Jews to Jerusalem, a nameless descendant of Ezra's priesthood, in 209 BC, reinstated the ritual, but did not reconstruct the chapel. Whereas the ritual associated with Solomon's chapel was administered at any time on any day except the Sabbath, the new reinstated ritual followed more closely the original ritual that had been administered by Zidok. This reinstated ritual was performed on behalf of those suffering from venereal diseases, during the Passover celebration, *only*. The ritual consisted of the diseased bathing in the waters of the brook. Into it had already been poured a mixture of sour wine, blood from a sacrificed animal, and water from the brook. A priest quoted the *"Lament of the Diseased"* over the diseased as they washed. It was not unusual for one or two of the diseased to be healed ever year.

Upon completion of the pool by Herod the Great, on the exact spot where Solomon's chapel had been constructed, the respected rabban, Joseph ben Rabenah, named the new pool The Pool of Bethesda, *"the pool of peace"* or *"place of peace."* The *Ritual of God's Grace*, conducted at the new and magnificently colonnaded Pool of Bethesda, continued to be a significant part of the yearly Passover celebration. That ended chapter one of the book.

I then began reading chapter two.

"By the time of Jesus' ministry, the *Ritual of God's Grace* had become one of the Passover celebration's most popular rituals. It had expanded to include not only those who were suffering from a venereal disease, but also all who were impotent, lame, or diseased. All of them were invited to come to the Pool of Bethesda to participate in the *Ritual of God's Grace*, which was administered on the High Sabbath preceding Passover. On the day before the Sabbath, the pool was used to wash the animals that were to be sacrificed. After they were washed, the gates to the pool complex were closed, so that the waters would not be defiled. At sundown, the pool complex was again opened, but the Temple guard, who would not allow anyone, under threat of death, to touch the water, strictly guarded the pool itself. All night long, until 6:00 a.m. the next morning, which marked the beginning of High Sabbath, the lame and the afflicted were brought to the pool complex with hopes of being healed of their affliction. Visitors who wanted to witness the ritual came and found a place so they could see the administering of the ritual. After 6:00 a.m., the beginning of High Sabbath, no more afflicted were allowed to come into the pool complex, and no more visitors were allowed into the complex."

The Pool of Bethesda actually consisted of two large rectangular pools. The two pools were separated by a stone wall. The top of the wall was about one foot above the surface of the water. The pool area was a large area that consisted of five covered platformed areas that stepped down from the Temple compound level to the pool level. Each of the first four large "porches," (each one was approximately 60' X 45') was covered by a magnificent Ionic, marble columned, granite canopy. The fifth canopied area was the pool level area. On the High Sabbath all the lame and diseased that had come to the complex crowded on to the first four canopied levels.

At the dawning of High Sabbath, which coincided with sun-up, the High Priest would leave the porch of the Holy Place (the Ulam) in the Temple, followed by a large number of priests, Sadducees, and other religious leaders, and in a great solemn processional he would slowly lead the procession to the pool, carrying a silver cup filled with a mixture of sour wine, lamb's blood, and water that had been taken from the Pool of Bethesda immediately after the washing of the sheep. Upon his and the processional's arrival at the pool, a long blast of trumpets would signal the beginning of the *Ritual of God's Grace*. As the High Priest stood at "street" level at the top of the first platform, he would begin to quote the 38th Psalm. He would then step down to the first canopied level and would begin to make his way through the crowd of the afflicted and diseased, as he continued to quote the Psalm. As he quoted the Psalm and walked through the crowd, he would take a small hyssop, dip it into the mixture in the cup that he was carrying, and would scatter drops of the mixture into the crowd of the afflicted. Priests who accompanied him would identify the ones on whom a drop of the mixture had fallen. These were selected to assemble on the fifth level, the pool area level, to await the High Priest. Traditionally there were about 50 or 60 on whom the drops had landed and who were chosen to assemble at the pool level. They were told to assemble around the two pools, with an equal number gathered around each pool. Temple guards carefully guarded the group to assure that none touched the water before the appointed time.

After the first level participants were selected, the High Priest would step down to the second level and repeat the process. He would repeat the process on all of the first four levels. By the time he reached the fifth level, the pool area level, he stopped quoting the 38th Psalm. He then began to recite a prayer as he walked out onto the center wall that separated the two pools. In the center of the wall, located about mid-way, was a hole that went vertically through the wall and exited at the very bottom of the wall, at the pool floor. The hole exited into both pools.

By the time the prayer had concluded, the High Priest was standing over the hole in the wall. At the conclusion of the prayer, he would shout in a loud voice, "The death has passed. Lord send your angel of healing and mercy and give life to the one chosen of the Lord to obtain His mercy." The High Priest would then pour the mixture into the hole in the wall. He would then wait and watch to see into which of the two pools the mixture would enter first. At the first sign of the bubbling up of the mixture, the High Priest (the word that has been translated "angel" in the John 5 setting was actually the classical Greek word *aeonos*. The word meant *"servant of God."* However, the King James translators wrongly translated it by using the Hellenistic Greek word *aennus*, which means *"messenger of the Lord; angel"*) would take the hyssop and stir it in the water of the pool into which the mixture had first appeared as he quoted Psalm 51. This stirring of the water was translated by the King James translators as *"troubling the waters."* After he had finished quoting Psalm 51, he would walk back down the wall to the covered pool area. Once he was safely back to the covered area, he would shout with a loud voice, "Give mercy O Lord," and then he would throw the hyssop into the pool into which the mixture had bubbled up and the one in which he had stirred the hyssop. The group that had been selected and had gathered around that particular pool only of the two pools were the ones who were eligible to be healed. As soon as the hyssop hit the water, the afflicted would rush to the pool. The first one into the pool would be healed.

Before the *Ritual of God's Grace* took place Jesus met a man who was ill lying by the pool.

In the John 5 portion, verse 5, the King James translators used the word "infirmity" to describe the man's affliction. The word was a translation of the classical Greek medical word *nyronus*. This word was used to describe a disease called *"the corruption of Venus"* or any of various kinds of venereal diseases.

The most identifying characteristic of this man was the fact that John said that he had had the disease for 38 years. This is significant in that the scribes and the Sadducees taught that if a man had venereal disease and if he had not been cured of his disease within a 38-year period that his disease was incurable and the sin that had been the cause of his disease was unforgivable. David was healed of the disease on the 38th year after the death of Samuel. Hence the scribes and Sadducees used this as a basis for their beliefs. Bath-Sheba, they say, had the disease for two years; hence, if a woman had the disease for more than two years without being healed, then her disease was considered incurable and her sin unforgivable.

In John 5, verse 6, Jesus asked the man who was lying on a "sick bed" on the same porch where Jesus and his disciples were waiting for the ritual to begin, if he wanted to be cured of his disease. Jesus was just one of the multitude of visitors who had found a place on one of the four porches to witness the ritual and miracle healing. Jesus used the word "whole" when he spoke to the man who was ill. The word whole is a root Persian word, *qiami*. It was used to encompass all aspects of life: physical, psychological, emotional, spiritual, and intellectual. In essence, Jesus was offering the man total and complete cleanings of both body and spirit.

The man misunderstood Jesus' question, feeling perhaps that Jesus was just making small talk. He responded by saying that he could not be healed because the ones who brought him would not get him into the water fast enough.

Jesus did not respond to the man's comments and excuses. He merely looked at him and told him to take up his bed and walk. The man obeyed without question or argument, and he was healed completely: body, soul, and spirit, and picked up his bed and walked away.

It appears that the ritual began shortly after Jesus healed the man for the Jewish religious leaders (the priests and religious leaders who had accompanied the High Priest in the processional) reprimanded the man for carrying his bed. In essence they told him, "You have had all night to carry your bed to this place. It is now too late. It is the High Sabbath and the ritual has begun. You cannot break the law of the Sabbath in the very face of the High Priest himself." The man immediately began to make excuses as he had done with Jesus. He said, "It's not my fault. The man who healed me told me to take up my bed. I was only doing what he told me to do. I don't know who he was, but he healed me completely."

Later, after the ritual and ceremony had concluded, Jesus searched for the man and found him in the Temple. Jesus said to him, *"You are whole—qiami—(body, soul, and spirit), go and sin* (the probable cause of his disease) *no more, or a worse thing will come upon you."*

Either out of fear of the Jewish religious leaders or out of total contempt or lack of respect for Jesus, and a lack of gratitude to him, the man immediately went to the Jewish religious leaders and told them that it was Jesus who had told him to pick up his bed on the Sabbath, thus purposely telling him to break the law of the Sabbath.

The Jewish leaders were so infuriated at Jesus for urging someone to break the law of the Sabbath that they began to justify why he should be killed because of his disregard for the law. The majority of these Judean Jewish leaders probably knew little about Jesus because the major portion of his ministry up until that time had been in the Galilee. Their only contact with him had been his relationship with John the Baptist, that he was the one who had caused all the problems when he drove the money changers out of the Temple compound, his very short ministry in the state of Judea after the Temple incident, and the reports of his conduct at the great religious conference that had been held in Capernaum [many of the religious leaders from Judaea probably had attended the conference and were eye witnesses to Jesus' teachings and his conduct]. In addition, all that was known about Jesus was by way of reports and hearsay concerning his activities in the Galilee. This "disregard and disrespect for the law" was a crime that up until the Roman occupation had been punishable by death by stoning if a religious leader (priest, Pharisee, Sadducee, scribe, rabbi, rabboni, or rabban) was found guilty. In fact, upon entering rabbinical school, a student had to sign a pledge that he would defend the Law with his life and that through penalty of death by stoning he would not disregard nor disrespect the

Law for as long as he lived. Thus, the Jewish leaders felt that their actions were justified according to the religious laws and according to the pledge that Jesus had signed.

"It seems quite strange that the Orthodox Jewish religious leaders would be so fanatical in regard to the Sabbath," Dr. Weizmann continued, "considering that up until the time of the giving of the law at Mount Sinai, the Sabbath was not a statute by which one must live and be governed. The word *Sabbath* (from the Akkadian word *shabattu* or *shapattu*) was originally used in connection with an Akkadian celebration called "the festival of the menstruating moon goddess." It was on this day, the day that the Akkadian's celebrated *shabattu*, that Moses led the people of Israel out of Egypt.

By the time of Jesus' ministry, the observance of the Sabbath allowed, according to the Pharisees, no exceptions. The law of the Sabbath was so strict and the Jews clung to its custom so rigidly, that during Pompey's siege of Jerusalem the Jews refused to bear arms on the Sabbath. This hastened the Roman victory. It was excesses such as this to which Jesus objected to so obstinately. In fact his opposition was so fervent that he disregarded most pettifoggeries of the Pharisees. The Pharisees had added so many restrictions to the law of the Sabbath instituted by Moses that the original law had become unrecognizable. Jesus did not object to the law of the Sabbath as instituted by Moses; he objected to the additional restrictions placed on the law of the Sabbath by the religious leaders. Jesus sought, in contrast to the Pharisees and religious leaders, to maintain the immunity from punishment and greater merit in the eyes of God. Faced with the choice between performing a good deed and at the same time violating some rule of the law of the Sabbath, he did not hesitate to do good on the Sabbath."

The Sabbath and the primary significance of the Sabbath was stated in Deuteronomy 5:15, *"And remember that thou wast a servant in the land of Egypt, and that the Lord thy God brought thee out thence through a mighty hand and by a stretched out arm; therefore the Lord thy God commanded thee to keep the Sabbath day."* In essence, the Sabbath celebrates and commemorates Jewish independence day. On that the people could stop, rest and reflect upon what God had done and how He had miraculously delivered the Hebrews out of slavery in Egypt. Work was not allowed on that day because God did not want the people to be so encumbered with work to where they would forget what things God had done for them and their ancestors. It was never intended to be the justification for placing unwarranted and unnecessary burdens upon the common people. This concluded the second chapter of Weizmann's book.

I skimmed the remainder of the book to confirm that there was no other information that I could use and then re-shelved the book.

For years controversy has raged regarding the Pool of Bethesda and this miracle associated with it. Some theologians argue that the pool itself never existed while others claim that although the pool may have existed, the miracle was not recorded in the original texts. Hence, it should not be consider as authentic. Still another group feels that the miracle along with its angel and the troubling of the water illusion, the 38-year mention, and the race to the pool to be the first one in are all symbolic images reflecting God's desire to rescue those who feel hopeless and helpless. Even those who feel that the miracle was a true and authentic miracle performed by Jesus don't agree on how, under what circumstances, and why. I must admit that until I read this small book by Dr. Weizmann, I had a multitude of doubts concerning the miracle that had never been satisfactorily answered. But when I read Dr. Weizmann's (a Jewish historical educator who made no claim to Jesus' divinity or professed to believe in anything except documented legitimacy) account of the healing miracle performed by Jesus at the pool, many, if not the majority, of my questions were answered. So much so that I am not only convinced of the validity of the miracle, but also that John's record of the event is genuine and accurate.

Jesus and his disciples stayed in Jerusalem and in the Judea area for a number of months after Passover. It was during this time that his disciples picked corn (or wheat) and ate it on the Sabbath day. The Pharisees confronted them for picking corn, or working, on the Sabbath. Jesus answered on behalf of his disciples. He first compared their actions to David's eating of the concentrated shewbread, implying equality to the most honored of all Jewish kings, King David. He then followed up this comparative allegory by teaching his "Lord of the Sabbath" lesson (Matthew 12:1-8; Mark 2:23-28; Luke 6:1-5).

It was also during these months that Jesus and his disciples spent in Jerusalem and the surrounding area that he healed a man on the Sabbath day with a withered hand (Matthew 12:9-14; Mark 3:1-6; Luke 6:7-11—Matthew seems to imply that this happened on the same Sabbath day that his disciples were confronted by the Pharisees for picking corn).

I had been researching for about twenty years when an archaeology friend of mine, Dr. Edgar Newman, professor of archaeology at the University of Texas at Arlington (he was excavating near ancient Heshbon in Jordan just east of the Dead Sea), introduced me to an Arab historian, Dr. Amed Kori, a retired professor of Ancient History from the University of Jordan in Amman, Jordan, while Dr. Newman and I were visiting Amman. Dr. Kori in turn invited me to accompany him to the university's Archaeological Museum located on the main campus of the University of Jordan. There he exhibited to me an ancient scroll whose subject matter was Jesus' healing of the man with a withered hand.

As he unrolled the fragile leather scroll, Dr. Kori said the scroll was most likely written in Arabia by an unknown monk or hermit, probably sometime in the 3rd or 4th century. Although it had originally been written in Latin, the museum translators had translated the Latin text into Arabic, Turkish, and English. He then walked just a few steps to a small bookshelf and retrieved the 3-ring binder that contained the translations.

He encouraged me to examine the scroll but said that if I wanted to make an in-depth study he would prefer I use the translation notebook. I understood and agreed.

Before I began reading Dr. Kori had said with a big smile, "You will be surprised at what you will discover in this manuscript. I cannot tell you, but just be content that you will be surprised."

So, after taking a few minutes to examine the original scroll, I let Dr. Kori return it to storage and I, not knowing what to expect, began to read the English translation of the manuscript text.

The Search

As I read and re-read the translated text, I was amazed with the author's depth of understanding and his knowledge of Roman/Jewish history and Jewish culture.

The monk or hermit author began his tutorial by quoting Luke's record of the event.

> *"And it came to pass also on another Sabbath, that he entered into the synagogue and taught: and there was a man whose right hand was withered. And the scribes and Pharisees watched him, whether he would heal on the Sabbath day; that they might find an accusation against him. But he knew their thoughts, and said to the man which had the withered hand, 'Rise up, and stand forth in the midst.' And he arose and stood forth. Then said Jesus unto them, 'I will ask you one thing; Is it lawful on the Sabbath days to do good, or to do evil? to save life, or to destroy it?' And looking round about upon them all, he said unto the man, Stretch forth thy hand. And he did so: and his hand was restored whole as the other. And they were filled with madness; and communed one with another what they might do to Jesus" (Luke 6:6-11).*

The author then began to create a foundation of historical background information that related to the healing of the man with the withered hand. Where the author got the information, he did not indicate. It was as if he just assumed that the information was common knowledge.

He began his background information by saying, "During the reign of Herod the Great, the magnificent Jewish Temple of worship in Jerusalem was enhanced and enlarged by Herod, making it one of the great architectural and engineering wonders of the eastern part of the Roman Empire. Herod spared no expense in its construction, hiring the most talented master builders in the world to work on the Temple. Among these master builders were 217 of the most masterful of Jewish stonemasons.

"Construction went smoothly until 5 BC, when Herod began to have a premonition that he would die before the Temple's construction was completed. At that time the majority of the substructure work that had not yet been finished was the work of the master stonemasons, the Jewish stone masters. In order to get the stonemasons to finish their work before his death, Herod ordered the work to continue around the clock, seven days a week, even on the Sabbath.

"Jeshu ben See, Herod's hand picked Jewish chief priest responsible for overseeing and supervising the construction of the Temple, gave his approval for the Jewish master stonemasons to work on the Sabbath. He said that it was permitted because it would benefit the Temple. Jeshu ben See then convinced the High Priest, Joazar, to agree with his decision, for the benefit of the Temple. Hence, the stonemasons worked even on the Sabbath, with the approval of the High Priest, the Sadducees, and the most powerful Jewish religious leaders in Jerusalem.

"Herod died in 4 BC without seeing the master stonemasons complete their work. Under Archelaus, Herod's successor, Jeshu ben See maintained his position as supervisor of construction. Within four years, the master stonemasons had completed their part of the Temple construction.

"Although the stonemasons had completed their work on the Temple itself, Herod's Tower of Antonia (located at the northern end of the Temple complex) had not yet been completed. The tower would become the administrative headquarters for the Roman military garrisoned in Jerusalem. The Roman governor, Coponius, demanded that Jeshu continue the seven-day workweek of the stonemasons until the tower was completed as well. Jeshu had no choice but to consent to the demand of the Roman governor. Jeshu convinced the new High Priest, Elazar, the brother of Joazar, to issue the *Sabbath of Weeks* proclamation. This proclamation allowed the stonemasons to work an additional 126 consecutive Sabbaths in order to complete their work on the Tower of Antonia. This was more than enough time for them to complete their work.

"When their work on the Tower was complete, all of Judea celebrated the completion of the stonemasons' work. The *Sabbath of Weeks* proclamation expired in March AD 2. On the Sabbath following the expiration of the proclamation, Jeshu invited all of the stonemasons and their families to the Temple complex so that he could, as he said, honor them for their great work.

"When the master stonemasons arrived with their families," the monk or hermit author continued, "Jeshu praised them and honored them for the beautiful work that they had done, even though they were forced to work on the Sabbath. But after the praises and the exaltation Jeshu's true character and the real reason for his calling the stonemasons together was revealed. As the stonemasons and their families were basking in the acclaim and praise of the moment, Jeshu stood in their midst and said, "Working on the Sabbath is forbidden, according to our law. But working on the Sabbath was permitted so that work on the Temple could be completed; and for that you will not be punished. But for working on the Sabbath to complete the Tower of Antonia, for the Romans, you will be punished." They were to be punished not because they worked on the Sabbath but because they worked for the Romans on the Sabbath. With that Jeshu had the right hands of all 217 master stonemasons smashed, instantly destroying the stonemasons' livelihood. This act of punishment was contrary to the laws of the Sabbath that forbade any type of cruelty to be inflicted that would destroy a man's livelihood. He then ordered that the eyes of the stonemasons' children be gouged out and that their wives have one eye gouged out and the fingers on their right hands cut off. The wives were then condemned to work in the garbage dump of Gehenna for the rest of their lives and the children were forced to beg on the streets. Never again were the stonemasons and their wives permitted to see each other or to see their children.

"The stonemasons were then commanded that from that Sabbath Day forward, they would have to spend every Sabbath, all day long, in a local synagogue of their town or village, wear sackcloth on their right arm and right crushed hand as an example to all who dare break the law of the Sabbath. They had to bow their heads at all times (they were not allowed to raise their heads in public or look at anyone for as long as they lived) and beg in the streets for their food. The excuse that Jeshu used to justify such cruelty was that it would have been far better for the stonemasons to have refused to work for the Romans and thus face death by them, and even break the proclamation of the High Priest than to break the law of the Sabbath by working for the Romans on the Sabbath.

"Elazar, the High Priest then issued the *Xena Reposa [Proclamation]*, or the *Masons' Disallowance*, saying that the proclamation had come directly from God. The proclamation said that these masons had greatly displeased God, and that He had chosen to abandon them and to forsake them forever.

"Although their families would be forgiven of the sin for which the stonemasons were responsible, the stonemasons would never be forgiven. In addition, if a stonemason took his life in order to escape the horror of the punishment, God would reverse His word concerning his family's forgiveness in the after-life and He would transfer the stonemason's punishment to his family and relatives for the next three generations.

"The stonemasons were forced to live the rest of their lives being convinced that God Himself (so declared by the High Priest, who claimed to be the 'mouthpiece' of God) had forsaken them and that they could never under any circumstances escape their life of horror or be forgiven. The proclamation further said that no one was allowed to talk to them, and they were allowed to talk to no one. If they did talk to someone or someone talked to them, God's curse that had been inflicted upon them would also be inflicted upon the one to whom they spoke or who spoke to them.

"When the Roman authorities were alerted to Jeshu's act of punishment they tried to stop the cruelty. But by the time the Roman soldiers arrived at the Temple compound, the carnage was over. Jeshu and the High Priest were arrested, but, upon Jeshu's insistence that the High Priest was innocent of any knowledge of the incident, the High Priest was released. Jeshu was convicted of inhumane abuse to his fellow man and was sentenced to three years in the Roman prison at Cadasa in Ulatha, north of the Galilee. But, the damage had been done and the lives of the stonemasons and their families had been ruined because even though Jeshu had been imprisoned, the High Priest's *Xena Reposa [Proclamation]* had not been revoked—it remained in force.

"It was one of the master stonemasons exampled by Jeshu ben See and the High Priest who Jesus confronted on a Sabbath so recorded in Luke 6. It had been almost 30 years since the man's right hand had been smashed. The hand was a *xera enpa*. It was dried out, withered and lifeless. Everyone at the synagogue knew what had caused the former stonemason's affliction and everyone knew that he had been cursed and forsaken by God (so the Sadducees, Pharisees, and priests taught). For almost 30 years the former stonemason had come to the synagogue every Sabbath as an example to all of how "God" treats those who work for the Romans on the Sabbath.

"Dare would this man, Jesus, countermand and blatantly disregard a 'divine judgment' by God's High Priest against a transgressor of God's Law regarding the Sabbath? It was blasphemous enough that Jesus would heal on the Sabbath, but to spitefully defy the proclaimed judgment of the High Priest was deplorable.

"In the Luke setting (verse 9)," the monk or hermit continued, "Jesus alluded to the original judgment proclaimed by the High Priest more than 20 years before. *'Is it lawful on the Sabbath days to do good, or to do evil? to save life, or to destroy it?'* Was it acceptable to do good by building the Temple on the Sabbath, but evil when the same type of work was done on buildings other than the Temple? Is it evil, as Leviticus says, to take away a man's livelihood on any other day, except the Sabbath, then it is permissible?

"Regardless of the controversy that would result, Jesus healed the man showing that this man had not sinned. He had never been nor was he at that time cursed. He had been a victim of the harshness and ruthlessness of the religious leaders. The healing vividly supported Jesus' message of doing good on the Sabbath by forgiving sin and healing the physically handicapped."

The monk or hermit concluded the message or teaching lesson by giving a personal and practical application to the miracle by Jesus. He said, "Jesus has not changed nor have his desires and priorities changed. Jesus is still more concerned with the individual than he is with the institution. He is still a Savior who can heal the unhealable and forgive the ones who are seemingly unforgivable and who have been cursed. Even if people feel that God has forsaken them—that God Himself had chosen to turn His back on them—and they are forced to live a life of emptiness and loneliness, Jesus can make a difference in their lives. He still heals the physically damaged. He still forgives, and he still recreates the life that has been smashed and destroyed."

After I had finished reading the monk's conclusion, I sat and talked to Dr. Kori for a few minutes discussing in amazement that this was perhaps one of the greatest sermons that I had ever "heard," and it was over 1700 years old.

Truly the Gospel has no time restraints. It is alive and relevant regardless of the time period, time passed, culture, or social system.

It was also during these months that Jesus and his disciples spent in the Jerusalem area that he chose 12 out of the ranks of the "army" of disciples and followers to be his apostles. He made this selection in the summer of AD 28. It was the first of two times that he selected 12 to be his apostles. Eleven of the 12 were chosen both times. The second selection was about a year after this first selection.

Dr. Stefus Kenwanjuni of Nairobi, Kenya, the president of East Africa School of the Bible, is the person who explained to me the character of each of these disciples who were chosen to be apostles. I met Dr. Kenwanjuni while attending a mission's conference in Houston, Texas. We both attended the same conference workshop where we became acquainted and became friends. After sharing with him my search for historical Jesus project, he explained to me about the 12 over dinner.

"There is not much background material of the selection event," he began by saying as we waited for our meals to arrive, " but what is available is important."

"In mid-summer of AD 28," he continued, "while Jesus and his followers were in the eastern part of the province of Judaea, he chose out of the ranks of his disciples or followers (which could have numbered into the hundreds), 12 who he would later call apostles. The event is recorded in Matthew 10:1-15 and Luke 6:13-49. At this time the chosen were commissioned, and sent out to minister to the Jewish people in Judaea only. This commissioning was the first of two times that 12 were commissioned and were sent out (11 of these 12 were chosen for both of the two commissionings). The second time that Jesus sent them out they were allowed to expand into the Galilee and the Decapolis. Jesus charged them to preach that the kingdom of heaven was at hand, to heal the sick and diseased, cleanse lepers, cast out demons, and raise the dead (Judas Iscariot even received this power). They were to travel by two's and stay in the homes of friends in Judaea as they ministered.

"According to Matthew 10, Mark 3, Luke 6, and Acts 1, the 12 selected at this time were Simon (later called Cephas by Jesus), Andrew (Simon's brother), the cousins of Jesus—the brothers James and John (the sons of Zebedee— called the sons of thunder by Jesus), Philip (the first called by Jesus), Bartholomew (the son of Tholemaios—perhaps the nathanael mentioned in John 1:45), Thomas, Matthew (Levi, the former tax collector), James (the son of Alpheus), Thaddeus, Simon the Canaanite, and Judas Iscariot (the only non-Galilean chosen). The Luke 6 and Acts 1 listings of the 12 apostles do not mention Thaddeus. Instead they name Judas, the son (or brother) of James. Over the years Catholic tradition has sought to clarify the differences by saying that Thaddeus was the surname of Judas, the son (or brother) of James. This may or may not be true.

"Let's look at each of these 12 men." He said.

"Simon (Shim'on) was a fisherman originally from Bethsaida. He was married and lived in Capernaum. Along with his brother Andrew, he was a junior partner in a fishing business owned by Zebedee. Zebedee's sons, James and John were also partners. Catholic tradition (they base their tradition upon the opinions of Clement, Ignatius, Dionysius, Irenaeus, Caius, Origen, and Tertullian) says that Simon went to Rome and established the first Christian community there and later died a martyr under Nero. The Bible seems to imply the opposite for it says that Simon went to Babylon, rather than to Rome. This Babylon could have been the ancient city of Babylon, hundreds of miles east of Judaea or it could have been the great Roman commercial fortress city of Babylon in Egypt, north of ancient Memphis. Clement of Alexandria says that Simon's wife's name was Perpetua and that they had three children. He said that both Perpetua and the children were martyred some time after Simon's death. A somewhat questionable Catholic tradition says that a disciple of Simon's wrote *The Gospel of Mark* (they claim that this Gospel is basically a re-write of Peter's sermons relating to Jesus and his ministry) and *I* and *II Peter*. More believable is that he personally authored both *I* and *II Peter* and had nothing what so ever to do with the writing of *The Gospel of Mark* (neither he nor any of his disciples). Both *I* and *II Peter* were written from Roman Babylon in Egypt. Simon was probably a seasonal or occasional follower of John the Baptist before being called by Jesus. Although Catholic tradition claims that Simon was crucified upside down by Nero in Rome, non-biased historical documents have not been able to confirm this tradition. Nonetheless, they do confirm that Peter was martyred and that he was probably crucified.

"Andrew was Simon's brother. At least one of their parents was probably Greek, based on the fact that Andrew was a Greek name. He was also a fisherman and a junior partner with Peter in the fishing business owned by Zebedee. Andrew too was probably a part-time disciple of John the Baptist. Eusebius says that he preached in Scythia. Jerome and Theodoret say that he preached in Achaia (Greece). Jacob Baradaeus claims that Andrew preached in and evangelized Arabia, Peter the Hermit says he founded churches in Dalmatia, and Nicephorus says that he preached in Asia Minor and Thrace. Tradition says that he was crucified at Patrae, Achaia on a cross "decussate" or an "X"-type cross.

"James (Ya'kob) was one of two sons of Zebedee, Jesus' uncle, who was called by Jesus. James was a cousin of Jesus. His brother was John. He and John were junior partners along with Simon and Andrew in Zebedee's fishing business. According to Acts 12:2, Herod Agrippa I in AD 44 ordered James to be killed. Up until the Council of Bishops, held in Toledo, Spain, in AD 1215, it was taught that Herod had also killed John at this time. It was at this council that John was proclaimed to have lived until AD 104, that he was boiled in oil during the reign of Domitian in AD 95, but survived the ordeal and was exiled to the Roman penal colony on Isle of Pathmos, that he died a natural death, and that he had authored *The Gospel of John, The Revelation* (The Apocalypse), and *I, II,* and *III John*. John was *a major* point of controversy and disagreement throughout the Middle Ages. While most Protestants believed that John died with James (John Foxe in his book entitled *Actes and Monuments of These Latter and Perillous Days*, printed in March of 1563, stated that both James and John were beheaded by Agrippa I), Catholics held to the belief that John survived until the age of 100. This belief gradually began to 'win over' the Protestants and by 1770 it had become a part of the *Congregational Creed*. This set the stage for its adoption into mainline Protestant doctrine.

"John (Yohanan) was the other son of Zebedee who joined Jesus. He too was a cousin of Jesus. He was the brother of James (Coptic tradition says that James and John were twins, although there is very little, if any, evidence to confirm this). As stated earlier, John did not 'become' the author of the biblical books attributed to him until the Council of Bishops in AD 1215. Although present day thought says that John had suffered persecution and was exiled to the Isle of Pathmos where he worked in the mines and died in AD 104 of natural causes. Nothing has been discovered to confirm this other than that claimed as authentic by the Church of Rome. Polycarp, Ignatius, and Papias were claimed by the Catholic Church to be disciples of John. As I (Dr. Kenwanjuni) stated earlier, it is most probable that John was killed along with his brother, James, in AD 44 by Herod.

"Philip was a Greek and was the first to be called by Jesus. In a letter written in AD 190 by Bishop Polycrates of Ephesus to Bishop Victor of Rome, there is mention of the fact that Philip, while living at Chenoboskion in Upper Egypt, wrote his own *Gospel of Jesus*. Proclus claims that Philip preached at Hierapolis in Phrygia (in modern Turkey). According to St. Epiphanius, after preaching in Scythia, Galatia, and France, Philip returned to Hierapolis where he was martyred by crucifixion.

"Bartholomew (bar-Talmai or bar-Tholemaios—the son of Tholemaios) does not appear in the *Gospel of John*, unless he is that nathanael that was confronted by Jesus in John 1. If so, he was introduced to Jesus by his friend, Philip. A late 5th century Coptic tradition says that he ministered in Arabia. Armenian tradition claims that he preached in India. It is said that he was flayed alive and then crucified up side down in Armenia.

"Matthew (Matthai, a contraction of Mattaniah) is generally identified with the name Levi, the tax collector from Capernaum. He was probably a mix of Hebrew and Greek. The tradition that Matthew was the author of one of the Synoptic Gospels is based on statements by Bishop Papias of Hierapolis, in Asia Minor, towards the middle of the 2nd century. Other than these statements, no evidence to support this assumption has surfaced. *The Gospel of Matthew* was probably written by a 2nd century or late 1st century, Jewish convert to Christianity, perhaps even an early church leader—a person who had a remarkable knowledge of Jewish manners, customs, and history. *The Gospel of Matthew* is far from being chronologically correct and leads me (Dr. Kenwanjuni) to believe that its major purpose was to preserve the teachings, character, and purposes of Jesus and his ministry. Eusebius says that Matthew preached for 15 years in Judea, and then traveled east. Socrates Scholasticus says that he preached for more than 20 years in Ethiopia. Ambrose says that Matthew left Jerusalem after the Lord's ascension and went to Persia where he preached for 40 years. Isidore says that he ministered in Macedonia where he founded a school. Clement claims that Matthew suffered terribly when he was martyred. Over a period of five days Matthew was slowly and methodically dismembered and chopped to pieces with an ax.

"Thomas (Toma; his Greek name was Didymos—both names mean *twin*) tradition says was a Zoroastrian philosopher of Syrian ancestry and that he eventually evangelized throughout Persia, Arabia, and India. He was most known for his unbelief regarding Jesus' resurrection. Since the 3rd century, an apocryphal Gospel has been ascribed to him, *The Gospel of Thomas*. Some biblical scholars feel that Thomas' Gospel warrants the position of 'the 5th Gospel.' I (Dr. Kenwanjuni) disagree. First century Christian tradition says that Thomas preached in Parthia and Persia. The Church in Malabar in India has traditionally claimed to be founded by Thomas. The Mar Thoma Church in Travancore and Cochin, now called Kerala, was claimed to have been founded by Thomas. Thomas was martyred by being ran threw with a spear first and then a sword.

"James (Yakob) was called 'the less' or 'the little,' either because of his physical stature or because he was a younger brother. It can be argued that in some places in the Gospels it appears that he is called the brother of Jesus. This assumption is implied by the Jewish/Roman historian, Josephus as well as Eusebius of Caesarea in his 4th century *History of the Church*, when he wrote, 'James, the son of Joseph, the husband of Mary, the mother of Jesus the Christ.' But by the 8th century, when the tradition that Jesus was an only child began to gain in strength, the rosters of the apostles in Mark and in Luke were amended by adding 'the son of Alpheus' to the name of James. If this James is in fact James, the brother of Jesus, he became the leader of the early church in Jerusalem and was considered the most authoritative of any and all Christians of the 1st century. All theologians and Christian historians agree that he authored the book that bares his name. There is enough circumstantial evidence to suggest that he also authored *The Gospel of Mark* and the *Letter to the Hebrews*. Hegesippus says that before the siege of Jerusalem by Vespasian, angry scribes and Pharisees threw James off of the roof of the Temple in Jerusalem. He was then stoned and his brains were dashed out by a fuller's club.

"Thaddeus (Taddai) or Jude Thaddeus is very mystical in that little is known about him. Legend says that he was sent by Jesus to heal Abgar, the king of Edessa. Matthew (Lebbaeus whose surname was Thaddeus) and Mark list him, but they do not list Judas, the son or brother of James. Some try to associate him with Jude, the brother of Jesus and James, the author of The Epistle of Jude, while others say that he is the one that John's Gospel refers to as Judas, not Iscariot. Tradition says that he evangelized Persia, Mesopotamia, and Arabia. He was said to have been martyred in Syria.

"Judas, the son or brother of James, was listed in Luke and Acts (both authored by Luke), instead of Thaddeus. Tradition says that he was a strong Roman sympathizer and that he founded the Church in Edessa. He was martyred in Mesopotamia.

"Simon (Shimon) was called the Canaanite (from the Aramaic *qana* which means 'daggerman' or 'assassin'). These 'daggermen' were the radical faction of the Zealots, a Galilean revolutionary group that had staged an unsuccessful attempt at revolting against Roman authority in AD 6. The Zealot revolt had been led by Judah of Gamala. From that time onward the Zealots were continually involved in harassing the Romans, Herodians, and the Sadducees through 'guerilla warfare.' Although there is no record that the 'daggermen' ever attacked a Roman after the AD 6 revolt, they did become ruthless assassins who struck Roman sympathizers and Sadducees without warning, usually in crowded areas such as a market place or a celebration. Considering Simon was a Zealot, it is very surprising that Jesus, perhaps a Roman citizen or at the very least an honored and respected friend of Roman authority, would have selected Simon to be an apostle. But, on the other hand, it is also surprising that he selected Judas. Certainly we are not qualified to second-guess Jesus' choices or to question his decisions on who should be selected to be his disciple. Tradition says that Simon ministered in Egypt, Cyrene, and Mauritania and that he was crucified in Judaea during the reign of Domitian.

"Judas (Yehuda), the only non-Galilean selected, is perhaps the best known of Jesus' disciples based on the fact that he betrayed Jesus with a kiss. He is called Iscariot. This may refer to the town that he was from (Keryoth, Karioth, or Sychar) or it could refer to the name '*sicarius*.' This is what the Romans called the Galilean 'daggermen.' By the 12th century it had become assumed that Judas was a Zealot, although no historical evidence supports this assumption.

"According to Luke 6:13-49," Dr. Kenwanjuni continued, "After Jesus commissioned these 12, he and the 12 went up into a mountain to pray. After spending time in prayer together, they came back down from off of the mountain into the valley plain. There Jesus taught the 12 (verse 20) what has come to be called the *Sermon on the Plain*, recorded in Luke 6:13-49. The instructions given to the 12 in this *Sermon on the Plain* were very similar to the instructions that he had given his six original 'called' disciples in what has become known as *The Sermon on the Mount*, which had been taught to the six some time before this in an effort to prepare them for what lay ahead and to give them a 'sneak-peek' at his doctrines before they actually began to travel with him as his follow workers. In this *Sermon on the Plain*, Jesus was attempting to prepare the 12 for ministry, before he sent them out.

"After he had finished the *Sermon on the Plain* lessons, he healed all who needed healing (Luke 6: 45, 47-49), showing by example how these selected 12 needed to minister to the needy in Judaea. Afterwards he sent them out to fulfill their commission (Matthew 11:1). Then leaving the 12 to minister in Judaea, he returned to the Galilee, alone."

In mid-July, after Jesus had commissioned the 12 and had sent them out to minister to Jews in Judaea, he returned alone to the Galilee. Upon his return huge crowds from all over Syria and Phoenicia again met him. He ministered to them all—teaching, preaching, healing their diseases and afflictions, and casting out demons. In the midst of this seemingly non-stop ministry, Jesus healed a man in Capernaum who was demon possessed. This resulted in Pharisees and scribes who had recently arrived from Jerusalem and who were seeking to discredit Jesus and his ministry, accusing him of casting out demons by the authority of Beelzebub (Matthew 12:24-30, 43-45; Mark 3:22-27; Luke 11:16-20, 24-26).

I found documentation that confirmed the Gospel records of this implausible accusation by the scribes and Pharisee while researching in the library of the old Norman church, Annunziata dei Catalani, in Messina, Sicily.

The majority of the manuscripts housed in the church library was from the Middle Ages period, and most dealt with church doctrine, church politics, and liturgy. However, one was of special interest to me—a letter written by the prophet Dorotheus the Younger, the founder of the monastery of Khiliokomos near the Black Sea. The letter was written in Latin.

A large, leather-bound book resting on a podium at the end of the manuscript display case described the history of each manuscript and translated each into French, Italian, and English.

This book indicated that this letter written by Dorotheus the Younger was in answer to a question asked of Dorotheus concerning the unforgivable sin. It seems that in 1037 Cunegund, the daughter of Siegfried of Luxembourg and Hedwig, and the wife of Henry, Duke of Bavaria, wrote a letter to Dorotheus stating that she feared her husband, Henry, could have committed the unforgivable sin. She said that since he, Dorotheus, was a prophet that he would be able to explain to her what was the unforgivable sin and could tell her whether her husband had committed that sin.

Dorotheus responded back to Cunegund by writing her a letter (the letter that was there on display), and was to be hand delivered to Cunegund by a trusted servant named Eloi. But, Eloi never made it to Cunegund. In route, he was robbed and killed. Among the items taken from him by his attacker was the letter for Cunegund. The whereabouts of the letter was unknown for more than four centuries. Then in 1499 it reappeared. An orphan boy gave the letter to Jerome Emiliani saying that he had found it in the bookcloset (a small bookcase that straddled a horse saddle) of an infidel (a Jew). Apparently he had stolen the bookcloset while the Jew was bathing in a stream in the forest. But because he had taken it from a Jew, he did not consider it stealing. The letter remained in Jerome's possession until his death in 1537. Upon his death, one of his student teachers, Malchus Marillo, took the letter with him to Annunziata dei Catalani, where in 1540 he founded an orphanage that operated until 1760, when it was closed permanently. Sometime during those 200 years the letter was placed inside an empty wine bottle and was sealed closed with wax. Obviously it had been sealed in the bottle in order to hide it for some unknown reason. The bottle in turn was hidden in a small carved-out hole in the wall of the wine cellar and was plastered over to hide the hole. It remained hidden until 1908 when the devastating 1908 earthquake cracked the walls of the wine cellar and the empty wine bottle with the letter inside fell from its hiding place and broke, revealing the letter. The letter was then placed in the church's manuscript library until 1958 when it was transferred to the manuscript museum.

I took the leather-bound book and sat down at a nearby table in order to read the English translation of the letter and to take notes.

The scripture portion that Dorotheus used in his answer to Cunegund is recorded in Matthew 12:22-45.

"Apparently after Jesus had sent the 12 out to minister in Judaea," Dorotheus wrote, "he returned to the Galilee, and more specifically, to Capernaum. Upon his entering the city, a man who was demon possessed manifested by blindness and muteness, was brought to him. Jesus immediately recognized the source of the man's aliment and cast the demon out of the man. The man was immediately healed.

"Shammaite Pharisees from Jerusalem along with some Temple scribes were in Capernaum at that time and witnessed the exorcism. But because Jesus had not followed the accepted practice for exorcism, they dismissed the healing contemptuously and claimed that the reason Jesus was able to exorcise the demon was because he was allied to and had received special permission from Beelzebub, or Baal-zebub. This god known to the early Canaanites as Ba al zebul, and worshipped by the early generations of Canaan dwelling Israelites, was the Canaanite god of excrement and filth. By the time of Saul, the Philistines called the god Baal zebub, the god of flies, corruption, and infection. It too was worshipped by the Israelites. The influence and worship of this god, now called Beezeboul, or Beelzebub, a Greek name, was still very much in evidence in the Galilee at the time of Jesus. But by now, the god had evolved into *a* prince (not *the* prince) of devils who was in command of demons that specialized in the spread of filth, corruption, disease, and putrefaction. As it had been from the time of the Canaanites, many people in the Galilee felt it was necessary for this god of filth to be propitiated in order for infection and corruption to be neutralized and for disease to be healed.

"Bell-zebub was worshipped little in Judaea and probably not all the state of Judea," he continued. "Thus, not being familiar with the worship of this god, the Judean Pharisees mistakenly used the name Bell-zebub to signify Satan and his kingdom.

"Whether the Pharisees really believed that Jesus believed in Beelzebub is arguable, but they knew without a doubt that many of the Galileans believed in the god. If they could convince the populous that Jesus had been able to exorcise the demon because he had received permission from Beelzebub, then they would discredit Jesus' position, his methods, his teachings, and his mission, because it would imply that Jesus was allied with the forces of evil and corruption.

"Because these Shammaite Pharisees were unfamiliar with the rituals of the cult of Beelzebub practiced in the Galilee at that time, they made fools of themselves when they identified Beelzebub as *the* prince of devils. Almost any Galilean would know that Beelzebub was not *the* prince of devils, but rather *a* prince of the devils, so needless to say, the Pharisees convinced no one.

"Although the Gospel's account does not say that these Pharisees actually verbally accused Jesus of casting out the demon through permission by Beelzebub but rather, that Jesus knew that they were thinking this and thinking about doing it, I

(Dorotheus) imagine that they had actually accused Jesus openly in front of the crowd and from that assumption, he made his case.

"After the Pharisees had made fools of themselves, Jesus forced them to wallow in their disconcertedness and disgrace by confronting them and their fallacious ineptness in front of the entire crowd; the ones who had just witnessed Jesus' miracle of exorcism.

"Jesus did not confront them from an emotional position, but rather he confronted them logically. He stated a matter of fact concerning the mandatory position of unity if any unit, nation, kingdom, group, people, organization, or institution, was to survive, rather than defend his position or his actions. Jesus went on and implied that the forces of evil could only be overcome by antithetical powers. It was through the power of God that Satan could be overcome. So to say that evil does battle against evil and the authority of evil can overcome that evil is blasphemy because it negates the need for God's intervention."

Dorotheus went on for many more sentences explaining God's unchallenged power over evil and about the lesson that Jesus taught about binding the strong man of the house. He then got back to the subject at hand, that of the unforgivable sin—blasphemies against the Holy Ghost.

Dorotheus approached the subject of blasphemies against the Holy Ghost by bringing back into focus the event that precipitated the statement made by Jesus concerning blasphemy: he had been accused by the Shammaite Pharisees of casting out a demon by the authority and the power of the prince of devils. It appears that Jesus responded in this way because the Pharisees had consciously attributed the work of God to the work of Satan.

"The Shammaite Pharisees knew that it was through the power of God that the demon was cast out, but they refused to believe that Jesus could be used by God in such a way. These Pharisees premeditatedly, willingly, and knowingly attributed the work of God (or more accurately, God the Holy Ghost) to the work of Satan although they knew that it was the work of God."

Dorotheus then went on to explain that the unforgivable sin, the sin of blasphemies against the Holy Ghost, was neither rejection of the Spirit's prompting nor habitual sin. Rather, it was to premeditatively, willingly, and knowingly ascribe the work of God the Holy Ghost to the work of Satan.

He assured Cunegund that unless her husband, Henry, Duke of Bavaria, knew and participated in and fully understood the things, workings, purpose, plan, and will of God the Holy Ghost and then made a conscious, premeditated, willing decision to reverse his spiritual beliefs and espouse a belief that all that he had known and experienced was through the power and the authority of Satan, he had not committed the unforgivable sin.

That concluded Dorotheus' letter.

Shortly after Jesus' confrontation with the Pharisees and scribes, a woman of the Murias or as the KJV says, *company*, from Caesarea Philippi, approached him with the Theophus identification declaration. He had probably left Capernaum for a few days when this happened, because the next we hear from him is during the first part of August when he was entering back into Capernaum. For the detailed information concerning this woman of the Murias event see the chapter entitled **The Rome of Tiberius**.

Soon, probably within hours, after he had returned to Capernaum, Jesus was approached by Jewish elders on behalf of a well-respected Roman centurion, whose servant was sick and near death (Luke 7:1-16). Although this story is similar to the story of Jesus' healing of Nehem (Matthew 8:5-13), the servant of the Roman centurion, Rustus Flabian, two years previous in AD 27, (both stories indicate that the centurion had built a synagogue—it is known from Roman Syrian history that Romans were responsible for the construction of 13 synagogues in the Galilee, Gaulanitis, and the Decapolis; four of these Roman funded synagogues were in the region of Capernaum/Julias-Bethsaida—of these four, two were funded by Roman centurions.) they are two different events performed at two different times.

Dr. Timothy Whaley, Head of the Department of History at Aiglon College in Chesières, Switzerland was the one who introduced me to information that confirmed the Gospel record of this event.

I become acquainted with Dr. Whaley while I was touring the campus of Aiglon College and stopped him to ask where the college's research library and museum were located. He told me that he would accompany me to the library/museum because he was going there himself. As we walked we both introduced ourselves and I briefly told him my purpose for being on the campus and about my research project. Before really realizing it, we had arrived at the library/museum.

The building that housed the museum was the former residence of the rector of the college. The building was originally built in the 16th century and was converted to a museum in 1777. The museum was connected to the college library, built in 1781, by a covered and enclosed 20 or 30-foot long walkway.

Dr. Whaley told me that although the college research library and museum was smaller than some of the more well-known research libraries, he felt they had an impressive collection of Roman artifacts from the early Christian era and Christian medieval manuscripts that were religious in nature. However he could not think of any specific artifact or document that would fit within my parameters of truth. But he told me to take my time looking at the artifacts and manuscripts, and that he would be in the research study lounge in the very back of the library portion of the library/museum, if I needed him.

After about an hour of exploring the early Roman section, I had just begun to tour the 1st century BC through 1st century AD Roman section when purely by chance I noticed a small fragment (maybe 3" square and 2" thick) of what appeared to be an olive leaf carved from marble that was displayed among 20 or 30 other small, similar fragments. In fact, the artifact was so inconspicuous that more times than not visitors and tourists did probably overlook it. As I glanced over the articles in the display case, there were three words printed on the identification plate in front of the artifact that caught my eye: *synagogue*, *Capernaum*, and *Jesus*. I stopped and read the identification plate more carefully. Printed in French, German, Italian, and English it read, *A fragment of a 1st century Jewish synagogue from Capernaum in the Galilee, in the Roman province of Syria—probably financed by Roman* centurion. Early Christians believed Jesus might have been involved in its construction.

I was totally taken aback by this chance discovery. I immediately rushed to the lounge to ask Dr. Whaley about the small marble fragment. He could not recall the artifact, so we walked back to the case so he could look at it.

He said that there were so many artifacts that it is difficult to recall all of the details concerning every fragment in the museum. But that we would get the reference number of the fragment from off of the identification plate and then go to the reference archives in the basement and see what information we could find about the fragment.

Dr. Whaley led the way downstairs to the reference archives. I sat down at a reference table in the large storage room and waited for him to retrieve the information about the fragment. Within a few minutes Dr. Whaley returned carrying a large bound volume about three inches thick.

He flipped through the pages until he found the reference number of the artifact. He began to read the information about the fragment. "It appears that this fragment has been in the museum for at least 100 years and maybe 200. In fact," he continued, "it looks like this fragment could be one of the original museum pieces that dates back to when the former rector residence was converted into the museum."

"It looks like," he continued, talking slowly as he skimmed page after page of the reference volume reading information about the fragment, "most of the reference notes regarding this piece were written in a French/Italian combination and that the latest information about the artifact dates back to April, 1814, making it one of the original museum pieces."

Dr. Whatley explained that the artifact was originally discovered in the ruins of what was believed to be a 1st century AD synagogue in the ancient city of Capernaum, by a crusader known only as Robert of Wakefield, in 1187 after the crusaders' defeat at the battle of *the Horns of Hattin*. Capernaum was originally located in the region of what was at the time of Jesus, the Galilee. Robert of Wakefield joined Duke Frederick of Swabia in an attack against Acre in 1191. Robert carried the artifact into battle with him. He was killed in that battle and the artifact was discovered by another crusader, a friend of Robert's known only as Martin, when he discovered Robert's body in the aftermath of the battle.

"It is assumed that Martin took the artifact back to France with him. After that the artifact disappeared. It reappeared at The University in Siena in northern Italy probably in about the year 1390, because in 1410 a monk at The University known only by the name of Hilary the Teacher wrote a book that cataloged all of the artifacts that were then owned by The University. In this book he traced the history of the artifacts and gave details on how they were discovered. This fragment was included in Hilary's book."

"It seems that," he continued, "in about the year 1774, the Bourbon ruler of the Kingdom of the Two Sicilies 'liberated' many of the kingdom's university artifact vaults and brought them to Naples, the capital of the Kingdom, to stock his new museum, the Museo Archeologico Nazionale. This artifact and Hilary's portrayal were brought to Naples from The University in Siena at that time.

"Sometime between 1796 and 1797, as Napoleon Bonaparte was rolling like a tidal wave over Italy, the artifact and Hilary's description disappeared along with many other treasures that had been displayed at the Museo Archeologico Nazionale. Most of those treasures remain lost up to this present day. But of the few that did reappear in various places in Europe over the next 200 years, this fragment and Hilary's description were discovered in the private collection of Pierre LeRue Emser, a municipal judge who lived here in the city of Chesières, after his death in 1814.

"In order to pay off debts that Emser left behind, his son, Johann Peter Emser, auctioned off his father's estate. All that was not sold at auction was donated to Aiglon College in an effort to reduce the estate's tax liability. This fragment and Hilary's description were items donated to the College by the younger Emser.

"From Hilary's original description of the marble fragment, these notes were compiled in 1814."

"Apparently," Dr. Whaley continued, "the fragment and Hilary's description were part of a Christian artifact and manuscript display that the college took on a European tour in 1851. Unfortunately, because the manuscript was handled so much during that tour, it began to disintegrate. What remains of Hilary's original description is currently locked in the museum's airtight storage vault. But," he continued as he slightly lifted the volume from off of the table as a jester to me, "we do have the notes compiled from Hilary's work at our disposal."

Dr. Whaley then began to read the notes taken from Hilary's description.

"Hilary began his description by quoting the Gospel of John (2:12).

> *"After this he went down to Capernaum, he, and his mother, and his brethren, and his disciples: and they continued there not may days" (John 2:12).*

"Hilary then continued, developing a convincing case for Jesus' construction of this synagogue in Capernaum—one of three synagogues that the Capernaum branch of Joseph's construction company (the construction branch administered and managed by Jesus) built in Capernaum for Romans, two of which were for Roman centurions. He (Hilary) claims to have collected his information from two specific early church sources and numerous unspecified sources.

"Hilary then begins to speculate upon why and under what circumstances Jesus moved to Capernaum. He said that in the winter (probably during the month of Tebeth) of AD 26, Jesus, his mother, some of his brothers (perhaps his sisters too, but according to the Gospel of Mark, it seems that his sisters may have stayed in Nazareth), and his two disciples (he had only two at that time) moved to Capernaum in the Galilee.

"He claimed that Jesus too was a master stonemason and engineer, having been taught the trade by his father, Joseph, the husband of Mary, not Joseph, his adoptive father. He went on to say that the reason why Jesus moved to Capernaum was to open a branch of Joseph's construction business.

"One of Jesus' first projects was the construction of a synagogue that was funded by Rustus Flabian, the senior Roman centurion of the 7th Legion, whose district included Capernaum, and whose servant, Nehem, Jesus healed (Matthew 8:5-13). The successful construction of this synagogue led to Jesus' Capernaum construction branch building three more synagogues in the Capernaum region that were funded by Romans, and four others funded by non-Romans. Germanicus Procluis Fatimus, a retired Roman provincial Administrator of Roads and Water Supply for the province of Syria, funded one of the three other synagogues built by Jesus and financed by Romans. His son had married a Jewish girl. Fatimus had the synagogue built in AD 27as a wedding present to his son and his new bride. A second of the three was funded by Gius Laquinus, a Roman silk and textile broker who was accused by a group of Jewish cloth merchants of fraudulent import and trade practices—a serious crime in Roman Syria; one punishable by imprisonment if found guilty. To prove his innocence, he funded the construction of a synagogue in the Capernaum area. The third of the three synagogues financed by a Roman was funded by a Roman centurion by the name of Lucus Quintus Libirycum. He was a centurion for the Roman 10th Legion stationed in Gergesa.

"Like Rustus Flabian, Lucus Libirycum also had a Jewish servant who became his most trusted financial administrator. His name was Judhal ben Hossai. In AD 26 Judhal got married. Upon the birth of Judhal's first son (either AD 27 or AD 28), Lucus Libirycum had a synagogue built in Capernaum in honor of the birth of Judhal's son. During the midst of the construction, Judhal was stricken with a disease that attacked different organs of his body in succession. Before long so many vital organs had been attacked that he was at the point of death.

"As Jesus returned to Capernaum," Dr. Whaley continued as he read from the notes based on Hilary's description, "after being away for a number of days, Capernaum elders representing the Jewish community, approached Jesus on behalf of Lucus Quintus Libirycum, asking him to heal Judhal (Luke 7:1-10). Since Jesus was contracted by Lucus to build the synagogue, his relationship with both Lucus and Judhal up to that time had been strictly business. However, it is most likely that Lucus had heard about Jesus' healing of Nehem, the healing of the Herodian's son, the raising of the Herodian's daughter, the numerous healings during the Bubonic Plague crisis, and many more miraculous events associated with Jesus. So, he had no hesitation about approaching the Jewish elders, demanding that they speak to Jesus on his behalf.

"We do not know whether they objected to this demand by Lucus. If they did, they dared not express it opening to Lucus, if they valued their lives.

"Jesus immediately and willingly prepared to follow them to Lucus' house in order to heal Judhal. But before he got to the centurion's house, Judhal sent friends to tell Jesus that Judhal was not worthy for Jesus to come into his house. The friends said the same thing to Jesus about authority that Rustus had said two years previous and again Jesus marveled at the centurion's faith, saying the same thing to them as he had said about Justus.

"There is no record that Jesus prayed for Judhal or said a prayer on his behalf. All that is recorded is that when the friends had returned to the centurion's house, the servant was totally healed."

Dr. Whaley and I talked about Hilary's description until the museum closed for the day. I left convinced that Hilary's portrayal seemed to be as authentic as many of the other confirmations that I had accepted as corroborating documentation.

For the next couple of weeks nothing is recorded about the life of Jesus. It is not until August 29, AD 28, the *Day of Tribute,* that the chronology of Jesus picks up again.

It was on that day that, accepting an invitation from a high ranking Roman administrator or military official, Jesus traveled to the Roman military town of Nain, followed by a large number of supporters and disciples (these did not include the 12 that he had commissioned—they were still ministering in Judaea). It was in Nain that Jesus raised the widow's son, a Roman military officer, from the dead (Luke 7:11-17).

For years I had assumed that the city of Nain was nothing more than a typical Galilean city and that the widow was a typical Jewish resident, whose husband had died some time earlier and now her young son had died. But then I began to carefully study the Luke 7 account and discovered some things that did not "mesh" with my assumption. Some of the unexplainable things that I discovered were: (1) the *gate* of the city—Nain did not have a wall around the city so how could it have a gate? (2) Much *people* were with her—the word translated people by the King James translators was *giiaoi,* which was a Phoenician word that meant *"armed horde"* or military personnel; (3) touched the *bier*—the word *bier* was a Latin word that described a ceremonial burial platform on which a sarcophagus would rest. It was used in connection with ceremonial burials *only*; and (4) *Young man*—it was a term of respect and honor used by non-military residents when addressing a Roman officer.

None of this made sense if Nain was a simple Galilean city occupied by some Jewish residents and this boy was nothing more than a young son of a Jewish widow. There had to be something more.

I found the "something more" in Thessaloniki, Greece.

I was visiting the Archaeological Museum of Thessaloniki. The museum had ten rooms where permanent exhibitions were displayed and one room for temporary exhibits. Room four—The Thessaloniki Room—was a room that specialized in the history of the city from the prehistoric period up through the late Roman era. Exhibits in the Roman period section included sanctuaries, the agora, the palace complex of Galerius, numerous artifacts, cemetery stellas, and miniature artwork from the period. One of the miniature art pieces was an ornamental piece of jewelry, probably intended to be worn as a necklace. Painted on an oval shaped silver ornament, probably about 2" in length by 1" wide, was a representation of a soldier rising from what looked to be a bier, with a man standing beside the bier with his arm outstretched over the bier. The ornament intrigued me so I asked one of the museum attendants if they had any information about the ornament.

He felt that they did have some additional information in the museum's research sector. The research sector was actually a large room that looked like a library with about a dozen or so bookshelves, all filled with three-ringed binders. The attendant told me that each item in the museum had a number that corresponded with one of the binders. The binders contained information about the history of the artifact. If the artifact was a sculpture or one of the miniature art pieces, it also gave a description of what was depicted in the miniature.

After finding the binder that gave information about the ornament, he welcomed me to sit at one of the small study tables in the room, and study the information for as long as I wanted.

According to the information in the three-ring binder—written in Greek, Turkish, English, and French—Jacob of Amphipolis had painted the ornament in AD 282 and had presented it as a gift to Theognostus, the head of the Catechetical School in Alexandria, who was at the point of death. The artwork commemorated the most renowned sermon ever preached by Theognostus—the rising from the dead of the widow's son in Nain.

After reprinting the Gospel text as recorded by Luke (7:12-17) the information addressed Theognostus' sermon and all appropriate historical background information connected to the sermon.

I will paraphrase Theognostus' sermon.

Nain was a Roman military garrison and encampment around which there arose gradually a town to service the garrison. By Jesus' time Nain was the size of a small city and served as the district and regional headquarters for a portion of both the 7th and the 10th Roman Legions and the families of the officers. It was only during the reign of Tiberius that families of officers were allowed to accompany the officers to the fort to which they were assigned. It was not allowed during a time of war or military action, but during times of relative peace it was a welcomed benefit for the officers.

Nain was located in the Galilee, near the northern border of the district of Samaria on the Roman imperial military highway called the *via Augusta*—the *Augustan Way*. The imperial military highway, the *Augustan Way*, originated in Damascus and ended in Alexandria. The highway was only one portion of the main two-part Roman military highway network in the East that converged at Damascus. One portion of the highway, the *via Egnatia*, originated in the Adriatic port city of Dyrrhachium in Illyricum, present day Durres, Albania. It went from Dyrrhachium to Thessalonice in Macedonia, present day Thessaloniki, Greece, through Thracia (Bulgaria) and on through the city of Byzantium (Istanbul, Turkey) across the Bosphorus through the city of Nicomedia in Bithynia (northwestern Turkey) through Asia (west-central Turkey) and Galatia (south-central Turkey), through the city of Tarsus in Cilicia (south-central Turkey) on to Damascus in Syria. The other portion originated in Sinope, a port on the southern shore of the Pontus Euxinus (the Black Sea) in Bithynia Pontus (northern Turkey). It traveled through Cappadocia (north-central Turkey) and Armenia (eastern Turkey), passing just south of agi Vanii (Lake Van) on through the city of Nisibis (Al Mawsil) in Mesopotamia (Iraq) through Palmyra (Syria) on to Damascus in Syria. In reality, the portion of the Roman military highway that stretched from Nisibis to Alexandria was part of the ancient Persian royal highway built by Artaxerxes that connected Persia (ancient Assyria [Isaiah 19:23 refers to this highway]) with Egypt. The two portions converged into one major highway in Damascus. From Damascus it went through the Galilee and Judaea, on through the city of Alexandria (the portion of the highway that stretched from Damascus to Alexandria was called the *Augustan*

Way.) in Egypt, the city of Cyrene in Cyrenaica (Lybia), the city of Carthago (Tunis) in Africa (Tunisia), the city of Caesarea (Algiers) in Caesariensis (Algeria) and ended in the city of Tingis (Tangier) in Tingitana (Morocco). Non-military traffic (trade and local traffic) was allowed on the highway, but was sparse due to the fact that the Roman military on all non-military travelers levied a large transit toll. There was no non-military travel allowed at night, at a time of military operations, or during times of celebration (an example of this would be a restriction on pilgrim traffic traveling to Jerusalem for Passover).

Only the Roman military and the families of the officers were allowed to stay in the city of Nain. Non-military people were not allowed into the city unless they were members of an officer's family that was stationed at Nain, or by special permission of the Roman authorities. The city of Nain and the garrison were located just over one mile east of the *Augustan Way*. The city was connected to the *Augustan Way* by a broad straight road. At the point of intersection between the *Augustan Way* and the road that led to Nain was a military checkpoint and toll station. In Roman terminology, which was repeated in the Bible, this checkpoint was called "the gate of the city." It was not actually a gate but rather an inspection station, military checkpoint, and toll station where the non-military traffic would pay a transit toll to use the *Augustan Way*. No non-military people were allowed beyond this "gate of the city" except for an officers' family members or by special permission of a high-ranking Roman official. In essence, a non-connected person was not allowed within a mile of the city.

Emperor Tiberius, because he was a military man and former commander and general, gave special recognition would be given to Roman soldiers who had been killed while serving in the military. Generally, Roman soldiers killed in action were cremated in the region where they were killed. But under Tiberius, every 100th officer who had been killed was given special attention and was honored with an elaborate ceremony and burial (rather than cremation) that was intended to honor those who had died while serving the Empire. One time a year the emperor declared a *Day of Tribute* wherein an officer was ceremoniously buried and special recognition was given to the Roman soldiers who died while serving in a particular region.

In essence, one day was set aside each year, on the "Day of Augustus," August 29, in each of the four regions that was under the rule of Rome in which Roman military were stationed: Africa, the East, Europe, and the city of Rome itself, to honor the military dead.

Each of the four ceremonies was under the direction of a Roman Senator sent from Rome with a lavish imperial caravan for the occasion, and was complete with an imperial burial processional called *Caesar's Processional of Honor*. The Roman Senator sent from Rome led this processional. This particular *Caesar's Processional of Honor* (the one held in Nain in AD 28) was led by Senator Lucenius Appolonius.

Along with the Senator, the processional also included members of the emperor's own personal guard (they carried the burial bier), two priests from Rome, one representing the Temple of Jupiter and the other representing the Temple of Mars, local priests, chosen officer's family members, a sorti (50 soldiers) guard sent by the governor of the province (in this case, Syria), a cohort (600 to 1,000 soldiers) representing the local fort (in this case, Nain), the Roman high command of that district, a cohort of soldiers from the auxiliary army stationed in the region, and the various dignitaries who wanted to be seen by the officials from Rome, giving honor (these included the local, regional, and interregional political leaders) to the Roman military, friends of the officer who had been given permission to attend the ceremony by Roman officials, and special guests that had been invited by the Roman authorities.

Each year the tribute would be at a different military location. In the year AD 28, the *Day of Tribute* ceremony in the east was held in the military city of Nain in the Galilee under the direction and authority of Senator Lucenius Appolonius, whom Jesus had likely healed of paralysis in Capernaum just months before, during the midst of the great religious conference that had been held in Capernaum.

Preparations for the *Day of Tribute* began 30 days before the ceremony actually began. The body of the dead officer who had been chosen to represent his fallen companions was taken and from it was removed the brain, spinal cord, heart, lungs, tongue, eyes, and liver. These organs were dried in the sun for 20 days. They then were placed in a bronze container in a vinegar/myrrh/honey/salt solution. The Roman Senator who led the processional carried this container. After the organs were removed the officer's body was drained of its blood and a vinegar/honey solution was pumped through the body filling the blood vessels and cavities with the solution, where the organs had been removed. The body was then immersed and soaked in a salt/olive oil/honey/myrrh solution until the night before the ceremony. On the night before the ceremony the officer's body was washed first in vinegar, then in a spiced/salt solution, and finally in a scented oil and wine solution. He was dressed in ceremonial military apparel and was placed on a gold, silver, and brass inlaid cedar bier upon which he would be carried by the emperor's guard to the district seat (in this case the district seat was the city of Scythopolis, some 12 to 15 miles southeast of Nain). There he would be buried outside of the city, in a carved marble sarcophagus.

The processional left the military garrison or encampment (in this case the processional left the city of Nain) promptly at the first break of daylight.

No one was allowed to speak during the processional. Once it began, it was forbidden for the processional to stop for *any* reason. *No one* was allowed to touch the bier or any member of the processional. To do so usually meant immediate, on the spot, death (Tiberius had said that to touch the bier or to interfere with *Caesar's Processional of Honor* would be viewed the same as if Caesar himself had been attacked and molested. He declared this ceremony to be *the most solemn* of all ceremonies officiated by a Roman official, throughout the Empire; one for which there would be *no* mercy and *no* forgiveness if defiled or hindered). For this reason, the citizens and local residents usually stayed far away from the processional so that there would not be a chance, not even an accidental chance, of such a thing happening. In fact, the locals usually made a point of going miles out of their way so as not to disrupt the processional and ceremonial burial.

On the *Day of Tribute* the section of the *Augustan Way* that passed near Nain would have been closed to all non-military traffic. The only exception would have been for those non-military friends and guests who had been given special permission by a high-ranking Roman official to be a part of the processional and burial ceremony. It seems that Jesus had received this special permission (perhaps from the centurion in Capernaum, the Roman general in charge of the Roman 10th Legion in Gaulanitis, or Senator Lucenius Appolonius himself), and was leading a group of dignitaries and friends, many of which were his followers (probably from Capernaum, Magdala, and Tiberias), to Nain in order to be a part of the processional.

However, according to Luke (7:12), it appears that Jesus and his companions arrived too late to be a part of the processional, for as they neared the "gate of the city," the Roman checkpoint where the road to the city met the *Augustan Way*; the processional was just clearing the checkpoint and was on its way to Scythopolis. It was now too late to join the processional and to try to do so would have meant instant death for him and all who accompanied him.

When Jesus saw the weeping mother of the dead soldier, he had compassion on her. Luke (7th chapter) says that this woman was a widow. It meant that with the death of her son, the Roman officer, she had no means of support. Normally the Roman government would allow family members to stay in the compound for 30 days after the death of an officer, and they would give the family a monetary compensation of an amount equal to two months of the officer's salary. But since this widow's son, the Roman officer who had died, had been chosen as the *Day of Tribute* designate, she would be allowed to live for 90 days in the compound and would receive the monetary equivalent of six months' salary as compensation. Afterwards, she was on her own.

Jesus looked on the sorrow of this Roman woman and realized that unless God intervened her probable fate would be tragic. Overcome by compassion, he literally placed his life on the line, as well as all who were with him, in order to give comfort to the woman. In the face of immediate death from any one of the hundreds of soldiers in the processional, *he not only spoke to the woman telling her not to cry, but he also touched the royal bier and stopped the most solemn of all ceremonial processionals.* The processional stopped and Jesus spoke to the dead corpse of the Roman officer (a corpse that had not had life for 30 days) and told the officer to arise.

Jesus knew about *Caesar's Processional of Honor*. He knew that the blood and organs of the Roman officer had had been removed, that the organs had been dried and then placed in the brass container that was being carried by Lucenius Appolonius, and that the body had been embalmed. Yet, in front of this great crowd of people, 99.9 percent of which were non-Jewish and non-believers in the God of the Jews, Jesus told the officer to arise. Instantly, the young man was restored to life. Not only restored to life, but had re-created blood in place of the vinegar/honey solution, and had created a new heart, lungs, brain and spinal cord, liver, eyes, and tongue so that he was able to sit up and to speak. All of this—instantaneously! It is little wonder that the soldiers dared not try to kill Jesus for interfering with the processional.

"Is it even logic to question why *'there came a fear on all?'*" Theognostus was reputed to have asked.

Justin Martyr in his *Dialogue with Trypho* explained the fear that spread over the crowd after Jesus' great miracle, "The participants in the processional feared greatly what Tiberius would do if he ever found out what had happened. The officers and the soldiers feared what would happen to them if word got back to Tiberius that they had allowed such a thing without so much as attempting to prevent it and without killing the man who had dared defile the emperor. The Roman authorities feared that such a man who possessed such great power could be the nucleus personality around which a rebellion could be fomented. The handful of Jews who witnessed the event feared because Jesus had the power to raise their enemy, the Romans, from the dead. The Roman army would be even more invincible than they were at that time. The Jews also could have been fearful that Tiberius would punish them, the Jewish nation, because one of their own religious leaders, a rabboni, defiled the solemn processional of Caesar. The people feared because they could not understand how the power of creation and power over death could be given to a man. The non-Roman, non-Jews feared Jesus' apparent good relationship with the Romans. Senator Lucenius Appolonius feared that he would not be able to get back to Rome quickly enough to convince Tiberius that he had truly found that Theophus. He knew that resentment against Jesus by his own religious leaders was growing stronger daily, so much so that he feared that Jesus may very well be delivered into their hands for chastisement before he had the opportunity to plead Jesus' case before Tiberius. So, among all who had witnessed this great event, fear spread and was all consuming. Thus Jesus was allowed to leave unmolested and unquestioned. His fame most definitely spread throughout Syria."

No wonder the Romans feared him and the Jewish religious leaders hated him—he was a Jewish/Roman enigma that defied all logic and reason.

Nothing more is recorded about the life of Jesus until the winter of AD 28. By that time word had reached John the Baptist, who had been imprisoned at Herod's Machaerus fortress since the summer of AD 27, about Jesus' exploits: performing healings for Herodians and Romans, disagreeing with scribes and Pharisees, and even asking a tax collector to join him as one of his disciples.

To say the least, John was confused at what he was hearing about Jesus. He had originally felt that Jesus was the one—the promised one who was to come—but Jesus' actions were uncharacteristic of what he presumed would be the character of that one who was to come. So, he sent two of his disciples to ask Jesus if he was to one, or if they should wait for another (Matthew 11:2-6; 20-24; Luke 7:18-35).

William Juxon, Archbishop of Canterbury, and personal spiritual adviser to King Charles I until Charles' execution in 1649, wrote a lesson focusing on John's confusion concerning Jesus. Apparently the lesson was one of dozens of personal lessons written by William Juxon for Charles I, who seemingly during the last few months of his life wanted to learn all he could about the life and ministry of Jesus. Charles I had been introduced to a personal Jesus by William Juxon in 1648. The lesson on John the Baptist's confusion appears to be the only one of Juxon's personal lessons for Charles I that has survived to the present day. It is one display at the London Bible College in Northwood, England.

The following are the most important parts of Luxon's lesson.

"When John was put into prison," Luxon wrote, "not only did his disciples scatter, but Jesus and his disciples left Judaea as soon as they could and returned to the Galilee.

"As John passed his time in prison at Machaerus, news of Jesus' actions and exploits began to filter down to him. Some of the news was exciting and encouraging, yet some was extremely unsettling. By no means was John known for his strict observance of the Jewish religious law or for his attempts to get along with the local religious authorities. On the contrary, John stood strong against any who he felt resisted the true plan, purpose, and commandments of God, whether they are religious leaders, Roman authorities, political authorities, or dignitaries.

"By the winter of AD 28, the reports that had come to John concerning Jesus were so disturbing that he not only began to doubt his own call and purpose, but he began to doubt the person, call, and purpose of Jesus.

"Did he make a mistake in announcing Jesus to be the Lamb of God? Did he miss the mark? Was there someone else who would come later? Jesus seemed to have been the Messiah who was to come, but if he was the one, why did he do the things that seemed contrary to what John perceived as being appropriate for a man called to be the Lamb of God?

"Was this a characteristic of one who had been chosen by God to be His perfect Lamb who would take away the sins of the world? He healed a man of paralysis at the religious conference, which was good, but he was a Roman official, which was questionable, plus he forgave the man of his sins, which was unacceptable. Only God can forgive sin. He silenced the Pharisees, which was good, but then asked a tax collector to follow him as a disciple, which was questionable, if not totally unacceptable. The same tax collector then gave a feast in Jesus' honor that was attended by all sorts of sinners and unbelievers. Jesus even at and mingled with them. However, the raising of a little girl from the dead immediately followed this. But the girl was the daughter of a Herodian, John's sworn enemy. He healed a man in Jerusalem at the Pool of Bethesda, which was good. But he then told the man to carry his bed that was contrary to the laws of the Sabbath, especially the High Sabbath. This was not all that he did on the Sabbath. He also allowed his disciples to pluck corn and he countermanded a direct declaration of the High Priest by healing a stonemason's crushed hand on the Sabbath. He silenced the woman of the Murias, but immediately thereafter he healed the servant of a Roman centurion. Not just a Roman, but a Roman centurion, an authority in the military presence that forced God's people into submission. Did he make a mistake by proclaiming prematurely that Jesus was the Lamb of God? Was it really true that Jesus raised a Roman officer from the dead at Nain? He was not an ordinary officer, but an officer who was being honored on the *Day of Tribute*? What was Jesus trying to do? Was he in reality a Roman and an ally of Rome rather than the anointed one, the Lamb of God? John began to lean toward the conclusion that Jesus must not be the one; there must be another who was supposed to come. John decided that as soon as his appeal was complete, in just a couple of months, and he was released, he would search the land until he found that one who was to come, the true Messiah.

"Before he jumped to conclusions, the confused and distressed John sent two of his disciples into the Galilee to find Jesus and ask him a direct question, *"Are you the one who is suppose to come? Or do we look for another?"*

"When the disciples of John found Jesus and asked Jesus the question, he did not answer them directly. Instead, he demonstrated to them that he indeed was that one by his actions. All that he did that day in the presence of John's disciples was demonstrate the characteristics, as taught by John, of the one who was to come. The writings of the doctor evangelist Luke (7: 21-22) tell how Jesus demonstrated who he was. He healed infirmities, cured plagues, cast out demons, raised the dead, cleansed the lepers, and healed the blind. Afterward he sent John's disciples back to John telling them to tell John about all that they had seen and heard. Jesus did not answer their question verbally, there was no need. He answered by his actions. That was sufficient enough to satisfy John. Never again was it recorded that John doubted that Jesus was who he claimed to be or allowed his faith to weaken.

In December AD 28 Jesus was invited to the home of Simon the Pharisee in Capernaum, to participate in the Feast of Dedication celebration (Luke 7:36-50; 11:45-53).

One of the most unusual representations depicting scenes from the life of Jesus and Luke's record of this Feast of Dedication in Capernaum in particular, I discovered at a little church in Ulm, Germany called the Chapel of St. Kilian.

I entered the chapel and followed the directional signs that led me down a small hallway into a larger corridor hallway that was more like a room, called the Hall of Feasts. There on display were four very large sandstone carvings. All four of the carvings dealt with Jesus' participation at various dinners, as recorded in the Gospels. A monk named simply, Brother Paulus, carved all four over a period of 53 years from 1411-1464.

A guide stationed in the Hall of Feasts was there to tell the story of the carvings and to explain what they depicted. I was the only visitor in the Hall that morning, so I received a private lecture, in perfect English.

One of the carvings depicted the feast given by Matthew in Jesus' honor; one that Jesus attended at Simon the leper's; and the other two were depictions of Jesus' dinner with Pharisees at two different Feast of Dedication celebrations.

As the guide told the story about the two Feast of Dedication carvings depicting Jesus' feast with the Pharisees, he repeated at least three times a statement that caught my attention. The statement was, "Contrary to Pope Gregory the Great." It seemed to me that the guide, by repeating this statement, had made a calculated effort to emphasis the point that Gregory the Great had made some assumptions regarding the events that the two carvings represented, that were not necessarily historically or culturally true.

I did not say anything while the guide was explaining. But when he finished and asked if I had any questions, I asked him about his reference to Gregory the Great.

"Sir, you are very observant." He responded. "I did make that statement on purpose. But I have learned by experience that few ever catch the emphasis and care enough to ask me. You are one of only a small handful who has ever questioned me about it; and I have been making that statement for nine years, since I first started working here after my retirement from the University of Cologne. I am a retired professor of Roman History. And yes, I will be pleased to expound and to explain what I meant by the statement."

The guide sat down on a bench and welcomed me to sit down with him. I asked if I could take notes and he did not object.

Before he began explaining, he introduced himself as Dr. Karl Richenburger. I in turn introduced myself and briefly told him about my research project and that I was most interested in any information that he had about the depictions of the two Feast of Dedication celebrations.

He nodded his head in agreement and began his explanation.

"The first carving—that one there," he said as he pointed to the first of the two carvings, "Is a depiction of the Chief Pharisee's (his name was Zerebell Hazzel) Feast of Dedication Sabbath meal, to which he invited Jesus. It is recorded in Luke 14:1-24. Jesus healed a man with dropsy at the feast and taught a parable whose origin was based on a wedding feast. The Feast of Dedication that the first carving commemorates took place in Jerusalem in December of AD 30. [I will cover this event in the chapter entitled **The Fifth Year of Ministry**.]

"The second carving—that one," he said as he pointed to the second carving, "is the one that commemorates a Feast of Dedication Sabbath meal that was held in Capernaum two years earlier in December of AD 28. Jesus was invited to this feast by Simon the Pharisee. It is recorded in Luke 7:39-50 and 11:37-53.

"Because both of these occasions to which Jesus was invited was the Feast of Dedication one (in AD 30) was celebrated in Jerusalem (this feast was celebrated in Jerusalem every year) and the other (in AD 28) in Capernaum (the feast was celebrated in Capernaum only in the years AD 27 through AD 29), I will first explain the celebration and how it came to be.

"The Feast of Dedication celebration, or *Hanukkah*, was celebrated annually on the 25th day of the month of Kislev (some time between the middle to the latter part of December). The Sabbath meal was served on the final day of the seven-day celebration. The seven-day feast and celebration commemorated the 164 BC re-consecration of the Temple in Jerusalem by the Maccabees. This was six and a half years after the Temple was polluted and the Temple's Holy Place was destroyed by the Syrian king Antiochus Epiphanes. Antiochus offered 400 boiled pigs on the altar of sacrifice. Herod later enlarged this altar when he constructed Herod's Temple. The altar that Herod built was large enough to offer one hundred sheep at a time. When the Romans destroyed Herod's Temple in AD 70, they destroyed the altar and used its stones to help construct the Temple of Ventanius, which was a temple dedicated to the god Mars and the goddess Venus.

"For the first seven days and seven nights of the celebration, the celebrants were abandoned to continuous uninhibited drinking, feasting and wild joyous celebration. Only on the Sabbath, at the conclusion of the celebration, were there peaceful and solemn festivities.

"Originally, the celebration was confined to Jerusalem and lasted two days. However, by the time of Jesus' birth the celebration had expanded to eight days and was celebrated by Jews throughout the province of Judaea, the Decapolis, and the Galilee—with the exception of the city of Capernaum. For years Herod Antipas feared that the celebration could lead to a riot in Capernaum, so it was not until AD 27 that he allowed Capernaum to participate in the celebration. In Judaea anyone who wanted to celebrate could participate—Jew and non-Jew alike, but in Capernaum, Herod insisted that: (1) all who planned to be involved in the celebration must register their intent well in advance of the celebration; (2) that the participants had to be Jewish born; and (3) that the celebration participants had to pay a celebration fee to Herod's tax representative equal to seven days' wages of a common laborer (if anyone sponsored a Sabbath meal, the sponsor had to pay an additional tax equal to one day's wage for every guest invited to the meal).

"In the year AD 20 the High Priest gave special permission for the Feast of Dedication celebrants to eat the concluding Sabbath meal and to be entertained during the feast, as long as the cooking, serving, and entertaining was done by non-Jews, and as long as the sponsors of the concluding Sabbath meal: (1) invite at least one stranger to the meal—this stranger could be a non-Jew; (2) invite at least one guest whom the sponsor considered to be an enemy or a threat; (3) open their doors to the poor, the afflicted, and/or outcast so that they could partake of the scraps of food not eaten by the invited celebrants; and (4) respect the viewpoint and the values of all those present by encouraging their verbal interaction and by not ridiculing or belittling the guests' viewpoint if it happened to be different from the sponsor's. The common method used by a sponsor to show displeasure or disagreement with the guests' viewpoints or values was to remain silent. Silence indicated to all present that the sponsor disagreed with a stated point of view. If the sponsor remained silent even though he was addressed directly by a guest, it indicated that the sponsor vehemently disagreed, to the point of repugnance, with the guest's point of view.

"In Jerusalem these stipulations were strictly honored, but during the three celebrations that were allowed to be held in Capernaum, the sponsors may or may not have chosen to honor them.

"There seems to have been a great difference between how the Sabbath feast was conducted in Jerusalem and how it was conducted in Capernaum (at least in respect to honoring the viewpoint of all who were present without ridiculing or arguing), yet the seven days of night-time festivities (there was no night-time celebration on the final Sabbath evening) was enjoyed with equal abandonment in both places.

"The seven straight nights of dusk to dawn celebration was sometimes called the Feast of Lights," the tour guide continued, "because the celebrants would carry torches as they celebrated in the streets and moved from place to place. The whole city, including the Temple courtyard, seemed to be 'on-fire' with spectacular illuminations.

"Now let's examine the carving that commemorates the Feast of Dedication in Capernaum." He said pointing to the sandstone caving.

"As I have already told you, this Feast of Dedication Sabbath meal took place in December of AD 28. At that time there were very few Pharisees, and only three 'inner circle,' or Shammaite Pharisees, who called the Galilee their home. These three Shammaite Pharisees lived in Capernaum or in the Capernaum area.

"One of these Galilean Shammaite Pharisees was Simon. He had invited Jesus to the Feast of Dedication Sabbath meal. Why? We do not know. But because we know that he held Jesus in utter contempt, he could have invited Jesus as the token enemy that he was required to invite. The story of the events of this Sabbath meal is recorded in Luke 7:36-50 and 11:37-54.

"The Roman manner of feasting, especially in the Greek/Roman dominated Galilee, was generally employed at this time. At the meal, couches were arranged in a 'U' shape, focused around a central serving area. The guests reclined, usually leaning on their right elbows, on couches with the head positioned toward the central area and the feet sticking over the end of the couch. The servers would stay in the central area and move from couch to couch serving the food and drink.

"While Jesus and the other guests were in the midst of eating, a woman, whom Simon identified as a *sinner* woman, knelt at the foot of the couch on which Jesus was reclining with his feet sticking out over the end of the couch. It is not recorded if Jesus knew this woman or if she knew him, had heard of him, or if this was the first time that she had ever seen him. Nevertheless, the woman came up behind Jesus, knelt at his feet, and began to cry, letting the tears freely fall on his feet. She then dried her tears off of his feet with her long hair. Afterwards she anointed his feet with an expensive ointment called spikenard. Jesus allowed this show of adoration without saying a word in objection. However, Simon and the other Pharisees and scribes, or lawyers, who were present were totally appalled.

"The Gospel of Luke does not identify this woman. Pope Gregory the Great in the 6th century identified the woman as Mary of Magdala, whom he ultimately identified with Mary of Bethany, although nothing in the Gospels even remotely suggests that the three women were one in the same. Contrarily, it seems quite obvious that the three were three different women who lived in three different areas. The only thing that Luke says was that the woman was a sinner.

"The word that was translated *sinner* by the King James translators was *eros caritus*. The word was used by the local non-Jewish Greco-Roman residents to identify four different women. (1) The word was used to identify a consecrated follower of the goddess, Venus. Some of these women, but not all, were religious prostitutes who dedicated themselves to the worship of the goddess. (2) The word was used to describe an entertainer who was hired to entertain (usually she was a dancer) at a celebration. After the entertainment, many of these women made themselves accessible to the men who attended the feast, for those who desired a more intimate relationship. The sponsor of the feast generally paid the fee charged by the entertainer for such intimacy. (3) The word was used to identify a household courtesan. She was normally an unmarried young lady between the ages of 12 and 35 who was in the paid employ of a household to provide sexual favors for the master of the house and other adult male members of the household, if the household wives were not able to provide for the men whenever they felt they needed such favors. She lived in the home and was considered to be an essential member of the household. In some cases she was as much of a family member as the wives of the household. Any children that she bore were considered children of the household and heirs of the estate, just like the children of the official wives. However, she could not inherit the family estate. It had to pass to a surviving wife

The Search

or to the surviving sons. Although it was not an accepted practice for her to share her favors with any man outside of the household, it was expected that she serve food and drink at feasts and at special occasions and to entertain the guests by dancing or playing musical instruments. Most Galilean households practiced this custom—even the households of the Shammaite Pharisees and scribes. The Pharisees justified the practice by referring to Abraham's relationship with Hagar. If a man who was not part of the household accepted her favors, or allowed himself to be touched by her, he too would be considered an *eros caritus*. (4) The final way that the word was used was to describe a widowed or single woman who for some reason had no means of support for herself. As such, she would typically wander the streets in search of something that she could sell in order to buy food or shelter for the night. This type of woman was allowed to enter the houses of the feast celebrants during the Sabbath meal of the Feast of Dedication (she was allowed to enter only once—she could not make multiple entrances) and she was allowed to take all of the scrap bread and meat that she could carry out with her.

"Considering the fact," the guide continued to say, "that the Galilean Pharisees condoned all four classifications, a clear picture of just who this woman really was will probably forever remain a mystery. But one thing is certain; she was neither Mary of Magdala nor Mary of Bethany, contrary to what Gregory the Great thought.

"As I have already said, we have no idea who this woman was or if she had known Jesus or had known of him before this time. Perhaps she was a relative or at least a recipient of Jesus' goodness and/or his power; we just don't know. However, we do know that she gave him the most precious gift that she could have ever given him.

"The ointment that she used to anoint Jesus' feet was probably spikenard, for in the ancient world, *it alone* was the precious spice gum ointment that was stored in small sealed alabaster boxes. Spikenard was at that time, and probably is still today, the most costly and the rarest ointment in the world. Today it would take one kilogram, or about 30 ounces, of pure spikenard gum (pure gum is no longer used, artificial fragrance is now used exclusively in place of pure spikenard) per 25,000 liters or about 18,000 gallons, of solution to make a vat of Faberge Brute cologne.

"There are two types of herb extract that is called by the name, spikenard. One comes from the root of a rugged herb found at the northern most vegetation extremities of the highest mountains of Nepal. The root of the herb is crushed and the odorous oil that is secreted is used in the production of incense. Although the herb oil extract is pricey (about one week's income for an ounce of oil), when contrasted to the cost of spikenard gum, there is no comparison.

"Seldom did this herb extract or the incense made from the extract make it way to the Roman commercial trade market.

"The second kind of extract—spikenard gum—is the one commercially traded in the Roman Empire.

"Pure spikenard gum comes from the Indus River valley in Pakistan and India. Approximately every eight to ten years, the Indus River floods. As the waters recede, a bacterium that resides in the water attaches itself to and attacks the roots of the rare river valley grass that grows predominately on the western and northern shoreline of the river. To fight off the attack of the bacteria, the roots of the grass secrete a sticky gum—spikenard gum. This gum dries and hardens into brownish transparent crystals. The crystals are gathered and melted in oil to form a sticky spikenard suave (about 150 pounds of crystals are needed to make less than a quart of suave).

"To make the jelly like spikenard ointment, a small amount of the suave is boiled with large amounts of oil and is mixed with myrrh oil.

"To make the thick spikenard oil, a small amount of spikenard suave is mixed with oil, dry spices, honey, and various spiced waters.

"To make pourable spikenard ointment, a small amount of spikenard oil is mixed with myrrh oil, frankincense oil, olive oil, spiced water, and clove oil. The mixture is then permanently sealed in either an alabaster box or an alabaster cask.

"The alabaster box or cask containing an ounce or less of spikenard anointing ointment was so precious that it cost two-years' salary of an average laborer to purchase it. By today's German standards converted to dollars," the guide continued to explain, "that would be about $24,000. Because of this expense, usually only the exceptionally rich could afford to purchase a container of spikenard (the extremely wealthy would give these containers of spikenard as presents to women to whom they wanted to show their undying love and devotion. The high priest of Jupiter and the high priestess of Venus would give containers of spikenard as presents to those women who had provided a special service for the god or goddess, such as bestowing uninhibited sexual favors upon a Roman official who was in a high political position such as a Senator or an emissary of Caesar. Roman officials would give the boxes to women who had risked their lives for the sake of the empire or whose actions had brought great honor to the official, to Caesar, or to the Empire).

"This alabaster box of spikenard was the type of gift that was so precious that it would be passed down from generation to generation, generally from mother to daughter. Because of the expense, it was a gift that to the average woman could never be replaced if it was ever lost or destroyed. Usually the only time that she would break the seal of the spikenard box (once the seal was broken, the box would forever be damaged beyond repair) was at a time of the death of one of her loved ones. If a loved one in her life died, one who she loved beyond what words could express and she wanted to show how much she really did love that person (usually a husband or a son) she might choose to show her love by breaking the box and pouring its contents on the body of the loved one. By this act, no word had to be spoken. When she broke the container of ointment, everyone present knew without her having to say a word just how much she loved the one who had died.

"Because we do not know who the woman was, other than the fact that Luke's Gospel calls her an *eros caritus*, we do not know how she came by this most expensive of possessions. But if logic is to prevail, once she broke the seal on the box, it could never be repaired nor replaced. She had most likely given to and used on Jesus, the most precious possession that she had or ever would possess.

"Simon and the others present did not verbalize their contempt, yet Jesus knew what they were thinking. This prompted him to tell them a parable about a creditor who forgave the debts of two different debtors. One owed an amount equal to 500 days of wages and the other owed an amount equal to 50 days of wages. Jesus then asked Simon which debtor loved the creditor more. Simon answered by saying that he supposed the one who was forgiven the most loved the most in return. Jesus then used Simon's own answer to condemn him by saying that he did not even give Jesus the bare minimum of respect according to the law of hospitality. Yet the sinner woman gave him her most precious possession. He then, in their presence, forgave the woman all of her sins. This caused quite a stir because the celebrants felt that only God could forgive sin and here was Jesus, trying to occupy a position reserved for God only, or at least God's representatives on earth: the current High Priest, the coming Messiah, the coming Messias, or that prophet who was to come.

"This in turn led to a verbal duel between Jesus and the Pharisees and scribes (lawyers).

"Part of this duel is recorded in Luke's Gospel, the 11th chapter, verses 45 through 53 in your King James Bible, but what I feel was the real meat of Jesus duel with them is recorded in Luke 10:25-37. This was when one of the lawyers asked Jesus how he could inherit eternal life. Jesus' response in turn led to another question that Jesus answered by giving the lesson that has come down to us today as the story of the *Good Samaritan*.

"This question was again asked of Jesus, except that time the lawyer asked it in a different way in that he asked him which was the greatest commandment, during his final week before he was crucified. His answer at that time, which was basically the same as it was at this time during this AD 28 Feast of Dedication Sabbath meal, except he quoted the commandments himself, is recorded in Matthew 22, Mark 12, and in Luke 20.

"But," the guide said, "going back to his confrontation at the Feast of Dedication, it seems that shortly after Jesus was anointed by the woman, the Pharisees and scribes began to confront him.

"One of the scribes or lawyers, those who interrupted the law, stood up and asked Jesus to explain to him what he had to do to inherit eternal life. I like what Irenaeus, the 2nd century disciple of Polycarp, said in his *Against Heresies*.

"He wrote, and I'll paraphrase what he said, that this lawyer, along with all Pharisees at that time, felt that he must prove that he was worthy to receive the distinction of the *chosen of the Lord*, guaranteeing him eternal life. He said that all Pharisees felt that if they were chosen to be a Pharisee that the selection meant that they were chosen to be the *chosen of the Lord*, who were the only ones that would automatically inherit eternal life. But in order to prove to the High Priest that they were worthy to receive such distinction, they had to do some great deed or give benevolently for a specific objective dictated by the High Priest. Since Jesus had just forgiven this woman of her sins and in essence assured her of eternal life, this lawyer was very curious about how is it that she can inherit eternal life, seeing that she had not done any great deed to warrant it. This seemed to imply that the lawyer had probably already done many good deeds in his quest to become worthy, and wondered which one, if any, was the one that made him worthy.

"Jesus answered him by saying that he, the lawyer, already knew what the law stated and that he was not ignorant of God's greatest desires. Jesus then told him to answer his own question and to tell him what the Law said. The lawyer quoted Deuteronomy 6:5 and Leviticus 19:18. '*Love the Lord your God with your whole heart, soul, strength, and mind; and to love your neighbor as yourself.*' Jesus told him that he was correct and that if he kept those commandments—God's great commandments—upon which all other laws and principles are founded, that he will live and inherit eternal life. But the lawyer wishing to put Jesus on the spot in order to show his, the lawyer's, superiority and hoping to have Jesus make a fool of himself by not being able to clarify his words or actions, asked Jesus a very simple but profound follow-up question. He asked him, *'If I am to love my neighbor, then who is my neighbor?'* Rather than stumbling and not knowing how to answer the lawyer, Jesus presented a short story after which he asked the lawyer to answer his own question.

"Irenaeus says that this story by Jesus was actually based on a true event. It seems that in AD 15, Valerius Gratus was appointed Roman Procurator of the province of Judaea. Gratus appointed to the post of Minister of Taxation for Judaea, Marcus Antonius Sparitacus, Gratus' nephew, the son of his older sister, Nicolina.

"Because of Gratus' ruthlessness and his extreme tax collection methods, opposition against his rule began to build within the first three years of his rule, reaching a climax in AD 21. That year rebels from the region of Samaria and the wilderness area of Judaea formed an allegiance. Their primary goal was to so disrupt the flow of tax revenues into Gratus and Rome's coffers, that Rome would be forced to recall him and replace him with a more compassionate Procurator.

"Marcus Antonius Sparitacus employed over 100 customs officers whose job it was to ensure that all tax receipts and revenues were collected and safely delivered to Caesarea. Maritima. However, by AD 21 the rebels had killed at least 60 customs officers and had so disrupted the flow of tax revenues in Judaea that the administration of Gratus was teetering on collapse.

"In September of AD 21, a large tax receipt shipment was due to arrive in Caesarea by the usual way of Lydda, Joppa and the coastal highway. The shipment was to be accompanied by 100 Roman soldiers. However, Gratus conceived a plan that he felt would safeguard the tax receipts. He would use the expected shipment route and the 100 soldier guard as a diversion and then he would send Marcus Antonius Sparitacus by himself with the tax receipts down the Jerusalem to Jericho to Antipatris to Caesarea Maritima highway at night, arriving a day after the expected arrival of the decoy procession. All went as planned and Marcus Antonius Sparitacus left Jerusalem heading for Jericho, on the evening after the decoy procession had left Jerusalem heading for Lydda.

"As expected, the decoy procession was attacked by the rebels. The ensuing fight was devastating to the rebels, with more than half their number killed or taken prisoner. The survivors escaped to the hills of the district of Samaria. By the time the decoy caravan was attacked, Marcus was well on his way, by cover of night, to Jericho, with the tax revenues.

"Before sun-up, while it was still very dark, Marcus became very uneasy about being alone on the dark highway. Since he was only an hour's ride from Jericho, he decided to hide the tax revenues and then continue on to Jericho and spend the rest of the night. He then would return when it became light, retrieve the tax funds, and continue on his way to Caesarea. But just as he had finished hiding the money and was preparing to continue on to Jericho, some scavenging robbers attacked him. Since he had hid the tax revenues, he had little money on him. But being a wealthy

Roman, his clothing was valuable, so the robbers stripped him of his clothes and beat him unconscious, leaving him to die on the side of the road.

"As morning dawned, a priest from Jerusalem was traveling to Jericho. But seeing the wounded and beaten man who looked as though he could be Roman, he chose not to stop to help. Instead he passed him on the other side of the road. Besides it was not socially acceptable, nor religiously demanded or expected for a priest to help the Roman oppressors, regardless whether the Roman was in need of help. The next to come along was a Levite, whom God had specifically directed through instructions by Moses, to show mercy to the enemy and comfort to the hurting, regardless of social order or nationality. However, Moses was obviously not referring to oppressive Romans. So, as did the priest before him, the Levite passed by on the other side of the road.

"Next came a Samaritan silk merchant by the name of Narciss. He had left Jericho at sunrise and was on his way to Jerusalem to appeal to the regional custom's officer about reducing his tax burden. Although he had no love lost for the Romans who had taxed his business to almost bankruptcy, he did have compassion for this one who appeared to be a Roman, but who had been beaten and was hurting. He stopped and mended Marcus' wounds and took him back to an inn in Jericho. He paid for Marcus' stay and his care and told the innkeeper that upon his return from Jerusalem, he would settle up with him. Narciss kept his word and did as he had said that he would do.

"It took Marcus a year to recover from his wounds, all the time Narciss paid for his stay, without knowing who he (Marcus Antonius Sparitacus) was or his position, other than that he was a Roman. However, Marcus had sent word to his uncle that he was alive and that the tax receipts were safe and where he had hidden them, but that he would stay in Jericho until he was recovered. Gratus sent officers to retrieve the receipts from the hiding place, but left Marcus in Jericho to heal without revealing his identity.

"Finally Marcus was well enough to travel. He invited Narciss to Caesarea, saying that he wanted to repay his generosity. Narciss reluctantly accepted Marcus' invitation, because Marcus insisted. Upon their arrival in Caesarea, Marcus revealed his true identity and told Gratus of Narciss' hospitality and generosity. Gratus responded by rewarding Narciss for his generosity to his nephew. He declared that Narciss' tax load would be relieved for life and pledged that from that day forward, the entire court of Gratus would buy their silk exclusively from Narciss. Needless to say, Narciss was not only surprised to learn who Marcus really was, but was flabbergasted to reap such rewards merely because he chose to show kindness and compassion.

"Jesus used this true story as a basis for his question to the lawyer. After reciting the story he asked the lawyer, who of the three was neighbor to the one who was attacked? The lawyer correctly answered saying that the one who showed mercy, the Samaritan, was neighbor to the one who needed help. Jesus told him that he was correct, but added that he must do likewise if he intended to fulfill the commandment to love your neighbor as yourself, thus fulfilling the second half of the two-part method through which he could inherit eternal life."

With that, the guide ended his explanation.

We talked for another few minutes and then tour visitors interrupted us. So, since he had to attend to them, I thanked him for his time and for the invaluable information that he had shared with me.

Nothing else is recorded about the life of Jesus until the commissioned 12 returned to him in the Galilee, sometime in either January or February of AD 29 (Mark 6:30; Luke 9:10).

However, there was an important event that took place in December of AD 28 and January AD 29 that affected Jesus' life and ministry: the birthday celebration of Herod Antipas that culminated with the death of John the Baptist (Matthew 14:1-2; Mark 6:14-28).

As I did when compiling substantiating information about the arrest of John the Baptist, I must refer to Dr. Mehmet Abassi of Ma'daba, Jordan, for the most accurate information that can be obtained anywhere about the death of John the Baptist.

I will back track a little bit and repeat part of what Dr. Abassi said about John the Baptist's arrest and then continue on through John's death.

Dr. Abassi said, "When Zolleras (the repudiated wife of Herod Antipas) returned to Machaerus after visiting her father, and discovered that John was in prison there, she ordered that he could have unlimited visits from his disciples and that he was to be fed from her own table. She also began a process of appeals to the Roman authorities on behalf of John to secure his release. However, the appeal process would not be complete until the late winter (December AD 28 or January AD 29).

"In December of AD 28, Zolleras received word that her appeal on behalf of John had resulted in a reversal of his prison sentence and that he would be released on *Caesar's Day of Amnesty*, January 9. Until then, John would still be under the jurisdiction of Herod Antipas. Zolleras, relieved and feeling that John was safe, then went to Nabataean to visit her father for three months.

"In her absence, as he had done many times before, Herod took up residence in the massive and magnificent fortress of Machaerus. It was there that Herod would celebrate his birthday, which was on January 3, with many of his officials and ambassadors. Over the years Capernaum, Sepphoris, Scythopolis/Beth-shan, and Jerusalem have been proposed as places where Herod held this particular birthday party, it was not held in any of these places. The party was held in Machaerus.

"With regard to John," Dr. Abassi continued, "Antipas did not hate him nor did he despise him. He admired him and his non-compromising faithfulness to his principles. On numerous occasions when Herod was in residence at Machaerus, he would visit John in prison or release him temporarily from his confinement and audience with him in his chambers. He probably really liked John in a fearful sort of way, but for the sake of Herodias, who absolutely despised John, he dared not release him. If Antipas released John by his own initiative, it would infuriate Herodias, who wanted John dead. But, if he was forced to release John because of a Roman judicial mandate, Herodias might be angry, but she could do nothing about it. The Roman High Court had overturned Herod's imprisonment of John. But John could not be released immediately.

"Roman law dictated that four times during any given year (January 9, April 9, July 9, and October 9) individuals whose conviction had been overturned by the Roman High Court, or if it was determined that an individual had been imprisoned for an unjust cause and the imprisonment declaration was overturned, could be released. The special days in which those whose sentences had been overturned were called *Caesar's Day of Amnesty*. On these days, those whose sentences had been overturned were physically set free from their imprisonment. So as of January 9, AD 29, John the Baptist would be a free man. But until that time, he would still be a ward of Herod. Roman law demanded that from the day that their sentence was overruled, amnestied offenders be released from chains and bonds and that they be placed either in a decorous holding cell used for Roman citizens or a private room within the imprisonment facility (house arrest), that they should receive preferential treatment, and that they receive the fitting protection exemplary to distinctive tenants.

"Herodias, knowing that John was to be released on January 9, and that he would most likely return to his non-relenting excoriation of her and Herod, had to move quickly while John was still under the jurisdiction and authority of Herod. She first tried to convince Herod that there was just cause for Herod to appeal the High Court's decision to Caesar himself, because without a doubt John was a threat to Roman stability and coherence in the area. But Herod resisted her claim and insistence.

"But, Herodias would not be denied. So, she hastily developed another plan to eliminate John once and for all—a plan that was as diabolical as she was resentful. She felt that if Herod executed John while he was still under Herod's guardianship, that he (Herod) with his oratory ability could successfully defend his actions before a Roman tribunal. Thus Herod would be cleared of any wrongdoing and John would be dead. On the celebration of Herod's birthday, just six days before John's scheduled release, Herodias had prepared her revenge upon John.

"During the last few days of AD 28 and the first few days of AD 29, Herodias threw a birthday celebration for Herod: a 10-day birthday celebration, commencing on January 3rd, Herod's birthday. According to some historians," Dr. Abassi continued, "there were more than 3,000 in attendance at this 10-day continuous drunken feast and orgy celebration. The guests included officials and administrators from the House of Herod, Roman officials and dignitaries, and some of the wealthiest merchants in all of Syria.

"On the day of Herod's birthday, January 3, the final day of the 10-day celebration, Herodias scheduled Salome, her daughter, to dance for Herod. Herodias was the stepdaughter and former wife of Philip, Antipias' brother who lived in Rome. She left Philip in Rome and returned to the Galilee with Antipas. Salome, Herodias' daughter, at that time 15 or 16 years old, remained in Rome with Philip, her stepfather and lover.

"Herodias had lived in an adulterous relationship with Antipas for more than two years before she married him. After the marriage, Herodias sent for Salome, who by then was 17 or 18 years old. In the two years since Herod had last saw her, Salome had blossomed into a radiant woman with beauty that was so dazzling that Lucian of Antioch, the 3rd century teacher, said of her beauty 'the grandeur of the sun, the moon, and the stars all pall in their luster when compared to the splendor her beauty.' Upon her arrival, Herod Antipas was dumbfounded by Salome's beauty. Almost immediately Antipas initiated a licentious relationship with Salome—with Herodias' knowledge and consent.

"The dance that Herodias told Salome to perform was what the Greeks called *The Dance of Eros* and what the Romans called *A Tribute to Isis*. According to Ovid, *The Dance of Eros* was the dance that Helen of Troy danced for Paris which convinced him that she (Helen) was the most beautiful woman in the world.

"The dancer began the dance dressed in a variety of translucent silken veils or scarves. The music began with a very soft and gentle melody (this dance and Salome's performance were Ravel's inspiration for the writing of his *Bolero*, Dr. Abassi interjected), but before long, the music gradually crescendoed and built to a frenzied epicurean climax. During the build up from a soft love melody to a pulsating sensuous apogee, the dancer's movements would gradually swell from a light and gentle fluid promenade into an arousing voluptuous gyration, as she peeled off veil after veil until all that remained between her and total nudity was one transparent gold silk veil.

"John Scholasticus, appointed Patriarch of Constantinople by Justinian in 565, says of Salome's dance, 'The prince of devils himself could not have performed more erotically arousing than did Salome to procure the head of John the Baptist.'

"So moved was the drunk and sensuously disconcerted Antipas and so aroused was he by Salome's dance that he, as was his character, offered her up to half of his kingdom as a reward. Anticipating this response by Herod, Herodias prompted Salome to ask for the head of John the Baptist as her prize.

"Herod was taken completely off-guard by the request. But, for the sake of his reputation so that he would continue to be honored as a man of his word, he ordered John the Baptist to be beheaded (the most honorable of deaths) that very night.

"Tradition says that Herod dismissed his birthday celebration after John was beheaded and that he sank into a long period of depression. The depression would eventually cause him to divorce Herodias. When Jesus was brought before him preceding his execution, some two years later, he still had not fully recovered from his depression.

"In AD 39 Herod was denounced to Emperor Gaius by his nephew, Agrippa, as a treasonous plotter against Rome. This resulted in Herod being deposed from his Tetrarchy and exiled. He died in exile.

"Tradition says that Herodias' hatred for John the Baptist was so intense that she took his head and had it 'pickled' in vinegar and honey and placed in a brass container. She slept with the container by her bed for the rest of her life.

"Shortly after John's death, Salome, not able to live with the coldness and ruthlessness of her mother, returned to her stepfather, Philip, in Rome. In AD 30, she married Philip who was 35 years her senior (some historians claim that he was 48 years her senior). Upon Philip's death in AD 34, she married Aristobus, who Caesar Nero made king of Asia Minor."

Dr. Abassi then paused and walked into the back room of his house. He returned a few minutes later carrying a small file. As he sat back down he said, "At the library of the University of Istanbul in 1690 there was a scroll discovered that was entitled, *Herod Antipas, Defense Before the Roman Senate in Regard to the Execution of John the Baptist.* The scroll was Antipas' answer to charges of insubordination, disregard for the authority of the High Court of Rome, and unauthorized declaration of war upon an ally of Rome, Aretas. The charges were brought by Caius, the presiding judge over the High Court tribunal that had declared John's innocence and had mandated his release for January 9 of AD 29.

"Apparently the charges were brought before the Senate after Herod's defeat at the hands of Aretas. The charges were supported by Agrippa, a junior magistrate who at that time was serving in Caesarea Maritima, and by Pontius Pilate, who seemed to be more concerned about Jesus of Nazareth and about how Herod's actions could potentially cause a jeopardous revolt than whether John had been an innocent victim of a revengeful woman. If you want, I will read to you Herod's defense."

I asked him to continue, so he began to read Herod's defense to the Roman Senate and Tiberius.

"The letter starts with an introduction: 'To Tiberius Augustus and the Senate of Rome' and then his defense begins.

> 'My Noble Lords, Greetings:
>
> It is true, as my enemy asserts, that I was defeated in battle with Aretas, King of Arabia, but I was forced to fight when unprepared for the conflict. I either had to fight or have the country overrun by this wicked people. It is true I was defeated, but it was owing to the want of time and better preparation. Aretas came upon me without warning. Notwithstanding my defeat, his army was so crippled that he had to withdraw his forces from the field, and has not been able to rally them since. So our country was saved from the devastation of a foreign foe.
>
> I understand that the superstitious Jews say my defeat was for my wickedness in the death of John, called Baptist. My understanding of the God of the Jews is, that He does not chastise the innocent for the crimes of the guilty. What did my actions have to do with the poor, suffering soldier?
>
> The facts in the case are about as follows: John, called Baptist, had set a new mode of religion altogether different from the Jewish religion, teaching baptism instead of circumcision; which had been the belief and custom of the Jews in all ages past. According to their theory, God appeared to Abraham hundreds of years before, and told him with His own lips how and what to do to be saved; and the Jews had lived according to this until it had become their nature, and all their holy prophets had gone to their God after their death in this way of their God's own appointment. Now, the question came to them, as they suggested it to me: has their God found that He is wrong? Has His wisdom failed Him? Or has the unchanged changed? Or is He wavering in His position and purpose? Such would be the natural conclusion of a sensible man under the circumstances.

Now, John, which is to say, Baptist, if I can say that agreeing with his Jewish religious tormentors I felt had no authority from his God to do what he was doing, as Abraham had. All his authority came from his words saying, 'He that sent me to baptize is true;' but he could not tell who he was. Then his going into the desert land: the Jewish God had by their myth spoken to Solomon to build the finest temple of its time in all of this part of the world, and made promises that whoever came to that temple with an offering and a sacrifice, his prayers should be heard and answered. This temple that was destroyed but rebuilt on the same foundation of Solomon's was made even more wondrous by my father. This temple had been the place of the Jews meeting for hundreds of years, for the Jews think that this temple is the presence of their God come to earth.

Now see the difference:
- John had no authority to preach a different religious practice
- He changed the place of worship to their God from the temple to the desert
- He changed the doctrines of Abraham and Moses
- He changed the mode of application from circumcision to baptism

...these troubles on the Jewish mind were very heavy, and gave such respected religious leaders of the Jews such as Hilderium, Shammai, Hillel, and others great concern. And no matter, for in their judgment it was vacating the temple of religious worship; it was blocking the road to heaven, and driving the poor and unsuspecting to ruin, as well as destroying the whole nation. So it was, by their request, as so ordered, that it was better to execute one to save many from a worse fate. And this is the true reason for the deed, and not to please the whim of a dancing girl, as you have heard. Now my Lords, if this were not satisfactory, I would ask my accuser, Caius, to write to any of the learned Jews, and learn if my statement is not correct.

As to Aripa's accusing me of having arms for 70,000, it is correct; but they were left me by my father. And as they were needed to defend the province, and I did not know it was necessary to report them, I never thought of keeping them secret. But as to my being in league with Sejonius, I appeal to the virtue of my conduct, and demand investigation.

As to what Pontius Pilate says in regard to my cowardice and disobedience in the case of Jesus from Nazareth and Capernaum in the Galilee, I will say in my own defense: I was informed by all the Jews that this was the same Jesus that my father aimed to destroy in his infancy; for I have in my father's private writings and accounts of his life, showing that when the report was circulated of ambassadors inquiring where was he that was born King of the Jews, he called together the Hillel and Shammai schools, and demanded the reading of their sacred scrolls; that it was he that was to be born in Bethlehem of Judea, as read and interpreted by Hillel. So when my father learned that there had been a birth of a male child in Bethlehem two years previous, under strange circumstances, and he could not learn who nor where the child was, he sent and had the male children slain that were near his age. Afterward he learned that his father and mother had taken him and fled to safety. For this attempt to uphold the Roman authority in the land of Judea, the Jews in Bethlehem and Judea have not ceased to curse him to this day, and yet the Caesars have done a thousand times worse things, and done them thousands of times, and it was all well. As to Pilate's saying that Jesus was a Galilean, he is mistaken. Jesus was born in Bethlehem of the state of Judea, as the records show, as the adopted son of his Roman Senator uncle. He traveled from place to place. He learned soothe-saying while with his rabban in Egypt and in Persia and the Indias, to perfection, in so much that the Theophus Commission of Ambassadors of Tiberius convinced themselves that he was he. So this is my defense.

I submit it for your consideration of the facts. I pray for clemency.

Antipater of the House of Herod
Tetrarch Servant of Augustus and of Rome'

"Whether the scroll is authentic or not," Dr. Abassi continued, "We probably will never know. But we do know that at that particular time Antipas escaped the wrath of the Roman Senate. According to almost all historical references that discuss the situation, Antipas talked his way out of this particular crisis to his administration by casting doubt upon the validity of the accusations and by shifting blame from himself to circumstances that could not be verified or challenged, just as this document seems to show. However, 10 years later he was no longer able to escape. In AD 39 he was stripped of his position and was exiled."

"It seems fairly obvious that Zolleras was influential in the reversal of the charges brought against John the Baptist and that she played a part in convincing Caius to bring charges against Herod before the Roman Senate. Caius was the brother-in-law of Zolleras, having married her half-sister. Some historians feel that Zolleras was in love with Caius and wanted to marry him, when for political reasons her father chose to give her in marriage to Antipas. Caius in turn settled for Zolleras' half-sister."

As Dr. Abassi concluded and I reviewed my notes, I could not help but wonder at Dr. Abassi's admiration for John and his respect for and admiration of Jesus. Although Muslim, he seemed to honor Jesus as much as most Christians and more than some. To me he seemed to be not far from converting to Christianity.

XVIII

FOURTH YEAR OF MINISTRY

(AD 29)

After the death of John the Baptist, his disciples were allowed to bury his headless body (his head had been given to Salome as her reward—she had given John's head to her mother, Herodias).

After John's burial (Mark 6:29) and a time of mourning for his disciples who were joined by the 12 who had been commissioned by Jesus, the 12 returned to Jesus in the Galilee (Mark 6:30; Luke 9:10). They told Jesus about the death of John.

Jesus was profoundly affected by the tragedy. Perhaps he thought that John's death was the beginning of a persecution against those who proclaimed his and John's message; or perhaps he just wanted to get away with his disciples and reflect upon the loss of John. But whatever the case and for whatever reason, Jesus led the 12 into a desert place, away from the continual press of the multitudes. During this desert time apart, the 12 shared with him all that they had accomplished.

We don't know how long Jesus was in the desert place with the 12, or what all they did there. In fact, nothing more is recorded about Jesus' life and activities until the spring of AD 29, when he led the 12 to a large fish-drying area, near the new city of Tiberias, which was being constructed at that time. It was there that he preformed the miracle of the feeding of the 5,000 (Matthew 14:13-21; Mark 6:33-44; Luke 9:10-17; John 6:1-14).

I found documentation that confirmed the veracity of the Gospel records of this most peculiar event while doing research at the Maximilian library in Innsbruck, Austria, the Alpine jewel of Tyrol Austria.

The renowned Maximilian library, known for its superb collection of German and Austrian history, is the largest of its kind in the world. The library, constructed in 1710, was Gothic in style and had somewhat of a plain exterior. But inside, it was fabulously decorated with crystal chandeliers; cherry wood bookshelves; mahogany study tables with holly, maple, and gold leaf inlays; and solid walnut chairs with black leather upholstery. By looking on the exterior, one could not have dreamed that the interior would be so luxurious.

I spent the first hour or so just getting aquatinted with the layout of the library. I then spent another hour or more studying the library's book catalog system.

Out of a dozen or so resources that I found, I narrowed my search down to a two-volume set that I felt would be helpful. The title of the two-volumes (each of the volumes was about 60-pages in length) was *Palestinian Travels*. The well-known Scottish adventurer, Devin Allkin, had written the books in 1786. In each of the volumes, which in essence were his Palestine area travel journals, Allkin described six (12 total in both volumes) historical sites that related to the life of Jesus.

As I studied the journals, I was intrigued how Allkin had given a short historical background on each of the geographic areas that he described. He not only portrayed the physical location, including its geography and any archaeological remains that existed, but he also gave a brief history of the area and told why and how it was significant during the time of the life and ministry of Jesus. Along with this history, he also included his own thoughts, feelings, and conclusions relating to the events in the life of Jesus that were connected to the site.

The 12 sites covered in the two-volume travel journal were Jerusalem, Capernaum, Jericho, the Jordan River crossing at Bethabara, Tiberias, Gadara, Mount Hermon, Nain, the Gennarset, Mount Gerizim, and the *basquaiia* of both the Galilee and Decapolis. I had already collected information on 10 of the 12 sites, but had no information on the two *basquaiia* sites. So, I was anxious to read what Allkin had to say about these two locations—the two sites where Jesus performed the miracles of the feeding the 5,000 and of the 4,000.

I first read Allkin's accounts relating to both sites. I then went back and began taking paraphrased notes of Allkin's accounts including his personal thoughts and conclusions.

The first *basquaiia* described by Allkin was the one associated with Jesus' feeding of the 5,000. This event was recorded in Matthew 14:13-21, Mark 6: 33-44, Luke 9:10-17, and John 6:5-14. Allkin primarily used the Mark record in his description.

"In the spring, probably the month of Adar, of the year AD 29," he wrote, "Jesus took his disciples to a desert fish-drying-field near the city of Tiberias which was under construction. The fish-drying field, called a *basquaiia*, was in reality a large exposed flat limestone rock upon which (for decades) fish had been dried. The huge flat rock, the only site used for this purpose in the Galilee, was ideal for drying thousands of fish at a time. Surrounding the *basquaiia* on all sides, were large grassy fields. In the spring, the fields were lush and green. But by summer, the fields were dry and the grass had turned into brown dry deserty stubble.

"Although the area was across the Sea of Galilee from the city of Bethsaida, the *basquaiia* was originally owned (before the Roman conquest) and operated by the city of Bethsaida, the principal community located on the shores of the Sea of Galilee whose income came primarily from the fishing industry. For multiplied decades, Galilean fishermen had used the basquaiia to dry fish and on which they spread their nets to dry and repair.

"Since the days of Pompey's conquest, according to Tipirius, the 1st century Phoenician historian, this Galilean *basquaiia* and the surrounding area had been under the control of the Roman military.

"Thousands of fish at a time were dried here," he continued, "making this *basquaiia* the primary food supply source for the Roman military in the Galilee and the primary source of food for the laborers working on the new imperial city of Tiberias. Herod Antipas bought *basquaiia* dried fish from the Roman military to feed to the laborers who were working at Tiberias. But not only did this *basquaiia* supply dried fish for the Tiberias laborers and the Roman legions stationed in the Galilee and the surrounding area, but the Romans also exported the fish to Roman legions throughout the eastern Roman Empire. By the year AD 27, the dried fish from the Galilee *basquaiia* was so plentiful that the Roman military began to export the fish commercially.

"So valuable was this Galilean *basquaiia* food source to the Roman military machine, that they kept a 100-man guard minimum at the site throughout the day and night to protect it. As such, special permission had to be granted by the Roman military commander before anyone who was not in the military or was not a Tiberias builder (both the members of the military as well as the laborers who were working on Tiberias had special identification that they carried at all times that allowed them to come and obtain food from the *basquaiia*) could approach the site. This Roman guard protected the site so fanatically that anyone who approached the site without proper identification, permission, or without being accompanied by Roman military commander, would be killed on the spot without question.

"It was quite extraordinary for Jesus to have had free access to the site, unless of course he had developed a close relationship with the Roman commander in charge of the *basquaiia's* security.

"Tipirius recorded that Jesus and his father, Joseph of Nazareth, worked in Tiberias as stonemason construction contractors before Jesus began his intense rabbi training and that both he and Joseph had gained quite a reputation with the local Roman authorities as exceptional and trust-worthy contractors. If this was the case, Jesus should not have had any problem in obtaining the needed permission to enter the site. It could be that because of Jesus' building reputation in Tiberias, he might have been granted permanent permission to enter the area. But whatever the case may have been, we know that he was allowed to enter the *basquaiia* site.

"Not only did the site provide dried fish for the Roman military and the laborers working at Tiberias, but Herod Antipas supplied daily bread to the laborers as well. The bread was delivered early in the morning and was stockpiled in huge storage tents that Antipas had erected, adjoining the grassy fields. Each shift of laborers sat on the grassy fields and ate at the beginning of their work shift. Livy wrote that during the city's early days of construction, 20,000 laborers worked in two shifts from sunup to sundown, every day, with no holidays and no days off.

"Jesus and his disciples appeared at the *basquaiia* at the beginning of the changing of the work shifts. The laborers who were getting off of work heard that Jesus was at the *basquaiia*. So upon receiving the blessings of the Roman military command, they gathered around him (Mark 6:33, Matthew 14:13-14, Luke 9:11, John 6:2) at the *basquaiia* and he ministered to them.

"As the day wore on and the sun beat down, Jesus and his disciples became concerned about the men's physical welfare because most had not eaten since early that morning (Mark 6:34, Matthew 14:13-21, Luke 9:12-13, John 6:5), plus they had worked all morning on the city of Tiberias.

"Jesus had them divide into their specific work force companies and sit down on the grassy fields. He then performed a miracle by feeding the 5,000 men laborers (Mark 6:35-44, Luke 9:13-17, John 6:6-14). In this incident the mention of women and children (Matthew 14:21) seems to be secondary or incidental. This was probably due to the fact that all of those gathered there were men laborers, and only a very few had family members with them.

"The miracle of the feeding of the 5,000 laborers is one of the most controversial miracles performed by Jesus. For centuries many people have accepted the miracle as literal, while others have argued that the story of the miracle could not be taken literal; it was purely symbolic.

"In reality," Allkin continued by interjecting is own opinions and supposition, "probably either one of two things happened. Jesus and his disciples were given bread and fish to eat by his Roman military friends, after eating they had two fish and five pieces of bread left over (the John 6 setting says that they got the fish and bread from a 'baker boy.' Baker boys were young boys who were hired by the Roman overseers to distribute food to the laborers at the beginning of each shift. They were paid a penny a day. The laborers would sit down in the grassy area divided into work companies and the boys would walk among them distributing the food. This particular boy recorded in John 6 probably stayed behind after the noon meal distribution to listen to Jesus). (1) Jesus did in fact take these remains, did actually bless them, and did literally divide them and feed the 5,000 laborers and the family members who were accompanying the laborers. Because nothing was impossible for Jesus in that he had power over anything and all things if he so chose, he certainly would have had the ability to literally break the fish and bread and feed 5,000 laborers plus family members. But what would be his purpose in doing such a miracle? Seldom did Jesus demonstrate his power just because he had the ability to do it. He always had a plan and purpose for everything that he did and all miracles preformed by him. So again, why would Jesus want to demonstrate this type of power? Was the Father glorified by the miracle? Was the Kingdom of God furthered? Was attention drawn to the Father so that He would be honored? If these questions can be answered positively, then Jesus well could have literally divided the fish and bread and fed the multitude. (2) Jesus did not literally divide the fish and bread and feed the multitude. Instead he used his influence to convince the Roman military authorities to release enough food from their stores to feed the multitude. However, from a practical and literal point of view, this was impossible. Under *NO* circumstances would the Roman military authorities ever release food from the Emperor's food stores to accommodate the needs of common laborers. From a logistics point of view, not even Jesus could do this—unless it was a miracle. So, what could have happened was that Jesus took the food that remained after he and his disciples had eaten, he blessed it and broke it symbolizing the Jewish hospitality custom and breaking bread and sharing with guests. He then used his influence with the Roman authorities to have all the food needed to feed such a multitude to be released. If this was the case, the miracle of dealing with the Roman authorities could have been even greater than a miracle of literally dividing the fish and bread and feeding the multitude.

"Whatever way or whichever method, both would have been a miracle of equal measure: one would have been a physical miracle and the other would have been a political and governmental policy miracle. Both were equally impossible without divine intervention.

"The second *basquaiia* described by Allkin was the one located in the Decapolis where Jesus' miracle of feeding 4,000 took place. This event is recorded in Matthew 15:30-38 and Mark 8:1-9. The Decapolis *basquaiia* was smaller than the one in the Galilee, but it was used for the same purpose and the Roman military controlled it also. It was used, however, to supply dried fish *exclusively* for the Roman 10th Legion stationed in the Decapolis area. Dried fish from this *basquaiia* was not exported. Jesus' feeding of the 4,000 took place a year later, in AD 30. We will discuss Allkin's record of this miracle in the chapter entitled **The Fifth Year of Ministry**.

After feeding the 5,000 plus woman and children, the disciples collected 12 baskets full of scrap remains—about 24 gallons of fish and bread leftovers.

After they had collected the leftovers, Jesus demanded that his disciples get into a passenger boat, sail across the inlet to Bethsaida, located on the other side (the northeast side) of the inlet of the Sea of Galilee, and wait for him there. He would first send the crowd away to their homes, and then he was going to go into the mountains and pray, before he joined them on the other side.

Reluctantly following his instructions, they got into a boat and began to sail across the inlet for Bethsaida. They had no idea how he was going to get over to them, or when he would join them—he had not told them. All he said was to go, and he expected them to obey without question. However, when they got to the middle of the inlet, a storm blew up and threatened to capsize them. Jesus saw the rowers toiling with the oars and that the sails had been dropped. So, he came to them walking on the water (Matthew 14:24-33; Mark 6:47-51).

It was at the University of Glasgow in Glasgow, Scotland that I was shown documentation by Dr. Christian Craddi, a physicist at the University, that confirmed what some theologians feel was the greatest of Jesus' miracles.

Dr. Craddi had been studying for years the unnatural and unexplainable phenomenon of Jesus' walking on water.

One particular resource that he had been studying for more than 10 years was a manuscript that was an Old English copy of a Latin copy drafted by Felix of Ravenna, of an original Latin sermon authored in 448 by Peter Chrysologus, Archbishop of Ravenna. The focus of the sermon was Jesus' miracle of walking on the water.

Dr. Craddi began explaining to me the work he was doing relative to the miracle of Jesus' walking on the water by saying that Jesus not only walked on the water once, but he actually walked on it twice and perhaps even three times.

Then rather than entering into a long theological expose and explanation, he began to point out to me all of the unnatural elements connected to the phenomenal miracle. I was with him for probably close to three hours, during which time I took pages of paraphrased notes on everything that Dr. Craddi said concerning the miracle.

"The scriptural references used in Chrysologus' sermon," he began his explanation by saying, "Were Mark (6:45-46) and Matthew (14:22-33) regarding the first record of Jesus walking on the water, and John (6:17-21) for the second record.

"The first reference, recorded in Matthew (14:22-33), took place immediately after Jesus had miraculously fed with five loaves of bread and two fish 5,000 laborers who were working on the construction of the imperial city of Tiberias (plus some of the families of the laborers)."

Dr. Craddi continued, "Having sent the laborers away Jesus *constrained*, as the King James Version states, or forcibly demanded, as if to cause great displeasure if they did not follow his instructions, his disciples to get in a ship. It was a large passenger ship in which people bought passage to travel across the lake. They were supposed to sail from their present location on the west side of the Sea of Galilee to Bethsaida, on the northeast side. The disciples were probably afraid to return to Herod's jurisdiction, following the expected commotion accompanying John the Baptist's death, and did not want to go without Jesus accompanying them. Plus, the last time they had been on the lake a great storm almost capsized them, and it appeared likely that another storm was going to hit them before they reached the other side. At least with Jesus on board they knew that they would arrive safely to the other side. So, why Jesus was so insistent for them to go without him is a mystery that we will probably never figure out. After the ship containing Jesus' disciples had departed, he walked up into the mountains west of the lake, about 10 to 12 miles west of the seashore, in order to pray.

"At about 3:00 a.m., as the disciples approached the mid-point of their destination, the storm that had been brewing and had caused them such apprehension, hit with all of its fury. Jesus was up in the mountains praying about 12 to 14 miles away from them, yet he somehow saw the oarsmen struggling with the ship trying to keep it afloat.

"This was the first of many mysteries that puzzles me about the story," Dr. Craddi said, "How could Jesus, deep in prayer and meditation, some 10 to 12 miles away from the shore and probably at least 14 miles away from them, know what was happening in the midst of the Sea of Galilee and see what was happening in the middle of the sea? It was three o'clock in the morning and pitch black with the wind blowing so hard and the waves breaking so violently that the huge passenger ship was being tossed back and forth. Jesus was no where to be found. Surely, a man who could predict the 'bubbling up of the sea' could have foreseen how violent this storm would have been? But rather than warning them, he insisted that they go.

"If Jesus could have run the distance that separated him from them at a rate of 10 minutes a mile, it still would have taken him almost two and a half hours to cover the distance. Even if he had ridden an animal—a horse, or mule, or camel—that ran at top speed the entire 14 miles, it still would have taken him at least an hour to cover the distance. However, the Bible says that he came to them walking on the sea. Aside from that phenomenal statement," said Dr. Craddi, "there is so much more there. Of all the miracles recorded in the Bible attributed to Jesus, this one is the one that bars all logic and explanation.

"First of all, Jesus was at least 12 to 14 miles away from them, yet he is able to see them struggling in the middle of a black sea. How did he see them? And how did he know what was happening? How did he know which ship, out of perhaps dozens that were on the lake, was occupied by his disciples? Second, he was more than a three-hour walk, or a one to one and one-half hour full gallop by animal from them, yet he appeared on the scene long before the ship was in danger of sinking. How did he get there so quickly?

"When Jesus' disciples saw him walking on the water, they became terrified. They were not terrified at Jesus' appearance, but rather that he came to them walking on the water. There was a myth that was prevalent at that time that the soul or ghost of a formerly drowned seafarer would appear to a sailor who was destined to die by shipwreck. The ghost was said to appear, walking on the water just moments before the wreck was to occur. So, when the disciples saw Jesus walking on the water, they immediately assumed two things: (1) Jesus had been drowned in the sea and his ghost was walking toward them to warn them of impending shipwreck; and (2) since the ghost of Jesus had appeared to them, their death by shipwreck was imminent. This is why they were terrified.

"Regarding the miracle of walking on water," continued Dr. Craddi, "it had never been done before in all of history, except for fabled accounts in myths. Food multiplying had been done under both Elijah and Elisha. Both had performed miracles of raising people from the dead. Healings of various kinds had been recorded on numerous occasions, and both Moses and Elijah dramatically illustrated power over the forces of nature. On more than one occasion the obstacle of water had presented itself as a challenge to Moses, Joshua, Elijah, and Elisha. In all of these cases, water was either separated or its flow was stopped so that passage on dry land could be made through the midst of the water. But, never was a man of God given the ability to walk on the water, as if it was stable ground. Never before had the law of gravity been totally canceled or neutralized so that gravity would be reversed and forced to hold up a man rather than pull him down.

"Some scientists believe that there are six *in* holes and six *out* holes that lead in and out of this universe and where gravity is zero, where it is totally neutral. However, these *in* and *out* holes have never been known to move. They are stationary. Jesus walked on the water, therefore the neutralizing or reversal of gravity had to move—it was not stationary.

"Therefore, there is neither any precedence in history from which to draw a comparison of such a miracle, nor is there a logical explanation that describes how it was accomplished. However, not once but twice in this one setting, did the miracle occur. Not only did Jesus come to them walking on the water, but Simon Peter walked to Jesus on the water and they both walked on the water back to the ship, together. Since there is no logical explanation on how the miracle was accomplished, the miracle can only reside in the realm of the miraculous phenomena that can neither be explained nor comprehended.

"Even if Jesus ad used ley lines, " Dr. Craddi continued after stopping to organize his thoughts for a few minutes, " to accomplish the miracle, ley lines do not move, nor is there any record that they have ever neutralized the laws of gravity, and even if they could, it is doubtful that they would follow a walking person that they are influencing. There is no doubt that Jesus did somehow and in some way utilize these geophysical forces to accomplish the miracle, but how he did it is a mystery that will probably never be revealed."

As Dr. Craddi tried to justify or tried to explain how the miracle was accomplished, I politely listened. I knew that this miracle was beyond the scope of explanation or comprehension, so anything short of accepting by faith that the event took place, was an exercise in futility. As Dr. Craddi continued to "think out loud," trying to make some logical sense out of the event, I wondered what it must have been like for the disciples to experience first hand an event that had never taken place before in all of history.

I allowed myself to fantasize for a few minutes, and then pulled myself back to the present just as Dr. Craddi was saying, "...and what was amazing about Jesus' character is that he did not chastise Peter for sinking, when he looked around him and saw the storm raging. All he said to Peter was *'Did you doubt? Why were you not completely sure of what you believed? Why did you not believe that I could come to you regardless of what circumstances seemed to dictate? Why were you not completely sure of what you wanted?'* This was truly amazing! Of course! Jesus was an amazing man! He and Peter then walked back to the ship together. Then as soon as they step back into the ship, the stormed ceased. I have always wondered why, if Jesus had the power to still the storm, didn't calm it before he walked out on the water to meet the disciples? Or why not calm the water it so that he and Peter could walk back to the ship together without taking the chance that Peter would again panic? All of this is conjecture and wonder. But the question is valid. Why did he subject his disciples to such danger if he had the ability and power to calm the storm?"

I could not answer the questions that Dr. Craddi was asking, and to be quite honest, I felt that he really didn't want answers to his questions. He seemed to be talking and wondering out loud. But Dr. Craddi did make one statement that intrigued me. He said, "I am not a religious man. But if I chose to be a religious man and if I chose to believe in anything of a religious nature, I would choose to believe in a deity that had the power to reverse and bewilder the universal laws of nature."

Dr. Craddi then began to formulate his opinions concerning the second record of Jesus walking on the water. The one recorded in John 6.

"After they had been blown off-course as a result of the first storm in which Jesus and Peter walked on the water, they landed in Gennesaret, on the northeast shore of the Sea of Galilee, or the Lake of Gennesaret, so called by the Roman military. Gennesaret was a fertile plain that extended from the sea to about three miles inland. It served as an unofficial buffer zone between the northern settlements (a few of which had a larger than normal—for that area—Jewish population), and the Roman military lands.

"There, Jesus preached, healed, and performed many miracles. Because of these miracles, the people wanted to take him by force and proclaim him as their king. Upon discovering their intentions, Jesus left the people and went up into a mountain alone to pray. As evening approached Jesus' disciples went down to the lakeshore to wait for his return. He did not send them; they went on their own. As it became dark, the disciples went on board a small ship, not as large as the one they had arrived on. The ship was probably a 20-passenger boat. There were several of these boats on the Sea of Galilee and they were used for short excursions. They were about 25 to 30 feet long, approximately 10 feet wide and a small sleeping and storage quarters underneath the main deck. On the boat they waited for Jesus to join them so they could sail back to Capernaum. When nightfall overtook them, Jesus still had not joined them. Of course he never said that he was going to join them and he never told them that he wanted to sail back to Capernaum. They just assumed that would be the logical course of action.

"With the fall of the blackness of night," Dr. Craddi continued, "the wind of another brewing storm began to howl. Before long the wind reached critical proportions. To prevent damage to the small ship or harm to the occupants, the disciples released the ship from dock and rowed out into the open water of the lake about two or three miles from shore, supposing that Jesus would understand that they had to leave and that he should meet them in Capernaum later on.

"As they struggled with the ship in the midst of the lake in the middle of the steadily increasing treacherous storm, Jesus came to them again walking on the water. When they saw Jesus this time, they were more surprised than they were frightened. 'Surely this could not happen twice in a lifetime, much less twice within a time span of two days? But twice it was!'

"As soon as Jesus entered the little ship, the storm ceased and the boat and all of its occupants were *instantly* and *immediately* transported about three miles to the northern shore. In an instant of time, quicker than a micro-millionth of a second, the boat and its entire load and occupants were transported more than three miles. One moment they were in the middle of the sea and the next they were at shore.

"How? Only God knows. Again it happened on the Sea of Galilee, the only body of water to ever witness the reversal of gravity and instantaneous transport—both totally contrary to the laws of the universe and nature—, and both happened within less than a week of one another. Strangely, this would never happen again—never! Truly what manner of man was this Jesus?"

I agreed, but felt it unnecessary to add anything to Dr. Craddi's obvious admiration of Jesus.

Sometime after Jesus and his disciples had returned to Capernaum, probably in late spring, Shammaite Pharisees and scribes from Jerusalem confronted Jesus demanding that he produce and show them the sign of his authority that gave him the right to teach and to perform miracles (Matthew 12: 38-42).

Although I had been searching for years for any information about the life of Jesus, I had never searched for anything that specifically addressed this event in Jesus life. So, it was quite by accident that I discovered supporting information confirming this event at the Rijksmuseum, the home of Rembrandt's famous *Night Watch*, as well as home to the world's largest collection of the Dutch masters' works from the 15th through the 19th centuries, and the difficult to enter The Sketch Repository, in Amsterdam, The Netherlands.

It was in The Sketch Repository room that I discovered the information.

Three walls of the windowless room were lined floor to ceiling with wooden bookshelves. The fourth wall, the one with the entry door, was lined with individual workstations. In the center of the room were four long wooden reference tables, each containing 10 wooden chairs. Adjacent to the large room was a smaller room that was the research and reference library. In this library were kept written synopses each telling the history of a particular sketch and an explanation of the sketches subject matter. These synopses were bound in large reference books and were shelved in the library.

Displayed on the bookshelves of the large room were hundreds of artist sketches. Many of the sketches were working sketches that the artists whose work were on display at the Rijksmuseum, had used to refine their ideas before they put their final ideas on canvas. However, many more were sketches from artists that were not on display at the museum. Most of the sketches had a reference number printed on a tag attached to the shelf, just below the sketch. This reference number referred back to the specific bound volume that accommodated the written synopsis of that sketch.

I was not allowed to take pictures, use recording devises, remove from the shelves more than one sketch at a time, or remove more than one reference book at a time that contained a sketch's accompanying synopsis from the research and reference library. However, I was allowed to take longhand notes.

Although I was fascinated by a number of sketches, I was especially interested in a sepia sketch that had been drawn by a relatively unknown 16th century Dutch artist by the name of Hendrik von Schappen.

The sketch was of three men. One of the men looked to be representative of Jesus. The other two were depicted as having an air of self-righteousness in their disposition. They probably represented Pharisees. One of the two men was holding up to Jesus a signet ring, seemingly wanting Jesus to answer a question relating to the ring.

I wrote down the reference number and went to the reference and research library to look up the written synopsis pertaining to the sketch. After searching for a while, I finally found the bound volume and the synopsis that matched the sketch number. According to the synopsis the sketch was entitled *Matthew 12:38—Signet ring authority*.

The synopsis explained that this sketch was the last sketch of von Schappen before he entered a monastery. For 38 years after entering the monastery, he was not heard from. Then just before his death, he showed up unexpectedly at Nieuwe Kerk (New Church) with a handful of 10 sketches and gave them to the local priest. He then walked away and was never seen again. Later it was discovered that he had died while attempting to walk to Brandenburg, while carrying a very heavy load of wood. Apparently, the wood represented his sins and his earthly ambitions, which he felt that he was forced to bear and to endure, until he had been forgiven and cleansed thoroughly through the penance of walking. The sketch that was on display in The Sketch Repository was one of the 10 that von Schappen had given to the priest at Nieuwe Kerk.

I read the synopsis through three times, and then I began to write notes that explained the synopsis.

The synopsis began by quoting the Matthew 12:38-39 setting.

> *"Then certain of the scribes and of the Pharisees answered, saying, Master, we would see a sign from thee. But He answered and said unto them, An evil and adulterous generation seeketh after a sign, and there shall no sign be given to it, but the sign of the prophet, Jonah."*

I then recorded the explanation presented by the synopsis.

"The scribes and the elite Jerusalem Shammaite Pharisees, the inner circle, who were in Capernaum at this time, challenged Jesus asking him to show them his signet ring of authority that gave him the right to do and say the things that he did and said.

"In essence, they said, 'What gives you the right to teach contrary to the traditions of our fathers and do things contrary to our accepted rules, standards, and regulations. Show us the ring that gives such authority to you.'

"Tradition said that Ezra wore the first signet ring that designated his spiritual authority. This authority was supposedly passed down from generation to generation and from father to son (or an appointed heir). It is not known if the actual ring was passed down or if some other identification that indicated God's spiritual authority was passed down. The practice continued in unbroken succession until the time of the Maccabees.

"The Maccabees appointed the Haesmon family to be priests forever. The Haesmon priests in turn dissected their inherited spiritual authority and distributed various portions of it to High Priest approved and qualified, Pharisees and Sadducees. Each was given a signet ring, much like Ezra's original, to declare publicly his right to function as the spiritual authority in a particular specified spiritual area. The appointed spiritual authorities inherited the title of *Father of the Law*—those who had been entrusted with the spiritual authority of the Jewish people.

"The scribes and Pharisees were demanding from Jesus proof of his authority to say and do the things that he said and did. They wanted to see his signet ring.

"Jesus, rather than showing them a signet ring of authority, called them an adulterous generation—a generation that says it is faithful to God, yet is having affairs with outsiders or harlot religions. A harlot religion is similar and it satisfies, yet it is far from truth."

Nothing more was written about the sketch, but I was gratified that I had found information about such an obscure event in the ministry of Jesus

Immediately after his confrontation with these Pharisees and scribes from Jerusalem, the same two disciples, James and John, his cousins again approached him about their inheritance, just like they had done two years before in AD 27.

It was in the same resource in which I found the first inheritance squabble between James and John, Hans von Dohnaniy's *Inheritances*, housed in the archives on the grounds of the Palace du Palais in Avignon, that I found confirmation regarding this second inheritance incident.

The setting of the second lesson on inheritance took place in the spring of AD 29. It is recorded in Luke 12:1-40. The occasion is that Jesus and his disciples had just returned to Capernaum from the Gennesaret.

I will paraphrase what von Dohnaniy wrote.

Upon Jesus' return, scribes and Pharisees demanding proof of his authority confronted him. He responded to them and then he and his disciples walked away. As he walked, he warned his disciples about the doctrines of the Shammaite Pharisees, telling them not to be afraid of those particular Pharisees. He then talked to them about their true worth to God, about the unpardonable sin, and about how

The Search

they should not be concerned about their lives or what they would say or do, that the Holy Spirit would take care of them.

Then in the very midst of this teaching about how much God cares and about how the Holy Spirit will take care of all situations and all circumstances of their lives, either James or John interrupted him and asked him to tell the other brother that he had to share their inheritance.

It seems evident that James and John did forsake all two years previously and had been following Jesus since then, and had not concerned themselves with the distribution of Zebedee's estate. Of course, it is also apparent that Zebedee had not died yet either. Now in this setting, it appears that Zebedee has died and James and John were about to inherit his estate, and one of the brothers did not like the way the estate had been divided. He obviously wanted more.

Jesus however refused to get involved in the family squabble and would not take sides or give an opinion. Instead he used the occasion to put them in their place and to remind them of their calling and their purpose.

Jesus used an analogy to teach James and John as well as all the disciples a lesson regarding true riches, on what a disciple's attitude concerning riches should be, and on how a disciple must trust God completely. In the analogy a rich man decided to build himself bigger barns in order to store all his wealth. But because he was selfish and did not give God the honor for his wealth and because he had not laid up treasures in heaven, he died before he had an opportunity to enjoy his wealth. The analogy is recorded in Luke 12:16-21 and the wealthy man to whom Jesus referred was his Uncle Zebedee.

In the middle of the lesson Jesus turned his attention to James and John and spoke to them directly when he said in verse 33 of Luke 12. *"Sell that ye have, and give alms: provide yourselves bags which wax not old, a treasure in the heavens that faileth not, where no thief approacheth, neither moth corrupteth."* He then concluded the lesson by telling them that they had to be alert always and ready to do good for their Master, they must guard against evil and an attitude that would steal away their vision and their appointed goal and purpose of ministry.

It is not recorded how James and John responded, but we do know that they remained with Jesus. So they must have accepted his rebuke and learned from it. However, Peter asked for an explanation of the teaching. Jesus responded by telling them an analogy based on a well-known true event.

When Herod The Great married his second wife, he went to Rome for his "honeymoon" without telling anyone when he would return. He merely said as he parted, *"Be ye ready for in such an hour as you think not, I will return."* Herod was known for his ruthlessness, yet after three months being away, some of the servants became careless, saying that Herod would be gone for several more months. They began to do things that would not be tolerated by Herod and to abuse their privilege.

Finally, Herod arrived unexpectedly and caught many of the servants unprepared for his return. Those who had prepared and had remained prepared, Herod rewarded with great riches and privilege. Those who had abused their position, he stripped of their position and punished them. Some were sent to prison and some were sentenced to death.

Jesus used the occasion to warn that they, his disciples, should always be aware and be ready for in such an hour as they think not; they will be confronted by their Master to give an account of their faithfulness.

Jesus went on to tell them that they were set apart from the world to do the work of God. As such, they would be at enmity to the world and to what the world considered important. In short, there would be a division between them and those who were still absorbed in the world's ethnic, political, and civil system. Because they were called to be set apart, they would naturally be at odds with their friends, families, and acquaintances who did not understand their commitment. Because the things of God and his message had become foremost in their lives, they would not be included in the world's activities nor be considered one of them. They would be considered outcasts.

If von Dohnaniy's interpretation of Jesus' lesson was correct, it was obvious that Jesus wanted absolute dedication to his cause—if a person had committed to and had vowed to be faithful to that cause. It seems that not everyone was devoted enough to fill the positions of absolute surrender to his plan, but for those who did make that commitment and who did dedicate themselves to his plan and purpose, he demanded adherence to that vow without compromise.

As I read this, my first impression was that this demand seemed to be harsh according to today's standards. Yet, as I thought more about Jesus' expectations, it dawned on me that today's standards are not the standards of Christ's original plan and purpose. Our current standards are diluted and compromised. The standards by which Jesus called disciples are those that were standard in the Roman world: absolute commitment and faithfulness to any vow made, with appropriate punishment for breaking that vow. Although his punishment would not be physical, it was just as severe emotionally and psychologically—he would eliminate that follower as an intimate disciple. The follower would not loose his or her salvation and he or she would continue to be his (Jesus') follower, friend, and servant. But his or her cherished position would have been compromised, and, another would either replace him or her or the position would be eliminated altogether.

The remainder of von Dohnaniy's *Inheritances* was good, but it dealt very little with any more of Jesus' teachings or lessons.

Nothing more is recorded about the life of Jesus until the early summer of AD 29. As he was talking to some people in the city of Capernaum (tradition says that he was teaching in a synagogue), Mary, his mother, and some of his brothers summoned him. Many Bible theologians feel that they came to Capernaum to find Jesus and to urge him to return with them to Nazareth because Joseph, his father, the husband of Mary, was either near death or he had recently died. If this was true, then Jesus, the elder brother, would have a family obligation to oversee the funeral and burial arrangements and as administrator, to settle Joseph's estate.

I discovered documentation that addressed this event in the life of Jesus at the world famous Rococo Library, an unparalleled medieval library that specialized in religious sources, in St. Gallen, Switzerland.

The library was located in an old abbey that was originally built by Gallus in the 7th century. Although much of the original abbey had been destroyed during the

Reformation, the magnificent library with its over 150,000 religious volumes, manuscripts, and documents, had been preserved.

When I walked into the library, I was awe-stuck. I found myself not being able to move. I just stood there and admired the entire ancient complex in wonderment. When I finally collected my composure and started investigating the library's vast collection of "literary gold," I felt as if I could have stayed for days. I ended up spending all afternoon studying the seemingly boundless array of medieval religious volumes—and I did not go beyond the first floor. No telling what treasures I would encounter on the second and third floors.

Late in the afternoon, I became thirsty and went to the front reference desk to ask the library assistant for the location of a drinking fountain. After the assistant told me the location of the drinking fountain, I noticed a sign on the desk written in German, English, and French, announcing that the library would be closing at 9:00 p.m. that day for inventory and re-cataloging, and would not re-open for two weeks. Needless to say, I was totally taken back. I had planned to spend at least a couple days researching at the Rococo Library, and now all of a sudden I was forced to realize that unless I was able to come back to St. Gallen sometime in the future, which was highly unlikely, I only had the remainder of that evening to do any type of research.

So, I quickly left the desk and walked to the card catalog files, mentally kicking myself for not noticing the announcement earlier and wasting the entire afternoon. After about an hour of investigating the card catalogue I realized that although there was a wealth of information that I knew without a doubt I would probably be able to use, I needed to narrow my search down to two or three and then study those two or three to see if they could be useful.

By early evening I had narrowed my search to one volume that I felt fit within my parameters of truth and that could perhaps be beneficial. This resource was a small leather-bound volume that had been written by Bernardino Realino, a lawyer turned Jesuit, from Naples, who served as Rector of Jesuit College at Leece in Apulia. In 1600 while serving as rector, he had written three opinions in a legal format, much like the opinions then being written in the courts of his day. This bound volume contained all three of his opinions.

It appeared as if the opinions were probably used as teaching tools or as opinion examples for students who were studying law at the college. The first opinion that Realino wrote concerned the death of Joseph, the earthly father of Jesus. The second and third dealt with events that occurred in Jesus' ministry while he passed through Jericho: the healing of blind Bar-Timaeus and the conversion of Zacchaeus. I will discuss what Realino had to say about the events that happened in Jericho in the chapter entitled, **Final Year of Ministry.**

The first brief about which Realino wrote dealt with the death of Joseph. In his argumentative opinion Realino used the writings of Cyprianii of Carthage very liberally. Cyprianii had written in AD 248, a brief history of Jesus' supposed relationship with his immediate family members.

Realino first wrote an introduction and synopsis and then began his opinion by writing, "Cyprianii said that Matthew records (12:46-50) an event that occurred immediately after Joseph's death. Jesus was in Capernaum. He had moved to

Capernaum, along with his mother, some time before, but Joseph had stayed in Nazareth because in Nazareth was located the stone quarries that were so vital to his business.

"Apparently Joseph had fallen ill or had been injured and Mary had gone back to Nazareth to care for him. The occasion of the Matthew record was set in early summer of AD 29, while Jesus was teaching in the synagogue in Capernaum. As he taught, Mary and Jesus' brothers arrived to urge him to return to Nazareth to help with the arrangements of either Joseph's imminent death or he had already died and Jesus, being the oldest son, had the responsibility of arranging for his burial and the distribution of his estate. This estate could have been extensive if Joseph did in fact (as Roman records of commerce from that period indicate) have branches of his construction business in Capernaum and Tiberias along with the home office in Nazareth.

"When those who were there listening to Jesus told him that his mother and brothers were there to see him, he told them that *'these are my mother and brothers,'* as he stretched his hand out and pointed to his disciples. This implied that his disciples had become his family, rather than his natural family, who for the most part had rejected him and his mission. Because Joseph was likely already dead and he (Jesus) could not (or chose not to) do anything about it, Jesus did not leave with Mary and the brothers. Instead he kept teaching. They responded to Jesus' apparent insensitivity by leaving and returning to Nazareth without him. The teaching message that Jesus delivered after Mary and the brothers had left is recorded in the Gospel of St. John (6:30-69).

"Some 2nd century manuscripts state that Mary responded to Jesus' seeming lack of concern by saying *'quoniam in furorem versus est,'* which essentially meant that she questioned his sanity. These same manuscripts give two speculations concerning Jesus' relationship with Joseph. One says that Jesus and Joseph were estranged and that they were not on talking terms. This is why Jesus did not return with Mary in order to heal Joseph or to raise him from the dead.

"The other speculation states that Jesus and Joseph were very close, in fact Jesus was the head of Joseph's Capernaum branch. Jesus and Joseph had a long standing agreement that if anything ever happened to Joseph, that Jesus would not intervene, but rather he would press forward in the mission to which he was called and that upon Joseph's death Jesus would close the Capernaum branch and would then go full-time into the ministry into which he was called. This speculation also claims that Mary knew of these arrangements when she came to get Jesus. But when Jesus honored the agreement, Mary became angry and returned home.

"A few days later, in order to honor Joseph's memory, Jesus did return to Nazareth, probably after closing or selling the branch business in Capernaum. By then, Mary had cooled down and had remembered Jesus and Joseph's agreement. From that time forward, Mary's relationship with Jesus was close. Which one, if either, of the two speculations is correct, is not known. But we do know that after teaching, Jesus did in fact return to Nazareth (Mark 6:1), presumably, in order to help Mary with the arrangements. He ended up staying in Nazareth for a number of months. Less than a year after Joseph's death, Mary and her children who were still living at home, moved to Jerusalem."

Realino concluded by saying, "The opinion that Joseph died at this time, some two or three years after Jesus had begun his ministry, was the generally accepted belief throughout Christendom until Gregory XII said in the 15th century, that Joseph died when Jesus was 14-years old and that at his death Joseph was a very old man. Gregory went on to say that after Joseph's death, Jesus took care of his mother until he launched his ministry.

"From the time of that declaration by Gregory, the church has taught and it has become accepted throughout Christendom that Joseph died when Jesus was in his teens, contrary to what was accepted, believed, and taught as fact for the first 15 centuries of the history of the Christian faith. I for one," Realino wrote concluding the matter, "Have chosen to believe Cyprianii's record."

By the time I had finished with Realino's accounts, it was time for the library to close. So, I reluctantly left. But I was thankful that I was able to find at least one document that I was able to use.

A few days after Mary and his brothers had left Capernaum to go back to Nazareth Jesus also went to Nazareth. During these few days, he probably closed or closed and sold Joseph's branch office in Capernaum. Then after the closing or closing and sale transaction was concluded, he and his disciples left for Nazareth.

He stayed in Nazareth until late October or early November, settling Joseph's estate and helping his mother.

It was during this time that he was in Nazareth, probably in early to mid-summer, that he again selected 12 out of his many disciples and appointed them to be apostles. As before, he commissioned the 12 and sent them out to minister. But unlike the first time when he restricted their ministry to Judaean Jews only, this time he told them that they could minister to anyone, anywhere (Matthew 10:16-47; Mark 6:1-13).

After the 12 had been sent out, he appointed 70 more and sent them out to minister in like manner as the 12 (Luke 10:17-22).

Nothing is recorded about the life of Jesus while he was in Nazareth during those months. It was not until September or October when both the 12 and the 70 or more returned to Nazareth and reported their accomplishments to him, that the next event in the life of Jesus is recorded.

With regard to the second commissioning of the 12 and the commissioning of the 70 and the reports of their ministry upon their return to Jesus in Nazareth, I discovered documentation that confirmed the Gospel accounts while researching at the Toledo Museum of Art in Toledo, Ohio, considered to be one of the top ten art museums in the world.

On the ground floor of the museum is the manuscript evaluation room. The room contains dozens of bound volumes that identify and describe manuscripts on which the museum's manuscript specialists have worked, but have not as yet be put on public display. In the volumes are pictures of the manuscripts, translations of the manuscripts into English, Italian, German, Spanish, and French, a history of each of the manuscripts, and an explanation describing the primary focus of each manuscript.

I was studying a volume in this room that contained the description of a manuscript written by Florentius Radewijnsa, when I discovered that the volume also contained information about a sermon written by the Welsh bishop, and Bible translator, William Morgan, in 1602, just two years before his death. The sermon's main focus was the commissioning of the 12 and the 70 or 72 (as some manuscripts indicate).

Morgan wrote, "In the summer of AD 29, while in his mother's home in Nazareth, in a valley just north of Nazareth and west of the city of Capernaum, Jesus again called 12 of his disciples together in order to commission them a second time (Mark 6:7-11). Eleven of these were also included in the first commissioning. Thaddeus was the one that may not have been included with this second commissioning. If in fact he was not included, then Judas, the brother or son of James was the one who was chosen in his stead.

"Again he told them to go two by two and gave them power to teach, preach, heal, and cast out demons. However, this time he gave them permission to minister throughout the Galilee and to minister to everyone, not just to the Jews, as was the case with the first commissioning in Judaea. Matthew 10:16-47 and Mark 6:8-11 record Jesus' instructions to them. They were gone all summer and into the early fall of AD 29.

"After the 12 had been sent out, perhaps a few weeks later, he commissioned and sent out (Luke 10:1-2) 70 more (some early manuscripts say 72 rather than 70) of his disciples to minister in the Galilee. According to early church tradition, Aristobulus—or Eubulus in the Greek language—(II Timothy 4:21, Romans 16:10), the younger brother of Herod Agrippa, (Agrippa was appointed king over the Galilee area by Caligula in AD 41), and father of Peter's wife, Peter's father-in-law, was one of the 70 or 72 commissioned by Jesus at this time. Jesus' instructions to the 70 or 72 are recorded in Luke 10:3-16.

"After the 70 or 72 had been sent out, Jesus remained in Nazareth until both the 12 and the 70 or 72 had returned. It was probably in September that the 12 returned and in October that the 70 or 72 returned. Both groups were exhilarated at what had been accomplished by using Jesus' authority (Luke 10:17-20). Jesus shared in their joy and their excitement, but when they began to tell him that they even had authority over evil spirits through his name, he gave a strange response, the wording of which is like no other or nothing else in the Bible.

"In Luke 10:18," Morgan continued, "he said in response to their excitement, *'I beheld Satan as lightning fall from heaven.'* The Anglo-Saxon translators translated it so, and it means literally *'I saw Satan fall upon the inhabitants of the earth unmercifully, but I have given you power over him and his power. However, you should rejoice because you are a child of God, not because you have power over Satan.'*

"The Anglo-Saxon translators translated the statement as if it had been written in Greek, but Jesus' statement was not spoken in Greek, rather he spoke it in Chaldean. The Chaldean translation is *'I caused Satan to fall, as quickly and as violently as lightning that falls on earth, from this [universe] to that [universe].'*

"Assosmeless, the renowned 3rd century Persian mystic explained this Chaldean statement by Jesus in his *Habitations of Gods*. A copy of this book—of course it is far removed from the original by probably at least seven or eight or more rewrites

The Search

and translations—is safely stored in the reference vault of the University in Tehran, Iran.

"Assosmeless explained that in the beginning, God created four interconnecting universes. They are the universe called *Faith*, the universe called *Hope*, the universe called *Satisfaction*, and the universe called *Love*. The universe of Love was the central universe where was located the home and the throne of God Supreme (Heaven), our God, known as The Trinity. A god who was a member of the Divine Council of Universal Governors governed each universe. This council was administered by the first person of God Supreme, The Trinity, God the Father. The third person of The Trinity, the Son, was the governor of the universe called Love. Lucifer was governor of the universe called Satisfaction.

"After time unlimited," Assosmeless continued to explain, "rebellion developed and war broke out between the universes called Love and Satisfaction. The governor of the universe of Love, the Son, who became Jesus the Christ on earth, defeated the governor of Satisfaction and cast him, Lucifer, and his followers out of Heaven and imprisoned them in the bowels of a small planet located in the universe of Love, Earth—a planet that would eventually be inhabited by Adam and his linage. The Son then closed light and communication passages to Lucifer's universe of Satisfaction resulting in it becoming the universe of Hate.

"When Adam sinned, Lucifer and his followers were released from their prison and again gained access to the universe that had become Hate, Lucifer's universe. From that home his spirit agents travel back and forth to Earth to torment man.

"What Jesus was telling his disciples who he had sent out to minister was *'I already have power over Satan. I was the one who threw him out of Heaven and I gave you my power so that you too could overcome him. Do not rejoice because you have power. It is not your power; it is mine that I allowed you to use. Rather be joyful that you are a child of God.'* He then finished by praying for them.

"If this is true or not," Morgan wrote, "we will never know until we get to Heaven. But, it does shed a different light on the traditionally accepted explanation. I for one lean towards believing it."

With that Morgan finished the material that he used to compile his sermon.

To say the least, my head was swimming in confusion. I had never heard of some of that information before. Yet I didn't have an acceptable alternative to what the good bishop had revealed.

In late October or early November of AD 29, Jesus and the 12 left Nazareth and traveled to Caesarea Philippi, located just south of Mount Hermon, about 25 or 30 miles north of the Sea of Galilee. It was there that Peter confessed that Jesus was the Christ, the Son of the Living God, and where Jesus was transfigured (Matthew 16:13-25; Mark 8:27-28; Luke 9:18-27).

Dr. Pil Klensberg, the Historical Research Director of the Kunstmuseum in Bern, Switzerland, introduced me to documentation that validated the Gospel records of these events in Jesus' life.

The Kunstmuseum, Bern's fine arts museum featuring works by Paul Klee and a host of French masters, was located downtown.

Dr. Klensberg told me that the museum itself had very little, if any, of the information for which I was looking, but that he had a private document in his office that might be of interest to me. It was a document that discussed Peter's confession at Caesarea Philippi.

I told him I was interested, so he led me into his private office, where he took a slim bound volume off of his bookshelf.

The volume contained about 10 leather leaves, bound between two oak boards. Peter of Tarentaise in 1147, when he was Archbishop of Tarentaise wrote the volume in French. Accompanying the volume was an ink sketch, also on leather, depicting Peter kneeling before Jesus. The sketch was entitled *Peter's Confession*. Dr. Klensberg did not explain how he obtained the document and sketch other than to say that for 32 years he had made the translation of the document and research regarding the document and sketch, his primary research focus.

Dr. Klensberg took a few minutes to collect his thoughts, and then he began.

"In late October or early November of AD 29, soon after the return to the Nazareth area of the 70 (or 72) that he had sent out, Jesus and his disciples left the area and traveled about 30 miles north of the Sea of Galilee to the Roman city of Caesarea Philippi, located in the Roman district of Panias. It should be noted that Jesus had returned to Nazareth after he helped his mother settled Joseph's estate.

"Caesarea Philippi was originally called Paneus, the city of Pan (the Greek/Roman god of wild animals, material goods, and sexual pleasure). The city had been built around the Paneion grotto, the source of the Jordan River. It was an open city in that anything and everything (except murder and stealing), was tolerated and accepted. It was also a religiously tolerant city and residents worshipped, respected, and honored virtually every god, goddess, honored patron, respected citizen, or religious philosophy known in the Empire, and others that were worshipped even outside of the Empire. All forms, customs, ceremonies, and rituals of worship were allowed and revered.

"Throughout the Roman Empire, Caesarea Philippi's nick-name was *The Gates of Hades* [*Hell*] (Matthew 16:13).

"Romans from all over the Empire would vacation in Caesarea Philippi in order to 'let their hair down,' so to speak, and to indulge in every, any, and all imaginable licentious and sexual pleasure. The entire city was completely given over to gross decadence and sexual debauchery in their vilest states. The sexual wantonness never stopped. It went on 24-hours a day, 365 days a year.

"At this time of the year, late October and early November, the *Festival of Pan* was in full swing. The festival lasted from the time of the first changing of the leaves (October or November) until the winter solstice in December. The festival was actually a 'mourning' festival in which the observers would celebrate the 'death' and hibernation of the earth (winter). It was a homosexual festival. Winter, or the time of non-productivity and non-reproduction, was set aside for blatant homosexual activity and bestiality because Pan had supposedly decreed that reproduction was not advisable during the time of non-production. The first sign of spring signaled the beginning of a carnival atmosphere of fun, music, love games, and wild heterosexual activity.

"I'm sure that the disciples were bewildered as to why Jesus had brought them to such a wicked and sexually perverted city. However, Jesus wanted to emphasis a point and to do so, although they did not stay in the city itself, they had to be close enough to the city so that the point could be driven home.

"Sometime after they had arrived in the area of Caesarea Philippi, Jesus went away by himself to pray (Luke 9:18). After a while, his disciples came to him as he was praying. As they gathered around him, Jesus asked them, *'Whom do men say that I, the Son of Man, am?'*

"They answered him and told him that some say he is the reincarnated John the Baptist, some say Elijah, and others say Jeremiah or one of the other prophets. The typical Jew believed and the Jewish religious leaders (excluding Sadducees) taught reincarnation; in fact, most all of the religions and religious philosophies at that time, with the exception of the hard-line Roman religions and the ancient Egyptian religions, believed in and taught reincarnation.

"He then asked them what they thought. *'Who do you think I am?'*

"Peter answered almost instantly, *'Thou art the Christ; the Son of the Living God.'*

"For the first time ever, Jesus was recognized for who he really was. For the first time he was recognized as the Messias, the Christ, and Messiah, the Son of the Living God, in one person. Up to this point, some identified Jesus as *Messias* and others felt that he was *Messiah*, but here for the first time Peter recognized him as both *Messiah* and *Messias* in one person.

"Jesus acknowledged that Peter could not have known the truth had not the Father revealed it to him (Peter), thus confirming Jesus' statement of Luke 10:22.

"Jesus then began to address him with the name that Jesus had told him a couple of years before that he would be called (John 1:42). He called him *Peter*, thus setting into motion the living analogy that Peter's spiritual maturation was indicated by his names: Simon (a reed) was transformed into Peter (a chip of granite rock). The seven levels of spiritual maturity was allegorized by a seven-step natural process of the evolutionary transmogrification of reed to rock.

"Jesus then said that Peter was a chip of the rock. He (Jesus) was *The Rock* upon which the church would be built, but Peter was a chip of that rock.

"Jesus, probably pointed to the city of Caesarea Philippi then said, *'And the gates of hell will not prevail against it (the church).'* The statement was one that indicated an offensive position. In other words, the church will become so powerful that its members will literally storm the gates of hell (symbolized by Caesarea Philippi) and lay siege to hell itself. They will be successful against any and all defenses thrown up by the forces of evil. The church as a powerful conquering offensive force was destined to break the defenses of hell and bring the forces of evil to its knees.

"He then said that he had given Peter as well as the other disciples the keys of the kingdom. He did not use the word *to*. He instead, used the word *of*. The word *to* represented something borrowed, or that it did not belong to the one who had the keys, but the word *of* meant ownership. The one who had the key owned the kingdom. And because they were heirs and owners, anything they loosed on earth would be loosed in heaven and anything they bound on earth would be bound in heaven.

"In other words, because they had the authority of the kingdom come down from heaven, authority that Jesus had given them and authority that they would continue to possess as long as they remained in him and he (Jesus) in them, they had the right to dictate when, where, how, how much, and under what circumstances, presently and in the future warfare with the forces of evil would take place

"Unfortunately," Dr. Klensberg interjected, "For the most part that authority was abdicated to the organized church with its dogmas, doctrines, and ritualistic traditions. The church crushed it and allowed it to drain away until all that was left was an empty shell that looked impressive on the outside, but inside it was and still is, empty and filled with void and/or corruption.

"Jesus went on and told his disciples that he was in fact the embodiment of the one that Peter had proclaimed, but that he (Jesus) would have to face death. Peter, perhaps prideful and confident because he was the one who had recognized Jesus for who he actually was, and perhaps believing he was now exalted in the eyes of Jesus far above the others present, openly and arrogantly corrected Jesus for making such a negative statement concerning his up-coming death.

"Jesus immediately responded to Peter's correction by sternly rebuking him in front of the others and rebuking the spirit that was influencing him. Apparently Peter's pride had left him vulnerable to the deceptions of Satan with regard to Jesus' true mission, thus blinding him from the truth.

"Jesus told Peter to get under authority and maintain the proper line of priority authority; and he demanded of Satan that he quit trying to detour the plan of God because it is going to happen, regardless of how he (Satan) might fight against it or try to disrupt its fulfillment.

"Jesus then explained what was expected of them if they truly wanted to be *born again*, He implied that they first had to die—emotionally, psychologically, and spiritually—a death that was excruciatingly painful, humiliating, and totally self-destructive. But after the death process was complete, they could be *born again*.

"Faced with the tremendous emotional upheaval that accompanied the *born again* instructions by Jesus and the continual licentiousness associated with the festivities going on in Caesarea Philippi, the disciples felt what they needed more than anything else to learn how to pray and to get a hold of God the Father. Jesus gave them an example of the perfect prayer structure and prayer priorities."

After Dr. Klensberg had finished reading, I spent another hour or so asking him questions about Caesarea Philippi, Peter's confession, and the church's current position with respect to the authority that Jesus had given them.

Six days after Peter's confession, Jesus took Peter, James, and John and traveled to Mount Hermon to be transfigured (Matthew 16:28-17:16; Mark 9:1-13; Luke 9:28-36).

I discovered documentation that confirmed the Gospel records of the transfiguration at the Church of St. George in Istanbul, Turkey, located within the Ecumenical Orthodox Patriarchate compound.

On display in the church was a four-leaf manuscript that had been written by Peter Damian in 1066, while he was in seclusion at Fonte Avellana. It seemed that some 20 years before, in 1046, Peter had supported Emperor Henry III's decision to depose two Popes and replace them with one of his own choosing.

Now 20 years later, Peter was forced to defend his support of Henry. In a letter to Pope Gregory VII, Peter not only defended his position, but he also brilliantly used the transfiguration of Jesus to support his position. Although most of the portion that explained the historical event of Jesus' transfiguration was intact, the portion dealing with his use of the transfiguration story as part of his defense had long since disintegrated.

The manuscript was written in Latin and it was one of four exhibits on display in a small room adjacent to the main church structure. In front of the display case where Peter's letter was displayed sitting on a tall narrow wooden table, was a leather-bound notebook with an English and Greek translation of the letter, along with an explanation about why Peter wrote the letter.

According to this notebook, Peter first related the story of the transfiguration; then he gave his defense using the transfiguration story as a justification for his stand. Since less than a third of the letter remained, I was not able to see how Peter used the transfiguration in his defense. But Peter did give an interesting re-telling of the transfiguration story.

Peter used as his text the Matthew (17:1-21) setting of the transfiguration story.

"Jesus and his disciples were still in the area of Caesarea Philippi. It was during that time that Peter proclaimed that Jesus was the Christ, the Son of the Living God. Six days after that proclamation or eight days after Jesus and his 12 appointed disciples had arrived in Caesarea Philippi (Luke 9:28), Peter, James, and John accompanied Jesus to Mount Hermon.

"Mount Hermon rose 8,500 feet above the city of Caesarea Philippi and the top most portion was covered with snow a good part of the year. This was the first time that Jesus had separated these three out from the others and took them with him to pray (Luke 9:28), or for any specific purpose.

"Although Matthew," Peter continued, "says that they went into the mountain, it is not known with certainty whether they went into a cave on the mountain, were nestled under a ledge or outcropping, or some other place of protection, or were on top of the mountain. Wherever it was, it was there that Jesus was transfigured (probably while the four were praying) and was launched into the last phase of his ministry.

"The word that Matthew used to describe this event was the Greek word *metamorphoo*. It meant *'to change form.'* I (Peter) am not quite sure what this meant. Did Jesus transform from flesh into spirit? Did he change from mortal to immortal and then back to mortal? We do not know. But we do know that while the four of them were there, Jesus was transfigured in their presence, right in front of them.

"Then suddenly, before their very eyes, appeared the forms of Moses and Elijah. The two men began to talk to the transfigured, or glorified, Jesus. According to the Luke setting, they talked to Jesus about his death and about his ministry from that time until his death. Moses probably represented the Law and the Old Covenant and the promise of salvation; Elijah probably represented the prophets and their message. Both gave honor and subservience to the glorified Jesus.

"As the disciples watched this event, Peter spoke to Jesus telling him that it was good that they were there to witness this event, perhaps implying that no one would believe this unless they saw it with their own eyes, or that they deserved to be there because they were the three out of all the 12 who were most qualified to be there to witness these events.

"Peter then suggested that he build three sanctuary shelters, much like the hundreds of sanctuary shelters scattered around the mountain, the grotto at the foot of the mountain with its accompanied morass which is the source of the River Jordan, and other places throughout the city of Caesarea Philippi, were dedicated to various gods, goddesses, demi-gods, holy men, deified personages, or philosophers, and were used in the worship of those to whom they were dedicated. The sanctuaries suggested that all three were worthy to be worshipped and should be objects of worship. It also indicated that although Peter had said that Jesus was the Christ, the Son of the Living God, he perhaps did not completely believe it. If he had believed it, then he would have been convinced that Jesus and Jesus alone was the *one* and *only* Christ and the *one* and *only* Son of God, who stands alone (not with Moses and Elijah) as worthy of honor and worship. As it was, Jesus' position, in Peter's eyes, most assuredly was exalted, but it was exalted to a level equal to Moses and Elijah in respect, adoration, and honor—not necessarily above them, but certainly equal to them.

"While Peter was speaking, a bright cloud engulfed them. Then out of the cloud a voice spoke (whether the voice was the personality of God the Father or God the Holy Spirit or both, we do not know; but we do know that the voice belonged to God.). It said that Jesus was His beloved son in whom He was pleased and that they should listen to him (Jesus) [only]. The disciples fell face down on the ground, terrified. This indicated that Moses and Elijah or the Law and the prophets were not equal to Jesus; but rather Jesus, his ministry, and his teachings were superior to both. He and he alone is the one who must be served, listened to, followed, exalted, and honored. All else and all others are subject to him—even the Law and the prophets.

"His instructions concerning discipleship (Matthew 16:24-25) are true and must be followed if one is truly a disciple of Jesus. That discipleship is more than a conversion experience or more than just being saved. It is a born again experience. Born again is not the same as conversion. Born again implies that there must be a death, and then a rebirth. It is a step beyond conversion. It is a step that leads to discipleship. The death is an awful death of suffering and of pain in which all will turn against you and all will forsake you. It is a devastating emotional death, just like a death on the cross. Being saved and being converted guarantees entrance into heaven and an eternal life with Christ.

"But for those who want to go further here on this earth and be his disciple on the earth and be identified as one of those true disciples here, then they must go through the born again experience which is in addition to the conversion experience. It is a disciplinary experience of emotional and spiritual pain and suffering unlike anything that a person has ever experienced. But once the pain, suffering, and devastation are completed, the person can be born again into a life of victory and power unmatched by any on this earth.

"This discipleship process is not the same as believing that he is the Son of God, that God raised him from the dead, confession of sin, and accepting Jesus as

Savior and Lord. This process insures salvation, but it is not the born again experience that brings the discipleship that Jesus is talking about in this Matthew portion.

"A person who has been saved does not have to move into the born again experience. It does not bring nor is it salvation; acceptance of Jesus as Savior, and it alone, brings salvation. Although a person cannot move into the born again experience unless they are saved, born again is not conversion. Born again is an experience beyond salvation into which only a small handful will choose to venture by accepting the challenge and the discipline necessary to achieve it. The instructions concerning the move from converted into born again are the instructions that the voice of God said is correct and must be followed to insure true discipleship."

I paused as I read this portion of Peter's letter and thought about what Peter was saying. This was the second time that Jesus had talked about the born again experience. The first time he was addressing Nicodemus. This second time he was addressing three of his disciples. Outside of these two times, expressed by the writings of two different men at two different times, the first by the Irish teacher, Malachy O'More in 1140 in reference to Nicodemus, and the second by Peter Damian in 1066 in reference to the disciples at the transfiguration, I had never heard this concept before.

I had always been taught that salvation and conversion *was* being born again—and that basically sins being forgiven, salvation, conversion, born again, acceptance of Jesus as Savior, names record in the Lamb's Book of Life, redemption, and believing on Jesus were all just different terms that meant the same thing and in essence explained salvation.

But both O'More and Damian said that there is conversion in which a person is saved. Then beyond that salvation experience there is an experience in which a person can choose to be involved: the born again experience. They said that born again has nothing whatsoever to do with salvation, rather it has to do with discipleship. If O'More and Damian are both right, how did the truth get so corrupted? After the Nicodemus explanation, I was not so convinced that conversion and born again were two different experiences, but now that the subject has been brought up a second time, it has caused my confidence at what I had always believed concerning this issue to be greatly challenged.

So, knowing that I could not resolve the issue right then, I returned to Peter's letter.

"The disciples remained face down on the ground terrified, until Jesus came and touched them and told them not to be afraid. When they looked up, Jesus was back to normal, Moses and Elijah were gone, and the cloud and the voice had left.

"Perhaps immediately or maybe even the next day, they climbed down the mountain. As they descend the mountain, Jesus told them not to tell anyone what they had seen until after he was raised from the dead. The reason for this caution was probably because Jesus did not want this experience to be identified with the mythological stories of the prevalent pagan religions. In Egyptian mythology, Osiris was transfigured and in his transfigured state Isis spoke to him telling him that he was chosen to live again. In Babylonian mythology Marduk was transfigured; and in Phoenician mythology Baal was transfigured. All three were worshipped and honored in Caesarea Philippi. What better way for Jesus to be discredited than for his disciples to begin spreading the news that he had been transfigured in Caesarea Philippi?

"As they descended the mountain (either walking or riding animals—we do not know which) the disciples asked Jesus that if he in fact was the Son of God, Messias—The Christ, Messiah, why did the teachers of the Law say that Elijah must first come before Messiah is revealed?

"The traditional eschatology teachings of the teachers of the Law at that time said that based on Malachi (4:5-6) Elijah must appear before the coming of Messiah. If Jesus was that one who was to come, why had not Elijah come first?

"Jesus answered that Elijah had in fact come before him; but that the religious leaders did not recognize him; instead they consented to and even applauded his death. The disciples realized that Jesus was referring to John the Baptist, and that he would die just as John the Baptist had died. Just like John was not recognized by the teachers of the Law, so Jesus would not be recognized by them, but instead would consent to and applaud his death.

"Jesus and the three disciples returned to where they had left the others. There is no record that the three told the others what had happened on the mountain, until after Jesus had resurrected."

Peter of Tarentaise then began his defense based on the transfiguration story, but only two lines of that portion of the letter had survived. A large segment of the letter was missing. Then the letter picked up again telling the story of Jesus' healing of the boy in Caesarea Philippi.

After the missing part, the letter continued, "Some time after the transfiguration, Jesus and his disciples were walking to Caesarea Philippi. As they approached the city a man ran out to meet him. The man had a son who the town's people classified as *lunatic*.

"The man pleaded for Jesus to heal the boy saying that he had asked some of his disciples (not the 12 but some of his other followers—perhaps some of the 70) to heal him, but they could not. The traditional belief at that time was that a person with the type of disease from which the boy was suffering was *lunatic*, or 'moon-struck.' The feeling was that the moon caused the disease and that the disease usually manifested itself during a full moon.

"Caesarea Philippi was known to be the center for those who suffered lunacy. It was the 'madness' capital of the Empire. Of course with open promiscuity and an 'international' city that welcomed all forms of religious worship and philosophy, it was not surprising.

"Yielding to the emotional need of the father, Jesus healed the boy. Knowing that the moon had not caused the problems, Jesus did not rebuke the moon. Instead he cast the demon that caused the disease out of the boy.

"Jesus then used the inability of the disciples to heal the boy as an opportunity to teach the 12 a lesson on faith.

"Pointing to a mountain, probably Mount Hermon, which was covered with mustard plants, Jesus used the mustard plant and the mustard seed as an example of faith. Jesus' primary focus was not the removal of the mountain, but rather the consistency produced through disciplined fasting and prayer and the never-giving-up type of faith and determination of the mustard seed and the mustard plant. Against overwhelming odds, the mustard plant becomes victorious over the mountain through patience, confidence, determination, discipline, and consistency."

The last three lines of this portion of the letter explained how Peter of Tarentaise was going to use Jesus' lesson on faith to show why he (Peter) supported Henry's decision. But, because the remainder of the letter was missing, Peter's explanation has been lost.

With regard to Jesus' use of the mustard plant and mustard seed to teach mountain removing type of faith, I found some very convincing information while researching at Texas A&I University in Kingsville, Texas.

At the Texas A&I University library I discovered a small book whose subject matter was the interpretation of and the history of an Italian manuscript that had been written in the year 1430, by Laurence Justinian, the former Bishop of Castello. Pope Nicholas V had appointed him the first Patriarch of Venice. The book was entitled *Venice Mustard Gold*.

Rev. Theodore McKinney, a 19th century Methodist pastor from Richmond, Virginia, had compiled the information in the book. This book explained in detail the implications of the mustard seed and mustard plant at the time of Jesus.

The book indicted that the Justinian manuscript was a sermon, or a lesson that Justinian had written, and was to be taught to the new inductees into the priesthood at Castello. The lesson was entitled *Lessons on the Seed of the Mustard*, and its subject matter was the four different instances (the first was at this time in AD 29, the second time was a couple of months after the first, the third was a year later in AD 30 when Jesus healed a woman who was stooped for 18 years, and the last time was a year after that in AD 31 when he cursed a fig tree) in which Jesus used the tiny mustard seed or the mustard plant to emphasize unwavering and consistent faith.

Laurence Justinian began by quoting three portions of Scripture, one after the other. There was no break between the three, and they were quoted chronologically out of order, based on the present day order of Scripture. In the present day Bible the portions are Matthew 21: 21-22, 13:31-32, and Luke 13:18-19.

> *"Jesus answered and said unto them, verily I say unto you, if ye have faith and doubt not, ye shall not only do this which is done to the fig tree, but also if ye shall say unto this mountain, be removed, and be thou cast into the sea; it shall be done. And all things, whatsoever ye shall ask in prayer, believing, ye shall receive. Another parable put he forth unto them, saying, the kingdom of heaven is like to a grain of mustard seed, which a man took, and sowed in his field: which indeed is the least of all seeds: but when it is grown, it is the greatest among herbs, and becometh a tree, so that the birds of the air come and lodge in the branches thereof. Then said He, unto what is the kingdom of God like? and whereunto shall I resemble it? It is like a grain of mustard seed, which a man took, and cast into his garden; and it grew, and waxed a great tree; and the fowls of the air lodged in the branches of it."*

Justinian then explained the historical background of the significance of the mustard seed, the historical setting in which each was spoken by Jesus, he gave an explanation of the character of a mustard seed and the mustard plant, and he explained how and why Jesus used these analogies within the context of that particular setting.

"In 63 BC Pompey conquered the Judean area for Rome. One of his most trusted companions was his director of engineering and construction, Albanus Gaius.

"After the conquest, Pompey felt that new harbors and ports needed to be built by Gaius on the Mediterranean Sea, the Sea of Galilee, and the Dead Sea (called Salt Sea at that time) and that the existing harbors and ports needed to be enhanced to better serve Rome's interests.

"Pompey petitioned the Roman Senate for funds to build the ports and harbors and asked permission to use nationals as slave labor to perform the task. Pompey and Gaius waited for two years and six months for a reply from Rome. During that time of waiting, Gaius discovered a process whereby stones that would be needed to serve as construction harbor fill, could be 'quarried' naturally, without the use of manual labor.

"As an amateur biologist, Gaius noticed that the rugged spice plant, mustard, a spice that had been imported from Asia and Africa by Rome over the past one hundred years, grew abundantly and effortlessly (many times it grew wild) in the Judean and the Galilee region. He discovered that the plant seemed to grow best in soil that had an abundant lime content. So he began to experiment by first planting mustard *plants* on mountains that were predominately limestone and then he revised his emphasis and began sowing the mustard *seeds* on the mountains.

"To his surprise, what he had speculated was true. Because of the abundance of lime that made up the mountain, the seeds sprang up immediately and grew rapidly and effortlessly. As the plants grew, pulling the lime out of the soil and rocks, Gaius noticed that the limestone became chalky and crumbled.

"Big boulders began to break away and rumble to the bottom of the mountain. The simple and weak mustard plant literally had the ability, over an extended period of time, to disintegrate a limestone mountain, regardless of the size of the mountain.

"Afterwards the stones were collected by laborers and hauled to the port and harbor construction sites—the mountains were literally being *'cast into the sea.'*

"So, as Pompey and Gaius waited for word from Rome, Gaius contented himself with knowing that daily more stones were being 'quarried' naturally, and as a bonus, a steady supply of mustard spice had now become available for export to Rome.

"The Roman Senate finally did respond, but the Senators denied Pompey's request and recalled him to Rome. He immediately returned to Rome, but he left Gaius in Judea, promising to send the needed funds when he (Pompey) arrived in Rome.

"Pompey never again returned to the Judean region, and Gaius never left it. Gaius died in Judea in 19 BC at the age of 84 without ever receiving any funds from Rome.

"Up until his death he experimented with plants. He discovered that a sycamore or mulberry tree also thrived in soil with large concentrations of lime. He planted mulberry trees on the mountainsides and found that they grew larger and stronger on the limestone mountains. He further discovered that if he planted mustard seeds within the proximity of a mulberry tree, mustard plants would emerge and flourish. But in time, the mustard plants had taken so much lime out of the rocky soil that the roots of the mulberry tree, regardless of how big or how old the tree was, would lose their grip in the soil and the tree would fall. Again from a tiny mustard seed sprang a fragile plant that could uproot a sycamore tree a thousand times its size.

"In 37 BC Gaius received orders from the Roman Senate to begin constructing harbors and ports in the Judea region, but he received no funds to pay for the construction.

"However, as a result of his experiments over the past twenty years, enough stones and timber had broken away from the mountains that very little quarrying and timber harvesting had to be done. All that the laborers had to do was to gather the material and haul it to the construction sites. By this method, years' worth of construction time and money was saved. In essence, he had already quarried most of the materials that he needed to fulfill Rome's construction demands without costing them any money.

"So successful was Gaius' process that it became the common practice in that entire area for the next 23 centuries. And," Laurence Justinian added, "the process is still practiced today, but on a limited scale.

"Albanus Gaius became," Justinian continued, "World renowned for his 'natural quarrying' process and he became extremely wealthy by exporting mustard spice, mulberry fruit, crushed lime, and timber.

"Next, Justinian turned his attention to a historical and biological explanation of Jesus' second allegorical use of the mustard plant. The analogy that Jesus spoke to his disciples and to the Pharisees and the Sadducees concerned the defilement of the kingdom of God—the religious system.

"While experimenting with the mustard plant, Gaius discovered that the mustard plant was not as puissant as he had originally thought; that it did have its vulnerability.

"He found that a healthy mustard plant grew to about two or three hands (10 to 18 inches) in height and had tender and fragile limbs and branches, and that the odor that was expelled by the plant not only repulsed insects but it also repulsed all birds except the ground habituating morning dove.

"However, he found that there was a type of fungus that attacked all mustard plants that he called *salvadora persican lolia,* a parasitic disease. If the plant was healthy and well rooted in the rocky soil or into a limestone rock, the fungus had little effect upon the plant and died soon after it had attacked the plant. Apparently the large amount of lime content in the fiber of the plant protected it from the fungus.

"However, if the plant was weak, was not well-rooted in the soil, and had only a limited supply of lime flowing through the branch fibers, the fungus would find an acceptable home and would live off of the plant's inner fibers.

"The disease caused the root system to distribute more and more nutrients to the branches to feed the disease rather than to the branch extremities to produce fruit. As the fungus deprived the plant of more and more life, the plant fought back by storing the nutrients in the branches, which increased the size of the outside branch fibers. This caused the plant branches to grow larger, as the branch sought to encircle the fungus. Eventually the plant's branches became extremely large, but they were hollow, with the center core of the branch filled with the black mushy fungus.

"Before long, the fungus began to seep out of the core of the branch. Eventually the plant no longer gave off its protective odor. Rather, the seepage gave off its own odor that attracted insects of all sorts. These insects in turn multiplied and lived off of the plant.

"The plant's lack of protective odor, coupled with its insect population, attracted birds.

"Ultimately the mustard plant, which by this time was large enough to be considered a tree, would almost overnight dry up and die of the disease. However, to those who did not know the character of the mustard plant, the large big-branched mustard tree looked healthy and strong.

" So, in essence, because the mustard plant became diseased and polluted, it attracted its natural enemy, which in turn caused its death, even though the people who knew little about the plant believed it looked healthy and strong. The mustard farmer, who knew the character of the mustard plant, knew immediately when a mustard plant was diseased: it was when it started to grow beyond its true character and began to give off the odor that attracted its natural enemies.

"One interesting point that even though an authority on the mustard plant like Albanus Gaius could recognize a plant that was diseased, he had to be careful about fighting the disease. He could not cut off a diseased branch or limb because that would cause the disease to spread very rapidly to other plants. The only way to fight the disease was to either cut down the entire 'tree' or cut off a diseased branch above the diseased portion. This too was risky because the cut portion would then be exposed and unprotected, totally vulnerable to any and all diseases, until it could grow a protective covering. It was so risky that most mustard farmers did not try to save a diseased plant. The farmer just left it alone let it grow to its enormous size, and then let it die."

Justinian again quoted the scriptural settings and began to explain what Jesus was trying to say with the two different analogies. "In the first analogy, the one that centered on the mustard seed, the emphasis was placed upon the seed, not the removal of the mountain. Basically he was saying to his disciples that consistency is the one thing that is mandatory. Regardless of how long it takes, if you are consistent in your belief and your faith and do not doubt, eventually the mountain in your life will be dissolved. Just as the tiny mustard seed has the potential to bring down a limestone mountain which seems unconquerable, so too do you (my disciples) have within you all that is needed to bring down the mountains that you now face or those you will be facing. Just do not give up; continue to be firmly grounded in my (Jesus') words and be consistent; and if you do not give up, you will see the unconquerable, conquered.

The Search

"The second analogy of Jesus dealt with the religious system. The system, allegorized as the mustard plant that became a tree that looked from the outside to be strong and growing and mighty, if it was not grounded enough to fight off disease, it would become diseased and a 'haven' for all kinds of evil, deception, and mendacity. If left unchecked, these will eventually be the system's ruin.

"Unfortunately," Justinian lamented, "we see this today in our own Christian religious system. Needless to say, Jesus was correct.

Justinian's conclusive hypothesis to this analogy was that if the religious system remains rooted and grounded in God's Word and His principles, although it may not become mighty in the eyes of the world, in God's eyes it will be powerful and undefiled. However, if it does not remain rooted in God's Word then the system will become compromised and diseased and will eventually be unrecognizable from other worldly systems."

A second manuscript written by Justinian and addressed in the book seemed to be a continuation of the mustard seed theme. It was entitled *Variations on the Mustard Plant*. But rather than a sermon, this lesson was apparently written as an apostasy warning and was sent to the church leaders in northern Italy and southern France.

Again he began by quoting Scripture. This time he quoted a portion of Luke where is also recorded the analogy of the mustard plant that grew to a huge size, Luke 13:10-21.

In this setting Jesus used the mustard plant lesson in connection with his using of the Sabbath in the true sense that it was intended to be used: to give freedom to the oppressed. We will discuss the event in which Jesus taught this allegory in the chapter entitled, **The Fifth Year of Ministry**.

In late November or early December, after the boy in Caesarea Philippi was healed and Jesus had given his lesson on faith as a grain of mustard to his disciples, they left the Caesarea Philippi area (Matthew 17:22; Luke 8:1-3).

As they journeyed Jesus warned his disciples that he would be delivered into the hands of those who considered him their enemy and that he would die. Nothing is recorded of their response. But, considering the scolding the Jesus had given Peter just days before when He questioned Jesus' comments, they probably dared not say anything.

The next recorded event in the life of Jesus is when he and his disciples had returned to the Galilee from Caesarea Philippi and his disciples came to him and asked him who of them were greatest or of more importance to Jesus and his ministry and in the kingdom come down from heaven? (Matthew 18:1-34; Mark 9:33-37).

Jesus responded by calling a *ta* child to him. He placed the child in the middle of the group and taught the disciples a lesson on who is truly greatest.

I discovered a unique painting that substantiated this event at The Cinquantenaire Museum of Art and History in Brussels, Belgium. The museum is part of the Royal Museums of Art and History, to which also belong The Hallepoortmuseum, The Japanese Tower, and the Chinese Pavilion.

When I arrived at The Cinquantenaire Museum, I spent at least two or three hours studying the various rooms featuring Roman, Greek, and Byzantine works of

Dr. Ron Charles

art, before coming to the Renaissance section. One of the rooms in the Renaissance section was the Taormina Room. The Taormina Room was a room that featured the 40-year efforts of Sulius of Taormina who in the 14th century produced a series of 11 paintings that he entitled *Daily Life of the Saviour*. Each of the 11 paintings depicted Jesus in a different daily activity. Below each painting was a brief description of the subject of each painting.

I spent quite some time studying the paintings. One, however, was of special interest to me. It depicted Jesus sitting on a stone wall that surrounded a wellhead, holding a young child on his lap, with four more children standing around him. In the background were four adult men looking on contemptuously. The title of the painting was simply *Becoming Ta*.

I did not understand the title, but I assumed that it probably had something to do with Jesus blessing the little children. I asked to be allowed to review the reference notes on the painting in the museum's in-house research library located on the ground floor. The museum security granted my request, but they only allowed me to be in the library for one hour.

Fortunately, the museum's research information was cataloged in chronological order, so the material that related to the painting was easily located. Dr. Jensin Ginozzi of Verona had written the reference description essay in 1851. He gave a convincing explanation and argument as he unfolded the mystery of the "Galilean Ta" of Jesus' day.

The biblical text that Dr. Ginozzi used was the entire 18th chapter of the Gospel of Matthew, however, the actual focal point was the first three verses:

> "At the same time came the disciples unto Jesus, saying, Who is the greatest in the kingdom of heaven? And Jesus called a little child unto him, and sat him in the midst of them, And said, Verily I say unto you, Except ye be converted, and become as little children, ye shall not enter into the kingdom of heaven" (Matthew 18:1-3).

Dr. Ginozzi then explained the background regarding the biblical text.

"The 12 disciples of Jesus were disputing among themselves about who was the greatest or which of them was the greatest asset to the kingdom come down from heaven. In other words, which one of them was the most indispensable to the kingdom that Jesus was proclaiming, or who among them was of greatest value to that kingdom. Jesus did not address their argument directly. Instead he took a little child and sat the child in the middle of the group. The child was a *ta* child. The KJV translated this word to mean 'little,' but the original word that was used was the Greek word *ta*. The word *ta* meant handicapped or mentally afflicted. It was usually used to describe a mongoloid child or one who was mentally handicapped.

"In the Greek culture dominated Galilee, *ta* children were usually responsible for washing the feet of visitors or gusts before they entered a home. Because this job was considered one of the most demeaning of all tasks, it was given to a *ta* child.

"*Ta* children were also used as 'sex slaves' by many brothels in the Galilee that catered to more of the upper class residents of the Galilee at this time. Because the *ta* children were outcasts, no one really cared.

"The name *tasim,* meaning *'one cursed with ta,'* was used to describe a person who is despised and regarded with utter contempt. In the Galilee, it was the most insulting name that one could be called."

It was Dr. Ginozzi's opinion that Jesus, through his actions and statement, was teaching his disciples to give up all pride, all worldly loyalties, and all selfish desires and be willing to be despised by the world and its society and its system in order to be acceptable in the eyes of God the Father. Then and only then can a person be truly great, either on earth or in the kingdom. Then and only then could they be fully exposed without the facade of pride, ego, self-exhalation, worldly ambition and flattery so that all could see and know them.

He went on to explain that Jesus wanted a person to go to the furthest extreme to avoid offending another person, especially one who was spiritually, mentally, or physically handicapped. It was a lesson that was contrary to the teachings of the Pharisees who taught that *ta* children had been rejected by God and were cursed by him. They had no worth and no feelings. Whatever was said or done to them was acceptable; they couldn't be offended no matter the insult or degradation.

Dr. Ginozzi continued with a long explanation concerning Jesus' lesson on forgiving others, forgiveness in general, and being forgiven. He emphasized that Jesus' teaching on these subjects was contrary to the teachings of the scribes and the Pharisees. Thus it was foreign to his disciples. Yet Jesus insisted it was truth and must be practiced in order for them to be part of the kingdom come down from Heaven.

Dr. Ginozzi concluded his essay by explaining how confusing such a teaching must have been to the disciples who had been taught, and the Pharisees had also taught their ancestors for generations past a totally different concept. These Pharisees also said, like Jesus, that their doctrine was given to them directly by God. How could both Jesus and the Pharisees be right when their doctrines were so different and opposite? Yet Jesus insisted that if they were to be his followers and be part of his kingdom, they would have to adopt his teaching as truth and reject the teachings of the Pharisees.

To say the least, I was fascinated by Dr. Ginozzi's essay. Although I had never heard this explanation about *ta* children before, Dr. Ginozzi had so much documentation to prove his point, that I accepted it as a logical possibility and certainly one that could not be dismissed without some serious thought and investigation.

Apparently after this lesson on greatness, Jesus and his disciples left Capernaum for a few days because the next we hear about him is that they have returned to Capernaum.

As they entered the city, some special Temple tax collectors approached Peter about whether Jesus and his followers were going to pay the special Temple tax (Matthew 17:24-27). Peter told them that Jesus would pay the tax. But when Peter returned to Jesus, Jesus implied that he really should not have to pay the tax, but so that he would not cause others to be offended, he would pay the tax. He then instructed Peter to go down to the sea and catch a fish. And the first fish that he was to catch he was to look in his mouth, and a coin would be in the fish' mouth that would amount to what was needed to pay the tax.

I found information that verified this event in Jesus' life at a small museum in Adana, Turkey called the Adana Ethnography Museum, a quaint little museum housed in a small crusader church.

Most of the displayed items in the museum were Roman or were from the Roman era. One of the displayed items was a silver coin, sitting alone on a small silver tripod, locked safely inside a glass front display case. Next to the display case was an audio box that when the front button was pushed, it would tell a story about the coin first in Turkish, then in Arabic, followed by French and English.

The audio recording claimed that the coin on display was the coin that Peter retrieved from the mouth of a fish that Jesus had told him to catch. The coin that was in the fish's mouth, Jesus used to pay their Temple tax.

The coin was supposed to have been paid to a tax collector on behalf of the Temple authorities by the name of Mathius in Capernaum. This Mathius was supposed to have been a friend of Matthew the disciple of Jesus and the former tax collector. Matthew told his friend, Mathius, the story about Jesus commanding Peter to go fishing and then paying the taxes with the coin found in the fish's mouth.

Mathius was so moved by the story that he kept the coin and hid it in a safe place in the floor of his home in Capernaum. Apparently he had made enemies of the Roman authorities for embezzling large amounts of tax money and they sought to have him put to death. Fearing for the life of his son, Mathius had him flee to Antioch, the home of his grandmother, Mathius' mother-in-law. Mathius and his wife were arrested on the day that his son fled to Antioch. They both were executed two days later. As the son fled, Mathius had him take the "fish coin" with him and commanded him to hide it in a safe place. Upon his arrival in Antioch, he hid the coin.

He remained in Antioch for the rest of his life, never disclosing where he had hidden the coin.

The coin remained hidden in Antioch until AD 365 when during the reign of Emperor Valens, Julian Sabas worked great miracles in Antioch as he refuted accusations that he was involved in Aryanism. One of the miracles attributed to Sabas was that he revealed the hiding place of the "fish coin". He later used the coin as an illustration to bring many people back to the true faith.

There was no explanation on how the coin ended up in the little museum. But by pushing the button a second time, I heard a modern paraphrase of Julian Sabas' message that he preached, using the coin as his illustration. I was amazed at Julian Sabas' depth of historical knowledge concerning the coin.

According to Sabas' sermon, Jesus and his disciples went to Capernaum in order to pay the special Temple tax (the tithe) that was demanded by the High Priest of all Jewish males. The tax was used to fund the seemingly never-ending Temple construction efforts. The deadline for the payment of this tax was December 30 of each year. The tax was actually due at the end of the month of Adar (March), but it had to be paid by December 30. This particular year was AD 29.

Jesus made it clear to Peter that he was not really required to pay a tax that was to be used to enhance a Temple that was supposed to be used for the worship of his Father. He decided to pay the tax so that no one would be offended and there would be no unnecessary trouble with the Galilean Jewish religious leaders. He paid it in the most unusual way. He told Peter to go down to the Sea of Galilee and to go fishing with a line and hook. This manner of fishing (this was the Persian method of fishing that had been adopted by the Roman aristocracy for recreational fishing) was foreign to Peter.

He was accustomed to fishing with a wide variety of nets that ranged from small personal nets to large multi-manned commercial fishing nets. Telling Peter to go fishing by using the fishing line and hook Persian method was a direct insult to his pride and ego, but it was necessary in order to teach Peter a lesson in non-compromising and absolute obedience. Angrily (Sabas said) Peter went down to the sea to do as Jesus had commanded. To his amazement the events unfolded just as Jesus had said. He cast in his hook and caught a fish. He opened the fish's mouth and there in his mouth was a coin, a *chrusous stater*. It was worth about 27 drachmas. Peter took the coin and paid the tax. Since the tax (tithe) was two drachmas per person, the coin was enough to pay for Jesus as well as each of his disciples.

How the coin got into the fish's mouth, is not known. Perhaps the fish had swallowed it after it had been thrown overboard by a rich merchant, or by a Greek priest of Poseidon, or a Roman priest of Neptune as a sacrifice to the god of the sea. Nevertheless it was in the fish's mouth. It was enough to pay the Temple tax and it taught Peter a very valuable lesson in obedience—that he must obey the command of Jesus regardless of how insulting it is, whether agreeable or not, or whether it is logical or not. Obedience without question or comment was what Jesus expected of Peter.

Although I was thankful that I had learned some background information regarding the coin, I was not sure whether I believed the story of the coin with regard to Sabas or whether I agreed with Sabas' conclusion that the main purpose for the coin experience was to teach Peter obedience. Sabas' conclusion was a supposition that I felt that I needed to think about for a while.

The day after Peter paid the Temple tax, Jesus and his disciples went down to the seashore. A great multitude followed him, so like he had done one time before when he taught from Peter's boat, he got into a boat and taught the people a number of parables from the boat, while they remained on shore (Matthew 13:1-52; Mark 4:1-32; Luke 8:5-18). These parables included the lesson of the sower, the tares, another lesson on the faith of a mustard seed, the lamp on a stand, leaven in a loaf of bread, household treasure, treasure in a field, the pearl of great price, casting out a net, and the householder.

While researching over the years, I have found dozens of different documents, essays, sermons, and books that focus on one or two of these parables, but it was not until I found a manuscript that had been written in 1167 by Peter Comestor, a priest at Norte Dame in Troyes, France, that I found a document that dealt with almost all of the parables spoken by Jesus at this winter time in Capernaum, seaside setting. I discovered a copy of the manuscript in a book while studying at the University of Southwestern Louisiana in Lafayette, Louisiana. Photocopies of Comestor's manuscript as well as other manuscripts had been bound in a volume entitled *The Folio of the Priests of Norte Dame—Troyes*. The original manuscripts are still housed at the church in Troyes.

The book was big and bulky, but not only did it have photocopies of the manuscript, but also an English translation, historical facts about the manuscript, cultural facts about the parables themselves, and the author's opinions regarding some of the parables. Peter Comestor's manuscript seemed to focus on the Matthew 13 setting of Jesus' teaching.

Comestor began by explaining the difference between the two kingdoms: the Kingdom of God and the Kingdom of Heaven.

The Kingdom of Heaven, he wrote, or literally "the kingdom from heaven or the kingdom that came down from heaven" was the kingdom about which both John the Baptist and Jesus proclaimed had come to pass or was at hand. It was the earthly kingdom that God the Father had planned to establish with the Messiah/Messias, Jesus, as the kingdom's monarch, at the time that Jesus began his ministry. However, by the time of Jesus' second year of ministry, it had become obvious that the physical and literal earthly Kingdom of (from) Heaven had been and would continue to be rejected by the people and that it could not be established as a physical identity with Jesus as king.

Comestor felt that it was at the time of Jesus' transfiguration that it was decided that Jesus' earthly Kingdom of (from) Heaven would from that time forward be a kingdom that would dwell within the hearts of those earthly inhabitants who accepted at that time and all who would accept from that time forward, Jesus as King and Lord. All of the parables spoken by Jesus relating to the Kingdom of Heaven were relative to this Kingdom of Heaven within the hearts of his followers.

The Kingdom of God describes the overall sovereign dominion of God the Father. This includes our universe and all therein, including the Kingdom of (from) Heaven. The most obvious difference between the two is that the Kingdom of God is not restricted to the earth and occupants of the earth like the Kingdom of (from) Heaven. It has no restrictions.

Comestor then turned his attention to the parables.

Although he began his dialogue on the parables with the parable about the tares, Peter first gave his opinion about sowing and reaping as recorded in Matthew 13:1-23.

Comestor wrote that there are three basic laws of nature concerning sowing and reaping: (1) you will reap what you sow; (2) you reap in a different season than you sow, and (3) you reap more than you sow. He then went on to explain what each meant in the life of an individual.

Comestor said that an established principle of God's nature is that we will reap what we sow. If we sow good seed, good fruit will grow and be reaped. If we sow bad seed, then bad will grow and be reaped. The unbeliever will reap the sinful seeds that he has sown for all of eternity. For this reason it seems sometimes to the believer that the unbelieving sinners get away with wrong doings and sinful acts during their life times. They will reap and they will pay, but their reaping is for eternity. But for the believer, we do not have an eternity to reap the seeds that we have sown, unless they are good seeds.

"For the sake of this lesson, I (Peter Comestor) will not discuss the good seeds that a believer sows, although they are far more fair to discuss. I instead will discuss only the bad seed that a believer sows and must reap during his lifetime.

"Because a believer," he continued, "Will not have all of eternity to pay for or reap the bad seed that he has sown, he only has this lifetime to reap the seeds that he has sown. This is why it seems that many times the good have to go through so much tragedy. It is because we must reap what we sow. That is a law of God established from the beginning of Adam's sin. So, because the believer has only a very short lifetime that he has been given to reap what has been sown, sometimes his sorrow in this life is unrelenting, because he will not have to reap it in his afterlife.

"Most times God does not pass individual judgment upon individual acts of the believer. Many times the judgment has been predetermined by the fact that a bad seed will grow and bad will be reaped. When it is reaped it will be many times worse than the initial sown seed, and it will be at a different time. Sometimes that different time will be one week from the time the seed was sown, sometimes two weeks, or two months, or maybe even six years. But however long it takes for the seed that was planted to grow, it will grow, it will come up in the life of the believer, and it will have to be harvested. The sorrow of that harvest will be so much greater than the seed that was planted. As an example, if I am angry with my brother and I lash out at him, then I plant a seed of anger and bitterness. That seed will grow and it will come up. When? I do not know, but it will come up. Let us say that six months later, the seed has grown and it is now ready to be harvested. You then have to harvest the seed that has grown. By harvesting, it may mean that many dozens of people become angry with you and lash out and ridicule you. So, you have harvested the seed that has grown, but it has grown to produce many times more anger and bitterness than you first planted.

"God always forgives us when we plant the bad seeds, but they still have to come up. The sin of planting has been forgiven, but the crop still has to grow and be harvested. Now, once the crop has been harvested, the believer has three choices. (1) He can harvest the crop, bundle it up, sit it in a corner, be depressed and disheartened because of the harvest, and never rise above his depression, in which state he is worthless for the kingdom. (2) He harvests the crop and looks at the harvest and says that it could not be helped, that it is just his nature, and he justifies the harvest and the planting, saying that he cannot change. By doing this, he plants the harvested crop all over again and down the road the seeds will come up again. But, this time it will be many times worse than the beginning. By doing this a few times the believer will have hundreds of times more sorrow than that he had planted in the beginning. (3) The last thing that he can do is to recognize that this hardship or trial or problem or misunderstanding or conflict is nothing more than the crop that he has to harvest resulting from the seeds that he had planted before. He gathers that harvest up and gives it all to God so that God can destroy the harvest. Admit what it is, and then give it to God for disposal."

After finishing his lesson on the law of sowing and reaping, Comestor began to explain Jesus' teaching regarding the kingdom of heaven as explained in the parable of the tares. He said that according to Jesus' own explanation (verse 38) the field in which seeds were sown, was the world. But Comestor felt that the word St. Jerome [translator of the Vulgate] translated *world*, was a misnomer. He felt the word should have been translated *church*. He said that Jesus would not contradict himself in his own parable. Considering the parable was relating to the kingdom of heaven, the field where the seed was sown had to represent not the world, or society, in general, but rather it represented the church or the church world. In essence, Jesus is saying that in the church world or within the ranks of Christianity, good seed or believers in and followers of Christ are in abundance. However, the enemy, Satan, has also sown bad seed or tares within the church world for the purpose of destroying the church.

Comestor then explained that as far back as ancient Assyria, conquerors sowed tares or weeds in the cultivated fields of their enemy. This was meant to destroy the crops of the enemy for perhaps years to come and to cause a famine among the enemy population. Both Alexander the Great and the Romans were notorious for doing this. The Romans used two kinds of tares. One was darnel (*lolium temulentum*) and the other was *zizania*. The *zizania* was the tare used most often by Pompey the Great, the conqueror of the East for Rome. So, most likely Jesus was referring to *zizania* in this parable.

"*Zizania* looked very much like wheat as it grew and the average person could not tell the difference between the wheat and the tares, *zizania*. Only the farmer who knew his wheat could tell the difference. As the tare grew, it would produce grain that looked very much like grains of wheat. But, as the *zizania* matured the grains would break open and release a black powdery fungus substance that was poisonous to the healthy wheat around them. Very quickly the healthy wheat grain would be eaten by the fungus leaving nothing but a dry empty husk.

"*Zizania* was also a parasite, getting its nourishment from a healthy wheat plant rather than from the soil. As the *zizania* plant grew, its root system would grow outward rather than down into the soil. It would wrap its roots around the roots of a healthy wheat plant, usually a young plant, and would actually 'feed' off of the nutrients that the wheat plant was pulling from the soil. Eventually the wheat plant would die because it had been robbed of all of its nourishment by the *zizania*. Upon the death of the wheat plant, the *zizania* would release its hold from the wheat plant that had died and would begin to grow outward once again until it came in contact with another wheat plant. The process would then be repeated again and again."

Comestor explained that Jesus was saying that in the kingdom of heaven, or the kingdom come down from heaven, the church world, there has been an infiltration of tares and spiritual parasites. The infiltration came from Satan while the church leaders—pastors, priests, and bishops—slept and were not in tune to the hazards of the enemy. Through their negligence the tares of the enemy were allowed to infiltrate. These enemies of the church, these tares, look spiritual and act like believers, but they are full of poison and bitterness. Unfortunately they are virtually undetectable until they destroy the spiritual life of a true believer. By then it is too late. However, these poisonous tares will be purged and they will receive their just reward, but not until the end of the age and not before they have damaged and ruined the spiritual lives of multiplied thousands of believers.

Comestor next described the parable of the mustard seed as recorded in Matthew 13:31-32. As I read Peter's description of what Jesus was trying to teach with the parable about the mustard seed I found that this part of Peter's argument seemed to be similar to information that I had collected about the mustard seed at

The Search

Texas A&I University. As I read Peter Comestor's account, I was amazed at how closely it followed what had been written by Laurence Justinian in the year 1430, yet Peter's was written in 1167, some 263 years before Justinian's record. I seemed that either Peter and Justinian used the same or similar source to obtain their information, or Justinian used Peter's information without crediting him. Whatever the case, Jesus used the parable to show that though the church world or the religious establishment may look strong and healthy from the outside, it will become corrupted from within and will become diseased so much that the birds of the air, representing evil or evil influences, will be able to take up residence within the system. Then by compromise the religious system or church world will adopt them as part of its own.

The next parable Jesus used to describe the kingdom of heaven was the parable of leaven recorded in Matthew 13:33. Comestor wrote that in this parable, the three measures of meal represent the church world whose identification is with The Trinity, the leaven represents sin and evil, and the woman represents the compromising church leadership. The meaning of the parable is that the church leadership will compromise the truth and will allow evil and sin to hide within its ranks, which in turn will infect and contaminate every area of the church.

The next parable that Comestor discussed was the one in which Jesus said the kingdom of heaven was like a treasure hid in a field, recorded in Matthew 13:44.

The parable had its roots in Greek history. Plato told this story about his teacher, Socrates, to his favorite pupil, Aristotle, who was the tutor of Alexander the Great. Plato said that Socrates discovered quite unexpectedly a treasure: that truth did exist and that moral virtue was essential for a perfect life. He then sold all that he had and bought the field in which he found the treasure. He forsook all and dedicated his entire life to the teaching and the preservation of that truth, or the preservation of that treasure. Unfortunately for Socrates, when he "bought the field" or dedicated his entire life to show his fellow Greeks the principle of the truth that he had discovered, he bought not only the treasure but also the weeds and thistles growing in the field. The weeds and thistles were his critics and enemies who eventually forced Socrates to take his life. Jesus used the well-known parable told by Plato to describe the kingdom of heaven. The kingdom of heaven is like a treasure that was discovered in the very midst of false religions, religious systems, and paganism. He gave all that he had to purchase the field, or the religious system, in which was buried the true treasure, the truth of his teachings. However, in the midst of the field that he purchased were the sins of weeds and thistles.

The next parable was similar to the parable about the treasure in a field. It was the parable of the pearl of great price recorded in Matthew 13:45-46. Instead of purchasing the place where the treasure was located, he purchased the treasure, or the pearl itself; implying that he had given all so that his truth would remain secure in the midst of the church.

The following parable recorded in Matthew 13:47-50, also describes how the church world is and has been infiltrated with all kinds of good and evil which will be separated from each other at the end of the age. At that time, the righteous and the unrighteous will be separated and each will receive their rewards or punishment, whichever is applicable.

The final parable about which Peter Comestor commented was recorded in Matthew 13:51-52. With this parable Jesus was saying that the kingdom of heaven, or his kingdom in the hearts of his followers, would be one that had a mixture of Godly truths. Some truths would be from the Law and the prophets while other truths would be those that he had introduced. They are found in both the Old and the New Testaments.

This concluded Peter Comestor's comments on the parables taught by Jesus in Capernaum in the winter of AD 29 and recorded in Matthew 13.

Not long after this teaching, at the end of December, AD 29, Jesus and his disciples entered a ship in order to sail to the other side of the Sea of Galilee. Again they are confronted by a terrible storm on the lake (Matthew 8:26-27; Mark 4:35-41; Luke 8:23-25). Jesus calmed the storm. But when they arrived on the other side, they were confronted by a demonic that has come to be called, Legion (Mark 5:1-21; Luke 8:27-40). Although this confrontation with the man who came to be called Legion did not take place until January, AD 30, because it was part of a story that began in December, AD 29, I will include it in AD 29, Jesus' fourth year of ministry.

I was shown supporting documentation concerning these events by Dr. Fredrick Koffman, director of the Swiss Guard Museum in Schwyz, Switzerland. Schwyz is a predominately Catholic town that regularly supplied the Vatican with the world-famous Swiss Guard.

The ancient manuscript that Dr. Koffman showed me had been written by Martin of Braga in the 6th century. Martin had served as Bishop of Dumium as well as Bishop of Braga. Although Martin of Braga was reputed to have authored several important works, his most enduring writing was a collection of thirteen biographical sketches that he had entitled *Portraits*. The manuscript that Dr. Koffman showed me was a small fragment of that original document.

The manuscript was written on parchment in Latin. The biographic sketch was the historical portrait of the man in the Decapolis who came to be called Legion. The subject included the time from Jesus' calming of a storm on the Sea of Galilee up to his confrontation with the man Legion.

Martin said that late in the afternoon of either December 30 or 31st of AD 29 or January 1 of AD 30, Jesus decided to take his disciples to the other side of the Sea of Galilee. (Clement of Alexandria said that the event occurred on either December 30th or 31st but Zaccheus the Elder of Ezarum said that it occurred on January 1st AD 30).

Once it was discovered that Jesus and his disciples wanted to go to the other side, they were invited by the Roman military commander to ride on one of the massive troop supply-transports that was being taken to the other side (a privilege that was only granted to Roman citizens and to those accompanying the Roman citizen or to honored and respected friends of Roman citizens). The transport that Jesus and his disciples were sailing on was one in a convoy of twelve transports that were sailing to the other side. Ten transports were filled with supplies and two were carrying replacement troops for the 10th Legion stationed in the Decapolis. Although the story of this event is recorded in both the Gospels of Mark (4:35-41 and 5:1-20) and Luke (8:23-39), Martin chose to concentrate on the Mark setting.

The convoy of Roman supply transports left the western shore of the Sea of Galilee at sundown. Soon after leaving port, a physically exhausted Jesus went below deck and went to sleep in the ship's troop sleeping-quarters. While he slept, an unexpected storm suddenly blew up. Clement of Alexandria claimed that this was the "bubbling up of the sea" that historically took place on the Sea of Galilee on December 30. However, Zaccheus the Elder said that this was a secondary squall that was spawned on January 1, in the aftermath of the December 30 "bubbling up of the sea." What is known for certain is that the storm appeared suddenly, catching them all completely off-guard.

No doubt the huge ship began to rock to and fro as monster waves began to break over the sides, causing the disciples to fear for their lives. However, Jesus seemed to be unaffected by the storm as he continued to sleep.

Finally the fear felt by the disciples so overwhelmed them that they ran downstairs and awakened Jesus with a question which was in reality an accusation, *"Master, carest thou not that we parish?"*

The question seemed to imply that they feared that perhaps God had sent the storm as punishment for something Jesus had done, or maybe because he had accepted the invitation to sail with Roman troops. It was within reason to assume that in order for God's wrath to be appeased, Jesus would have to be thrown overboard, much like in the case of Jonah, with whom God had been angry enough to send a storm that could have sunk the ship that he was on and destroyed all of the inhabitants.

It is possible that their unspoken comment was, "Jesus if you care about us, you would not have displeased God. Now, you must do something about it or else we will perish; even if that means throwing yourself into the sea."

Upon awaking, Jesus knew what they meant and what their judgmental question implied. He became aggravated and corrected them harshly for their lack of confidence in him and their doubts concerning whether he cared for them. After the harsh rebuke, he went up to the deck and calmed the storm.

Once the storm quieted, the disciples became frightened because of their accusations and Jesus' subsequent rebuke of them. They were more terrified of his power and authority than of the storm that he had just calmed. This fear also extended to the on board Roman troops and their commanders.

The convoy came to shore on the far southeast side of the sea.

The most dominate city in that area of Gaulanitis/the Decapolis was the Roman occupied Greek/Syrian mountain city of Gadara (Mark 5:1). The city was located about 10 to 12 miles inland from the seashore in the Decapolis. Gaulanitis was the Syrian district of the Roman province of Coela Syria; the Decapolis was the independent Greek area of that province. The border of Gaulanitis and the Decapolis was just north of the city of Gadara. Hence Gadara had both Syrian and Greek inhabitants, as well as a very large population of Romans (no Jewish inhabitants—they were not allowed to live in either the city of Gadara or in the area surrounding Gadara), who were the friends and family of the Roman 10th Legion under whose military authority the province was governed. The 10th Legion had the effigy of a wild boar on its standard.

Within the 10 to 12 mile distance between the seashore and the city of Gadara, were hundreds of hills and cliffs that contained caves that had been used as tombs for hundreds of years. At this time, they served not only as tombs but also as hideouts for the many anti-Roman rebels who had unofficially declared "war" on the Roman military.

As soon as Jesus stepped foot on shore, a maniac who lived in the tomb caves, came running out from his tomb home to challenge him. The maniac was suffering from *lycanthropy*, or werewolf disease. It was the same disease from which King Nebuchadnezzar of Babylon had suffered centuries before.

Martin then asked a thought provoking question; yet he provided no answer for the question, "How did this man know that Jesus had arrived? Jesus may have been many, perhaps 10 or even 12, miles away from this man, yet as soon as Jesus stepped foot on the shore, he knew about it and ran out to challenge him."

After asking the question without giving an answer, Martin returned to Mark's account.

Martin said that no one really knows who this man was. Perhaps he was one of the rebels who occupied some of the caves. Perhaps he was a resident of Gadara who had been confined to the cave tombs by the citizens of the city.

Alexus of Sepphoris (14 BC – AD 68), the Roman mayor of the city of Sepphoris/Beth-shan from AD 25 to AD 44, a man who considered himself a learned historian, wrote in his *The Legion of the Boar*, a history of the Roman 10th Legion written in AD 62, that the locally-known maniac was a man by the name of Marcelus. His healing by Jesus caused quite a stir among the high command of the Roman 10th Legion.

Marcelus had been an officer in the 10th Legion. During the Jewish rebel uprising of AD 29, he went mad and became a wild man. For no apparent reason he began to kill and to violently mutilate everyone and everything in sight, both man and animal, screaming day and night that he was encompassed by "demons of evil."

The Roman military police imprisoned him in a narrow cave near the city of Gadara, chaining him naked to the inner wall of the cave. Twice a week they fed Marcelus a whole pig, which he devoured raw. Also about twice a week they would have to re-chain him to the inner wall of the cave because he would break loose from his chains.

Alexus said that Marcelus would scream in anguish continually, day and night, and would break free of his chains and would run into the walls of the cave in an effort to kill himself. Locally he became known by the name of Legion because it was claimed by the locals that he had evil spirits equal to the number of troops that made up the Roman 10th Legion.

Jesus confronted this man, who Mark said was demon possessed and cast out the demons.

Faced with the horror of having no place to go or having no one to possess, the demons asked permission from Jesus to go into a herd of pigs that were grazing on the near-by hillside. Tradition says that the pigs were feeding so close to the city of Gadara that the townspeople heard the tormented squeals of the pigs when the demons entered the pigs. If so, it means that the pigs were grazing a good 8 to 10 miles from the seashore.

Jesus gave the demons permission to possess the herd of pigs that numbered about 2,000. The pigs became so terrified that they went completely insane and ran violently the 8 to 10 miles to the sea and drowned.

The citizens of Gadara were so upset with the loss of their pigs that they told Jesus to leave their region, because he was responsible for the destruction of their livelihood. Perhaps they were afraid of what the Roman military commander would do to the residents once he discovered that 2,000 of the pigs that they were raising for food for the 10th Legion had been destroyed. Such destruction under normal circumstances would have been justification for the city's total destruction by the occupying Roman army. However, these were not normal circumstances.

According to Alexus, the commander of the 10th Legion was one of the officers that had been an eyewitness to Jesus' calming the storm just a few hours earlier. Therefore, he dared not challenge Jesus over this incident. Instead, he encouraged Jesus and his disciples to leave the region, citing that for the time being, it would probably be best.

Marcelus asked Jesus if he could join him, but Jesus told him to remain in the Decapolis and tell the residents of the area what great things God had done for him. Marcelus did such a good job of evangelizing the region on Jesus' behalf that a few months later when he returned to the area, Jesus had one of the greatest cooperative responses of his entire ministry.

Alexus said that after his deliverance, Marcelus rejoined the 10th Legion and became an excellent officer. He would eventually command the Legion in the Decapolis and he became the first true Roman evangelist who stated publicly, the message of Jesus.

In AD 60, Alexus continued, Marcelus was transferred to the court of Porcius Festus in Caesarea Maritima. There, Marcelus met Paul, a Jewish Roman citizen of Tarsus who was being held in chains by Festus. Paul had converted to Christianity and claimed to be a disciple of Jesus. Marcelus gave Paul special privileges while he was being held in the imperial prison of Festus.

XIX

FIFTH YEAR OF MINISTRY

(AD 30)

The next major event in Jesus' life was the raising of Jarius' daughter as recorded in Mark (5:22-43). It took place in the winter of AD 30, about two years after the raising of the Herodian's daughter. Jesus and his disciples had just returned from Gadara in the Decapolis where he had healed a man of demon possession. This man has become known as Legion.

With their return to Capernaum, Jesus and his disciples were welcomed by a huge crowd of joyous people. Jarius, a ruler, or an official ritual overseer of the people in a local synagogue, was among those who met him as he docked.

Upon Jesus' exit from the ship, Jarius immediately approached him and told him that his 12-year-old daughter was sick and was dying. Jesus did not answer him or speak to him; he merely turned and he and his disciples began to follow Jarius to his house. A huge crowd followed them as they made their way to the house. For details concerning this miracle see the chapter entitled **Third Year of Ministry**.

Not long after the miracle of raising Jarius' daughter, scribes and Pharisees who had come to Capernaum from Jerusalem, approached Jesus and began to complain to him about his disciples—seems quite ironic that the numerous times that the Jerusalem Pharisees and scribes were upset at Jesus, instead of confronting him, they complained about or to his disciples; they were either afraid of Jesus or were not sure how he would respond—not washing their hands before they ate.

This washing involved scooping the water up in their cupped hands and letting the water run down the arms and drip off of the elbows. This was a tradition established by the scribes in Jerusalem some 100 years before this time.

By this time the tradition of the scribes was generally accepted by them to be more important than the words of the prophets and the Law. Hemjal the Third, the great 1st century BC Jewish Rabban said, "The words of the elders as recorded by the scribes is more weightier than the words of the prophets."

But his assertion was only one of several such contentions recorded in the Talmuds. Dishonoring the tradition of washing hands and the ritual that accompanied the tradition was considered a grave iniquity to the Jerusalem Pharisees. So much so, that these visitors from Jerusalem could not let it rest. They felt compelled to confront Jesus on this great iniquity of dishonoring the traditions of the elders.

Jesus did not make excuses for his disciples; instead he turned the tables on the Pharisees. He told them that they were just as guilty as his disciples, because they choose to keep the traditions of the elders but dishonor the commandments of God.

He then told the people that had assembled around him to be careful what they are taught by the Pharisees because they are like the blind leading the blind. They, who know nothing, are trying to teach those who know nothing. Eating with unwashed hands does not defile the spirit man but rather listening to the teachings of the Pharisees defiles the spirit man.

Soon after this confrontation, Jesus felt that he needed to leave Capernaum and go someplace where he and his disciples could rest without being a public spectacle or without having to minister to multitudes. He decided to bring them to the most unexpected place that he could think of bringing them—Phoenicia, and in particular the cities of Tyre and Sidon (Matthew 15:21-29; Mark 7:24-31).

While researching at Wheaton College in Wheaton, Illinois, I was studying one of the many biographies written about Charles Albert Blanchard (Charles Blanchard was president of Wheaton College for 43 years), that the college library had housed in a special school history section, when I ran across a statement that interested me. It said that when Charles was pastor of Chicago Avenue Church in Chicago from 1891 to 1893, he had written three long treatises about the life of Jesus, but that all had been lost except a small portion of the second treatise. The small portion dealt with Jesus' trip to Phoenicia. The statement went on to say that the surviving portion of the treatise was reproduced in the appendix of the volume that I was reading. So, I turned to the appendix and read Blanchard's account. It was so fascinating that I read it twice before I began taking notes.

Blanchard began the surviving portion of his treatise by introducing Jesus' journey to Tyre and Sidon.

The event of Jesus and his twelve disciples traveling to Phoenicia on the Mediterranean coast and what is now Lebanon, in April of the year AD 30, was recorded in both Matthew 15 and in Mark 7. However, Blanchard referred to the Mark setting only.

> *"And from thence He arose, and went into the borders of Tyre and Sidon, and entered into a house, and would have no man know it: but He could not be hid. For a certain woman, whose young daughter had an unclean spirit, heard of Him, and came and fell at His feet: the woman was a Greek, a Syrophenician by nation; and she besought Him that He would cast forth the devil of her daughter. But Jesus said unto her, 'Let the children first be filled: for it is not meet to take the children's bread, and to cast it unto the dogs.' And she answered and said unto Him, 'Yes, Lord: yet the dogs under the table eat of the children's crumbs.' And He said unto her, 'For this saying go thy way; the devil is gone out of thy daughter.' And when she was come to her house, she found the devil gone out, and the daughter laid upon the bed"* (Mark 7:24-30).

The port cities of Tyre and Sidon were the principle cities of Greek/Roman and Greek/Phoenician dominated Phoenicia. They were located on the Mediterranean coast and were about 20 miles apart. Tyre, the closer of the two to the Galilee, was about 40 miles northwest of Nazareth. Both served as important seaports for Rome, but Tyre was probably the more important of the two. Tyre had a long and distinguished history, and had served as an important seaport colony for a variety of empires. It was also an independent state for almost two thousand years, up to the time of Jesus' visit. In addition, both Tyre and Sidon were centers of worship for the

Roman deities Venus, Isis (adopted from Egypt), Mercurius (Mercury), and Neptune as well as numerous other Roman and Phoenician deities.

The Romans called the residents of this area of Phoenicia *Syrophoenicians*, in order to distinguish them from the Phoenicians of the North African coast, who were called *Libyophoenicians*. The vast majority of the population was Greek, Greek/Roman, or Greek/Phoenician and was very pagan. In Tyre, the center of worship for Mercury, the priestesses and female devotees who dedicated themselves to the worship of Mercury, together with the associated immoral and sexually perverse rituals, were, according to Petronius in his *Trimalchio's Feast*, called *Syrophenician* or *Syrophenicias* by the local inhabitants. This was the name used to identify the woman who approached Jesus about her possessed daughter recorded in Mark 7 and Matthew 15.

Because of the intense hatred and contempt the Syrophoenicians had for the Jews and the Jews for them, the Roman authorities ruled that no Jew (unless the Jew was a Roman citizen) was allowed to enter any city or village in all of Phoenicia except for the cities of Tyre and Sidon, and then only if the Jew was a male merchant. The ruling was made to preserve the peace. However, even as a merchant, the Jew was not permitted to stay for more than two days, or else the Roman authorities would imprison him. The only exception or exemption to this ordinance was by order and special approval of the highest ranking Roman military authority, as well as the highest-ranking Roman civil authority in Phoenicia. According to Philo, this approval to non-Romans was granted only two times from the conquest by Pompey to the death of Tiberias (a period of almost one hundred years).

It seemed that for some unspecified reason, Jesus felt it necessary to hide out for a while and that neither the Galilee, Judaea, Peraea, nor the Decapolis was where he and his disciples needed to be at that time. He had to find a place that was so inconceivable that there would be no thought that he could possibly be there. He could have gone north into the mountains or south into the desert, but instead he chose the most illogical of all locations and destinations: the most morally depraved region in all of the eastern Mediterranean—Phoenicia, and by far the most corrupt and profligate region in all of Phoenicia was the region of Tyre and Sidon.

So, crossing the rugged spurs of the Anti-Lebanon Mountains, he and his disciples crossed the border into Phoenicia.

Jesus and his disciples stayed in the region for at least two months and perhaps three, so he had to have been either a Roman citizen or he had been granted permission to stay in the region by the Roman authorities. There is no way that he could have otherwise stayed for such a long period of time.

Jesus and his disciples stayed with a friend, probably in Tyre (although they might have stayed for a time in Sidon also), and except for the one incident with the lady recorded in Matthew 15 and Mark 7, their presence seems to have been kept at least semi-secret.

How the woman discovered Jesus' whereabouts is not known, but it is obvious that she told no one of his presence. So, except for the woman, her daughter perhaps, and the Roman authorities, Jesus' furtive seclusion remained non-compromised for as long as he stayed in the region.

How long Jesus and his disciples had been in the region before the woman approached them is not known. The fact that the woman was called a *Syrophenician* indicates that she was a priestess or at least a female ceremonial devotee affiliated with the massive temple of Mercury located in Tyre. Therefore, when she approached Jesus, they were most likely in the city of Tyre.

The religious devotees or sacred courtesan dogs (as they were called by Gabriel ben Haddiel, a renowned rabboni of the 1st century AD, who lived in Damascus at the time of Jesus' ministry, but who came to greatly admire Jesus) were scorned and held in contempt by the majority of the Jewish population. Most Jews had never seen a Syrophenician, yet they held them in contempt purely because of their reputation, calling them dogs or ravenous vultures. "After all," they probably reasoned, "these vile creatures were nothing more than religious harlots who indulged in all manner and kinds of immorality and sexual perversion in dedication to a pagan god, Mercury. So they should expect to be disdained by civilized people."

This same attitude seemed to be in evidence with Jesus and his disciples. Perhaps it was an inherent animosity that seemed to naturally come out.

On the other hand, maybe in Jesus' case he was exasperated because he had been discovered, which threatened his and the disciples' secret time apart.

Whatever the case, when the woman approached Jesus requesting help for her daughter who was at home and was possessed by an evil spirit, both Jesus and the disciples treated her contemptuously—at first. In fact, Jesus just ignored her until his disciples asked him to send her away. It was after this that Jesus acknowledged her presence and when he did speak to her, he addressed her with the typical contempt that a Jew had for a woman of her vocation. He told her that it was not right for him to share the blessings of God that come from him with dogs.

The woman likely anticipated Jesus' answer and was prepared with a comeback that so impressed him that he not only spoke to her in admiration but he also healed her daughter from demon possession—long distance. In fact, Jesus spoke about this woman having great faith. He only said this about three people, and none were Jews. Two were centurions in Capernaum and the other was this immoral devotee to the god Mercury from Tyre. However, all came to him with the absolute faith that he would meet their individual needs, and they refused to allow doubt to overrule their confidence in him.

The age of the daughter is unknown nor does scripture say how she became demon possessed, but considering that it was a normal practice for a Syrophenician to dedicate her children to the god Mercury (while in the midst of a wild and frenzied ritual that was probably a squalid celebration of depravity and evil that openly invited and welcomed demon possession of both the participants and those who were offered), it is quiet reasonable to assume that the daughter became demon possessed during a dedication ceremony. Hence, the mother knew that her daughter was demon possessed and had no hope for deliverance or of recovery. Then she heard that Jesus was in town, and Jesus did not leave her in despair. He healed the daughter by delivering her from the evil spirit.

That ended the portion of Blanchard's treatise that had survived and had been reprinted in the appendix of the biography.

Nothing else is recorded about the two or three months that Jesus and his disciples spent in Phoenicia.

The next we hear about Jesus is when he and his disciples left Phoenicia, traveled to the Sea of Galilee, and sailed to the Decapolis, where just months earlier he had been asked to leave, after healing the man who came to be called Legion. There in the Decapolis, Jesus ministered to and healed all who came to him, including a man who was deaf and could not speak (Matthew 15:29-31; Mark 7:31-37).

It was while touring the Stuttgard State Gallery, a gallery that was known for its medieval paintings, sculptures, and manuscripts, in Stuttgard, Germany that I discovered a painting that authenticated the healing of the deaf-mute in the Decapolis.

The museum had an impressive collection of Medieval European art, especially French and German. But what made the museum unique was that the entire museum was divided into numerous small rooms. In each room was displayed from four to as many as eight paintings, depending on the size of the paintings. All of the paintings in the room seemed to relate to one another. An individual whom they called a Museum Art Rectorite serviced each display room. These rectories were positioned in the rooms to answer questions and to explain details relating to the paintings on display in the particular room that they serviced.

The room that impressed me the most was called the Room of Miracles. In it were displayed five paintings that depicted various miracles of healing attributed to Jesus and recorded in the Gospels. One painting dating back to 1617 was done by the French painter, Mureaux Martise, showing Jesus looking like he was about to spit into the mouth of a man who was standing in front of him with his mouth open. The caption below the painting read, *Jesus heals a mute in Decapolis*. The painting interested me so I asked the room rectorite to explain the scene to me. He was delighted to comply with my request.

He went into great detail explaining the event about which the painting depicted, including the historical background and beliefs of the day (Jesus' day). As he talked, I sat down on a small leather padded bench in the room and began to take notes.

The rectorite began by explaining the event depicted in the painting. "The event itself is taken from the Gospel of Mark 7:32-37 in our current King James translation English Bible," the rectorite explained.

> *"And they bring unto him one that was deaf, and had an impediment in his speech; and they beseech him to put his hands upon him. And he took him aside from the multitude, and put his fingers into his ears, and spit, and touched his tongue; and looking up to heaven, he sighed, and saith unto him 'Ephphata,' that is 'Be opened.' And straightway his eyes were opened, and the string of his tongue was loosed, and he spake plain. And he charged them that they should tell no man: but the more he charged them, so much the more a great deal they published it; and were beyond measure astonished, saying, he hath done all things well; he maketh both the deaf to hear, and the dumb to speak."*

After quoting the passage in Mark 7, the rectorite gave a brief comment about the painting itself followed by an explanation of the event in Jesus' life that the painting represented.

"There was nothing of note relative to the history of the painting, except that for some reason it had been banished by the church in France back in the 17th century. Had it not been for the efforts of the Duke of Lorinesheim the painting would have been destroyed long ago. In 1816, the Duke, going against a direct order of the church to destroy the painting, took it to his home near Nancy and preserved it.

"After Jesus and his disciples had spent a few months in the region of Tyre and Sidon, they left there and traveled all the way through the Galilee and across the Sea of Galilee to the Decapolis, where just months before Jesus had been asked to leave because of his conflict with the locals over the healing of the man possessed with demons. Jesus had sent the demons into a herd of pigs, which ultimately led to their demise.

"The man that was healed of demon possession, the one whom we now call Legion, wanted to go with Jesus, but Jesus had not allowed him to come. Rather, he told him to stay in the Decapolis and to tell the good news about Jesus.

"Obviously, the man who came to be called Legion had been successful in his mission on behalf of Jesus, for when Jesus landed in the Decapolis, probably near Gadara, he was met with open-arms by the people. He responded by ministering to the people and healing all who came to him.

"One of those brought to him for healing was a man who was deaf and could not speak. Why this particular man's healing is recorded and not any of the other healings is quite significant—the man was a Zoroastrian priest.

"In the Decapolis lived a vast array of people groups and cultures, the least of which were Jewish. In fact, only a small percentage of the people, probably less than 1 percent, were of Jewish ancestry, and few, if any, of these people were active participants in Judaism. Most residents were Greek, Syrian, or Roman, and their religious beliefs were a combination of Syrian Zoroastrianism and Greek traditional, with a major emphasis on Syrian Zoroastrianism."

The rectorite continued by describing a practice that was performed by Zoroastrian priests on a Zoroastrian priest, if the priest was afflicted with '*a sensory affliction*' (so called by the Zoroastrian priests), or a disease that affects one or more of the sensory functions (sight, hearing, smell, touch, and taste) He said, "Since Zoroastrianism was the dominate form of worship and religious practice, it seemed quite logical for Jesus to capitalize on the man's (who was most likely a Zoroastrian priest) faith in that form of religious worship and to use practices and rituals to which the priest could relate, in order to bring healing to him.

"The common healing practice of the priests was typical for all priests who were blind, deaf, or mute. The priest who was afflicted stood in silence before the priest who was performing the healing rite. The priest who was performing the ritual would then lick his finger and touch the eyes, ears, nose, and tongue of the priest who was coming to be healed. The priest who needed to be healed would then look into the eyes of the priest who was performing the healing ritual and would open his mouth. The priest who was performing the ritual would then spit into the mouth of the priest who wanted to be healed and would look up into the sky and say in the ancient Chaldean/Persian language, *Ephphata.* Which means, *'Open now.'* He then would stick his fingers into the ears of the deaf, pinch the tongue of the mute, or pull the eye lids of the blind while saying a prayer invoking the will of Innanu, the son of Aramuk, the invisible Father God of all gods, for the person's healing.

"Jesus followed this same procedure. Not because he needed to follow a ritual; but rather, it was for the benefit of the priest who wanted to be healed, in order to relate to him and to encourage his faith to be released. However, when Jesus got to the part of the ritual where he suppose to plead to Innanu, he instead healed the priest himself, signifying that *he*, Jesus, was the divine one and that *he alone* possessed the power that the Zoroastrian priests could only invoke. *He* (Jesus) and *only he* had the power of life and restoration. Jesus showed the priest that he truly was divine and that he should be honored, respected, and praised.

"Jesus then instructed the priest who was healed and those who were witnesses to the healing not to tell anyone about the healing procedures that he used to heal him. Jesus was not saying that they should not tell others that he healed the priest, nor was he trying to keep the healing a secret. That would have been impossible because he had already healed all who had come to him. Rather, Jesus did not want them to tell how he (Jesus) had done it. He either did not want to be identified with the Zoroastrian priests or he did not want any attention directed toward him, which could have added fuel to the fire of speculation that he was The Theophus. But whatever the case, Jesus did not want them to tell others how the Zoroastrian priest was healed."

After the rectorite finishing explaining the painting, he asked me if I had any questions. I had never heard this explanation before. There were hundreds of questions to ask, but none came to mind, so I shook my head no, and thanked the rectorite for his time and his explanation. The rectorite then excused himself and walked away. I remained seated on the bench, staring at the painting, trying to comprehend what I had just been told and how different this rectorite's explanation was than what I had always believed to be true. I thought that this man was a Jewish man and that his healing was no different than hundreds of others that Jesus had healed. But if that was true, then why out of hundreds of others was he and his healing recorded and the others were not? There had to be something special and unique about the healing of this man. To suggest that this man was a Zoroastrian priest, would certainly qualify as special and unique.

Finally after a while, perhaps another hour or so, I left the room and continued touring the rest of the museum. However, there was nothing more there that I felt could help my research efforts.

While in the Decapolis at this time, Jesus repeated a miracle that he had performed a year previous when he fed 5,000 laborers at the Galilean *basquaiia* (see the chapter entitled **Fourth Year of ministry**). This time the miracle was performed at the Decapolis *basquaiia.*

In the two-volume set in which I found information about Jesus' feeding of the 5,000, I found information about his feeding of the 4,000. It was a two-volume set entitled *Palestinian Travels*, written in 1786 by the Scottish adventurer, Devin Allkin.

The first *basquaiia*, or a large flat granite rock surface used for drying fish, was the *basquaiia* in the Galilee where the miracle of the 5,000 was performed. The second *basquaiia* described by Allkin was the one located in the Decapolis where Jesus' miracle of feeding 4,000 took place. This event is recorded in Matthew 15:30-38 and Mark 8:1-9.

This *basquaiia* was smaller than the one in the Galilee near Tiberias, but it was used for the same purpose, was controlled by the Roman military, and was used exclusively by the Roman 10th Legion which was principally stationed in the Decapolis area. Dried fish from this *basquaiia* was not exported; it was used exclusively by the Roman military stationed in that area. It too was guarded around the clock by a guard of 100 soldiers.

The first feeding, the feeding of the 5,000, took place in the spring of AD 29, this second one took place a year later in April of AD 30. This particular *basquaiia* was located near the Yarmuk River, just north of Gadara, not far from where Jesus was ministering. Jesus was probably ministering to the multitudes near the banks of the Yarmuk River, but the *basquaiia* was located on the hillside overlooking the river. So, it was only a five or ten minute walk from the river to the *basquaiia*.

Whereas with the feeding of the 5,000 Jesus was ministering primarily to Jewish laborers of the Galilee, on this occasion he and his disciples were ministering to the Greek/Roman/Syrian residents of the Decapolis, many of who were probably Roman officials or military men.

By the time of this miracle, Jesus had been ministering for three straight days to the multitudes, which numbered 4,000 plus women and children, making a total of probably near 10,000 or more. It is unclear whether they were without food for the entire three days, or they ran out of food and on that day, the day that they had become hungry.

But whatever the case, when the disciples suggested that he send the people away so they could buy food, he was concerned that they would collapse before they had a chance to buy food. So, he led the people up the small hill containing the *basquaiia* and had them set down. There he again, as he had done a year before, feed the people.

Again, it is not clear how and under what circumstances this miracle was performed. If he took a few fish and a few loaves of bread and multiplied them in order that thousands could eat until they were filled, then the physical miracle is self-evident. But if he took the food that he had left and broke it, as was culturally accepted, signifying that he was preparing to eat with the multitude and then used his influence to convince the Roman authorities to release the food from their stores there at the basquaiia (again at this basquaiia, as with the basquaiia in the Galilee, Herod had set-up bread storage tents), then that too would have been a political miracle of equal standing.

We don't know how long this took, but after feeding the people Jesus sent the crowds away and then he and his disciples crossed the Sea of Galilee and landed in Dalmanutha, just south of Magdala, between Magdala and Tiberias (Matthew 15:34-39; Mark 8:5-10).

It is not recorded how long Jesus stayed in Dalmanutha, for the next time we read about him he has just arrived in Bethsaida, just northeast of the northern shore of the Sea of Galilee. The last fixed date of Jesus' chronology was in April AD 30 when he fed the 4,000. The next fixed date is September AD 30 when he went to Jerusalem for the Feast of Tabernacles. So, it was between April and September that Jesus went to Bethsaida. In Bethsaida Jesus healed a blind man (Mark 8:22-26) and a boy possessed by an evil spirit (Mark 9:15-29).

I found information about Jesus' healing of the blind man from Bethsaida at the Antalya Museum in Antalya, Turkey.

It was while I was studying the museum's small collection of Christian art objects and Christian manuscripts, that I saw an ancient manuscript that caught my eye. There were no identifying plates with the displayed material so I had to find a museum custodian in order to get information about the manuscript. The young lady custodian I found spoke perfect English and said that she would be honored to help me in response to my request. As we walked back to the Christian section, she introduced herself as Simir Othman. She was a student at the University of Istanbul, but during the summer she worked at the museum. When I commented on how well she spoke English she said that her father was a professor of Turkish history at Heilman University in England, and that she had received both her elementary and secondary education in England.

I pointed out the document to her. She responded by telling me the history of the manuscript and explained it's content.

The manuscript was written in Greek by Anthanasius the Athonite, who lived from 920 AD to 1000 AD. He was a professor at Constantinople and later founded the celebrated monasteries located on Mount Athos, which are still active to this day.

The manuscript itself was written as an answer to a question to him by one of his students. The student's father had developed a disease that left him blind. The student had prayed for God to restore his sight, but it had not been restored. It seems the student had made comments to his professor, Anthamasius, that God's son chose to heal only when it was convenient for him and only when he would receive the praise of men by performing the healing. The manuscript was Anthanasius' answer to the student.

The manuscript itself had been discovered rolled up inside a sealed pottery jar, which had been buried in an 11th century Christian grave. It was discovered in 1937 during excavations at Konya. It had been brought to the Antalya Museum in 1958.

Simir gave me permission to take the manuscript to a small study room adjacent to the manuscript display room. She accompanied me to the room. There, with Simir's translating help, I read Anthanasius' letter and make paraphrased notes.

Anthanasius started his letter by thanking the student for his question and his observations concerning Jesus' healings. He then referred to the Gospel of Mark and quoted a portion that I recognized as chapter 8, verses 22-26 of Mark.

> *"And he cometh to Bethsaida; and they bring a blind man unto him, and besought him to touch him. And he took the blind man by the hand, and led him out of the town; and when he spit on his eyes, and put his hands upon him, he asked him if he saw ought. And he looked up, and said, I see men*

as trees, walking. After that he put his hands again upon his eyes, and made him look up: and he was restored, and saw every man clearly." (Mark 8:22-26).

Anthanasius began his explanation by first describing Bethsaida and the people who lived in Bethsaida. He then went into a description telling about the form of worship that was practiced by most of the residents of Bethsaida and how Jesus showed that he was the fulfillment of their object of worship. He then explained the healing and concluded by explaining how healing is an act of grace rather than an act of faith or a reward to show that God hears prayer.

He wrote that Bethsaida was a Roman city that had a population mix of predominately Greeks, Parthanians, Persians, and Syrians with a few Jews. The occupation of most of its residents centered on the fishing industry. They fished, packed, dried, pickled, salted, exported, cleaned, and sold fish.

In Bethsaida, Judaism was such a minority religion that it was, for the most part, non-existent except for a small handful of devotees. In fact, Anthanasius continued, Judaism and the Jewish religion was so insignificant that it was not even acknowledged when Herod Agrippa made a report to Nero concerning the religious practices of the region.

The primary religious observances were divided between the Greek and Roman religions, Greek philosophy, and Zoroastrianism, with Zoroastrianism claiming the lion's share. There were two Zoroastrian temples in Bethsaida at this time. The larger of the two was used for public worship. The smaller temple was attached to a school for Zoroastrian priests. There they learned the arts and performance of prophecy, physical healing, emotional and spiritual healing, and exorcism. The temple attached to the school was a private temple used by the priests in their special education rituals.

Once every 100 days each priest would go into the streets of the city and seek out and select two residents—one who needed to be healed of a physical ailment and one who needed to be healed emotionally. This emotionally handicapped person could be insane, depressed, possessed by evil spirits, or suffer from any number of mind (emotional or psychological) problems. After they were selected, the priests would bring them to the priests' private temple. There they became the object on which the priest performed his rituals. For this reason, the local Roman authorities had to place a continuous guard around the temple, day and night, on the day that the residents were selected, to prevent the temple from being over run by those (and their friends and family members) who wanted to be healed of their ailments. This mad rabble and their deranged rush to the priest's temple could very well be the cause for Jesus' condemnation of Bethsaida recorded in the Gospel of Matthew (11:21).

While the priests performed their rituals, the doors of the temple were closed and sealed. No one was allowed into the temple except the priests and their ritual subjects. Outside however, hundreds would set-up an all-day and all-night vigil that lasted the entire six days that the rituals inside were being performed. This crowd generally became unruly, unrestrained, and licentious as the days passed and the vigil usually turned into a drunken debauchery.

If a priest was successful in performing a healing, the person who had been healed was presented to the crowd waiting outside of the temple. The one healed would then be honored and showered with gifts and exaltation. In addition, the priest who had performed the healing would be exalted to the position of the highest of honors and esteem. For the remainder of his life he would be the object of homage just short of worship in the city, and would be given gifts and the title of *Venerated Priest*.

Anthanasius explained that there were different rituals that were performed for each aliment. Because his student who asked the question was concerned with physical healing, Anthanasius would restrict his remarks to the physical healing rituals.

Zoroastrian priests taught that Ahura-mazda, the one supreme god, the god who created all things that are good, including man, created all in six creative phases in six-days time. Therefore a re-creation or a restoration, a physical healing, must also follow the original six phases of creation. If performed correctly, the ritual of the six phases of good creation would result in a re-creation of the physical part that needed to be healed.

The priests taught that Ahura-mazda took a full six days to create man. The first day he spat on the ground and with the resulting clay he formed a man. This is why in the healing or re-creation ritual, the priest first spat on the part of the body that needed to be healed. After forming man Ahura-mazda placed his hands on the man image and transferred intellectual, emotional, and spiritual life into the imagine and the formed man was made alive. In the healing ritual, the second thing the priest did on that first day was place his hands on the person to be healed in order to transfer life into the physical part that needed to be healed.

Over the next five days of creation, Ahura-mazda created the five senses that govern the physical body: sight, smell, taste, feel, and hearing. None of the five came to maturity and fruition until day six, when Ahura-mazda again placed his hands on the man. He then became perfect and all of his senses and all the parts that the senses governed were made perfect.

Even so, during the healing ritual the priests believe that the entire re-creation and healing process took six days, passing through six phases. They believed that on each of days two through six a different sense and the parts of the body that the sense governed were presented to Ahura-mazda for re-creation. If no physical aliment was present that needed to be healed, the ritual proceeded to the next sense the following day. If there was a physical ailment that needed to be healed, the body part was "awakened" and began to be restored. On day six the priest laying his hands again on the person to be healed concluded the entire ritual. At that time, if Ahura-mazda so willed that the healing was to be completed, the body part would be healed and restored completely whenever the priest again laid his hands on the one to be healed.

It is obvious that the friends of the man whose eyesight Jesus restored were believers in the Zoroastrian religion. They brought the blind man to Jesus because to them he (Jesus) was a priest (because of his acts of healing in the past and his reputation), and was qualified to perform the healing. It also was obvious that they were trying to by-pass the traditional selection process by going directly to a priest (Jesus) rather than hoping that a priest would select their blind friend.

Anthanasius then began to explain the details surrounding the healing performed by Jesus.

The Zoroastrian priests always presented the person who had been healed to the great mass who had gathered outside of the temple. It was done to show that the person had been healed and to bring praise and honor to the priest. But Jesus led the blind man outside of the city and there he healed him away from the crowd and thereby avoiding praise the crowd would have conferred on him (Jesus). In addition, it is possible Jesus did not want to be associated with the Zoroastrian priests or be identified as a Zoroastrian priest. It is also true that Jesus had cursed this city some nine months before, and he was not going to compromise that curse by performing a healing within the city.

The blind man was a believer in Zoroastrianism, yet Jesus had compassion on him. Note that he did not criticize the man's beliefs; rather he showed him that he (Jesus) was the true Ahura-mazda, the true creator and restorer of all things. Then to show him who he was and that he truly did have the power to heal and to restore, Jesus related directly to and became the fulfillment of the man's religious views. He did this by following to a degree the healing ritual with which the man was acquainted. However, Jesus showed him that rituals did not heal, rather, healing is accomplished by the grace of God through His servant and that the healing did not take six days to be realized. Jesus went through the entire healing process in a matter of minutes, and the man was completely healed.

Jesus did not want any attention to be directed toward him, especially from the mass that would have exalted him in the position of *Venerated Priest*. Rather he wanted the attention to be directed to the healing and to the fact that the man was healed because of God's grace. Thus he instructed the man not to tell anyone in the city how he was healed or the process that brought about his healing.

So, contrary to the student's accusations, Jesus did not perform healings so that he could and would be exalted by men. If that were Jesus' motive, he would not have performed this healing in the manner that it was performed. Rather he healed so that God's grace would be manifested upon man and so that the Father would be glorified and exalted.

Anthanasius next explained that healing was by God's *grace* rather than by man's *faith* or *ritual*. He said, "Healing is not the end result of *faith*, but rather it is a product of God's *grace* bestowed upon man. The entire process of physical healing consisted of three elements. The first element is *trust*. A person must have unwavering trust in the power and the authority of God the Father and the authority and power of the name of Jesus the Christ—God the Son.

"Upon this first element of trust must be built the second element: *faith*. The element of faith says that the person knows without a doubt that God the Father through the power and the authority of Jesus Christ can provide the physical healing needed. There is and can be no question about this fact. *No doubt*. The person knows and is convinced that God *can* heal. Once that element has been fully realized, the third and final element becomes visible: *grace*. Grace is God's unwarranted favor bestowed upon a man because of His love and because by bestowing this grace, His plan and His purpose will and can be furthered. Healing is purely, totally, and completely an end result of God's grace. *Solely God's grace—not man's faith.*

"Trust says I trust God's power, His plan, and His purpose. Faith says I know without a doubt that He can perform the miracle of healing. But by God's grace is healing realized. The healing is not provided because God feels that a person deserves it, is faithful, or is worthy. The healing is provided for one purpose and one purpose only: so that God's plan and purpose will be realized and furthered, thus bringing glory and honor to Him."

Anthanasius concluded the letter by giving words of encouragement and comfort to his young student. He urged the student to reconsider the accusations he leveled at the Savior, repent of his faithlessness, recommit himself to fulfilling the will of God, and re-submit himself to Christ without further condemnation of either himself or Christ Jesus.

I thanked Simir for her help and was prepared to return the letter to its display case, when Simir asked me to stay for a while because she wanted to hear more about Jesus and about his miracles and his life. I was happy to oblige. Simir was Muslim, but she was somewhat acquainted with Christianity having lived in England for a good portion of her life. For the next few hours, until the museum closed for the day, I shared with her the life of Jesus and the person of Jesus Christ. Even after the museum closed she and I walked down to a little park not far from the museum and talked until well past sundown. By the time I left her that night Simir had become convinced that Jesus the Christ was the missing component in her life, that only he could fill the emptiness deep inside, and that only he could gratify her aspirations. So convinced in fact that I had the privilege of introducing her to Jesus.

Shortly after Jesus healed the blind man in Bethsaida, he was walking in one of the cities when he came upon a crowd of people and some scribes were talking to them (Mark 9:15-29). Jesus asked the scribes what they were talking about to the people. They did not answer him but someone from the crowd answered him telling him that he had brought his possessed son to Jesus to be healed by him. We are not told whether the scribes were preventing the man from coming to Jesus or they had tried unsuccessfully to cast out the demons. But considering Jesus' response, it seems that either assumption could be correct. But whatever the case, Jesus healed the boy and cast the evil spirit out of him.

The next we hear from Jesus is in September, when some of his brothers came to him in Capernaum, taunting, ridiculing, and mocking him and asked him contemptuously, if he was going to go to the Feast of Tabernacles in Jerusalem, scheduled for September 15th through the 22nd that year, AD 30. He told them that he was not going to go to Jerusalem with them.

But after the celebration had already started, about two days after the brothers had left to go to Jerusalem, he led his disciples secretly to Jerusalem in order to celebrate the feast celebration.

It was at this Feast of Tabernacles celebration that Jesus caused such a ruckus with his "rivers of living water" proclamation (John 7:11-44), forgiving a woman caught in the act of adultery (John 8:3-11), and his "light of the world" proclamation (John 8:12-58).

I discovered an informative manuscript that discussed these events while researching at the University of Nottingham in Nottingham, England.

The manuscript was a five-page velum text written on front and back in Latin. The author was William VII of Troyes, written sometime before 1490, the year of his death.

The manuscript was entitled *Feast of Tabernacles* and traced Jesus' activities in Jerusalem during the last Feast of Tabernacles that he was to attend before the combined feast during the year of his crucifixion, as is recorded in the Gospel of John (7:2 - 8:12). Although I was not necessarily surprised with William's theology and philosophy, I was intrigued by the historical background and Jewish custom background that he used.

I will paraphrase some of the manuscript and directly quote other portions.

"Sometime in early September of AD 30," William began, "Some of Jesus' natural brothers came to him while he was ministering in the Galilee and asked him if he was going to attend the Feast of Tabernacles that year. He told them that he was not going to go to Jerusalem that year with them. About two days after the brothers had left to go to Jerusalem, he led his disciples to Jerusalem to celebrate."

After the feast began, the religious leaders began looking for Jesus, but as yet he had not arrived in the city. Two days later, when Jesus did arrive, he went immediately to the Temple and began to teach.

He repeated this process of going to the Temple, teaching all day, and then leaving at sundown, everyday of the feast until the last day.

On the final day of the eight days of the Feast of Tabernacles, the day that was called the *Great Day*, for it was on that day that sacrifices were made for the Jewish people and the Jewish nation (on the seven previous days sacrifices were made for other people groups and other nations), the day's celebrations and activities began at sunrise with the solemn ceremony that they called *"the libation of water."* This ceremony was one in which God (addressed as *Ani-wehu* in this setting) was thanked for the harvest and for sending rain. The climax of the ceremony was when the High Priest entreated God pleading for Him to not allow the rain to fail. He also pleaded for God to have mercy upon the people of Israel.

At dawn on the eighth day, just moments before sunrise, long drawn-out trumpet blasts announced that a chief priest had been selected (a once in a life-time honor) to draw water from the Pool of Siloam [some 0.6 to 0.8 kilometers south of the Temple area].

Then, at the first glimpse of the sun exploding over the eastern horizon, William continued, another trumpet blast signaled that the priest was kneeling at the pool and was drawing water from the pool into a golden vial. After drawing the water, the priest would rise and hold the vial of water.

Again a series of long draw-out trumpet blasts were sounded, announcing that the priest had begun his slow solemn walk back to the Temple from the pool. Along his return route to the Temple compound, the priest was met by thousands of cheering and shouting celebrants. The priest slowly walked to the Temple from the pool, carrying the vial of water with both hands to prevent spillage.

At the foot of the great staircase that led to the Temple compound's massive courtyard, the priest stopped and stood still. As he stood perfectly still, the multitudes that had lined his route as well as the many thousands who had gathered in the Temple compound to celebrate the occasion, cheered and shouted with a voice so loud that historians who witnessed the event said that the shouts sounded like rolling thunder. After an extended period of time, allowing the people to cheer and to celebrate, the trumpets again sounded a series of long drawn-out blasts. This signaled the beginning of the priest's solemn ascent up the grand staircase. It also was a signal for the multitudes to stop cheering and to remain silent because the priest was about to ascend into the Temple courtyard.

As the chief priest entered the Temple courtyard, there was total silence, except for the rustle of the priest's feet as he ascended the stairs and on into the courtyard. Holding the golden vial of water, he walked in a deliberate hieratic pose until he arrived at the altar of sacrifice, where the High Priest, dressed in full ceremonial vestments awaited him. The High Priest took the vial of water and poured it into two silver cups. Into one of the silver cups, which now contained half of the water that had been brought from the Pool of Siloam, the High Priest poured wine, mingling the wine with the water. Into the other cup with the other half of the water that had been brought from the pool, he poured olive oil, mixing the oil with the water.

The High Priest then walked up the ascending ramp that led to the top of the altar of sacrifice, where the sacrifices were offered. When he arrived at the top, the High Priest set one cup on the altar's east side and the other on the altar's west side. The sacrifice had already been placed on the altar. It lay between the two silver cups.

After the cups had been placed by the High Priest, a single long blast by a trumpet signaled that a pre-selected company of seven priests should begin to solemnly ascend the ramp to the top of the altar. As they ascended, they softly recited pre-selected Psalms. The reciting by these priests was the only sound that was permitted. Everyone else was to remain silent. Upon reaching the top of the altar, the company of seven priests was joined by the High Priest. They, along with the High Priest, walked around the top of the altar seven times, as they continued to recite the Psalms. After circling seven times, the company stopped and stood still with the High Priest standing directly in front of the sacrifice. The High Priest then took both cups and held them up to heaven and quoted a portion of Isaiah (the 12th chapter). Then he took the water and wine mixture and poured it into the cup containing the oil and water mixture. He then poured the mixture of water, wine, and oil upon the altar and the sacrifice as he quoted another portion of Isaiah (the 55th chapter). All this time the people stood still and remained silent. After the High Priest had poured the mixture onto the altar and the sacrifice, he set the sacrifice on fire. As the sacrifice began to burn, the High Priest removed a portion of the Law from a small golden chest that had been hidden in the top of the altar the year before, and read it aloud. He then threw the animal skin on which a portion of the Law had been written into the sacrificial fire and shouted to the Lord with a loud voice. This was a signal for the entire multitude to begin cheering, shouting, and singing praises to the Lord.

The Search

After corporate praising and singing, the High Priest concluded the ceremony by hiding the Law for the up coming year. He placed the small animal skin on which a portion of the Law was written in a gold, jewel-encrusted chest and then hid it under stones in the top portion of the altar. There the animal skin on which a portion of the Law had been written, remained until the next year's Feast of Tabernacles celebration.

On this particular year, as the High Priest began to pour the water, wine, and oil mixture onto the sacrifice, in the midst of the stillness and silence, the solemn hush was shattered by the thundering voice of Jesus, who had come to the Temple courtyard to witness the celebration along with the thousands of others. Jesus shouted at the top of his lungs, *"If any man thirst, let him come unto me...*(alluding to the Isaiah portions [12:3 and 55:1])...*and out of his belly shall flow rivers of living water."* Indicating that he, Jesus, was the giver and the provider of the indwelling of the Holy Ghost, which the Saducees and Pharisees taught could be provided only by God. Thus, in the audience of thousands, he claimed equality to God.

A great disturbance followed. A disturbance that could have imprisoned him had it not been for the sake of his high Roman standing or his citizenship. While many celebrants began at that time to believe on him, the Pharisees and the religious leaders began to earnestly plot how they could use the Roman political system and his standing with them against him, assuring that the Roman authorities themselves would put him to death.

Although in the minds of these religious leaders some actions by Jesus could be overlooked, this one could not. This event became the catalyst that convinced the moderate Shammaite Pharisees in Jerusalem to join the most conservative Jerusalem Shammaite Pharisees in demanding that Jesus either had to change, repent, and make amends for all the damage he had done, or he would have to be removed from the public eye. From that time forward they began to aggressively search for a way to force Jesus from the public stage—by death, if not by any other means.

Jesus remained in the Temple teaching for the rest of the day.

The religious leaders wasted no time in trying to eliminate Jesus from the public eye. Later during that same day, the day he made the *rivers of living water* proclamation, some scribes and Pharisees brought a woman to him while he was in the Temple compound. They said that she had been caught in the act of adultery. They brought her to Jesus not because they wanted her to be punished or because they respected and honored Jesus' opinion and wanted him to pass judgment upon her, but rather, they brought her to Jesus in order to trap him into acting against the authority of Rome.

Their argument was that the Law of Moses demanded that the woman be stoned.

If Jesus confirmed that the woman (the Greek word that was translated *woman* in this John setting, is *anakom*; the word was used to describe a Roman lady of high social rank) should be stoned, he could be held in contempt of the local Roman court, which was the only authority that could carry out capital punishment, especially if this woman was a high society Roman citizen. But if he indicated that the woman should not be punished, the scribes and Pharisees could use that against him with the people saying that he was undermining the Law of Moses, even though the Law of Moses was applicable to Jews *only*.

This accusation in turn could be used to foment sedition against him, which then would be forcibly crushed by the Roman authorities. So, although the suppressing of this sedition would most likely cost the lives of hundreds of innocent celebrants, Jesus would have been stopped. Thus, the religious authorities felt the sacrificed innocents were worth the cost in order to get rid of Jesus. However, Jesus refused to be trapped.

William next explained the historical background regarding this particular woman. He said, "The woman who was caught in adultery was a young lady by the name of Livia. She was the 22-year-old daughter of Plinius Coponicus, the Roman Governor General of the region of Peraea. It was common knowledge and well known in Jerusalem that Livia was having an illicit sexual relationship with Justus, the married adopted son of Annas, the former High Priest and father of Caiaphas, the current High Priest, and adopted brother of Caiaphas. This was the woman that the scribes and Pharisees brought to Jesus. These religious leaders were so determined to eliminate Jesus, that the very day they pledged to get rid of him, they sought out Livia, the daughter of a Roman governor, forcibly brought her to Jesus, and tried to provoke him into passing judgment upon her.

They were so blinded by their rage that it seemed that they considered the probable vengeance that the Roman governor would likely heap upon them for humiliating and dishonoring his daughter, to be worth the cost it if it meant that their actions would guarantee the eradication of Jesus.

"This caused the entrapment scenario to thicken even more. Would Jesus condemn a Roman citizen of high rank? Would he say that Livia was not guilty and allow blatant sin with the brother and son of God's anointed to go unpunished?"

Before William addressed Jesus' response, he included some additional background material concerning the Gospel of John. He wrote, "This portion of John's Gospel (7:53 - 8:11) was not included in the earliest biblical manuscripts of the first three centuries. For this reason, many Bible historians of the 4th century through the 10th century believed that the story of Livia, was added to the Gospel either by a disciple of the real author of the Gospel of John in the 3rd or 4th century or by St. Jerome in the 4th century. We know from the Roman historian, Practicus, who was a court historian for Plinius Coponicus and who was in Jerusalem for the Feast of Tabernacles celebration that year, AD 30, that the events of the story themselves are true and factual—that a Galilean Jewish rabboni of some distention, who as the adopted son of Joseph, the Roman Senator representing Britannica, and who was the only rabboni in Syria who was a Roman citizen (Practicus does not mention the name of the rabboni), did in fact during the Feast of Tabernacle celebration of the year in which he attended and witnessed the events (AD 30), challenge the Pharisees who had brought Livia to him in the Temple compound, having caught her and Justus in one of the eastern chambers of the Temple annex within the Temple compound in the midst of sexual fornication. Why Justus was not brought also, is not known.

"This Roman/Jewish rabboni did not defend Livia. Instead he challenged those who had brought her to him, that they should take her life only if they had no sin within them for which they could be charged. None who had brought Livia to him, sought her death any further. Then, left with no accusers, the Roman Galilean rabboni dismissed Livia with a charge to commit no more acts of fornication—yet, even with this overwhelming proof by the Roman court historian of the authenticity of the story, it was not included as part of Jesus' Feast of Tabernacles week activities, as recorded in the Gospel of John, until the 4th century.

"Even after the 4th century, when the story was included in the Gospel of John, the portion where Jesus said, *'Neither do I condemn thee. Go and sin no more'* (8:11), was not read in public because it seemed to suggest a lax attitude with regards to adultery."

William then returned to Jesus' response, as it was recorded in John's narrative. "Jesus did not respond in judgment to the Pharisees' and scribes' accusations. He merely stooped down and began drawing in the sand and said that he that is without sin; let him cast the first stone.

"The concept and the spirit of the statement that Jesus made to the Pharisees and scribes was at that time being taught in the Rabbi School of Helliel. However, the Stoic philosopher Lucius Annaeus Seneca in a letter that he wrote to Cornelius Tacitus originally spoke the statement. '…if one is to fully understand this law of forgiveness then one cannot be first to cast a stone if he too has that deficiency or fault that itself would be worthy of stoning…'

"Afterwards, Livia's accusers one by one, walked away without casting stones or making further accusations.

"We are left with confusion." William continued, "Although we know for a fact that Livia was forcibly brought by Pharisees and scribes to Jesus while he was in the Temple during the Feast of Tabernacles celebration in AD 30, and that she and her adultery were objects of assertion between them and a respected and feared Roman/Galilean rabboni of some renown, and that the rabboni responded to their accusations by quoting and challenging them with a well-known Stoic proverb, we do not know without a doubt that the Galilean rabboni was Jesus, or that the event can be attributed to Jesus.

"However, no other event confirms Practicus' record than that recorded in John's Gospel relating to Jesus' dealing with a similar issue at the same time and on the same day."

After this event, nothing more is written in either the Gospels or in William of Troyes manuscript about Jesus' activities until later in the evening that same day.

Although William wrote nothing more regarding the actual event of Jesus' refusal to condemn the woman caught in adultery, he did go into a lengthy discussion about the difference between sin, iniquity, transgression, and trespass. Although he gave no New Testament references, he used the 51st Psalm to confirm Jesus' position on the subject and to show that there are four different offenses for which we must ask God's forgiveness daily.

As I began to read William's explanation, I found myself feeling that once again we of the current Christian society had somehow been "left in the dark" concerning some key foundational truths: truths that centuries ago were taught as basic doctrines of the faith, but now, in our modern world, they are no longer taught at all.

my life I had been taught that sin is not acceptable to God—which is true—sin is sometimes called transgression, sometimes iniquity, and sometimes trespasses. But in essence, they are all the same thing—sin. But according to William, this assumption is far from correct.

I will paraphrase William's explanation.

He said that Psalm 51 shows that there are differences of offense and diverse wrongdoing that require us to deal with each differently. Jesus recognized the difference between the four primary offenses—sin, iniquity, transgression, and trespass—and taught that we must in prayer deal with each, daily.

William then explained the difference between the four offenses. I will quote him direct.

"Sin is an offense that if left unconfessed and unforgiven will condemn to hell. These are offenses that damn the soul. These could include conscious rejection of Jesus as Savior, blasphemy against the Holy Ghost, trying to purchase salvation with deeds rather than accepting it by faith as a gift from God, and maliciously taking the life of the innocent.

"Iniquity is a lack of righteousness or justice. It is an unjust action or word that is hurtful. An example would be that I hurt another brother in Christ and I knew that I hurt him, but I justified it by saying that he needed to be hurt or that he needed to hear what I had to say even though he was offended by it and it hurt him. So, it is willful hurting. This willful hurt, if left unconfessed and if no attempt is made to rectify the hurt, will eventually evolve into sin.

"Transgression is overstepping or breaking the established rules, law, or principle. It means to go beyond the limits, most times unknowingly or without realizing that the rule or law has been broken. Sometimes this means that I may offend another with my speech or actions, but I did not realize that I have offended. For this reason we must ask our Lord to forgive our transgression daily just in case we have offended and are not aware that we have offended.

"The last of the four is trespass. Trespass means to knowingly (compared to transgression which means, unknowingly) go beyond the limits of what we know to be right, lawful, moral, ethical, and right. It is also an encroachment or intrusion upon or against another person. This means that the person offends, but they usually try to justify the offense as needed, wanted, or necessary. This is similar to iniquity but not entirely the same. Iniquity results in hurt, sometimes deep and lasting hurt. Trespass results in offense, or a small hurt ,that only lasts for a short period of time. However, each must be confessed daily to prevent them from evolving into sin."

With that, William ended his description and explanation of the four offenses, and continued where he had left off, with his record of Jesus' activities for the remainder of the day.

As an introduction to Jesus' next event that day, William again elaborated on the historical background and customs.

He wrote, "By the year AD 25, the Jewish religious leaders had added a ninth day to the Feast of Tabernacles celebration. The common people did not customarily observe this ninth day, but for religious leaders, its observance was expected. The ninth day was called *The Day of the Lamp of the Word.*

"At sundown on the eighth day, the observers gathered in the Temple courtyard around the altar of sacrifice. As the observers watched in silence and stillness, the High Priest carried a small wooden chest (this was not the same golden chest into which a portion of the Law had been placed earlier that morning) and a small-lighted oil lamp to the top of the altar. In the chest was a small scroll with a portion of the Law, a portion of the Psalm, and a portion of the prophets written on it. While the observers looked on in complete silence, the High Priest opened the chest and removed the small scroll and replaced it with the small lighted oil lamp, commemorating the sayings of Psalm 119:105 and Proverbs 6:23. This was followed by the High Priest leading the observers in the singing of Psalm 119. The lamp stayed in the chest all night. Then at sun-up the following day, the ninth day, the High Priest replaced the small scroll into the box and took out the oil lamp.

"It was while the High Priest placed the oil lamp into the chest, and before the singing began, that Jesus again, as he had done that morning, broke the silence with his thundering voice, *'I am the light of the world.'*

"The phrase used by Jesus was the same Hebrew phase that was used by God when He gave a description of the definition of His name to Moses, *I AM*. It was a phrase that was never heard or never mentioned verbally in public, because it was so holy. The term was spoken by the High Priest only one time, once a year, on the Day of Atonement, while he was secure and in solitary in the Holiest of Holies of the Temple. So, no one heard him say the name. As the High Priest lay upon his deathbed, he would whisper the name into the ear of his successor. In this way the name was ***never*** spoken in public.

"With the exception of the High Priest, of those who witnessed this interruption by Jesus, none had ever heard the term that he used and no one had any idea what Jesus was talking about. If they would have known, Jesus would have been torn apart immediately. But because they were ignorant of the implications of the phrase, they, especially the scribes and the Pharisees, instead criticized Jesus for interrupting the ceremony.

"Why the High Priest did not object is unknown, unless perhaps he had no explanation as to how and why Jesus knew the word that no one on earth knew, except him (the High Priest).

"Jesus defended his position, which in turn evolved into a full-fledged verbal war of accusations and counter-accusations between Jesus and the accusing religious leaders.

"Finally after perhaps an hour or so of this back and forth arguing, the religious leaders had had enough, so they picked up stones intending to stone him to death, with little concern about their action being prohibited by Roman law. However, Jesus escaped the stoning. How he escaped, we do not know. Did he hide? Did he supernaturally escape? Did the Roman military, which sought to prevent a major riot, instigate his escape? Did his disciples, or friends, or followers, or even his brothers rescue him? Any of these could have been true. However, we are not told by either historical records or by the Gospel of John, so all assumption is nothing more than speculation.

"Afterwards, Jesus walked to the Mount of Olives. The following morning he returned to the Temple area."

With that statement, William VII ended his manuscript with in-depth historical documentation.

For the next few weeks nothing is recorded about the life of Jesus other than the fact that we know he stayed in the Jerusalem area. In late September (the Feast of Tabernacles ended on September 22, and this next event took place after the Feast of Tabernacles had concluded) or early October Jesus and his disciples saw a man who had been blind from birth.

His disciples asked him who had sinned; the man or his parents in that he was born blind? Jesus told them that neither he nor his parents had sinned. But, so that the works of God would be glorified, the man would be healed. He then spit on the ground, made mud, and smeared it on the man's eyes. He then told him to go wash in the Pool of Siloam. The man's healing caused quite a stir because Jesus healed him on the Sabbath Day (John 9:1-37).

I found important authentication dealing with this miracle while researching at the Synagogue of El Transito in Toledo, Spain.

Although the Synagogue of El Transito was no longer used as a synagogue (during the Spanish Inquisition the synagogue had been converted into a Christian church and most of the Jewish worshipers had been killed), it housed a museum that had numerous Sephardic Jewish religious articles on display as well as numerous artifacts and manuscripts dealing with the doctrines and rituals of the Catholic church throughout the centuries.

The authenticating documentation that I discovered at the synagogue museum was a four-leaf manuscript written in French and bound between two pieces of thick leather.

According to the director of the museum (who helped me by translating the Latin text), all that remained of the document's original 100 leaves or more were the four leaves that were bound between the two pieces of leather.

Gregory Makar, an austere 11th century hermit who resided at Pithiviers in Orleans, had written the document. Makar had entitled the original document, *Pagan Practices Made Truth*.

Makar feared that the decrees of the then existing Pope, Alexander II, would forever eliminate from the annals of history any and all references to the fact that Jesus had been knowledgeable of the ritualistic healing practices of the non-Jewish nations that were part of the Roman Empire of Jesus' day. Apparently Pope Alexander had set out on a crusade to search out and to destroy all documents that did not confirm the existing doctrinal position of the Church concerning the healing miracles of Jesus.

In Makar's introduction, he claimed that Alexander had destroyed hundreds of non-replaceable Roman, Greek, Syriac, Babylonian, and Egyptian documents in a nine-year purge.

Makar's stated purpose was to document from memory what he had discovered about some of Jesus' miracles of healing and how many of his healing techniques paralleled some of the practices of the non-Jewish healers. Over a 20-year period, he wrote by hand three copies of the more than 100-leaf document. After his death, all three copies disappeared. That particular copy, with only four-leaves remaining, re-appeared in Toledo in 1602, and there it had remained.

The Search

The director then explained that these four-pages included the introduction and the first three pages of the document. "Although we have no idea what Makar said in these missing sections or how many different miracles of healing he addressed, in the pages that have survived, he discussed the opening of a blind man's eyes in Jerusalem.

"In the four pages, Makar did not identify any scriptural references, although he did quote the biblical portion that relates to this miracle. The quote comes from John 9:1-38 of our current Bible."

Because of the length of this scriptural portion, I have chosen to inscribe only portions of the reference.

> *"And as Jesus passed by, he saw a man which was blind from his birth. And his disciples asked him, saying Master, who did sin, this man, or his parents, that he was born blind? Jesus answered, neither hath this man sinned, nor his parents: but that the works of God should be made manifest in him....*
>
> *When he had thus spoken, he spat on the ground, and made clay from the spittle, and he anointed the eyes of the blind man with the clay. And said unto him, go wash in the pool of Siloam, (which is by interpretation, sent.) He went his way therefore, and washed, and came seeing....*
>
> *Therefore said they unto him, how were thine eyes opened? He answered and said, a man that is called Jesus made clay, and anointed mine eyes, and said unto me, go to the pool of Siloam, and wash: and I went and washed, and I received sight....*
>
> *They brought to the Pharisees him that aforetime was blind...therefore said some of the Pharisees, this man is not of God, because he keepeth not the Sabbath day. Others said, how can a man that is a sinner do such miracles? And there was a division among them...then again called they the man that was blind, and said unto him, give God the praise: we know that this man is a sinner. He answered and said, whether he be a sinner or no, I know not: one thing I know, that, whereas I was blind, now I see....*
>
> *They answered and said unto him, thou wast altogether born in sins, and dost thou teach us? and they cast him out....Jesus heard that they had cast him out; and when he found him, he said unto him, dost thou believe on the Son of God? He answered and said, who is he Lord, that I might believe on him? And Jesus said unto him, thou hast both seen him, and it is he that talketh with thee. And he said, Lord, I believe. And he worshipped him"* (John 9:1-38).

The director then began to read the document.

"At the feast, Jesus had created a spectacle by twice disrupting the solemn celebration rituals of the feast, by comparing himself to Moses, and by claiming equality to God. So incensed were the Jerusalem Pharisees that they plotted with the Temple scribes to have Jesus arrested and to have him condemned to death. Therefore, Jesus was already on the Pharisees' enemy list by the time this miracle took place. They were looking for any excuse in order to accuse him of blasphemy or sedition.

"Some time after the feast, probably in early October, Jesus and his disciples were walking in the Temple area on the Sabbath day when they noticed a blind man begging. Jesus and his disciples may have seen this man before, because he was likely just one of the many beggars who would sit at the Temple compound gate, Beautiful, every day and beg for money from the Temple visitors. But on this day, Jesus looked upon the man differently than he ever had before.

"At this time in the Roman province of Judaea it is estimated that one out of every 30 people suffered from some kind of eye disease, many of which caused blindness. In fact, blindness at this time was the most widely spread and one of the most common afflictions in all of Syria.

"The Jerusalem Shammaite Pharisees believed and taught that at death pious and righteous souls were reincarnated as a reward, not as a punishment. However, the wicked were either put into eternal prisons to be tormented forever or they would be forced back into an imperfect, diseased, or afflicted body as a penalty for sins either committed by them in a former life or by their parents or grandparents before the person was born. The presence of physical infirmities (especially blindness, deafness, and lameness) were held by these Pharisees to be outward signs that sin was present and that the person must pay the full penalty for that sin (marks on the body proves that there is sin in the soul).

"The Shammaite Pharisees considered these afflicted to be cursed by God. Jesus' disciples even believed this. Why should they doubt it or question it? It is what they had always been taught from childhood and what the Jewish religious leaders had taught the people for generations.

"When Jesus' disciples questioned him as to who had sinned, the man or his parents, Jesus told them that neither had sinned. In other words, he said the Pharisees were wrong in their teachings. This implied that all teachings on re-incarnation, pre-existent sin, and physical infirmities proving the existence of sin, all taught by the Pharisees, were false teachings. This man was blind, Jesus said, because he was born blind. It was a physical reason. He was not born blind because of sin or a curse.

"Jesus then spat on the ground, made clay and rubbed it on the man's eyes, and told him to go to the other side of town and wash in the pool of Siloam. This pool was a large deep pool, deep enough to dive into. Hezekiah had built it. It was located on the far south extremity of the city, quite a distance from the Temple compound. In fact, it was so far from the Temple that unless the man had help, it probably would have taken him (in his blind condition) two or three hours to walk to the pool.

"For centuries it has been a mystery why Jesus," the director interjected, "rubbed mud on the man's eyes or why he had him walk so far in order to wash. There were other pools much closer. However, the man obeyed and was healed of his blindness. That mystery is cleared up by this document."

The director then continued translating the manuscript, "There has been for centuries much speculation that this blind man was from Roman heritage or at the very least he was a non-Jew. Like all beggars, he was permitted to beg at the gate called Beautiful regardless of whether he was a Jew or non-Jew. But the thing that seems to indicate that he was perhaps of Roman or non-Jewish heritage was the ritual of the clay that Jesus performed on him.

"The Romans taught in their schools, that Janus, the twice-born son of Jupiter, God Supreme, created man by spitting on the ground and making clay. From the clay he formed man and breathed life into him. The priests of Janus had had since 107 BC a 'healing school and healing clinic' in Rome where they performed various rituals of healing and treatment for those who were afflicted and/or diseased. It was still active at the time of Jesus' ministry. One of the healing rituals was for healing for the blind.

"In this ritual, the Roman priest would spit on the ground and make clay. The clay would then be rubbed on the blind person's eyes. This was known as *the ritual of the clay*. After the clay was rubbed on the eyes, the blind person would then be escorted to the Tiber River where he or she would wash off the clay off. If Janus found favor with the person, he or she would be released from the curse of blindness. If the victim did not find favor, he or she would remain blind. There are records that claim healings from blindness through this ritual. Why and how the person was healed, is not known, or whether the records are accurate, one cannot say for sure.

"What makes believers in the theory that the man was a non-Jew and perhaps even a Roman feel that their assumption is correct is the fact that Jesus performed the same *ritual of the clay* that the priests of Janus followed. It was a ritual with which all Romans or Roman-educated people were acquainted. As such, the man would have obeyed Jesus' instructions without question, especially if the man believed that this Jesus was a holy man or an agent of the god Janus.

"The Tiber River was considered by the Romans a holy water source, one that was sacred to the gods. In the same sense, the pool of Siloam was also considered a miracle pool of water whose source location was claimed by the Jews to have been given to Hezekiah by God in a vision. Thus, it too was considered sacred and to a certain extent, holy.

"If the man was a Roman or a non-Jew, Jesus would have received immediate cooperation from him, if he (Jesus) had used the generations old ritual of healing to gain the man's confidence. At the same time Jesus would show the man that he (Jesus) was the one who had the power to heal and to neutralize a perceived curse, not by the gods proclaimed, taught and worshipped by the Romans.

"Jesus sent the man on his way with mud over his eyes to struggle to the pool of Siloam, and to be healed of his blindness, while he and his disciples went on about their business.

"The Shammaite Pharisees were furious with Jesus for healing the man on the Sabbath. He was already considered their devout enemy because of his interruption of the Feast of Tabernacles celebration rituals and was looking for any excuse to accuse and to condemn him. It was bad enough, they thought, that Jesus healed on the Sabbath, but he healed a man whom they classified as cursed by God. For this man to be healed of blindness (according to the Jerusalem Shammaite Pharisees) the man's sins first had to be forgiven and his curse revoked. Then as an outward sign that the sin had been forgiven and the curse reversed, his blindness would be healed. The fact that the blindness was healed was a sign that God's curse had been reversed. Only God or God's anointed could reverse His curse. They could not accept the fact that Jesus was God's anointed or that he was sent from God. He broke the Sabbath regularly and disrupted the sacred celebrations, so obviously he could not be God's representative with the power to reverse a curse on behalf of God. They considered Jesus a sinner because he did not honor the rules, regulations and traditions, which they say had been established through God's inspiration. They were thoroughly confused over the question of Jesus, and this confusion led to their contempt for him.

"Because they would not accept that Jesus had the authority and the power to reverse the man's curse, resulting in the healing of his blindness, they mercilessly interrogated the healed man about Jesus and about what technique Jesus had used to heal the man's eyes.

"The man told them what Jesus had done and that he had used the technique used by the Janus priests. Immediately they labeled Jesus a sinner. They then searched out the man's parents to confirm his blindness. They were of little help to the Shammaite Pharisees' cause. Finally, out of sheer frustration, they threw the man out of the Temple compound. If he was Jewish, this action was contrary to their own established rules and regulations. If he was a non-Jew, then this action by the Shammaite Pharisees was permitted.

"The episode must have caused quite a stir in Jerusalem. The Feast of Tabernacles had just concluded so there were probably still some 200,000 visitors in Jerusalem in addition to the residents of the city. The Temple compound was probably still a beehive of activity with thousands utilizing the various facilities. Yet in spite of the mass of people and the precipitance, Jesus and his disciples heard the very day that it happened that the healed man had been thrown out of the Temple compound. The news prompted Jesus to actively search out the man.

"When Jesus found the healed man, he revealed himself to him as the Son of God. The man responded by falling down and worshipping him. Apparently, Jesus accepted this show of adoration. It was the first time in the state of Judea that Jesus directly implied that he was the Son of God.

"Jesus then exposed the sinfulness of the Shammaite Pharisees and gave the analogy of he being the door to the sheep-fold and that he was the good shepherd (John 10:1-42), before again verbally pouring his wrath out upon them (John 10:19-39). Afterwards, the religious leaders tried to detain him; but again, as in times past, he escaped (John 10:39). After this Jesus and his disciples went to the east side of the Jordan River (John 10:40) and from there they apparently went to the Galilee because the next record we have of him is when he was leaving the Galilee, about a month after these events in Jerusalem."

With that, the director finished and closed the document.

Although Makar had mentioned Jesus' analogies of him (Jesus) being the door to the sheepfold and the good shepherd, he did not go into detail regarding the analogies. I didn't discover corroborating information dealing with these analogies until I visited the Ny Carlsberg Glyptotek (New Carlsberg Sculpture Museum) in Copenhagen.

The museum had an impressive collection of Greek and Roman sculpture, Egyptian artifacts, and medieval art and manuscripts.

As I toured the museum's manuscript section, I came to an abrupt halt in front of a 2-page velum manuscript written on the front and back in Latin, entitled, *The Feast of Tabernacles—The Good Shepherd*. I was not so much surprised by the title of the manuscript, but rather by its author, William VII of Troyes. The same author whose work I had studied in Nottingham.

I asked one of the museum guides to explain the manuscript to me, because I had seen a manuscript authored by William VII of Troyes in Nottingham. The guide told me that William VII's original 27-page Latin manuscript had been the property of King Christian IV, who reigned from 1588 to 1648. The manuscript was housed in Copenhagen's historic Round Tower. The great fires of 1728 and 1795 destroyed most of the city. It was during the clean up after the fire of 1795 that it came to the attention of Christian IV's descendants that the manuscript was missing. The manuscript remained lost until 1957, when seven of the manuscript's original 27-pages turned up at the University of Nottingham.

Arrangements were made with the University of Nottingham to return a portion of the manuscript to Copenhagen, the portion that is now on display in the Ny Carlsberg Glyptotek. The remaining portion remained in Nottingham. Then every ten years, the Ny Carlsberg Glyptotek and the University of Nottingham exchange the portions of the manuscript that they house.

Satisfied with the explanation, I asked the guide if I could be permitted to study the manuscript.

He retrieved the manuscript from its display case along with a small volume that was the translation of the manuscript into German, Danish, French, and English that was located beneath the case.

I immediately recognized William's writing style. Once again as with the portion of the manuscript that I had studied in Nottingham, this manuscript went into great historical depth. I first read through the manuscript translation and then went back and read it again while taking notes.

William's setting was the Gospel of John (10:1-18) and again he did not quote the scriptural portions, he merely referred to them.

"Jesus was addressing the Pharisees," William wrote, "after their objection to his healing of a blind man when he told them that he was the *door to the sheep fold*, and that any shepherd or porter who did not go through him, the door, but climbed over the wall of the sheepfold was a thief and a robber. He then said that he was the *good shepherd*, a shepherd who would give his life for the sheep.

"Sheepfolds were low sheds or lean-to's opening into a central court, surrounded by a low stone wall or fence with a layer of thorns on top for protection. These were used as shelters for flocks where they could repose at night and be safe and secure. There was only one opening to the sheepfold and the chief shepherd stretched out across that opening, called the gate to the sheepfold. He served as the primary protector for the sheep. Nothing or no one could enter the sheepfold without going over him. If any apprentice shepherd or porter shepherd that worked for or was associated with the chief shepherd wanted to enter the sheepfold, he had to go through the gate where the shepherd was stretched out. If the apprentice had a good relationship with the shepherd and was no threat to the sheep, the shepherd would let him in. However, if he was an enemy or was not trusted by the shepherd, the shepherd would not let him in. If such was the case, the rejected porter or shepherd sometimes chose to jump over the fence in order to steal or harm the sheep. Such people were thieves and robbers. They were like (in allegory) false teachers who really did not care for the sheep or care to instruct them correctly, but instead used them (the sheep) for personal profit and gain.

"Another meaning to this analogy could be that through Jesus and his disciplined path of self-crucifixion, death, and the born-again experience that spiritual fulfillment, inner peace, divinely inspired intellect and wisdom, and spiritual awareness and power can best be assured. Yet it can also be attained through other means. Nevertheless, to do so, the person would have to 'sneak over the wall,' or come into the fold of spiritual awareness, power, and peace through an alternate route. For a time that person would indeed be in the fold, or the inner place of peace and power. But because he came in from an alternate route, or over the wall, he eventually would suffer loss of all that he gained by such means because he chose the alternate route, rather than the disciplined route of spiritual maturity, self-denial, and the divine progression of supernatural instruction and education.

"Jesus also said that he was the good shepherd; a shepherd who would give his life for the sheep. This was a direct indictment of many of the priests and religious leaders of Jesus' day.

"In 176 BC, Antiochus III," William continued, "the Seleucid Syrian Emperor, plundered the Temple in Jerusalem of its treasures, installed a garrison in Jerusalem, and systematically desecrated the Temple and the holy places. Prostitutes were imported by Antiochus to live in the Temple, using the Temple as a brothel, a pig was sacrificed on the altar, a statue of Zeus was set up in the Temple, Jews were not allowed to enter the Temple, and Jews throughout the region suffered wholesale persecution. While all of this was going on, most of the Jewish priests and religious leaders, for the sake of self-preservation, compromised their position and station and went along with Antiochus in his depravity and his abuse of the Jewish people. However, there was a small remnant of priests that did stand against the desecration and the abuse. They eventually had to flee for their lives, although some gave their lives trying to protect the people. Nonetheless, these priests were respected, loved, and honored by the Jewish people. The people called these priests who stood against Antiochus, *Good Shepherds*.

"Jesus, in this sense, was accusing the Pharisees, Sadducees, scribes, and priests, of being like the compromising priests during the days of Antiochus. They abused the people, they treated them with utter contempt, and refused to even help them with the lightest of burdens, much less give their lives for them. But he, on the other hand, was the one remaining Good Shepherd, who was trying to defend the common people in the face of their (the religious leaders) abuse and contempt. He was trying to lead them and teach them, and he and he alone of all of the religious leaders was willing to give his life for them.

"After the continuance of this heated exchange between Jesus and the religious leaders, it became apparent that they again had had enough. So, for the second time in as many days, they attempted to take Jesus and put him to death. But again, as before, he somehow escaped. But, no one knows how."

After this heated confrontation with some of the religious leaders in Jerusalem, Jesus and his disciples first traveled to the east side of the Jordan River, and then continue on back into the Galilee. Nothing more is recorded about the life of Jesus until late October, when Jesus and his disciples leave the Galilee and traveled back to Peraea and Judea Beyond Jordan (Matthew 19:1-2; Mark 10:1).

Although there is nothing recorded about the life of Jesus during this time does not mean that there was not a whirlwind of activity focused upon him—the lest of which was the arrival of Valleus Paterculus and his Theophus Commission of Ambassadors in Syria to investigate the Jewish rabboni from the Galilee—Jesus.

Some of the most authentic documentation relating to Valleus Paterculus and his Theophus Commission of Ambassadors I found while studying at the library at The Monastery of St. Catherine in Sinai. The library is housed in the new (built in 1951) southwest wing of the monastery. Hundreds of the library's more than 6,000 volumes and manuscripts have been translated into 12 languages including English, French, Arabic, Syriac, French, and Spanish, including one that I discovered that was older than the monastery itself. It was a manuscript written by Pachomius (292-348) who built a monastery on the banks of the Nile known as Tabennisi about the year 320. It was while he was at Tabennisi that he wrote the manuscript that I discovered at St. Catherine's.

Although the library would have allowed me to study the manuscript itself, I choose not too, opting instead to study its English translation.

Pachomius' manuscript was about Valleus Paterculus and Tiberius' Theophus Commission of Ambassadors. He claimed to have been given the information from a scribe (who was a secret Christian) who had been ordered in 302 by Emperor Diocletian to chronicle into the *Senate Annuals of the History of Rome* all that had been written by Rome's historians, scribes, and recorders, of all that had transpired in the Empire from the time of the death of Augustus up to the present (302)—the annuals had not been updated since the death of Augustus.

Tradition says that upon learning that the scribe had secretly included information about the life, death, and resurrection of Jesus and the spread of Christianity into the official *Senate Annals of the History of Rome* (Roman law forbade the removal of any entry recorded in the official *Senate Annals of the History of Rome*; not even the Emperor could remove or have removed an entry once it was written), Diocletian became violently and uncontrollably angry and ordered (in 303) a general persecution of all Christians everywhere within the Empire. Following the declaration, the scribe fled for his life to Egypt, taking with him some of the historical documentation that he had used as authenticating sources for what he recorded in the official *Senate Annuals of the History of Rome*. The scribe showed this documentation to Pachomius. The primary focus of Pachomius' manuscript was the information given to him by the runaway scribe.

Information that accompanied the manuscript translation indicated that well over half of the manuscript had disintegrated over the years and that what had survived was Pachomius' chronicle of two letters that the scribe had used as authentication sources regarding Valleus Paterculus and the Theophus Commission of Ambassadors. "These letters", so wrote Pachomius, "had been delivered to Valleus Paterculus by Judaean Procurator Pontius Pilate and by Tetrarch Herod Antipas in January AD 33, one year and 10 months after the death and supposed resurrection of Jesus, the son by adoption of Rome's Senator to Britain and imperial administrator of the district of mining for Caesar, the rabboni from the Galilee, who was under scrutiny by Valleus Paterculus and the Theophus Commission."

Pachomius then gave some background information concerning the letters. "Valleus Paterculus was a Roman historian who was 19 years old when Jesus was born. He is the author of *Historia Romania*. After the Theophus dream by Tiberius, he (Tiberius) created a commission of 130 ambassadors whose responsibility was to investigate claims from all over the eastern Empire of The Theophus sightings. Tiberius appointed Valleus Paterculus to be the chief ambassador commissioner, over the 130-member The Theophus Commission of Ambassadors.

"The Herodians of Syria reported to the commission that Jesus, a Roman Jew who was a rabboni from the Galilee, had performed miracles consistent with what would be expected from The Theophus. One such was his raising from the dead a young child, the son of a prince of Herod Antipas. Just over two years from the original report made by the House of Herod, two ambassadors from the commission arrived in Capernaum to investigate Jesus and his works. Three months later the two returned to Rome to report to the commission and then continued on to Capri to report to Tiberius, amazing stories about this man, Jesus, a Roman citizen by adoption, of Jewish birth from the Galilee who had become a Jewish rabboni. The commission suggested that Valleus Paterculus journey with all speed to the Galilee of Syria and to investigate for himself the inference of the ambassadors.

"Valleus arrived in Jerusalem in October, AD 30, less than seven months before Jesus was to face death by crucifixion. He questioned the Roman officials in Jerusalem about Jesus' whereabouts. They did not know much about him, other than they had heard that he was a Jewish rabboni of Roman citizenship due to his being adopted by Caesar's Senator to Britain and Imperial Minister of Mines, who also represents Rome and her interests before the Jewish Sanhedrin in Jerusalem, and that he [Jesus] was highly regarded in the Galilee.

"Valleus Paterculus then questioned the Jewish religious leaders and Jewish civil leaders about his (Jesus') whereabouts. They told him that they had received word that Jesus could either be in the Galilee or in the territory of Herod Antipas on the east side of the Jordan.

"This marks the beginning of the Jewish religious leaders' determined resolve to eliminate Jesus. They were convinced that if Jesus were somehow identified as The Theophus, that the Romans would dissolve their nation and they would become a ward of the Emperor (John 11:48 and 50). Hence, it was better for the Jewish people as a whole that Jesus, even though he was Roman by adoption, die rather than for their whole nation to vanish. So although many of the Shammaite Pharisees wanted Jesus dead because they held him in utter contempt, the Sadducees, the chief priests, the legal scribes, and the High Priest felt, on the other hand, that Jesus must be removed as a matter of national identity and security.

The Search

"Even as the day of his death approached, although many of the Sadducees became white-hot angry at him over his disturbing incidents in the Temple that caused disruptions, they generally all agreed that it was best for their nation that he be eliminated in order that the Jewish nation could maintain their national identity, not necessarily because he was a threat to their religious institution or form of worship.

"Valleus Paterculus left Jerusalem, traveled to the Galilee and met with Herod Antipas and the Herodians concerning the report given to the ambassadors by the House of Herod. There Valleus Paterculus was told that Jesus was somewhere on the east side of the Jordan River in either Peraea, Judea east of Jordan, or Nabataean Arabia, whereupon Valleus Paterculus immediately left the Galilee in search of Jesus. Herod Antipas sent four of his officials and 20-armed soldiers to accompany him.

"Finally, about a month after he had arrived in Jerusalem, Valleus found Jesus in the village of Machaerus, at the foot of the mountain upon which Herod Antipas had built the fortress of Machaerus. The events leading up to Valleus' encounter with Jesus are briefly recorded in the Gospels of John (12:21-27) and Luke (13:31-33), but the encounter itself is not recorded in the Bible. The encounter is recorded in the writings of Valleus Paterculus, Priscian, Tacitus, Dio Cassius, and Petronius."

Pachomius then explained Valleus Paterculus' impression of Jesus. "That of Valleus Paterculus' four-page record to the Theophus Commission and to Tiberius Caesar of his encounter with Jesus, only one small paragraph has survived." He then paraphrased the surviving paragraph.

> "Valleus Paterculus said that in the Syrian region of the Galilee/Judaea he interrogated and witnessed the character of a Roman Jewish religious figure named Jesus from the scoria city of Nazareth in the Galilee, by ascendancy of Tiberius Caesar's Theophus Commission of Ambassadors. He followed him and witnessed and testified to his character, his works, his actions, and his teachings for 20 days and then reported his findings to a special calling of the entire commission in Rome and then to Tiberius Caesar in Capri. Valleus Paterculus wrote that Jesus was one of the most remarkable characters he had ever met and that he was more afraid of Jesus and his influence with the unseen powers that control the destinies of both men and nature, than an entire army of our (Rome's) most elite guard. He cured disease of all manners. He raised the dead of Jew, Roman and Greek. His command was reported to subjugate the winds, the sea, and the elements of nature. He is feared, respected and hated by his Jewish religious countrymen, but honored by his Roman fellows. Yet, even though it is reported or rumored that his uncle and conservator is none other than he who represents our Senate in Britain and is Minister Administrator of Mines and Mining for our beloved state, Jesus seeks no authority, recognition, reverence, nor office."

After this, Pachomius wrote that the remainder of Valleus Paterculus' testimony was missing except his conclusion and his return commission, which he quoted.

> "It is my opinion that it is within Jesus' power that if he chooses, an entire army could be raised by him in a single hour, which could sweep the world in conquest in a single day. Yet, he denounces all earthly claims to rule or reign. I feel that of all who have been interrogated by this commission, Jesus only has the idiosyncrasy and the qualifications to fulfill the required Theophus character. However, we cannot suppose that he is in fact that Theophus. I proffer to your most excellent Augustus Tiberius, son of our most divine Augustus, that there must be another thorough interrogation of Jesus before representation from this commission, from our treasury, and from our honored Senate, under the protection and authority of our military magistrate, before such a proclamation is affirmed upon any man. I propose to this commission and to your most excellent Tiberius Caesar that after the winter celebration, two years thence, I will lead this delegation to the region in order to interrogate further this man Jesus. If he will not submit to this investigation, we must not distinguish him as that Theophus of whom your most honored esteemed Augustus Tiberius and this commission seek."

"Although we have no record of Tiberius' response or the response of the commission, we know that Valleus Paterculus did lead a delegation to Judaea in January, AD 33. The delegation questioned Procurator Pilate at his palace in Caesarea Maritima, Tetrarch Herod Antipas at his palace complex in Capernaum, and Caiaphas the High Priest in Jerusalem on the matter of Jesus. After hearing of Jesus' death, Valleus demanded that Caiaphas, Pilate, and Herod report their actions in the matter and justify their actions, addressing both the Commission and Tiberius Caesar, and that he, Valleus, would hand-deliver the reports to the Commission in Rome and to Tiberius in Capri. In addition, we know that Valleus did in fact deliver the three letters to Tiberius in Capri sometime in early AD 35.

"We also know that Tiberius recalled Pilate from Judaea in AD 36 or 37 for the offense of brutality in that Pilate had had hundreds of Samaritans slaughtered who had gathered on Mount Gerizim having been lured there by a false prophet who had declared that he would reveal the hiding place of the sacred vessels used by the priests, that Moses was supposed to have hidden. Pilate, fearing insurrection, had them all massacred.

"The personal chronologer of Tiberius Caesar, Priscian, wrote that the true reason why Pilate was recalled was because his justification before Tiberius of the death of The Theophus candidate, the Roman Jewish rabboni from the Galilee, was insufficient for even Tiberius to excuse. Although," Pachomius continued in referring to what Priscian had written, "'Tiberius should have beheaded Pilate, he instead exiled him to the southern regions of Rhaetia, near a lake that is today called Lucerne [Switzerland]. There Pilate died, never again to see Rome.'

"The court historian of Emperor Maximinus, Protoian Anticlius, said that Tiberius recalled Pilate from Judaea because he had ordered the death of The Theophus of Tiberius' obsession, who he claimed was a rabboni from the Galilee of Syria. Tiberius then had him exiled to Veinne in Gaul where he committed suicide during the rule of Nero Augustus."

Pachomius next paraphrased the report letters written by Pilate, Caiaphas, and Herod. Because chronologically the events on which these letters focus are regarding Jesus' death, I will highlight these letters when the crucifixion, death and resurrection of Jesus is covered in the chapter entitled **Arrest and Crucifixion**.

So, although there may not be any record of Jesus' activities during this period, attention was being focused on him by the highest authority in the Empire (so mandated by Tiberius)—Valleus Paterculus and his Theophus Commission of Ambassadors.

The next recorded event in Jesus' life took place in late October when Jesus and his disciples left the Galilee and returned to Peraea and Judea Beyond Jordan (Matthew 19:1-2; Mark 10:1).

A week or two after he had returned to Peraea, he was approached by some people who told him about Pilate's killing of Galileans and mingling their blood with the blood of their sacrifices. This event had occurred in October, so Jesus may or may not have heard about it before they told him. Jesus' response to them sheds no light on whether he knew it already or not.

While I was touring the El Muallaka Church in the Coptic Quarter of Old Cairo, I came across a painting that confirmed Pilate's killing of the Galileans.

Gamal, one of my best friends in Cairo, had driven me to the El Muallaka Church, called the Hanging Church, at my request because I had never visited the church for any other reason other than as a tourist. But this time, I wanted to see if the church housed anything that could be useful for my research.

Although there were 20 or so paintings and carvings on display for tourists, Gamal had told me that there were more paintings, icons, and etchings in a storage vault deep beneath the main floor of the church.

A friend of Gamal's was the security guard at the church, so we had no problem getting access into the deep basement vault. The security guard led us down a dark narrow stairwell that had at least 70 or 80 narrow, well-worn steps. We finally got to the bottom of the stairs, which opened into a large dimly lit granite block room.

Hanging on the block walls, were about dozen icons and etchings that were of obvious Coptic origin. They looked to me that they dated from sometime between the 2nd and probably the 7th centuries. In front of three of the displayed icons stood very small stands. On each stand had been placed a typed three-page tri-language Arabic/French/English document that explained what that particular icon depicted. It was obvious that the three-page explanatory documents were produced as part of the study efforts of educators and religious icon experts who had been for years studying and investigating these particular icons.

Most of the icons were interesting, but I felt that most were of little value to me with regard to my research project, however, one was of special interest to me. It was a 4th century Coptic icon that depicted a brilliantly dressed, royal-robed, figure standing in front of a large group of long-bearded, long-robed men, who were standing in front of an altar of sacrifice and were surrounded by soldiers. The royal dressed man was holding a scroll and was reading to the group of bearded men. Feeling that the icon could have illustrated almost anything, I studied the three-page explanatory document for some clarification.

The document not only explained what the icon depicted but it gave a historical background about the depicted event, as well. The icon portrayed an event that was recorded in Luke 13:1-2:

> *"There were present at that season some that told him of the Galilaeans, whose blood Pilate had mingled with their sacrifices. And Jesus answering said unto them, Suppose ye that these Galilaeans were sinners above all the Galilaeans, because they suffered such things?"*

The massacre as portrayed in Luke 13:1-2 was told to Jesus in November 30 AD, while he was ministering on the "east side of the Jordan," having just recently arrived from the Galilee where he had been the month before. Apparently, the massacre had occurred just days after he had departed the Galilee.

According to the historical records, 600 Galilean Jewish *patriots*, or more likely revolutionaries, in October 30 AD, during the Yom Kippur celebration, had crossed the southern border of the Galilee and had gathered in the small city of En-gannim, one of the northern most cities in the province of Judaea.

They said that they had gone to the city in order to celebrate Yom Kippur (the Day of Atonement), yet they had been given strict orders by the Roman military officials not to cross the border into Judaea. They also claimed that they were on their way to Caesarea Maritima to confront the Roman authorities concerning what they felt to be unjust taxes imposed upon the Galileans by Herod Antipas; and that they had stopped in En-gannim to celebrate Yom Kippur, before continuing on their way to Caesarea.

Pilate had a different opinion as to why these revolutionaries had defied strict orders not to cross the border, and had gathered in the Judaean city of En-gannim.

Upon receiving word in Caesarea that the band had gathered in a synagogue in the little northern Judaean city, Pilate immediately set out from Caesarea for En-gannim with a force of 1,000 crack Roman soldiers intending to arrest the 600 rebels and take them forcibly back to the Galilee.

Pilate and his elite force arrived in En-gannim just as the band of revolutionaries had begun to participate in the Yom Kippur sacrifice celebration. Pilate's choice troops broke into the synagogue and arrested the revolutionaries on the grounds of unlawfully assembling for the purpose of sedition. His intent was that after leading them bound back into the Galilee, he would release them with a stern warning that if they crossed the border again without permission, they would be imprisoned.

But, rather than submitting peacefully to the arrest and being transported back to the Galilee, the rebels violently resisted the Roman arrest by force of arms. The ensuing scuffle left six Roman soldiers dead. So infuriated was Pilate, that he had all 600 of the rebels slaughtered right there in the synagogue. Pilate justified his actions to Tiberius by saying that the slaughter was necessary in order to defuse an imminently violent revolt.

Upon hearing the news, Jesus used the occasion to teach that just because something bad happens, it does not necessarily mean that something wrong had been done or that God is displeased in some way. Sometimes, bad things happen because all people live in a world where both good and bad can occur unexpectedly and without notice.

Shortly after this, perhaps the next Sabbath Day, while Jesus and his disciples were still in the vicinity of Judea East of Jordan, they visited a synagogue located in the village that had built-up around the foot of the mountain atop of which housed Herod Antipas' luxuriously fortress of Machaerus. In the synagogue that Sabbath, with members of The Theophus Commission of Ambassadors there as eyewitnesses, Jesus healed a woman who had been stooped over for 18 years. But as I was to discover, the healing of this particular woman was no ordinary healing.

As I had mentioned back in the chapter entitled **Fourth Year of Ministry**, while researching at Texas A&I University in Kingsville, Texas I discovered a small book entitled *Venice Mustard Gold* whose subject matter was the interpretation of an Italian manuscript entitled *Lessons on the Seed of the Mustard*, that had been written by Laurence Justinian, the former Bishop of Castello. The book was the work of Rev. Theodore McKinney from Richmond, Virginia.

Along with the interpretation of *Lessons on the Seed of the Mustard*, discussed in the aforementioned chapter, Rev. McKinney also interpreted a second lesson written by Justinian entitled *Variations on the Mustard Plant*. This second lesson written by Justinian seemed to be a continuation of the mustard seed theme. But rather than a sermon like his first lesson, this second lesson was written as an apostasy warning and was apparently sent to church leaders in northern Italy and southern France.

Again, as with his first interpretation, Rev. McKinney began by quoting Scripture. This time he quoted a portion of Luke where is also recorded the analogy of the mustard plant that grew to a huge size, Luke 13:10-21.

"And He teaching in one of the synagogues on the Sabbath. And behold, there was a woman which had a spirit of infirmity eighteen years, and was bowed together, and could in no wise lift up herself. And when Jesus saw her, He called her to Him, and said unto her, Woman thou art loosed from thine infirmity. And he laid His hands on her: and immediately she was made straight, and glorified God. And the ruler of the synagogue answered with indignation, because that Jesus had healed on the Sabbath day, and said unto the people, there are six days in which men ought to work: in them therefore come and be healed, and not on the Sabbath day. The Lord then answered him, and said, thou hypocrite, doth not each one of you on the Sabbath loose his ox and his ass from the stall, and lead him away to watering? And ought not this woman, being a daughter of Abraham, whom Satan hath bound, lo, these eighteen years, be loosed from this bond on the Sabbath day? And when He had said these things, all his adversaries were ashamed: and all the people rejoiced for all the glorious things that were done by him. Then said He, unto what is the kingdom of God like? And whereunto shall I resemble it? It is like a grain of mustard seed, which a man took, and cast into his garden; and it grew, and waxed a great tree; and the fowls of the air lodged in the branches of it. And again He said, whereunto shall I liken the kingdom of God? It is like leaven, which a woman took and hid in three measures of meal, till the whole was leavened."

McKinney began interpreting Justinian by writing, "The setting for this event and teaching was in a synagogue on the Sabbath Day, on the east side of the Jordan. Jesus and his disciples had been on the east side of the Jordan River for about two or three weeks. He was probably in Peraea, Judea Beyond Jordan, or perhaps even in Nabataean Arabia. Peraea and Judea Beyond Jordan were both in the Tetrarchy of Herod Antipas. Aretas, the Nabataean king of Arabia, ruled Nabataean Arabia, the kingdom that bordered Peraea on Peraea's south border, with its capital at Jahaz.

"In Peraea, as well as Judea Beyond Jordan, the Jewish population was less than 10 percent of the total, with more than 80 percent made up of Greeks, Syrians, Arabs, Nabataeans, Ammonites, and Edomites. In Nabataean Arabia, the Jewish population was less than 2 percent.

"In the state of Judea, west of the Jordan, the Jewish synagogue was *off limits* to anyone who was not Jewish. However, on the east side of the Jordan, much like in the Galilee, there was no such restriction.

"In fact, the leaders of the Jewish community on the east side actively solicited synagogue worship and education participation from the local population, regardless of ethnic background, race, or national identity. In essence, everyone was welcome. It was well known that in most Jewish synagogues on the east side, only the leader and some of the elders were Jewish; almost all other attendees and worshipers were non-Jewish. These worshipped their own gods and participated in their own religious rituals and observances, as well as Jewish worship and rituals. During this time on the east side, the population was so cosmopolitan that it was not unusual to find a person or a family or a clan worshipping 10 to 20 different gods and observing a dozen different religious customs, rituals, practices, and celebrations, including Judaism.

"Because of this liberal policy, the Jewish leaders in Jerusalem looked upon the leaders east of the Jordan with contempt, calling them collaborators, and ignoring them unless they were guilty of defiling the Sabbath or defiling the provisions of the laws of circumcision.

"In evaluating pure Judean Judaism, the leaders in Jerusalem were probably right. Judaism in the region east of the Jordan was not pure Judaism. It was Judaism in name, but in practice it did not maintain the rigid standards and requirements that were consistent with Judean Judaism. Although worship was observed on the Sabbath Day, consistent with traditional Judaism, that was about the only thing that had not been compromised. On the east side of the Jordan, diverse traditions, teachings, observances, customs, manners, and rituals of all of the represented people groups had slowly crept into Judaism's worship, rituals, and ceremonial observances until the Sabbath day observance was pure Judaism in name only—not in practice."

McKinney continued, "Justinian said that at the time of the healing of this woman, Jesus was in a synagogue in the village that surrounded the foot of the mountain upon which the massive and luxuriously impressive fortress of Machaerus was positioned. The mountain fortress was located near the border of Nabataean Arabia and Peraea. Herod Antipas, the Tetrarch of Peraea and the Galilee, built it.

"Justinian then went into a long dissertation describing and explaining what he felt was the accurate and factual historical background concerning the healing of this woman. Justinian did not reveal the source of his historical information, nor did he elaborate upon its authenticity. He merely presented the information as a matter of fact, as if his audience was well acquainted with the particulars of the event.

"He said," McKinney continued, "that Herod Antipas had married Zolleras, the 12-year-old daughter of Aretas, king of Nabataean Arabia, in AD 13, to form a non-aggression political alliance. It was said that her beauty was extraordinary and without comparison in all of the Tetrarchy of Herod, yet she was flawed in that she had a disease that caused a slouching of her shoulders and back. With each passing year, her condition worsened. Unfortunately, the disease made its first physical appearance in the very year that she married Herod. Herod never really loved her and married her only for political reasons. It seems that the more the disease physically affected Zolleras, the more Herod despised her physical appearance, refusing to have a marriage relationship with her. This in turn caused Zolleras to become embittered and calloused.

"In AD 26, leaving Zolleras in Sepphoris, Herod Antipas traveled to Rome. He stayed with his half-brother Herod Philip, who had a residence in Rome (this *was not* the same Philip that was Tetrarch of Hauran and Gaulonitis). In Rome, Herod Antipas fell in love with Herodias, the wife of Herod Philip. Herod Antipas approached his half-brother about marrying Herodias. After Antipas had offered his brother a large amount of money [equivalent of $2 million in today's money], Philip consented. They then confronted Herodias. She also consented, but she demanded that Antipas divorce Zolleras, even though she and Antipas did not marry immediately (they lived together a number of months before marrying).

"So, before they left Rome to return to Capernaum, Herod was granted a Roman divorce from Zolleras, even though she knew nothing about it; and Herod Philip was granted a divorce from Herodias (women could not divorce in Rome; only men could divorce. In the event of a divorce, according to Roman law decreed by Augustus, a divorced woman could not remarry as long as her former husband lived. If she did, she would be considered an adulteress. So, in reality, Herodias broke the law of Augustus by marrying Antipas.). Antipas and Herodias then returned to Capernaum.

"Zolleras was never officially notified of the divorce; however, she did find out when Antipas did not return to Sepphoris from Rome, but instead he returned to Capernaum. Antipas had no contempt for Zolleras as a person and invited her to stay as his guest in his Tetrarchy as long as she cared to—for life if she wanted. However, Herodias had other plans.

"The divorce was considered official in Rome, but in Nabataean Arabia it was not. There, a wife had to consent to a divorce before it was considered official. Nevertheless, if ten years after the husband had filed for the divorce, she still had not consented to the divorce, the divorce became official. Rome acknowledged and accepted as legal the regional divorce proceeding and provisions of Nabataean Arabia.

"Zolleras probably would have granted Antipas the divorce had he consulted with her first, but because he had secretly divorced her, she refused to consent to the divorce. Herodias became furious at her refusal to consent to the divorce and demanded that Antipas imprison her or put her to death. Antipas was probably not a very good administrator, nor was he an honorable ruler, but he was not stupid. If he ordered Zolleras killed, it would have meant war with Aretas, plus he would have had to answer to the Roman authorities. So, he resisted Herodias' insistence.

"Zolleras was notified of Herodias' threats and appealed to Antipas for permission to move her estate to the fortress of Machaerus, located near the border of her homeland. Herod Antipas quickly gave his unconditional approval, and even sent an escort to accompany her and to protect her entourage.

"With Zolleras now out of the way, Antipas and Herodias could live as they so desired. Later that year, 27 AD, Herod married Herodias, without being legally divorced from Zolleras. Now not only was Herodias a breaker of the laws of marriage, but so was Antipas. In the strictest legal eyes of Rome (not the social rules of acceptance), both were lawbreakers and guilty of adultery.

"When John the Baptist railed on them for their incestuous and adulterous marriage, he was referring to the breaking of the laws of Rome, as per the decree of Augustus, rather than any laws of the Jews or the Nabataean Arabs.

"Zolleras stayed at Machaerus for the next ten years" McKinney continued to write. "She could not leave the Tetrarchy of Antipas or else he, as a Tetrarch of Rome, could claim abandonment to the Roman Senate and demand a Senate judgment of divorce in his favor. So, Zolleras was content to reside at her private palace located within the mountain top fortress compound of the massive Machaerus; however, Antipas did grant her permission to visit her homeland two times a year for as much as three months at a time.

"Outside of the enormous fortified walls of Machaerus, a small village developed at the foot of the mountain to serve the needs of the fort. Eventually the village grew to about one thousand people and there were merchant shops, trade depots, private homes, and places of worship, including a Jewish synagogue. It was at the synagogue in this village located at the foot of the mountain where stood the fortress of Machaerus, that Jesus performed his healing and taught his lesson of the mustard plant and leaven.

"It seems that although Zolleras never became a Jewish convert, she did develop an appreciation for the religion of the Jews and their form of worship and religious practice during her years of living in Sepphoris with Antipas. Although Sepphoris was a Roman city, it did have a Jewish synagogue that was open to all ethic groups. Zolleras attended Sabbath day observances at this synagogue, on occasion. She practiced the same tradition in Machaerus—occasionally, she attended the Jewish Sabbath day observance held at the local synagogue.

"The synagogue leadership of the village of Machaerus reluctantly welcomed her. They were honored by the fact that the wife of the Tetrarch would come to their Sabbath day observances, but they did not want to draw any gratuitous attention from Antipas because of her attendance. Since Antipas had spies everywhere Zolleras went, the synagogue leadership had to develop quite a balancing act. On the one hand, they did not want to do or say anything that would draw attention to them by Antipas, because he had been known to not only close synagogues, but to also imprison the leadership of synagogues and levy a heavy fine on the attendees, if they offended him or Rome in anyway. On the other hand, they did not want to offend Zolleras. She was still the wife of a Roman official and she still had many friends that were Roman officials. She was also the daughter of Aretas, the king of Arabia, whose army that was amassed on the border just a few miles away, far surpassed in number that of Antipas', and he would not hesitate to use it to protect the dignity of his daughter.

"This one particular Sabbath was no different than any other, except for the fact that Jesus was present at the observance on this Sabbath—the same Sabbath on which Zolleras decided to showed up. Herod Antipas had put the word out throughout his kingdom that if anyone knew the whereabouts of Jesus, that they were commanded to bring Jesus to him immediately, because representatives from Rome sought an audience with him. But, if the report of Commissioner Valleus Paterculus, the head commissioner of Tiberius' The Theophus Commission of Ambassadors, is true, then Valleus Paterculus and his entourage had pre-empted Herod with regard to locating Jesus, for they were present that Sabbath Day intending to interrogate Jesus concerning members of the House of Herod's claim that Jesus could well be The Theophus. Instead, they became first hand observers and eyewitnesses to one of Jesus' truly great miracles.

"The story of Zolleras was well-known throughout Syria. Some sympathized with her, realizing that her misfortune was no fault of her own, while others despised her because of her seeming insensitivity and lack of concern for the welfare of the people. At times she was compassionate, distributing caravans of gold, food, and clothing to the people of Machaerus and the surrounding area. Yet at other times, especially when she felt that one of the residents had mocked her physical appearance or had scoffed at her, her wrath could become sizzling in an instant, and she would order the death or imprisonment of all who she suspected of insulting her.

"Because she was so unpredictable, most of the residents were cordial to her, yet they held her at a safe distance. As such, she and her entourage usually occupied a separate section of the synagogue whenever she attended, and they usually did not arrive until the worship observance was under way.

"On the Sabbath Day of Jesus' attendance, Zolleras decided to go to the synagogue, not knowing that Jesus would be there. It had been 18 years since the disease had first made its physical appearance in Zolleras. By now she was so bent that she could not straighten up—she was so permanently bent that her face continually looked at the ground.

"The leaders of the synagogue were probably very uncomfortable when Jesus showed up; were probably beside themselves when Zolleras arrived; and were terrified when Valleus Paterculus and his commission representatives entered the synagogue. They felt they had to maintain a perfect balance or else they could be *snuffed-out* in one quick and fatal sweep. Never before had so few been face to face with so much power and political might.

"We do not know at what time the event took place, but sometime during the Sabbath Day observance, Jesus called attention to Zolleras and healed her. What her infirmity was, no one knows. Some have speculated that satanic oppression had crippled her. Others claim that a bone or muscle disease had crippled her. Still others claim that the whole crippling scenario was nothing more than an allegory that showed that Zolleras had been under the evil oppression of Herod Antipas for 18 years and it had crippled her ability to function properly. Whatever the case, whether it was a literal physical infirmity or an allegorical oppression, Jesus set Zolleras free from her oppression, and Valleus Paterculus was so astounded that it is recorded that he became weakened at his knees and staggered when he left the synagogue.

"Justinian interjected at this point," McKinney wrote, "that the records he had read reported that from this time until the end of her life, Zolleras became one of the most compassionate and benevolent women in the history of Nabataean Arabia. It is assumed that she became a believer in Jesus and was the first to bring that belief into Arabia. She also believed and convinced her father of the truth that Jesus was in fact The Theophus of Tiberius' search.

"Within two months of her healing, under the protection of her father's personal guard, and with the permission of Antipas, she moved her entire estate to the court of her father in Jahaz. There she remained until the divorce-waiting period was complete.

"It was while she was residing at Jahaz that she first heard of the death of Jesus. So weighed down by sorrow was she that her father feared for her life and/or sanity. Aretas sent messengers to Jerusalem to inquire about Jesus' welfare. It was there that the messengers heard the story of Jesus' resurrection.

"When word was brought back that Jesus had risen from the dead, Zolleras' life returned, and she became thoroughly convinced that he (Jesus) was The Theophus. So much so, that she became the primary witness for the sake of Christianity in Arabia until her death in 58 AD.

"Zolleras' temper was appeased by Jesus' miracle, but Aretas' was not. He was angry because of Herod Antipas' illegal divorce from his daughter, Zolleras. Added to this was his revulsion of Herod because of the death of John the Baptist, who was killed in Zolleras' residence at Machaerus, while his daughter was visiting him (Aretas), and because of Jesus' death. Aretas blamed Herod for not defending Jesus before Pilate, and for not demanding further inquiry into accusations against Jesus. Aretas was probably not a believer in Jesus, but his daughter was, and she claimed that Jesus would have been saved if Herod had spoken in Jesus' favor. Because she believed that, Aretas too believed it.

"So intense grew Aretas' bitterness for Herod that on the day the divorce was legally recognized, which was ten years after Herod had requested his divorce while in Rome, Aretas declared war on Herod and soundly defeated him.

"Many at that time attributed Herod's defeat to God's displeasure with him for executing John the Baptist. Others said that it was because of God's displeasure with him over his divorce from Zolleras and marriage to Herodias. Still others said that it was because of his refusal to claim that Jesus was The Theophus or to even defend Jesus before Pontius Pilate. But, if facts are the governing standard, the superior forces of Aretas, whose appetite for vengeance was propelled by anger and bitterness, defeated Herod.

"If the story is correct, Valleus Paterculus, representing The Theophus Commission and who witnessed Jesus healing Zolleras in the synagogue of Machaerus, claimed that his eye witness account and the account reported to him by the Commander of the Roman 10th Legion in the Decapolis regarding Jesus' calming of a storm on the Sea of Galilee, were the two miracles associated with Jesus that he reported to the Commission that were unexplainable and non-comprehendible. These convinced Valleus Paterculus that Jesus, out of all others interrogated, might very well be that Theophus.

"In January or February, AD 31, Valleus Paterculus returned to Rome and reported his findings concerning Jesus to The Theophus Commission. In late April, AD 31, he reported his finding and his Theophus conjecture regarding Jesus to Tiberius in Capri—but by then, Jesus had been crucified.

"The miracle spectacle created a dilemma for the leaders of the synagogue of Machaerus. If ever there were an event that would draw attention to them by Herod Antipas, it was this miracle of healing. First there was the healer—Jesus—for whom Herod was searching. Then there was the recipient of the miracle—Zolleras—her healing would generate kingdom-wide attention. Last there were The Theophus Commission representatives from Rome who witnessed the miracle—their report could attract international attention.

"If the leaders of the synagogue said nothing about the miracle, it would imply their acceptance of the spectacle and the Jewish leaders in Jerusalem would call them into question for allowing the Sabbath day regulations to be violated. If they rebuked Jesus for his actions and for the miracle, they risked igniting the temper of Zolleras and the suspicion of The Theophus Commission.

"The leaders felt trapped, yet they realized that something had to be done. They decided to not attack Jesus directly but to condemn the act of healing on the Sabbath as a violation of the laws of Sabbath observance.

"Jesus scoffed at their attempts at self-preservation and called their complaint and position hypocritical. He knew that they were liberal in their observances and he knew that their complaint was nothing more than a desperate grasp for sustentation. But he also knew that they were terrified of a censure by the Jewish religious leaders in Jerusalem.

"He reprimanded them and told them why they were hypocrites. He said that there was no better day than the Sabbath for Zolleras, a daughter of Abraham (she, being an Arab, was in fact from the line of Abraham through Ishmael and the historical Nabatareans were from the line of Abraham through Isaac and Esau), to be delivered from her bondage, since the Sabbath was originally designated to be a commemoration of Israel's deliverance from Egypt.

"Justinian then deviated from his line of thought and related the origin of the Sabbath Day. He quoted Deuteronomy [5:15] and referred to Exodus [12:17]:

"And remember that thou wast a servant in the land of Egypt, and that the Lord thy God brought thee out thence through a mighty hand and by a stretched out arm: therefore the Lord thy God commanded thee to keep the Sabbath day" (Deuteronomy 5:15).

"Justinian explained that the Sabbath Day commemorated the people of Israel's deliverance from Egypt. In fact, they began their journey out of Egypt on the

Sabbath Day, April 15 [Exodus 12:17]. However, at the time of their deliverance, they did not regularly commemorate the Sabbath. The Sabbath at that time was a day that was set aside for rest. Any day could have been chosen. Whenever the leaders of the slave nation of Hebrews felt that they needed a rest, they would petition the Egyptian authorities. They in turn would either grant the request or deny it. It was on one of these days of rest, April 15, that the Hebrews began their exodus.

"Because it was a Sabbath, God told Moses to tell the people that they had to dedicate the Sabbath to the memory of their deliverance, doing no work nor involving themselves in any business. Instead, they were to spend the entire day in contemplation and reflection upon God's miraculous deliverance of them from Egypt.

"From these honorable and simple beginnings evolved over the centuries an elaborate set of rules and regulations that were designed to regulate the Sabbath observance. The rules and regulations in reality became an unbearable burden upon the people; a burden that was so heavy that the people usually chose to ignore the Sabbath. So, an observation that was originally intended to commemorate a day of deliverance from oppression, turned out to be oppressive itself.

"Jesus used the Sabbath in the true sense that it was intended to be used: to give freedom to the oppressed. Zolleras had been oppressed for 18 years, so on the Sabbath, the day to commemorate deliverance and freedom; Jesus set her free from her bondage and oppression.

"It was after this healing," McKinney continued, quoting Justinian, "That Jesus gave his analogy of the mustard plant that symbolized the religious system that will be corrupted. In addition, Jesus taught that the entire religious system would become corrupt because corruption had hidden itself within its ranks originally. The analogy that he used is recorded in Luke [13:20-21].

"In this analogy, Justinian reasoned, Jesus indicated that there would be three measures of meal, or three separate systems, that would be born out of the same original seed meal. If the original becomes corrupted with leaven, or evil and compromise, then all three would become corrupted. In this he allegorized that the three measures were the three religious systems that had their roots, both physical and spiritual, in the seed of Abraham and the Law of Moses: Judaism, Muslim, and Christianity. Each of the three has become and is still, corrupted because rebellion and sin compromised the original seed. That compromise was never corrected to the point of removing the evil permanently. So, we are left with defiled religious systems that will continue to be defiled. The only solution will be to destroy them all and start over.

"Justinian concluded by saying that because it is highly unlikely and illogical to dissolve the existing defiled and corrupted religious systems, our only recourse is to work within and through the system, attempting to prevent the corruption from spreading and encompassing the entire world."

McKinney wrote in conclusion, "There is no known record of how Justinian's warning and indictment was received. But chances are, it was not received with enthusiasm. Whatever the case, this explanation ended Justinian's manuscript."

After Zolleras was healed, Jesus and his disciples began making their way toward Jerusalem in order to participate in the Feast of Dedication celebration. As they progressed, he ministered in the villages and towns along the way. We only have one recorded event that happened during this slow journey to Jerusalem—the lesson of entering into the straight gate recorded in Luke 13:24-30.

This is the second recorded time that Jesus spoke about entering the straight gate in order to attain eternal life. The first is recorded in Matthew 7:13-14 when he was teaching his disciples. This first lesson is detailed in the chapter entitled **The Second Year of Ministry**. This second teaching is directed to the people at large who had come to listen to him teach.

About the middle of December, Jesus and his disciples finally arrived in Jerusalem. There he was invited to participate the Feast of Dedication at the home of a Shammaite Pharisee.

The Feast of Dedication, Hanukkah, actually had its origin in 164 BC. The feast was celebrated annually on the 25th day of the month of Kislev, about our mid-December. It commemorated the reconsecration of the Temple in Jerusalem by the Maccabees in 164 BC.

While at the feast, he healed a man of dropsy and for the first of two times he gave his teaching on the wedding feast (Luke 14:1-24). The second time is during his last few days in Jerusalem before his crucifixion (Matthew 22:1-14)—see the chapter entitled **Final Year of Ministry**.

The first time that Jesus was invited by a Pharisee to attend the Feast of Dedication was in Capernaum two years previous. I detail that event in the chapter entitled **The Third Year of Ministry**. However, the same documentation that I used for the first time that Jesus was invited by a Pharisee to attend the Feast of Dedication, I used for the second time. As you may recall, I came across this unusual validation at the small Chapel of St. Kilian, in Ulm, Germany, in a room called the *Hall of Feasts*. In that room were located large sandstone carvings that depicted these two Feast of Dedication celebrations. The tour guide at the Chapel of St. Kilian, Dr. Richenburger, explained to me the significance of the carving that depicted this Feast of Dedication celebration in Jerusalem.

"The seven straight nights of night-time celebration was sometimes called the Feast of Lights because the celebrants would carry illuminated lights and torches as they celebrated in the streets and moved from place to place. The whole city, including the Temple courtyard, seemed to be 'on-fire' with spectacular illuminations.

"It was to the concluding Sabbath feast of this Feast of Dedication celebration in the year AD 30, to which Jesus was invited by the chief Shammaite Pharisee in Jerusalem, Zerebell Hazzel (he was the chief Shammaite Pharisee in the state of Judea from AD 27 to AD 32). Zerebell Hazzel was a very powerful man. He was a friend of the Romans (this probably prompted him to invite Jesus to The Feast of Dedication celebration) and under his leadership he somehow mended, or at least partially mended, the rift between the Pharisees and the Sadducees. Under him, for the first and probably the only time in the history of the two religious sects, there was maintained a fragile peace and semi-harmony between the two religious sects.

"As they were eating, a handicapped man appeared, as was the custom for that feast, in order to partake of the food scraps left by the celebrants. The man had a disease that the King James translators identified as *dropsy*. Dropsy, or *dropsical* (the Greek word that was translated dropsy was *hudropikos*), was a kidney disease that caused the body to swell to grotesque proportions because of excessive water retention.

"Luke said that Jesus asked the guests whether it was good to heal on the Sabbath. This seems to indicate that the man may have asked Jesus to heal him. If so, he recognized Jesus and perhaps he had even followed him to the feast.

"They did not answer Jesus when he asked the question. They remained silent, which indicated displeasure or disagreement.

"Jesus then healed the man. Afterwards, (perhaps the swelling went down immediately confirming the healing) he asked them another question regarding what is acceptable practice to do on the Sabbath Day. Once more they all remained silent, showing their disagreement and their displeasure with him.

"Knowing that they held him in contempt for healing a physical outcast on the Sabbath, Jesus told them a parable that was intended to show the host as well as the guests just how dangerous it was to hold anyone in contempt and to show favoritism.

"The parable is recorded in Luke 14 of the Holy Bible.

> *"And He put forth a parable to those which were bidden...but when thou art bidden, go and sit down in the lowest room; that when he that bade thee cometh, he may say unto thee, friend, go up higher.... Then he said unto him, a certain man made a great supper, and bade many:..... So that servant came, and showed his Lord these things. The master of the house being angry said to his servant, go out quickly into the streets and lanes of the city, and bring in hither the poor, and the maimed, and the halt, and the blind...for I say unto you, that none of those men which were bidden shall taste of my supper" (Luke 14:7-24).*

"The incident that led to Jesus' telling of the parable was that Jesus had made special note of how the guests tried to manipulate themselves into a higher seating position, or a position that was nearest the host, so that they could be recipients of the host's favoritism.

"At this time, especially in the homes of the Pharisees, there was an elaborate social 'pecking order' associated with any feast or celebration, in that the ones who were chosen to sit closest to the host were the ones who where the most influential to the host and the most respected by the host. These in turn would receive the most valuable gifts, when the host gave gifts to the guests. This caused the guests to 'manipulate for position' in their attempt to be chosen to sit close to the host.

"Upon seeing this 'show of favoritism,' Jesus, in his non-threatening manner, scoffed at their prideful decadence, and reprimanded both the host and the guests for their self-assertiveness and self-idolization.

"This was quickly followed by Jesus telling a parable about the wedding feast. This wedding feast parable was based on a true story. Although both this Luke 14 setting and the later Matthew 22 setting (see chapter entitled **Final Year of Ministry**) are two different parables spoken at two different times, both had their foundation in the same historical event.

"The history behind the parable took place in AD 5. In April of that year, the Britton tribal chief, Cymbeline, king of the Catuvelliums, a northern tribe, proclaimed himself king over all of the tribes of central and northern Britain (this *did not* include Roman controlled southern Britain—he dared not challenge Rome's supremacy in the south). To secure his claim, he kidnapped and held captive 30 of the most powerful and most respected and honored of the Druid priests in central and northern Britain. He then spread the word from one end of central and northern Britain to the other that he would 'fill the land with a sea of blood, fresh from the throats of Druid priests,' if the High Council of Priests did not confirm his rulership claim and proclaim him king over all of the tribes of central and northern Britain.

"Having no other alternative, the Druid High Counsel proclaimed Cymbeline king of all of the tribes of central and northern Britain.

To 'seal the arrangement,' Cymbeline's son, Cymbellic, married Ullima, the daughter of the Druid Grand High Priest of Britain (the Druid religion was the common bond that bound almost all the tribes of central and northern Britain). A dual celebration was declared by Cymbeline—a celebration that would honor the marriage of his son to the daughter of the Druid High Priest and one that would honor his coronation as king of all of the tribes of central and northern Britain. The date for this celebration was scheduled for September 13.

"Invitations were sent to all patriarchal chiefs, tribal heads, officials, stations of honor, tribal chieftains, and heads of families of all of the tribes of central and northern Britain, giving instructions that his servants would arrive on a particular date ('the day of the first budding of the fall rose of the forest') to accompany the invitee and his family to the dual celebration. And although he was officially the king of all of the tribes of central and northern Britain, Cymbeline was greatly despised and hated because of the method by which he secured the throne.

"As the story goes, because Cymbeline gave them no alternative, to the last tribe, they all agreed that when the servants came back to accompany them that would send representatives to attend the wedding and the celebration. So, the wedding celebration progressed as planned. As the celebration day approached, Cymbeline sent his servants to accompany the officials to the celebration, telling them that all was prepared for them to join in the celebration. But Cymbeline was despised and hated by his subjects because of the method he secured the throne. So to the very person, the officials refused to accompany the servants to the celebration, citing any number of dozens of excuses for not being able to attend; and in some cases the servant was ridiculed and abused. Cymbeline was angered by this abuse of his servants and the refusal of the one's invited to join in the celebration. However, he said that there was still enough time left to try again. Two days later he tried again, but this time he sent his own trusted household servants to accompany the guests. These servants were treated even more ruthlessly than were the original servants. In fact, not only did the guests refuse to come, but also they took Cymbeline's servants and beat all of them, permanently impaired many of them, and actually killed some of them.

"This abuse of his servants and the tribal leader's disdainful attitude concerning his coronation so infuriated Cymbeline that he went totally berserk. He commanded his armed servants and his personal body guard to go out into the villages and the encampments and into the highways and the out of the way haunts, and compel, and if they had to, bind the people, the ones whom the tribal officials considered unworthy or undesirable, and force them to come to the celebration, so that the ceremony would be attended to its maximum capacity.

"However, after the seven-day celebration (some historians claim that it was a 10-day celebration) was completed, Cymbeline had his revenge. He led his army on a killing and destruction rampage that up until that time had not been matched in all of Britain's history. Hundreds of Britons were beheaded, skinned alive, burned, impaled, or dismembered. In fact, 22 of central and northern Britain's 38 tribes were totally exterminated, and 115 villages, cities, towns, and encampments out of the 190 in central and northern Britain at that time were destroyed and their inhabitants exterminated.

"So shocking was the extent of this ruthless revenge by Cymbeline, that when word of his actions reached Rome, both Augustus and the Senate agreed that no attempt would be made to subjugate Cymbeline's kingdom until after his death (they were content to control southern Britain for the time being. It was not until after Cymbeline's death that Rome resumed its conquest of central and northern Britain), and that no effort would be made to punish him for his actions.

"It was this historical event that Jesus eluded to in the presence of all those gathered there in the chief Pharisee's house. It is not clear the lesson that Jesus was trying to teach, nor does the Gospel tell what was their response. Perhaps Jesus was trying to teach that not everyone who is invited is worthy of acceptance. Or that the Jews had abused the servants sent by the king, so they will be scattered and slaughtered, and others who they might consider unworthy will be invited to participate in the celebration of the king, instead of them. But, because Luke's Gospel says nothing of their response, all assumption regarding Jesus' intent can be nothing more than conjecture.

After the completion of the Feast of Dedication, nothing more is recorded about the life of Jesus. The next we hear about him is in mid-January AD 31, when he and his disciples leave Jerusalem and travel back to Judea Beyond Jordan (Matthew 19:2-30; John 10:40-42).

XX
FINAL YEAR OF MINISTRY

(AD 31)

Jesus and his disciples left Jerusalem about mid-January and traveled back across the Jordan to Judea Beyond Jordan. While there multitudes came to him. He taught and healed all who came to him. Pharisees from Jerusalem also came to him confronting him on a number of issues.

I discovered confirming documentation about Jesus' January AD 31 ministry in Judea Beyond Jordan while researching at the library of the University of Illinois at Urbana-Champaign. It was there that I came across an essay that had been written in 1600 by Dutch Reformed theologian Conradus Vorstius. The essay was entitled *Stephen's Account of Jesus' Ministry Beyond Jordan*. The primary focus of the essay was to bring attention to Stephen of Hungary's (crowned the first king of Hungry in 1001) excellent account of Jesus' ministry in Judea Beyond Jordan.

The scriptural setting used by Conradus Vorstius in his 11-page essay were Matthew 19:16-30 and Luke 14:25-35.

He began his essay by writing, "King Stephen, commenting on Jesus' ministry, said that while in Judea Beyond Jordan ministering to a multitude of local residents as well as many hundreds of his disciples, not just the 12 but many more disciples as well, a rich man approached him. The man was a rich young ruler.

"The same term that Luke used to describe the man as a rich young ruler was at that time commonly used when describing Herodians, Roman officials, representatives of Tiberius, Syrian officials, or Greek consultants to Roman officials. Because there is no explanation, the man could have been anyone of these. However, it appeared that both Luke and Matthew identified the man by recording what Jesus said to him. The man approached Jesus and asked him, *'Good master, what good thing shall I do, that I may have eternal life?'*

"Jesus responded to him by quoting Aeschylus, a Greek dramatist who died in 456 BC. In his *Prometheus*, Aeschylus wrote that the Persian fleet commander, just before the battle of Salamis, which resulted in the defeat of the Persian fleet by the Greek fleet led by Eurybiades of Sparta, had addressed Eurybiades by calling him Good Master. Eurybiades responded back immediately by saying, 'Why call me good? There is none good, but the great unknown God who created the earth and all therein, and I, most honorable fleet commander, am not He. So, bear to arms. If eternal life in the after-life is your desire, then I trust most honorable commander that you have kept the commandments of your youth, for by them will you share and be assured of life eternal, once yours here, has been relieved by your most humble adversary, myself at your service.'

"At this time, during the reign of Tiberius, reading the writings of Aeschylus was an educational requirement for all ambassadors appointed by Tiberius who represented Rome and Tiberius in the eastern Empire. Because Jesus quoted the work of Aeschylus that all ambassadors appointed by Tiberius were required to learn, and one that probably only he out of all who were gathered there could understand and comprehend, this very well may indicate that this rich young ruler was a Tiberius appointed Roman ambassador representing Rome in the eastern Empire.

"Jesus continued in this same sequence in regard to this ambassador by quoting Publius Vergilius Maro's (Virgil), the Roman poet who lived from 10 to 19 BC, *Eclogues*. Virgil's *Eclogues* was another mandatory educational requirement for Tiberius-appointed ambassadors to the eastern Empire. In *Eclogues* Virgil writes, 'If one shall enter into life after death until all time has become no time, then he must keep the commandments and laws established before the forming of the laws, established by the fathers of law—the laws established by the gods. If one should enter into true life—life after this life—life forever and everlasting, he must keep the commandments, honor the law of the gods and of his appointed rulers in our society, and give to the poor the whole of ones earthly treasures, for they are of no small value in this life but are valueless in true life everlasting.'

"Jesus used the ambassador's own Roman education to show him that his motive for asking his question was wrong. The Romans had no concept of eternal life gained by faith. So, Jesus could not approach this Roman from that standpoint. However, their poets and authors did point out time and time again that people who keep the commandments of the unknown and unseen god and of nature, keeps the laws established by the Roman authorities, and gives possessions to the poor, they will qualify for life eternal. They further 'preached' that it was the attitude of the heart and the motive behind an act that was more critical than the act itself. To have that perfect balance between motive, attitude, and trust, a person couldn't love the possessions of the world and eternal life equally. In essence, the person could not love God and the eternal life He gives and mammon, or a substitute god. The person either loved the things of the world or loved eternal life. They couldn't co-exist.

"The rich young ruler who came to Jesus was not arrogant" Conradus Vorstius continued as he quoted King Stephen. "He was just ignorant of the concept of attaining eternal life strictly by faith, which was being taught by Jesus. Therefore, he came to Jesus on the only level at which he could relate—doing some great thing in order to qualify to attain eternal life.

"Jesus met him at his point of need, on the level that he could comprehend and understand. Jesus used the man's own Roman education to show him that his attitude was wrong, and his motive was unsuitable. Both Jesus and Virgil had taught that a person could not serve both God and mammon, or a substitute God. A person could not love the world's materialism so much that he was not willing to give it up in order to gain eternal life.

"It soon became obvious to Jesus that what he had originally suspected about the man was in fact true; he was too much in love with his material possessions to give them away, even if such was the path that he had to follow to attain eternal life. If he had not loved the materialism, more, would not have objected to giving his possessions to the poor or to anyone else.

When the rich man went away from Jesus feeling sorrowful, Jesus used the occasion to teach the multitude of his disciples gathered there a lesson on attitude and motive. But, they did not understand what he was trying to get across to them.

They felt that wealth was a mark of God's blessings and approval and that poverty was a mark of God's curse. A rich man, they believed, could more easily enter heaven because it was obvious that he was more blessed of God and God was more pleased with him. This was all that they saw, just the outer facade. They did not comprehend what Jesus was saying.

"Jesus then recited an old classical Periclesian Greek proverb to them ('a camel can pass through an eye end of a needle for sewing easier than can a man of wealth who loves his wealth can enter into the dwelling of the gods'—Pericles 485 BC), that had been borrowed by the Jewish rabbis during the past century, *'that it was easier for a camel to go through the eye of a needle than for a rich man to enter into the kingdom of God.'* Jesus was implying that a man who is rich in pride and in love for materialism and riches, would probably never see the kingdom of God because his attitude, his motives, and his focus are contrary to what God expects and demands.

"King Stephen explained the old Jewish proverb that Jesus used. He compared ivory needles to metal needles and then wooden needles to bone needles. Not once" Vorstius continued, "Did he suggest that Jesus was talking about a small door that had been placed in a gate where camels had to kneel to pass through."

I paused for a moment and remembered that throughout my adult life it had been taught and accepted as a matter of fact that this eye of the needle was a small door in a larger gate. This teaching, which I concluded had obviously been a recent creation, suggested that a camel could indeed enter a gate through the *'eye of the needle,'* the small door located within a larger gate, but he had to kneel and crawl through it. This was generally used as an allegory to suggest that a rich man could enter into the kingdom of God, but he had to do so on his knees, humbly.

However, King Stephen did not even give a hint of confirmation of this type of teaching. This suggested to me that this teaching had probably been a mid-20th century creation used by some ministers to justify becoming wealthy at the expense of unsuspecting Christian masses—"It is God's will for you to be wealthy. If you are not, then you need to re-evaluate your relationship with God" seemed to presently be the norm more than the exception.

The style of writing and subject tone of the essay then changed, suggesting that perhaps Conradus Vorstius interjected his own thoughts regarding the subject. He described in detail the difference between the kingdom of heaven (or the kingdom come down from heaven) and the kingdom of God. He discussed how the kingdom of heaven is the kingdom that is within believers and the kingdom of God is this world, the heavens, and all therein. He said that all who are saved are members of the kingdom of heaven, but that only true disciples can be a part of the kingdom of God. This is the group who are chosen by God to rule for all of eternity following the second coming of Jesus.

Conradus Vorstius then returned to his examination of King Stephens's account. "The king went on to explain that just like a physical camel cannot pass through the physical eye of a physical needle, without a direct miraculous intervention from God, so a man who is rich in pride and is in love with riches cannot enter the kingdom of God without the miraculous intervention from God. This would apply to both a man who is rich in material possessions and who loves his wealth, and a man who longs for, covets, and lusts after material wealth but has little in the way of material possessions. It would also apply to a man who is rich in pride and in self-righteousness. These will not enter into the kingdom of God.

"The lesson that Jesus was trying to point out was that if a man is rich in the things of God and in the kingdom of God, then he has no earthly possessions because he would have transferred ownership of all to God. He may have at his disposal great wealth, but his attitude is that the wealth is not his. It is God's and he is nothing more than a steward of God's possessions. He has been given the responsibility of managing the possessions that God has given him to manage. With this type of attitude, the man will be rich in God's favor his riches will be stored up in the kingdom, and he will not be concerned about the things of this world because they are not his, they are God's, so he need not worry or be anxious about them. With this attitude and motive, the man can qualify for entrance into the kingdom of God.

"Even after this great lesson by Jesus, the 12 disciples still did not comprehend what Jesus meant. They believed that in order to receive an earthly or eternal reward they must give away some physical possessions, which they claimed as their own. They did not see themselves as stewards of goods and possessions that God had entrusted to them to manage. This was typified by Peter's comment and question to Jesus. He said that they had given up all for him and then he asked what their reward would be? Knowing that they had not understood and probably would not understand until after his death and resurrection, the meaning of his lesson, Jesus pacified them by saying in general terms that those who had given up everything to follow him would sit, after the regeneration (his own resurrection), sit on 12 thrones judging the 12 tribes of Israel. It was an evasive answer, but it was probably the only one that their spirit was prepared to receive; and Jesus recognized that fact."

Conradus Vorstius again paused from his examination of Stephen of Hungary's account and inserted some of his own thoughts and opinions. He said, "I feel that it is impossible to understand what Jesus was talking about with his answer to Peter. Was he saying that these 12 disciples (which included Judas at that time) would sit on 12 physical thrones in heaven and judge the 12 tribes of Israel, which at that time, the time of Jesus, did not exist? They had not existed in their original state since one generation removed from the conquest of Canaan by Joshua. Or was he saying that after his resurrection, the disciples would be raised to an exalted position (giving the appearance of royalty or sainthood) by the followers of Jesus, the Christians down through the ages from his resurrection until the time of his return? Was he saying that they would be the exalted Jews who would be the super-structure built upon the sub-structure of Christ, upon which his Church would be built—a super-structure that would act as an indictment against the Jews for their rejection of Jesus? If so, then they in essence would be responsible for the spread of the Gospel that would result in the pronouncement of judgment upon the Jewish people. Beyond these elucidations, I cannot not understand what Jesus was trying to tell them. Maybe he was just pacifying them because they could comprehend what he was saying. A statement made by Jesus seemed to solidify the pacification assumption. He said that if they followed him and gave up all, they would receive great rewards in life everlasting. It is interesting to note that none well after his resurrection."

Conradus Vorstius then returned to the focus of his es[...] seemed to be satisfied with Jesus' answer, even though it did question. They were pacified because they were on a different Jesus. They were still on the physical, material, and carnal plane. Jesus teach them motive and attitude from the spiritual plane, but they were too preoccupied with the physical and material to grasp what he was saying. Jesus made one last statement to the 12. He quoted an old parable first cited by Lucretius, the Roman poet and philosopher (96-55 BC), one that concluded with' *The first will be last and the last will find their position as it were to be first.'*

"After that, King Stephen stated, Jesus concluded his lesson to the 12 and began to teach the multitudes gathered around him. His teaching to the multitude is recorded in the Gospel of Luke (14:31-33). Jesus began to explain to them that if they want to be his disciple (in this case, disciple meant not only to be a follower, but also a follower who was totally and completely dedicated and committed to his master teacher—one who willingly forsakes all earthly possessions, pleasures, and relationships for the privilege of following his master/teacher.) they had to go through the born-again experience. This was the third time that Jesus had drawn attention to the born-again experience. The first time was when he addressed Nicodemus. The second time was when he addressed Peter, James, and John after his transfiguration. Now this third time he was addressing a group of dedicated followers.

"This experience, King Stephen continued, was not salvation or eternal life guarantee. Rather, it was an experience related directly to devoted *discipleship*. In essence, Jesus was implying that the salvation, eternal life guarantee, and born-again experiences were different and distinct experiences. First there is repentance (this is a conscious act of making an about face and desire to go in a different direction that one was going), then there is confession of sins, and confession that Jesus is Lord and that God raised him from the dead. This is followed by forgiveness of sin by way of redemption; this brings conversion, which guarantees salvation.

"However this process is not the born-again experience. The born-again experience is an experience that is strictly related to discipleship. Salvation assures eternal life. Redemption provided by Christ's death guarantees forgiveness of sin, salvation, and eternal life. A person does not have to be born-again to be guaranteed eternal life, but he does have to be saved in order to achieve eternal life and become a part of the Kingdom of Heaven.

"The born-again experience," Conradus Vorstius continued quoting King Stephen, "is one in which a person chooses to be involved. *It is not mandatory for salvation.* However, it is one that is absolutely required if one wants to become a stanch and steadfast disciple of Jesus and an integral part of the Kingdom of God. One does not have to be a devout disciple of Jesus in order to achieve eternal life; but they have to be saved to obtain eternal life. Just because a person is saved does not mean that they automatically advance to the position of disciple.

Discipleship is a spiritual maturing process in which only a small number of verts choose to become involved. If a person chooses to be a fervent disciple of esus (not a follower, a person can be a follower of Jesus, he can be their Savior, Lord, God, and King, they can be guaranteed eternal life because of their belief in him and be guaranteed a place in the Kingdom of Heaven and still not be a veritable disciple) he must submit to the emotionally agonizing born-again experience—the emotional and spiritual death and re-birth experience. This is the experience that Jesus told Nicodemus that he must choose to do if he wanted to see (be integral part of—used to convey rulership, administration, or overseer) the Kingdom of God. In essence, Jesus is saying that if a person chooses to submit to the born-again experience and successfully passes from death of the old person into life of the new and becomes a dedicated disciple, then they will qualify to be part of the ruling and governing body of God, called the Kingdom of God. These will rule and reign with Christ and will govern all of God's creation. However, people who do not choose to become involved in the born-again experience will still be saved. They will be guaranteed eternal life because of their faith in Jesus. But, they cannot qualify to be God's eternal rulers and governors. They cannot be part of the Kingdom of God, God's ruling body of administrators and governors.

"The born-again experience, King Stephen continued to elaborate, must first be preceded by a death experience. This is not a physical death, but rather an emotional, a psychological, and a spiritual death. It is just as agonizing as a physical death. It is as agonizing to the spiritual, psychological, and emotional man as crucifixion is to the physical man. When Jesus told the dedicated disciples gathered around him that they had to take up their cross daily and follow him, or follow in his footsteps, in order qualify to be one of his true disciples, it was an invitation that few would choose to accept. All aspects of physical death on the cross would be experienced in their own emotional, psychological, and spiritual lives. It was a type of commitment that only a few would attempt to fulfill and at which only a small number would succeed. Such is also the case to this day (King Stephen's day).

"Jesus then explained to them," Conradus Vorstius continued quoting King Stephen, "that before they made an impulsive decision and said yes to his invitation to commit to the born-again experience and to become one of his fervent disciples, they needed to count the costs and carefully contemplate the circumstances. He first accentuated his point by telling them that they needed to know exactly what they were doing and know exactly what it would cost them. He used the construction of the Beca Tower, located on the road that connected Julias in Peraea with Jericho, as his example (probably pointing to the unfinished tower as he spoke). This route was the main caravan route traveled by textile and linen traders traveling from the Galilee and Gaulanitis to Peraea. By the side of the road, Proclutius, at one time the wealthiest textile and linen merchant in Syria, began construction in AD 27 on a tower that he called the Beca Tower to commemorate his success in the textile trade industry. But, the construction of the tower cost him far more than what he had anticipated. Then in AD 28, Proclutius lost his entire fortune. The tower was left unfinished and became an example to all in the area that unless people count the cost before they begin a project, they very well may end up being a failure and open themselves up to ridicule and mockery. Jesus said to his disciples that if any one of them wanted to be one of his devout disciples and commit to the agony of the born-again experience, they first must count the cost of such a decision; a cost that was far greater than most followers of Jesus were willing to pay.

"Next, Jesus used a well-known historical event to emphasize the point that if they were not willing to give all to the born-again experience it might be better to back off now rather than say yes and then quit in the middle of the ordeal. The historical incident that he used was an event that took place in Tiberius' campaign in Pannonia, in 8 BC. King Aqentius, king of some of the tribes occupying Pannonia, had an army of 10,000 facing Tiberius' 20,000. When Tiberius was still a day's march away, Aquentius sent ambassadors to Tiberius to sue for peace. Tiberius accepted Aquentius' surrender, thus preventing the sure annihilation of his army and the probable destruction of all of Aquentius' villages and the tribes that he ruled. Tiberius left them in peace and they continued to survive in peace for another 100 years.

"What Jesus was telling his potential disciples with this analogy was that they are now at a critical juncture. They had to decide if they were willing to pay the tremendous price that it took to become one of his faithful disciples. If they decided to become true disciples, accept the challenge, and pursue the anguish of the born-again experience, then they should expect war with their enemy—Satan. However, he also warned them that most, if not all, of them would sue for peace with the enemy before the completion of the born-again experience. This action would not damn them nor would it weaken their assurance of eternal life, it would disqualify them from becoming one of his dedicated disciples, which would in turn disqualify them from being included in the Kingdom of God, the governing body of God's universal rule. In suing for peace, the follower of Christ would simply reach a bargain with the enemy—a bargain that said that the follower would not pursue the born-again experience and true discipleship, if the enemy would allow him to live in relative peace with the assurance of eternal life guaranteed.

"Jesus ended the challenge by telling them that if anyone did choose to be his true disciple and submit to the pain and suffering of the born-again experience, they would be like the salt of the earth: good, necessary, and mandatory. However, if they began the born-again discipleship training and then decided that it was too much and choose to quit, they would be like salt that had lost its savor. They would no longer of value to the Kingdom of God. They would still provide a service for the Kingdom of Heaven, but they would be of little value to God's eternal plan relative to the kingdom of God."

That concluded Conradus Vorstius' re-telling and examination of King Stephen of Hungary's account of Jesus' ministry in Judea Beyond Jordan.

I reshelved Conradus Vorstius' essay and sat at the study table for a long time thinking about the confusing question of the meaning of born-again. It seemed that every time I read something else about it, I became more confused and my conventional belief seemed to erode a little bit more. It made so much sense that the born-again experience should be a different experience from salvation, but how could all of these multiplied thousands of pastors, evangelists, teachers, and theologians over the past century have been and continue to be wrong? Such deception on that large a scale would seem to have been near impossible. Yet, when

Dr. Ron Charles

Jesus explained that those disciples who had chosen to submit to the born-again ordeal had to take up their cross and follow him daily, it seems that he was talking about more than just confessing sins and asking Jesus to come into your heart. Jesus carried his cross in agony and suffered one of the most agonizing deaths ever invented by humankind. So, if that same type and intensity of anguish and suffering in the psychological, emotional, and spiritual life realms rather than the physical are what is to be expected in a born-again experience, then the simple act of confession of sins and asking Jesus to be one's savior to ensure salvation, that we today claim is born-again, is far from what Jesus originally intended when he introduced the born-again model as a prerequisite for stanch discipleship.

After Jesus had finished his teaching about the born-again experience, Shammaite Pharisees and scribes began to complain that he received and associated and even ate with sinners, or commoners. Jesus answered them by relating a number of parables directed at them and their attitudes (Luke 15:1-17:10).

It was at the beautiful Eglise des Cordeliers cathedral, the church where the Dukes of Lorraine are buried, in Nancy, France that I discovered information that confirmed the truth of the Gospels regarding these parables spoken by Jesus.

I had been touring the church for about an hour admiring the cathedral and the artwork, when I heard a lady calling me by name. Needless to say, I was shocked that anyone in Nancy, France knew me by name. I turned to find out who was calling me and discovered that it was the young lady from the hotel where I was staying who had shown me to my room.

She introduced herself to me again, which was good because I had forgotten her name. Her name was Marquette Lebeaux. She said that her off days at the hotel were Friday and Saturday, and on those days she served as a tour guide for the church. It was on a Friday that I visited the cathedral.

She asked me if she could help me with anything. I told her a little about my research project and then asked if the church had a research library or a documents room that was off of the beaten path of the tourist.

She told me about the church's private research library that was made available to church scholars and educators, but was off-limits to tourists. She said that there were several bound medieval period volumes stored in the library. She said that if I wanted to look at what they had, she would gladly show me the library.

I told her that I was interested, whereupon Marquette led me to the far back wall of the church and out an exit that led into a cloister. We walked around the covered walkway and entered another building directly opposite the church door that we had exited. Upon entering the building we immediately walked down a very long staircase that opened into a large room. The room had about a dozen glass-covered wood cases, which housed a total of about 20 or 25 bound volumes, with two or three volumes in each case. Each book had a card in front of it with a number on the card and a brief explanation about each volume. The number cross-referenced a 40-volume set of typed reference notes that explained the contents of each of the books on display, a translation into French, English and German and a reprint of each so that the original need not be touched by a researcher, and gave the historical setting and explanatory notes relating to the volume.

Although most of the volumes were religious in nature, only one volume in one case dealt exclusively with the ministry of Jesus. This volume was a small thin bound volume of less than one hundred pages entitled *Parables Given to the Pharisees in the Presence of Sinners.*

The explanation reference volume where the text was reprinted and historical explanatory notes were included, revealed that the small volume was probably a sermon that had been written by Heribert the Archbishop of Cologne in the year 1021, in an effort to neutralize a growing belief in the Church that Jesus used myths, fables, and tales as the foundational basis for his parable teaching lessons. Therefore, his parables could not be trusted as lessons of truth and holiness. Heribert's sermon was intended to put a stop to this false teaching about the parables of Jesus.

I did not study the original document; instead I read the English reprint.

Heribert began his sermon by explaining the definition and meaning of a parable. He wrote, "At this time in Jesus' ministry the typical didactic teaching methods of the rabbis and rabbonis consisted of them stating to their students a *halakah*, a precept or a rule, and then explaining the halakah by analogies, making inferences to various possible cases, or generalizing from a particular current or past instance. These analogy commentaries were called *haggadah*. But on most occasions Jesus went further than the typical, for the sake of clarity, and resorted to using imaginative illustrations called *mashals*, a complex descriptive form of figurative speech that incorporates comparison, metaphor, historical fact, allegory, and comparisons that were called *parabole*. The combination of all four: *halakah, hagadah, mashal,* and *parabole*, was called a *parable*."

With that definition, I understood why Heribert became so irritated when some of the religious leaders of his time tried to discount Jesus' parables as nothing more than fables or myths that could not be trusted as doctrinal truth.

Heribert continued, "The setting for Jesus' parables is recorded in Luke's Gospel (15:3 - 17:10) when Jesus was invited to a gathering of Pharisees. Before long, sinners joined the gathering. Jesus welcomed them and began to eat with them. The Pharisees became furious at Jesus because he 'mixed' with these sinners and ate with them, even though their own most respected leaders 100 years before taught that they must have compassion on the sinner in order to bring him back into righteous standing before God. Their reactions, which were in stark contrast to the teachings of their most honored Pharisaical leaders—that all of them had been taught—is what prompted Jesus to relate these particular parables to the Pharisees. Of these that Jesus told, I (Heribert) have included six in this sermon: the lost sheep, the woman who lost a coin, the prodigal son, the rich man and his unjust steward, one cannot serve two masters, and the rich man and Lazarus. All six were based on well-known historical events, customs, or beliefs."

As Heribert was quick to point out, Jesus had an uncanny knack of being able to instantly sift through the annals of history and immediately come up with an historical event or teaching around which he would form a relevant parable that implicated himself in that immediate situation and that directly related to the situation and to the people involved in the situation. Such ability had never before been exercised, nor has it been since.

The first of Heribert's six concentrated parables told by Jesus was the parable of the lost sheep told by Jesus in Luke 15:3-7. Heribert apparently chose not to quote the entire text, but just enough to identify the parable.

> *"What man of you, having an hundred sheep, if he lose one of them, doth not leave the ninety and nine in the wilderness, and go after that which is lost, until he find it?"*

After quoting the scripture portion, Heribert began his sermon.

"This first parable by Jesus, the parable of the lost sheep, was a well-known allegory at that time based on an historical event.

"The record of the Kings (II Kings 22) records the reign of the righteous king of Judah, Josiah. The legend connected with Josiah says that before he left Jerusalem with his army to go out and meet on the field of battle in Megiddo, the invading army of Egypt under the command of Necho, Pharaoh of Egypt, he related this story of the lost sheep to his advisors, relating a personal event in his life when he was a young boy tending sheep for the family. In allegorizing the story, King Josiah said that the Lord's chosen people who dwelt in the villages of Megiddo, the people who had drifted from the Lord and who were being threatened by the Necho ravaging wolf, whose intent it was to devour them, needed to be brought back into the sheepfold of Judea.

"With that, King Josiah set off to meet Necho, protect the villages, and restore them to the place God had intended for them. Unfortunately, King Josiah was killed and the villages came under Egyptian subservience.

"In 160 BC, just before Judas Maccabees left Jerusalem to meet the Syrians in battle, he related this same allegory to his military council and family that centuries before had been spoken by King Josiah, and applied the allegory to himself. He said that he had been chosen to rescue the wandering few, who had not as yet joined his cause to throw off the yoke of Syrian oppression, from the bloody jaws of Antiochus IV, the lion of Syria. He said that these wanderers thought that the lion would be their friend because they did not join in the fight against him, but he was not their friend. He was coming to break them and to devour them as a lion devours a lost lamb.

"Judas left Jerusalem confident of victory, but he was killed in battle against the Syrians, and the inhabitants of the three towns in the region of lower Samaria, the ones he went out to protect, were annihilated by the Syrians.

"Jesus repeated the same parable to the Pharisees. Why? What was he trying to imply? Jesus insinuated that the Pharisees who were critical of him for receiving sinners, the sheep of God's fold who had wandered away and had been trapped into a life of sin, were comparable to Necho the wolf and Antiochus the lion, whose purposes were to devour the defenseless sheep that had wandered from the fold? Jesus implied that they (the Pharisees and scribes) should try to rescue sinners, yet they had not, nor would they. However, he would rescue them. With each lost sheep that he brought back into God's sheepfold, there would be great rejoicing by God the Father and by all the righteous in heaven, because they, the sinners, were lost

The Search

but had been found and had been returned safely to the fold before they could be devoured by their enemy while they were lost.

"With this parable Jesus most likely was implying that he was the shepherd who had been sent by God to bring his wandering sheep back into the fold before they could be devoured by their enemies, the ravaging Pharisees and religious leaders.

"The parable that Jesus used had a tragic end to both shepherds who had originally allied it: King Josiah and Judas Maccabees. The devourers of the lost sheep killed both. 'Is this an indictment against the Pharisees and the religious leaders and a prophetic message that says that they too will deliver him, the shepherd, to be devoured?'" Heribert questioned.

On the heels of the first parable, Heribert began his explanation of the second parable spoken by Jesus, without further comment on the first.

The second parable is recorded in Luke 15:8-10. It dealt with a woman who had lost a coin and had become very distraught. Upon finding the coin she became overjoyed and went out and told her friends and neighbors that she had found the coin that she had lost. Jesus concluded the parable by saying that the joy expressed by the woman is the same type of joy that the angels in heaven express over one sinner (one who was once a part of the family but who had wandered away from the family and had become involved in a life of sin) who repents and is restored into the family of God.

"Again," Heribert wrote, "this parable is based on an allegory founded in historical fact. The allegory was well known because it was taught in the school of the rabbis and rabbonis at that time. Hyrcanus II, the High Priest of Judea, appointed to his position by Pompey in 63 BC, originally spoke the allegory. Upon his appointment to the position of High Priest, Hyrcanus addressed the crowd of well-wishers and related the allegory. He said that it was based on a true story relating to his poverty-stricken, widowed grandmother, the mother of his mother.

"Hyrcanus II said that his grandmother, some time after the death of her husband, lost a coin off of her generations shawl. From the time of Alexander the Great's occupation through the Roman occupation (a period of almost 500 years), a generations' shawl was presented to a daughter by her mother. During that 500-year period, if a husband divorced his wife, all of the wealth and assets that they had accumulated became the property of the husband. If a husband died, the wealth and assets that they had accumulated would go to the sons. The sons then would be responsible for the care of their mother. If the couple had no sons, the wealth and assets would go to the family of the husband and they would be responsible for the care of the widowed wife.

"The only thing that actually belonged to the divorced wife or widowed wife was whatever she had brought into the marriage or what she possessed before the marriage. To safeguard a daughter from a potential life of poverty if she was ever divorced or widowed from her husband, the mother presented her with a generations shawl on the day on which her marriage was consummated. This generations shawl was linen or silk shawl that had coins fastened to it. The coins that were used during the Roman era, or at the time of Jesus' ministry, were Roman *denarius*. A *denarius*, during the reign of Augustus and Tiberias, was equal to one day's salary for a typical laborer.

"If the family was rich," Heribert continued, "the daughter would receive a shawl with multiplied dozens of coins. If the family was poor, she might have only received a dozen or two.

"In the case of Hyrcanus' grandmother, because of the extreme Syrian oppression of Judea, the family had been reduced to poverty by the time her husband had become a victim of Syria's ruthlessness. Since she had two daughters and no sons, and the members of her husband's family had either been killed or imprisoned by the Syrians, she was left impoverished with only her generations' shawl containing 100 coins to guarantee her survival.

"Within about five years of her husband's death, the coins had been reduced to 10. These coins were all that prevented her from being cursed to a life of begging, so when she lost one of them, she became frantic and 'tore the house apart,' sweeping it clean in an attempt to find the lost coin. Finally she did find it. She was so excited when she found the coin that she ran throughout the entire village telling everybody that she had found the coin that she had lost.

"Hyrcanus used his grandmother's joy at finding her lost coin as an allegory to express the joy that he felt over every one of the Jews of the Diasporas who were lost in the world of the Syrians, Greeks, and Romans. They had been found and were returned to the God of their fathers. Jesus, however, used the story of the lost coin to express the joy felt by God the Father when one of the sinners who was an object of the Pharisees' criticism, was found by him (Jesus) and joined again to the family of the Father.

"The conclusion to Hyrcanus' story was much more pleasant than the conclusion to the true story concerning the lost sheep. The day that the grandmother found the coin and went throughout the village telling everyone about it, a wealthy Greek merchant was passing through the village and became curious about all the excitement.

"Upon hearing the widow's story from some of the residents, he became so impressed by her persistence and her stewardship that he sought her out and made a marriage proposal to her, even though it was the first time that he had ever laid eyes on her. He remained in the village and 'courted' her for another few months. Afterwards they married and he took her back to his magnificent estate in Corinth. There they lived happily and wealthy until her death some 16 years after their marriage."

The third parable of the ones that Jesus spoke to the Pharisees that Heribert included in his sermon was recorded in Luke 15:11-32. It is now commonly called the story of the prodigal son.

According to most literary experts, this story, as told by Jesus, has come down to us in the 20th and 21st centuries as the most famous story and the most repeated and retold story of all time in all of literature.

"Yet again," Heribert continued with his sermon, "this parable was based on historical fact. The history behind the story dates back to 800 BC and was taught throughout the eastern Roman Empire during the time of Jesus as part of a student's mandatory world history curriculum. The story's setting was the Kingdom (in present day eastern Turkey, northern Iran, and western Armenia).

"The king of the Kingdom of Urartu was Cherimachinus. His older Urrais, was the governor of the city of Tushpa, which was located on the eastern shore of Lake Van. He also served as chief administrator of Urartu's western provinces. The younger son, Arrias, was the chief of the palace defenses of Cherimachinus' royal palace, located on a high cliff overlooking the Araxes River and the capital city of Sehvanes, which stood on the northern shore of the river.

"King Cherimachinus and his two sons ruled with distinction and honor for many years. Then an event took place that set the stage for a complete remolding of Urartu's future.

"When Arrias was 33 years old, his wife and infant son accidentally drowned in the Araxes River. Arrias went into deep depression. In this state he determined that he would leave Urartu and leave the painful memory of his wife and son behind. Because he was determined never to return, he demanded of his father the king an 'inheritance settlement.'

"The right of an 'inheritance settlement' had been the 'law of the land' for more than 1,000 years, since the adaptation of the code of Hammurabi's laws by the kingdoms of the Mesopotamian region, centuries before. The law stated that a younger son of a king could demand an *'inheritance settlement'* anytime after the son's 25th birthday.

"Once the settlement was granted, it was final and irreversible. By this *'inheritance settlement'* a younger son would forfeit his right to rule, his position as heir or joint-heir, his inheritance estate, his right of succession, his family name, and all of the rights and privileges bestowed by the family from that point on and for all succeeding generations.

"In return the king would 'buy out' the younger son for an amount equal to five years' family income.

"Arrias had the legal right to demand the *'inheritance settlement'* from his father the king, and he acted upon that right; to which the king was obligated to grant—in effect, disinheriting and disowning his youngest son.

"Upon receiving his inheritance," Heribert continued, "Arrias immediately left Urartu and moved to Ashur in Assyria. There he 'lived it up' for three years, spending his entire fortune and running up a tremendous debt that he could not pay. It landed him in a debtor's prison.

"While in prison, a local official who had been befriended by Arrias a year previous, felt that he needed to return the favor, so he paid off Arrias' debt and had him released from prison into his charge.

"But upon his release from prison Arrias had to pay off his debt to the official. So, Arrias was obliged to work for the official on the official's farm, until his debt was paid in full. Actually the official was a supplier of meat to the Assyrian army, so Arrias' job was to tend the pigs, cattle, and sheep prior to their delivery to the Assyrian army.

"Arrias worked at the job for four years until the debt was paid in full. After the debt was paid, the official asked him to stay on as a paid overseer of the meat production portion of the farm. Arrias agreed.

"Shortly thereafter, however, the official died and his estate was sold. The new owner kept the farm employees intact, so Arrias maintained his job. But, in less than a month the new owner became ruthless and overbearing and began to treat the employees harshly. Arrias objected to this type of treatment. The new owner responded by stripping Arrias of his position and assigning him the job of feeding the pigs and cleaning the pigpens. Even in this state Arrias was vocal about how the owner was mistreating the employees and threatened to report him to the authorities. The owner responded by imprisoning Arrias in a pigpen with no food and no water.

"Considering there was a drought and famine in the area at that time, it would not have been too many days before Arrias would have starved to death. But, somehow Arrias escaped and fled north to Urartu.

"All the time that Arrias was gone (more than eight years) he had no communication with his father. From the first day that Arrias had left Urartu the King became depressed over the loss of his younger son. He would sit in the in an upper most chamber of the cliff palace and look out of the window to the south, all day every day, month after month, and year after year, hoping to see his son return.

"The law and social custom of the time would not allow the king to go after his son since he (the son) had renounced his princely position, however, the king could allow the son to return, if he returned voluntarily.

"During Arrias' absence, the king, who had ruled so brilliantly with wisdom and foresight, began to neglect his kingdom. Within a year after Arrias had left, the kingdom had fallen into a state of rebellious anarchy floundering without a leader, like a ship in the midst of the sea in the middle of a storm without a rudder.

"Finally the older son, Urrias, fearing for the welfare of the kingdom, left his governorship in Tushpa in the hands of trusted associates and moved to Sehvanes in order to govern the kingdom in his father's stead. King Cherimachinus did not protest, but allowed his older son to take over the leadership 'reins.'

"Under Urrias' brilliant leadership the kingdom not only survived and recovered, but it thrived; becoming a strong rival to Assyria on Assyria's northern border. Within six years of taking control of the kingdom, Urrias had brought the Kingdom of Urartu from a state of ruin and destructive revolution to one that was strong enough to be reckoned with and influential enough to be feared by the Assyrians, the Phrygians, and the Lydians.

"All the while Cherimachinus spent his days in a depressed trance-like stooper, gazing for hours out over the highlands to the south, hoping to once again see his younger son before he, the king, died.

"One day while Urrias was away from the capital city on pressing business for the kingdom in the city of Musasir on the Urartu/Assyrian border, Arrias returned home to Sehanves.

"King Cherimachinus saw him approaching from afar and miraculously his depression broke. He ran from his upper chamber and ordered the palace to prepare a great feast in honor of his returning son.

"Cherimachinus, who was greatly over-weight, then ran all the way down the steep road that connected the palace to the capital city, almost dying of exhaustion in the process.

"When he got to the city, he ordered his personal guard to accompany him as he rode out to meet Arrias. The homecoming celebration that followed lasted for 21 days, but Cherimachinus was unable to enjoy it to its fullness because he was still trying to recover from his ordeal of running to meet his son.

Nevertheless, in the midst of the celebration, the king called Arrias to him and contrary to the law restored his position as son and gave him a family signet ring to 'seal the deal.' Yet, his heir position was not restored.

"News reached Urrias about his brother's return, his father's miraculous recovery, the celebration, and the restoration of Arrias by his father. He was pleased to hear that Arrias had returned and that his father had recovered from his depression, but he became furious when he heard that Arrias had been restored to his former position as son of the king.

"Urrias immediately returned to Sehanves in order to reason with his father about his unlawful decision: a decision that very well could again usher in lawlessness. Urrais' pleadings fell on deaf ears.

"Cherimachinus, who had not fully physically recovered from his running ordeal and was still confined to bed, in order to appease Urrias, offered to abdicate the throne and to proclaim Urrias king and governor of the Kingdom of Urartu and heir to all that belonged to the king, if he would but forgive his brother and welcome him back home.

"Urrias refused and hurriedly returned to his city of Tushpa. There he quickly gained the support of the people and seceded from the Kingdom of Urartu and founded the Kingdom of Van.

"In Sehvanes, Cherimachinus finally recovered physically and again began to govern with pride and dignity, with Arrias by his side. Because Arrias had given up his right of rulership, he was not permitted to hold a royal position of leadership; however Cherimachinus restored him to his former position as chief of the defenses of the royal household and the royal palace.

"In the meantime, Urrias raised an army and marched against his father and the Kingdom of Urartu. He conquered all of the land between Lake Van and the capital city of Sehvanes, and then laid siege to the city. He conquered the city after an 80-day siege. It was completely destroyed; never to rise again as a place of dwelling, and every occupant in the city was either killed or enslaved.

"Next, Urrias laid siege to the royal palace, although taking the palace would have been an impossible task. Not fearing Urrais or his siege, Arrias attempted to reason with his brother by leaving the security of the palace and walking out to meet him, unarmed.

"Urrias refused to talk to him and instead cut his body in two with his sword and then cut off his head. Upon seeing Arrias killed, the king threw open the gates to the palace and ran out and fell upon his son's mutilated body. Then while holding the decapitated head of Arrias in his hands, he begged Urrias to forgive, forget, and to start anew.

"Urrias responded by decapitating his father. Afterwards his army entered the impregnable palace by marching through the door that the king had left open. Thus the Kingdom of Van conquered the Kingdom of Urartu. The palace was partially destroyed and remained unoccupied for almost 500 years.

"In 320 BC, Alexander the Great conquered the area and restored the palace and used it as an observation fortress.

"It is unclear," Heribert questioned, "why Jesus told the Pharisees the parable of the prodigal son. It must have related to the issue of the sinners that the Shammaite Pharisees refused to accept. It seems quite obvious that Jesus was comparing Arrias to the sinners who had rebelled against God and had strayed from the 'family' of God.

"It appears that he was comparing Urrias to the unforgiving Shammaite Pharisees who reject sinners as being to impure and not worthy enough to be accepted into the family and/or the kingdom of God. They felt that the family of God was exclusively for those who had never rebelled against God or strayed from God's Law and had proven themselves worthy to be a part of the family (the Jewish religious leaders). They also believed that the Kingdom of God would be an earthly kingdom established by the Messiah, and composed approved family of God members. They felt that God had no intention of welcoming sinners into either the family or the kingdom, or welcoming any who had strayed from His established Law. In essence, they felt that if a 'family' member turned away from the family, they could not return to God and again be a part of God's family. If they did, however, return in humility, they could eventually be forgiven if they proved themselves worthy of forgiveness, but they would always be subordinate servants to the rightful family of God members.

"It also appears that Jesus compared God's and well as his own forgiving nature, to the compassionate forgiveness of King Cherimachinus. They forgive rebellious sinners and joyfully welcome them back into the family of God.

"The unsaid implication by Jesus was that the Shammaite Pharisee's bitterness, unforgiveness, self-righteousness, blind hatred, and unmotivated attack against sinners and those who had strayed from God, yet whom God loved, would not only result in the destruction of the sinners, but their hatred would ultimately tear apart the very family and kingdom that they were so desperately tying to preserve and keep pure.

"So, although the parable has been used for centuries as an allegory of a father's unconditional love in the face of rebellion and bitterness, Jesus' primary purpose for telling it to the Shammaite Pharisees seems to be one of indictment against their self-righteousness, unforgiveness, and judgment."

The fourth of the parables spoken by Jesus and used in Heribert's sermon was the story about the rich man and the unjust steward recorded in Luke 16:1-12. It is also based on a true story.

"The story," Heribert wrote, "was told by Mark Antony to Antipater. It was a true story about Antiochus IV, the king of Syria. Antony told the story to Antipater to encourage him to make friends with not only his own countrymen, whom he represented before the Roman government, but also with the Roman officials themselves, whom he may or may not have respected. Even if he did not respect them, if he appealed to their honor and good graces, he would always have friends in places of authority, if ever such friends were needed.

"The story behind the parable involved Antiochus IV, the king of Syria. In 192 BC, Antiochus III was killed in a battle against Egypt. Seleucus IV succeeded him.

"In 175 BC, Seleucus IV died under mysterious circumstances. His cousin, Antiochus IV Epiphanes, succeeded him.

"Shortly after securing the throne of Syria, Antiochus IV appointed the son of Seleucus IV, Demetrius, Antiochus' second cousin, his personal steward over all of his household and personal possessions. Demetrius served in that position until 166 BC when Antiochus discovered that Demetrius was 'skimming money off the top.' Not only would he take money from the treasury to buy goods, but also the goods would never be delivered. He then would sell them to other unsuspecting customers. In addition, he sold goods and materials from the king's warehouses to local nobles and officials for bartered goods rather than for money, and then he never collected on the agreed upon bartered goods.

"Antiochus had determined to relieve Demetrius of his position and to exile him for four years. At that time under Syrian and Roman law, four years was the maximum length of time a royal steward could be exiled for embezzlement, if the king chose to exile rather than to behead the steward. Because of Syria's close relationship with Rome under Antiochus, made arrangements for Demetrius to be exiled to Rome for four years.

"Over the years, Demetrius had purchased from numerous merchants from all over the known world and had made special arrangements with many more merchants, nobles, and officials that in essence cost them nothing, but produced for them great wealth, at the expense of the household of Antiochus.

"When Demetrius heard purely by accident that the king intended to dismiss him and exile him, he quickly moved to protect himself and his future. He contacted all of the merchants, nobles, and officials who owed the household of Antiochus money or undelivered bartered goods and revised the actual amount owed to a lesser amount. This not only assured that Antiochus' household would at least get something rather than nothing at all, and because the debt owed to Antiochus was reduced considerably from what it was originally, the merchants, nobles, and officials become obligated to Demetrius thus assuring him of a life long friendship with those merchants, noblemen, and officials. So, by the time Demetrius was stripped of his position and exiled to Rome, he had secured his future and his friendly acceptance by these same merchants, nobles, and officials upon his return from exile in Rome.

"After Demetrius had been sent to Rome, Antiochus discovered what Demetrius had done. Unfortunately, he could do nothing about it. At the time that Demetrius revised the debt, he had the authority to do so because he still held the position of royal steward to Antiochus' household, and was in charge of making debt repayment arrangements. Antiochus admired Demertius' shrewdness and his foresight in making friends with those who owned him, in order to secure his future.

"The story involving Antiochus IV and Demetrius as it was told by Marc Antony became the basis for Jesus' parable of the rich man and the unjust steward. Through it Jesus implied that the Shammaite Pharisees were not of God and that they were not even faithful over the very least of God's mandates—showing mercy to the widows and the fatherless and accepting the lost. So how could God trust them with the greater things in His kingdom, like leadership?

"This being the case, Jesus told them that they needed to develop friendships with the godless societies of the world and with the lord of this world because they would be with the godless and the lord of this world for all of eternity. In turn they would be accepted by the godless and they would live in harmony with the lord of this world. Although in doing so they would become enemies of God and outcasts of the kingdom of God, they would be accepted by the godless societies of the world."

The fifth parable used in Heribert's sermon was one that Jesus used in connection with the fourth parable. It is recorded in Luke 16:13 and it deals with serving two masters. Of the six parables that Heribert examined, the fifth is by far the shortest. In fact, Heribert explained it in one short paragraph.

According to Heribert, "The word used by Jesus in the parable that was translated 'mammon' by St. Jerome in the Vulgate, was actually a Chaldean word: *majarian*. The word meant 'a god who is a substitute god for the one served in truth.'

"In essence, Jesus was saying to the Shammaite Pharisees that they could not serve God and a substitute god. They could not serve two masters. They could not harbor bitterness, hatred, envy, unforgiveness, and non-acceptance and serve a God of forgiveness, acceptance, holiness, and love at the same time. They had to serve one or the other. They could not serve God and a substitute god (bitterness, hatred, anxiety, hopelessness, guilt, job, wealth, pleasure, family, immorality, entertainment, faithlessness, religious ritualism, pride, self-righteousness, lust, etc.) at the same time."

The sixth and final parable is also one that many have felt through the years was based on a true story: the parable of the rich man and Lazarus and is recorded in Luke 16:19-31. Most of the proponents feel that because Jesus said, *"there was a man,"* that this related to a true story. Opponents feel that because no name was given to the rich man, the story was nothing more than an allegory, not an actual event. *"But considering the fact that all of the other parables were based on true stories, why should this one be different?"* questioned Heribert.

"The parable" he continued, "Was based on a true story, it is suspiciously similar to an allegory told in 210 BC by the great, and at the time of Jesus, highly respected Jewish religious leader from Alexandria, Meleshia.

"The allegory was related to another religious leader also from Alexandria, who had died about 50 years before that time in 260 BC. His name was Zeruthem. Although Zeruthem was a Jewish religious leader and a friend of Ptolemy III, Pharaoh/king of Egypt, he was far from holy, godly, friendly, or compassionate.

"Zeruthem demanded that tithes, worship tax, and offerings be paid to him directly. But instead of using the funds to help the widows and the needy, he used them to finance his own lavish lifestyle. He held the widows, orphans, homeless, and needy in the utmost contempt.

"The Law demanded compassion for sinners, which would encourage them to forsake their life of sin and return to the family of God, to give to the poor, and to have compassion for the widows and orphans. To Zeruthem, they were a nuisance that needed to be removed from sight.

The Search

"When Zeruthem died, he received a fabulous Egyptian funeral. However, as Meleshia said of Zeruthem when he told the story to a group of scholars who were charged with writing commentaries relating to the Greek translation of the Hebrew Scriptures, *'he lifted up his eyes in the world of darkness and intense heat, being in torment in Hades.'*

"From that place of torment, Zeruthem could see a man who used to beg for alms at his gate and who had died before him. This could have been the beggar Lazarus, featured in Jesus' parable, because Lazarus was in fact an Egyptian name.

"The beggar Lazarus was in a place of peace, whereas the rich, man was in a place of torment.

"Meleshia said that Zeruthem requested from the governor of the place of peace to have the beggar place one drop of water on his tongue in order to quench the horrible torment, but the governor refused his request.

"Next, he asked the governor to send someone back from the dead to warn his family so that they could avoid such a horrible place. But the governor told Zeruthem that they had the prophets, the Law, and the scriptures. If they believed them, then that was all they needed and all that they would receive.

"Meleshia used the story as an allegory to show the scholars that although they were working daily with the Holy scriptures, if they did not believe the scriptures and did not practice what the scriptures said and live according to what was written, they would end up in the same place as Zeruthem because they would have proven that they had the same heart as he.

"Jesus had just told the Pharisees about the truth of the scriptures, implying that they must live according to the whole Law and the entire Word of God, which by their contempt for sinners and their contempt for Jesus for showing these sinners love, compassion, and acceptance, they were forsaking and to which they were living contrary.

"Almost to the last detail, the parable that Jesus spoke to the Pharisees was the same as what the great Jewish holy man, Meleshia, related to the Alexandrian scholars more than two centuries before. However, Jesus did add a portion to Meleshia's allegory. He added that the rich man said that if someone who had risen from the dead would come back and speak to his family that they would listen and would avoid that place of horror. But Abraham said that even if someone rose from the dead and came back and preached to them, they still would not believe. Heribert felt that this portion directly related to the fact that the Shammaite Pharisees would not accept or believe Jesus, even after his death and resurrection.

"The sad realization regarding the historical story is that after Meleshia related this story to the scholars, some of them, the ones who had been offended by his judgmental implications, attacked him and killed him. The story had been told and retold in the Pharisaical Rabbi and Rabboni schools to impress the need for remaining faithful to every aspect of the Law—even to show compassion to sinners and to those who had drifted from the fold.

"With Jesus' last statement, he too implied that the Pharisee's rejection of the truth of the scriptures in favor of their own rules and regulations which served to compliment their self-righteousness and non-conforming self-gratifying and self-exalted position, as well as their rejection of him, would result in his death, just like it resulted in Meleshia's death.

"Without a doubt the Shammaite Pharisees and the scribes became furious with Jesus for using the parable to implicate them and to condemn them."

With that statement, Heribert concluded his sermon.

The next time we read about Jesus, it is late January and Lazarus, his friend from Bethany, the brother of Mary and Martha, had become sick.

Jesus was still ministering in Judea Beyond Jordan or Peraea, when he received word from a messenger sent by Mary and Martha that Jesus needed to come quickly or else Lazarus would die. Yet, he delayed his return to Bethany. By the time he reached Bethany, Lazarus had died (John 11:1-46). With Lazarus' death, the stage was set for one of the greatest miracles in Jesus' ministry.

The information that I needed to confirm the truth of John's Gospel account of the death and resurrection of Lazarus, I found at the El Azhar Muslim University in Cairo, Egypt. El Azhar was *THE* major university for Islamic studies in the entire world.

The information that I needed to confirm the truth of John's Gospel account of the death and resurrection of Lazarus, I found at the El Azhar Muslim University in Cairo, Egypt.

The manuscript vault at the university was impressive and beautiful; with Islamic manuscripts that dated all the way back to the 8th century. But what was most amazing to me were the 3rd and 4th century Coptic Christian manuscripts that were hidden away and stored in dark, underground, air-tight granite and steel vaults.

As I descended the narrow stairs that led to the underground vaults, the university guide explained that the Christian manuscripts had been originally placed in the university's storage vaults in 980 AD, after the vizier Yacub Ibu Killis had prophesied that Christianity would be extinct within one millennium from that time. To insure that the memory of Christianity would not be totally eliminated, he demanded that 100 Christian manuscripts and documents be preserved, so as to sustain the memory of the existence of Christianity for the benefit of future generations. Of the 100 manuscripts and documents originally preserved, almost 40 still remained intact, with an additional 20 or so preserved in fragments.

The area was very dimly lit, so it was difficult to see. Each vault had a description plaque on the vault door that briefly described the manuscript or document that it held.

Considering the fact that all but two were written in a language that I could not read, perhaps an early Christian/Egyptian dialect or some other local dialect that had long since been lost, I could only read two manuscripts: one that had been written in Greek, and one written in Latin.

The first manuscript I studied was the Latin text. It appeared to be a letter written by Cyprian of Carthage, addressed to the "beloved sufferers for Christ at the hand of Emperor Decius." This meant that the manuscript, if original, would have been written sometime between 246 and 258 AD, because Cyprian had been converted to Christianity in 246 and had suffered martyrdom in 258.

The letter was one of encouragement to the families and friends of those who had become victims of Decius' purge, as well as his personal testimonial of how he had been converted to Christianity through the influence of the presbyter, Caecilianus. The manuscript was fascinating because of its historical significance, but it was of little value to my research efforts.

The second manuscript was a four-leaf document written in Greek. Although the author identified himself in the introduction, it was not until I had studied the document for a while that it finally dawned on me what it was. It was a sermon (not just an essay) written by Tertullian, who was also from Carthage, but who had died 12 years before Cyprian was born.

What confused me most was that over the centuries there had been stories, suppositions, and speculation that although Tertullian had primarily written his 30 books and countless sermons in Latin, some of his sermons could have been written in Greek. Yet, all of his writings that had thus far been discovered, identified and used by the western world of Christian theological education had been written in Latin. As a result, most western Bible educators and theologians assumed that all of Tertullian's writings were in Latin and the Greek supposition was nothing more than a fable.

Because of this teaching and assumption, I did not recognize this Greek manuscript as being originally authored by Tertullian. I thought that it was probably a Greek re-write of one of Tertullian's original Latin sermons. But, there it was, in so-called "black and white." This manuscript was one of the mysterious long lost, hotly debated and speculated upon, original Greek sermons of Tertullian.

I sat down on the woven-rug-covered floor of the study room, and began to study the document. The manuscript was a sermon written by Tertullian for the local church at Carthage. The subject of the sermon was Jesus' rising of Lazarus from the dead.

Tertullian was reputed to have had the greatest mind in all of Christendom, if not of all of humanity, during the first seven centuries after Jesus' death and resurrection. Although that distinction may be at the very least, argumentative, it is non-argumentative that his range of interests was far greater than any Christian writer before 1000 AD. Tertullian was brilliant, having distinguished himself in history, literary education, legal matters, philosophical education, medicine, and theology.

Knowing Tertullian's background, I should not have been surprised when I read the sermon. What Tertullian wrote about the resurrection of Lazarus was so amazing and so inspiring that nothing that I had ever seen, heard, or read, matched the incredible sermon that Tertullian had written about the raising of Lazarus. In his exposition, Tertullian used to perfection his diversified background.

I read and re-read the sermon a second and a third time.

Tertullian began by quoting portions of the scriptural setting where the story of Lazarus was recorded. In our Bible today it is John 11:1-44.

> *"Now a certain man was sick, named Lazarus, of Bethany, the town of Mary and her sister Martha.... Therefore his sisters sent unto Him, saying, Lord, behold, he whom thou lovest is sick. When Jesus heard that, he said, This sickness is not unto death.... When he had heard therefore that he was sick, he abode two days still in the same place where he was... Then said*

> Jesus unto them plainly, Lazarus is dead.... Then when Jesus came, he found that he had lain in the grave four days already...And said, Where have you laid him? They said unto him, Lord, come and see...Jesus said, Take away the stone....And when he thus had spoken, he cried with a loud voice, Lazarus, come forth. And he that was dead came forth, bound hand and foot with grave clothes: and his face was bound about with a napkin. Jesus saith unto them, Loose him, and let him go."

After quoting the scriptural passage, Tertullian began his sermon.

Apparently, according to Tertullian, Lazarus either lived with or lived in the same town, as did his sisters, Mary and Martha, the town of Bethany, on the eastern slope of the Mount of Olives, near Jerusalem. It seemed to Tertullian that Lazarus was well known and was well respected by the political leaders, Roman and non-Roman alike, and the religious leaders of Bethany, as well as the entire Jerusalem region. He also said that Lazarus, the Roman Egyptian/Jew, was the best friend that Jesus had in the Jerusalem area.

Jesus was neither present nor was he in the area, when Lazarus became sick. He was in either Peraea or Judea Beyond Jordan, east of the Jordan River. Tertullian concluded that Jesus was east of the Jordan because he was fleeing from and/or hiding from Herod Antipas, who sought to detain him on behalf of The Theophus Commission of Ambassadors.

When Lazarus got sick to the point of death, it was a natural reaction for his sisters to send a messenger to find Jesus and to have him come back to heal their brother. It did not enter their minds that Jesus would hesitate. It was unthinkable to them that Jesus would refuse to come to the aid of his best friend, Lazarus.

Unbeknown to the messenger who had been sent by Mary and Martha, Lazarus died the very day he left to go search for Jesus. According to the record of John [verse 14], Jesus knew that Lazarus had died even before the messenger had arrived. The day following the day that he had left Bethany, the messenger found Jesus and told him that Lazarus was sick and was near death. Jesus, knowing that Lazarus was already dead, sent the messenger back to the sisters with the message that Lazarus' sickness was not unto death, but rather it was so that God would be glorified.

"Imagine the excitement that the messenger would have had," Tertullian interjected, "When he arrived at the home of Mary and Martha and told them that Lazarus was not going to die, but that he would recover so that God would be glorified. This then was immediately followed by the depths of despair, when he realized that Lazarus was dead already and had been dead since the day that he had left to find Jesus, perhaps three days before Jesus had said that Lazarus was not going to die—yet he was now dead.

"And to make matters worse, Jesus did not even return with the messenger, but rather he sent the messenger away, telling him to return to the sisters with news that ended up being nothing more than a false hope, that ultimately turned into an untruth.

"If Jesus had returned with the messenger immediately, he still would have been three days too late. However, Jesus did not leave immediately. Instead, knowing that Lazarus had died already, he chose to stay two more additional days before he began his journey back to Bethany. By the time Jesus arrived in Bethany, Lazarus had already been dead for five days, and had been entombed for four days."

Tertullian then paused in his presentation and began to recount his discovery of a papyrus containing a Greek text that he had found while visiting the ruins of the ancient Jewish settlement of Elephantine during the days of his early manhood.

Tertullian said, "That he had found a Greek papyri that had been written during the period of the community of Elephantine's re-settlement into Judaea, and more particularly, the establishment of Bethany by these displaced Elephantine Egyptian/Jews. Elephantine was an island in the Nile River at the first cataract of the river in southern Egypt [close to what is present day Aswan].

"When Babylon was closing in on Jerusalem, some of the Jerusalem Jews fled to Egypt. Many of them settled in the northern part of Egypt, but some fled to southern Egypt and established a settlement on the island of Elephantine. There they lived a life of relative peace under the dominion of first the Babylonians, then the Persians and then the Greeks. They even built a temple of worship on the island.

"By the time the Romans began to make an impact in the area, the community had evolved into an Egyptian/Jewish syncretistic community with worship offered to the traditional God of the Jews, Yahwe, as well as to Anat-Bethel and Anat-Yahwe.

"However, for some unknown reason, the community chose not to cooperate politically with the Roman/Greek Egyptian coalition. This led to the dissolution of the settlement and the dispersion of its inhabitants. Many of the former Elephantine Egyptian/Jews settled in the Jerusalem area and established the community of Bethany. In fact, for almost 300 years, from near 100 years before Jesus' birth to almost 200 years after his birth, the families and descendants of these Elephantine Egyptian/Jews occupied the town of Bethany (the town and region was permanently deeded to the Egyptian/Jewish residents and their descendants by Caesar Augustus in AD 12). Since the names of Lazarus and Mary are typical and traditional Egyptian names, and because they lived in Bethany, most likely they were of Roman/Egyptian/Jewish decent.

"Lazarus, Mary, and Martha were third generation descendants of the displaced settlers from Elephantine, Egypt. Bethany was unique in that the residents exercised a form of Judaism in their worship practices and religious observances and celebrations, yet they were very much Greco-Roman/Egyptian in their customs, traditions, manners, rituals, observances, and manner of dress. This consummate Greco-Roman/Egyptian influence extended into the realm of burial practices and myths, as well. Thus, when Lazarus died, he was not buried in the typical and traditional Jewish manner, but rather he was embalmed and entombed in the traditional Greco-Roman/Egyptian/Jewish manner, with all of its rituals and uniqueness.

"The first day of the death and burial ritual, the day of death (from sundown of the day of death to sundown of the day following death), was set aside for family mourning.

"That first day and the day following death were also the days that the body was prepared for burial.

owing the traditional rituals and arrangements that their ancestors had in Egypt for hundreds of years, Mary and Martha prepared Lazarus' body. First, the heart, the brain, the tongue, the eyeballs, and the lungs were removed and placed in a honey, wine, and olive oil filled pottery jar. The jar was then sealed with bees wax. The body was drained of blood, coins were placed in the empty eye sockets, and the cavity where the organs had been located was filled with a mixture of honey, olive oil, and spiced wine. Afterward, the body was sewn up and was coated with thick layers of resins, salts, and gums with aromatic spices, and wrapped 'mummy-style' with dozens of wide strips of linen. The wrapped body was then placed in a tomb.

"The typical Roman/Egyptian/Jewish tomb of the residents of Bethany was a tomb that had two compartments or rooms. The first room was an area about six or eight feet square. In this first room was placed on day one, the day of death, the pottery jar that contained the removed body parts. The pottery jar remained there in the first room for four days. Also in the room was placed a loaf of bread and a vile of water, to feed the spirit as he prepared for the afterlife."

At this point Tertullian deviated from his sermon text to explain a Hellenistic Greco-Roman/Egyptian/Jewish tradition that had been brought from Egypt and was still believed and practiced at the time of Lazarus' death. The tradition said that the soul of the dead person wandered about in the small room of the tomb for three days looking for it's removed body parts and seeking an opportunity to return to the body. After four days, the body began to decompose. At that time, the soul would depart from the room and would begin its journey into the afterlife. A Jewish Pharisee persuasion had been added to the traditional Egyptian/Jew belief, and was much postulated at the time of Lazarus' death. The Jewish belief said that for four days following death, if God chose to, He could resurrect a person who had died. But when the body began to decompose, after four days, even God Himself could not resurrect the dead person. Death at that point was irreversible.

Tertullian then returned to his sermon, "From the first room of the tomb, a steep stairway, consisting of 40 steps that commemorated the exodus of the Israelites and their 40 years of struggle before they entered Canaan, descended down to a larger second room—the burial chamber. Here, in this larger underground second room, on day three or four, the wrapped body was placed in a stone vault or sarcophagus, which was then overlaid with a heavy stone or brick lid, and sealed with tallow or hardening wax.

"From day two through day four, the family accepted visitors, friends and relatives. Many gifts of condolences were given and many visits were made to the tomb.

"On day five, the day that the body began to rapidly decompose, the official public funeral took place. The final burial benediction was pronounced, gifts were given to the Temple representatives by the family, the pottery jar holding the remains of the organs was placed in the second chamber, the larger underground room, and the tomb was closed by a huge stone that was rolled in front of the tomb opening. The huge tombstone was then sealed airtight with tallow and bees wax. This was followed by a Roman official's sealing of the tomb, it was unlawful for any unauthorized person to break the seal.

"Afterwards, the family accepted hospitality visits from the public at large for the remainder of that day, day five, and on into the following day.

"It was on this day, day five, the day that the tomb was sealed, ending Mary and Martha's last hope, sealing out life forever, that Jesus appeared. He was not met with much enthusiasm. In fact everyone received him somewhat contemptuously, except Mary and Martha. The two sisters received him with a combination of astonishment, sorrow, and faithlessness.

"Jesus then requested that Martha remove the stone from the tomb opening. The request was not only an impossible physical task but it was an almost incomprehensible emotional and psychological task. It was the day that the public was invited to pay their respects to the deceased and there was perhaps hundreds of friends, acquaintances, business associates, political and religious leaders and acquaintances, neighbors, and out-of-town visitors gathered at the tomb of Lazarus and at the home of Mary and Martha. These people witnessed Jesus' extraordinary request.

"It is not known how long it took Martha to roll the stone away, or who helped her do it. But, we do know that it would have been impossible for her to do it herself, and we know that Jesus did not help her. Why did he not help her? The answer is not known.

"Finally, after the stone had been rolled away, Jesus stood before the open tomb and after giving thanks to the Father in advance for the miracle that was about to be performed, he cried in a loud thunderous voice, *'LAZARUS, COME FORTH.'* Then Jesus waited.

"The next scene that is recorded in John's Gospel is Lazarus standing at the entrance of the tomb still wrapped in his burial bandages with a separate wrap over his face. But, how did he get there?

"It is unlikely that Lazarus just appeared instantaneously—one moment he was lying in the sealed sarcophagus and then the next moment he was standing in front of Jesus in the opening of the tomb. Jesus did not work that way. Jesus raised Lazarus from the dead, but he did not make him disappear from the bottom chamber of the tomb and reappear in the top chamber doorway, instantly."

Tertullian went into a long explanation of how Lazarus somehow probably "kicked" the heavy lid off of the burial sarcophagus, and somehow managed to struggle, still bound tightly from head to toe and not able to see what he was doing or where he was going, out of the vault. Lazarus then had to find a way to stumble up the 40 steps that led to the upper chamber, so that he could appear in the door opening, still bound and not able to see. In essence, Lazarus had to rely completely upon the voice of Jesus (who spoke only once) in order to know how to get up to the upper room and the tomb opening and freedom. Yet, all of this was done after Jesus had raised Lazarus from the dead and had re-created for him a new physical body to replace the one that was decomposing, blood, a heart, lungs, a brain, eyes, and a tongue, and set them into motion to function properly and to sustain the new body.

"We do not know," Tertullian continued, "how long it took Lazarus to struggle out of the vault and stumble up the stairs in order to appear still bound at the tomb opening. It could have taken hours, during which time Jesus waited silently and the crowd of spectators watched. Doubtless many of those watching and waiting were curious. Others stayed and watched because they held Jesus in utter contempt and were certain that he would make a fool out of himself. Still others stayed because they did have a deep, but somewhat skeptical, hope that Jesus really could do something miraculous.

"No doubt many waited and waited, and seeing nothing happening, they turned away thinking that Jesus was nothing more than a fool and a failure. Others perhaps turned away with their confidence in Jesus shattered, while still others perhaps turned away thinking that this attempt was just too big, even for Jesus. But, those who remained and waited with hope and confidence became eyewitnesses to one of the greatest miracles ever recorded in the history of man."

Tertullian continued by describing the release of Lazarus from his bonds. "Lazarus had been given a new body, a new mind (the brain), new breath (the lungs), a new speech (the tongue), a new vision (the eyes), and a new heart, yet he was still bound and had to rely upon the help of his friends and his family members to help release him from his bonds and blindness. We today can do no lesser a service for our brothers in Christ. He gives them new life, but we must loose them from their bonds and accept them into the brotherhood of the living."

After I had finished reading the manuscript, I just sat there on the floor rug in amazement. This was probably the most powerful sermon that I had ever read, heard, or experienced. I could certainly understand why Tertullian was considered the most intelligent and the most powerful representative for Christ of his day. But in my opinion, Tertullian could easily stake a claim as the most powerful representative for Christ, of all time.

Nothing more is recorded about the life of Jesus until March, when Jesus and his disciples left Ephraim and began to make their way to Jerusalem "the long way around" (Matthew 20:17; Mark 10:32; Luke 9:51; John 11:54-55). When they had originally traveled to Ephraim, or just how long they stayed there is not known.

As Jesus and his disciples traveled from Ephraim to Jerusalem, they first went north and passed through Phasaelis and Archelais in the district of Samaria, and then proceeded on north into the Galilee before turning back south passing through Jericho and continuing on to Jerusalem.

In 22 BC, the cities of Phasaelis and Archelais were given to Salome, the sister of Herod the Great, by Herod. Upon her death in 2 BC, possession of the cities was passed to Livia, the wife of Augustus, and then in 14 AD to the emperor, Tiberius. These particular cities had been set aside by Herod the Great as leper cities.

Tradition says that Salome's mother-in-law became a leper not long after Salome's marriage. Because Salome was disgusted by the manner in which lepers were treated, she appealed to Herod, her brother, for help in treating her mother-in-law. Herod in turn gave the cities of Phasaelis and Archelais to Salome and declared them to be cities where lepers who were Roman citizens could come and receive the best treatment available at that time in the Empire.

Until Salome's death, she saw to it that the residents of the city received all that was needed for the treatment of their disease, including religious instruction.

Upon her death, the cities became the possession of Livia. She opened the cities to all who were suffering from leprosy, not just Roman citizens. Along with hospitals, residence housing, and extensive food preparation and service, Livia had constructed dozens of temples, places of worship, and residences for priests of all religions whose devotees where resident in the cities. Before long the cities' populations swelled to unmanageable levels, forcing the Roman military to set up permanent occupation camps outside of the city walls.

With the death of Augustus, possession of the cities passed from Livia to the new emperor, Tiberius.

Tiberius gave jurisdiction of the cities to the Syrian governor. Under the Syrian governor, the cities degenerated into a leper "dumping-off" place for the province. The hospitals, food service, and residence housing facilities were closed because of lack of operating funds.

By the time of Jesus' childhood all that remained of the once noteworthy leper treatment cities were the dozens of religious facilities, resident priest housing, and hundreds of suffering lepers from all over Syria who had been dumped in the cities. Treatment for the disease was no longer available in the cities.

By the time of Pontius Pilate, the cities had become a walled prison where lepers from every city in the region were placed during times of celebration and festivities, in order to get them off of the streets.

It was through these cities that Jesus and his disciples were passing when 10 lepers pleading that he would heal them, confronted him (Luke 17:12-18). Jesus did heal the 10 lepers who had approached him by telling them to go show themselves to the resident priest. As they were walking to the priest's residence, they were healed. But only one came back to thank Jesus for healing him.

Mankind has not changed much since that time. God still answers pray and meets our needs but seldom receives the thanks and praise worthy of His supply and provision.

Nothing more is recorded about Jesus' travels from Ephraim through Samaria, into the Galilee, and then back south toward Jerusalem until he prepares to pass through Jericho.

As Jesus and his disciples approached (or were leaving) Jericho, he healed a blind man named Bar-Timaeus, or the son of Timaeus (the Mark setting indicates that Bar-Timaeus was healed as Jesus was leaving the city—for simplicity sake we will address the healing of Bar-Timaeus after addressing the conversion of Zacchaeus). In the city itself he confronted the tax collector Zacchaeus, and as he left the city he healed two blind men (Matthew 19:29-34; Mark 10:35-52; Luke 18:35-19:10).

The same confirming documentation that I found at the great Rococo Library in St. Gallen, Switzerland, concerning the death of Joseph, the earthly father of Jesus, addressed in the chapter entitled **Fourth Year of Ministry**, I also used to confirm two of the three recorded events in Jericho: the healing of Bar-Timaeus and the conversion of Zacchaeus.

If you will recall, the confirming documentation was a legal brief written in 1600 by Bernardino Realino, a lawyer turned Jesuit, from Naples, who served as Rector of Jesuit College at Leece in Apulia, expressing his opinions concerning the two above-mentioned events.

Realino began his opinionated brief by describing the city of Jericho. "The city of Jericho is one of the oldest cities in the world. It has been continually occupied for more than 4,600 years (up to Realino's time). In the years of the conquest of Canaan by Joshua, the city was the center of worship for Tai-Innanu, the Canaanite moon goddess.

"Jericho had been called the City of Palms for centuries before the rise of the Roman Empire, because of its location in the midst of a large oasis of leafy palms (the main city center shifted many times over the centuries, but it always maintained its relationship to the oasis). The Jericho of the time of Jesus was located on the slopes and valley of a rugged 'horseshoe' shaped mountain range north of the city. It had a tropical climate, which made it ideal for the growing of numerous types of tropical fruit. Herod the Great built a magnificent summer palace in Jericho. At the time of Jesus' ministry, Herod the Great's son, Herod Archelaus, occupied the great palace.

"Herod the Great made Jericho into a wonderland of beauty. It was the 'eastern playground and recreation center of the exceptionally wealthy,' with many of the richest Romans in the east having residence there. It was one of the wealthiest cities in all of the Roman Empire and probably *the* wealthiest city in the eastern Empire.

"The city stretched southward from the mountain slopes. At the time of Herod's death, the city's length was more than 100 stadia (100 stadia was approximately equal to a five-hour walk at a brisk-pace) from the northern limits of the city to the southern limits. It had straight wide avenues [the width of the streets varied from 50 feet to 140 feet] that ran north to south and northwest to southeast.

"Jericho enjoyed a pleasant semi-tropical climate year around and it boosted of having the Empire's most elaborate irrigation network. Because of these," Realino continued, "The streets of the city were lined with gorgeous palm trees, almond trees, orange trees, African fig or African mulberry trees [the KJV of the Bible translated these trees as sycamore], lime trees, and lemon trees. North of the city the mountain slopes were covered with groves of almonds, oranges, lemons, limes, pomegranates, date palms, balsam (from which was extracted myrrh), and bananas. On the ground growing between the groves of trees were thousands of vanilla orchids. The sweet aroma of all of these combined fragrances caused Ovid to comment that *'Jericho must be inhabited by the gods for its sweet smell betrays them.'* Antony was so enchanted by the city that he gave it as a gift to Cleopatra. She in turn built a dazzling summer palace there, which she never occupied.

"Augustus fell under the spell of Jericho and was convinced that the city had been chosen by the gods as a sacred city. Consequently, by decree of Augustus Caesar, Jericho became a 'city of religions' or a 'city of the gods' also called 'a city of priests,' wherein all religions and all forms of worship were respected and honored and all were equally allowed to function and practice. No religion was acknowledged or proclaimed as superior to another. All were equal and were equally honored.

"It is estimated that at the time of Jesus' ministry in Jericho, there were temples and places of worship for at least 240 different gods, religions, religious philosophies, and/or religious sects. Out of a total population of near 200,000 residents (this did not include 25,000 slaves) there were 5,000 Jewish priests, 1,700 Pharisees and Sadducees, 400 scribes, and 700 nathanaels. Along with these, there were 42,000 other priests, religious leaders, and religious personnel representing numerous other religions from Greece, Parthia, Persia, Syria, India, Rome, Edom, Arabia, Ammon and other places. There were also at least 20 religious instructional institutions in Jericho representing religious training in 17 different religions.

"In addition, Augustus decreed that the religious leaders who lived in Jericho were exempt from paying taxes; however the city's tax liability did not decrease. Hence, the non-religious leadership, the common citizens of Jericho, had to pay far more taxes that average in order to make-up the tax difference. For this reason, only the extremely wealthy typically had a home in Jericho. For the average Judaean or Galilean family, the tax load in Jericho would have prohibited them from living there. But even with this tax load, the enormously wealthy wanted to live in Jericho because of its openness, its continuous holiday festival atmosphere, its beauty, and the international prestige and eminence of 'living in Jericho.'

"The Gospel of Luke (19:1-10) tells us that as Jesus and his disciples were walking through Jericho, a tax collector climbed up into a tree to see him.

"Jesus' reputation followed him everywhere he went, including in Jericho. In Jericho, Jesus would be highly respected because of his Roman standing and accepted as an equal to the other religious personalities who lived there because of his religious leader's position. A crowd of these contemporaries would have quickly developed as soon as it was discovered that Jesus was visiting the city.

"Zacchaeus was one of the ones who wanted to see Jesus.

"Zacchaeus was a chief tax assessor for the province of Judaea. He was employed by and under the direct supervision of the Roman tax authorities in Caesarea Maritima. Although he lived in Jericho, he was the director of all tax assessment and tax collection for the entire province, which meant that he might have been Roman by birth or a Judaean who had been granted Roman citizenship.

"Jesus would call Zacchaeus a son of Abraham, but nothing indicates that he was Jewish, although he could have been. On the other hand, a son of Abraham could have been Arabic, Edomite, Ammonite, Moabite, or any number of other nationalities or people groups who could trace their ancestry back to Abraham. Zacchaeus could have been any one of these.

"A 3rd century tradition said that Zacchaeus was the wealthiest native Judean who lived in Jericho. It seems quite obvious that he was very wealthy in that he lived in Jericho. The common Judean would never be able to afford a home in Jericho. Many non-Judean native Romans considered Jericho *the most* expensive city in which to live in the entire Empire.

"Because of Zacchaeus' height," Realino continued with his opinion, "he was unable to see over the crowd of fellow religious admirers of Jesus representing religions from all over the known world, and ran on ahead of the crowd in order to climb up either an African fig or African mulberry tree, so that he could see Jesus as he passed under the tree.

"When Jesus came to the tree that Zacchaeus had climbed, he stopped, looked up into the tree and told Zacchaeus to come down because he wanted to go to Zacchaeus' house. This was a privilege that any Roman royalty or Roman citizen with administrative or legislative authority traveling through a city, could demand. Zacchaeus quickly came down out of the tree to honor Jesus' demand (this too was accepted practice by any resident who had demanded hospitality from a Roman royalty or authority—obviously Jesus had been given this right and authority by the highest levels of Roman administration). When his disciples and some of his more orthodox followers realized that Jesus was going to the house of Zacchaeus, they became angry with him. But Jesus went anyway.

"At the feast [Realino suggested that Zacchaeus had a feast] that was given in Jesus' honor, Zacchaeus stood and without provocation by Jesus or even a suggestion that such a thing should be done, announced that half of all that he owned would be given to the poor. Whether or not Zacchaeus gave one half of his wealth is not known. However, Tantautius, an Arabic historian living in Jericho at the time, write a history of Roman Jericho from the first Triumvirate of Caesar, Pompeius, and Crassus to Vespasianus, and in it he recorded that Zacchaeus gave what today (Realino's day) would be the equivalent of $27 million to the poor, and another $17 million to those who he had taxed falsely.

"Zacchaeus gave all of this before he had acknowledged the salvation principal established by Jesus. Truly Jesus' influence was most powerful," said Realino concluding that portion of his opinion.

Realino then began the next portion of his opinion.

"We do not know how long Jesus stayed with Zacchaeus, but upon leaving the house of Zacchaeus, Jesus with his disciples and followers, left the city, and headed for Jerusalem.

"As they exited the city gates, Jesus was confronted by a blind man screaming to him, *'Jesus, thou son of David, have mercy on me'* (Mark 10:47). The man was called Bar-Timaeus or the son of Timaeus. Neither his given name nor his sir name was recorded in the Gospel of Mark. All that is obvious from the Gospel record is that the man was blind. He was begging outside of the city walls (begging was not allowed within the city limits of Jericho) along with several other beggars who found it profitable to beg from the rich residents traveling to and from Jericho. The Gospel further records that he *regained* his sight, indicating that he had sight previous to his blindness—he was not born blind.

"From the writings of Tantautius the Arab," Realino continued, "we discover that the healing of Bar-Timaeus by Jesus caused quite a stir in Jericho among the Roman officials. In fact, Jesus' exalted and respected position with the Roman authorities began to immediately crumble. By the time Jesus had reached Jerusalem, just a few days later, he had fallen from his lofty political position with the Roman authorities to the level of a common radical whose actions had to be closely monitored.

"According to Tantautius," Realino continued, "The event behind the blindness of Bar-Timaeus took place in the year AD 22, under the procuratorship of Valerius Gratus. It seems that Valerius Gratus, like most high-level Roman aristocrats, maintained a place of residence in Jericho. Attached to the residence was a private armory of arms and military supplies that were used by Roman troops in case of a local disturbance.

"His personal residence steward was a Greek/Roman whose name was Timaeus. In AD 22, Timaeus' 24-year old son, Infatius, led a nighttime raid on the armory in an attempt to steal the arms. He was going to sell them to rebel Galilean factions. He had no loyalty to these factions nor did he have any anti-Roman sentiments; his actions were strictly a business venture—steal and sell to the highest bidder. However, he was caught in the act and was found guilty of profiting by sedition (he was not accused of sedition or rebellion, rather he was accused of making a financial profit stimulated by sedition. This crime was not punishable by death, if the accused was a Roman citizen.)

"Infatius' 17 non-Roman accomplices were crucified on the northern hilltop overlooking the city. But because Infatius was Roman, he could not be crucified. Instead, his eyeballs were burned out with a red-hot sword blade and he was forced to wear a red-stained tunic to indicate that he was suffering punishment for making a profit by actions against Caesar and Roman authority. Although he was not allowed to leave the Jericho area, he was not permitted inside the city of Jericho again. Instead, Infatius, identified as Bar-Timaeus in the Gospel of Mark, had to stay outside of the city and beg for his survival for the rest of his life.

"When Infatius heard that Jesus was passing through the city gate, he cried out loud *'Jesus, thou son of David.'* This was a Messianic title. It's use implied that Infatius felt that this Galilean Roman/Jew, Jesus, whom many had said was that Messiah that would in fact neutralize the great and indomitable Roman authority and would set-up his own governmental structure. He screamed out for Jesus to come and touch him.

"Jesus asked for the man to be brought to him. The man responded by immediately casting off the tunic that the Roman authorities had *sentenced* him to wear and *demanded* he wear for the remainder of his life. In total defiance to Roman authority, he threw away this symbol of Roman judgment, punishment, and mark of ridicule. Jesus did nothing to prevent this contemptuous insult to Roman authority and its Imperial judicial decision. Instead he asked the man what he wanted. The Gospel of Mark says that the man said that he wanted to receive his sight. But Tantautius said that Infatius replied, *'That I may avenge my sight.'* It was political statement suggesting that he wanted reprisal upon his adjudicators.

"Perhaps not knowing what Infatius meant, or not fully recognizing the depth of his hatred for the Roman authorities who had condemned him, Jesus healed him. By doing so, Jesus interfered with the official punishment sentence of the Roman authorities and placed himself in a dangerous political position.

"Jesus then turned to continue his journey to Jerusalem, with the man who had just been healed following him.

"When word reached the Roman authorities that Jesus, their friend, had countermanded the judgment of the Imperial tribunal of Rome by healing the physical sign of punishment inflicted by the high court of Rome upon a rebel who was guilty of seditious profiteering; had encouraged the man to throw-off the symbol of Roman judgment, his tunic; had actually helped the imperial convicted criminal to escape the lifelong judgment that had been inflicted upon the 'sedition leech' in that he was never suppose to leave the Jericho area; and had encouraged him to join his group of followers, they became furious.

"Word of this affront by Jesus quickly spread to all of the Roman authorities in the area. In so much that by the time Jesus reached Jerusalem, word of his insult to/contempt of/disregard for Roman authority had already reached the Roman officials in Jerusalem. They were waiting for him upon his arrival in Jerusalem and carefully monitored and scrutinized every move that he made—just in case.

"Jesus' enemies would soon capitalize upon the Roman mistrust and suspicion of Jesus and use it to accuse him of and have him convicted of sedition.

"Before entering Jericho," Realino concluded, "Jesus was honored and respected by Roman authorities from Syria—the Galilee, the Decapolis, and Peraea—to Judaea and even extending as far as to Rome itself. After exiting Jericho, he was held in derision by those same high-ranking Roman officials and looked upon with suspicion."

As the group traveled to Jerusalem it appears that Jesus had some insight as to what might lay ahead and the responsibilities that his followers would have after he was gone. His followers thought that the kingdom that he was to establish would be forthcoming immediately. But Jesus delivered a parable to them that indicated that it would not be immediate. The parable is recorded in the Gospel of Luke (19:11-27) and it is based on a true incident that took place during his lifetime—the parable of the ten servants and the ten pounds.

I found confirmation of this story while researching at North Park Theological Seminary in Chicago, Illinois. It was there that I found an essay that had been written in 1878 by Rev. Theodor Christlieb from Bonn, Germany. The essay was entitled simply, *The Truth Behind the Parable.*

Rev. Christlieb began by saying, "After the death of Herod the Great in 4 BC, Herod's son, Archelaus, left quickly for Rome to lay claim to the succession of Herod's throne. He was unsuccessful in his efforts because the Jewish leaders themselves sent ambassadors to Rome with a message to be delivered to Augustus saying, *'we will not have this man to rule over us.'* Augustus reacted to this, as well as to the threat of war with an eastern confederacy for which Herod was primarily responsible, by dissolving Herod's kingdom and dividing it up into Tetrarchies. Archelaus received only a small portion of Herod's former kingdom.

"The well known story that was circulated at the time was that Archelaus was so certain that he would be successful in his attempt to secure the throne of Herod, that before he left for Rome, he divided the kingdom (Herod's old kingdom) into ten tax districts (Rome allowed Archelaus to do this, until Augustus had settled the issue permanently). Over each district, he placed one trusted guardian. Each guardian was given 10 talents of gold [worth $2,950,000 in Christlieb's day] and ten talents of silver [worth $19,200 in Christlieb's day]. With this money as seed money, each guardian was to *'increase the treasury of the kingdom in his district, better it's conditions, and increase its revenues by trade and commerce.'* The guardian, who was most successful in the accomplishment of the commands left by Archelaus, would be the new king's chief administrator. His administration would include the top fifteen cities in the kingdom. The other nine guardians would be rewarded according to their successes.

"As the story goes, Antonious, Archelaus' cousin, was given charge of the tax district of Areopolis Rabba. Antonious was terrified of Archelaus' temper and his ruthlessness. Consequently, he isolated himself in his palace in the city of Rabba. While the other nine guardians' funds increased in value, Antonious' did not. Although the funds did not lose value, they also did not increase in value.

"When Archelaus returned from Rome, he was furious with his cousin and had him exiled to and placed in prison in Ituraea. There Antonious died of starvation. Although Archelaus did not attain the entire kingdom of Herod, he was given control of Judea (including the area of Samaria) and Idumea. It remained under his control until AD 6, when his Ethnarchy was placed under the Judaean procuratorship of Rome. Nevertheless, Archelaus kept his promise.

"The guardian whose funds increased the most was Bertenius. He was appointed chief administrator over all of Archelaus' Ethnarchy. Bertenius divided the Ethnarchy into 15 tax districts, with one major city in each district. Over 10 of the districts, Bertenius appointed Appinoni (with Archelaus' approval) because his increase was second to Bertenius'. Three of the remaining districts were given to the third place finisher, and the final two were given to the fourth place finisher. The four remaining guardians were given jurisdiction over individual cities within the tax districts.

"It was to this true story that Jesus alluded with his parable as he and his followers approached Jerusalem," Christlieb wrote as he concluded the background information regarding Jesus' parable.

Nothing more is recorded about the continuation of Jesus' journey to Jerusalem, until Tuesday, March 13, when he made his first (Matthew 21:1-11; Mark 11:1-10; Luke 19:29-44) of two (John 12:12-19) triumphant entries into Jerusalem.

It was while I was researching at Southern Methodist University in Dallas, Texas that I discovered a thin bound volume, edited in 1829 by Dr. Wilkins Boothe. The book was entitled *Letters from the Cedron*. It was a compilation and translation into English and Spanish of 15 letters written in Latin by a Cappadocia born monk, who simply went by the name, Sabas. The letters were written in about the year 485, when Sabas was in seclusion in a cliff cave overlooking a gorge of the Cedron, in what became known as Palestine. Later, in 499, Sabas built a hospice in Jericho.

The letters that Sabas wrote were letters of clarification and instruction that were distributed to and read by the 150 or so monks who were also living in seclusion in the cliff caves of that area.

Dr. Boothe began by writing, "According to tradition, these 15 letters are but a fraction of the hundreds of letters of instruction that Sabas wrote as teaching lessons to the Cedron monks. Apparently from about 470 until about 492, neither he nor the community of monks said a word, except in vespers at prayer. All instructions and teachings were in writing. Eventually, against his will, Sabas became recognized as the priest and religious authority of the cave seclusion community.

"These 15 surviving letters are teachings that dealt with the last couple of weeks of Jesus' life before he was crucified. They specifically covered Jesus' first and second triumphal entries into Jerusalem."

At this point I paused and re-read what Dr. Boothe had written. "First and second triumphant entries...." That was the first time that I had ever heard or read of a first and a second triumphant entry. The only thing I had ever heard was Jesus' one triumphant entry into Jerusalem that we celebrate today as Palm Sunday. However, if there were two entries, it would certainly explain the conflicting given by the Gospels of Matthew, Mark, and Luke and the one given by ›el of John. With two entries, there is no conflict.

ı continued reading Dr. Boothe's compilation, "I (Dr. Boothe) have compiled all of the letters as if they were a single document. I will not separate them into individual letters. However, there appears to be a letter or two missing between the aftermath of Jesus' first entry, to the beginning of his second entry in that one letter begins to describe the events of Jesus' second Temple cleansing and then the description stops abruptly. The next page picks up as a completely new letter, and describes the second entry.

"The first of Jesus' two triumphal entries took place on what would be our Tuesday, March 13, AD 31. The incident is recorded in the Gospels of Matthew 21:2-8; Mark 11:2-10; and Luke 19:30-40. The second triumphal entry took place on what would be our Friday, March 23, AD 31. This one is recorded in the Gospel of John 12:12-19.

"Sabas began his letters by saying that in this particular year (AD 31), because of a well justified fear of rebellion in the Galilee and in the state of Judea, Pilate had declared in January, AD 31, that the Jewish celebrations of the Feast of Tabernacles, Yom Kippur (the Day of Atonement), and the Feast of Dedication were not to be held in the city of Jerusalem or in all of the Galilee.

"To counter this unjust infringement upon Jewish religious traditions, the Sadducees in Jerusalem decided to incorporate the celebrations of the Feast of Tabernacles, Yom Kippur, and the Feast of Dedication, into an expanded Passover celebration—a celebration that would last for 17 days, rather than the typical seven days of unleavened bread. When the proposal was submitted to Pilate for approval, he willingly approved it in order to discourage any kind of rebellion. So, for the first and only time in the history of the Jewish people, four Jewish celebrations were combined into one national celebration—one that was approved by the Roman authorities. So, on Tuesday, March 13 of the year AD 31, Jesus found himself approaching the city of Jerusalem, at the time that the Feast of Tabernacles portion of the 17-day celebration was about to begin.

"As Jesus and his disciples approached the city of Jerusalem's municipal customs post or customs station, Jesus sent two of his disciples on ahead into the little village that had grown up around the custom's station. The name of the village was Bethphage and it means *district customs house*. The disciples who were sent into the village were to secure a donkey on which Jesus could ride into the city of Jerusalem.

"It is at this point," Dr. Boothe interjected with a personal comment, "That the author of Matthew's Gospel quoted what he said was a portion of Zechariah. Actually what he quoted came from Zechariah 9:9. It was in reality a prophecy that related to a deliverer who would come and who would deliver the children and descendants of Abraham from the yoke of Persia. Nonetheless, the writer of Matthew used it to describe this event.

"One of the primary traditional celebrations associated with the Feast of Tabernacles," Dr. Boothe said as he returned to Sabas' letters, "Recorded in Leviticus 23:40, began at sunup, and was carried out on both the first day and the last day of the celebration. The people would gather at the Pool of Siloam where a chief priest gave them green tree branches. They then would slowly walk to the Temple while waving the branches. As they walked and waved the branches they lamented, mourned, and cried, begging for the Messiah to come and to save them. This was called the *Great Hosanna*. The Great Hosanna literally meant, *'Save us; we beseech you.'*

"It was not a shout of joy or celebration, but a loud lamenting beseechment accompanied with crying and wailing as if loved one had just died."

This was another surprise to me. I had always been taught that *Hosanna* was praise and a shout of joy and exultation. Now I find out that *Hosanna* was a lamentation and a cry for mercy. How could the word make an 180° change in definition from that time until today?

I then returned to Dr. Boothe's evaluation of Sabas' letters. "While the lamenting celebrates were making their way from the Pool of Siloam to the Temple, Jesus and his followers were moving toward the Eastern Gate of the city, which exited into the Temple compound.

"As Jesus and his followers began their descent from the Mount of Olives toward the Eastern Gate, his disciples and followers began to spontaneously spread their clothes in front of the donkey that he rode, and began to shout praises to him.

"Upon entering the Eastern Gate, Jesus and his disciples, who were shouting praises to Jesus, met the lamenting Feast of Tabernacles participants. As the two groups joined they became a huge lamenting and praising throng. The disciples then joined the participants in shouting the *Great Hosanna*, however, they directed it to Jesus, indicating that they recognized him as that great delivering Messiah. Eventually the outer court of the Temple was filled with the massive crowd, crying and shouting and directing the *Great Hosanna* to Jesus.

"Jesus allowed this adoration to continue for quite some time. He did not try to stop it.

To the Sadducees, this was blasphemy. Some years previous, this same Galilean rabboni, this Jesus, had caused a stir in the Temple when he drove some merchants and moneychangers out of the Temple compound with a small whip, which attracted the negative notice of some of the more powerful Sadducees. Since that time, there had been no other incident with regard to Jesus that they, the Sadducees, felt was worthy of their investigation. But now, once again, Jesus had drawn attention to himself. This act of receiving praise and adoration within the Temple compound was *the act* that caused the powerful Sadducees to begin to look at Jesus as someone more than just another itinerant Galilean, and some say, Roman, rabboni, who claimed to have been sent from God.

"From that time onward, every action and every word would be evaluated with (extreme scrutiny—added Dr. Boothe). The Sadducees were the ones that Jesus had to fear. They, not the compelling Shammaite Pharisees, had the power and prestige to influence his arrest, his imprisonment, his trial, and perhaps even his death. The Sadducees were very tolerant of the hundreds of self-proclaimed Messiahs and saviors who were at that time traveling throughout the Galilee and the province of Judaea. These self-proclaimed saviors did not overly concern them because they knew that they were nothing more than religious fog—here this moment and gone the next.

"However, when festival celebrants who had come to Jerusalem from all over the Roman world, began to direct the *Great Hosanna* toward Jesus and to proclaim his Messiahship, by incorporating that conviction into the sacred ceremonies instituted by Moses himself, special attention had to be given to that man. Then when Jesus refused to silence those who were giving him adoration but instead allowed it to continue for perhaps hours, it was more than the Sadducees could take.

"It was one thing to dispute with the Shammaite Pharisees, the scribes, and the Galilean Sadducees; but it was quite another thing to become an enemy of the extremely powerful state of Judea Sadducees and the Sadducee leadership in Jerusalem. In comparison, whereas disputing and arguing with the Pharisees would be like dealing with an obnoxious fly, contending with the Jerusalem Sadducees was like wrestling a wild bull or an angry Nile crocodile.

"Finally after the praises died down, Jesus made his way back through the Temple compound, heading toward Solomon's Porch. However, the more he walked, the angrier he became until he exploded into a fit of anger that resulted in the second of the three times that he cleansed the Temple [for details concerning Jesus' first cleaning of the Temple see the chapter entitled **Second Year of Ministry**].

"Hours later, after things had calmed down," Dr. Boothe continued, "Following Jesus' expulsion of the moneychangers, children who were in the Temple compound began shouting praises to Jesus. Whether they did this on their own or were simply mimicking the adult lamenting/praising celebrates, we cannot say. But we do know that the chief priests and the scribes were quite upset because Jesus did not stop them from praising him.

"Shortly after this, he went to Bethany and spent the night.

"On perhaps the next morning, but most likely the morning following that one, on Thursday, March 22, Jesus and his disciples left Greco-Roman/Egyptian/Jewish Bethany and traveled back to Jerusalem. While they were traveling, Jesus noticed a single fig tree a far off. Because he was hungry, he was expecting figs to be on tree, but as he approached the fig tree, all it had was leaves—the tree had no fruit on it. Since figs normally appeared before leaves, it was understandable why Jesus would expect the tree to have figs. When he saw that it did not have any figs on it, he cursed the tree (Matthew 21: 18-22; Mark 11: 12-26), which immediately began to wither and die from its roots up.

"They then continued on their way to Jerusalem.

"Upon their arrival into Jerusalem, they first went to the Temple. When they arrived at the Temple, again they saw merchants selling and moneychangers exchanging money. So, for the third and final time Jesus drove the merchants and moneychangers out of the Temple compound; again causing a stir with the scribes, chief priests, and the Sadducees.

"Nevertheless, the merchants and moneychangers *did not* return to the Temple to sell their goods or to exchange money until after the death of Jesus.

"Later in the day, Jesus and his disciples left the Temple compound and returned to Bethany for the night. On their way back they passed the fig tree that Jesus had cursed and noticed that it had already died and withered away. Some of the disciples commented about how quickly it died.

" Jesus responded by teaching them a lesson on faith by using the example of a mustard seed for the 3rd time (Matthew 21:18-22; Mark 11:12-26). [For details relating to the first and second lessons on having faith as a mustard seed see the chapter entitled **Fourth Year of Ministry**].

"On all three occasions in which Jesus used the mustard seed analogy, he emphasized the importance of a person's faith by comparing faith to a mustard seed and/or mustard plant. All three occasions took place at different times in two different years.

"Later that evening (Thursday, March 22, AD 31) Jesus and his disciples were invited to eat at the home of Mary and Martha, the sisters of Lazarus, whom Jesus had raised from the dead (John 12:3-8).

"After dinner, Mary knelt behind Jesus, who was reclining on one of the feast reclining couches that was so typical of Roman culture or Egyptian/Roman/Jewish culture, as was the case with Mary, Martha, and Lazarus, and anointed his feet with spikenard.

"It appears that Martha was doing the serving for the reclining Jesus and his disciples and Lazarus. We do not know what Mary was doing until we see her come up behind Jesus and begin to anoint his feet that were sticking out over the foot of the reclining couch. The ointment that she used was the same kind of ointment with which he had previously been anointed by a sinner woman at Simon the Pharisee's house in Capernaum [see the chapter entitled **Third Year of Ministry**], except it was a different consistency. The sinner woman had used liquid spikenard ointment and Mary used spikenard salve. John's Gospel says that Mary used a pound, or about 12 ounces, of the salve to anoint Jesus. Considering that this was the most expensive salve in the world at that time, 12 ounces of it would have been worth a two years' income on the wholesale merchants market and a five to seven years' income on the retail market. This anointing of Jesus' feet with spikenard was the second of three times that he was anointed and the first of two times in the last week before he was arrested.

"After anointing Jesus' feet with the salve," Dr. Boothe continued as he explained Sabas' letter, "filling the whole place with the aroma of the ointment, Mary dried them with her hair.

"The apostle Judas was incensed at what he considered a waste of good and expensive ointment, saying that the ointment could have been sold for a wholesale minimum of one year's income and the proceeds given to the poor. Perhaps he mentioned the poor because shortly before this Jesus had given his great challenge to them about feeding the poor, helping the orphans, and visiting those who were in prison—*'In that you have done it to the least of these, you have done it unto me.'* Judas felt safe in challenging this 'waste' by riding on the 'coattails' of Jesus' own credo and probably expected Jesus to credit him for being so synchronal with Jesus' ideas and philosophy.

"However, Jesus knew that Judas' underlying motive was one of selfishness and greed. Instead of venerating Judas, Jesus defended Mary, implying that honoring him (Jesus) was a higher form of service than was service to others, even the poor and needy. This stern rebuke of Judas in front of all those present was humiliating and infuriating to Judas.

"It was probably after this open rebuke that Judas decided to 'get even' with Jesus for this degradation. This leads us to believe that perhaps greed and revenge were the primary motives for Judas' loathsome betrayal of Jesus.

"That is all that this letter written by Sabas contains. Obviously the rest of it has been lost." Dr. Boothe wrote, "So, I'll go on to the next letter.

"This next letter starts with Jesus and his disciples traveling back to Jerusalem from Bethany on Friday, March 23, AD 31, at the same time of the day that he had traveled to Jerusalem 10 days before. On this day, the last day of Feast of Tabernacles' portion of the 17-day combined feast celebration, and the day that the second *Great Hosanna* lamentation took place, Jesus found a colt himself, sat on it, and led his disciples toward the Eastern Gate (John 12:12-19). Jesus again intercepted the *Great Hosanna* participants just as they were approaching the Eastern Gate. This time though, his disciples did not have to lead the way in worship and adoration to Jesus. The lamenting celebrants themselves recognized Jesus from 10 days previous and they began to praise him and to direct the *Great Hosanna* toward him. Again, Jesus accepted the praise and adoration, refusing to restrict it.

"Without a doubt, this was *the* final slap in the face to the powerful Sadducees. From that time forward until the time that Jesus suffered his death on the cross, these Jerusalem Sadducees were determined to take Jesus' life.

"Ten days later, their determination was realized in the death of Jesus the Christ." With that closing statement Dr. Boothe concluded his examination of the Sabas letters that he had compiled.

After the second triumphant entry, Jesus and his disciples spent the day in the Temple compound. At nightfall they returned to Bethany.

The next morning [Friday, March 23] they again traveled to Jerusalem and went to the Temple. This time there where no merchants, animals, goods, or money changers in the Temple. For the remainder of the day Jesus stayed in the Temple and taught the Pharisees, scribes, and priests who would listen, and the combined feasts celebrates who were in the compound and who wanted to hear what he had to say, a number of lessons including the parables of the two sons, evil servant, marriage feast (the second time Jesus told the parable of the wedding feast), and the wedding garments; the lesson on rendering unto Caesar that which is Caesar's, the greatest commandment (the second time Jesus taught this lesson), the question of marriage in the afterlife, and the question about who is David's son?

Although all of these (Matthew 21:23-22:46; Mark 11:27-12:37; Luke 20:1-44) were spoken by Jesus in one day—Friday, March 23 as he taught in the Temple—I had to rely upon more than one source in order to find corroborating documentation confirming the truth regarding these parables and lessons as recorded in the Gospels.

I found authenticating documentation for some of the parables and lessons spoken by Jesus on that day while researching at the Merton College, Oxford in Oxford, England.

I had been studying for just over two days at the library of Merton College when I came across a book edited in 1841 by Sir Oliver Stewart entitled *A Day of Parables*. The book was Sir Stewart's commentary on Rev. Charles Simeon's sermon series focusing on Jesus' response to challenging questions conveyed to him in the Temple by religious leaders on Friday, March 23, AD 31, just twelve days before Jesus' death, which was on Monday, April 2, AD 31.

Sir Stewart began his commentary on Rev. Simeon's sermons by writing, "As Jesus was in the midst of teaching in the Temple, Sadducees and officials of the Temple came to him asking by what authority he thought he could disrupt the accepted Temple practices and traditions, and could accept adoration and praise from the people?

"Jesus answered them by asking them by what authority did John baptized? When they chose not to answer, he responded by saying that he too would not answer them about his authority. He then followed that statement by telling (in the company of many on-lookers) them five parables that were all based on true, well-known historical events. These were intended, perhaps, to show that they, the religious leaders, had been rejected as the approved and the chosen of God, and that God had in fact chosen others to take their places; those whom they (the religious leaders) probably considered unworthy to be chosen.

"The first parable was one about two sons being asked by their father to work [Matthew 21:28-32]. One said that he would not work, but then he changed his mind and did work. The other said that he would work, but he did not.

"Cicero first spoke this parable as he addressed the Roman Senate on April 6, 46 BC.

"It seems," Sir Stewart continued, "that the Senate was quite upset because Julius Caesar had discharged the eldest general in his army, Marcus Porcius, the former chief general of Pompey's Illyricum defenses, but who had abandoned Pompey in Epiru and had defected to the side of Caesar. Marcus Porcius had been quite instrumental in assuring Caesar's victory in Egypt at the Battle of the Nile. When Caesar was called to Syria to re-secure Pontus, a Roman province just south of the Black Sea near Lake Van, which had been invaded by Pharnaces, the son of Mithridates the Great, he left Marcus Porcius in charge of the occupation forces of Egypt and hastened to Syria.

"Arriving in Pontus, Caesar found the situation much more critical than he had anticipated, so he sent word to Marcus Porcius that he should hurry in joining him at Zela. Marcus Porcius sent word back that he would come with all speed. However, his life in Egypt was too comfortable, and he did not come as Caesar had commanded. In fact, he assumed that if he did not come to Caesar's aid that Caesar would probably be killed and the Roman Senate, where he had some powerful friends, would appoint him, Marcus Porcius, governor of Egypt.

"When Caesar discovered that Marcus Porcius was not coming to his aid, he secretly swore revenge and then sent a request for assistance to Perge Alexandrus, the chief of a small band of mercenary fighters from the mountains of Armenia. Caesar said that if he would join forces with him, that he would grant Roman citizenship to both him, Perge Alexandrus, and to his mercenary army, and that he would pay each member of the army a talent of silver and give Alexandrus two talents of gold.

"Perge Alexandrus sent back word refusing Caesar's request for aid, stating that he did not desire Roman citizenship, nor did he want Roman gold and silver.

"Yet, in the heat of the battle at Zela, at a time when it was uncertain whether Caesar would be victorious or defeated, Perge Alexandrus' little band of 400 fierce fighters came running down the mountainside and turned the odds of victory in favor of Caesar. After the battle, Caesar greeted Perge Alexandrus and thanked him openly before his entire army. This is also when Caesar made the famous statement that he eventually spoke again before the Roman Senate, *Veni! Vidi! Vici! —I came! I saw! I conquered!*

"Caesar again offered Roman citizenship, gold, silver, and even gave Alexandrus' fighters permission to loot as they pleased. Perge Alexandrus refused all of these. Caesar asked him why he had changed his mind and decided to help him, if not for the rewards and loot.

"Perge Alexandrus responded that he hated Pharnaces because he had destroyed his city and his family, as well as every member of his army's families. So when he discovered that Pharnaces was the one Caesar was fighting, every one in his army, to the man, wanted to help Caesar in order to take vengeance upon Pharnaces.

"When Caesar returned to Rome he relieved Marcus Porcius of his command, dismissed him from his position, and brought him before the Senate on charges of insubordination and treason in that his refusal to obey a direct order had jeopardized the stability of the Republic.

"The Senate friends of Marcus Porcius rushed to his defense, citing that a goal of personal glory on the part of Julius Caesar was his justification for even going to Syria in the first place.

"Cicero stood firmly on the side of Caesar and gave a moving speech before the Senate, a speech that condemned Marcus Porcius. He was convicted of both treason and contempt for the Republic. Two months later Marcus Porcius, while under house arrest awaiting sentencing, committed suicide.

"The parable told by Cicero in the Senate was used to defend Caesar and condemn Marcus Porcius. Jesus used the same parable to condemn the so-called chosen of God, the Sadducees and the Temple officials.

"Imagine how the Sadducees felt," Sir Stewart interjected, "when Jesus used a well-known, well-documented event in 'barbaric-paganistic' Roman history to condemn them—God's chosen people.

"This parable," Sir Stewart continued, "was quickly followed by another: a parable about an evil husbandman [Matthew 21:33-41]. This was a parable in which Jesus used another historical event to emphasize his point that because the chosen had abused the messengers of God, including himself, they would be rejected.

"The great Rabboni, Hillel, spoke this same parable as he addressed Herod the Great in 21 BC. He spoke it in reference to the abuse the Diaspora Jews had suffered at the hands of their Hasmonean overlords. This parable by Hillel so moved Herod that he increased his 'war on the Hasmonean until he had virtually annihilated their very bloodline, and had redistributed their wealth to the Diaspora Jews in his kingdom.

"This parable by Hillel, repeated and used very effectively here by Jesus, had its historical foundation in Persian history.

The Search

"In 480-479 BC, Xerxes I, emperor of Persia, invaded Greece by land and by sea in an attempt to subjugate Greece. Xerxes was known throughout the world as 'the wine king' because of the huge vineyards that he possessed and the huge amount of wine produced by him. While in Greece, he had left his 'master of the household,' Xerubelle, in charge of tending his vineyards. The Greek campaign became much more costly than Xerxes had anticipated, so he sent servants back to Persia at harvest and wine processing time to collect some more funds from the worldwide sale of his wine, in order to continue to finance his war efforts.

"But Xerubelle, who had visions of Xerxes being killed in battle and he (Xerubelle) becoming the 'master of the wine trade' throughout the world, had the servants sent by Xerxes killed. Thus, Xerxes did not receive the funds that he needed to purchase supplies and reinforcement weaponry. Four times Xerxes sent servants and each time the servants were killed.

"Finally, Xerxes sent Arathexar, his own son, to collect the money, feeling that surely his son would be honored and respected. But when Xerubelle saw that it was Arathexar who had been sent to collect the funds, he felt that Xerxes was probably near defeat or else he would not have sent his own son. So, he had Arathexar killed, like he had had all of the servants killed.

"Finally, Xerxes agreed to a 20-year peace with Greece and returned home. Upon his return, Xerxes impaled Xerubelle. He was left on the stake until wild beasts had consumed his body. Xerxes then took Xerubelle's entire family and either imprisoned them in the salt mines of Achmetha (these mines were called 'outer darkness' by the people of Persia) or had them impaled.

"The parable based on this story, spoken by Hillel and repeated by Jesus, was probably one of the best-known and most widely circulated parables in any Jewish school of thought at this time in Jewish history.

"Again, Jesus' use of this well known 'Jewish' parable was extremely effective in his dealings with the Sadducees and other religious leaders who had gathered around him."

Sir Stewart continued with his commentary on Rev. Simeon's sermons, "Attached to this parable about the evil husbandman was a parable that had its origin in ancient Egyptian folklore, although Jesus used it as an analogy to show how the Jewish religious officials had rejected him, and that their decision to reject him would come back on them and would likely crush them [Matthew 21:42-45].

"This story involved the rejection of the capstone at the time of the construction of the Great Pyramid of Cheops, near ancient Memphis in Egypt. This was an edifice that had been standing for as many as 2,500 to 3,000 years by the time Jesus was born. It is likely that he saw it many times while he lived in Egypt and that he heard numerous and varied stories and fables about it.

"One of those stories was a tale, which may or may not have been true, about the selection of the Great Pyramid's capstone.

"This particular story was passed down orally for centuries before being written down by a scribe some 1,000 years before the birth of Jesus. As such, it was taught as part of an Egyptian student's folklore education.

"The story begins with Father Universe, the father of the sun, Ra, giving to Ora, his representative on earth and the builder of the Great Pyramid, the plans for the building of and the placement location of the Great Pyramid. The story continues by saying that the capstone, the chief cornerstone, was the first stone to be quarried. It was formed from a solid piece of hard and precious marble, different from the rest of the Pyramid, which was made of limestone and granite.

"The capstone was made with two pointed projections: one up and one down. The one pointed up would serve as a finish to the project and the one pointed down would serve as the head of the four corners and would hold the Pyramid together.

"It was said that the stone was polished; it was treated with fire to purge out all impurities; it was abused with stones and hammers to see if it would crack; and after all of the abuse and all of the testing, it proved to be truly worthy to serve as the chief cornerstone and capstone of the world's greatest structure. After the stone was formed, it was set aside so that work could begin on the Great Pyramid itself.

"As time passed and construction on the Great Pyramid progressed, the importance of the capstone was forgotten. Consequently, it was not guarded, nor was it cared for; it was instead neglected and forgotten.

"Finally, the Pyramid was complete except for the capstone, the chief cornerstone. But instead of using that stone that had been tried and tested, the builders rejected it and chose instead to make their own cornerstone out of pure, solid, polished brass. It would be much more beautiful and much easier to handle. It would not resist; it could easily be poured into a mold that the builders had prepared for it. So, the original cornerstone was rejected in preference to one of the builder's own creation. The result was a beautiful structure capped by a beautifully radiant cornerstone.

"But this beauty was short lived, for within two generations, invaders from the east laid waste the land of Egypt and the brass capstone was removed and melted down to be used in the forming of weapons.

"After another two generations, a new Pharaoh came to power and drove the eastern invaders out of Egypt. The new Pharaoh attempted to restore the Pyramid to its past glory, except this time he insisted upon the placement of the original capstone.

"A nationwide search followed, but the original capstone was never found. The conclusive assumption to the story was that the Father of the Universe had taken the stone from the Egyptian people because of their rejection of it, and only He could replace it. Hence, to this day, the Great Pyramid is minus it's originally designed, quarried, and tested capstone.

"After Jesus had told this parable, the Sadducees and the Temple officials became furious and wanted to take him and probably stone him, but they feared what the people would do if they did.

"Again Jesus immediately followed that parable about the capstone with another parable. This one was about king Cymbeline, king of all of the tribes of central and northern Britain, who gave a combination marriage feast in honor of his son's wedding and a coronation feast to celebrate his, Cymbeline's, coronation [I have already alluded to the historical background concerning this story in the chapter entitled **Fifth Year of Ministry**]. This was the 2nd time that Jesus told a parable focusing on the wedding feast of Cymbeline. However, when he related it this time, Jesus added another allegory to the parable that he had not included the

The Search

first time. This addition had to do with the providing of the wedding garments [Matthew 22:1-14]. Once again, Jesus used well-known Roman history as a basis for his parable.

"It seems that this parable was based on a true event that took place at the marriage of Marcus Antonius (Mark Antony) and Cleopatra in 36 BC.

"Antony and Cleopatra had sent wedding invitations to all of the officials and dignitaries throughout Egypt and in all of the surrounding countries. However, because Antony was still married to Octavia, the sister of Octavian, the soon to be Augustus Caesar, most of the officials in the surrounding countries feared Octavian's retaliation wrath if they were to attend the wedding. So most of the dignitaries outside of Egypt refused the invitation.

"Antony and Cleopatra had prepared a large wedding celebration and they were left with much more food than the guests could consume and far more empty places than occupied. So, Cleopatra told her servants to go out into the city and bring in the citizens of the city so that the celebration feast would be fully attended. So common citizens by the hundreds were obliged to attend the ten-day wedding celebration.

"These unusual circumstances allowed the opportunity for a plot against Antony's life, which had been in the planning stages, to come to maturity.

"Somehow, however, Antony discovered the plot to take his life during his wedding celebration. Yet, the celebration preparations were too far advanced to cancel, so he and Cleopatra devised a plan whereby everyone would be searched and no one would be allowed to wear garments in which weapons could be concealed.

"As the guests arrived, they were ushered into preparation quarters. There the guests' old garments were taken from them. They were bathed in perfumed water and pampered like royalty. They then were given a special wedding garment. The women were given a transparent gold or blue silk toga that was held in place by a gold woven rope belt, and a gold necklace. The men were given a blue or white linen toga with a gold chain to place around their neck and gold woven sandals. Each guest was allowed to keep the garments, which to the common citizen of the city of Memphis could have been worth more than ten years' wages. However, to wear anything other than the accepted wedding garments would be a direct insult to Antony and Cleopatra. Such impertinence would be dealt with in severity.

"The wedding celebration went as planned and everyone wore the appropriate wedding garments. However, on the sixth day of the celebration, three guests arrived. Thinking that Antony would be so drunk by then that he would not know anything, they silently and secretly seated themselves in the back of the banquet hall, among the servers and prepares of food. Two were dressed in typical military garments and one was wearing a course homespun toga. They had weapons hid beneath their garments; weapons meant to be used for the murder of Antony.

"Antony had been waiting for such an incident. He immediately noticed them as they entered the banquet hall. He responded by acting drunk and incoherent while he watched the three gradually make their way over the next couple of hours, closer to where Antony and Cleopatra were reclining on their gold threaded couches, being entertained by the celebration dancers.

"Finally, the three had advanced so close that they were only a few feet from Antony. Thinking that Antony was far too drunk to notice them, they silently eased their hands under their garments to retrieve their weapons.

"At the very instant that they were about to expose their weapons, Antony suddenly jumped up and stood on his couch. He pointed to the three men and asked, 'How is it that you insult my wife and queen and dishonor your lord by attending my celebration without proper attire?' He then told his guards to seize them and strip them, whereupon the weapons intended for Antony's murder were discovered. One of the conspirators was named Sejus Rufus, the captain of the palace guard of Cleopatra.

"Antony accused them of treason and of plotting to assassinate the queen. He then ordered that they be bound and thrown into *outer darkness,* a term often used by Antony to mean that they would reside forever in the regions of darkness. In essence, the men would be put to death, but rather than being buried and their souls committed to Seth, (according to Egyptian beliefs) the god of the underworld, for passage into the realm of the dead, their bodies would be burned, thus assuring them of no bodily life after death. No sacrifice would be given to Seth on their behalf and there would be no commitment of their souls to Seth. This meant to the Egyptians that the condemned souls would fall hopelessly and aimlessly in intensely hot total darkness for all of eternity.

"Again Jesus had the audacity, so thought the religious leaders who were present, to use a historical event of the pagan Romans to rebuke the 'God chosen guardians' of 'God's chosen people.' How dare he? To imply that perhaps they had been called, but had not been chosen by God, was unforgivable. They could not, would not, and did not tolerate this from Jesus. The parables directed against the powerful Sadducees, as much as anything else in Jesus' last two weeks, led to his death." That statement ended Sir Stewart's commentary.

After replacing the book in the bookshelf, I wrote a concluding note. "I had wondered for years concerning these particular parables of Jesus and now I have discovered that the parables were more than just stories or tales invented by him. They were based on actual events that were used by him as tools for teaching; much like allegories or analogies. By using actual historical events, Jesus made the parables come alive with meaning, significance, and importance."

Luke 20 implies that the Pharisees, scribes, and the chief priests left the Temple for a while and collaborated with some Herodians who were in Jerusalem (they were probably in Jerusalem to investigate Jesus as a probable Theophus candidate), in an attempt to catch Jesus at some inconsistency which they could use to judge him (The Jewish religious leaders were the ones who wanted to catch Jesus at some inconsistency, not the Herodians. But they did join with the Herodians, who had their own agenda concerning Jesus). So, with a new determination and with the support of the Herodians, they approached Jesus again later that day with a question about whether they should pay the mandatory Roman poll tax. Jesus responded with his famous, *"Render unto Caesar the things that are Caesar's..."* (Matthew 22:15-22; Mark 12:14-17; Luke 20: 19-26).

I discovered documentation supporting the Gospels account of this event while studying at the University of California at Berkley. It was during the Vietnam era, and Berkley was a political boiling pot of protests against the campus ROTC program and America's involvement in the Vietnam war, and a magnet for eastern religious, metaphysical awareness, and spiritual consciousness. But, to the best of my ability, I tried to stay away from all of the crowds and demonstrations and concentrate on my research

At the Berkley library I investigated and evaluated dozens of resources that seemed to have potential, but out of all of those that I investigated only one seemed to fit into my parameters of the key of truth.

The resource was an art commentary compiled by German activist, Jack Bonnern, entitled *Politics, God, and Government*. In this book, published in 1939, Bonnern reproduced miniature copies of ten lesser known church altar paintings from Medieval German times, and gave a one to three page semi-detailed explanation describing each painting.

All of the miniature reproductions were intriguing and the history behind each was fascinating, yet I felt that only one miniature, with its accompanying notes, could actually be beneficial to my research. This one painting depicted Jesus standing in front of a group of well-dressed, arrogantly pious-looking men. He was holding a coin in his hand. The title of the painting was *Render Unto Caesar* and the painting was an alter piece for the small but ornate Church of St. Lidwina in Hirsau, Germany. The church was built in the 16th century.

Of all of the paintings reproduced by Bonnern, this one, *Render Unto Caesar*, is the one about which he wrote the most. In fact, he went into three or four times as much detail with this painting as he did with any of the others.

Bonnern first explained the history of the painting and how it came to be housed in Hirsau, and then he described the depicted scene itself.

According to Bonnern, "On Friday, March 23, AD 31, after ineffectively confronting Jesus in the Temple earlier in the day, the chief priests, many of the Shammaite Pharisees from Jerusalem, and some of the Jerusalem scribes met to decide how they were going to eliminate Jesus. But since they were afraid of the people and Jesus' reputation with the people, they decided that the best way to eliminate Jesus was to let the Roman government pass judgment on him, especially since it had become known to them that Jesus' exalted position with the Roman authorities had begun to rapidly deteriorate since his visit to Jericho.

But regardless of their growing suspicion of Jesus, the Roman authorities would not pass judgment upon him unless he was found guilty of sedition or treason. So, in an attempt to accuse Jesus of saying something treasonous or of doing something unlawful, or something that could be interpreted as seditious, the Jerusalem Jewish religious leaders sent spies to the Temple to observe him, attempting to catch him doing or saying something forbidden by Rome (Matthew 22:15-22; Luke 20:22-26).

"Later in the day, the conspirators met with some Herodians who were in Jerusalem to investigate and to observe Jesus. Together they plotted how they could determine whether he truly was qualified to be that Theophus, and if not how they could catch him saying something or doing something whereby he could be judged and accused. They came up with a plan that they felt would reveal Jesus' true nature and would identify whether or not he had a Theophus temperament—they would question him on the issue of taxes and the law of Rome.

"They went to the Temple where he was teaching and confronted him concerning the Roman poll tax.

"One of the most hated of all mandatory Roman taxes was the controversial poll tax," Bonnern continued. "The poll tax was a tax that was applied to each family member of each non-Roman family in Judaea. It was used to support the Roman auxiliary military units in Judaea. The larger the family, the higher the tax that had to be paid. By their questioning Jesus concerning this most hated of all taxes, his inquisitors sought to trap him into making a statement that would implicate him as being rebellious to the Roman authorities. If Jesus denied the legitimacy of the poll tax, they would have grounds to denounce him and to call him up on charges of inciting sedition against Rome. If he said that the payment was legitimate, he would lose prestige with the Jewish and non-Roman populous, and they could accuse him of collaborating with the Romans; hence, he would be portrayed as a false prophet.

"The conspirators questioned Jesus by saying, *'Tell us whether or not it is lawful to pay the poll tax, or tribute tax.'*

"Jesus did not answer their question directly, except to ask them why they were tempting him or why they were trying to trap him. He then asked them to give him a coin.

"They handed him a silver denarius. On one side of the coin bore the head and/or the bust of Tiberius, surrounded by the inscription of Tiberius' official name and title: TI (for Tiberiuu) CAESAR DIVI AUG (for Caesar Divi Augusti) F (for Filius) AUGUSTUS. The inscription actually meant, *Tiberius Caesar, Son of the Divine Augustus, Augustus.* On the reverse side of the coin was the image of the empress Julia Livia (symbolizing peace, or Pax) holding a scepter and flowers, along with the inscription: PONTIF (for Pontifex) MAXIM (for Maximus). The inscription meant *High Priest*.

"Taking the coin and looking at it, he asked them whose image and superscription or identifying inscription was on the coin. They told him that it was Caesar's. He then told them to, *'Render unto Caesar the things that are Caesar's and to God the things that are God's.'*

"Jesus' answer so disarmed his agitators that they had no response. They walked away amazed and left him alone. Never again did these four—the chief priests, the Shammaite Pharisees, the scribes, and the Herodians—cooperate together in an effort to trap Jesus. In fact, this was the last involvement against Jesus by *any* of the Herodians. From this time forward, the Herodians washed their hands of any plot against Jesus. This seems to imply that Jesus' answer convinced them that there was a very strong probability that Jesus truly was that Theophus of Tiberius".

Bonnern concluded the matter of *Render Unto Caesar* by giving a personal comment. I will quote Bonner's conclusion directly. "Although it is quite obvious that Jesus' answer was his true political philosophy, to understand what he meant by his answer is far less obvious. Was Jesus saying that there needed to be a sharp division between religion and civil governments? Was he saying that one's moral and civil duties are on equal basis? Was his statement a transitory acceptance of the civil authority of Rome or of civil power and authority in general? Was he saying that religion should be subordinate to civil authority? Was he saying that civil authority should be subordinate to religion? Was he saying that God does not intervene into the affairs of governments? Was he saying that God does only intervene into the affairs of government whenever He receives what is due Him? All of these explanations have been used over the past centuries by monarchs, political leaders, military leaders, dictators, and religious leaders to justify their actions. But, no one really knows exactly what Jesus meant. However, we do know that his antagonists never again tried to trick him with questions regarding civil authority." With that conclusion, Bonnern ended his description of the painting.

In light of the extreme scrutiny that the Roman authorities had placed upon Jesus' every action since the "near treasonous and unfortunate incident regarding Bar-Timaeus" (so states the Syrian/Roman court transliterator, Justin Ponticus, who was on assignment in Jericho when Bar-Timaeus was healed by Jesus), Jesus' answer was masterful for it afforded no reason for added Roman suspicion or animosity, and offered no ammunition that his adversaries could use against him.

Soon after this incident, while he was still teaching in the Temple, Sadducees approached Jesus with a question about the resurrection, in which they did not believe (Matthew 22:23-33; Mark 12:18-27; Luke 20: 27-38). They tried to trap him by setting up a hypothetical situation in which they said a woman married seven brothers, one after the other, and had no children by any of them. So in the resurrection, whose wife would she be? The typical Pharisee teaching at the time said that widows who remarried would be the wife of her first husband in the afterlife. Jesus responded by telling them that they were wrong in their beliefs—that there was no resurrection and that there is marriage in the afterlife, the same as in this life. He then went on to say that in the afterlife the resurrected would be like the angels in heaven. They were created in the beginning and live forever. They do not marry. Since marriage's primary purpose is to ensure that descendants are produced and to replenish the earth, then angels who live forever need not marry. Such is the case with the resurrected. Upon their resurrection, they will live forever, so marriage is irrelevant in the afterlife.

He then challenged the Sadducees with an enigma. The Sadducees believed in the Law of Moses only and accepted only the books written by Moses as authoritative. They identified God as "The God of Abraham, Isaac, and Jacob." However, they did not believe in angels, Satan, or the resurrection. But Jesus put them on the spot by telling them that God was not a God of the dead, but rather a God of the living. If there is no resurrection then Abraham, Isaac, and Jacob will remain dead for all of eternity. So, if they only acknowledge that God is the God of Abraham, Isaac, and Jacob, then they needed to reevaluate their position. If there is no resurrection then Abraham, Isaac, and Jacob will remain dead, never to be resurrected. But, God is a god of the living, not the dead. So, if there is no resurrection, then there is no God. But, if there is a God, who is the God of the living, then logic must concluded that there is a resurrection.

Needless to say, the Sadducees were speechless, offering no response to his answer, except to say that it was a good answer. The people on the other hand were amazed at his logical answer and his doctrinal line of reasoning.

As soon as the Shammaite Pharisees and scribes had heard that Jesus had silenced the Sadducees, they decided that they would try one more time to trap him. So, while Jesus was still in the Temple teaching, the group of Pharisees and scribes approached him. The spokesman for the group confronted him asking him which of the commandments is the greatest commandment (Matthew 22: 23-46; Mark 12:18-37; Luke 20:27-44)?

Jesus' answer was similar to the answer he had given to a scribe who had asked him the same question at the Feast of Dedication dinner held at the home of Simon the Pharisee in Capernaum three years previously, in AD 28. See the chapter entitled **Third Year of Ministry** for Jesus' response concerning which is the greatest commandment.

After Jesus had answered the scribe, he turned the tables on the group and asked them a question (Matthew 22:41-46; Mark 12:38-40; Luke 20:40-44) concerning whose son is Christ. The scribes responded that Christ was David's son. Jesus' response to them caught them completely off-guard to the point that they were totally silenced. Never again did the Pharisees and scribes try to trap Jesus, and from that day forward, they asked him no more questions.

Shortly thereafter Jesus and his disciples left the Temple compound and returned to Bethany for the night.

The following morning, Saturday March 24, Jesus and his disciples again left Bethany early, traveled to Jerusalem, and went to the Temple. One of the first things Jesus did that morning in the Temple was to call his disciples attention to how people were giving their offerings. This led him to pay special attention to a widow who gave only two mites, which was all that she had to give (Mark 12:41-44; Luke 21:1-4).

While I was touring the Courtauld Institute Galleries in London, England, known more for its amazing collection of impressionism art, I came across a unique display that served to confirm the Gospels account of Jesus' lesson focusing on the widow's giving of the two mites.

Upon exiting the stairs on the second level of the gallery, I immediately noticed a glass display case about six feet long standing in the middle of the walkway, about ten feet from the stairs. The display was filled with Christian religious relics related to various saints. One artifact in particular intrigued me. It was a small coin. The inscription below the coin, written in English, German, and French identified the coin as *Bartholomea Capitanio's teaching coin.*

I asked the upstairs gallery assistant the meaning of the inscription. The assistant told me that the coin was one that was used by Bartholomea Capitanio of Lovere to teach children about the story of the widow's mite recorded in the Gospels of Mark and Luke.

"In 1827," the assistant continued to explain, "Bartholomea Capitanio and Catherine Grosa founded the Sisters of Charity of Lovere, headquartered in Milan. She died at the age of 26 but left behind this coin, two volumes of writings, and a number of letters."

The assistant then abruptly excused herself and returned a few minutes later carrying a bound volume. The assistant said that the volume was one of the two volumes that had been written by Bartholomea Capitanio. She then to explain more about the coin from what was written in the volume.

"The coin that was called in the Bible a widow's mite was probably either a Roman *gerah* or a Greek *lepta*; it was not a Hebrew coin. Both were almost worthless, about 1/50th of a penny.

"At that time, giving to the Temple treasury (called at that time the *Lord's gift of devotion*) was to many a prideful function. There were basically three ways whereby a giver presented the *Lord's gift of devotion* to the Temple. The first was to bring a large gift of gold, silver, or jewels to the Men's Court and place the gift in the hands of the priest who stood just inside the Men's Court side of the Nicanor Gate. The priest would accompany the giver to the jewel encrusted gold receiving box and deposit the gift, accompanied by numerous trumpet calls, ram's horn blasts, cymbals crashing, and a loud proclamation of blessings by the priest upon the giver. [For more detailed information see the chapter entitled **Second year of ministry**.]

"The second method was to give a smaller gift of gold and silver to a priest who was standing next to a silver plated receiving box located on the Court of Women's side of the Nicanor Gate. The priest would proclaim blessing upon the giver as he placed the gift into the box, accompanied by one long trumpet or ram's horn blast.

"The third method was to bring a small gift and place it into a wooden receiving box located in the north corner of the Court of Women. It was into this box that the widow placed her two mites that Saturday. The gift was not proclaimed.

"Although unnoticed by anyone else, she was noticed by Jesus. The others were giving from their abundance, but she gave all that she had, and Jesus took note. No doubt she received her great reward from Jesus himself, when she passed from this earth and was received into heaven's paradise.

"We do not know this woman's name, but because Jesus took note of her, she has become one of the most well-known widows in the history of the world. So too must we give all that we have to our Heavenly Father, leaving nothing in reserve, and we will obtain our just reward."

"And that is all she wrote about that particular subject," the assistant said as she closed the volume.

Jesus spent all day in the Temple teaching. As he and his disciples were leaving the Temple compound that day, his disciples called his attention to the magnificence of the Temple. Jesus responded that the Temple would soon be so destroyed that one stone would not be left upon another. So shocked were the disciples with his answer that they did not speak again until they had crossed the Kidron valley, climbed the Mount of Olives, and had sat down to rest.

As they rested, they asked Jesus to explain what he meant. When would it happen? What will be the sign of his coming as Messiah? What are the signs of the end of the world? Jesus' response is what we call today his *Olivet Discourse* (Matthew 24:1-51; Mark 12:41-13:2; Luke 21:5-36).

I remember coming across a compilation of sermons while studying at Southeastern Seminary in Louisville, Kentucky. Dr. Alfredo Mozzini edited the book in 1938. It was a compilation of the sermons of Elijah Coleman Bridgman (1801-1861), America's first missionary to China. The entire book was fascinating but the sermon that looked to me like it would most easily fit into my research criteria was the one entitled, *"The Olivet Discourse."*

The sermon began with Elijah Coleman Bridgman setting the stage for the sermon and giving some historical background. This background information was what, in my opinion, was more important to my research efforts than the sermon itself.

He said, "Jesus actually began this discussion with his disciples while they were still in the Temple compound, but were just about to exit. As they admired the grandeur of the Temple Jesus told them that not one stone would be left on top of the other. It is not clear if Jesus was alluding to a physical future event or a symbolic event. Physically, this did take place with the destruction of the Temple in AD 70, when the Roman soldiers dismantled the Temple. They dismantled the Temple stone by stone to get to the gold that had melted, because of the intense heat after the Temple was set ablaze, and had ran down and had lodged between the joints of the stones.

"Symbolically it also was fulfilled. Jesus could have been alluding symbolically to a time when the existing Jewish religion would perish and be replaced by a new, purer, and less formal observance that was more in accordance with Jesus' own teachings. After the destruction of the Temple, Jewish worship as they knew it, disappeared. It was displaced with a different form of Jewish worship that was simple and far less ritualistic. In addition, the seeds of Christianity began to grow and blossom and spread throughout the known world.

"We do not know who besides the 12 disciples heard Jesus make these statements. Most likely, it was only the 12 because if more had heard Jesus' remarks, it could have caused a panicked uproar.

"Fact in point, a man by the name of Jesus of Ananius stood in the Court of Men in AD 70, just weeks before the actual siege of Jerusalem, and publicly prophesied the same things that Jesus had told his disciples. Jesus of Ananius was dragged from the Temple and was flogged to unconsciousness. Yet, nothing was done to Jesus of Nazareth when he prophesied the destruction of the Temple.

"After Jesus made his statement, he and his disciples left the Temple area and began to travel back to Bethany. Upon reaching the Mount of Olives, they stopped to rest. Peter, James, and John came to him and asked him three questions: When will the destruction of the Temple take place? What will be the signs of your coming (or when will you set up your kingdom and reign as Messiah)? And when will be the end of time? Jesus responded in Matthew 24 with what has been called the *Olivet Discourse* or the *Eschatological Discourse*."

Elijah Coleman Bridgman went into great length describing the various logical aspects of the discourse that did not seem to fit into the accepted theology of his day with regards to their interpretation of the discourse.

"Many Bible scholars," he continued, "think that major portions of Jesus' discourse have been lost. The primary reason for thinking this is because the Matthew 24 portion does not flow smoothly or clearly, which is different from most other discourses spoken by Jesus.

"Another theory is that rather than some of the discourse bein
of Matthew's Gospel did the same thing with this discourse as he h
Sermon on the Mount. He picked out parts from many differe
teachings over the entire length of Jesus' teaching ministry and put
into one discourse as Matthew 24.

"Within the discourse can be found end-time catastrophes, judgment, the siege of Jerusalem, natural disasters, and the persecution of the Christians in the Roman Empire. They are all thrown together in disorderly fashion. Hence, we must extract from this literary hodgepodge, some type of coherent flow of events.

"But, one thing is for certain," Mozzini interjected. "Very little, if any, of the discourse had to do with future events that would be fulfilled in our time (Mozzini's time) or some time beyond our time, regardless of what the reformers and revivalists have said over the past one hundred years.

"They have tried to mold this Matthew 24 portion into a predetermined theory, which has evolved into eschatology doctrine. This doctrine then must somehow fit into the prophecies of Ezekiel, Isaiah, Jeremiah, Daniel, I Thessalonians, and the Revelation, and reveal events that are supposed to take place at the end of time and usher in a world-renowned Anti-Christ [In our modern society this particular idea was introduced by the Anglican priest turned preacher, Rev. John Nelson Darby, in 1862. However, it was Darby's disciple and associate, Rev. Cyrus I. Scofield, with the publication of his *Scofield Reference Bible* in 1909 that raised the hitherto radical and unconventional philosophy to the level of fundamentalist doctrine].

"But I feel that this reasoning and manufactured doctrine is absolutely ridiculous!" Mozzini continued with his commentary, "All one has to do is to read this Matthew 24 portion and it becomes obvious that this revivalist inspired end-time prophecy teaching is nothing short of heresy.

"To me," Mozzini returned to Elijah Coleman Bridgman's sermon, "it seems obvious that the statements Jesus made have been enmeshed with many successive layers of revisions at different time periods.

"The additions were not affixed to the beginning or to the end of the original discourse. Instead, they were added to the discourse in places where they would best conform to and emphasize the current doctrines of the church at that particular time in church history. As a result, we can readily recognize numerous 'out of place' statements by just reading the discourse.

"One such example is the statement *'Now learn a parable from the fig tree.'* The entire portion from *'Now learn a parable'* in verse 32 through the statement *'Truly I say unto you'* in verse 34 was added in the 10th or 11th century. This portion had to do with the lives of the disciples not passing away before they would experience much of the horror that Jesus told them about. It is not the rebirth of the nation of Israel or the recalling of the Jewish people to their homeland.

"Jesus' original discourse dealt primarily with the immediate future. Jesus warned that the persecutions would begin soon after his resurrection and would continue for centuries. He also said that Jerusalem would be destroyed before the death of all of them who were there with him. After Jesus' resurrection and ascension, these disciples expected Jesus to return immediately and to set up his kingdom, meaning that all of the things that he had spoken would be fulfilled.

"Certainly during the 1st century, there were numerous times when the early church believers could have concluded that Jesus' words were becoming a reality. For example, the atrocities (*to bdelugma tes eremoseos*) to which Jesus referred in Matthew 24:7-8 could be seen everywhere in Roman Judaea and throughout Roman Syria.

"In AD 44 there was a widespread famine throughout Roman Syria including Judaea. This ushered in numerous epidemics that before the famine subsided in AD 48, had claimed the lives of one out of every three adults and three out of every four children under the age of 12.

"In AD 44, Claudius expelled all of the Jews from Rome. Jews who had been converted to Christianity or who had publicly denounced Judaism were allowed to live in the underground sewer tunnels and catacombs of the city.

"In AD 53 a series of disastrous earthquakes occurred in Phrygia, Galatia, and Cappadocia destroying over 300 cities, towns, and villages, and killing tens of thousands.

"In AD 54, the Black Death struck Syria, Cilicia, and Cappadocia taking the lives of over 1.5 million people—the cities of Jerusalem, Antioch, Iconium, and Tiberias (a Jewish and Christian stronghold at that time), were hit the hardest.

"In AD 61, an earthquake recognized as the strongest earthquake ever to hit that part of the world, perhaps even the strongest earthquake ever to hit the earth, struck Asia, Phrygia, and Macedonia. It destroyed the twin cities of Laodicea and Colosse along with 110 other cities and towns and it killed from 50 to 75 percent of the population of the region. The earthquake was followed by epidemics that were worse than any epidemic or any series of epidemics that had ever been up to that time. In the entire history of mankind only the plagues that ravaged Europe in the 14th century was worse than these that struck Asia, Phrygia, and Macedonia.

"In AD 64 a tremendous fire broke out in the city of Rome. Nero blamed the Christians for the fire and had hundreds of them put to death by the most horrible means.

"In AD 66 the Judeans revolted. Vespasian savagely crushed the rebels. Thousands were crucified, flayed alive, and killed by the most torturous means; and many thousands more were sold into slavery as labors for the Isthmus of Corinth canal.

"In AD 70 the son of Vespasian, Titus, besieged the city of Jerusalem when Vespasian was called back to Rome to secure his position as Emperor. Rebels had again taken up positions in the city, including the Temple compound. The siege of Jerusalem began in April, AD 70. The lower city fell on July 7. On August 7, Titus secured the Temple and it was set on fire. On September 8, the upper city fell to the Romans and Titus ordered the upper city to be totally leveled and plowed under.

"However, this was not the only time that Jerusalem was besieged or destroyed, nor was it the last time.

"I'm going to list the sieges and the conquests of Jerusalem that Elijah Bridgman listed," Mozzini wrote as he continued his commentary on Bridgman's sermon, "This will show how utterly ridiculous it is to try and place the events discussed by Jesus in the *Olivet Discourse* at some time in the far future, centuries after the death of his disciples. It would be obvious to anyone who knows even a fraction of world history that the events spoken of by Jesus have already been fulfilled, for the most part.

"In 2000 BC Jerusalem was besieged and destroyed by Manechur; in 1800 BC it was besieged by Issachur; in 1535 BC by the Canaanites; and in 1370 BC by Habiru. In 1000 BC Jerusalem was besieged and conquered by David. He who made it his capital. In 922 BC Egyptian Pharaoh Sheshonk conquered it, followed in 850 BC by the Philistine. In 786 BC Jerusalem was conquered and sacked by the Arabians; in 701 BC it was besieged by Assyria. This was when Hezekiah was king and when God destroyed the Assyrian army that was besieging Jerusalem. In 594 BC and again in 588 BC Jerusalem was conquered by Babylon. In 198 BC and again in 167 BC it was conquered by Syria. In 63 BC it was conquered by Rome. Again in AD 70 Jerusalem was besieged and conquered by Rome (this Jerusalem that the Romans conquered in AD 70 was the Jerusalem of Jesus' day). In AD 135 Rome again conquered and totally destroyed Jerusalem and built a Roman city, Aelia Capitolina, on the spot where Jerusalem once stood (no Jews or Christians were allowed in the city). In AD 324 Constantine laid siege and partially destroyed the city and in AD 614 the Persians conquered it. In AD 638 the Muslim Caliph Omar conquered Jerusalem and in AD 969 Shi'a of Egypt conquered it. In AD 1010 it was conquered by Caliph Hakim; and then 61 years later in AD 1071 by Seljuk the Turk. In AD 1099 Jerusalem was besieged and conquered by the Crusaders and in AD 1187 Saladin re-conquered it for the Muslims. In 1229 the Crusaders again besieged and conquered the city; but in 1244 Khwarizmian Taters drove them out of the city. In 1247 the city was conquered by Egypt and in AD 1517 Selim I, who built the current walls of the Old City, conquered it. The last conquest that Bridgman listed was the 1832 conquest of Jerusalem by Mohammed Ali of Egypt.

"So, out of 29 sieges and conquests of Jerusalem, 16 of them have taken place since Jesus gave his *Olivet Discourse*; and in all of these, multiplied thousands of Jews and Christians alike were killed and tortured. [And Mozzini's list did not even include the battles of World War I and II and the Jewish wars against the Arabs in this 20th century]."

"Now continuing, in AD 81 Domitian began the most far reaching general persecution of the Christians to date and for the first time Christians were persecuted in all Roman provinces and in every region where Rome ruled. It is estimated that during this persecution the Christian community throughout the Empire dwindled from 6 million at the time of Domitian's assent to the throne to less than 2 million at the time of his death in AD 96."

Mozzini then approached Bridgman's treatment of the subject of the false prophets that revivalists say will be a sign of the end of time. "Bridgman felt that there many false prophets during the lifetime of the apostles.

"A disciple of John the Baptist, a man by the name of Dositheus of Samaria, claimed in AD 34 to be the Messiah. Simon Magus, who was confronted in Samaria by Peter, succeeded him.

"In AD 56 Menandrus of Antioch claimed to be the incarnation of Jesus. His claim was said to be accompanied by 'wisdom beyond his natural ability and by acts of healing and miracles beyond the natural means.'

"In AD 63 Theudas of Hebron not only claimed to be the returned Messiah, but he actually acquired a following of over 4,000 dedicated disciples who went two by two spreading his message throughout the Roman world.

"Joachim of Floris said in 1130 that during the first century after Jesus' death and resurrection, no fewer than 380 men and three women claimed to be either the Messiah, the returned Messiah, or the reincarnated returned Jesus.

"So, although Jesus may well have referred to events that were to lead to the 'end-times,' the majority of his *Olivet Discourse* was centered around the immediate future and directed to his disciples and how they were going to survive the immediate future.

"The concept of the end of the world with a final judgment was not unique to Jesus." Bridgman continued, "The Babylonians, Persians, Assyrians, Hittites, Syrians, Greeks, Mayans, the ancient Jews, and other peoples, taught a future end, judgment, rewards for the righteous, and punishment for or destruction of, the wicked and evil. But what made Jesus' message unique was that he did not concentrate on the punishment side of judgment. Rather, he sought to open the hearts of his followers so that they would be spared punishment and be received into his new kingdom through faith in him and through forgiveness from God the Father and by being vigilant in their dedication to being 'doers' of what he had taught them."

Mozzini then breaks from his commentary on Bridgman's sermon and begins to talk about the times in which he lived. "When Bridgman wrote this sermon, the Darby inspired fundamental dispensational movement with its six or seven dispensation periods, rapture, and end-time prophecy was in its infancy. So it did not make much of a stir until after his death and after the Scofield stimulated dispensational movement 'caught hold' in America and spread like a wild fire until it became the dominate thinking among American Protestants; then Bridgman's writings were met with extreme hostilities.

"By the end of the World War I, Bridgman was considered a heretic in American Darby and Scofieldian and dispensational premillennialist circles, as well as with European fundamentalists, primarily because the truth about which he wrote was contrary to their view of truth based on the dogmas of Darby and Scofield."

After reading his commentary on Bridgman's sermon, it seemed obvious to me that Dr. Alfredo Mozzini not only believed Bridgman, but also he was "death" on Darby and his Premillennial Dispensationalism (Darbv's name for his philosophy) and Scofield's prolongation of the philosophy. The last ten pages of Mozzini's book were assigned to refuting the Darby/Scofield doctrine.

As I read his argument against Darby and Scofield, it was so blatant that Dr. Alfredo Mozzini despised everything that they stood for.

Although I knew some of the teachings that had originated with Darby and Scofield, there were others that I did not realize derived with them. Some of these teachings were original thoughts, while others were borderline dogmas that for centuries had not been rejected as false, but also had not been accepted as truth. These were recognized as undeniable truth by Darby and Scofield.

"Although it was difficult to separate truth from bitterness and antipathy, I feel it my obligation to point out some of the things that were either formulated by Darby and Scofield or brought into the realm of truth by them," wrote Dr. Mozzini.

Mozzini claimed that some of the Old Testament Darby and Scofield fabrications included: a godly line of Seth and an ungodly line of Cain (all were ungodly because both lines were destroyed in Noah's flood); it took Noah 120 years to build the ark (ancient Babylonian documents indicate that it probably took Noah two to five and no more than twelve years to build the ark); Noah preached to the people and tried to convert them (he did not try to make converts—God had already predetermined and had already told Noah that Noah, his wife, his sons and their wives were going to be the only ones saved from the flood); Ham was cursed black (Ham was not cursed—Canaan, Ham's son, was cursed); Abraham always worshipped the God of the Hebrews (Abraham originally worshipped the gods of Ur); Melchizedek was a priest of the God of Abraham; God's covenant with Abraham was passed down to and through the Jews only (Darby and Scofield followers felt that present day [20th and 21st century] Jews and residents of present day national Israel are God's chosen people); David was righteous and was a godly man (far from it—David was one of the most ruthless warriors who ever reigned over the people of Israel); world history is divided into dispensations of 2,000 years each; and much more.

Mozzini then turned his attention to the New Testament. These falsehoods included: three wisemen visited Jesus at the manger in Bethlehem; Jesus, Mary, and Joseph stayed in Egypt for 2 years; Jesus knew from before age 12 that he was the Son of God and that he knew his mission; Jesus began his earthly ministry immediately after his wilderness experience; Jesus was crucified on Friday and arose on Sunday; the Harmony of the Gospels dogma; the Rapture of the Church in which Jesus appears in the sky and the dead in Christ will rise to meet him in the air and the ones who are alive will go meet those in the air—they all return to heaven with Jesus and will return with him at his 2nd coming; Jesus' *Olivet Discourse* is end-time prophecy that is to be fulfilled at the end of this dispensation and it somehow fits into The Revelation 4:1-22:21, I Thessalonians 4:13-5:11, II Thessalonians 1:5-2:13, Ezekiel 38-40, Daniel 12, and more "end-time" prophet passages; seven years of tribulation—3 years of lesser tribulation and 3 years of greater tribulation; the marriage supper of the Lamb will be held in heaven while tribulation is on earth; the nation of Israel will be attacked by Russia; a world leader will arise who is The Anti-Christ; the Battle of Armageddon in Israel will be fought against either an Anti-Christ or China; a second return of Christ to the earth in which he as well as those who were with him at the marriage supper, will step foot on the Mount of Olives; saints will have a literal millennial reign on literal earth with Christ; Satan released for a season and then he will be bound again and cast into bottomless pit; a new Temple is to be built in Jerusalem; Temple rituals and sacrifices are to be re-introduced; and it went on for two more pages.

"Not all of these teachings that have become doctrines," Mozzini continued, "Were invented by Darby and Scofield. Some had been fringe beliefs for centuries that were not considered worthy of serious consideration. However, once they were introduced as fact in his 1909 dispensational, premillennial Scofield Reference

Bible, they became verity so solid that a doctrine could be built on them, irrespective of the foundational doctrines upon which the church fathers fomented their beliefs more than 1900 years earlier."

As I thought about Mozzini's rebuttal of the Darby/Scofield theology, I felt that I had been deceived. All of my life most of these "doctrines" had been taught to me as truth. My father seemed to be the only exception. He did not swallow the dispensational teaching because God's Word did not confirm it. But because I had been taught this doctrine by every pastor and every Sunday School teacher in my life (except my father), I was faced with confusion that bordered on frustrating anger.

Nevertheless, it sparked my awareness and taught me that under no circumstances could I believe something to be true just because I had been taught that it was true. Truth—*ABOSULTE TRUTH*—is only attainable by studying the Word of God. Not what some one says that the Word of God says, or what they interpret that the Word of God meant when it said a particular thing, but rather, what it actually says. God's Word does not need extra interpreters to explain what God meant when He spoke. It is complete within itself. So, I chose from that time forward to believe completely and without question only one source, the Word of God. All other sources would be evaluated and scrutinized and its contents thoroughly analyzed against the Word of God before I accept it or any part of it as truth. Unfortunately, many of Darby and Scofield's dogmas did not pass the test.

After Jesus' *Olivet Discourse* teaching, he immediately began to tell his disciples three parables: the 10 virgins, the 5 talents, and how important it is to show mercy. I discovered confirming information about the first two parables in one source and information about the third and last one in another source.

I found the first source at the University of Norte Dame in South Bend, Indiana. The source was an essay written in 1899 by Dr. Leslie Pfeiffer commenting on a sermon written by Thomas Becket, Archbishop of Canterbury, using these two parables as his focal point.

Dr. Pfeiffer said that Becket used as his text the Gospel of Matthew portion that we now identify as chapter 25, verses 1-46. The first portion of this Matthew setting records Jesus' parable of the ten virgins and the second portion deals with his parable of the five talents.

After an introduction and a short history of the life and death of Thomas Becket, Dr. Pfeiffer began her commentary. "The historical setting for both of these parables is the Mount of Olives. As Jesus concluded his *Olivet Discourse*, he told both of these parables to his disciples. The time was Saturday, March 24, AD 31.

"Although Thomas Becket was a Archbishop, he was a historian before he was a clergyman. As such, he had extraordinary knowledge of the historical background of each of these parables. In his commentaries he spent more effort trying to understand the historical setting of Jesus' parables rather than the analogy illustrated by the parable. He felt that if the people could understand the historical setting in which the parable was based, then they could understand the sermon rooted in the parable and the analogical teaching exemplified by the parable.

"The setting of the first parable was a wedding. Becket felt that Jesus could have been an eye witness to the events that set the stage for the parable of the five

The Search

wise virgins (friends or personal care-maids of the bride) and the five foolish virgins, however, he believed that Jesus was probably eluding to the marriage of Demeter, the daughter of Annius Rufus, the former governor of the province of Judaea. The details of this wedding were well documented and well known to the populace of Judaea. Demeter's marriage took place in Caesarea Maritima in AD 13.

"As the story goes, Demeter's wedding was scheduled for a specific day, March 15. However, her bridegroom, Sethius Octavia Seneacus, the commander of the Roman military forces on the island of Rhodes, had to sail from Rhodes to Caesarea Maritima. Because of a perilous storm, Sethius was delayed from departing from Rhodes by almost two days and he was unable to send word that he had been delayed. The guests could only speculate what had happened to Sethius.

"After a day of waiting, most of the guests became frustrated and left the wedding celebration. Among the ones that stayed were ten of the bride's best friends, who also served as the bride's personal care-maids. They would be participants in her wedding.

"As the second evening wore on with no word, discouragement began to sit in. Then suddenly a messenger arrived declaring that Sethius had been blown off coarse and had arrived unexpectedly in Tyre and that he was on his way to Caesarea Maritima and should arrive sometime that very night to take his bride.

"Demeter told her ten friends to travel up the main highway toward Tyre with a military escort and when they meet Sethius to escort him back to the wedding. Because it was night, the friends had to take lamps with them. Five of the friends had enough oil in their lamps to leave immediately, but the other five had to go into town and buy additional oil before they could leave. But, while the five were gone to buy oil, yet before the other five had left to go and meet him, Sethius suddenly arrived at the palace where the wedding was to take place. Upon his arrival he ordered the doors of the celebration hall to be closed, allowing no one else into the celebration. Those who had gone to buy oil were locked out, even though they were supposed to have been part of the wedding ceremony. Consequently they were not permitted into the wedding ceremony.

"Jesus used this historical event to show that regardless of how secure a people feel that they are with the bride (the church, its doctrines, and its leaders) if they are not ready to enter into the joy of the Lord at the time of his return, they will not be allowed to participate. Closeness to the bride (the church and the established Christian religion) is and always must be secondary to closeness to the groom (Jesus).

"Jesus then told another parable," Dr. Pfeiffer continued as she commented on Thomas Becket's sermon background information. "It too had a historical foundation. This story was a favorite that was told in the Roman Imperial Schools of Economics and Finance, which were located in the cities of Rome, Cyrene, Thessalonica, Ephesus, Tyre, and Aquileria. The story was told in order to show economics students the absolute necessity of investing tax receipts (tax revenues that were collected in the provinces—they were delivered to Rome every five years) in income producing investments or into interest bearing bank accounts so that the revenues would grow in value.

"Graduates from these schools became Rome's 'tax lords' (a tax governor or economics director over an entire Roman province). The tax lords in turn had various levels of tax assessors, tax collectors, and tenure officers who were subject to them.

"If he was a Roman citizen, a common tax collector could work his way up through the tax collection ranks so that he could qualify to be enrolled into one of the economics schools. No one could be a tax lord unless he had graduated from one of the schools.

"This particular story has to do with one of these tax lords. His name was Craverius. He was the tax lord of the Roman province of Achaia, during the reign of Augustus. Because of his unique ability to invest the province's tax revenues and to always make a huge profit that was at least double what he had collected and in some cases as much as 1000 percent more than the amount that he had collected, Augustus in 10 BC appointed Craverius the honored position of tax lord over four additional provinces, Macedonia, Epirus, Thrace, and Dalmatia.

"Because of the added responsibility, in order to continue servicing Augustus in the manner in which he was accustomed to being serviced, Craverius divided the assessor responsibilities of the province of Achaia among his five district tax assessors (Craverius had divided Achaia into 5 tax districts) with instructions that the five assessors were to continue in Craverius' footsteps of investing and providing Augustus with many times more resources than were collected in taxes. Afterward giving the five final instructions, Craverius left Achaia in order to visit his other four tax realms.

"He told them," Becket continued (so writes Dr. Pfeiffer), "that if they were successful in their task that they would be in a position to be selected to attend one of the schools of economics and to eventually qualify to become tax lords.

"Craverius was gone from Achaia for five years, expecting things to run under his five assessors as well as they had under his direct leadership. Upon his return, one of his first acts was to demand an accounting of the tax revenues and investment revenues.

"Four of the assessors had been successful in making income on their investments. They went on to the schools of economics and eventually became tax lords themselves. But one did not want to risk the tax revenues on investments nor did he trust the banks, so he did nothing with the revenues. Although he did not lose any money, the tax revenues that he collected did not grow. This assessor was condemned as a traitor by Augustus and was exiled to Moesia, where he worked in the unbearably hot and miserable sulfur mines (called *outer darkness* or *utter blackness* by the locals) for the remainder of his life, never seeing the light of day again.

"Jesus used this event as a basis for his allegorical teaching which emphasized that his disciples should not be satisfied with the status quo. They, as his followers, must go beyond the expected ministry to ones of like social standing and minister to the hungry, the naked, those in prison, and the hurting. In so doing, they would be investing revenues into interest bearing accounts. The small investment that they would make would be multiplied far beyond their expectations because they would be investing in him and laying up treasures in heaven. Every time they did good for those who needed help would be an investment in him, and his rewards were greater than anything that they could imagine.

"Becket said that Jesus taught these lessons," Dr. Pfeiffer explained, "as they paused to rest on the Mount of Olives on their way back to the little town of Bethany."

"In the meantime the religious leaders and the elders were conspiring with the High Priest on how to silence Jesus, even if it meant his death. But, they had a problem. If they arrested Jesus in the open in the daylight hours, his many followers would start a riot in his support. This would bring the wrath of Rome down upon them. At night he could not be arrested because he had been staying with influential friends in Bethany, the Roman/Egyptian/Jewish settlement just east of Jerusalem on the eastern slopes of the Mount of Olives.

"Bethany had special protection from the Roman government," Dr. Pfeiffer interjected. "And it was outside of the jurisdiction of the Jewish Sanhedrin. Because it had freely given supplies and laborers to Valerius Gratus in AD 18, in preparation for the construction of the city of Tiberias, Bethany had from that time forward been exempt from paying taxes and had been given the distinction of being named a city of the governor. This meant that its town council and its residents did not have to answer to anyone or any authority except the Roman authority. However, to be a resident of Bethany, a person had to prove that he or she was of Egyptian/Jewish ancestry and that his or her family had lived in Bethany for at least two generations, including the present.

"The residents of Bethany had no love for the arrogant Jewish religious charlatans, especially those from Jerusalem. In fact, a Bethany town governor (mayor) by the name of Cleopaulas Ceophus in AD 23 forbade (with Roman procurator approval) any Jewish religious leader from entering Bethany, under penalty of death, unless a resident of Bethany invited them to the town. A Jewish religious leader was permitted to pass through Bethany without an invitation, but he could not stop without an invitation. At the time of Jesus' ministry this restriction was still being practiced.

"Now let's get back to the plot against Jesus as described by Becket, " Dr. Pfeiffer said, "The Jewish religious leaders in Jerusalem, especially the powerful Sadducees, were convinced that Jesus had to be silenced. Yet, as stated, they feared a riot by the people and the wrath of Rome. They needed to get Jesus alone, away from the people, away from the Temple (it was forbidden to arrest a religious leader within the Temple compound grounds), and away from Bethany. What they needed was someone close to Jesus who could monitor his every move and tell them when he was going to be alone.

"They put the word out that they would be willing to pay handsomely anyone who would be willing to cooperate with them. The Matthew setting says that they were willing to pay up to 30 pieces of silver ("Eight years' salary for a common laborer in Old Testament [Zechariah's] times or the equivalent to $88,000 by today's standards," Dr. Pfeiffer added). The author of Matthew says that he got the number of the silver pieces from a prophecy found in Jeremiah. But in reality, the prophecy to which the author of Matthew referred is found in Zechariah (11:13). We can only speculate as to how much the 30 pieces of silver was worth. But, chances are the amount offered was substantial enough that the loyalty of his most trusted followers would be portentously tested.

"The other Gospels do not specify the 30 pieces of silver, they only say that the religious leaders offered money.

"The [apocryphal] *Gospel of Andrew*," Becket continued, "says that Judas was given a large sum of money—enough to make him among the ten wealthiest men in Jerusalem, thus rivaling the most wealthy Romans in Jerusalem.

"This 'gospel' also says that Judas himself bought the field referred to in Zechariah. The Gospel of Matthew records that the field was bought by the chief priests, with the money that was returned to them by Judas, and was converted into a potter's field. However, if this were true, it would have been quite unusual because under Tiberias, non-Roman citizen Jews in Jerusalem (only in Jerusalem) were not allowed to buy land or property. If it was inherited or was part of a family estate, they could keep ownership, but they could not buy new land or property. And if by chance they did get an opportunity to buy property (land was not included), it was expensive because taxes had to be paid to the Roman authorities on all newly purchased property at 250 percent of either the value or the purchase price of the property."

"I think," Dr. Pfeiffer said expressing his own opinion, "that Andrew may have stretched the point a bit."

"And that ends Thomas Becket's sermon background information," Dr. Pfeiffer said in clusion. "The remainder of the text is his actual sermon."

The third parable that Jesus taught at this time was one that dealt with the need for showing mercy. I discovered corroborating documentation about this parable while studying at Central Michigan University in Mount Pleasant, Michigan. The documentation was a book written in 1861 by Sir Isaac Pearmon, a professor of Ancient History at the University of Liverpool. The book was entitled, *Mercy for the Sake of Mercy*. The primary focus of the book was showing how mercy had been granted or shown by different historical figures, most of which were not religious, upon unsuspecting, and in many cases, unknown to the grantor, people. The introduction of the book is what interested me most for in it Sir Pearmon used this particular parable spoken by Jesus and recorded in Matthew 25:31-46, as a basis for his focus.

In the introduction Sir Pearmon wrote, "I have approached the subject of showing mercy by comparing Paul the Apostle's lesson on the subject of sowing and reaping as found in his letter to the Roman Galatians (recorded in Galatians 6:7—these Galatians were not Jews; they were Roman converts to Christianity) and how the law of sowing and reaping applied to the lesson on mercy that Jesus taught to his disciples on the Mount of Olives on Saturday, March 24, AD 31, just 10 days before his crucifixion".

He continued by giving some brief background information, "Both Jesus and Paul quoted and used as a reference and a basis for their respective teachings a drama written by Publius Terentius Afer (Terence), a Roman dramatist who lived from 186 BC to 159 BC. The drama was entitled *Era Imperator Conquirere*. The drama was about Cyrus the Great, the Persian emperor. Cyrus died in 530 BC. He was the founder of the great Persian Empire that stretched from India to Greece. He was also the one who allowed all the Jews who so desired, to return to their homeland. But, only a small percentage of the Jews actually did return to their homeland, opting instead to live under subjection to Cyrus, who was known throughout the world for his justice, mercy, and compassion.

"The drama exalted Cyrus to the highest level of honor and respect as if he were a god. Terence presented Cyrus in a manner that brings to mind the myths of King Arthur and how the land and Arthur were one. As Arthur prospered, so the land prospered. So also, as Cyrus prospered, the Empire prospered. Although Cyrus probably was the most compassionate and merciful emperor in all of the ancient world, the drama portrayed him more immortal than mortal."

Sir Pearmon then quoted the portions of Terence's drama that Jesus and Paul quoted. In the case of Jesus, he semi-quoted a portion of the drama (Jesus basically adapted the quote to fit his lesson). Then he added to the quote his own words to emphasize not only the concept of sowing and reaping but also the responsibilities of the individual disciple. Paul quoted his portion to the Roman Galatians to emphasize his lesson on sowing and reaping as presented by one of their own authors.

Sir Pearmon continued, "The portion of the drama that Jesus quoted and adapted for his own lesson purpose began with, '…and before him [Cyrus] did representatives from all nations under his rule gather. And he separated the one nation ambassador from the other as a shepherd divides his sheep from goats who have joined his flock, according to how well they had embraced his policies of mercy and justice into their administration. The ones who honored his policies were set on the right of his seat of judgment; those who had not honored them were placed on the left. To the ambassadors who had been placed on the right he said, *'As you have shown mercy upon your poor and downtrodden, you have shown mercy unto me. I now will show mercy unto you, enter into the inheritance of your king.'* With that he gave a portion of his collected wealth to the ambassador to share with the inhabitants of their nations. To those representatives on the left he said, *'As you have shown no mercy but have instead showed contempt for my statutes and have abused your people, so too have you abused me. I then will abuse you.'* With that he had each representative flayed, with pieces of his body sent to all members of the ruling administration of the abusing nation as a warning of what was to come. He then sent his armies into that nation and utterly destroyed the ruling administration and their families and bound their governors and their families, blinding them, and forcing them to work in the sulfur mines in utter darkness. He said, *'Depart from me you worker of evil, for in that you have abused the least of those over whom I gave you authority, you have abused me. Depart into death and into darkness. Your state will be given to those who you abused.'* With that Cyrus appointed a new ruler and new governors to rule, from the ranks of the ones who had been abused.'

"From the foundation of this drama by Terence, Jesus made an adaptation that related to him and to his kingdom and his dealings with the nations of the world and with the individual authorities of those nations.

"Jesus' lesson was this: If governing leaders of a nation shows mercy to their own people and to strangers, they have sown mercy. If they have sown mercy, they will reap mercy. If they have been benevolent and have involved themselves in humanitarian efforts, they will receive benevolence. If they have sown compassion by supporting the abused and have helped to feed and clothe the oppressed, they will reap wealth, blessings, and honor, because showing compassion to the oppressed is the same as showing compassion to him, the King of kings. Not only will they reap the rewards of what they have sown on this earth, but also at the end when all nations are judged, they will receive a higher reward because of their selfless support of the abused, the poor, the hungry, and the victims of oppression.

"The rulers," Sir Pearmon continued with Jesus' analogy, "Of nations who sow abuse, selfishness, oppression, and terror upon their people, they will reap in this life abuse, poverty, heart-ache, oppression, ridicule, and desolation. Plus, at the final judgment they will receive their reward of pain and destruction at the hands of the King.

"Jesus then implied that because Cyrus sowed seeds of good by showing mercy not only to the Jews but to all of his subjects, contrary to the historical trend of the emperors at that time, he and Persia reaped wealth. The Persian Empire created by Cyrus stretched from Africa to India; it was larger than any empire up to that time. So any nation who followed Cyrus' example of sowing good seeds of compassion would reap the same kind of rewards. In Persia's case, as long as those seeds of good were planted, the Persian Empire prospered and was influential. It was not until Persia forsook the policies of mercy established by Cyrus, that the Persian Empire fell into corruption and decay and was destroyed by Alexander.

"Paul," Sir Pearmon continued, "quoted the last few lines of Act IV of the drama when he said, *'Be not deceived, the gods are not mocked; their laws from the beginning are established and cannot change: for whatever a man does sow, that will he also reap. Yet it will be in a season different than the season of sowing, and the sown will be reaped far greater than what was sowed.'* With these words Paul sought to explain to the Roman Galatians that whatever they sowed, be it good or bad, they would reap. If they sowed good then they would reap good. If they sowed bad and evil, then they would reap the same."

Sir Pearmon then explained the three principles of sowing and reaping: what is sown will be reaped, what was sown will be reaped in a different season than when it was sown, and what is reaped will be far greater than what was sown. This is a repeat of a lesson that I have already covered in detail in the chapter entitled **Fourth Year of Ministry**.

Sir Pearmon continued in his introduction by saying, "Contrary to current beliefs, everything that happens is not caused by either God or Satan. Sometimes things, especially bad things, that happen are the result of reaping what had been sown some days, months, or years previous. This was a law that God brought into existence from the beginning. If thorns are sown, thorns will be reaped, not roses. If roses are sown, roses will be reaped. For every one seed that is planted, a hundred more seeds will be produced. The consequences of sowing seeds will not be immediate, be it good or evil seed. But, in a month, or six months, or a year, or six years or more, the planted seeds will grow to maturity and will have to be reaped.

"If bitterness, harshness, selfishness, anger, and hatred are sown, then that is what will be reaped, but what will be reaped will be far greater in quantity than what was sown. If goodness, patience, and love are sown, so will the same be reaped, but much more than what was sown."

That concluded Sir Pearmon's introduction. I was thankful that I ran across this book because it cleared up a lot of questions that I have had for years concerning the separation of nations into merciful nations and non-merciful.

Nothing more is recorded concerning Jesus' activities until Tuesday evening, March 27.

We can speculate that he and his disciples stayed in Jerusalem and followed the same routine that he had followed days previous: going to the Temple to teach each day and then returning to Bethany at night. But we do not know for sure.

What we do know is that on Tuesday evening Jesus and his disciples were invited to the home of Simon the leper to have dinner. There Jesus was anointed for the third and last time.

I discovered confirming information concerning this event in beautiful Garmisch-Partenkirchen, Germany, the site of the 1936 Winter Olympics.

It was while I was visiting the Alte Kirche, or Old Church, on the Garmisch side of the twin city, that I unexpectedly found my confirming information. Because I was not actively researching, this came as sort of a shock to me.

I had gone to the Alte Kirche to view their large collection of 15th and 16th century murals and tapestries. As I was viewing the displayed murals and tapestries, one caught my attention and was especially interested me. The tapestry appeared to be depicting a woman rubbing something on Jesus' head.

I asked the director of the exhibit, Dr. Josef Wycerman, if he could explain the depiction on the tapestry to me.

He willingly obliged.

"This tapestry depicts the last of three times that Jesus was anointed. The first two times his feet were anointed; the last time an unnamed woman anointed Jesus' head while he was at the home of Simon the leper just before his crucifixion.

"The tapestry was woven in the 15th century by an unknown artisan, however, it became the property of Mary Frances of Naples, the Neapolitan mystic who was said to experience the pains of the Passion during Lent each year. She owned the tapestry from 1751 until her death in 1791. After her death, the family sold the tapestry to an Italian carpet merchant to pay-off her personal debt. In 1830, the merchant in turn sold the tapestry to a German wine producer, who gave it as a gift to the church.

"As I have stated the tapestry depicts a woman pouring ointment on Jesus' head. This event is recorded in Matthew 26: 6-16. Historically it took place on Tuesday evening, March 27, AD 31, at the home of Simon the leper of Bethany, who had invited Jesus and his disciples to a meal.

"It appears," Dr. Wycerman continued, "that Simon was a former leper who was both wealthy and well-known in Bethany. Perhaps Jesus had healed him, although nothing in the Bible even remotely suggests such a healing. However, if he was not a cured leper, it would not have been permitted for Simon to associate with those that were clean, much less invite them to dinner. If Simon was not clean, then Jesus and his disciples might have been invited to his home by members of his family, in which case Simon would not have been present at the dinner.

"Another possibility is that the early translators mistakenly confused two similar Hebrew words (although mostly written in Greek, the Gospel of Matthew does use a few Hebrew words and phrases). If the translators did not pay close attention, it would have been easy for them to mistranslate the phrase, *the humble one*, for the word, *leper*.

"But, whatever the case, apparently after the meal, an unidentified woman approached Jesus and anointed his head with spikenard salve while he reclined on the dinner couch. This was his second anointing in less than a week.

"Again the disciples objected to this 'waste' of this most precious of ointments. Scripture does not say which disciples, but taking into consideration that Judas immediately left the dinner upon its conclusion and visited with the chief priests in order to make arrangements to betray Jesus, Judas may well have been the leader of those who objected.

"Jesus defended the actions of the woman. He suggested that it is far greater to minister to him rather than for him, and openly rebuked the disciples who had objected, humiliating them as he had humiliated Judas just days before.

"Immediately after the meal, Judas, burning with resentment and wanting revenge for being humiliated in front of his peers twice in less than a week, went directly to the chief priests. He made a deal with them to tell them where Jesus would be on a certain day, when and how they could take him alive, and where he would have the least number of his followers present with him.

"John's Gospel implies that Judas betrayed Jesus because he wanted to make a profit out of Jesus' arrest, but it seems unlikely that this was his only motive. Judas may have justified his actions by convincing himself that Jesus would again escape as he had so many times before, to which Judas had been an eye witness, so he could sell information about Jesus' location for a few pieces of silver, Jesus would escape arrest like he had several times before, and Judas would be that much richer, and no one would get hurt—least of all Jesus. Or perhaps Judas, the only non-Galilean in Jesus' group of 12 close followers, was disappointed that the Kingdom about which Jesus had so often proclaimed was imminent, had not as yet materialized. This coupled with Judas' judgment that Jesus appeared to be more concerned with receiving exaltation and personal honor than he was with helping the poor, may have convinced him that Jesus was a false prophet, or at least a prophet who could not produce as he had claimed and did not practice what he preached.

"Yet again, perhaps Judas was afraid," Dr. Wycerman said with a shrug of his shoulders.

"Since Jesus had recently become an enemy of the powerful Sadducees and had come under the suspicious eye of the Roman authorities, it was probable that his disciples could also be suspect. In fact, it seemed quite likely that both Judas and the other 11 disciples would also be classified as enemies of the Sadducees and of the Romans through their association with Jesus. Hence, he moved quickly to align himself on the side of the 'winners.'

"Paulus of Damascus said that Judas betrayed Jesus because as a former zealot, who still harbored deep within the rebellious spirit of a zealot, he sought to strike the first blow for independence by having Jesus arrested. Then by using Jesus'

The Search

arrest as a rallying point, the faithful masses would revolt and rescue their Messiah, thus launching the long awaited revolution against Roman tyranny.

"The 1st and 2nd century Cainite sub-sect of the Gnostic religious faction taught that since the death of Jesus was essential for the salvation of man, Judas, following divine guidance and understanding better than any of the other disciples the need for Jesus to die, sacrificed his own pride, reputation, and position and submitted to the will of God. In essence, he, Judas, had been divinely chosen to bring salvation into the world. Through his (Judas') sacrificial actions, Jesus' death would assure salvation for all of mankind. Hence, Judas became the victim who sacrificed himself so that man might receive life eternal and salvation.

"Another 1st century speculative assertion maintained that Judas believed Jesus was determined to get rid of him. He believed that Jesus decided he had made a mistake in choosing a non-Galilean, or that Jesus suspected him of some financial indiscretion. So, Judas acted against Jesus before Jesus had an opportunity to act against Judas.

"Of course we could go on and on speculating and discussing dozens of other opinions that have been brought forward over the years regarding why Judas betrayed Jesus, but in the end, all of the opinions would have to be placed in the same bin of presumed conjecture because none can be proven to be correct.

"Well," Dr. Wycerman concluded "That is all that I know about this tapestry and all the information that we have."

The following day, Wednesday March 28 was the preparation day for Passover portion of the expanded celebration. Like it was for most devout Jews, this was an exciting day for Jesus and his disciples.

One of the most intriguing accounts of the Passover preparation was written by the early 18th century British nonconformist Philip Doddridge. Doddridge claimed to have gotten his information from Hilary, Bishop of Poitiers' (315-368) *De Trinitate*.

Then again, the portion of *De Trinitate* that I have read does not mention the information that Doddridge claims he found in the document. That is not to say that it is not there because I only read about half of the document, but in the half that I read, it was not there.

I discovered Doddridge's book at Harvard University library in Cambridge, Massachusetts. The name of the book was *Studies on the Opinions of the Fathers*, published in 1749. The book was hard to follow, but it seemed to be a rough outline of the last few days of Jesus' life. Considering Harvard was such a liberal institution, I was surprised the find this book there.

But contrary to my initial supposition, it seemed obvious that Harvard was more concerned with providing a well-rounded education than they were with advancing liberal indoctrination.

Doddridge did not go into detail with his outline, but it seemed to follow a logical series of events, even though the events seemed to be contrary to the traditional and the accepted western Christianity viewpoint of the last days of Jesus' life.

Doddridge began by giving an assumptive opinion concerning the difference between the present [Doddridge's day] method of counting days compared to the method that was in use during the time of Jesus' life. Nevertheless, I am not absolutely convinced that Doddridge assumptive opinion, which he said came from Hilary of Poitiers, was totally correct. But because his opinion is inter-twined into his true and correct content, I felt I needed to include it in my notes.

Afterwards he continued by saying, "Typically the seven days of unleavened bread and the Passover celebration began the evening of the 14th of Nisan (using the Jewish lunar calendar) and ended on the evening of the 21st of Nisan. Even though it was an expanded 17-day celebration in the year AD 31, the Passover portion of the expanded celebration remained the same. The daytime period of the 14th of Nisan was called the *Day of Preparation*. During this daytime period of the 14th of Nisan, the Passover lamb was killed. The evening of the 14th of Nisan was when the *Feast of the Passover* was observed.

"The next day the *Feast of Unleavened Bread* was observed. This first 24-hour period was called a special Sabbath. Six days later, on the evening of the 20th of Nisan, the *Feast of the Lord* was observed. This feast frequently lasted all night. The following day, the 21st of Nisan, was the last day of the seven days of unleavened bread. This last 24-hour period was a High Sabbath because it was a special Sabbath that overlapped a weekly Sabbath. Jesus ate the 14th of Nisan *Feast of Passover* with his disciples, but he did not eat the 20th of Nisan *Feast of the Lord.*

"The typical Jewish day was a 24-hour period that began at 6:00 a.m. (the 1st hour) and ended at 6:00 a.m. (the 1st hour) 24 hours later. Each 24-hour period was divided into two 12-hour parts: the day period of 12 hours was from 6:00 a.m. (the 1st hour) to 6:00 p.m. (the 12th hour). The night period of 12 hours was from 6:00 p.m. (the 12th hour) to 6:00 a.m. (the 1st hour). Therefore when we refer to Tuesday, we think of a period that began at mid-night on Monday and ended at Tuesday's midnight, 24 hours later. But in the Jewish time frame the same period of time (our Tuesday—midnight Monday to midnight Tuesday), would be composed of the last 12-hour night period of Monday and the first 12-hour period of Tuesday."

Doddridge then explained the traditions and the history of the differing chronological time periods of Jesus' last week. He said "For the past two centuries all of the events of Jesus' last few days from the last supper to the resurrection have been compressed into four days (from Thursday evening to Sunday morning).

"However, the traditionally accepted viewpoint of the first 10 centuries placed the events from the Last Supper to burial in a five-day period with resurrection occurring *THREE FULL 24-HOUR DAYS* after burial.

"During the next five centuries the traditional viewpoint of the time period that covered these events fluctuated between three days and seven days, with resurrection of the body occurring two days later. This tradition carried with it the belief that Jesus had two resurrections: one was body resurrection and the other was the spirit resurrection. The two resurrections were separated by eight 24-hour days.

"It's amazing that over the centuries all three of these viewpoints have been official doctrines of the church, and all others, including each of these three at one time or another, were considered heresy.

"So, this leads us to acknowledge that we really don't know how many days it took for all of the events from the Last Supper to the final (or only—whichever is right), resurrection to take place. And I guess it really doesn't matter. All that matter's is that it happened and he arose from the dead."

After explaining these differences, Doddridge began his confusing outline, and although he did not state which of the three traditions he believed to be true, his summarization seemed to reveal his true belief.

He began his summarization by saying, "On the day of preparation of the Passover portion of the 17-day expanded celebration, Jesus sent Peter and John into the city to prepare a setting for the *Feast of Passover*. (This would have been our current Wednesday, March 28, daytime period.) That evening, the 14th of Nisan (our Wednesday evening, March 28, AD 31), the first day of the observance of the seven days of unleavened bread began. The *Feast of Passover* was eaten after sundown, as the night period of the 14th of Nisan (6:00 p.m. on our Wednesday, March 28), the 12th hour, began. Jesus ate this with his disciples. This is commonly called *The Last Supper*.

"At the feast there arose a strife between the 12 over personal greatness (Luke 22:24-30).

"Jesus did not reprimand them for arguing and comparing, he merely showed them true humbleness by washing their feet (John 13:4-17). By washing their feet he was implying that in order to obtain greatness you must be a servant and be willing to humble yourself and become a servant. He, being the Messias/Messiah, humbled himself and became a servant. He was not only a regular servant, but the lowest of servants—the one who washed the feet of guests.

"Some time after this Jesus foretold Judas' betrayal (Matthew 26:20-25).

"After the meal, it was customary for the host of the meal to take bread, sop out the meat dish, give the bread sop to different ones in the group, and give them a blessing as he fed them a piece of bread by hand. One of the ones that Jesus picked to give a sop was Judas. As he gave it to him, Jesus told him to go and do what he felt he should do. Because the blessing was always given to an individual so that only he could hear it, none of the other disciples knew what Jesus had said to Judas. They just assumed that when Judas left, since he was the treasurer of the group and it was up to him to distribute funds as Jesus dictated that he was going to give money to the poor, which was customary and practiced annually after the Feast of Passover meal had concluded. Or they assumed that Jesus had sent him to buy the goods that would be needed for the *Feast of Unleavened Bread*, which would be held the following day.

"After the sop, Judas left the supper and went to the chief priests to betray Jesus. He took their money and told them where Jesus would be later that night. He later led them to the spot where Jesus was praying. After Judas left, John 13:2, 27-30 tells us that Satan entered into him. He probably became demon-possessed at that time.

"The chief priests had decided that if they could arrest Jesus, that he had to be interrogated before the *Feast of the Lord*, which was to be held on the 20th of Nisan (our April 2, AD 31). The 21st of Nisan (our April 3, AD 31) was the High Sabbath.

"After Judas had departed, Jesus gave the remaining disciples a new commission and a new commandment that they should love one another (John 13:31-34). He also instigated the *Lord's Supper*, which commemorated and became a permanent reminder of his sufferings and death. He also indicated that he would not eat the Feast of the Lord with them, which they were to eat on the 20th of Nisan, six days from then (Matthew 26:26; Mark 14:22-25).

"Finally they were finished, it was time to leave. He asked about their weapons (Luke 22:35-38). They then sung a hymn and departed to the Mount of Olives (Matthew 26:31-35; Mark 14:26-31; Luke 22:31-39; John 13:36-17-26).

"On the western slope of the mount was located the Garden of Gethsemane, where Jesus was going to pray (Matthew 14:26-30). It was a garden owned by a friend of Jesus.

"As they walked to the Mount of Olives," Doddridge continued, "Jesus foretold that all of them would forsake him that night. Peter brazenly stated that he (Peter) would never forsake him, even if all the rest did. That is when Jesus said that he (Peter) that very night before the peacock crowed two times, would deny at least three times that he knew Jesus. Peter refused to believe that; stating his emphatic loyalty.

"As Jesus and the 11 continued to walk to the mount, Jesus encouraged them with a discourse that is recorded in John 14. As they approached the mount, he continued his discourse to his disciples. It is recorded in John 15 and 16. Climbing the mount and approaching the garden he finished his discourse. It is recorded in John 17. So, the entire chapters of 14 through 17 of John record his conversation with his disciples as they walked from the place where they had the *Feast of Passover* to the Garden of Gethsemane."

"Upon their arrival at the garden, Jesus and his disciples entered.

"Leaving the rest of his disciples near the entrance to the garden, he took Peter, James, and John with him further into the garden. Jesus and the three disciples walked a ways into the garden, and then he left them, asking them to watch and pray, while he walked by himself even further into the garden in order to pray. Jesus prayed probably until about 8:00 or 9:00 the night of the 14th of Nisan (our Wednesday, March 28)."

"Jesus had been praying in the garden when Judas arrived with a mob of at least 600 to as many as 1,000 or more, to arrest Jesus." This was the concluding statement of Doddridge.

Although Doddridge's description and summary was confusing and difficult to follow, it did shed some light on the assumed method of time reckoning during the time of Jesus' ministry—information that I had not found anyplace else—and it provided a logical progression of events that culminated with Jesus' time of intensive and emotionally heart-wrenching prayer on the night of his arrest.

XXI

ARREST AND CRUCIFIXION

(Wednesday March 28 through Monday April 2, AD 31)

"On the eve of Passover they hanged Yeshu of Nazareth. And a herald went before him forty days, saying, 'Yeshu of Nazareth is going forth to be stoned, since he has practiced sorcery and cheated, and led people astray. Let everyone knowing anything in his defense come and plead for him.' But they found no one in his defense, and they hanged him on the eve of Passover"—from the Babylonian Talmuds.

Jesus taught his disciples numerous lessons as they walked to the Garden of Gethsemane located on the Mount of Olives. Most of the lessons are recorded in the Gospel of John, beginning with chapter 13 and on through chapter 17. But once they arrived at the Garden of Gethsemane, Jesus' long ordeal of pre-crucifixion torture actually began.

One of the foremost confirming accounts of Jesus' agony in the Garden of Gethsemane was a letter written in 457 by Leo I (the Great), addressed to a "Cornelius of Carthage, sufferer for Christ." I discovered the letter while researching at the University of Manchester. It was one of several letters written by Leo the Great that had been reproduced and translated from the original Latin into English, French, and Spanish and had been bound into a volume in 1817, and edited by the staff of Trinity College. The volume was entitled *Great Letters of Leo the Great*. The letter that interested me most was this letter addressed to Cornelius, about Jesus' passion in the Garden of Gethsemane.

Leo quoted portions of all of the Gospels in his letter; portions that we now can identify as being taken from Matthew 26, Mark 14, Luke 22, and John 18.

Leo began his letter by greeting Cornelius and praying for God's grace to be granted to him and that healing would visit his household.

He then praised Cornelius for keeping the faith against overwhelming obstacles.

Afterwards he began to explain Jesus' passion in the garden, saying, "As Jesus went through so much for our sakes then we too must be willing to go through the same for him. For as Jesus entered the Garden of Gethsemane, a large garden that fronted an immense olive grove (which contained an olive press), that covered the entire north and most of the west side of the Mount of Olives, he left eight of his disciples in the garden near the entrance to the grove and proceeded further into the grove, perhaps as far as the olive press, located well within the grove, with Peter, James, and John.

"When they got to the olive press, Jesus left Peter, James, and John there and continued on further into the olive grove in order to pray.

"Matthew's Gospel says that Jesus asked the three to pray for him, and to keep watch, as he went further into the grove to pray. Apparently he was expecting to be arrested that very night. He told the three that he felt like he was dying of emotional anguish.

"As he got to the place where he was going to pray," Leo continued, "he collapsed in spiritual torture and emotional agony. On two different occasions, about an hour apart, he returned to the three and found them sleeping, probably because the filling meal that they had just consumed had made them sleepy. He warned them to "pray, that you enter not into temptation." Although they were probably willing, the physical body would not cooperate.

"Luke's Gospel recorded that as Jesus prayed, his sweat became as great drops of blood. (Luke was a physician so he was the only one who recorded this event)

"I feel," Leo interjected, "even though I am not a doctor, that this was caused by Jesus' great emotional stress. This type of condition was, in my opinion, a physical phenomenon that was known to the Greeks as *hematidrosis*, or bloody sweat. The condition occurs when a person is under extreme emotional stress to the point that tiny blood passages in the sweat glands break and mix with the sweat. This condition is rare, but it has been documented to occur amongst the Greeks, Romans, and Egyptians. Accompanying this condition is comes extreme fatigue, weakness and the possibility of shock."

Leo then continued with his account of Jesus' passion, "Jesus prayed and asked the Father that if it be His will, for the cup to be taken from him. This cup could have been the cup of intense suffering (Luke [22:42] John [18:11]). However, Jesus knew that he was going to go through the most intense suffering that had ever been inflicted upon any man in history, so although he may not have been prepared for it to the fullest, he was aware that it would happen and that it was supposed to happen. Therefore, I am not sure that this cup was the cup of Jesus' suffering.

"The cup could have been the cup of death by the most inhumane means.

"It could have been the cup of betrayal in that he knew that not only would Judas betray him but also that every one of his closest follows would forsake him in a matter of hours.

"It also could have been the fact that he knew that his Father would literally turn His back on him, leaving him totally and completely alone.

"It could have been the cup of shame in that he would be crucified naked, shamed, and exposed to everyone.

"It could have been the fact that he knew that his death would eventually culminate in the persecution of those whom he loved so dearly.

"Or it could have been that the cup was the cup of death by Satan before he got to the cross, right there in the olive grove. If Satan could kill him before he got to the cross, then God's redemptive plan could be short-circuited.

"Although we do not know for sure," Leo continued, "we do know from Luke [22:42] and John [18:11] that Jesus did partake of the cup and submitted to all that God the Father had planned concerning the redemption of mankind.

"The third time that Jesus came back to the olive press, he again found Peter, James, and John sleeping. But this time he did not ask them to pray as he had the other two times. This time he told them to sleep on because the hour was at hand for him to be arrested.

"Shortly thereafter, but well into the night, Judas arrived leading a huge procession of armed guards and civil and religious officials. The Gospel of John [18:31] indicates that an armed guard of 600 to 1,000 temple guards (this action may or may not have been with the Roman authorities approval) was sent by the High Priest to arrest Jesus. These, along with the local civil authorities and religious leaders, could have numbered well over a thousand who had marched to the Mount of Olives to arrest Jesus in the Garden of Gethsemane.

"It was predetermined that Jesus would be identified by Judas, who would greet him with the traditional kiss on each cheek."

Leo then talked about the admirable courage of Peter, "Who when he realized what was happening, drew his sword and attacked Malchus, the servant of the High Priest, in an effort to defend Jesus.

"For almost four centuries there has been confusion about this attack. The Gospel of John [18:10] says that Peter cut off Malchus' right ear. This could represent three different scenarios: (1) Peter was left handed, and he attacked Malchus while facing him; (2) Peter was right handed, but he attacked Malchus from the back; or (3) Peter attacked and killed Malchus and then cut off his right ear as a trophy of conquest (which was a typical action for victors of duels or arena blood games of contest.).

"I (Leo) feel that Peter was left-handed. However, the other scenarios could also be true, especially since many in the Church are now beginning to suppress any and all reference to Peter killing an unarmed man, even though he was protecting Jesus.

"Rather than thanking Peter for risking his life to save him, which Peter fully expected, Jesus instead rebuked him in front of this huge crowd and his companions, Jesus then healed (and perhaps raised from the dead) the man who Peter had attacked (Gospel of Luke [22:51]).

"Without a doubt," Leo continued to write, "this caused Peter to become angry with Jesus. Peter's anger turned to resentment, which culminated in revenge, prompting him to repeatedly deny Jesus a few hours later.

"From the garden, the multitude led Jesus bound, to the palace residence of Annas, a former High Priest (AD 6-15) and the father-in-law of Caiaphas, the current High Priest. Nothing is recorded of what happened at the residence of Annas.

"None of Jesus' followers supported him at the time when he needed them most. Perhaps they were afraid of the Temple guards, feeling that if they could arrest Jesus, the leader, surely they would arrest his followers too. Or maybe they were afraid of Jesus and how he would react if they tried to support him. After all, look at what happened to Peter! Or maybe they were afraid of the Roman authorities, especially if they had approved this arrest.

"Although for years Jesus had been a friend of the Roman authorities, it had become obvious to them, his followers, that ever since his healing of the son of Timaeus in Jericho, Jesus had become an object of suspicion and a concern to the Roman authorities. They could have felt that Jesus was a chief threat to the peace and security of Jerusalem during the extended Passover celebration time. Therefore, it was determined that he needed to be arrested and detained; at least until the extended Passover celebration had concluded.

"Since Jesus was a Jewish religious figure, the Jewish religious authorities in Jerusalem were granted precedence in dealing with him. Hence, it is most likely that they were given permission to arrest and detain Jesus. However, if the one arrested was highly regarded by the Roman authority, as was Jesus, the Jewish religious leaders, while still allowed to make an arrest and to deal with the problem up to a limit, were not permitted nor were they granted permission to inflict punishment that would be considered excessive.

"Little did the Roman authorities realize that the detention of Jesus would quickly lead to the conviction of Jesus.

"Jesus had already suffered intense emotional anguish which left his body and spirit weak and vulnerable. But it was on the beginning of an unprecedented journey of pain, torment, and agony that Jesus would endure over the next few days until his death and resurrection."

With that, Leo concluded his account of Jesus' passion.

The rest of the letter was an encouragement for Cornelius to use Jesus' passion as his example to press forward and not to falter in his faith.

The remainder of Leo's letters were doctrinal, with none containing any more events of Jesus' life.

For documentation that I hoped would provide the necessary authentication of the continuation of Jesus' chronology on the night that he was arrested, a reproduction of a medieval manuscript that I discovered at the London Bible College research library, in London, England, proved to be invaluable.

Raymund of Penafort had written the original 60-page Latin manuscript entitled *The Historia Chronicon Pascale*, in 1237. Raymund of Penafort was a successful lawyer before becoming, in AD 1222, a Dominican monk at the age of 47. He is credited with compiling the first collection of cases of conscience and was one of the founders of the Mercedarian order.

In a volume entitled *The Order of the Mercedarian*, edited in 1937 by Sir Thurmon Kane of the University of London, the four surviving pages of Raymund's original (along with hundreds of other manuscript pages from dozens of ancient manuscripts) had been reproduced and translated into Greek, French, and English. Along with the translations, Sir Kane had also added his own comments and background information.

The original surviving velum leaves of Raymund's manuscript are safely stored in The Vatican II library.

According to the background information included in the volume, the main focus of Raymund's original 60-page manuscript (written on front and back) was to provide an exhaustive and extensive treatise recounting the passion, arrest, trail and crucifixion of Jesus. The surviving four pages reproduced in *The Order of the Mercedarian*, covers primarily a portion of Jesus' trial. It is written in the form of a legal summarization of events, much like the summarizations used during Raymund's time in preparing a defense for a client.

The Search

"It appears that Raymund," Sir Kane began with his background information about the document itself, "had quite some insight into the judicial practices of both Jew and Roman at the time of Jesus' crucifixion.

"In his original manuscript, Raymund first summarized in chronological order, the last days of Jesus' life before crucifixion. He then went back and for the remainder of the document, described in detail the events of those last days. Nothing from the last part, the detailed description part, of the manuscript has survived. These four surviving pages, written on the front and back, represents but a small portion of the first part, the summary part.

"Raymund moved from point to point, with little concern about maintaining a non-hindered flow. But, as he moved from point to point, he stopped occasionally to explain a particular part of the summary in more detail, without going into minute elucidation. Therefore, although some points are explained painstakingly, other points are either just touched on or are totally ignored."

Sir Kane then began explaining Raymund's document. The document seemed to begin in the middle of a sentence. "...The mob led Jesus, bound, from the Mount garden to Annas' palace. Annas was the father-in-law of Caiaphas, the High Priest. We know nothing about what happened during this time.

"From the palace of Annas, Jesus was led, still bound, to the palace of Caiaphas, the High Priest (John 18:13-14). There he appeared before the preliminary Court of Elders and Priests and was interrogated.

"As Jesus was being led into Caiaphas' palace, a disciple known by the High Priest (John 18: 15), probably Judas, Nicodemus, or Joseph of Arimathea, followed Jesus into the palace. Peter stood outside of the palace. Not long afterwards, the disciple that the High Priest knew and who had followed Jesus into the palace went out to get Peter and brought him inside (John 18:16).

"At the same time that Peter was entering the palace, the lady door keeper asked him if he was one of Jesus' disciples. Peter said, 'No!' (John 18:17).

"Inside the palace, Peter joined a group of servants who were warming themselves by a fire. As he warmed himself by the fire, a girl said to the people gathered there that he (Peter) was with Jesus. Peter denied it (Luke 23:56 & 57).

"As Jesus was being interrogated by the preliminary court, Peter was again asked if he was a follower of Jesus and for the third time he denied that he was a follower of Jesus (John 18:25).

"Not long thereafter a man said to Peter that he (Peter) was one of the followers of Jesus. Peter denied for the fourth time that he was one of Jesus' followers (Luke 22:58). Then a relative of Malchus, who Peter had confronted in the garden, challenged Peter. Weren't you in the garden with Jesus? He asked. Peter denied it. Immediately following the denial, Peter's fifth denial, the cock crowed (John 18:27) for the first of two times about which Jesus had warned Peter."

Sir Kane at this point paused to interject some of his own comments concerning the cock referred to in Scripture. "This cock was not a poultry rooster which we see so often depicted today. Chickens and roosters that we westerners so readily picture when we think about a cock, were not native to the Middle East, they were native to the Far East. The chicken as we know it, did not appear in the Middle East until the

2nd or 3rd century AD. The cock in this story was a peacock, or the 'fowl of conscience,' as Cicero called it.

"The trained peacock was used throughout the Roman Empire by the aristocracy and the wealthy for two reasons: (1) they served as night time clocks. From the setting of the sun until the rising of the sun the following morning, the peacock was trained to crow approximately every two hours. So, approximately two hours after sunset, the peacock crowed for the first time and continued throughout the night every two hours until sunup. (2) Peacocks were trained as burglar alarms. Peacocks were allowed to roam freely throughout the house and throughout the grounds. If at anytime during the night a stranger or anyone that was unfamiliar to the bird tried to enter the home or the grounds without being accompanied by a family member or a resident of the home, the peacock would start screeching and screaming its blood-curdling shriek, effectively waking the members of the household while at the same time frightening off the bugler or intruder. In addition, the peacock had an uncanny ability to recognize anyone who had ever tried to enter the home uninvited or had tried to harm a household member in any way. And if the peacock did recognize a person who had tried to break-in but had escaped, the bird would begin its shriek, warning the household that this person had at one time been an uninvited guest to the house. Thus, Cicero called the bird the fowl of conscience."

Sir Kane returned to Raymund's manuscript. "So, the fact that the peacock crowed twice meant that from the time it crowed the first time until it crowed a second time two hours has elapsed. Sometime after Peter denied that he knew Jesus for the fifth time and the peacock crowed the first of the two times, another man said that Peter was one of Jesus' disciples. Again he denied it and this time he cursed to emphasize that he was not a follower of this Jesus (Matthew 26:74; Mark 15: 70-71; Luke 22:60). Immediately thereafter, the cock crowed a second time (Mark 15:71; Luke 22:60). As the cocked crowed the second time, Jesus turned and looked at his disciple. Peter, remembering the words of Jesus as well as his own words of guaranteed faithfulness to Jesus, ran from the palace of Caiaphas, and went out and wept bitterly (Matthew 26:75; Luke 22:61-62).

"There is an interesting point that Raymund brings out about cursing," Sir Kane continued, "is that he says that cursing is not part of a Christ-like character. So, the best way to convince people that one is not a follower of Christ is to curse. The act of cursing will show to all that regardless of what comes out of a person's mouth in the form of praises, worship, respect, commitment, or admonition, that person is not Christ's. Cursing is the identifying act that more than anything else distinguishes whether or not a person truly belongs to Christ.

"Late that night, Raymund continues, the preliminary court reached a consensus of accusation and sent Jesus to Pilate, the ranking Roman authority (who was obligated to be in Jerusalem for the 17-day expanded Passover), for his approval to proceed with a trial.

"After a brief interrogation, Pilate gave his approval for them to proceed with a *civil trial*—not a criminal or capital trial. Up until that time, there had not been even a hint that this was but the beginning of a process that would lead to the death of Jesus.

"The Jewish religious authorities had no intention of honoring Pilate's authorization of proceeding with a civil trial. They insisted on a criminal trial. So, from Pilate, Jesus' accusers led him back to the High Priest for a private interrogation, as they began to build their case for a criminal trial rather than a civil trial."

Again, Sir Kane paused from the chronological events of Jesus' interrogation and interjected personal comments concerning the typical Jewish judicial procedures under the Romans. "The Sanhedrin, the legislative body of the Jewish nation, was divided into two bodies, the greater, which had 70 members, and the lesser, which had 24 members.

"The Court of Elders and Priests had 12 members and its chair was the High Priest. This court decided all appeals, and its judgment could not typically be appealed. This court was the one that made the final judgment against Jesus. It had exclusive jurisdiction for capital crimes, although under the Roman occupation, it could not carry out sentencing. Only the Roman authorities could carry out capital sentencing.

"When an accused person was brought before the members of the Jewish judiciary, he first appeared before a five-member preliminary interrogation panel made up of members of the Court of Elders and Priests. They held a preliminary interrogation in order to force a plea. If they could not obtain a plea, the accused was sentenced by the five members of the Court of Elders and Priests and was sent to the ranking Roman authority for his authorization to proceed with a trial.

"The Roman authority in turn ruled on whether the accused would receive a civil or a criminal trial. He could overrule the Jewish religious leader's petition indicating that a trial is necessary, but he could rule whether the trial would be civil or criminal. Civil trials usually resulted in a moderate to heavy fine being accessed against the convicted, a period of incarceration in one of the many prisons or at the very least a period of closely scrutinized probation, and in some cases scourging. Criminal trials usually resulted in the convicted being scourged, imprisoned for a lengthy period of time, the assessment of a very hefty fine, or in extreme cases, execution by any number of methods, including crucifixion.

"After the Roman authorities determined what kind of trial would be allowed, the accused was then taken to the High Priest who questioned him privately (although it was said to be private, in reality the priest had three observers who witnessed the questioning). If the trial was to be a *criminal trial*, after the High Priest had finished his interrogation, the accused was sent to the Sanhedrin where he was again accused and interrogated. There the charges were written in the official records and collaborating witnesses were introduced and interrogated separately and independently. Regardless of how many witnesses were introduced, there had to be a collaboration of two independently questioned witnesses before the criminally accused could be forwarded on for conviction.

"If there were not two witnesses who testified the same and collaborated each other's witness, the accused was usually set free. If two witnesses were found, then the Sanhedrin approved the recommendation of the preliminary interrogation panel of the Court of Elders and Priests and the accused was sent back to the High Priest.

"At sundown on the day of approval by the Sanhedrin, the High Priest and the remaining seven members of the Court of Elders and Priests who had not participated in the original preliminary panel's interrogation would again interrogate the accused. They could either find the accused innocent of all charges or blameworthy by suspicion. If found innocent, he would be released immediately. If found blameworthy, he would have to stand criminal trial before the entire Court of Elders and Priests. This Court was required to fast and pray for an entire day before the trial commenced.

"At sunrise on the morning after the members had fasted, the High Priest brought the Urim and Thummim out of the Holy Place of the Temple where they were kept, and placed them before the High Priest's seat of judgment.

"The High Priest then excused himself and closely veiled himself in a dark room with his back turned away from the accused. This act represented the uncompromising impartial justice of God. He then would be led out and seated in the seat of judgment. The seat of judgment where upon sat the High Priest was then totally draped in a solid black veil so that it was completely impossible for the High Priest to see the accused.

"The High Priest then released the *lactees*. The *lactees* consisted of two men. One stood at the door of the court with a red flag in his hand, and the other sat on a white horse some distance on the road that led to Gehenna, the place of execution. Each of these men would continually cry the name of the accused, his alleged crime, and the names of the witnesses who had sworn against him, followed by an appeal for any person, who was a non-family member, who knew anything to be said in the accused's favor, to come forward and to testify on the accused's behalf. The *'lactees' cry'* would last for at least one day and up to a maximum of seven days, at the discretion of the High Priest.

"If two persons, who were non-family and unrelated, came forward to testify in favor of the accused, the witness of the accusers would be neutralized and the accused would be granted an immediate appeal that was scheduled one year from that date (in Jesus' case not a single witness came to his defense). During that one year period, the accused was set free with a promise from him, sworn before God and the High Priest, that he would return the following year on that date to be re-interrogated by the preliminary court, thus starting the process all over again.

"These two new favorable witnesses could come forward at any time during the trial of the accused by the Court of Elders and Priests, which could have lasted from one day to months. After all accusing testimony was heard and the accused interrogated, if no one came forward on the accused's behalf, the eleven-member (the High Priest was not included) court would cast lots or vote and the decision was presented to the High Priest.

"A member could abstain from voting, but if as many as two abstained, it indicated that there was enough doubt that the accused could not be convicted. If this happened, the accused instead would be chastised by flogging, fined, and placed on suspicion probation.

"Suspicion probation meant that the accused would have to report to the Court six times yearly for seven years. Each time that he reported he had to pay a fine, and once a year he was again chastised by flogging.

"The accused could only be convicted if 100 percent of the Court members who voted, voted guilty.

"When the verdict was presented to the High Priest," Sir Kane continued, "He then would call for another vote of the members for their recommended penalty for the accused. Again the vote had to be 100 percent of the voters in favor of death, if the accused was to be sentenced to death; but a simple majority, if the punishment was other than death. The result of the vote was then handed to the High Priest.

"He then would remove the veils and would pronounce sentencing to the convicted based on the two votes. If the verdict was for death, the High Priest followed his pronouncement by washing his hands in a basin or ewer, as a token of the court's innocence, thus testifying to the fact that the convicted's own actions had condemned him.

"As soon as the High Priest had washed his hands, the Temple guards led the convicted to the Roman authority (in Jesus' case, this was Pilate), with the Court's recommendation for death.

"Even though the Roman authority (in this case, Pilate) had authorized a civil trial only, if 100 percent of the voting Jewish judiciary chose to reject the civil trial mandate in favor of a criminal trial, the Roman authorities generally agreed with their decision in order to preserve peace.

"The Roman authority would then determine whether the convicted was worthy of death. The Roman authority could not change or overrule the verdict, but he could decline the death penalty in favor of scourging or imprisonment it they felt that the accused had done nothing worthy of death.

"If the Roman authority determined that his crime was not worthy of death, he would transfer the convicted to a lesser Roman authority and civil court (in Jesus' case, Pilate referred him to Herod).

"That civil court would then interrogate the accused and either pass judgment and carry out a lesser sentence, or would send the accused back to the higher Roman authority (Pilate) with either a no recommended judgment or with a judgment of agreement with the conviction of the Jewish court.

"If the accused was returned with no recommendation, this signified that the lower court felt that there was not enough evidence for conviction or it did not have the authority to act on the matter, thus the higher Roman authority must act on the conviction and sentencing.

"If the higher Roman authority (Pilate) could find no justification for the recommended sentencing, he could either dismiss the case or he could demand that the Jewish Court justify its judgment and sentencing.

"If he felt that the accused was guilty of a crime, but that the crime was not worthy of a sentence of death, he could have the convicted flogged in an attempt to force an admitted guilt. If there was no admitted guilt, and if the accused lived through the flogging, he could either choose to set the accused free, feeling that he had paid for his crime, send him back to the Jewish Court for re-trial, imprison him, or ratify the Jewish Court's recommendation and send him away to face the death penalty. If the accused died during flogging, it indicated that he must have been guilty.

"If the Roman authorities sent the convicted away to the death penalty, the authority (Pilate) would wash his hands indicating his and the Roman government's innocence in the matter.

"After this, the street and road leading to the place of execution was cleared of all traffic and observers (only those who had a residence on that street or road, or guests staying at inns on the street or road, were allowed to witness the walk to the place of execution) and the convicted would be led away by an 8-member escort and a 25 to 100-member Roman guard to the place of execution.

"If the convicted was guilty of sedition, treason, or crimes against Caesar or the Roman State, he would face crucifixion.

"If the crime was not a crime against Rome but was still a crime worthy of capital punishment the convicted would either be 'shot' by an archery 'firing squad,' run through with a sword, beheaded, or run through with a spear.

"After death, all victims of crucifixion were forced to stay pinned to the stake or cross for 21 days or until their bodies were either greatly decomposed or had been eaten by scavenging animals and fowl.

"The body and bones that remained were then burned in the refuse fires of Gehenna.

"Other victims of capital punishment (other than those crucified) were usually claimed for interment by family or friends, but if no one claimed the body by two days after death, they too were burned.

"It was very unusual for Jesus' body to have been allowed to be entombed. If fact, it was so unusual that in the official Roman court records from all over the eastern Empire from one hundred years before and one hundred years after the death of Jesus, there were only three confirmed cases out of a total of 9,784 who had faced capital punishment by crucifixion, in which permission had been granted for the victim to be buried or entombed immediately after death, rather than letting the body be devoured and then the remains burned."

Sir Kane ended his personal comments and returned to explaining and commenting upon Raymund's manuscript. It appeared as if Sir Kane was setting a stage to conclude whether the Jewish authorities followed correct procedures when they convicted Jesus.

He continued, "At sun-up the following morning (our Thursday, March 29) Jesus was again interrogated by the High Priest. Afterwards he was sent to the judgment hall of the Sanhedrin for further interrogation. It was at this time that witnesses were allowed to make their accusations and Jesus was subjected to mockery and physical abuse. After all of the witnesses were heard, the Sanhedrin confirmed the findings of the preliminary court from the night before. At sundown, the second preliminary Court of the Elders and Priests sent him back to the High Priest for additional interrogation.

"The following day (our Friday, March 30) was a fast day for the Court of Elders and Priests. No interrogation of Jesus was allowed or litigation was conducted on that day. Jesus however, remained bound.

"The day following the fast day (our Saturday, March 31) was the Sabbath during which typically there was no litigation. However, on this particular Sabbath, because it would occur during the Passover week portion of the 17-day expanded celebration in which a High Sabbath would be observed, the High Priest gave permission for the Court of Elders to convene and for Jesus to stand trial.

"At the trial Jesus was found guilty and was sentenced to death. However, the Jewish court had no authority to carry out sentencing, so they had to send Jesus back to Pilate so that he would ratify the decision of the Court of Elders and Priests.

"Pilate was totally taken back that the Jewish Court of Elders and Priests would dare to suggest that Jesus was guilty of a crime that was punishable by death. True, Jesus was antagonistic to the religious leaders in Jerusalem and he certainly had dropped in respect in the eyes of most of the Roman authority, these did not warrant a death condemnation. Pilate decided to personally interrogate Jesus. This was unheard of with anyone who was a non-Roman. Roman procurators and governors personally interrogated *only* Roman citizens. Jesus remained silent during this interrogation.

"Appalled by the Jewish religious leaders unwarranted condemnation of Jesus and disagreeing with the ruling of the Jewish court, Pilate found nothing worthy of death for which to sentence Jesus. So, Pilate sent him to Herod Antipas, who was in Jerusalem for the first and only expanded 17-day Passover celebration. Pilate and Herod decided that Jesus should be tried on civil offenses, in which Herod would officiate.

"The following morning (our Sunday, April 1) Jesus stood trial before Herod for civil offenses and for claiming to be The Theophus of Tiberias. Jesus was vindicated of all charges and wrongdoing and after Herod's soldiers had mocked and made fun of him and physically abused him for hours, was sent back to Pilate. Before Pontius Pilate once again at the Praetorium of the Fortress (Tower) of Antonia, the residence and governmental seat of Pilate while he was in Jerusalem, Pilate personally interrogated Jesus. Again, Pilate could find nothing wrong with Jesus, or at least nothing worthy of death."

"At this point the story of Jesus' ordeal becomes cloudy and inconsistent." Sir Kane again interjected. He then began to explain the confusing Gospel accounts of Jesus' trial and conviction.

"The Matthew setting suggests that Jesus was accused of blasphemy, a crime that to the Jews was punishable by death, yet the Romans did not consider blasphemy a crime punishable by death. In fact, the Romans considered blasphemy nothing more than an irritation. So, considering that the Roman authorities were the only ones permitted to condemn a man to death and to carry out a death sentence, especially if the accused was in high standing with the Roman authorities, the Jewish religious leaders had to come up with something with which to accuse Jesus, that would fit within Rome's narrow parameter of crimes that should be punishable by death, preferably death by crucifixion. The Jewish religious leaders felt that if they could convince Pilate that Jesus was a threat to the political power and rule of Rome, or that he was actually an insurgent posing as rabboni, who could incite the people to revolt against Rome, then they would accomplish their purpose. Consequently, they accused Jesus before Pilate of trying to depose the ruling authority of Rome by claiming to be the King of the Jews.

"However, when the Jewish religious officials accused Jesus before Pilate of claiming to be King of the Jews, Pilate considered their accusations of Jesus only a minor offense. Since Pilate had been faced over the past four years with no less than 28 different men who had proclaimed themselves to be the King of the Jews or the rightful heir to Herod, he not only showed little to no concern regarding this accusation against Jesus. In fact, he was noticeably aggravated with the Jewish religious leaders and annoyed that they would waste his time by bringing such a case to his judgment seat. Of the 28 self-proclaimed kings of the Jews, all had enjoyed a following and all said that God had appointed them to be the king of the Jews. Pilate dealt with each one with contempt and quickly squelched each movement. Seven of the self-proclaimed kings had large rebellious followings. These 'kings' were each sentenced to eight to ten years in solitary prison. Once a 'king' was imprisoned, the movement ceased to exist. Seventeen of the self-proclaimed kings were flogged mercilessly with from 20 to 50 strikes and were released after being sternly warned against inciting rebellion among the people. That ended those particular movements. One very ruthless 'king' who was a murderer and took pleasure in disemboweling Roman women who were with child and dismembering innocent Roman male residents, had to be executed, which then ended his movement. Thus, Pilate was in no mood to deal with another self-proclaimed king of the Jews. However, this one, Jesus, had no radical following and those who he considered his followers, fled and forsook him and one of his most trusted insiders even betrayed him. He had no army in waiting, no political allies, and no one on whom he could call for any type of support, be it military, political, moral, or social. He had nothing and no one. Surely, the Jews wanted him dead for spite. Although Pilate was not known for his compassion, (in fact, the opposite—his ruthlessness, his numerous murderous attacks on the innocent, and his iron-fisted merciless dealings with the populous—was widespread and well-known throughout the region) he also was not one to put to death an innocent rabboni in order to satisfy the resentful jealousies of the troublesome Jewish religious hierarchy. But if past history was any indication of what Jesus should expect from Pilate, then a flogging of 20 to 50 strikes would be typical and then he would be released.

"The Mark setting seems to be non-committal. In one sense it implies that the Jewish religious leaders did in fact accuse Jesus before Pilate of claiming to be the King of the Jews and then in another sense it seems that they accused Jesus of sedition and treason, a crime that was punishable by death—if it could be proven. All accusations of treason were taken seriously and were investigated by the procurator, Pilate. If Pilate found the accused guilty of treason and insurrection, the accused would be flogged with 100 strikes and then crucified or he would be flogged with 200 strikes, which usually caused death long before the flogging was completed, and was not crucified.

"The false assumption that the Romans restricted themselves to 40 strikes is a misnomer. That was a Jewish custom and the Romans did not honor the Jewish customs. Roman floggings were dependent upon the severity of the crime. But generally, the floggings ranged from a minimum of 10 strikes up to a maximum of 200 strikes. On the average, a man that had been sentenced to death by crucifixion for any other reason besides treason received 30 strikes and then he was crucified. A man who was sentenced to death by crucifixion for treason was first flogged with 100 strikes and then he was crucified, if he survived the flogging.

The Search

"The Luke setting indicates that Jesus had been brought before Pilate as a rebel who tried to incite the people to rebellion and who provoked the people to rebel against paying taxes to Caesar. This might be the most accurate account of why Pilate made his decision to flog Jesus and to have him crucified as a treasonous enemy of the state. This sentencing by Pilate was confirmed by Seneca, Livy, Plutarch, Cornelius Tacitus, Pliny the Younger, Suertonius, Thallus, Phlegon, and the satirist Lucian of Samosata, who all wrote authoritative records regarding the crucifixion of Jesus and the cause for which he was crucified. Some of these historians also said that the incident that sparked the fire that resulted in Jesus be condemned to crucifixion was the last of his three times that he cleansed the Temple compound of merchandisers. The first time it took place (John 2:14-15), Pilate was not in Jerusalem and no action was taken against Jesus. Almost four years later it happened again (Matthew 21:12-13). At the very beginning of the 17-day expanded Passover celebration (Pilate had not as yet arrived in Jerusalem for the celebration and most of the celebrates who would eventually arrive in town for the celebration, had not yet arrived) Jesus stormed into the half-empty Temple compound and violently kicked over the tables of the money changers, and drove the moneychangers out of the Temple area, knocked over the cages containing animals thus setting them free, and caused a major ruckus that somehow was brought under control with little damage. However, if he had done that in the middle of the seven-day Passover portion of the expanded celebration, during the days of sacrifice, when the Temple area was packed full of celebrants and worshipers, there would have been a major disturbance, which could have only be suppressed by the intervention of the Roman military. So thought the High Priest and the powerful Sadducees, who up to this point had considered Jesus little more than a wearisome annoyance, but who quickly would become his most powerful enemies—enemies so powerful that they may have been the major voices and influences in his being condemned to death. Then two days after Jesus cleansed the Temple a second time (Mark 11:15-17) the nightmare that the Sadducees feared most occurred. At the height of the seven-day Passover portion's days of sacrifice, at a time when the Temple compound very well could have been 'bursting at the seams' with over one million worshipers, celebrants, sight-seers, money changers, animals, merchants, priests, religious leaders, temple guards, and Roman military, Jesus for the third and final time came storming into the Temple compound and repeated the same 'cleansing ritual' that he had done two times before. Neither of the two previous Temple cleansings had been carried out in this type of setting with so many people and so much potential for a major uncontrollable insurrection. (As Jesus cleansed the Temple there must have been thousands of people trying to get the money that was being scattered about, frightened animals running and bucking trying to escape, people screaming and running wild and hundreds of soldiers carrying out their ruthless mob control tactics.) Had it not been for the mercies of God (so thought the Sadducees) Jesus' insanity would have caused the entire city to erupt into a violent insurgency, which would have been violently crushed by the Roman authorities, killing thousands of expanded Passover celebrants, and subjecting the city of Jerusalem and the state of Judea to the pitiless iron fist of Imperial Rome. This time Pilate was in Jerusalem. From his residence at the Fortress of Antonia, he could have seen what was transpiring in the Temple compound. As such, it may not have taken too much persuasion to convince him that Jesus was a troublemaker who had the power, the personality, and the charisma to incite the people to rebellion. If Jesus were not dealt with immediately, next time he did something like this there very well could be a major revolt.

"It is possible that Pilate and the temple officials, the Sadducees, had an understanding that if there were any trouble during these religious celebrations—especially this 17-day expanded Passover celebration which he had personally approved—it would be dealt with immediately and mercilessly and that the perpetrator of the trouble (whether Jew, Roman, Greek, or another nationality) would be dealt with swiftly and in severity. If this was the case, all the Jewish officials had to do was secretly arrest Jesus, so that such an arrest would not incite his followers, quickly convict him and send him to Pilate for sentencing. This would be done quickly, secretly, and conclusively.

"Considering the information recorded in Luke, one could conclude that the Sadducees controlled Sanhedrin, using the incident of Jesus' third cleansing of the Temple, found Jesus guilty of sedition and inciting the people into riotous behavior (Joseph of Arimathea abstained from voting. This was either because as a Roman appointee to the Sanhedrin, he had no vote in matters that involved Jewish religious leaders accused of capital offenses or as the adopted father of the accused, he was automatically disqualified from casting a vote). He was then sent to Pilate for ratification of the Sanhedrin conviction and for sentencing. The conviction had already been agreed upon by Pilate and the High Priest or Sadducees and the sentence would be death for the perpetrator by crucifixion.

"The John record is like Mark's record, confusing and non-committal. It first implies that Jesus was accused by the Jewish leaders before Pilate of blasphemy, which to them was worthy of death, as well as treason. However, Pilate decided to try to satisfy the Jew's thirst for Jesus' blood by ordering Jesus to be mercilessly flogged, implying that this was an optional punishment that Pilate could have chosen to implement for the crime of treason, rather than crucifixion. This is contrary to Matthew, Mark, and Luke as well as Roman history which records that all who were accused of treason were crucified and all who were condemned to crucifixion were first flogged and then if they survived the flogging they would be crucified within 24 hours after the flogging.

"Later, the Gospel of John begins to emphasize that Jesus had been accused and sentenced to death by crucifixion because the Jews had threatened Pilate saying that if he did not convict Jesus and condemn him to death, then he was not Caesar's friend, implying that they would accuse Pilate of treason. Pilate, fearing that he would be accused of treason before Sejanus' tribunal reluctantly submitted to the wishes of the Jews and sent Jesus away to be flogged and crucified. Knowing the type of person Pilate was and based on his record in dealing with the Jewish people, I (Sir Kane) personally cannot imagine Pilate succumbing to blackmail instigated by the Jewish religious leaders. I can see him ordering his troops to kill them all on the spot for trying to blackmail him and for tying to browbeat him into submitting to their demands, but I cannot see him cowering down to their demands." With that Sir Kane finished his comparative commentary and returned to Raymund's record.

"Nevertheless," Sir Kane continued, "Pilate sends Jesus away to be flogged, or scourged, as the KJV of the Bible says. Floggings for those convicted of crimes against the state of Rome were carried out in a lower, or below street level, room in the Fortress of Antonia. Every non-Roman who was condemned to death was first flogged and every Roman who was condemned to death by crucifixion for treason or sedition was first flogged—this was a preliminary punishment demanded by Roman law. The only exceptions would be women and auxiliary soldiers serving with the Roman military (unless a soldier was condemned for desertion or treason).

"The instrument generally used in flogging was a short whip called a *flagellum* or *flagrum*. The whip had several (from 10 to 30) single or braided leather thongs of variable lengths, in which small iron balls, iron chips, pottery shreds, and sharp pieces of bone were tied at intervals. Although the Bible does not record the number of strikes to which Jesus was subjected, we do know that 100 up to a maximum of 200 strikes was generally the number reserved for those convicted of treason and condemned to crucifixion. If in fact the *flagrum* had the larger count of 30 thongs and Jesus suffered the generally prescribed strikes of 100, Jesus would have been subjected to 3,000 individual stripes.

"In preparation for flogging, the prisoner was stripped of all clothing and was restrained in one of two ways. He was either tied with his hands above his head to an upright post, hanging by his wrists tied above his head; he was then pulled up until his toes slightly cleared the floor; in effect, the weight of his entire body was held by this tied wrists; or the convicted was forced to bend over a stone or wooden bench type base or pedestal, exposing the back and buttocks; the hands were then tightly chained to the feet, not allowing the victim to move.

"Before using the *flagrum*, a Roman legionnaire would beat the victim (only in cases where the condemned had been convicted of treason) with a thick wooden stave. The number of blows was not consistent, so it could range from 10 blows to as many as 50. The purpose for the beating was to force the blood from the muscles to the surface of the skin, so that the whip could inflict the maximum amount of damage.

"When the Roman legionnaire in charge of the flogging determined that the blood had risen close enough to the surface of the skin to maximize flogging by the *flagrum*, he stepped aside and directed the flogging. Four strong slaves administered the flogging. The process involved all four slaves. Each slave was allowed 10 strikes at a time until the strike allotment, determined by either the Roman governor, Pilate, or the administering Roman legionnaire (the legionnaire who had beaten the prisoner with the wooden stave), had been administered, or the prisoner died. After each strike, the flagrum was dipped into salt water, which was intended to increase the agony on the prisoner. The Roman government was generous when it came to the slaves who were chosen to administer treason floggings, for if a slave could kill the condemned with his allotted strikes, the slave would receive either a talent of gold or the condemned's weight in silver—the slave's choice. Either would have been enough for him to buy his freedom and then live comfortably for the rest of his life on what money remained. Thus, each of the four slaves tried to the best of his ability to kill the prisoner with the strikes that he had been allotted.

"There was no reprieve if the prisoner collapsed into unconsciousness. If this happened, the prisoner would be revived and then the flogging would be continued. The heavy whip was brought down with full force again and again across Jesus' naked shoulders, back, buttocks, and legs; reaching around the body on the sides as well as the face, causing deep contusions and lacerating the skin and subcutaneous tissue. Before long the skin was hanging in quivering ribbons, exposing the underlying skeleton, backbone and skull, and some internal organs. In essence, the entire area that was being flogged became an unrecognizable mass of torn, bleeding tissue. After the flogging was complete, the victim was unshackled. Victims that were not killed during the flogging were destined to face death by crucifixion. So, in order for as much blood to be spared as possible, at least enough to keep him alive until he could be crucified, they rubbed his entire body with rock salt or they bathed it with salt water. The pain was excruciating, but the process did check the unimpeded flow of blood.

"In Jesus' case, after the beating, the Roman soldiers, (approximately 600 strong) amused that this weakened mass of torn tissue and blood had claimed to be a king, began to mock him by placing a scarlet or deep purple robe (perhaps a cloak of one of the legionnaires) on his shoulders, a crown of thorns on his head, and a wooden staff as a scepter in his right hand. They knelt before him and mockingly paid homage by saying, *'Hail, King of the Jews.'* They spat on him (imagine how he looked after 600 had spit on him for any length of time), they beat his head that contained the crown of thorns that covered the entire scalp with the wooden staff, driving the 2 inch long thorns deep into the scalp and forehead, causing severe bleeding and agonizing headaches, and they ripped out his beard by the handfuls, exposing his jaw bone and teeth. Finally the Roman soldiers tired of their sadistic sport and tore the robe from Jesus' back. Already having adhered to the clots of blood and serum in the wounds, the robe's removal caused excruciating pain.

"The severity of the beating is not detailed in the Gospels." Sir Kane continued explaining Raymund's writing, "However, the Old Testament book of Isaiah (chapters 50 and 52) mentions that Jesus was beaten so severely that his form did not look like that of a human being. People were appalled to look at him. Isaiah implies that Jesus was more marred than any man who had ever been marred and yet lived and more marred than any man who will ever live. He was so severely beaten that people were sickened to look at him.

"After the beating and the mockery, Pilate brought him out to the people and said *'Behold your king.'* In other words, look at him. Isn't this enough? The people demanded that the sentencing be carried out—death by crucifixion.

"So, as the day came to an end, Jesus' condemnation was confirmed by Pilate. The Roman governor then washed his hands clean of all guilt associated with the death by crucifixion of Jesus, indicating that Rome did not condemn the man to death—he condemned himself, for the crime of treason. After that he released from prison Barabbas, a revolutionary that the Sadducee incited people chose to have released, rather than Jesus. The beaten and flogged Jesus was then returned to his prison cell to await crucifixion early the following morning, Monday, April 2, AD 31.

"At 6:00 the next morning, Jesus was taken from his cell, and Gehenna, called *the place of bones, the place of death*, or *the place o*̷ be crucified, along with 25 to 50 others who had been condemned crucifixion.

"The narrow street that turned into a wider road outside of the city gate and led to the place of crucifixion, was cleared of all traffic and observers early Monday morning, if in fact there were any observers that early in the morning. The only people who were allowed to observe were those who lived along the route or had places of business along the route, or visitors who were perhaps staying in inns located along the route. Generally, very few people were allowed by the Roman soldiers to witness the transfer of prisoners from prison to the place of execution. So, contrary to tradition, only a few people actually witnessed Jesus' journey to the place of crucifixion.

"Before the victims left the prison compound," Sir Kane continued, "each of the condemned was obliged to carry across his shoulders the crossbar, the *patibulum* (with his hands chained to the crossbar) of the cross upon which he would be crucified, to the place of crucifixion. The wooden crossbar probably weighed from 75 to 100 pounds (slightly less than 50 kilos), and was treated with an oily creosote-type of mixture. A Roman guard of seven soldiers escorted each condemned prisoner; with an eighth soldier who walked in front of the prisoner carry a *titulus*, which was a sign that announced the crime for which the prisoner had been condemned. In the province of Judaea the *titulus* was written in Hebrew, Greek, and Latin (Matthew 27:37; John 19:19-22). This *titulus* was attached to the top of the cross at the crucifixion site (Jesus' read, *Jesus of Nazareth, King of the Jews*). Along with the eight-member personal escort for each prisoner, the entire processional was escorted by an additional Roman guard of from 25 soldiers to 100 soldiers (depending on the number of prisoners being crucified). A centurion led the procession. So, if there were in fact 50 who were being crucified, then the entire processional that walked to Gehenna or the golgotha (the calvary) that morning, including the Roman military escort, could have numbered in excess of 500.

"From the prison compound, according to Roman tradition, the condemned walked naked to the place of crucifixion; carry their crossbar, escorted by the Roman soldiers. The fact that Jesus' garment was parted and then gambled away at the crucifixion site indicates that Jesus, being a religious leader (or perhaps because he was a citizen), was allowed to wear it to the site.

"Somewhere along the way, because of exhaustion Jesus was unable to continue carrying his *patibulum*. Falling under the weight of the *patibulum* (some historians claim that he fell down a flight of stone steps; others claim that he did not fall at all, he merely stumbled) could have led to a contusion of the heart, predisposing his heart to rupture on the cross. Simon of Cyrene (Cyrene is presently North Africa [Tripoli]) was compelled to help Jesus carry the crossbar (Matthew 27:37; Luke 23:26) to the crucifixion site.

"Crucifixion was used by the early Babylonians and Assyrians but the type of crucifixion used by the Romans probably began with the Persians. Alexander the Great introduced the practice to Egypt and Carthage, and the Romans appear to have learned it from the Carthaginians. While the Romans did not invent rucifixion, they perfected it as a form of torture and capital punishment. It was designed to produce a slow death with maximum pain and suffering. It was one of the most disgraceful and cruel methods of execution ever devised by man.

"The cross commonly preferred by the Romans was called the low *tau* cross. In this cross the vertical piece did not extend beyond the horizontal piece. The Roman crucifixion practices adapted and conformed to the accepted practice of a particular area. Therefore, conforming to the traditional crucifixion practice of a particular area, the Romans used the Latin cross (with the vertical piece extending above the horizontal piece), the tau cross, and the single impalement upright pole as instruments of crucifixion.

"In the province of Judaea, the place of crucifixion was located outside the city walls, in an area called Gehenna, which served not only as the place of crucifixion, but as the garbage dump for the city of Jerusalem. Only the immediate family members (no more than three at a time) and in some cases a few of the condemned's accusers (in the case of Jesus this would be the priests and Sadducees), could be present at the actual crucifixion site. These accusers would only be allowed at the crucifixion site after the condemned prisoners had been crucified and only for the first three hours after crucifixion. As many people as wanted to could watch the proceedings from the cliff tops that surrounded the area of Gehenna."

At this point Sir Kane again paused in his explaining of Raymund's manuscript and inserted observations from a totally different source. He wrote, "Before we go further with Raymund's document, I feel that it is crucial that for a accurate understanding of Gehenna and Calvary that I include comments made less than a century ago by the Danish thinker Sören Kierkegaard, who lived from 1813-1855 and whose influence was most critically felt in post-World War Europe. He has become known as the 'father of existentialism.'

"In 1848 Kierkegaard wrote two books and one discourse that revolutionized established Danish religious thinking. The titles of the books were *The Sickness Unto Death* and *Training in Christianity*. The discourse was entitled, *The Disease of Tradition*. The discourse is what I will refer to.

"Although a number of different historical and traditional Christian rituals and traditions were attacked in the discourse, the segment entitled 'Golgotha' is the one that I will include in these commentaries. It is about the crucifixion of Jesus.

"According to Kierkegaard, early, probably about 6:00, on the morning of Monday, April 2, AD 31, Jesus carrying the cross member of his own cross, began his walk to the valley locally described as the calvary (Greek) or the golgotha (Hebrew and Aramaic). Calvary meant *'a place of death* or *a place of burnt bones* or *a place of the skull.'* Golgotha meant *'the place of skulls* or *the valley of bones* or *the place of death.'* At the time of Jesus' death neither word was used as a proper noun or as the name of a place, but rather the words were used as adjectives describing a deep ravine that was located south of Jerusalem. It was called *'the valley of (the sons of) Hinnom'* in the Old Testament. During the reigns of Ahaz and Manasseh, human sacrifices were offered in the valley to the god, Molech. For centuries the valley had been associated with and had been central to the worship of numerous pagan gods. In Roman times, the proper name for the valley was *Gehenna* (during this time the local Jerusalem populous still generally referred to the valley by its descriptive name—the calvary or the golgotha—rather than by its proper name), and it was used as the city garbage dump and was where the Romans carried out capital punishment. In the New Testament the name *Gehenna* was many times translated *hell* or *hades* because fires were continually burning in the valley to dispose of garbage and maggots and all kinds of vermin were always present—a typical picture of what hell was perceived to be like at that time."

Sir Kane continued with his record of Kierkegaard's comments, "The Romans carried out capital punishment three times per year: in the spring, (April 2) in the summer, (June 2) and in the fall (September 2). Either crucifixion or impaling was the typical method of punishment for those persons convicted of crimes against Rome or the citizenry of Rome. The condemned included those convicted of treason, rebellion, or sedition (whether Roman citizen or non-citizen made no difference in the case of treason—Jesus was convicted of treason); malefactors (non-citizens only) or homosexual prostitutes (Luke 23:33) who had killed their Roman citizen lovers; and thieves (Matthew 27:38 and Mark 15:27—non-citizens only). These thieves were not just robbers, they were robbers of the Roman treasury—those convicted of tax evasion, embezzlement of tax money, theft of collected taxes, or those convicted of the sabotage of or interference with tax collections or tax receipts.

"Capital punishment was scheduled three times per year, yet Roman law dictated that there had to be at least 25 who had been sentenced before sentencing could be carried out. If there were not at least 25, the sentence was postponed until the next scheduled time. This was repeated until at least 25 were available. Though generally, the Romans waited until there were at least 30 to 100 who had been sentenced before sentencing was carried out.

"This being the case, Jesus was most likely crucified with a minimum of 25 people who had been convicted of crimes against Rome and its citizenry, and most likely from 30 to 100; and he was crucified in the valley or ravine of Gehenna, the place of bones—the garbage dump of Jerusalem, south of the city.

"At the place of crucifixion, Gehenna—described locally as the calvary or the golgotha—pot holes had been chiseled out of the exposed rock, about 18 to 20 inches deep. The holes were carved out of the rock in a half-moon design and arrangement, about 8' to 10' apart. The far back row of holes began the half-moon design with each row thereafter following the same pattern until the half-moon design was filled. The vertical portion of the cross had already been fitted and secured in the holes by the time the execution processional arrived at the crucifixion site. Most of the vertical poles extended upward from the ground to a height of about seven to eight feet. Some of the vertical poles were made of wood while others were made of stone. The ones that were made of stone had a hollowed out hole at the bottom near the ground. In this hole was placed a wooden plug, which served as a nail backing for the feet. Another plughole was located about mid-way up the pole. This served as the nail backing for the stake that was driven through the hip and pelvic regions of the condemned. At the top of the pole was cut a U-shaped groove into which the horizontal portion of the cross was affixed. If only the vertical pole was used, the top groove was used to affix the condemned's hands to the pole, above his head.

"Kierkegaard did not describe the methods of crucifixion," Sir Kane continued, "he did make a revealing statement. 'Although death by crucifixion was by far the most painful death that was inflicted by the Romans, many times death was not directly caused by crucifixion itself. More times than not the condemned died from exposure and from being eaten alive by scavengers. Gehenna was filled with vultures and other flesh eating birds as well as wild dogs and jackals that would eat the flesh off of the dying prisoner, long before he was dead. Considering that a condemned usually stayed fixed to the cross from two to 14 days before finally dying, and 21 days before removal from the cross, this slow ravaging of the flesh would have been more torturous than any mind can imagine.'

"Kierkegaard then turned his attention to proving that the exact location of the site of crucifixion as well as the burial place of Jesus has long since been lost.

"In AD 70 when the Romans sacked Jerusalem, Titus had every tree in and around Jerusalem cut down and every building torn down. This included the trees in the present Garden of Gethsemane and in the Jerusalem locations of the various events connected to the life, ministry, and death of Jesus. He then had the city scraped clean down to the foundations. All that remained was a portion of the retaining wall of the Temple compound that Titus left as a permanent memorial to the memory of the race of the Jews and to their religion. Over the next few decades the remaining Jews began to rebuild, with the Roman's approval, some of the homes. In time other Jews returned to Jerusalem and stayed.

"In AD 135 the Jews again rebelled. This time Hadrian had no mercy. Not only did he completely wipe out the city and scrape it clean to its foundations, but also he built a Roman city upon the former city of Jerusalem's foundations. The name of the city was Aelia Capitolina. By AD 139 the rebellion had been crushed and the city's construction was complete. Neither Jew nor Christian was allowed in the city and pagan temples dedicated to Jupiter, Venus, Mars, and other Roman, Greek, Persian, and Egyptian deities were built over the sites of the crucifixion, the burial of Jesus, the Temple of Herod, and other locations considered holy or honored and revered by either or both the Jews and Christians. For the next century and a half Christian activity in Palestine was centered in Caesarea Maritima, the Roman capital of the Palestine area.

"In AD 313 Constantine, the emperor of the Western Empire, issued the *Edict of Milan* which moved Rome's recognition of Christianity from hostile neutrality to friendly neutrality. It was also in that year that the city of Aelia Capitolina was opened to Christians and Jews. Soon thereafter, Constantine declared himself an admirer of the God of Christianity. In AD 324 Constantine became emperor of the entire Roman Empire and published his *Edict of Tolerance*, which officially encouraged the adoption of Christianity throughout the Empire.

"For nearly three centuries, the actual crucifixion and burial sites of Jesus were lost, then Constantine had his dream. In the dream a man in white showed him the location of the two sites and told him to build churches or shrines on the sites to preserve their locations.

"In AD 326, Helena, the mother of Emperor Constantine and a very strong Christian, traveled to Aelia Capitolina, which by then was unofficially called

Jerusalem once again, to confirm Constantine's dream and to find the locations associated with Jesus' nativity, crucifixion, and burial.

"Upon her arrival, Helena found it difficult to find anyone who could help her locate the sites. Finally, after offering a huge amount of money as a reward to anyone who could help, a young Jewish boy by the name of Judas came forward and told her that he had old family records that described the true location of Jesus crucifixion and burial. He took her to the location of the crucifixion and burial site. A pagan shrine dedicated to Venus stood on the site and all around the shrine the ground had been recently plowed. Judas told Helena that she should dig there and perhaps she would find something that would confirm his family's records. So, she had her servants dig in the freshly plowed soil next to the shrine. Miraculously they 'discovered' three crosses in a state of perfect preservation. Constantine claimed that the site was the same as the one in his dream, so he proclaimed it to be Golgotha, the true and actual location site of the crucifixion (it was at this time that the word *golgotha* changed from a descriptive adjective to a proper name) and ordered the Venus shrine to be destroyed and removed and a church to be built on the site. The Church of the Holy Sepulcher covers both locations proclaimed by Constantine to be the actual crucifixion and burial site of Jesus.

"Eusebius, the Bishop of Palestine at the time, strongly objected to Constantine's proclamation, stating that the location was not the crucifixion and burial site of Jesus. He said it was the burial site of the Maccabean priest/king John Hyrcanus. He pointed out that a shrine dedicated to the memory of John Hyrcanus had been erected over the site and that in AD 135 Emperor Hadrian had desecrated it by demolishing it and building a Venus shrine there.

"Constantine did not listen. He had the church built. Judas was converted to Christianity and Constantine offered him the position of Bishop of Jerusalem, in Eusebius' stead. He was also given the name Judas Quiriacus. This same Judas over the next ten years accompanied Helena as she traveled throughout the entire 'Holy Land' area—Nazareth, Bethlehem, Cana, Capernaum, Bethany, and so on. They 'discovered' many other locations associated with Jesus and his life and ministry, and in most cases, they built churches on the sites.

"In AD 614, the Persians attacked the area of what had then began to be called Palestine and destroyed all of the churches and shrines that Helena had constructed, except the Church of the Nativity in Bethlehem.

"In the 12th century, Crusaders ruled Jerusalem for 88 years. During this time, most of the churches that had been destroyed were rebuilt. The Church of the Nativity was modified to its present state during this time.

"The existing walls of present day (Kierkegaard's day) Old Jerusalem were built from 1537-1541 by the Turkish Sultan Suleiman the Magnificent. It was after this that the *Via Dolorosa* (Way of Sorrows) and the *Ecco Homo* gate (where Pilate was said to have condemned Jesus) were built and were established as 'shrines' to Christ's suffering.

"Although this ended the portion of Kierkegaard's discourse entitled 'Golgotha,'" Sir Kane inserted as he ended Kierkegaard's comments, "I need to add a few explanatory notes of my own concerning this topic.

"In 1867 Dr. Conrad Schick excavated an ancient tomb that had been hidden for centuries in an area north of the present Damascus Gate just outside of the current 16th century walls of Old Jerusalem. The tomb had been cut in a rocky wall and was unusually large, signifying that the owner had been wealthy. Dr. Schick found evidence that the Crusaders had used the tomb, but the tomb itself was much older. Near the tomb was found an ancient wine press and a large underground water collection system. The property was later converted into a beautiful garden with protective walls. The tomb became known as *The Garden Tomb* and is identified today by many Protestants as the tomb of Jesus.

"In 1883 a British General Gordon visited the tomb and noticed as he surveyed the rocky cliff outside the tomb, a skull-shaped depression in the cliff with sunken eye sockets. Due to the proximity of the tomb he declared the place to be the actual Calvary (it was at this time that the word *calvary* changed from a descriptive adjective to a proper name). He also identified an area just across the street from the tomb as the place where Stephen had been stoned.

"This ends my personal notes on this subject." Sir Kane wrote, "I now feel that I must return to the place in Raymund's document where I exited.

"Vertical upright poles or *stipes*, were permanently fixed in holes that were either drilled or chiseled in the exposed granite rock of Gehenna. At the top of the *stipe* a *mortise* or *tenon joint* was cut. Into this joint the crossbar would fit and be attached to the *stipe*.

"At the site of execution, by law, the victim was offered a bitter drink of wine mixed with myrrh as a mild analgesic. Jesus refused this drink. The offender was then violently thrown to the ground on his back, with his arms outstretched along the *patibulum*. Heavy, square, wrought iron nails were then driven through the wrists deep into the wood, firmly attaching the wrists and hands to the crossbar. After the arms were fastened, the *patibulum* and the victim were lifted, together, onto the *stipes*.

"After the crossbar was attached to the *stipes*, the titulus was attached. Next, a *sedile* or *sedulum*, a round wooden stake that served as a crude and cruel seat upon which the hip bones rested, was added. There were two ways a *sedile* used by the Romans. The Romans would drive a *sedile* through the bladder area just below the hipbone and above the groin area of the offender, into the *stipe*. Upon this round wooden *sedile*, the raw hipbones and pelvic bones would balance. Or the Romans would take the body of the condemned and twist it 90° opposite his outstretched arms. Then the *sedile* would be driven through the fleshy part of the side of the buttocks, just below the hipbone, into the *stipe*. Again the raw hipbone would balance on the round wooden *sedile*.

"If the offender was twisted 90° opposite the outstretched arms, the feet were nailed to the vertical *stipe* in one of two ways. One way was to straddle the vertical *stipe* with the criminal's feet and nail one ankle to each side of the *stipe*. The other way was to press one foot backward against the other foot, and with both feet extended, toes pointing down, a nail was driven through the arch of each into the *stipe*. If the victim was crucified with the *sedile* in the front, the left foot was pressed backward against the right foot, and with both feet extended, toes down, an iron nail was driven through both arches of the feet into the *stipe*.

"One of the most agonizing aspects of nailing the feet was that it affected every organ of the crucified person. The nerve endings that connect to every internal organ in the body collect at the bottom of the feet. When a person walks, the nerve endings are massaged and the nerves send messages to the organs encouraging them to function properly. If a foot is severed and the nerve ending severed, there is little effect upon the organs of the body. If the foot is punctured from beneath, it also has little effect upon the organs because the puncture follows the route of the nerves. But if the foot is punctured from the top down, like with nailing the feet at crucifixion, the nerve endings are violently split apart and frayed. This sends an instant message of malfunction to the organs affected. Thus, when the nail(s) was/were driven into the feet of Jesus, instantaneously and simultaneously, Jesus had the symptoms and the affects of every malfunction, every disease, and every injury known to man to every internal organ in his body.

"Instantly and at the same time," Sir Kane continued, "Jesus had the symptoms and the pain of hundreds of malfunctions and diseases (not the disease or malfunction itself, but the pain and the symptom associated with the disease or malfunction) such as heart attack, brain cancer, gallbladder problems, migraine headache, coerces, diabetes, lung cancer, and so on. Yet Jesus said not a word. He remained silent as a lamb being slaughtered.

"Jesus was crucified in the midst of at least 25 and perhaps as many as 100 condemned offenders. In his immediate area were four offenders, probably one on each side, one in front of him, and one in back, or two on each side. Two of these condemned criminals were thieves (robbers from the Roman treasury or revolutionaries who had stolen Roman tax receipts—this was an act of treason) and the other two were malefactors. *Malefactor* (a Latin word that meant *'squalid exploiter of a man'*) was a word used by the Romans to describe a non-Roman male prostitutes with whom a Roman official had died while involved in immoral activities. A malefactor was not punished for being a homosexual prostitute, but because a Roman high official had died while he and the malefactor were engaged in homosexual sex. This made the malefactor guilty of murdering a Roman high officer—this too was considered an act of treason.

"Both thieves railed on Jesus, but only one of the malefactors did. The other malefactor believed that Jesus was who he said he was. Jesus told the believing malefactor that he (the malefactor) would die that very day [a miracle within itself because it normally took from 2 to 14 days for a man to die from crucifixion], and that Jesus would meet him in paradise. Obviously Jesus forgave him of all sin, allowing the malefactor to enter paradise, the abode of the righteous dead at that time.

"It was 9:00 in the morning, and Jesus was now crucified. Jesus was naked, bleeding, an unrecognizable bloody mass of torn flesh, weak, and broken-hearted. He knew that none of his followers stood by his side, and realized that soon even his own Heavenly Father would be turning His back on him. But he hoped against hope that this would not happen. Yet, the first words that Jesus uttered after being raised and suspended between heaven and earth were, *'Father, forgive them for they know not what they do.'*

"As Jesus slowly sagged down applying more and more weight on the nails in the wrists, excruciating pain shot through the median nerves, along the fingers, and up the arms to explode in the brain. As he pushed himself upward to avoid this torment, he placed his full weight on the nail(s) through his feet causing searing agony as the nail(s) in the feet tore through the nerves between the metatarsal bones and the bottom of the feet. This in turn renewed the symptoms of trauma in his internal organs.

"As the arms began to fatigue, waves of cramps followed in quick succession that ran up and down the arms, knotting them in unimaginably throbbing pain. With these cramps came his inability to push himself upward. Hanging by his arms, the pectoral muscles became paralyzed and the intercostals muscles became enabled to act. Although air could be inhaled, it could not be exhaled, causing Jesus to fight desperately to raise himself in order to release even one short painful exhale. This caused the lungs to begin to collapse. Finally, carbon dioxide built-up in the lungs and in the blood stream and the cramps partially subsided. Spasmodically, he became able to push himself upward to exhale and to breathe in oxygen. It was during these short periods that Jesus uttered the last six messages before his death.

"After hours of waves of cramps, intermittent asphyxiation, and searing pain as tissue was torn from his back as he moved up and down the rough *stipe*, another pain began deep inside his chest as the pericardium slowly filled with serum and began to compress the heart. Eventually the loss of tissue fluids reached a critical level; the heart began to struggle more and more to pump the thick, sluggish blood into the mass of bloody tissue. Meanwhile the lungs struggled desperately to gasp small gulps of air.

"Finally Jesus realized that death was upon him and in a tortured whisper he said, *'It is finished.'* Then as he felt his last breath oozing from his body, with one last surge of strength, he once again pressed his ripped and torn feet against the nail(s), straightened his legs, took a deep breath and with all the strength that he had left he cried, *'Father! Into thy hands I commit my spirit.'* Then he died. It was 3:00 in the afternoon. Jesus had been on the cross for six hours.

"His death was accompanied by an unusual pitch darkness and a great earthquake that historians who lived at that time recorded. It was felt throughout the world. It was felt in Rome, Greece, China, Africa, in the Ural mountains of Russia, and in the Pyrenees of Spain.

"Jesus was a rabboni," Sir Kane continued, "and even though the Sadducees and High Priest may not have liked it, his position had been granted him by the High Priest after he had met all the qualifications and his position had been ratified by the Sanhedrin. That fact could not be denied. Because he was an official religious leader in the fact that he was a Jewish rabboni, Jewish religious law would not allow a religious leader to profane the High Sabbath by remaining on the cross. No such restriction was relevant with regard to the other crucified criminals.

"As far as the other criminals was concerned, it was standard practice for the Roman soldiers to inflict *crurifracture* (the breaking of their legs) upon those crucified after the victims had been crucified for 12 hours. This prevented a victim from pushing himself upward; thus the tension could not be relieved from the muscles of the chest. This increased the process of suffocation. With the breaking of the legs, the victim usually died within two to 14 days. However the body stayed on the cross for a total of 21 days and was usually devoured by birds, dogs, and other scavenger animals. The legs of all of the victims who were crucified with Jesus that day were broken. Jesus was already dead by the time they got to him. Apparently to confirm that Jesus was actually dead, the legionnaire responsible for breaking the legs, drove a lance through the fifth interspace between his ribs, upward through the pericardium, and into the heart resulting in a flow of water-fluid (from the sac surrounding the heart) mixed with blood. This indicated that Jesus had not died of suffocation, which was the typical cause of death for victims of the type of crucifixion inflected by the Romans. He died of heart failure, or a ruptured heart (broken heart—literally) due to shock and constriction of the heart by fluid in the pericardium.

"Seeing that their law forbade a religious leader (Jesus) from hanging on the cross past 6:00 in the evening," Sir Kane continued, "Because that was the start of High Sabbath, and Jewish religious law forbade the desecration of the body of a religious leader (being scavenged by animals), regardless of how much they hated the victim, the representatives of the High Priest approached Pilate about taking Jesus from the cross, since he was dead already. Pilate was surprised that Jesus was already dead, so he granted their request to remove Jesus from the cross.

"Soon thereafter, one of the most powerful men in all of Syria, the Roman Senator representing Britain, the Imperial Minister of Mines for both Augustus and Tiberius Caesar, the Roman representation and appointee to the Jewish Sanhedrin, and the adoptive father/grandfather of Jesus, Joseph of Arimathea, approached Pilate and demanded that he release the body of Jesus to him. Nicodemus, one of the wealthiest men in the state of Judea, joined him. Without hesitation, Pilate released the body of Jesus to Joseph. He had no choice if he wanted to stay in the good graces of Tiberius, whose adoptive father, Augustus, had appointed Joseph to his post.

"Nicodemus supplied expensive spices to temporarily preserve the body until after the High Sabbath, when they could return and prepare the body for burial more professionally. Jesus' body was then entombed in Joseph's family tomb. In essence, Jesus was the first family member to be laid to rest in the family tomb of the family in which both Jesus and Mary were adopted members." [For additional information regarding Joseph of Arimathea see the two chapters entitled **Essential Golden Nuggets** and **Son of the Law**.]

That concluded Sir Kane's comments, explanation, and transliteration of Raymund of Penafort's manuscript.

I remember after reading Sir Kane's and Raymund's account that I sat at the study table in the university library for what was perhaps an hour or more with tears in my eyes, letting their words run over and over in my mind. I couldn't believe the utter gruesomeness of the tragedy. Jesus did all of this and went through all of this suffering for me. And not only for me, but also for every person who has ever lived. Perfection submitted to death so that imperfection—me—could have a hope of being able to live for eternity with Him—King of Kings and Lord of Lords.

Although Jesus' death had a sobering affect upon his disciples and followers, it caused major repercussions in the highest levels of Roman authority.

Upon his return to Rome after witnessing the healing of Zolleras in Machaerus, Valleus Paterculus presented his findings concerning Jesus to The Theophus Commission of Ambassadors in Rome. But, by the time he had presented them to Tiberius in Capri, Jesus had been crucified. It is not known when Tiberius and Valleus Paterculus found out about Jesus' crucifixion, but from the manuscript written by Pachomius that I discovered at The Monastery of St. Catherine at the foot of Mount Sinai, it appears that perhaps neither knew about it until Valleus Paterculus and his delegation returned to Judaea in January AD 33.

Pachomius wrote that Valleus Paterculus lead a delegation to Judaea in January, AD 33, and that the delegation questioned both Pilate at his palace in Caesarea Maritima, Caiaphas the High Priest at his residence in Jerusalem, and Herod Antipas in Capernaum, on the matter of Jesus. It was while questioning Pilate that Valleus Paterculus discovered that Jesus had been crucified. Pachomius, quoting the 1st century Roman court historian scribes, Dio Cassius and Petronius (they both similarly recorded the same event), wrote that upon hearing of the death of Jesus, Valleus Paterculus became furious and told Pilate that he would see to it that he (Pilate) would personally pay for the death of Jesus with his own life. These court historians also reported that after his confrontation with Valleus Paterculus, Pilate sunk into deep depression and became extremely ruthless, brutal, and irrational, loosing his ability to properly govern Judaea.

After hearing of Jesus' death Valleus demanded that Pilate, Caiaphas, and Herod not only report to him their actions and the part they played in the death of Jesus, but also he demanded that they write letters, addressing both The Theophus Commission and Tiberius Caesar, justifying their actions and detailing the part they played in Jesus' condemnation. Valleus said that he would hand deliver the letters to the commission in Rome and to Tiberius in Capri.

He returned to Rome in March AD 35 and delivered the letters to the Commission. In April AD 35, he delivered the letters to Tiberius in Capri.

We do not know how the Commission reacted or how Tiberius reacted upon hearing the news that the one person who could have fulfilled all qualifications of and who probably was in fact The Theophus, Jesus of the Galilee in the province of Syria, had been put to death. All we know is that in June AD 35, Caiaphas was removed from his High Priest position by Roman authorities; in either AD 36 or 37, Pilate was recalled from Judaea; and Herod was exiled by the Romans in either AD 38 or 39 on the charge of treasonous incitement—a vague offense that could have encompassed any number of justified and unjustified charges. In less than a decade after the crucifixion of Jesus, Valleus Paterculus had succeeded in avenging the death of the man whom he was convinced was The Theophus.

After supplying his background information, Pachomius recorded the letters the three officials were commanded to write to The Theophus Commission of Ambassadors and Tiberius Caesar.

The first letter that he recorded was that of the Jewish High Priest, Caiaphas. Caiaphas not only addressed The Theophus Commission and Tiberius, he also addressed the Sanhedrin in Jerusalem. Although it was Caiaphas' official report, he dictated it to a Sanhedrin scribe named Eliezer Hiran, who was the actual writer of the letter.

Pachomius began with his record of Caiaphas' letter.

> "Joseph Caiaphas, High Priest of the Most High God, to the Theophus Commission of Ambassadors, our most honored of statesmen Valleus Paterculus, our most respected Augustus, Tiberius Julius Caesar Augustus, and Masters of Israel, greeting.

In obedience with our demands by Valleus Paterculus for a reason for my action in the case of Jesus, a directed rabboni from Nazareth of the Galilee, and in defense of my conduct, I beg leave to submit the following for your consideration: I would assure you that it was not on account of personal malice, envy, or hatred, that in my own nature, nor for the want of a willingness upon my part to conform to the Jewish law in its strictest sense. I have but very little personal knowledge of the man from Nazareth of the Galilee. The most I knew of this man was from outside sources; more specifically from reports from the Galilee. Nor was it because I had been told that he claimed to be Roman or as to the King of the Jews claim, nor because it was reported that he is reported to have accepted exaltation as the Son of God, not that he prophesied or ignored the holy Temple. No, nor all of these in combination. There is a cause, and a more weighty matter, back of all these things that determined my action in the matter. Therefore, I hope you will investigate strictly on legal principles the reasons that I may give.

In order that you may be able to see and weigh the question fully, and remember the responsibility that rests upon me according to the laws of our nation, I will ask you to go back to the chronicles of the history of our people. First, our dedication is pledged to one living and true God, this God being indescribable, unchangeable, incomprehensible, and unnamable. But yet in our daily communions with, and our applications to Him, He has been pleased to give us His name, or His several names, according to His relations to us, and they are found nowhere, only in the ark of His holy temple—there where He presents to us His strength and power. He is called Eloi, almighty strength; that He can do what He will without effort; that He does the greatest thing as easy as He does the least. In His Holy Ark He records Himself Elaah—existence without beginning or end. Again He says of Himself, Hhelejon—unchangeable. Again He says His name Jah—knowledge that comprehends without being comprehended. Again He says of Himself, Adonai—full and free. A man cannot pronounce His name in its comprehensive sense. It is the want of being able to pronounce this name in His comprehensive sense that causes and has caused so much dissension among us. Jesus could pronounce His name in His comprehensive sense, but he stole it out of the Holiest place of the Temple, so I am creditably informed.

But the object in calling your attention to pronouncing His name, with all of His bearings, may be seen in the preparation of the Law wherein is the special order made by Him to Moses, that to make atonement for offenses must be by fasting for seven days, by an offering of oil and flour, and the sacrifice of a young bullock. Now, unless Moses was deceived, he has deceived us, or this Jesus from Nazareth in the Galilee is a false teacher; for he teaches metanoeite, as though a man's being sorry for an offense could make restitution to the offended. A man might repent every so much, but what good would that do toward healing the man he had injured? None in the least. This mode of making atonement was ordained of God and revealed by Moses; but if man has nothing to do but repent, the disease carries its own remedy. So a man can sin as often as he may wish. Jesus was called by his followers, although I have not heard him so say, that he is called the Son of God; and claims that he has been born of almah; that he and his Father, God of whose name can not be uttered, are one and equal. These things will establish the conclusions: if he and his teachings are right, his Father is false. If they are one, then their teachings are one; and if his teachings are true, God's must be wrong, or there are not those perfections in Him that is learned by knowing to pronounce His name. By tolerating the teachings of Jesus, we say to the Romans that all of our former teaching are false; that our God is not to be trusted; that He is weak, wanting in forethought; that He is vacillating and not to be trusted, much less to be honored and obeyed.

Jesus ignored God's holy Temple, where He promised to dwell with His children, to hear their prayers, and to be pleased with their sacrifices. This is the grandest gift of our God. He sneers at the priests and scoffs at our holy ordinances and boasts that the gift will be destroyed. No doubt he would attempt the destruction himself if his prophecy would not come to pass.

According to our laws I was made responsible, and stand before God between the people and God, to protect them from His consuming fire by doctrine and the Law. Now the insinuating plan that was Jesus' was well qualified to deceive the people. It had already led many to forsake the Temple, to hold the High Priest, the delegated authority of God to the people, in contempt, to hold the ordinances of the temple in derision, and to neglect the tithe to the temple, but still encourage the payment of tax to the Romans. He appealed so to the unsanctified flesh of the pagan Galileans and the deceived Judeans that although he preached for less than five years he had more followers at his death than did Abraham during his life.

So it seemed to me of necessity for him to be removed. That this may be evident to your minds, I ask you to contrast our present condition with the past. Jesus from Nazareth left his father's business of constructing for

The Search

Caesar in Judaea and the Galilee and spent two years or more in Egypt under the instruction of Rabban Joshua bar Yeddesi, and learned the art of thaumaturgy to perfection. If the reported miracles of Jesus are true, he must have learned how from Horus and Serapis, as practiced by those pagan priests. He came back to the Galilee from Egypt a physician. He became a sympathizer of John the Baptist. As an itinerant teacher and physician he roused the pagans of the Galilee to metanoia, to bring about a restoration of the kingdom of heaven on earth.

Jesus embraced the doctrine of the Hillelites, presenting conspicuously the cosmopolitan spirit of the Jews. He taught that the dead would rise again and would live again in a future state of happiness or misery according as they have lived on earth in this present life. Which doctrine is the doctrine of the pagan Egyptians and Indus [Hindus]. He taught future rewards and punishments; but he being present, how could he reward in the future? He taught the revelation of the prophets, but contradicted their teachings. He taught the eternity of God's laws and promises, but attempted to supersede them by living a life free from the rituals established by the law of God. Even as rabboni, the highest of level of instruction, he so far cut himself loose from the others of his rabboni rank that he ate with unclear hands, publicans, and lepers, and permitted the living dead, the unclean, and the harlots to address him and to touch him, and had little regard for the rituals of cleansing and of sacrifice. These certainly were the doctrines of the Hillelites, except he presented his message on the style of the pagan Solon.

He seemed to take little notice of the political affairs of our nation and would as soon be governed by one nation as another. In fact so much friendship was afforded the Roman that it seemed that he had preference for rule by Caesar. His idea concerning Rome was that they are here among us to stay, do not fight that fact. Leave them alone. It matters not who rules or governs the nations; if they abuse, love them, and they cannot be enemies for long. Honor them by not speaking evil of them and by paying your taxes owed to them. 'It is only Caesar's money that you pay, which is unlawful because of its images, for you to have anyway.'

He said that we could not conquer Rome so honor them instead, and then they no longer would be enemies. Indeed the conduct of Jesus was so strange and incompatible with the interests of the Jews that it seemed to me, upon hearing the reports of his position presented to me, that he was a subject employed by Rome themselves to keep our nation submissive.

As the people became more and more confused and divided, the authorities of Caesar became increasingly hostile, fearing sedition. So to preserve our cause and our nation, I ordered that Jesus be taken into custody and brought to me for interrogation. But understand I did not act rashly or illegally. I passed sentence only after intense interrogation in which Jesus refused to cooperate by remaining silent or spoke few words of little worth on his behalf. Thus I was forced to pass judgment. It was not a voluntary act, but a legal one and one in accordance with the Law. So after much more and multiplied repeated interrogation and questioning by myself, the Court of Elders and Priests, and this most honored Master of Israel directorate, in which no one spoke on his behalf, only those spoke to his detriment, I was forced to pass a sentence worthy of death, for if he was to continue to promulgate his pernicious heresies and refuse to deny that he was that Theophus to whom the Herodians claim him to be, of which the honored Valleus Paterculus has choice of but to believe, the Jews, as a nation, would perish at the hands of Rome. I thus sent him to Pilate for interrogation with my written conviction, and for his ratification. Although the preservation of our nation was true reason for my conviction, the following is the purpose of his conviction that I sent with him to Pilate:

Caiaphas, High Priest of the Most High, to his most honorable and worthy Pontius Pilate, Procurator of Judaea:

'Jesus from Nazareth of the Galilee is thus charged by the Court of Elders and Priests:

1. Teaching a doctrine that there are more gods than one, which indeed he feels is himself, and by his silence refuses to desist from proclaiming even to the presence of this high court.
2. Through silence he acknowledges that he is The Theophus so sought by Tiberius Caesar Augustus, by his refusal to either confirm to refute such claims.
3. He teaches baptism is the seal of God, instead of circumcision, which is contrary to our law.
4. He teaches asceticism as the means of salvation, contrary to our law, the law of the nation of the Jews.
5. He has abrogated the priesthood and the laws and rituals of our law and our fathers, and has set the temple at naught.
6. He has proclaimed himself to be a king, while his followers have said that he is the king of the nation of the Jews, and through his silence has confirmed that such is the case of both.
7. He says that he will destroy our Temple, God's gift to His children, and by his silence he has admitted that such is true. Others have testified which he will not deny that he will destroy the temple and will rebuild it in three days.
8. He says that his kingdom will be a kingdom that will sweep away all other kingdoms and empires, present and future, and will last forever more in the hearts of his followers. Such seditious blasphemies against the administration of Rome must not be tolerated.

For this cause is Jesus from the Galilee charged, convicted and sentenced to death. We plead this resolve to our most honored governor Pontius Pilate.'

With these reasons for my actions, I submit my case favorably to The Theophus Commission of Ambassadors, most honored Valleus Paterculus, domain regulator governor Tiberius Julius Caesar Augustus, and most esteemed Masters of Israel."

In God's will and service—Joseph Caiaphas, High Priest of One God"

> After recording Caiaphas' letter, Pachomius went directly into recording Pilate's letter without comment.
>
> "To my most noble Sovereign Tiberius Julius Caesar Augustus and the honorable The Theophus Commission of Ambassadors and Valleus Paterculus—Greetings.
>
> The events that coincided with the trial and death of one Jesus, a Galilean Jew from the scoria of Nazareth, in my province a year and some months ago have been such that I will give details in full as they occurred. Concerning these events, I should not be surprised if, in the course of time, they may change the destiny of our nation, for it seems of late that all the gods have ceased to be propitious. I must say that cursed be the day that I succeeded Vallerius Flaceus; since that day my life with these Judaeans has been one of continual uneasiness and distress.
>
> On my arrival in Jerusalem I took possession of the Praetorium, and ordered a splendid feast to be prepared, to which I invited the tetrarch of the Galilee, with the High Priest and his officers. At the appointed hour no guests appeared. This I considered an insult offered to my dignity, and to the whole of Rome. A few days after, the High Priest deigned to pay me a visit. His deportment was grave and deceitful. He pretended that his religion forbade him and his attendants to sit at the table with authorities from Rome. Although I thought it expedient to accept his excuse, from that moment I was convince that the conquered had declared themselves the enemy of the conquerors. It seems that of all conquered regions, Judaea, and especially the state of Judea, is the most difficult to govern. So turbulent are the people that I live in momentary dread of an insurrection. I secluded myself from the masses in Caesarea Maritima, for I did not know what or who might influence the rabble to do; yet I endeavored to ascertain the mind and the standing of the people.
>
> Among the rumors that came to my ears, there was one in particular that attracted my attention. A young stonemason having been educated as a rabboni of the Jew's religious authority, who was said to be a legal ward by adoption and right of our state's Minister of Mines of Sovereigns Augustus and Augustus Tiberius and who represented your most excellent Sovereign Augustus Tiberius and the state's Senate in/for/on behalf of the

conquested territories of Britain, appeared from no one knows, although his boyhood home was in the refuse guardian of Nazareth. He was a preacher of a new religious law in the name of the God of the Jews, who said he was sent by Him. At first I was apprehensive that his design was to stir up the people against our authority, but my dread was soon dispelled. This man, whom his followers call Jesus of Capernaum and whose friends call Jesus from Nazareth, spoke as a son and as a friend of Rome, rather than as one of the Jews. To further focus my attention upon him, the Herodians from the court of Herod, whom your most excellent Tiberius has appointed to investigate for the honored Commission of Ambassadors, sent to my seat in Caesarea, a court messenger informing me that they had petitioned the Commission in the name of Tiberius Caesar for representation to come as quickly as can be possible to the Galilee of Syria to perform a Theophus interrogation of this man of the Galilee, this Jesus. My own attention proved that this man had no malice intended for your Sovereign's authority, his words seemed to be more wisdom and philosophy in the tradition of our own Cato, Suetonius, or Posidonius of the Grecians. It was on this account that I granted him much liberty; for it was in my power to have him arrested upon his visits to Judaea. I must conclude that he was neither seditious nor rebellious, except perhaps to the brothers of his own religious consanguinity. This liberty provoked the Jewish leaders of their religion. It is true that Jesus was severe on these leaders, and this was a political reason for not restraining the liberty of him while his leave was Judaea. At times of celebrations of the Jews in Judea and in Jerusalem, complaints were many against his insolence.

His most honorable Valleus Paterculus presented himself to my seat in Caesarea as representative of The Theophus Commission of Ambassadors in October before the events of this report, inquiring of the whereabouts and the activities of the Galilean of the emperor's citizenship called Jesus. I received him and sent him to the magistrate of Jerusalem to inquire of knowledge and the whereabouts of Jesus. From there I was told that he was instructed to appear before Herod.

In December before the record reflected in this report, soon after the return of our most honorable Valleus Paterculus to Capri, the enemies of Jesus addressed themselves to Herod, to wreak their vengeance upon him. Herod, unsure of The Theophus investigation concerning Jesus, and not willing to offend neither our most excellent Tiberius nor this Commission made no judgment concerning the welfare of his fate, nor of his actions or message. Instead he requested my audience in Caesarea. Whereupon he asked my opinion concerning the matter of Jesus and of his identity. I told him that I could not judge on the matter on behalf of the commission but that Jesus appeared to me to be a great philosopher and that his message was neither seditious nor did I consider him a threat to the authority of Rome. I further stated that the intentions of Rome were to leave him to his freedom of his proclamations and actions, unless such actions threatened the peace of the state of Judea or gave way to cause for seditious actions from the masses. At which to insure the peace and the authority of Rome, he would needs be dealt with according to the severity of his actions and motives.

In February before the events of this report, I arrived from Caesarea in Jerusalem to insure the peace of the masses during the Jews' celebration of the Passover. I was instructed by informants that during the celebration misfortune would likely befall Jesus and an insurrection would follow. Not having enough force in Jerusalem during the celebration to suppress a state insurrection, I resolved upon adopting a measure that promised to assure tranquility of the city without subjecting Rome to concession. I would not allow anything or any man to be the subject of or cause for sedition whether he be philosopher or a child of the gods.

The permitted extended Passover solemnization of the Jews, a 17-day celebration, was approaching and my emissaries had warned that because of Jesus' attribution to that Theophus, the religious leaders of the Jews, especially those of the sect of the Sadducees, whom say they that Jesus disrupted the traditions of their temple ordinances and practice, were intent to raise a sedition on Jesus' account and force his execution either with or without our approbation, to prevent your Sovereign from selecting their state as your ward. My emissaries had further informed me that the treasury of their temple had been employed in bribing certain vial characters to swear witness against him and to incite calls for his execution and if not execution then rebellion against the authority of your Senate's appointed procurator, your servant who now reports his actions. I feared the worst and was assured by my informants that sedition against our authority was inevitable if execution was not forthright. I sent a messenger demanding of the governor of Syria reinforcements, anticipating an unremitting crisis. The governor sent back word that reinforcements could not be sent until 20 days thence. I felt myself alone with but less military might than must be needful to subdue such an melodiously incited rabble of rebels, who knew nothing of Jesus, but rather were being inflamed by gold given them by contemptuous religious Jews who held Jesus in utter disdain. So in my attempt to keep order in the face of indubitable rebellion, I determined that if this Jesus had to be sacrificed for the advantage of peace and to secure the authority of Rome, then that expiration had to be heavily weighed.

Very late on the first night of their 7-day Passover portion of the 17-day celebration, the preliminary court of the Jews on instruction by the High Priest of the Jews asked permission to proceed with a trial. Knowing that for spite they had brought his arrest, I felt that before a court Jesus would be released for lack of condemning testimony. I gave my approval. But my wife bid me leave the decision to the Jews and give no judgment. Three days later, the day of their Sabbath, which they chose not to observe because of another Sabbath associated with their celebration four days thence, Jesus was presented to me for condemnation. I interrogated him and found in him nothing worthy of death. So not qualifying for execution, and he being from the Galilee, I sent him to the lower civil court of Herod who was in Jerusalem for the celebration, so that judgment for a less minor offense would be passed.

Herod, whose intent was more to prove whether Jesus was that Theophus, demanded of Jesus miracles to prove his Theophus character. Jesus refused all opportunity to show his position. Herod, then convinced that if Jesus would remain silent in the very midst of a possible exaltation, then he could not be that Theophus; so Herod mocked his silence and his position as a false Theophus, although he had no call or reason to do so. Herod then in disgust released Jesus as deserving nothing more than minor punishment for the crime of insolence for remaining silent before his authority. He sent Jesus back to me.

Again I interrogated Jesus and found in him nothing worthy of death, yet I knew that if he were released without a punishment, rebellion would likely encompass the city and spread to the regions. The Jewish religious leaders and the rabble that they had paid to solicit his death, demanded his crucifixion and proclaimed that I, your most loyal of servants, would no longer be a worthy governor for my Sovereign and that they would register a complaint to our Senate and with Segirus that my actions incited a riot and that my lack of action expanded the riot to rebellion.

I feared not their complaint or their accusation but I did dread that if a spark of rebellion was allowed to smolder, then only a small wind of defiance could cause it to spread into a consuming fire of revolution and anarchy. Yet, I found nothing in Jesus' character worthy of his death, nor so to give judgment for punishment by crucifixion.

After fruitless attempts to release him or to send him back to the Jews for a lesser crime, I adopted a measure that appeared to me to be the only action that would both save his life and satisfy the Jews for his blood. I proposed to them as was their custom, that Jesus be proclaimed as their scapegoat, as they so called, and let him to be released into the desert and to dwell among the rocks, never being allowed into the region again. They chose instead another criminal, one Barabbas being held for robbery of their temple offerings and a murderer, and appealed to me to offer this man if I was content to offer a man for a scapegoat. I could not withdraw my offer, so the criminal was set free. I then had Jesus mercilessly scourged so as to satisfy their demand for his life. But they wanted him dead; these riffraff wretches had no cause against Jesus nor did most know anything about him

The Search

except for his words and his works. But gold persuaded them to be his enemy, at least until after his death.

My Sovereign, to avoid rebellion and regional revolt, I condemned Jesus to death, washing my hands and Rome's involvement forever of the blame and responsibility of his death. As you see I had no choice. Yet, I fear that I have condemned to death the one man who in all of the world could have and must have qualified for the distinction as The Theophus of my most excellent Augustus, Tiberius Julius Caesar.

Before the dawn of the second day of the 4th month after the month of winter solstice celebrations, in the 18th year of the rule of my most excellent Tiberius who is in truth Augustus Caesar, Jesus was led with 46 others condemned for crimes against your Sovereign and our state, by my guard through the deserted streets to the scoria hollow of death, Gehenna, so called by the Jews, outside of the city, south, where matters of capital punishment are forever concluded.

By the time the sun had risen over the hills, the condemned were being raised to their post of death. To my astonishment, by mid-afternoon of that same day amid blackened clouds and terrible natural circumstances, I received word that Jesus had died. An earthquake that was later said to have been felt as far as Egypt and Parthania followed this announcement. Our most honored Minister of Mines and Senator of our holding in Britannia, Joseph Marmore from the region of my dominion, Judaea, claimed the body of Jesus as his own son by adoptive guardianship, demanding his immediate release into his care. Whereupon I hastily released his body to our state's most honored. At the request of the Jews I placed a guard of six to guard the tomb, but at the insistence of our Minister of Mines I raised the number by 60 to secure the tomb from robbers for seven days.

Benius Ishamius, my commander of the guard, later reported, three days after the guard was set, an incredible story about how this man Jesus had likely risen from his death. I do not doubt my commander, but I cannot believe in myths and stories. But if it is true that he has raised from death and his tomb failed to hold himself, then Jesus is of a truth that Theophus so sought by my Sovereign.

Now, noble Sovereign, honored statesman, and most respected Commission, this is as near as I recall the facts concerning the trial and condemnation of this man, Jesus, from the Galilee. With the promise of faithfulness and hopes for good to my noble Sovereign, I am your most obedient servant. —Pontius Pilate."

After Pachomius had recorded Pilate's report, he again without further comment, began to address Herod's letter.

"To Tiberius Julius Caesar Augustus and to The Theophus Commission of Ambassadors.

My Noble Lords, Greetings.

As my most gracious and honorable Valleus Paterculus, Chief Ambassador of The Theophus Commission has demanded in the name of my most excellent Sovereign, Tiberius Caesar Augustus, the following is to my best recall the matter of the events concerning the trial and death of the builder of stone, whose work has been witness to even residents of Capernaum, whom his followers call Jesus the Christ of the Galilee of the dross disposal city of Nazareth.

About two years before his trial by the Jews, a prince of my house reported to my chamberlain that his son had been raised from the bed of sickness unto death by Jesus a rabboni of the Jews whose father by adoption was our most honorable Senator representing the frontiers of Britain, whom we had heard nothing of fact, but only myth and rumor. The report of Caprinaius, the prince whose son was raised, claimed that Jesus was a distance of one day from the palace when the son was healed from his death. I called for Caprinaius to interrogate him on the possible Theophus connection between the said and Jesus. After much debate, in which he felt strongly that Jesus was qualified to be questioned about his position, I demanded of Caprinaius that he appoint 25 aids and gather for six months all information as could be found concerning this Galilean stonemason turned rabboni of the Jews.

Six months to the day Caprinaius again appeared before my seat with a detailed report of all that could be found concerning this Jesus. It seems from this information that this Jesus was perhaps the same that my father, the Great of all the house of Herod, aimed to destroy, during the time under Augustus that the massive array of eastern ambassadors from the greatest confederation that has ever been assembled in the history of our kind, inundated Jerusalem seeking a new king of the world that had been born among the Jews. War was averted with them by Augustus whom divided my father's kingdom to appease those whom they say my father had killed the king to whom they had given allegiance and the Gifts of Ramses. Of course it cannot be left proven that this Jesus is the same who had caused such turmoil in our state at the time of his birth and two years after. It was claimed that Jesus as a young man spent much time in Egypt where he learned the arts of soothe-saying and necromancery. There were also claims to his wide travels as an accompanying vassal of his father by adoption, our most honored Minister of Mines, whose residency is both in Rome and in our region.

There were other records of his defiance of the natural laws: of walking on water, reprimand of storms, of taking water and it becoming wine, of miracles of restoration and reversals of death. He also has been a friend to Rome and has many among the citizenship likened to himself and among our state's authority who look upon him in high regard. With so much that had been observed, I felt it justified sending for him to interrogate him and prove by some miracle that he is that one whom we seek. I too sent my finding to the Commission of Ambassadors, requesting representation for an investigation. Jesus never honored my demand for his presence and two years and four months past the time of my request, two ambassadors representative of the commission, arrived at my seat demanding to investigate the substantiation gathered from which I made my request to them.

The representatives of the commission followed Jesus' activities and witnessed his actions and words for three months. They then returned to Rome with their findings. Some months after their return, I received a messenger sent from the commission stating that our most honorable Valleus Paterculus and his assemblage would be arriving soon to conduct an interrogation of Jesus, and demanding that I give notice to Jesus of their arrival. But Jesus was not of a kind that would submit to the interrogation demands of the commission. Even though such notice was forwarded to contacts that instructed Jesus of the matter, nothing came of it. When his most honored chief ambassador arrived in Capernaum, demanding the whereabouts of Jesus, I informed him that he was beyond the river Jordan, and sent my own counsel to accompany him in his search for Jesus. Within a month my counsel departed from our Chief Theophus Ambassador and returned to me with news that they had found Jesus and had been witness to many of his deeds and teachings. They were without question that he was that Theophus of your most Sovereign.

I arrived in Jerusalem for the 17-day distended celebration of the Passover observance, one day removed from its first feast. To my astonishment it came to me through report from my emissaries that Jesus whom we were investigating on behalf of the Commission of Ambassadors was arrested. I assigned five servants the task of collecting the happenings of his arrest and to report to me anything that would characterize a justification for a pronouncement of The Theophus.

On the day following the general Sabbath, which had been repudiated for the sake of a High Sabbath two days thence, Pilate sent Jesus to me for judgment of a lesser crime than one worthy of death. At last I was to meet this man face to face. But for me to rule and to declare that he was to be released on fear that we had detained The Theophus, he must needs to show cause for his release by executing a miracle of proof. Yet he did nothing and said nothing. He retained silence, contemptuous silence. After many attempts to break his silence, I turned him aside to my guard for insulting treatment knowing that if he in fact was that Theophus that he would speak it plainly and would be proud to be proved correct and right within the eye of approval of our great and Sovereign Tiberius Caesar. But having found nothing worthy of death and having found no cause to judge on a lesser act of offense, I returned him to Pilate for his judgment.

I knew not the outcome of Pilate's judgment until the day before the Jew's High Sabbath, a great and terrible earth shaking caused damage to my estate, and when my chief steward gave notice that Pilate had condemned Jesus, that Theophus, to death and that even the earth and the heavens are now in mournful revolt against his death. Such an state could have been prevented and the death of such a just man would have been avoided.

As to the rumors of his raising from the tomb, if he is that Theophus, it cannot be beyond his powers. But if he is not, then how easy can a lie become truth, if the lie is more to be believed than truth.

These facts and causes I submit to my most excellent Caesar and our most honored Theophus Commission of Ambassadors for your consideration, praying for clemency if by chance justification has not come forth from the facts of my actions concerning this matter. —Antipas of the House of Herod, most humble Tetrarch of my most excellent Sovereign."

Although it would be impossible to confirm the validity of the three letters recorded by Pachomius because neither the originals nor copies of the originals have survived. But because the letters confirm known and undisputed historical facts regarding Jesus' crucifixion, I am inclined to accept their authenticity currently.

One thing the letters did show, however, is that Jesus' death was not just a local interest story that would be easily justified and forgotten. For not only did it cause confusion and upheaval among his disciples and followers, threatening the very foundation of their faith, it sent shock ways throughout the highest levels of Roman government.

Dicrecitmus, a court historian for Caligula, documented the finality of the issue of The Theophus when he recorded that in Valleus Paterculus' final interview with the Senate in April AD 40, he proudly declared, "My work is now complete. My retribution on his behalf is finished. Those who were responsible for the murder of my lord Tiberius' Theophus have now been abolished. The small flicker of light and hope that once was, is no longer. Such a one as he will never again rise among us. Now those who are responsible for his light being extinguished are no more."

Then again, the conclusiveness of The Theophus issue for Valleus Paterculus was in reality *not* the final chapter in the story of the *true* Theophus—Jesus. For when it became known and word began to spread that Jesus had risen from the dead, a succession of events was put into irreversible motion that ultimately resulted in the crumbling of the mighty Roman Empire, the destruction of the proud Jewish state, and the creation of a new religion founded upon the life, teachings, death, and resurrection of Jesus which became the most influential religion that humankind has ever experienced.

XXII

THE BEGINNING

"Nero fabricated scapegoats...and punished with every refinement the notoriously depraved Christians (as they were popularly called). Their originator, Christus, from whom they derive their name, had been condemned to death in the reign of Tiberius by the Procurator [of Judea], Pontius Pilate."—*The Annals of Imperial Rome*, written by Roman Senator and historian Cornelius Tacitus (56-117 AD).

"It was at that time a man appeared...if it be lawful to call him a man...who had all the attributes of a man but seemed to be something greater. His actions, certainly, were other than human, for he worked such wonderful and amazing miracles that I cannot regard him as a man; yet, in view of his likeness to ourselves I cannot regard him as an angel either. Everything that some hidden power enabled him to do he did by authoritative word, he was a teacher of such men as receive the truth with pleasure. Some people [the Jews] said that their first Lawgiver had risen from the dead and had affected many marvelous cures; others thought he was a messenger from heaven. However, in many ways he broke the Law ...for instance, he did not observe the Sabbath in the traditional manner. At the same time, his conduct was above reproach. He did not need to use his hands: his word sufficed to fulfill his every purpose.... He was the Messiah (this statement may have been added by later Christians)...Returning to his usual haunts he resumed his normal work. When the crowds grew bigger than ever, he earned by his actions an incomparable reputation. The exponents of the Law were mad with jealousy, and gave Pilate 30 talents to have him executed. Accepting the bribe, he gave them permission to carry out their wishes themselves. So they seized him and crucified him in defiance of all Jewish tradition.... he appeared to them alive again the third day, as the divine Prophets had foretold these (this statement may have been added by later Christians) and ten thousand other wonderful things concerning him, and the race of Christians, so named from him, are not extinct even now."—*The Jewish War* by Joseph ben Matthias, who took the Latin name of Flavius Josephus, from a chapter entitled "Antipas and the Two Agrippas"—Williamson translation.

[NOTE: Flavius Josephus lived from AD 63 to 100. His four principle works were: *The Jewish War, Antiquities of the Jews, Life*, and *Against Apion*. G.A. Williamson was the translator who actually brought Josephus' writings into modern light. Williamson's translation is called *Josephus: The Jewish War*. Mr. Williamson discovered that most of the common writings of Josephus had been back-edited during the reign of Domitian, to remove any and all statements pertaining to Jesus. However, Williamson uncovered an early Greek variation of Josephus' *The Jewish*

War. This text was a Slavonic version that had survived Domitian's cut, and had been circulated in Russia and Rumelia. This version included discussions about Jesus, John the Baptist, James the brother of Jesus, and the original apostles. The above quote is taken from that Slavonic version.]

Although the common tradition that Jesus was crucified on a Friday and rose from the dead on a Sunday has little foundational authenticity, his resurrection, whenever it happened and regardless of how long after his death it occurred, was the next major event in the life of Jesus.

I discovered an unusual authentication of the Gospel records while I was visiting the library of the Bordeaux Abbey located in Orléans, France. Orléans' primary claim to fame is tied to the conquest of Orléans by Joan of Arc, the Maid of Lorraine, The Maid of Orléans, in the 15th century. The loss of Orléans (at that time under the control of the English) to Joan's French army brought her to the forefront of England's formidable foes—a foe that they vowed to destroy; a vow realized when the English burned her as a witch in 1431.

Portions of the Bordeaux Abbey dated back to the 13th century, but during the Hundred Years War it was damaged so badly that it had to be abandoned for almost two hundred years, during which time it was repaired inconsistently. The library attached to the abbey was originally built in the 17th century and housed a beautiful collection of artwork and sculptures, but only a few books and documents. When I first saw it, I wondered why they called it a library and not a museum. As I was slowly walking through the library, admiring it, the head librarian asked in French first, then in English followed by German, if he could help me.

I introduced myself and told the librarian that I was looking for information about the life of Jesus. We talked in English the remainder of the time I was there. The librarian said that they did not have many documents or manuscripts because most had been destroyed during the September 12, 1789 revolutionary riot, when the library was partially burned. When the rioters ransacked the abbey and library, they left the works of art virtually untouched, but they destroyed every book, document, or manuscript that had not been hidden.

The librarian told me that I was welcome to review the documents that they did have and to view the artwork as long as I wanted

I wandered around for a while looking at the books they did have, but found nothing that would be of benefit to my research efforts. I then started reviewing the impressive collection of Renaissance art.

One painting in particular caught my eye. It was a large painting compared to most of the others and it was divided into four squares. Within each square was a different scene of what appeared to be the story of the resurrection of Christ. I studied it for a while, and became so intrigued by it that I went to the librarian's desk to ask for his help.

The librarian told me that the painting did in fact depict different accounts of Jesus' resurrection and that there was a more in-depth interpretation of the meaning of the painting on microfiche film that I could review in one of their sound proof private viewing rooms, but the film did not tell the history of the painting. "If you want to know that," he said with a smile, "you will have to ask me."

I was interested, so I asked him to tell me the history. He led me into one of the microfiche research rooms so we would not be disturbed.

I sat down at a desk and prepared to begin taking notes while the librarian searched the microfiche file that was in a central location near the rooms and selected the film that explained the painting in which I was interested.

After studying the film for a few minutes, the librarian began to speak. "This artwork was produced by Ambrogio Lorenzetti, the Italian story painter, and was presented to Pope Boniface XII on Christmas Day, 1342, on the occasion of the dedication of the Pope's new palace and residence in Avignon. Although the papacy court, under Clement V, had moved their seat of government from Rome to Avignon thirty years before, the new papal palace was not completed and ready for occupancy until 1342.

"Boniface XII admired the painting and placed it near his private altar in the palace. However, within two weeks, Clement VI succeeded him.

"Because of the subject matter and the controversy associated with the four separate options on the subject of Jesus' resurrection, Clement claimed that the painting offended him, so he had it removed and placed in storage.

"It remained in storage throughout the papacy of Innocent VI and Bl. Urban V. In January 1377, for fear of losing control of the Papal States, Gregory XI, Urban's successor, abandoned Avignon and re-established papal residency in Rome. Gregory had never seen the painting; nonetheless he wanted it destroyed. However, purely by accident, when Gregory had most of the artwork and treasures that were in store sold to finance his move back to Rome, unknown to the Pope, this painting by Ambrogio Lorenzetti was among those that were sold. Henry, Duke of Orléans, had bought, sight unseen, 25 works of art and trusted his steward, Andrea of Tours, to correctly pick the ones that Henry had bought. One of the paintings that Andrea claimed for Henry was this painting.

"Once Henry realized that one of the paintings that he had brought was the painting that Gregory wanted to have destroyed, he brought the painting to this abbey for safe keeping. It remained hidden until 1859, at which time the abbot placed it on display in this library. It was hidden again when the Nazis invaded, and then brought back out of hiding and put on display in 1950."

The librarian (he told me that his name was LeSaul) then inserted the film in the microfiche. Unfortunately, it was written in French. So, I asked LeSaul to translate for me.

He said that before he explained the painting itself, he first wanted to explain the atmosphere that was prevalent at the time of Ambrogio Lorenzetti.

"As I said," he began his explanation; "Clement V had moved his papal court to Avignon in 1309. This was in an effort to neutralize the growing power and insolence of King Philip the Fair of France. Philip had accused the former pope, Boniface VIII, of adultery, blasphemy, sacrilege, and maintaining a brothel in the papal residence in Rome. In addition, Philip had arrested, tortured and killed numerous Knights Templar (claiming that they were homosexual and that they were soldiers of the devil) because not only was he deeply in debt to them, but also they were staunch and uncompromising supporters of the Pope (by eliminating the Templar he could wipe the slat clean of the enormous debt that he owe them, while at the same time eliminate the Pope's last dependable line of defense, leaving the Pope totally defenseless).

"For four years after he was confirmed as Boniface's successor, Clement made numerous trips to France in an effort to defuse the political controversy between Philip and the papacy. Finally in 1309, Philip showed willingness for reconciliation and both Philip and Clement accepted a very weak truce. To insure that the truce would not deteriorate, the Pope moved his seat to France. So, at least for the time being, there seemed to be political peace between Philip and Clement, but doctrinally and theologically they were still miles apart.

"Because Philip's hatred for Boniface was so deep, Philip the Fair developed a posture against Boniface, much like the posture that the Arabs had developed against Pope Gregory, that if the Pope says it and believes it, then the direct opposite must be true. Philip found fault in *ALL* that Boniface claimed and taught.

"At this time, the big theological controversy in the Church was whether Mary Magdalene went to the tomb to see Jesus one last time in order to prepare his body for a delayed decomposition, or to worship him and to pray for him to be released from Paradise, so that he could ascend back to his Father.

"Along with this argument, the Church was also beset with controversies that were rooted in 'new revelations' that had come to light with the study of non-Christian commentaries on previously unknown Talmuds that were claimed to have recently been discovered. These were commentaries that told a different story from the Bible story about the women who came to the tomb. In fact, these commentaries, which were said to be based on actual eye-witness accounts of the events concerning the resurrection of Jesus, were not the record of an eye-witness report of a single event, but rather a compilation of several differing records of the same event: the resurrection of Jesus."

LeSaul then paused and interjected, "it seems quite obvious that these commentaries on the different accounts were produced for the purpose of causing confusion and polarization within the church. They were probably produced by either scribes in the employ of Boniface or in the employ of Philip in an effort to discredit the other in the eyes of the clergy and religious leaders."

He then continued with his explanation, "Although the differing stories of the account of Jesus' resurrection, if believed, could have totally destroyed the very foundation of the Catholic theology of that day, that did not seem to matter to the writers. This is why I (LeSaul) feel that these reports were circulated chiefly for political reasons. Yet some of the information may have been grounded in truth, even though that truth seemed to be contrary to the accepted resurrection doctrine that had been recognized by the church."

Again LeSaul interrupted his explanation to interject his own thoughts. "I feel that the events that surrounded the resurrection of Jesus have been extremely confusing ever since the first century.

"On the one hand, we have the modern, or the last four hundred years', tradition of the resurrection, and on the other hand we have the first eight centuries' tradition of the resurrection. Both of these traditions have chosen to leave out some very important scriptures that would have either refuted or confirmed the tradition. A third tradition arose in the 9th century. Its most popular period of acceptance was the 300 years from the 9th century to the 12th century. In reality, this tradition actually used more scriptural justification than the other two more commonly accepted traditions. The non-contested centuries, the 13th through the 16th, brought a multitude of other traditions, some of which were logical and some were so controversial and mystical that they bordered on the ridiculous. It was during this period that this painting was produced, which addressed some of these resurrection story controversies."

LeSaul then turned his attention back to the painting. "According to tradition, each of the small pictures illustrated in the painting represents four different versions of the same event: the women's post-Sabbath visit to the tomb of Jesus.

"In our present day Bible," he interjected, "This would be the story as is recorded in John 20:1-18, Luke 24:1-11, Mark 16:1-8, and Matthew 28:1-10."

He then explained that he would first point out the three most obvious areas of controversy of the differing opinions. Second, he would explain the four different sequences of events that the pictures depicted. In conclusion, he would explain the three traditions that the four different versions portrayed, drawing from information that he discovered in commentaries on 1st and 2nd century Christian Greek texts. He said that he particularly used these commentaries when he was trying to determine the names of the women who went to the burial site of Jesus.

LeSaul began his explanation, "The three areas where differences in the pictures are the most obvious are: the day and time of day; who the women were and how many women came to the tomb; and upon their arrival, where was the tomb sealing stone. I have to again interject something here," LeSaul said. "I was very impressed with the 19th century scribe or monk or educator who translated the pictures and wrote the explanation that was then preserved on the film that we were studying. Unfortunately, his name has long since been forgotten.

" Another thing that I will say is that the tomb sealing stone being placed in the mouth of the tomb played a very important part in this resurrection story. Traditionally at that time, the stone did not close the tomb opening for at least four days and in some cases five days. Still in other cases, after four days the stone was rolled in front of the tomb opening, but it was not sealed permanently until all of the burial spaces had been occupied. This could have taken months or even years. However, in Jesus' case the stone was rolled into the mouth of the tomb the same day that he died, and it was sealed. Very unusual, unless Joseph of Arimathea's influence was far greater than the church has traditionally given him credit."

LeSaul continued with his explanation by comparing the day and the time of day depicted in the four painted versions. "John's account," he said, "represented here in the first picture, said that the women came to the tomb on Wednesday morning, the 22nd of Nisan, while it was still dark. Luke's account, represented in picture number two, also indicates Wednesday morning, the 22nd of Nisan. But it shows the time to be the earliest dawn. The Mark version, represented in the bottom left picture, picture number three, also depicts that the day as Wednesday morning, the 22nd of Nisan, but the time was later dawn, implying that the sun had already risen. The Matthew version, represented in picture number four, in the lower right side, indicates that the day was Thursday evening, the 30th of Nisan, after sundown."

The Search

LeSaul then gave his explanation concerning the number of women who came to the tomb and the names of the women. "In the John setting, the top left picture, only one woman came, Mary E. Magdalene. In the Luke version, the second picture, upper right, at least five women came: E. Magdalene Mary, Joanna, Mary E. James, and others. In the Mark version, lower left picture, there were three women who came: E. Mary E. Magdalene, Mary E. James, and Salome. The Matthew version has two women coming: Mary E. Magdalene and the other Mary."

After this he explained the various depictions of the location of the sealing tombstone. "In the John version the stone had already been rolled away before the women arrived. In the Luke version as well as the Mark version, the stone had also been rolled away already. However, in the Matthew version, the stone was still in the mouth of the tomb and the women witnessed the angel rolling the stone away."

Next he described the probable sequence of events of the four different versions of the women coming to the tomb of Jesus:

"John's version:
1. Mary E. Magdalene came to the open tomb but she did not enter the tomb.
2. She reported what she saw to Peter and John. They went to the tomb.
3. Mary E. Magdalene returned to the tomb and after Peter and John had left, she entered the tomb.
4. When she came out of the tomb, Jesus met her. She thought he was the gardener. He made himself known unto her.
5. Jesus emphatically told her not to touch him because he had not yet been resurrected to the Father.
6. She again reported everything that had happened to the disciples.

Luke's version:
1. The five women entered the open tomb and then came out.
2. They saw two men in shining clothing who told them that the resurrection had taken place.
3. They reported all that they had experienced to the 11 disciples. The disciples did not believe them.

Mark's version:
1. The three women entered the open tomb and found a young man sitting inside.
2. The man, or angel, spoke to them and told them to report to the disciples.
3. The three women were terrified and did not report anything to anyone.

[This version indicates that it was after this event that the soldiers sent by Pilate replaced the stone in the mouth of the tomb, and sealed it.]

Matthew's version:

1. The two women did not enter the tomb because the tombstone was still in the mouth of the tomb and soldiers were guarding it.
2. The women witnessed the stone being rolled away.
3. They saw one messenger of the Lord outside of the tomb. He told them that the resurrection had taken place.
4. The two women ran from the tomb to report to the disciples. Jesus met them in route. They touched him by embracing his feet. He told them to go tell his disciples that he would meet them in the Galilee.
5. The women reported all of these things to the disciples."

After LeSaul had given the four opposing sequence of events, without personal comment, he began to relate the three most commonly accepted, yet different, traditions concerning the resurrection and the women's visit to the tomb site.

"Tradition number one, the tradition of the last four centuries, or the tradition of our modern era, says that Jesus was crucified on Friday morning, he died on Friday afternoon and was entombed on Friday evening. He descended into Hades, where those who had been non-righteous on earth went, and there he ministered to those who were in captivity, setting those who believed on him free from their captivity (this tradition also held that the righteous went to Paradise at death, which was a separate place of peace and rest annexed to Heaven. There they remained until they were judged. Jesus released the righteous from Paradise and allowed them to go to Heaven.) he was there in Hades for two nights, Friday night and Saturday night, and one day, Saturday. Before sunrise, early Sunday morning, there was a great earthquake: an angel rolled the tomb stone away and Jesus arose from the dead and came out of the tomb. The guards fell as dead men (Matthew 28:2-4). Saints (the ones who were released by Jesus from their captivity in Hades) who were in the graves arose and went into the city (Matthew 27:53), followed by their ascension into heaven with Jesus. A short time thereafter, when it was still dark, Mary E. Magdalene left her house alone to go to the tomb (John 20:1). A short time after this, just as day began to break, Mary E. James, the mother of James (the cousin of Jesus), Joanna, the wife of Chuza (a steward of Herod), Salome, the wife of Zebedee, and other women, met Mary E. Magdalene at the tomb (Mark 16:1-2, Matthew 28:1, and Luke 24:1). As they approached the tomb, they discovered that the tombstone had been rolled away (Luke 24:2, Mark 16:3-4). Mary E. Magdalene turned at this point and immediately ran back to Peter and John and told them that Jesus' body had been stolen (John 20:2). Peter and John ran to the tomb to see if what Mary had said was true (John 20:3-7). In the meantime, after Mary had left, some of the remaining women went into the tomb. Inside two angels met them. One spoke to them and told them that Jesus had risen and that they were to go and tell his disciples (Luke 24:3-8, Mark 16:5-7). They ran out of the tomb terrified and ran away (Mark 16:8). By the time Peter and John arrived at the tomb, the women had already left. All they saw was what remained: an empty tomb and empty grave clothes (John 20:7-9). They then believed Mary's story that someone had stolen Jesus' body. They returned to where they were staying (John 20:10). Mary E. Magdalene had followed them back to the tomb, but she did not return with them. She was left alone. She remained on the outside of the tomb, weeping. After a while however, she did go into the empty tomb. There she also saw the two angels. One of them talked to her (John 20:11-12). As she was talking to the angels, maybe thinking that they were gardeners or grounds keepers, Jesus walked up behind her and spoke to her (John 20:13-14). Jesus then revealed himself to her (John 20:15-17). She immediately turned and ran back to tell the disciples that he had risen. In the meantime, the other women were fleeing back to their homes, terrified. As they fled, Jesus appeared to them and confirmed to them the instructions that the angel had given to them (Matthew 28:8-10). They then went to the disciples and told them what they had experienced and what Jesus had told them. As they reported to the disciples, Mary E. Magdalene arrived with her story about seeing Jesus. At this, Peter again ran back to the tomb and again found nothing (Luke 24:12). That same day, Jesus appeared to two disciples in the country (Mark 16:12). They in turn returned to the disciples and told them what they had seen. The disciples did not believe (Mark 16:13). That night Jesus appeared to the ten disciples (John 20:19-20). Eight days later, he appeared to two going to Emmaus (Luke 24:13-32). As they were telling their story to the disciples, Jesus appeared to all of them (John 20:24-29, Luke 24:33-35, Mark 16:14). After this the disciples went into the Galilee as Jesus had instructed (Matthew 28:16) and waited. Jesus delayed his coming, so they went fishing (John 21:1-23). Jesus did eventually arrive on the seashore and taught them. Forty days after his resurrection he gave his final instructions before ascending into heaven.

"Tradition number two was the tradition that was believed and accepted for the first eight centuries after the resurrection of Jesus: This tradition is basically the same as tradition number one except the time differences between the burial of Jesus and his resurrection. Tradition number two held that Jesus was crucified Friday morning, died Friday afternoon, and was entombed on Friday evening (although in the 5th century and the first part of the 6th believers in this version said that Jesus was crucified and died on Monday and in the latter part of the 6th and 7th century, the believers in this version said that Jesus was crucified and died on Wednesday). Immediately after death, he descended into Hades, which was divided into two compartments: The Abyss and Paradise. The Abyss, commonly called at that time, Hell, is where the souls of the non-righteous dead, the damned, were held in torment until the Day of Judgment. Paradise was the place where the souls of the righteous dead from the time of Adam until Christ, were held in peace. This tradition says that Jesus descended into the Abyss and preached to the damned. He then went into the compartment of Paradise where he released the souls of the righteous dead who was being held there. He later took them to heaven with him when he ascended to the Father. The church at that time taught that the Abyss (Hell) was still occupied by the souls of the non-righteous and was increasing daily. Concerning Paradise, they felt that Paradise was emptied by Jesus and that it is now unoccupied and will never again be occupied. They believed that after Jesus emptied Paradise from that time forward the righteous dead go immediately to heaven at death. This tradition held that Jesus was in Hades for three full days. On Tuesday (or Friday if he was crucified on Monday and Sunday if he was crucified on Wednesday), he arose from the dead. The remaining events and those concerning the visit of the women, followed the same sequence as tradition number one.

"Tradition number three was the tradition that was believed and accepted from the 9th century through the 12th century: This tradition was much more radical than the two other traditions, yet it seemed to utilize more scriptural truth within a more logical sequence of events than did tradition number one or number two. Tradition number three said that Jesus was crucified on Monday morning, died on Monday afternoon, and was entombed on Monday evening, the 20th of Nisan, the stone probably being rolled in front of the tomb by Joseph of Arimathea. This tradition strongly emphasized the physical death of Jesus on this day, the day of his death, in that he died as a perfect sacrifice for sin. Upon death he descended into the Abyss portion of Hades. He stayed there the evening of Monday and all day Tuesday. On Wednesday morning, the 22nd of Nisan, the physical body of Jesus arose from the dead. This was the first resurrection. Early on the morning of the 22nd of Nisan, Wednesday, while it was still dark, the physical Jesus arose from the dead. Shortly thereafter, also while it was still dark, Mary E. Magdalene came to the tomb. She saw that the stone had already been rolled away from the tomb. She did not enter the tomb, but instead, she reported to Peter and John that someone had stolen the body of Jesus. Peter and John ran to the tomb and found that Mary was correct. They returned to where they were staying. Mary stayed behind and lingered outside of the tomb as she wept. She then entered the tomb and saw two angels. One of them talked to her. She exited the tomb and met the physical Jesus, whom she mistook for the gardener. He revealed himself to her. He emphatically forbade her from touching him because he had not yet ascended to his Father. She left him and again reported to the disciples (John 20:1-18). Mary E. Magdalene left to go report to the disciples just as dawn had barely begun to break. Soon thereafter, five other women including E. Magdalene Mary, Joanna, E. Mary James, and two others came to the tomb. They too discovered that the stone had been rolled away. They went inside, then came right back out, but as they were exiting the tomb, they were met by two men in shining clothing who told them that the physical Jesus had risen from the dead. They hurried to the 11 disciples and told them what they had experienced. The 11 did not believe them (Luke 24:1-11). Later that morning, as early morning was in full dawn, and while the five women were on their way to tell the eleven disciples what they had experienced, three more women arrived at the tomb: E. Mary E. Magdalene, Mary E. James, and Salome. When they arrived they too noticed that the stone had already been rolled away. They entered the tomb and found a young man sitting inside. He spoke to them and told them to go and report what they had seen to the disciples. The three became terrified and ran off. They did not go to the disciples, nor did they say anything to anybody (Mark 16:1-8).

"At mid-morning, the 22nd of Nisan, the guards that Pilate had agreed to post arrived. Finding the stone removed, they replaced the stone in the mouth of the tomb and sealed it (Matthew 27:62-66; 28:11-15). Since typically the body was placed deep within a tomb, or on occasion even in a separate chamber of the tomb, the soldiers did not go in, they probably just assumed that the stone had not been placed in the mouth of the tomb yet; a natural and typically logical assumption for that time. Later that day, the physical Jesus appeared to two people (it is not certain whether these were men or women), in the country (Mark 16:12). That evening the physical Jesus appeared to his disciples behind closed doors. Thomas was not with the disciples (John 20:19-25). After this, the physical Jesus appeared no more to anyone for almost an entire week, fanning the flames of unbelief resulting in the disciples concluding that what they had seen was nothing more than a vision and that Jesus really was dead after all.

"Here this tradition number three gets a little mystical, yet it does have enough merit to be considered. Six days later, on the very early morning of the 28th of Nisan, Christ died spiritually to sin (Romans 5:8, II Corinthians 5:21). This was the second death. Jesus became The Christ when he died to sin. Christ descended into the Paradise section of Hades and there he remained for two days and one night. This makes a total of three days and three nights that he, Jesus who became The Christ, stayed in Hades (Luke 24:45-47, Mark 9:31, Matthew 12:40): two nights and one day in the Abyss and two days and one night in Paradise. At the 12th hour, the very end of the day period, eight days after the first resurrection of the physical Jesus, the second resurrection took place: The Resurrection of Christ: the Resurrection of Justification.

"Accompanying this resurrection is when Christ set those who had been in Paradise, free. As the day grew to a close and a new day began (6:00 p.m.), Mary E. Magdalene and the other Mary went to the tomb, probably like they had done every day, since all hope had died that he really was alive; they too probably were convinced that their witness of Jesus alive was nothing more than a vision or a dream. The stone was in the mouth of the tomb and the Roman guards were guarding it, the same as it had been for well over a week. Suddenly, there was a huge earthquake, and an angel rolled the sealed tombstone away from the mouth of the tomb and sat upon it. They and the soldiers that were there were eyewitnesses to this event. The guards became terrified and fell as dead men. The angel told the women that Christ had risen and for them to go and tell his disciples to meet him in the Galilee. The women ran from the tomb to report to the disciples. Christ met them in route and confirmed to them what the angel had told them, and he told them to tell his disciples to met him in the Galilee. At this point they embraced his feet and worshipped him. They then ran off and reported all of these things to the disciples (Matthew 28:1-10). Later on in that 24-hour day (the next morning before 6:00 a.m.), Christ appeared to the two who were going to Emmaus. He spent all day with them. They then went to Jerusalem to tell the disciples about their experience (Luke 24:13-35). The disciples did not go to the Galilee as Christ had instructed; they as yet did not believe. So, he, Christ, appeared to them behind closed doors at the very instant that the two who were going to Emmaus were telling their story. This time Thomas was with the disciples (Luke 24:36-37, John 20:26-29). After this, the disciples did go into the Galilee. There they waited for Christ to join them; however, he did not arrive as quickly as they had anticipated. They decided to go fishing (John 21:1-23). This was followed by his joining them and his spending forty more days (after his 2nd resurrection) with them, teaching and instructing them. Afterwards, he then ascended into heaven to take his place as advocate and mediator."

LeSaul then concluded by saying, "Each of these three most dominant resurrection traditions, among numerous traditions, has taken their turn as *THE ACCEPTED LAW AND DOCTRINE OF THE CHURCH* during the past 20 centuries. Each has taken its turn at being the accepted without question or argument version; as the factual and truthful version; and as *'God inspired and revealed'* doctrine, for hundreds of years, wherein all other traditions were rejected as heresy. So, over the centuries all three traditions have taken their turn as heresy and each has taken its turn as truth. But all three *CANNOT* be correct. So, we are left with a decision. Which of these three traditions or some other version is true and factual?"

"I must conclude this whole thing because I must attend to a pressing matter. But I will conclude by simply saying that what really matters is not which tradition is right but that each confirms the fact that Jesus rose from the dead, whether one resurrection or two, it matters little, and is living even to this day. As far as I am concerned, I accept neither of the three as absolute fact, yet I accept all three as conditional fact. All three have strong points and all three have gaping theological and doctrinal holes in them. But tradition number three seems to have a more consistent flow and a more logical sequence of events."

Upon his conclusion, LeSaul had to leave. But I took the opportunity to just sit there in silence wondering about how all of that could have been depicted in that one painting. No wonder the Pope wanted it destroyed. It would have been far too controversial for those of that era. In fact, it's probably even too controversial for this modern era.

So, we are left with many questions that have not yet been answered satisfactorily. The primary question that must be answered is: How long did Jesus stay in the tomb before he rose from the dead? If we take the words of Jesus literally, then he was to remain in the tomb for three days and three nights. So, if he was entombed on Monday evening and he stayed in the tomb for three days and three nights, then he rose from the dead on Thursday evening before the dawning of Friday. What about the two resurrections—one physical and one spiritual separated by six days? In my research, I have not discovered enough information to affirm the reality of two resurrections. Yet, it seems to be the only explanation that justifies the inconsistency between Matthew's account of the resurrection and the other three Gospels' accounts. So, I will continue to research and search for the truth regarding the two-resurrection question. But until I discover enough truth to warrant a re-evaluation, I have chosen to stick with the words of Jesus—that he will remain in the tomb for three days and three nights (three FULL days and three FULL nights) and then he would rise from the dead.

After the resurrection of Jesus, he remained on the earth for 40 more days. Numerous eyewitnesses testified to his appearance. Much of that 40-day period Jesus spent with his disciples and followers preparing them for the time, that was fast approaching, when he would no longer be with them. He instructed them and gave them power to minister as he had ministered and with the same authority with which he ministered, and commissioned them to spread his teachings, his doctrines, and the truths exemplified by his life to the far corners of the earth, to every culture, and to every people group.

When the 40 days had expired, he led the 11 to Bethany. There he gave them two last commands (Acts 1:4-11): (1) *tarry in Jerusalem until you receive the gift of the Holy Ghost and power from on high* (this was realized 10 days later on the Day of Pentecost); and (2) *be witnesses in Jerusalem, Judea, Samaria, and to the utter most parts of the earth.* After giving these two commands, Jesus ascended into heaven and took his rightful place—seated on the right hand of the Father. As the disciples looked into the sky as him descend into heaven, two men dressed in white apparel (perhaps angles) stood by them and told them that Jesus would return (the Second Coming) in like manner in which he left.

After the ascension, the disciples did do as Jesus had commanded—they returned to Jerusalem and tarried in the upper room waiting for the promise of the Holy Spirit.

Although Jesus had ascended into heaven, his work did not stop. In fact over the next two centuries his message was taken to the far corners of the known world. Though to cover the spread of Christianity with the detailed concentration deserving of such a subject would take another book this size or larger or even a series of books, I did come across some interesting information while researching the life of Jesus, that directly relates to Jesus' Great Commission command and the disciple, because of his letters of canon, who is most easily recognized by modern Christianity: Paul the Apostle. Although this information is not intended to give a detailed account of Paul's ministry, it does shed some light on some of the areas of Paul's ministry that have for years been a mystery.

While researching the life of Jesus at the Toledo Public Library in Toledo, Ohio, I came across an essay entitled *Boyd's Paul* written in 1953 by Dr. Clive Emerson, a professor of Roman History at Dallas Theological Seminary. The essay was a commentary on a treatise written in 1795 by history professor Richard F. Boyd from the New College in Edinburgh, Scotland. Boyd's treatise was entitled *Paul Unveiled.*

Dr. Emerson's essay was divided into two parts. Part one was called "Boyd's opinion." The second part was called "Boyd's flummox." The first portion of the essay was a general commentary and evaluation on Boyd's treatise. This part seemed to be a typical commentary like one would find with any theological evaluation of any historical treatise. There was nothing that "stuck-out" enough in this first part to make me want to take notes. The second part of the essay was what intrigued me the most. In almost the entire latter portion of the essay, Dr. Emerson commented on Boyd's uncovering of previously unknown information concerning Peter and Paul's (especially Paul's) connection to the new Christian church in Rome.

Dr. Emerson established a historical setting for the second part of his essay by quoting Boyd directly. "...Because Jesus was a ward and son by adoption of Joseph of Arimathea, he probably traveled with Joseph all over the Roman Empire—from Britain to Arabia and from the North Sea to Egypt. He could have even traveled by caravan as far east as the Himalayan Mountains. Joseph of Arimathea was one of the richest men in all of Syria and probably the richest Jew, if not the richest man, in the province of Judaea.

"He owned virtually all of the metal and mineral trade between Syria and Europe and exclusivity controlled metal and mineral trade between Syria and Britain.... because Joseph was the Imperial Minister of Mines and Mining for the Roman Empire as well as a Roman Senator representing Britain, a great deal of time was spent in Britain. Joseph, hence Jesus if he traveled with Joseph, could travel anywhere mines were being worked to sell ore and minerals to the Roman Empire, especially in Britain.... making Jesus a virtual stranger to the area that is now called Palestine...that would explain why most of the Jews had questions about who he was. Even his cousin, John the Baptist (if in fact they were related) did not recognize him (John 1:31)...Jesus was required to pay the 'stranger and wanderer's tax' (Matthew 17:24-27).... Bartholomew the nathanael who lived close to Nazareth had no idea who Jesus was...in short, Jesus was known by very few in the region of his own home town.... that could explain why a 13-year old boy could so astound the great educators of the Law, yet nothing more is recorded about him in the Gospels until he neared age 30. If he had remained in the Judaea or the Galilee area, surely more would have been written about him.... Jesus at age 30 was more of an Roman/British subject than he was a Galilean resident...."

"The traditions of Glastonbury, Boyd continued, say that Jesus had blue eyes and either auburn or medium brown hair and was kept somewhat short according to the Greco-Roman standards of that day. These traditions also say that he and Mary, his mother, had built a home on the south end of Lake Glastonbury and lived there for some time on two different occasions. The city of Glastonbury is located near the headwaters of the Thames River near Bristol, within the region of the Silurian Kingdom, the center of Druidic worship...."

At this point Dr. Emerson made a few comments and then continued to quote Boyd directly, but further on in the treatise.

"...When Peter was put into prison (Acts 12:2-4).... according to tradition that originated at that time, Joseph of Arimathea, along with a handful of Jesus' followers, including Mary his mother, were cast adrift off the coast of Caesarea by the Jewish Sanhedrin in January of AD 37.

"Without sails or oars, they drifted with the currents until they arrived at Cyrene on the coast of Africa. After obtaining sails and oars in Cyrene, they sailed to Rome....Emperor Caligula was infuriated with the Jewish Sanhedrin who had dare treat with such disdain an official of his administration and a Senator of Rome who had been appointed to a position of membership in the Jewish Sanhedrin by Tiberias himself. So as to keep the actions of the Sanhedrin under extreme examination on behalf of Rome, Caligula ordered the death of 112 members of the Jewish Sanhedrin and the death of 33 Jewish priests who had supported Joseph's dismissal. Joseph was immediately returned to his position in the Sanhedrin in Jerusalem by the High Priest under direct orders from Caligula.... some three years after his reinstatement (in AD 40), Joseph, Mary, and a small band of followers sat sail from Caesarea...following the Roman trades they sailed, with a Roman military escort of 50 soldiers, as far west as Massilla (present day Marseilles) in Gaul and what is now called the coast of France.

"Cardinal Caesar Barinius," Boyd continued, "Who served as head librarian to the Vatican from 1538 to 1609, wrote in his *Ecclesiastical Annals*, a history of the Christian church from the resurrection of Christ up until AD 1198, that those accompanying Joseph to Massilla (Marseilles) included the sisters Mary and Martha of Bethany, their brother Lazarus, Eutropius, Salome, Cleon, Saturninus, Mary Magdalene, Mercella the maid of Mary of Bethany, Maximin, Martial, Mary the mother of Jesus, and Trophimus or Restitutus. Along with the 50-guard Roman escort, Joseph had in his company 67 souls.... ultimately Lazarus, the brother of Mary and Martha, became the first bishop of Marssilla (Marseilles). Both Lazarus and the sisters remained in France until their death. They all are buried in Gaul (France).... Joseph and Mary and 11 others plus the Roman escort crossed the length of Gaul following the Rhone and then the Liger (Loire) Rivers and then on to what is known as Brittany, to what became the city of Brest. From there they traveled by military transport to Britain. In Britain they traveled to Glastonbury where Jesus had established a home for he and his mother, Mary, some years before in that Celtic-Druid region.... Joseph built the first physical 'Christian' church in Glastonbury.... Hence, although Christianity was eventually confessed throughout the Empire, the region that proclaimed it as their religion first was Roman Britain....

".... Among the first converts of Britain was the royal house of Siluria, including the king of Siluria, Caradoc. Also converted were his daughter Gladys, his father Bran, and his brother (or brother-in-law) Aviragus who became king.... In 1086 King William the Conqueror had all the previous historic records accumulated into several volumes called the *Doomsday Book*.... 'King Aviragus is recorded as having granted to Roman Senator Joseph of Arimathea and his followers, 12 hides of land or approximately 1900 acres, tax free, in Yniswitrin, afterwards called the Isle of Avalon. This notable act of the King gave the recipients many British concessions, including the right of citizenship with its privileges of freedom to pass unmolested from one district to another in time of war...both Joseph of Arimathea and Mary the mother of Jesus (according to local tradition) are buried in the church courtyard of Glastonbury.... our most honored and reverend King Arthur has traced his lineage directly to the daughter of Joseph of Arimathea, Anna, the cousin of Mary the mother of Jesus.'

".... Paul was not converted into Christianity until about AD 37 or 38, shortly before the first Christian church in Britain was founded by Senator Joseph in Glastonbury. It is the letters that Paul wrote between AD 55 and 69 that establishes the fundamentals of today's Christian doctrine.... the remarkable letter that Paul wrote to the church in Rome contains the full essence of Christianity, but to whom was Paul writing when he wrote this letter around AD 59 and what was the occasion in which he wrote the letter?

"...Most historians agree that the letter to the Romans was written either from Paul's prison cell in Corinth or from Corinth just before he was imprisoned. The recipients of the letter were the 2,300 Christians living in Rome. For the most part these were Roman Christians, not Jews or Jewish converts. Claudius had expelled all of the Jews from Rome almost a decade before the time the letter was written (Acts 18:2), so most of the Christians in Rome were Romans or other non-Jews with no background whatsoever in Judaism.

"The occasion for the writing of the letter was that because of his imprisonment, Paul was unable to come to Rome in person to set things right doctrinally with the Roman Christians, so he sent this letter of compassion and discipline to the Romans by way of Phebe. She was the sister of a Roman Ambassadorial representative, Zephyrinus, a proconsul, and a member of the church in Cenchreae, but while in Rome both Phebe and Zephyrinus kept their Christianity secret. Paul did not expect to stay in prison long because he felt the need to go to Spain. The letter also served as his pronouncement that he would come to Rome on his way to Spain....

".... In the sixth year of Nero's reign, AD 59, something snapped inside of Nero," Boyd continued. "This man who had for five years ruled so admirably now made an abrupt about-face. By his seventh year, Nero had bankrupted the Roman central bank with his lavish lifestyle and building projects. In a six-month period, he raised taxes throughout the Empire 16 times, and for the first time ever in the history of the Empire, Roman citizens were taxed. By the end of his seventh year as emperor, Rome's citizens, except the nobility, the military hierarchy, and members of the Senate, were paying 60 percent of their earnings to the Roman treasury in taxes and non-Roman residents were paying upwards to 75 percent in taxes. During that seventh year, inflation grew in Rome from just under two percent to well over 300 percent....

"Apolodius, the leader of the 2,300 Roman Christians, began to stir up discontent over the forced payment of tribute money or taxes (Romans 13:6-8) to Nero. Procluius, a one-time Jew who had denounced Judaism and had converted to Christianity, rebelled against Apolodius' authority and demanded submission to Nero's order. A major rift developed between the two leaders and a seemingly non-repairable split developed in the Roman Christian community.

"Hearing of the unrest, Nero, using as an excuse that he wanted to squelch a rebellion before it began, had all of the leaders of the Christian sect arrested throughout Italy, Macedonia, and Greece, including Procluius and Apolodius who were imprisoned in Rome, and Paul who was arrested and imprisoned in Corinth.

"About a year and a half after the leaders' imprisonment, Nero had the middle city of Rome burned. To shift suspicion from himself, he blamed the Christians for burning Rome. What followed was the first, and according to some historians, the most ruthless, of the many Christian persecutions at the hands of Roman authorities.

"At first, the persecution was restricted to Christians who were slaves. But within two years the persecution had expanded to include all non-Roman Christians. One year later, it had expanded to include Roman citizen Christians as well. During the persecution, it is estimated that 1,700 Christians in the city of Rome and another 3,000 throughout Italy were victimized.

"Shortly after the terror was expanded to include Christians who were Roman citizens, Paul wrote his letter to the Romans. As stated earlier, Phebe, the sister of Zephyrinus, the Roman proconsul, carried the letter to Rome.

"About a year after Procluius and Apolodius were arrested, Zephyrinus arranged for the release from prison Procluius, who served as a tutor to Zephyrinus' children. However, Apolodius remained in prison. Therefore, with Apolodius still in prison, Procluius became the sole, unchallenged leader of the Christians in Rome.

"Many atrocities were associated with the persecution by Nero," Boyd continued, "Most were in violation of the Law of Moses. Procluius began to teach the surviving Christians that the blood of Jesus was mandatory for salvation from hell and damnation, but that adhering to and obeying the Law of Moses was necessary in order to guarantee a resurrection and a place in heaven. If people accepted Jesus as Savior they would not go to hell when they died, but if they had not kept the Law of Moses, then they would forever remain asleep in the grave those people would never be resurrected and allowed to go to heaven.

"...He further taught that God always responded to prayers that were prayed in the Hebrew language since Hebrew was the language of God. He responded to non-Hebrew prayers only after Hebrew prayers had been answered, which could take months or even years to complete. He also taught adherence to the old law of Augustus which said that if a woman's husband died, she could never marry again or else she would be considered an adulteress and claimed that God had also adopted that position. In addition he taught that both men and women had to submit to circumcision, along with keeping the Law of Moses, in order to be assured of a resurrection.

"...His primary emphasis was that it is better to commit suicide than to submit to the persecution of Nero, which was contrary to the Law of Moses. He went on to say that even if the atrocities are forced upon them or they are forced to participate, they would be judged guilty before God and would not receive a resurrection; so they must commit suicide in order to be guaranteed a resurrection and a heavenly reward.

"Among other things, the atrocities that the Christians were forced to endure, yet were contrary to the Law of Moses, were rape, homosexuality, bestiality, eating the flesh of boiled babies, drinking blood, eating internal as well as sexual organs of animals, and all kinds of forced sexual perversions.

"Procluius further said that if the Christians submitted to these, even though they were forced to do so and even though they faced death because of them, then not only would they not have a resurrection but because those things were contrary to the Law of Moses, but also the persecution would continue and would even intensify, because God would use Nero, as He used Nebuchadnezzar and Sennacherib of old, to purge and to punish all those who break His Laws as given to Moses.

"This teaching caused an eruption of suicides within the Christian community and caused an even greater rift and polarization among the Roman Christians than had the tax issue. The Christians were so busy fighting each other that they had no strength to fight off the spiritual attacks of evil.

"...When Paul heard about what was happening, he became furious and wrote a stinging letter of rebuke (Romans 2:1) to Procluius and within the same letter comforted the embattled Roman church.

"In the letter, Paul said that even in the midst of evil, suffering, and persecution, good will overcome evil. Christ is the common denominator that holds all Christians together. He is the common strand that runs through each Christian, so look to him and only him for hope and assurance. Even as the forces of evil are waging an all-out-war to prevent the Gospel from being spread, Christ will have the ultimate victory.

"...As he felt the unction [so he said as justification for his actions] to do so in AD 370, St. Gregory of Nyssa removed all references to Procluius by name from the letter to the Romans written by Paul. In place of the name of Procluius, so that his name would never be remembered, St. Gregory inserted words like *O man* or *that Jew*....

"...Paul ended the letter by telling them who precisely they should greet on his behalf. 'Greet Andronicus and Junias my relatives, and my fellow captives, who are well known among the apostles, and were in Christ prior to me' (Romans 16:7). Paul had relatives living in Rome who had became Christians before he had been converted. Most historians place Paul's conversion about AD 37 or 38. This means that his relatives, living in Rome at the time of his writing the letter to the Roman Christians, were among the earliest converts, and Paul said that they were well known to the original apostles. Who converted them?

"*'Greet Rufus, the chosen one in the Lord, and his mother and mine'* (Romans 16:13). In the Greek it would read *kai ten metera aytoy kai emoy*, which means *'and the mother of him and of me.'* Paul's own mother and Rufus, his brother or half-brother, were living in Rome at the time of his writing. Rufus was called *'the chosen one'* by Paul and appears to be a man of some significance in the early years of the church...

"...Some of the first converts made by Joseph of Arimathea were the royal household of Caradoc and Aviragus, Kings of Siluria...among the converts were Caradoc's daughter Gladys, and Bran their father. Bran was the son of King Lear, the character figure of one of Shakespeare's famous works.

"Caradoc was the grandson of the Silurian King Lear. Caradoc was an absolute terror to the Roman forces that invaded Britain from AD 40 to 43. In 40 battles the Romans never defeated Caradoc, he was always victorious; he was betrayed and was brought to Rome in chains. In AD 51 he was brought before the Roman Senate. In a speech before the Senate, Caradoc was so impressive that the Senate pleaded with Claudius to spare his life.

Claudius reprieved Caradoc and his family, but required that they remain in Rome for seven years. Caradoc and his family were paroled to a personal friend of Claudius by the name of Aristobulus. They remained in Aristobulus' palace as houseguests the entire seven years. When Paul wrote his letter to the Roman Christians, the seven-year parole period of Caradoc and his family was nearing an end. Paul had made sure that the letter arrived in Rome before the British king was freed and was allowed to return home.

"...Aristobulus' name means *'best counselor.'* He was the younger brother of Herod Agrippa, the same Herod that was appointed King over the area that became known as Palestine, by Caligula in AD 41. Aristobulus or Eubulus (in Greek) is mentioned in II Timothy 4:21 and Romans 16:10. He was the father of the apostle Simon Peter's wife, Peter's father-in-law. It was his wife that Jesus healed of the plague as recorded in Luke 4:38-39. Aristobulus was one of the 70 that were sent out by Jesus and he was in Jerusalem on Pentecost when the church was founded and when Peter preached his first sermon. Aristobulus could have been the first Gentile after Peter's sermon to openingly espouse the new Christianity.

"...The household of Aristobulus was the household in which Christianity had its first foothold in Rome. The members of Aristobulus' family was all Christian converts, and was well-known by both Caligula and Claudius. Aristobulus was both a good friend and a wise advisor to both Caesars....

"Joseph of Arimathea had converted the Silurian king's family to Christianity some years earlier," Boyd continued with his amazing chronology. "Caradoc's daughter, Gladys, was among the first British converts. She soon became engaged in Regnam to a young Roman Praetor named Rufus Pudens. She was responsible for the conversion of Rufus Pudens. They were married in Rome. Rufus, who became the husband of Gladys, was the younger brother or half-brother of the apostle Paul. Paul was the brother-in-law of Gladys, the Silurian princess. As such, he was well known to the Silurians.

"In Rome, because of Claudius Caesar's close relationship with the family, Gladys was adopted by Claudius. He changed her name to Claudia. II Timothy 4:21 records Paul's forwarding of greetings sent by her, along with Pudens and Linus and all the brothers.

"...Caradoc had sons: Selinus succeeded his father on the Silurian throne; Simon, called Lane or Linus, was consecrated the first Bishop of Rome by Paul around the time of the writing of the second letter to Timothy by Paul. Linus and Paul were both staying with Pudens and Claudia when Paul wrote the letter.

".... Claudius Caesar adopted Gladys. Paul was her brother-in-law. Paul and Claudius were well acquainted with each other. Claudia remained in Rome as the wife of Rufus after her father and brothers had returned to their homes in Britain.

"From the marriage of Rufus and Claudia came children: Timithus, Novacus, Podenciana, and Proxcedus. They were all later sainted by the Roman Catholic Church. Hermes became the pastor of the church in Rufus' house. Bran, Caradoc's father, was responsible for introducing velum to Britain and was responsible for taking some of the first copies of the early Christian writings back to Britain, when he returned."

Dr. Emerson again paused to make some personal notes. He then skipped further into Boyd's document and commented on an assumption Boyd had made (based on information originally written by C.S. Sonnini) that a portion of the book of Acts had either been lost or was purposely eliminated. As he commented on this assumption by Boyd, he made a personal observation.

"Some years ago," Dr. Emerson inserted his personal note, "I was privileged to read a portion of the Sonnini document (C.S. Sonini's *Sonnini's Travels in Turkey and Greece*) myself. After reading it, I too was amazed at the possibility that a portion of the Acts of the Apostles had perhaps been purposely altered to dislodge from history Paul's trip to Britain...Sonnini's document seems to me (Dr. Emerson) to be an accurate record as he has reported to have discovered it during his investigation in the ancient city of Constantinople.

"Allow me (Dr. Emerson) to quote the presumed missing Acts 29th chapter, the final chapter of the Acts of the Apostles, by beginning my quote with the familiar Acts 28:28 and then going directly into the 29th chapter. Acts 28: 29-31, as Sonnini speculated, was probably added (in my [Dr. Emerson's] opinion), by Emperor Phocas of Rome in AD 610, after he had the 29th chapter stricken from the permanent record of the Acts.

> *'Be it known therefore unto you, that the salvation of God is sent unto the Gentiles, and that they will hear it. And Paul, full of the blessings of Christ,*

and abounding in the spirit, departed out of Rome, determining to go into Spain, for he had a long time proposed to journey thitherward, and was minded also to go from thence to Britain. For he had heard in Phoenicia that certain of the Jews, about the time of the Assyrian captivity, had escaped by sea to the Isles afar as spoken of by the prophet Ezdra and called by the Romans, Britain. And the Lord commanded the Gospel far hence to all of the Gentiles and to the lost sheep of Israel. And no man hindered Paul; for he testified boldly of Jesus before the tribunes and among the people; and took with him certain brethren which abode with him in Rome, and they took ship at the harbor of Ostrium and having winds fair, were brought safely to Spain. And much people were gathered together from the towns and villages and the hills country, for they had heard of the conversion of the apostle, and the many miracles that were wrought at the hands of the apostles. And Paul preached mightily in Spain, and great multitudes believed and were converted, for they perceived he was an apostle of Jesus sent from God. And they departed out of Spain, and Paul and his company finding a ship in Amorica sailing into Britain, they were therein, and passed along the south coast, they reached a port called Raphinus. (Amorica was on the Western coast of what is now Bretagne, France. Raphinus was the Roman name for Sandwich-in-Kent, north of Dover and east of London.) Now when it was voiced abroad that the Apostle had landed on their coast, great multitudes met him, and they treated him with honor, and he abound and preached Christ unto them.... And Paul abode in his lodging three months in Raphinus confirming in the faith and preaching Christ continually.... And after these things Paul and his brethren departed Raphinus and sailed to Atium (modern day Boulogue) in Gaul.... And they went forth and came to Illyricum and strengthened Titus and the church in Dyrrhachium (present day Durres, Albania) *intending to go by Macedonia into Asia, and grace was found in all the churches, and they prospered and had peace. Amen!'*

" *With so enormous a congregation of reputable witnesses, dare I not accept as fact the document as I (Dr. Emerson) read it?*"

With that statement Dr. Emerson concluded that portion of his essay. The remaining three pages were nothing more than personal commentaries in which he attempted to lessen the shock factor, which he obviously knew would accompany any attempt to seriously dissect his essay, especially the latter portion.

As I concluded the essay, I sat for a while in total amazement. Although in my research I had found numerous entries regarding Joseph of Arimathea's connection to Glastonbury, never in my wildest imagination would I have thought that—if Boyd's facts were true—Peter and Paul had such a direct connection to not only the church in Rome, but to the royal court of Rome itself.

It would take a lifetime to explain in writing the history of the spread of Christianity and influence that Christianity played in shaping the post-resurrection history of the world, so I have chosen instead to conclude by quoting Pliny the Younger's *Epistles* (Number 10:96) written in about AD 115 or 117.

While governor of Bithynia and Pontus, in a letter to Emperor Trajan in which he sought advice about the treatment he (Pliny the Younger) should pursue with the Christians in his province, Pliny wrote:

> "...In the meantime, respecting those who were referred to me as Christians, I have followed this course. I have asked them whether they are Christian: if they confessed it, a second and third time I asked them threatening torture; if they persevered ordered them to be led away to the penalty. For I had no question, whatever that might be which they professed, that this fixed determination and inflexible obstinacy ought to be punished. Others there were of like unreasonableness, which, because they were Roman citizens, I made a note of to be remanded to the city. Straightway, when this policy had been inaugurated, the crime extended itself, as is often the case and several varieties arose. An anonymous list containing the names of many was published. Those who denied that they were, or had been, Christians, I thought ought to be dismissed, when in my presence they invoked the gods and to your statue, which for this purpose I had ordered to be produced together with the images of the deities, did homage with incense and wine, and moreover renounced Christ...a course to which, it is averred, those who are in verity Christians and soon denied it, indeed had been, but had ceased to be, some three years ago, some several years ago, and an occasional one even twenty years since. These all also worshipped both your statue and the images of the gods, and renounced Christ. They affirmed also that the sum of their guilt, or error, was to assemble on a fixed day before daybreak and sing in responses a song to Christ as to a god, and to bind themselves with an oath not to enter into wickedness, or commit thefts, robberies, or adulteries, or falsify their word, or repudiate trusts committed to them: when these things were ended, it was their custom to depart, and, on coming together again, to take food, men and women together, and yet innocently; which thing they had ceased to do after my edict by which, according to your injunctions, I had forbidden secret societies. Wherefore the more necessary I deemed it to seek, even by torture, from two maidens, who were called deaconesses, what was true. I found nothing else than an immoderate, vicious superstition. And so, the investigation concluded, I have hastened to consult you."

This letter as much as any other documentation from that period shows that not only was Christianity here to stay, but its numbers and influence were growing go rapidly in the Empire that it was safe to say that Rome's traditional and historical religions' days were numbered and the political power of the once mighty Roman Empire was rapidly and incessantly losing ground to the followers of Christ.

XXIII

EPILOGUE

MY SEARCH CONTINUES

I have been searching for fragments of information and documentation that would confirm the authenticity of the Gospel accounts of the life of Jesus for more than 33 years. For 15 of those years, while I still continued to research, I assembled my notes and the documentation that I had collected into manuscript form in anticipation of perhaps sometime in the future publishing my findings. Now, four 4-drawer file cabinets and four floor-to-ceiling bookshelves full of notes and compiled information later, I felt that it was time to stop researching long enough to compile it all into a book.

But even as I conclude this autobiographical account I have come to the realization that my work has just begun. Even as comprehensive as this book has become, it is obvious that I have not even scratched the surface of the life of Jesus. In fact, I look upon this book as somewhat of an outline of the events of the life of Jesus. In each division of the outline is so much information that needs to be investigated that it would take five lifetimes to cover just the major points. So, needless to say, once the final period has been placed in this book, my research efforts will resume.

All that has actually been covered in this volume is the chronological order of the life of Jesus, which included some interpretive notes that explained a particular subject within a specific setting. There is little mention of: (1) the character of Joseph and Mary, (2) Jesus' relationship with his parents and siblings, (3) Jesus' personality and his character, (4) his mission to man and how he intended to fulfill that mission, (5) the historical relationship and social implications of his parables, teachings, and sermons, (6) the theological and doctrinal implications of his parables, lessons, and sermons, (7) how each affected his followers, (8) Jesus' relationship with the common non-Roman resident in the region, (9) Jesus' relationship with the Roman residents of the region, (10) Jesus' relationship with Roman authority, (11) Jesus' kingdom messages, (12) his miracles, (13) his authority and power, (14) his battle with the forces of evil, and (15) inexhaustible other subjects to which an entire book could be devoted to each.

Since in my years of research I have discovered authenticating documentation confirming the truth of the Gospel records in less than one-tenth of one-tenth of a percent of all that the life of Jesus would include, I have no choice but to devote the rest of my life in pursuit of my quest to *"know him, and the power of his resurrection"* (Philippians 3:10).

APPENDIX: JEWISH CALENDAR
JEWISH CALENDAR

JEWISH MONTH SEASON *CELEBRATION* OR *FEAST*	CORRESPONDING MONTH	
1st—Abib or Nisan and flax harvest *Passover*; *Unleavened Bread; First Fruits*	March-April (latter rain)	barley
2nd—Ziv (Iyyar)	April-May	barley
3rd—Sivan	May-June	wheat
Pentecost		
4th—Tammuz (very dry)	June-July	vine tending
5th—Ab	July-August	ripening olives, figs, grapes
6th—Elul	August-September	processing figs, grapes
7th—Ethanim (Tishri) *Trumpets, Atonement,* (early rains) **Tabernacles**	September-October	plowing
8th—Bul (Marcheshvan)	October-November	sowing wheat and barley
9th—Kislev	November-December	winter rain; snow
Hanukkah (Dedication)		
10th—Tebeth	December-January	winter
11th—Shebat	January-February	winter
12th—Adar	February-March	almond trees bloom;

Purim citrus harvest

13th—Adar Sheni—Extra month added every three years so lunar time will correspond with solar time.

Dr. Ron Charles

APPENDIX: IDENTIFICATIONS and DEFINITIONS

All of these have been either mentioned or alluded to in the book

ABODAH ZARAH—One of the tractates of the fourth division of the Jewish Mishnah and Talmud.

ABOTH or PIRKE ABOTH—A collection of ethical maxims. One of the tractates of the fourth division of the Jewish Mishnah.

ACELDAMA—The name of the Potter's Field purchased by the "blood money" that was returned to the priests by Judas.

ACTS OF THE APOSTLES—A book in the New Testament traditionally written by Luke. Its focus is the founding of the Church and the ministry career of the Apostle Paul.

AGRICOLA—Roman governor of Roman Britain who died in AD 93. He was the father-in-law of the Latin historian Tacitus. He entered into the official records of Rome the establishing of Glastonbury and the first Christian church in Britain by Roman Senator Joseph of Arimathea.

ALLELUIA—From the Hebrew *hallelujah* meaning, "Praise the Lord."

ANDREW—A fisherman from Bethsaida. He introduced his brother, Simon Peter, to Jesus. He was originally a disciple of John the Baptist but became an apostle of Jesus.

ANNA—An aged prophetess, widowed for 84 years after only 7 years of marriage. When Jesus was presented at the Temple, she spread the word throughout Jerusalem that she had seen the Messiah.

ANNAS—The former Jewish High Priest to whom Jesus was brought for questioning before being sent to Caiaphas, Annas' son-in-law.

APOCALYPSE—From the Greek word meaning *revelation*. It is a prophetic description of the end of the world.

APOCRYPHA (of the New Testament)—From the Greek word meaning *hidden away*. Early Christian and quasi-Christian writing that resembled New Testament writings but where not admitted as New Testament Canon.

APOSTLES—Those 12 whom Jesus selected from the ranks of his many disciples to be his chief disciples and whom he anointed and sent out to minister on his behalf.

The Search

APPEARANCES OF THE RISEN JESUS—This includes all of Jesus' appearances after he was resurrected from the dead. He appeared to the women at the tomb, to two in the country, two on the road to Emmaus, to the 11 disciples on numerous occasions, to 500 on two different occasions, and to James his brother.

ARAMAIC—A Semitic language, which in Jesus' time was the common speech of the Jewish residents of the state of Judea in the province of Judaea.

ARISTOTLE—Greek philosopher (384-322 BC) and tutor to Alexander the Great.

ASCENSION—The doctrine that after Jesus' resurrection from the dead, he was taken up into heaven bodily.

ASSUMPTION OF THE VIRGIN MARY—The dogma that at the end of Mary's life, she was taken up to heaven bodily. It became a doctrine of the Catholic Church in 1950 by papal mandate by Pope Pius XII.

ATONEMENT—The doctrine that Jesus died to atone for the sins of all humankind.

AUGUSTUS—Augustus Gaius Octavius (36 BC-AD 14). He was emperor of the Roman Empire at the time of the birth of Jesus. He has been acknowledged by many historians as the best and wisest of all Roman Emperors.

BARA MEZIA—One of the tractates of the fourth division of the Jewish Mishnah and Talmud.

BARABBAS—A Jewish revolutionary who was in prison at the time that Jesus was tried and convicted. The people choose to release Barabbas instead of Jesus.

BARTHOLOMEW—One of the 12 that Jesus chose out of the ranks of his disciples to be an apostle. He was likely the nathanael (John 1:47-51) that Jesus called to be a disciple.

BAR-TIMAEUS—The son of Timaeus. He was healed of blindness by Jesus in Jericho during the last year of Jesus' ministry.

BATH-SHEBA—The wife of Uriah with whom King David committed adultery. After Uriah's death, she became David's wife and birthed Solomon.

BEATITUDES—The nine blessings of Jesus, recorded in Matthew's Gospel, presented at the beginning of the Sermon on the Mount.

BEEL-ZEBUB—"The Lord of the flies." The god of the Philistine city of Ekron. The Pharisees claimed that Beel-zebub was the prince of devils.

BERAKOTH—The first tractate of the first division of the Jewish Mishnah and Talmud.

BETHANY—A village located on the east side of the Mount of Olives. It was a Greco-Roman village inhabited by Jews of Egyptian lineage. It was the home of Lazarus, Mary, and Martha.

BETHESDA—A twin pool in Jerusalem near the sheep market that contained five porches. It was there that Jesus healed a crippled man on the Sabbath.

BETHLEHEM—A small town about five miles south of Jerusalem. David was traditionally born in Bethlehem, as was Joseph, the earthly father of Jesus. It was also the birthplace of Jesus.

BETHSAIDA—A fishing village located near the north shore of the Lake of Gennesaret (Sea of Galilee). It was the probable home of Peter, Andrew, and Philip.

CAESAR—A title of the Emperors of Rome derived from Caius Julius Caesar who died in 44 BC.

CAIAPHAS—Joseph Caiaphas was Jewish High Priest AD 18-37. He was the son-in-law of former High Priest, Annas. Caiaphas resided over the Sanhedrin when Jesus was brought to trail. After the resurrection of Christ, Caiaphas continued to persecute the church until he was relieved of his position in AD 37 by order of Tiberius. This was one of the last actions taken by Tiberias before he died.

CALVARY—Called the place of death, the place of bones, and the place of the skull. In Hebrew the name was Golgotha. The name was a descriptive adjective that identified the valley of Gehenna, the garbage dump of Jerusalem (located south of the city), and in particular identified the part of Gehenna where offenders whose crime was against Rome were put to death.

CALVINIST—A person who accepts the theological viewpoints and dogmas expounded by John Calvin (1509-1564). The primary focal point of Calvin's teaching was predestination. Some are predestined to everlasting life and others are predestined for damnation.

CANA—A village in the Galilee, northeast of Nazareth. At a wedding celebration held here, Jesus turned water into wine. This was his first recorded miracle.

CANAAN—Originally the designation for Phoenicia but subsequently used to describe the whole of what came to be called Palestine.

CHARLEMAGNE—King of the Franks (742-814). He was the first Emperor of the Holy Roman Empire. He is acknowledged to be the first of the royal saints because he was canonized by the antipope Paschal III (1164-1168) to placate Frederick Barbarossa.

CIRCUMCISION OF JESUS—Following the Law of Moses, Jesus was circumcised at the end of the eighth day after his birth (Luke 2:21).

COCK—A male peacock. Called the fowl of conscience. It crowed twice while Peter was denying Jesus.

CONSTANTINE the GREAT—Roman Emperor who died in 337. He issued the *Edict of Milan*, which gave religious tolerance to Christianity. He rebuilt the city of Byzantium and renamed it Constantinople. He then moved his capital from Rome to Constantinople. He, along with his mother Helena, did much to further the acceptance of and the influential spread of Christianity. He was baptized a Christian shortly before his death.

COUNCIL OF TRENT—The general council of the Roman Catholic Church, held at Trent in the Austrian Tyrol, 1545-1563. At this council many doctrines of the Catholic Church were established. Among these were the insistence on the Seven Sacraments, the Real Presence and Transubstantiation, Purgatory, and the invocation of the saints and the veneration of their relics and images.

DANIEL—A 6th century BC Jew who was a Chaldean magus and rose to prominence in both the court of Babylon and Persia. He was *the* most respected magus of the ancient world. After his death, he was deified by most ancient societies including Persia and Media. He prophesied the coming of the Messianic world leader. It was his prophecy that convinced the magi who came to Judea in search of the King of the Jews, to continue their search until the new king was found. An Old Testament book written about 166 BC tells of some of his experiences and prophecies.

DAVID—Second king of the united nation of Israel (1085-1015 BC). He ruled for 40 years. He was an ancestor of Jesus. He was considered the greatest of Israel's kings.

DECAPOLIS—A league of 10 Greek cities in Syria. Although far removed from the region, Damascus served as their capital. In Roman times Damascus was capital in name only—most Roman administration for the Decapolis was located in Scythopolis. A major portion of the Decapolis was under the direct Roman military control.

DEMON—One evil spirit designation. Many theologians feel that these evil spirits are either the disembodied souls of those who joined in Lucifer's original rebellion, of those who died during Noah's flood, or are the fallen angels who joined Lucifer's rebellion.

Dr. Ron Charles

DEUTERONOMY—The fifth and last book of the Pentateuch in the Old Testament. Jesus used quotes from Deuteronomy to combat the tempter during his wilderness experience.

DEVIL—Another level of the evil spirit world. They serve as observers and direct demon activities.

DIASPORA—Jewish communities living outside of the area that came to be known as Palestine.

DIONYSIUS EXIGUUS—The 6th century Scythian monk who when he lived in Rome miscalculated the date of Jesus' birth.

ELIJAH—A Tishbite of Gilead, a 9th century BC Hebrew prophet who did not die of natural means. He was taken to heaven without dying. He was considered one of the greatest of the Hebrew prophets.

ELISHA—The successor to Elijah's prophetic ministry. He was considered another of the Hebrew's greatest prophets.

EMPERORS—Roman rulers of the Roman Empire. Augustus was the first Emperor, under whose rule Jesus was born. The second Emperor was Augustus' adopted son, Tiberius. Under his reign Jesus was crucified.

ERUBIN—One of the tractates of the second division of the Jewish Mishnah and Talmud.

EUSEBIUS—(AD 260-340) He was Bishop of Caesarea Maritima. He wrote *History of the Church*.

EXORCISM—An injunction addressed to evil spirits to force them to abandon a person they are possessing.

EZRA—A Babylonian Jew who in the4th or 5th century BC led a group of Jews back to Jerusalem. He re-established the Jewish religion in Jerusalem. He is featured in an Old Testament book that bears his name.

FRANCIS OF ASSISI—Founder of the Order of Friars Minor. He was born in Assisi in 1181. He ministered to the poor and to lepers.

FRANKINCENSE—A sweet smelling resin of the balsam tree, originating in Arabia. It was one of the gifts given to the child Jesus, by the magi.

GABRIEL—An archangel who carries out special assignments on behalf of God. He announced the birth of both John the Baptist (to Zacharias) and Jesus (to Mary).

He is also revered in Islam because he was said to be the one who dictated the Koran to Mohammed.

GALILEE—The northern region of the province of Syria. It lies north of the province of Judaea and predominately east of the Sea of Galilee and the Jordan River. Jesus and all but one (Judas) of his apostles were from the Galilee.

GEHENNA—A valley south of the city walls of Jerusalem. In Jesus' time it served as the garbage dump of Jerusalem. Both of the words, calvary and golgotha, were descriptive adjectives that identified this valley. It was used by Jesus as an allegory defining hell.

GATHSEMENE—A garden on the eastern slopes of the Mount of Olives in which an olive press was located. Here Jesus prayed before he was arrested. He was also arrested here.

GENTILES—From the Latin *gentes*, meaning races or nationalities. It is the same of the Hebrew *goyyim*. Non-Jews were classified by Jews as Gentiles.

GLASTONBURY—Called Avalon during the Middle Ages. On this plot of land, Joseph of Arimathea built the first Christian church in Britain.

GNOSTIC—A doctrine that taught that salvation was to be obtained through "knowledge" of the secrets of the universe. Gnostics authored many of the apocryphal writings. The period in which they had the largest following and greatest influence was the 1st through the 3rd centuries.

GOSPEL—In general, the "good news" of the life, ministry, and redemptive work of Christ; in particular the record of his work as written by the authors of the first four books of the New Testament, called "The Gospels."

GREGORY THE GREAT—He was pope from 590 to 604. He, more than any other pope, was responsible for the spread, through force of arms, of the "Mary, mother of God" dogma. As a result of his insistence that unless one accepts Mary as mother of God, then they cannot accept Jesus as Son of God, Mary became to be viewed as a pagan goddess by Arabs, an idea that they rejected. As a result of his non-compromising Mary, mother of God stand, the seeds for the formation of Islam were planted. He was considered one of the most influential popes in the history of the Catholic Church.

HASMONAEANS (MACCABEES)—The name of the Jewish family who descended from Haesmon. They led a successful Jewish revolt against the Seleucids in the 2nd century BC and established a dynasty that lasted until the rule of Herod the Great.

HERMIT—One who chose to live alone in a hermitage in order to devote himself to prayer, fasting, meditation, and spiritual consciousness.

HEROD—The family name of many rulers in the region that came to be known as Palestine. Herod the Great was king when Jesus was born. Herod Antipas was Tetrarch of the Galilee when Jesus was crucified.

HERODIANS—Members and, to a lesser extent, political supporters of the House of Herod. Their loyalty was to Caesar and to Caesar alone. They were selected to represent Tiberius' The Theophus Commission of Ambassadors in Syria. Some respected Jesus while others displayed hostility to him.

HERODIAS—She was the daughter of Herod Aristobulus, son of Herod the Great and Mariamne. She was first married to Herod Philip, and then to Herod Antipas. She instructed her daughter, Salome, to demand from Antipas the head of John the Baptist as a reward for dancing for him.

HERODOTUS—A 5th century BC Greek historian called "The father of history."

HOLY GHOST (SPIRIT)—God the Holy Ghost (Spirit); the third person of the Trinity, along with God the Father and God the Son—coequal and coeternal but distinct. Also called the Holy Paraclete or Comforter.

HOSANNA—From the Hebrew *hoshi'a na,* meaning, "save us" or "save me, please." It is a beseechment for salvation or a lamentation pleading for Messiah to come and to save and deliver. The Great Hosanna was during the Jewish Feast of Tabernacles when palm branches and myrtle are waved and the people lament and plead for deliverance by the Messiah.

IGNATIUS OF ANTIOCH—Second or third bishop of Antioch said to be a disciple of either John the Evangelist, Peter, or Paul. He was martyred in the Coliseum of Rome in 107.

INQUISITION—An ecclesiastical tribunal set up in 1229 by Pope Gregory IX to enquire into cases of heresy and to prevent its spread. Pope Innocent IV sanctioned torture to procure evidence in 1252. The notorious Spanish Inquisition began in 1479. It lasted until 1808 when Joseph Bonaparte suppressed it. It was briefly revived under Ferdinand VII from 1808-1814.

INRI—The initial letters of Ieusus Nazarenus Rex Judaeorum, "Jesus of Nazareth, King of the Jews," the Latin phrase, together with a translation in Hebrew and Greek, which Pilate had inscribed on the titulus and secured above his head to the cross of Christ (John 19:19).

IRENAEUS—Lived 130 (40) – 200. He was the Bishop of Lugdunum (modern Lyon, France). He was the first one to accept Matthew, Mark, and Luke as the only true Gospels. All other records of the life of Jesus he rejected. John Chrysostom said in 380 that the spirit of Irenaeus had appeared to him in a dream saying that John's Gospel should be added to the other three as the only true Gospels and that the authors of the four Gospels were those whose names the Gospel bore. So, from the time of John Chrysostom it became historical fact that Matthew the tax collected was the author of the Gospel of Matthew; John Mark, the companion of Paul, was the author of the Gospel of Mark; Luke the physician and companion of Paul, was the author of the Gospel of Luke; and John the evangelist, the disciple of Jesus, and cousin of Jesus, was the author of the Gospel of John. The 1215 Council of Bishops held in Toledo, Spain, confirmed and upheld John Chrysostom's declaration as truth and fact. From that time forward, by Council proclamation, these four were the true unchallenged authors of the four Gospels.

ISAIAH—One of the greatest of the Hebrew Old Testament prophets. He lived in Judah in the latter part of the 8th century BC. He prophesied of the virgin birth of Jesus.

ISHMAEL—The son of Abraham and Hagar. His wife was an Egyptian and he was the ancestor of the Arabic tribes.

JACOB'S LADDER—Jacob, the son of Isaac, had a dream at a place called Luz. In the dream he saw a ladder or a stair reaching from heaven to earth and saw angels ascending and descending on the ladder to and from heaven. Jacob named the place Bethel. In Jesus' day, it was taught by the schools for priests that if a nathanael, one who was studying to be a priest, slept under a fig tree in Bethel and had a dream of Jacob's ladder, then that nathanael would become the High Priest who would identify and introduce the Messiah to the Jewish people.

JAMES THE APOSTLE (THE GREAT)—A disciple of Jesus who was selected by Jesus to be an apostle. He was the brother of John. Jesus called then "the sons of thunder." They were Jesus' cousins. James was killed in 44 AD by order of Herod Agrippa I.

JAMES THE BROTHER OF THE LORD—He has been called James the less, James the younger, and James the twin. He was the brother of Jesus. He may or may not have been a follower of Jesus before Jesus' death and resurrection, but after his dearth and resurrection, James became the leader of the Christian sect. He was considered up until the Council of Bishops to be the greatest of the early church leaders. He was martyred in 62 AD. He is unchallenged as the author of the Epistle of James. Some theologians claim that he also authored the Gospel of Mark, the Epistle to the Hebrews, and a last ¾ portion of The Revelation.

JEREMIAH—Old Testament Jewish prophet (650-585 BC). He warned Judah about their destruction at the hands of Nebuchadnezzar. He was spared by the Babylonian king and was allowed to stay in Jerusalem. He later was forced to flee to Egypt where he died. His tomb is located in the Coptic region of the city of Cairo.

JERICHO—An ancient Canaanite city. One of the oldest cities in the world. In Roman times it was a very wealthy city where only the extremely rich lived. There Jesus confronted Zacchaeus the tax assessor, two blind men, and Bar-Timaeus.

JERUSALEM—The ancient and holy city sacred to three religions: Jewish, Christian, and Islam. It's original name, which dates back to before the days of Abraham, was Salem. David conquered it and made it his capital. It has been destroyed and rebuilt numerous times. Jesus was crucified outside of the city walls of Jerusalem, in Gehenna. Mohammad was reputed to have been taken to heaven from Jerusalem.

JOHN THE APOSTLE—A disciple of Jesus who was chosen to be one of his 12 apostles. Jesus called him and his brother, James, "the sons of thunder." He and James were cousins of Jesus. He was called 'John the Evangelist' by some early church writers and 'John the beloved' by others. At the Council of Bishops in 1215 it was declared that John had lived to be near 100 years old, that he had been exiled to a Roman penal colony located on the island of Patmos, were he died of natural causes, and that he wrote the Gospel of John, the Epistles of John, and the Revelation.

JOHN CHRYSOSTOM—Born at Antioch in 347, he became one of the Four Greek Doctors of the Church. He became Bishop of Constantinople in 397. Throughout his life his passion was ministering to the poor. He was one of, if not *the* most, influential bishop in the first 500 years of Christianity.

JOHN THE BAPTIST—He was the last of the Old Testament prophets and the forerunner of Christ. He baptized Jesus and proclaimed him to be the Lamb of God. He was imprisoned by order of Herod Antipas and later beheaded by his order. At least one and perhaps more of John's disciples became disciples of Jesus.

JOSEPH THE CARPENTER—Joseph was a descendant of the House of David. He was the husband of Mary, the mother of Jesus, and was Jesus' earthly father. Early church tradition says that he was a master stonemason. Later church tradition says that he was a wood carpenter. Early church tradition says that he died during the time of Jesus' ministry. Later church tradition says that he died when Jesus was a child.

JOSEPH OF ARIMATHEA—A respected member of the Jewish Sanhedrin, by Roman appointment. Provincial Senator representing Britain and the Imperial Minister of Mines for the Roman Empire under Augustus and Tiberius. He was the younger brother of Mary's (the mother of Jesus) father. Tradition says that he adopted Mary and her unborn child after the death of Mary's father and before her marriage to Joseph. Tradition says that he built the first Christian church in Britain.

JOSEPHUS—A Jewish historian (AD 37-95). He fought in the first Jewish revolt and was captured by the Romans. He was released and then commissioned by the Romans to write a history of the Jewish people. He authored the *Jewish War, Jewish Antiquities, Against Apion,* and *Life.*

JUDAEA—The Latin name of the central part of what became known as Palestine annexed by the Romans as a province under a perfect (procurator), which resided at Caesarea Maritima. By the 3rd century the area had become known as Syria Palaestina. The Roman province of Judaea was formed in AD 6. Before AD 6 the area that became the province of Judaea was called Judea. After AD 6 the Roman province of Judaea was divided into states. Judea became one of the states in the province of Judaea.

JUDEA (ROMAN)—Under Roman occupation the province of Judaea was divided into states. The state that included the city of Jerusalem and its immediate area was Judea. Most of the Jewish residents of the province of Judaea lived in the state of Judea.

JUDAEO-CHRISTIAN—Christians of Jewish origin. After the death and resurrection of Jesus, James, the brother of Jesus, led them. After the death of James, Peter led them.

JUDAS ISCARIOT—An archetypal traitor. Although the most recognized apostle by name, his notoriety comes from the fact that he betrayed Jesus for money and identified him with a kiss. He was the only one of Jesus' apostles who was not from the Galilee. Tradition says that he was a member of the Zealot revolutionaries. After his betrayal of Jesus, he hanged himself.

JULIAN THE APOSTATE—Roman Emperor AD 361-363. Under his rule the empire, which had converted to Christianity under Constantine, the Great, reverted back temporarily to paganism.

JUSTIN MARTYR—One of the greatest of the early Christian Apologists.

LAMB OF GOD—John the Baptist identified Jesus as the Lamb of God, traditionally because he was the first to recognize Jesus as the suffering servant.

LAST SUPPER—The final meal recorded in the Gospels that Jesus had with his disciples before his crucifixion. It was during this Last Supper that he instituted the Lord's Supper or the Eucharist.

LAW (THE TORAH)—In the Jewish religion, it signifies the Pentateuch and at times denotes the entire Hebrew Scriptures, including oral interpretations.

LAZARUS—A beggar who was the central focus of a parable spoken by Jesus. The parable is commonly called, "The rich man and Lazarus."

LAZARUS OF BETHANY—One of Jesus' best friends in the Jerusalem area. He was the brother of Mary and Martha. Jesus raised him from the dead.

LIVY—(59 BC-AD 17). A Latin historian who wrote a history of Rome in 142 books, of which only 35 have survived.

MAGI—The plural of the Latin magus, meaning "magician." They were ambassadors of their respective eastern empires who came to Judaea in search of the "new born King of the Jews." When they found Jesus, they gave him gifts of gold, frankincense and myrrh (The Gifts of Ramses).

MARY—The virgin mother of Jesus. She and her unborn son, Jesus, were adopted by her uncle, Joseph of Arimathea, before Jesus was born and before her marriage. Her husband was Joseph the carpenter. It is not known whether she believed that Jesus was the Messiah, although the scriptures do imply that she supported his ministry and believed that he was able to perform miracles and that he was a servant of God. She was present at the cross when Jesus was crucified and she was in the upper room on the day of Pentecost.

MARY MAGDALENE—She was a woman from Magdala out of whom Jesus cast seven demons. She supported Jesus' ministry materially and followed him throughout the Galilee and Judea. She was at the cross when Jesus was crucified and was the first person to which Jesus revealed himself after his resurrection.

MESSIAH—The anointed one. The deliverer. The son of David. The Christ. One of the two anointed personalities the Jews were expecting at the time of Jesus' birth. They were expecting a Messiah and a Messias.

MESSIAS—The anointed one. The sacrifice for sin. The suffering servant. Savior. Redeemer. The Son of God. One of the two anointed personalities the Jews were expecting when Jesus was born. They were not expecting Jesus to be both Messiah and Messias in one person. They were expecting two people: a Messiah and a Messias.

MIDRASH—A term applied to methods of biblical exposition and to Jewish writings using these methods.

MISHNAH—A collection of Jewish traditional precepts that forms one of the two main parts of the Talmud.

MOSES—One of, if not the, greatest figure of the Old Testament. He was the one who was given the Law by God and who in turn presented the Law to the Jews. He led the Israelites out of Egyptian slavery and led them to the borders of the Promised Land.

The Search

MOTHER OF GOD—A designation and title given to Mary the mother of Jesus, by papal and council proclamation.

NABATAEANS—People of Arabic descent that occupied the region east of the Jordan River.

NATHANAEL—A student who had been approved and was studying to become a priest. The most prominent nathanael in scripture was the one introduced to Jesus by Philip. This nathanael could have been Bartholomew.

NEBUCHADNESSAR—King of Babylon (605-562 BC) He destroyed Jerusalem and carried off most of the inhabitants to Babylon. Daniel, one of the Jews carried to Babylon, became the most prominent magi in Nebuchadnezzar's court.

NERO—Roman Emperor (AD 54-68) who was responsible for the first of many persecutions of Christians.

NICODEMUS—A Pharisee who was a member of the Sanhedrin. He came to Jesus at night to question him. Jesus told him that he must be born again. He defended Jesus before the Sanhedrin after Jesus' arrest.

NIDDAH—One of the tractates of the sixth division of the Jewish Mishnah and Babylonian Talmud.

ORIGEN—(AD 185-254). He was one of the most outspoken defenders of Christianity to the Greeks, especially in Alexandria.

PACHOMIUS—(AD 292-346) A disciple of Antony of Egypt, he founded the Nile community of monks at Tabennisi. He was the "father" of Egypt Christian hermit living.

PASSOVER—A Jewish feast celebrating the most momentous event in Jewish history, the Exodus. It commemorates the night when Jewish homes in Egypt were spared by the death angel. The traditional feast lasted 7 days.

PAUL THE APOSTLE—A Pharisee from Tarsus and an enemy of the Christian sect who was converted to Christianity. Partly through Paul's efforts, Christianity was spread to every corner of the Roman world. His writings more than any other became the foundation upon which present day Christian doctrine in built.

PETER—A fisherman from the Galilee who was in business with James, John, and their father, Zebedee. He became a disciple of Jesus after the miracle of the multitude of fish. He was the first to recognize Jesus as "The Christ, the Son of the Living God," or the Messiah and the Messias. He denied Jesus when Jesus was being tried. He repented and became one of the pillars of the early church.

PHARISEE—A Jewish religious sect that originated in the 2nd century BC. The Pharisees were largely responsible for the creation of synagogues. They were the main ones responsible for the introduction of oral interpretations into the Law, the Talmud. Jesus' rabboni training was likely in the sect of the Pharisees.

PHILIP THE APOSTLE—A Greek fisherman from the Galilee. He was the first disciple to be called by Jesus.

PHILO—(30 BC-AD 40). The outstanding Jewish philosopher/historian of the Dispersion. He was largely responsible for insisting that the Jewish religion be more Hellenized.

PONTIUS PILATE—He was the extremely ruthless Roman procurator of the province of Judaea during the time of Jesus' ministry (appointed in AD 26). He condemned Jesus to be crucified, even though his wife, Claudia Procula, granddaughter of Emperor Augustus, warned him not to have anything to do with Jesus.

POLYCARP—Bishop of Smyrna who was martyred in 155. He was said to have been converted by the Apostle John and became a disciple of John.

PRESTER JOHN (JOHN PRESBYTER)—A legendary (it is not known whether or not he actually ever existed) priest and king said to rule over a fabulously wealthy Christian kingdom somewhere in the east. Tales of his existence began to circulate about the 3RD century and continued up until the 17th century.

Q (standing for German Quelle, meaning "source")—The designation given to a possible source which the Gospels of Matthew and Luke have in common but do not share with the Gospel of Mark.

QUMRAN—A community of semi-monastic Jewish hermits residing in the region of the Dead Sea. These hermits are thought to be the authors of the Dead Sea Scrolls. They existed between about 140 BC until the first Jewish revolt against Rome in AD 66.

RABBI, RABBONI, RABBAN—Level designations of Jewish teachers based on years of educational experience and training, during the time of Jesus' life. These three different level designations were originally established about the year AD 2 and continued until just after the first Jewish rebellion in AD 70.

REBELLION (Jewish revolt in the Palestine area against Rome)—The first rebellion started in AD 66 under Nero and ended in AD 70 under Vespasian with the destruction of the Temple by Titus and the fall of Masada in AD 73. The second rebellion took place in AD 132-135 under Hadrian. He ruthlessly suppressed it and totally destroyed Jerusalem.

SADDUCEES—A conservative Jewish religious sect who were pro-Roman and centered around the Temple cult. They did not accept the oral interpretations, the Talmud, as authorities. They also did not believe in a resurrection, demons, or angels. Most of the Jewish Sanhedrin was made up of Sadducees and generally chief priests and High Priests were Sadducees. They were extremely powerful because of their working relationship with the Roman authorities. Although they were tolerant to the extreme, when their patients ran out, they were inexorable in their callousness. They ceased to exist after the AD 70 destruction of the Temple by Titus.

SALOME—The daughter of Herodias, the wife of Herod Antipas. Her dance on the celebration of Herod's birthday so pleased Herod that he offered her up to half of his kingdom as a reward. Having been prepared in advance by her mother for such a situation, she demanded the head of John the Baptist. Herod reluctantly honored her demand.

SANHEDRIN—from the Greek synedrion, meaning "council." It was the highest Jewish court at the time of Jesus' life and ministry. It existed until the AD 70 destruction of the Temple. Most of the members were pro-Roman Sadducees; although there was also representation by the Pharisees and at least one Roman-appointed representative. During the life and ministry of Jesus, Joseph of Arimathea was the Roman appointed representative. Their authority was recognized by Rome in the state of Judea only and their actions were limited to Judea. Therefore as long as Jesus was in the Galilee, the Decapolis, Judaea (except for the state of Judea) or Peraea, they could not touch him. But once he entered their jurisdiction, they could act, subject to the approval of the Roman authorities.

SCRIBES—Doctors of the Law (lawyers). These were Jewish preservers, expounders, and experts of the Law. Although most scribes were Pharisees, there were some Sadducee scribes.

SELEUCIDS—A dynasty of Greek monarchs founded by Seleucus, one of Alexander the Great's generals. There empire included the region that came to be called Palestine from 200 BC until the Maccabean revolt in 168-142 BC.

SEPTUAGINT—The earliest Greek translation of the Old Testament, made during the 3rd and 2nd centuries BC. This was the "Holy Scriptures" of Jesus' day.

SHABBAT—One of the tractates of the second division of the Jewish Mishnah and Talmud.

SIMON OF CYRENE—A man from Cyrene who was in Jerusalem during the Passover in which Jesus was crucified. When Jesus could not carry his cross member, Simon was made to carry the cross member to the place of crucifixion.

SIMON THE LEPER—It was at a dinner at Simon the leper's house in Bethany that Jesus was anointed one of two times during his last week before crucifixion.

SOTAH—One of the tractates of the third division of the Jewish Mishnah and Talmud.

SUETONIUS OF HIPPO REGIUS—(AD 69-132) The Latin biographer of the *Twelve Caesars.*

SYNAGOGUE—A meeting place for the Jewish community where they assemble to pray, read the scriptures, and worship. After the destruction of the Temple in AD 70, the synagogue became the central focus of Jewish places for worship.

TACITUS—(AD 55-117?) He was a Latin historian who mentioned the Jews and the ministry of Jesus.

TALMUD—The written down oral interpretations of Jewish law and ethics. Revered by Jews as sacred. It comprises the Mishnah and the Gemara.

THEOPHUS, THE—The world leader about which Emperor Tiberius dreamed. The Theophus Commission of Ambassadors were investigating Jesus at the time of his death.

THOMAS (GOSPEL OF)—An apocryphal Gospel found in 1945 near Nag Hammadi in Egypt, reputed to have been written by Thomas, the apostle of Jesus.

VIRGINITY (PERPETUAL) OF MARY—A doctrine originally proposed by John Chrysostom and then adopted by the Catholic Church that Mary was, is, and always will be a virgin. Even at the point of the birth of Jesus she maintained her virginity. This teaching claims that Mary remained a virgin her entire life.

VULGATE—The Latin version of the Bible. It was mainly the work of Jerome at the request of Pope Damasus I (366-384).

YEBAMOTH—One of the tractates of the third division of the Jewish Mishnah and Talmud.

ZACCHAEUS—A rich tax assessor who lived in Jericho. After his confrontation with Jesus, he gave of his wealth to the poor.

ZACHARIAS—The father of John the Baptist. The husband of Elizabeth, the mother of John the Baptist. He was a priest from the line of Aaron.

ZADOK—High Priest of the Jews in the time of King David (10th century BC). The name of the Sadducees was probably derived from him.

ZION—The most easterly of the two hills of ancient Jerusalem. It is often used as a poetical designation of earthly Jerusalem as well as the new heavenly Jerusalem.

Dr. Ron Charles

About the Author:

Dr. Ron Charles is well qualified to write a book about the search for historical Jesus. Although he earned a B.S. in Civil Engineering and worked as a structural engineer for 12 years, and a B.A. in Theology and pastored for 14 years, his passion has always been history and archaeology, particularly New Testament and Roman era history. As such, Dr. Charles continued his education by earning an M.A. in Ancient History, an M.A. in Historical Theology, a Ph.D. in Ancient History, a Ph.D. in International Relations, and a Th.D. in Historical Theology.

Dr. Charles spent 33 years, traveled to over 50 countries, and was involved with numerous archaeological investigations in five different countries, in his pursuit for authenticating information regarding the life of Jesus.

Dr. Charles was a co-founder of the Albania-American Archaeological Society; serves on the Board of Directors of Pacific International University, Final Frontiers International, and as a member of the Board of Governors of Cambridge's Biographical and Historical Division; and has recently been a recipient of Cambridge's *One Thousand Great Americas* award. Dr. Charles has Mitten six other books.

Dr. Charles has been married to his wife. Paula, for 32 years, and is currently employed as a Miter for Crown Financial Ministries in Gainesville. Georgia.

Nov 08 second reading
July 16 third reading